Android for Java Programmers

Abdul-Rahman Mawlood-Yunis

Android for
Java Programmers

 Springer

Abdul-Rahman Mawlood-Yunis
Physics and Computer Science
Wilfrid Laurier University
Waterloo, ON, Canada

ISBN 978-3-030-87458-2   ISBN 978-3-030-87459-9   (eBook)
https://doi.org/10.1007/978-3-030-87459-9

This Springer imprint is published by the registered company Springer Nature Switzerland AG.
The registered company address is: Gewerbestrasse 11, 6330 Cham, Switzerland

I would like to dedicate this book to my family: my wife Arkhawan, my daughter Sara, my son Sipan, my youngest daughter Zylan, my dad Mawlood-Yunis, and my mom Saadia Abdullah Haydar.

I would also like to dedicate this book to the friends of my youth Hawaz, Zana, Arsalan, Nazir, Shapoor, and Qabil who were martyred very early in life because of the war in Iraq, political dictatorship, and extremism. Their memories will stay with me forever.

Preface

Android for Java programmers is about learning Android and developing native apps using the Java programming language. The book reflects my expertise and experience in teaching software engineering, Java, and Android application development, as well as 10 years of IT work experience developing stand-alone Java, Web, and Business Intelligence applications.

Target Audience

The book intends to be a textbook for introductory or advanced Android courses to be taught in one or two semesters in universities and colleges. It uses code samples and exercises extensively to explain and clarify Android coding and concepts. The book will benefit students and programmers who have no prior Android programming knowledge. It is also useful for those who already have some Android programming skills and are excited to study more advanced concepts or acquire a deeper knowledge and understanding of Android programming.

The book can be easily read and used by instructors. All the apps in the book are native Android apps and do not need to use or include third-party technologies to run. The book differs from others that spend substantive time explaining third-party software, such as React Native, Ionic Framework, Flutter, and App Inventor to create and run apps. Our approach is to stay focused on using Android and native apps, something important when learning Android for the first time.

Topics and Teaching Approach

For each chapter, one or two demo apps are developed to demonstrate the concepts discussed. The source codes of the demo apps are available for download from the book's website (https://github.com/amawloodyunis). The executable codes, i.e., .apk (Android application package), are also available for download. I recommend that you re-create the demo apps following the instructions provided in the book instead of just opening the source codes in Android Studio and running them. You will learn more by doing it yourself, i.e., by re-creating the demo apps incrementally and using the provided source codes as a reference to debug and fix any issues you might face. Once you are done reading this book, I expect you to be able to develop and publish apps on Google Apps Store, Samsung Apps Store, Amazon Online Store, and F-Droid.

Each chapter of the book is dedicated to one or more Android development topics. Each app has a main interface with two or more buttons on the first screen. When clicked, each button starts a stand-alone app. We followed this approach to consolidate all apps for each chapter into one project. However, if you wish, you can create multiple small projects by copying parts of the chapter app and using the code to create each separate stand-alone app. Although we cover the important features of each topic, they are not all-inclusive. There is space for further expansion of each topic. The topics covered include Activities and transitions between Actives, Intents, Bundle objects, Activity lifecycles, callback methods, Android user interfaces and Widgets, Activity layouts, Toolbars and Menus, Cursor objects, the Android Profiler, the Device File Explorer, Android Debug Bridge (adb), Toast and Snackbar message objects, the Log class and the LogCat utility, testing, Parcelable objects, Fragments, Date and Time Pickers, Shared Preferences, databases, XML and JSON processing, the Content Provider, the Room library, the Android directory structure and access to local and external files, Services and broadcasting, AsyncTask and threading, Broadcast Receivers, MediaPlayer, VideoView, location and motion Sensors, Android map and tracking, language and Locale settings, Android measurements, etc.

Content and Explanation

The book is unique in terms of its content, content explanation, approach, and structure. To emphasize the importance of app design, documentation, code maintenance, and evolving code, we include class structures for most of the apps created in the book. We also explain concepts such as code profiling, test coverage, and reverse engineering. While these topics are important to create high-quality business apps, they are rarely discussed in Android books. My objective is to go beyond the simple app explanations that are typically found in Android development books. Here, we help the reader to think of all aspects of software engineering to create robust and maintainable apps.

The book provides a deep explanation of what is beneath Android concepts in terms of Java. For example, while it is fundamental for Android app development to have a layout and create the layout for Activities in the XML file, we show how you can achieve the same results without creating a layout in the XML file. This approach deepens the reader's understanding of what is beneath the Android hood, something not often found or addressed in Android books.

Some of the apps included in this book solve real-world problems. For example, in Chap. 11, the live streaming app created using URLs enables one's favorite radio stations to be grouped in one place and, hence, easily played and switched from another. It is an app that turns your device into a radio and lets you listen to live streaming stations while in the office, on the road, or in any other setting. The app is similar to Spotify but on a smaller scale. Other apps in the book provide you with real-time weather information for all the cities in Canada and Covid-19 data. We also add further guidance to create apps that obtain news information, currency exchange rates, information about your local political representation in government, etc.

The structure of the book follows Java and Object-Orient (OO) programmers' expectations. Java and OO programmers are familiar with concepts such as classes, interfaces, methods, method calls, and passing values and objects between methods, and when they come to learn Android, they look for mapping between what they know and what they are trying to learn. That is, they look for equivalent concepts in the new API they are about to learn. Our book is structured in a way to help Java and OO programmers easily map Android concepts to their own. For example, in the early chapters of the book, we cover Parcelable objects, which are equivalent to object serialization for passing objects between Activities. We also introduce going back and forth between Activities, which is equivalent to navigating back and forth between Java frames or HTML webpages.

Latest Code

An important aspect of teaching and learning is to stay up to date. This is especially the case for a field of study that has been going through a lot of changes, where some of these changes are philosophical ones. For example, Google recently made changes to the way services run in the app's background, how the permission is checked to read/write the files, and how to access local resources and location services. These changes make explanations provided in any Android book written before them, some of these changes being made in 2018, invalid and their associated code to be unusable without a substantive redo. All codes of this book are up to date. They are implemented in the latest Android SDK version and the latest published Android Studio.

Enjoy.

Additional Resources for Users and Instructors

Users can download the source codes of the demo apps from here: https://github.com/amawloodyunis. In addition, instructors can download chapter presentations in PTT and PDF formats by request. The email for contact is droidforjavaprogrammers@gmail.com.

Convention Used in the Book

We use ... notation to indicate that the user should write their code in this place.

Waterloo, ON, Canada   Abdul-Rahman Mawlood-Yunis
July 2021

Acknowledgments

I would like to thank my daughter, Sara Mawlood-Yunis, for the reviews and contributions she made. Her input has been priceless. I would like to also thank my colleague, Professor Ilias Kotsireas from Wilfrid Laurier University, for his help and encouragement to write this book. I also would like to thank Ralf Gerstner, Sharanya Sakthivel, Ramya Prakash, and others from Springer who worked tirelessly to improve the manuscript of this book.

Contents

1 Java Review 1
  1.1   Introduction 1
  1.2   Language Basics 1
        1.2.1   Variables 2
        1.2.2   Type of Variable 2
        1.2.3   Java Primitive Data Types 3
        1.2.4   Default Variable Initializations 5
        1.2.5   Typecasting 6
        1.2.6   Type Assignment Example 6
        1.2.7   Java String Class 7
        1.2.8   Java Operators 8
        1.2.9   Control Flow Statements 11
        1.2.10   Arrays 11
        1.2.11   ArrayList 12
        1.2.12   Java Iterator Interface 13
        1.2.13   For-Each Loop 13
  1.3   Object-Oriented Programming Concepts in Java 15
        1.3.1   Classes 15
        1.3.2   Objects 17
        1.3.3   Interfaces 20
        1.3.4   Package 22
        1.3.5   Inheritance 22
        1.3.6   Inheritance Example 23
        1.3.7   Polymorphism 24
        1.3.8   Hiding Fields 28
        1.3.9   Using the Keyword Super 28
        1.3.10   Subclass Constructors 29
        1.3.11   Using Preserved Keyword *"this"* 30
        1.3.12   Java Exception Handling 32
        1.3.13   Generic Types 33

        1.3.14   Type Parameter Naming Conventions   35
        1.3.15   Autoboxing   36
        1.3.16   Parameterized Types   38
        1.3.17   Anonymous Classes   38
        1.3.18   Object Serialization   40
        1.3.19   Lambda Expressions   44
        1.3.20   Variable Argument (Varargs)   45
    1.4   Chapter Summary   48
    Further Reading   49

2   Getting Started with Android   51
    2.1   Introduction   51
    2.2   Starting with Android   51
        2.2.1   A Brief Android History   52
        2.2.2   Android Is Open Source   52
        2.2.3   Android Libraries   52
        2.2.4   Android Popularity   53
        2.2.5   Android Development Environment   53
        2.2.6   Android Developer's Skills   54
        2.2.7   Model View Controller and App Development   55
        2.2.8   Android's Main Program   55
        2.2.9   Java and Android   55
        2.2.10   Why Use Java for Android?   56
        2.2.11   Android and Linux   56
    2.3   Download and Install Android Studio and Android SDK   57
        2.3.1   Download the Android Studio   57
        2.3.2   Install Android Studio   58
        2.3.3   Update Android Files   63
        2.3.4   Release Note   64
        2.3.5   Android SDK   64
    2.4   Create a New Android Project   67
        2.4.1   Start New Project   67
        2.4.2   Select an Activity Template   67
        2.4.3   Fill in Application Requirement   69
        2.4.4   Define SDK Requirements   70
        2.4.5   Finish the Project Creation   70
    2.5   Compiling and Running Android Apps   71
        2.5.1   Running HelloWorld on Your Phone   71
        2.5.2   Running the Android App in Android Studio   73
        2.5.3   Issues Starting First App   74
        2.5.4   Running HelloWorld on Emulator   75
        2.5.5   Setting Up the Emulator   75
        2.5.6   Do It Yourself   77

2.6 Compiling, Building, and Packaging Technologies 78
  2.6.1 Compiling Android Code 78
  2.6.2 Android App Bundle 79
  2.6.3 Do It Yourself 79
  2.6.4 Install Android Apps 80
  2.6.5 Install APK from Online 80
  2.6.6 Install APK from Files 81
  2.6.7 From Dalvik to ART Runtime 81
  2.6.8 Gradle Build 81
  2.6.9 Software Versioning Using Local or Remote
        Repositories 85
2.7 Android Stack and Framework 87
  2.7.1 Android Architecture 87
  2.7.2 User and System Apps 88
  2.7.3 Java API Framework 88
  2.7.4 Native Libraries and Android Runtime 89
  2.7.5 Hardware Abstraction Layer (HAL) 89
  2.7.6 Linux Kernel 90
2.8 Chapter Summary 90
Further Reading 92
References 92

3 Your First Android Application 95
3.1 Introduction 95
3.2 Android App Development 96
  3.2.1 Early Android Development 96
  3.2.2 Android Versions 97
  3.2.3 Android Application Characteristic 98
  3.2.4 Android Activity 98
  3.2.5 R File 100
  3.2.6 Android Context 101
  3.2.7 Application Manifest Files 102
  3.2.8 Opening Android Project in Android Studio 102
  3.2.9 Cleaning Android Project Builds 102
3.3 Create Your First Mobile App 103
  3.3.1 Your App Specification 103
  3.3.2 Create Activity Layout 103
  3.3.3 Invoke Message on Activity 107
  3.3.4 Intent Class 107
  3.3.5 Using StartActivity 110
  3.3.6 Create Second Activity 111
  3.3.7 Project Manifest Update 114
  3.3.8 Running the App 117
  3.3.9 Receiving Messages/Data from an Activity 118
  3.3.10 Responding to the Messages from an Activity 119

3.4   Debugging Information   123
       3.4.1   Debugging Using Log.d()   124
       3.4.2   Using Logcat to View Log Messages   125
       3.4.3   Do It Yourself   126
3.5   Localize Your App and Resources   127
       3.5.1   Create a Resource File for Second Language   127
       3.5.2   Create Resource Entries for Languages Supported . . .   130
       3.5.3   Set Device Language   130
3.6   Chapter Summary   131
Further Reading   133

4   Debugging and Testing Using Junit, Espresso, and Mockito
     Frameworks   135
4.1   Introduction   136
4.2   The Android Studio Debugger   136
       4.2.1   Fault Handling Methods   136
       4.2.2   Enable Debugger   137
       4.2.3   Inspecting and Modifying Variable Values   139
       4.2.4   Android Profiler   141
       4.2.5   Device File Explorer   142
       4.2.6   Android Debug Bridge (adb)   144
       4.2.7   Do It Yourself   145
4.3   Toast and Snackbar Messages   146
       4.3.1   Toast Messages   146
       4.3.2   Snackbar Messages   150
       4.3.3   Do It Yourself   156
       4.3.4   The Log Class and Logcat Window   156
4.4   Android App Testing   159
       4.4.1   Create a Test Class   159
       4.4.2   Assert Methods   163
       4.4.3   Hamcrest Assert Methods   164
       4.4.4   Espresso Testing   165
       4.4.5   Unit Testing   167
       4.4.6   Unit Testing with Mockito   169
       4.4.7   Code Coverage   172
       4.4.8   Code Inspection and Refactoring   173
       4.4.9   Reverse Engineering   174
4.5   Chapter Summary   178
Further Reading   179
References   180

5   Activity Lifecycle and Passing Objects Between Screens Using
     Parcelable Interface   183
5.1   Introduction   183
5.2   Activity States   185

	5.2.1	Activity and States	185
	5.2.2	Transition Between States	186
	5.2.3	The Launcher Activity	187
	5.2.4	Implementing onCreate()	188
	5.2.5	Bundle Class	191
5.3		Understanding Activity Lifecycle	193
	5.3.1	Understanding the onDestroy Method	193
	5.3.2	Pausing and Resuming an Activity	194
	5.3.3	Stopping and Restarting an Activity	194
	5.3.4	Restoring Activity State	196
	5.3.5	Do It Yourself	199
5.4		Lifecycle Illustration App	199
	5.4.1	Lifecycle Callback Methods	199
	5.4.2	Callback Methods for the MainActivity	200
	5.4.3	Callback Methods for the DisplayMessageActivity	201
	5.4.4	Do It Yourself	205
	5.4.5	Callback Method Implementations	206
	5.4.6	Trigger the onPause() Method	208
5.5		Creating and Using Parcelable Objects	212
	5.5.1	Passing User-Defined Objects Between Activities	212
	5.5.2	LifeCycle with Parcelable Object	213
	5.5.3	Parcelable Example	214
5.6		Chapter Summary	225
		Further Reading	226
6		**User Interface Essential Classes, Layouts, Styles, Themes, and Dimensions**	**227**
6.1		Introduction	227
6.2		Essential UI Classes and Properties	228
	6.2.1	Android Project Structure	228
	6.2.2	Views	228
	6.2.3	View Class Examples	230
	6.2.4	Widget	232
	6.2.5	ViewGroup	234
	6.2.6	App Layout	236
6.3		Writing XML Layouts	239
	6.3.1	Declare UI Elements in XML	239
	6.3.2	Android Studio's Layout Editor	241
	6.3.3	Defining UI Programmatically	242
	6.3.4	LinearLayout Java Class	243
	6.3.5	LayoutParams Java Class	244
6.4		Details of the LayoutApplication Demo	245
	6.4.1	MainActivity Layout	245
	6.4.2	Activity with Linear Layout	248
	6.4.3	Linear Layout XML File	250

          6.4.4   Using Android Studio Design Option   252
          6.4.5   strings.xml File   253
          6.4.6   String Editor   254
          6.4.7   String Resources   254
          6.4.8   RelativeLayout   256
          6.4.9   Other Layouts   258
          6.4.10   Parent-Child Relationship Between Activities   262
    6.5   Styles, Themes, and Dimension   264
          6.5.1   Defining a Style File   265
          6.5.2   Applying Styles   267
          6.5.3   Defining the App's Theme   268
          6.5.4   The Difference Between a Theme and Style   271
          6.5.5   Padding and Margin View Properties   273
          6.5.6   Gravity and Weight View Properties   273
          6.5.7   Dimensions of a Phone and UI   274
    6.6   Chapter Summary   276
    Further Reading   277

7   ListView, ScrollList, Date and Time Pickers, and RecyclerView . . .   279
    7.1   Introduction   279
    7.2   List Views   280
          7.2.1   Adapter and ArrayAdapter Classes   280
          7.2.2   ListView and ListActivity   280
    7.3   Date and Time Pickers   289
          7.3.1   Date and Time Pickers   289
          7.3.2   Set Date Using the DatePicker   292
          7.3.3   Set Time Using the TimePicker   295
          7.3.4   Pickers and Anonymous Classes   296
    7.4   Scroll Views   298
          7.4.1   The ScrollView Class   298
          7.4.2   Top-Level XML Element for a Scroll View   299
          7.4.3   Scroll View Activity   303
    7.5   RecyclerView   304
          7.5.1   Using RecyclerView, Adapter, and ViewHolder
                    Classes   305
          7.5.2   RecyclerViewActivity   313
          7.5.3   Adapter and ViewHolder   315
          7.5.4   Using Recycler View with Older SDKs   321
    7.6   Chapter Summary   323
    Further Reading   324

8   Toolbar, Menu, Dialog Boxes, Shared Preferences, Implicit Intent,
    and Directory Structure   325
    8.1   Introduction   326
    8.2   More User Interface   326
          8.2.1   ActionBar   326

8.2.2 Toolbar............................... 326
8.2.3 Add androidx.appcompat Library to the Project..... 327
8.2.4 Extending AppCompatActivity................. 329
8.2.5 Specify a Theme with NO ActionBar............. 329
8.2.6 Adding Toolbar Element to the Layout........... 330
8.2.7 Menu Interface......................... 331
8.2.8 Options Menu and App Bar.................. 331
8.2.9 Context Menu.......................... 337
8.2.10 Popup Menu........................... 338
8.3 Dialog Boxes and the Camera App..................... 341
8.3.1 Dialog Boxes........................... 341
8.3.2 Custom Dialog Boxes...................... 344
8.3.3 Access a Phone's Default Camera App........... 344
8.3.4 Starting Activities for Results................. 347
8.3.5 Activity Result in AndroidX.................. 349
8.4 Saving Data with SharedPreferences..................... 351
8.4.1 SharedPreferences Interface.................. 351
8.4.2 Layout for Shared Preferences Activity........... 355
8.4.3 How SharedPreferencesActivity Code Works....... 356
8.5 Directory Structure and Saving Data in Files............... 361
8.5.1 Internal Storage Location................... 362
8.5.2 External Storage Location................... 362
8.5.3 Standard Public Directories for Data/Files......... 362
8.5.4 Android File IO Classes and Methods............ 367
8.5.5 Accessing External Storage Files............... 368
8.5.6 Permission to Access External Directory.......... 368
8.5.7 Examples Using External Methods.............. 369
8.5.8 Environment Class and
getExternalStoragePublicDirectory............... 372
8.5.9 Locate Apps on Emulator File System........... 374
8.6 Chapter Summary............................... 376
Further Reading...................................... 377

9 Fragments, Dynamic Binding, Inheritance, Pinching, and Screen
Swiping.. 379
9.1 Introduction.................................. 380
9.2 The Fragment Basics............................. 380
9.2.1 Fragment Uses......................... 380
9.2.2 Why Using Fragments..................... 381
9.2.3 Fragment Lifecycle....................... 383
9.3 Creating an App with the Fragments.................... 386
9.3.1 Create a Fragment....................... 386
9.3.2 One Activity and Multiple Layouts.............. 388
9.3.3 Detecting Device Size and Orientation........... 388
9.3.4 Fragment Development Steps in Details.......... 389

	9.3.5	The MainActivity Class and Demo App Demonstration	401
	9.3.6	Inserting Fragments in the Activity	405
	9.3.7	Fragment Static Binding Example	406
9.4	Inheritance in Android		408
	9.4.1	Create a Base Activity	408
	9.4.2	Layout for the BaseActivity	410
	9.4.3	No onCreate() Method for Child Class	413
	9.4.4	Layout Reuse	414
9.5	Density-Independent Pixel and Screen Sizes		416
	9.5.1	Naming Scheme	416
	9.5.2	Supporting Different Screen Sizes	417
	9.5.3	Density-Independent Pixel (dp)	419
9.6	Pinching and Screen Swiping		420
	9.6.1	Pinch to Zoom Image	420
	9.6.2	Swiping Gesture	423
	9.6.3	Swiping Gesture App	423
9.7	Chapter Summary		429
	Further Reading		430

10 Parsing Remote XML and JSON Files, Using HTTPUrlConnection, XmlPullParser, and AsyncTask 433

10.1	Introduction		433
10.2	Parsing Remote and Local XML Files		434
	10.2.1	XML Parser Review	434
	10.2.2	Push Parsing	434
	10.2.3	Pull Parser	435
	10.2.4	Remote XML Parsing	436
	10.2.5	Parsing Events	439
	10.2.6	Reading Image from Local File	442
	10.2.7	Retrieving Image from Remote Server	443
	10.2.8	An Example of Reading Image File	444
	10.2.9	A Demo App	445
	10.2.10	Parsing Local XML File	448
	10.2.11	Asset Folder	451
10.3	AsyncTask and Thread Handling		451
	10.3.1	AsyncTask Class	451
	10.3.2	Using AsyncTask Class	451
	10.3.3	AsyncTask and Varargs Type	452
	10.3.4	Input, Progress, and Result Parameters to AsyncTask	453
	10.3.5	AsyncTask Execute Methods	454
	10.3.6	AsyncTask Method Sequence Calls	454
10.4	App Implementation Details		456
	10.4.1	WeatherForecast Class	456

	10.4.2	Complete Code for Weather Network App Activity	459
	10.4.3	Parsing JSON Files	465
	10.4.4	Other XML Feeds	466
10.5	An App for Information on Covid-19		467
	10.5.1	Covid-19 App Development Steps	468
	10.5.2	Data Extraction and Conversion	469
	10.5.3	Testing and Production Development Environments	470
	10.5.4	Covid-19 Source Code and Class Structure	471
10.6	Chapter Summary		471
Further Reading			473

11   Android SQLite, Firebase, and Room Databases 475
11.1	Introduction		476
11.2	The Android SQLite Database		477
	11.2.1	SQLiteOpenHelper Class	477
	11.2.2	SQLiteDatabase Class	478
	11.2.3	Overriding Methods of the SQLiteOpenHelper Class	478
	11.2.4	The Class Constructor Method	478
	11.2.5	The onCreate() Method	479
	11.2.6	onUpgrade Method	481
	11.2.7	onDowngrade Method	482
	11.2.8	onOpen() Method	483
	11.2.9	Read and Read/Write Access	483
	11.2.10	The execSQL Method from SQLiteDatabase Class	484
11.3	Content Values and Cursor Objects		484
	11.3.1	Content Values and Insert Method	484
	11.3.2	Cursor	487
	11.3.3	Query Data	489
	11.3.4	rawQuery	490
	11.3.5	More Methods of the SQLiteDatabase Class	491
11.4	DatabaseDemo Project		492
	11.4.1	The Data Component	492
	11.4.2	The Middle Component	495
	11.4.3	The View Component	499
	11.4.4	Test Your Database Using SQLiteBrowser	505
	11.4.5	Use SQLiteBrowser for Database Design	506
	11.4.6	Android Database Inspector	507
11.5	Realtime Firebase Database		509
	11.5.1	Firebase and JSON Tree File	509
	11.5.2	Firebase Account and Project Setup	510
	11.5.3	Register Your Project Using the Firebase Console	510
	11.5.4	Adding Dependency to Your Project	510

11.5.5   Connecting to Database   511
11.5.6   Inserting Data into Database   511
11.5.7   Retrieving Data from Database   514
11.5.8   Deleting Data from Database   516
11.5.9   Query Data from Database   518
11.5.10   DataSnapshot and Query Classes   518
11.5.11   ChildEventListener Interface   519
11.5.12   Querying Firebase Database Using User-Defined
            Classes   520
11.5.13   Querying Firebase Database Example   522
11.6   Other Data Storage Options   524
11.6.1   Room Database   524
11.6.2   Content Provider   527
11.6.3   Internal and External Storage   527
11.7   Chapter Summary   528
Further Reading   530
References   530

12   **Content Provider, Service, Message Broadcasting, and
     Multimedia Player**   531
12.1   Introduction   531
12.2   Content Provider Component   532
12.2.1   Content Provider   532
12.2.2   Creating a Content Provider   534
12.2.3   Provider in Manifest File   542
12.2.4   Run and Test Content Provider   544
12.2.5   Content Provider Client   545
12.3   Media Content Streaming Apps   547
12.4   Android Service   549
12.4.1   Service   549
12.4.2   Communication with Service   550
12.4.3   Services Lifecycle   550
12.4.4   Creating Service   550
12.4.5   Service Binding   554
12.4.6   OnCreate() Method for Service   555
12.4.7   OnDestroy() Method   556
12.4.8   Stopping Service   557
12.4.9   Android Rules to End Service   558
12.4.10   Declaring a Service in the Manifest   558
12.4.11   Intent Service   559
12.4.12   Service Summary   560
12.4.13   Do It Yourself   560
12.5   Message Broadcasting in Android   561
12.5.1   Android Message Broadcasting Types   561
12.5.2   BroadcastReceiver Class   562

        12.5.3   Do It Yourself   566
  12.6 Android MediaPlayer for Streaming Radio Stations   566
        12.6.1   App Structure   567
        12.6.2   Android Media Player   568
        12.6.3   Power Manager and WakeLock   570
        12.6.4   WifiLock   571
        12.6.5   Other App Components   571
        12.6.6   Stopping and Restarting Service   572
        12.6.7   The New Restriction on Background Service   573
        12.6.8   Do It Yourself   575
  12.7 Remote and Local Video Playback   576
        12.7.1   Playback Video Using Implicit Intent and URL   576
        12.7.2   Playback Live Streaming Video Using URL and
                 VideoView   577
        12.7.3   Playback Embedded Video in Your App   580
        12.7.4   Playback Video Outside Your App Directory   581
  12.8 Chapter Summary   582
  Further Reading   583

13 Sensors, Location-Based Service, and Google Maps   585
  13.1 Introduction   585
  13.2 Android Sensor   586
        13.2.1   Accelerometer Sensor   587
        13.2.2   Accelerometer App   587
        13.2.3   Using Accelerometer   588
        13.2.4   Get List of Sensors   595
        13.2.5   Do It Yourself   597
  13.3 Location-Based Services   597
        13.3.1   Demo App Interface   598
        13.3.2   Location Service APIs   598
        13.3.3   App Development Steps   599
        13.3.4   App Implementation Details   601
        13.3.5   Revising Weather App   611
        13.3.6   Do It Yourself   613
  13.4 Use Google Maps in Your App   614
        13.4.1   Create a Google Maps Project   614
        13.4.2   Obtaining App Key   616
        13.4.3   Update Manifest File   617
        13.4.4   Google Maps API   619
        13.4.5   GoogleMap Class   620
        13.4.6   OnMapReadyCallback Interface   620
        13.4.7   SupportMapFragment Class   620
        13.4.8   Map Fragment Layout Example   622
        13.4.9   MapView   624
        13.4.10 UiSettings   627

13.4.11   Configure Initial State   627
13.4.12   Setting Map Initial State Programmatically   630
13.4.13   Covid App Revised   630
13.5   Chapter Summary   632
Further Reading   633
References   634

Index   635

Chapter 1
Java Review

What You Will Learn in This Chapter
This chapter includes reviewing Java language basics and Java classes and objects. If you have no prior experience with Java, by the end of this chapter, you will learn Java fundamentals. If you have prior experience, this chapter will help you gain more knowledge in Java and learn the latest developments in the Java world.

1.1   Introduction

This chapter presents a brief review of Java programming syntax and concepts as well as object-oriented programming terminology. The emphasis has been put on the part of Java that will be used for Android development. These include topics such as anonymous classes, the lambda expression, varargs, generic classes and methods, for-each statements, object serialization, etc. All the code snippets listed in this chapter are included in a file, the **JavaReview.zip** file, which you can download from the book website. Downloading and running the code is part of the learning material for this chapter. We start this chapter by reviewing the language basics.

1.2   Language Basics

In this section, we will review Java programming language basics. These include Java variables, data types, operators, and basic Java data structures and control flow operators.

1.2.1   Variables

The Java programming language uses both instance "variables" and "fields" as part of its terminology. In Java, to declare a class variable/field, you need to specify the access modifier, field type, and field name. The name of the variable must be unique within a class. The variable modifier is either public, protected, or private, where a public modifier means the field is accessible from all classes, a private modifier means the field is accessible only within its class, and a protected modifier means the field is accessible only within the class package. If you do not declare the field access modifier explicitly, the field will have a default modifier which will be accessible within the class package only. The default modifier is like the protected modifier except that the protected field can be accessed inside the package and outside of the class package through inheritance. Below are examples of variable declarations where access modifiers are private, protected, public, and default, respectively, and variable types are int, char, double, and String.

```
private   int     student_number ;
protected char    student_gender ;
public    double  grade_point_average ;
          String  student_name ;
```

1.2.2   Type of Variable

Java differentiates between four types of variables. The types are instance, static, local, and parameter variables. They can be described as follows:

- Instance variables (non-static fields) are unique to each object or an instance of a class.
- Class variables (static fields) are fields declared with the static modifier; there is only one copy of a static variable regardless of how many objects you instantiate from the class.
- Local variables hold temporary state values inside a method.
- Parameters are variables passed to methods. They are local variables to the method and are used within the methods.

Both local and parameter variables are not properties or fields of an object. They are local variables like x, y, and z that are used within the method. We will see examples of using these variables later in this chapter.

1.2.3 Java Primitive Data Types

Java has eight primitive data types. Unlike user-defined types, these are system-defined types. These are fundamental types that enable you to write programs and do computation/calculations. The types are listed below.

1.2.3.1 Integers

Java has four different variable types to hold whole numbers. The types are:

1. byte: its length is 1 byte or 8 bits.
2. short: its length is 2 bytes or 16 bits.
3. int: its length is 4 bytes or 32 bits.
4. long: its length is 8 bytes or 64 bits.

The types are different from each other by the range of the value they can hold. For example, when you declare a variable of type **byte**, the variable can have 2^8 (256) possible values. The value range of a byte is between -2^7 **and** $2^7- 1$, **i.e., −127 and 127**. It is for this reason that if you declare byte b = 127, it will be fine, but if you declare byte b = 300, the compiler will not accept it without casting (byte b = (byte) 300) which results in an expected outcome.

1.2.3.2 Real Numbers

Java has two variable types to hold numbers with fraction values. Like integers, the types are different from each other by the size of the value they can hold. The types are:

5. float: its length is 4 bytes or 32 bits.
6. double: its length is 8 bytes or 64 bits.

Double is used more often than float. This is because nowadays storage memory is cheap and anything you can do with the float you can do with a double as well.

When lining up Java primitive data types based on their size, they can be arranged in this order: byte, short, int, long, float, double. Values of any predecessor type can be assigned to any successor type (e.g., int to double, long to double). This is because larger types are big enough to hold the value of smaller types. To learn about Java variable types and how variables of small size types can be assigned to another type with a larger size, see the example in Listing 1.1:

Listing 1.1 Java primitive data type declaration and assignment.

```
public class PrimitiveTypes {
        public static void main (String args []) {
                byte b = 100; short s = 10000;
                int i = 100000; long l = 1000000;
                float f = 123.4f; double d = 1.234e2;
                s = b;
                i = s;
                l = i ;
                f = l;
                d = f;
        }
}
```

To assign a value the other way around, i.e., assign variables that can hold a large value to a variable that can hold a small value, you need to do explicit typecasting. This is because larger types cannot be saved in a smaller space. A value needs to be shortened to fit into a smaller location. See the example in Listing 1.2:

Listing 1.2 Primitive typecasting in Java.

```
public class PreimativeTypes2 {
        public static void main (String args []) {
                byte b = 100;
                short s = 10000;
                int i = 100000;
                long l = 1000000;
                float f = 123.4f;
                double d = 1.234e2;
                b = (byte) s;
                s = (byte) i ;
                i = (int) l;
                l = (long) f;
                f = (float) d;
        }
}
```

Note that the range of values that can be represented by a float or double type is much larger than the range that can be represented by a long type. This is because both float and double types use exponent to represent values. For more information about this topic, see the link that is called *widening primitive conversion* provided at the end of this chapter.

1.2.3.3   Char and Boolean

In addition to the whole and real numbers, Java has two other primitive variable types:

7. char
8. boolean

The char length is 2 bytes or 16 bits, and boolean is 1 bit of information and takes a true or false value. Variables of type int can be assigned to char. For example, char a = 97; is a valid Java expression, and when a is printed, it will produce "a." This is because the ASCII value for a small "a" is 97. In Java, you cannot assign int values to boolean variables, nor you can assign a true/false value to an int variable.

The Java class *String* represents character strings and is often used along with primitive data types to declare Java class fields. But remember String is a Java class and not a primitive type.

Note that in Java, you cannot assign one and zero to a boolean type; the value must be true or false. This is possible in other programming languages like C++, but not in Java.

1.2.4   Default Variable Initializations

Class instance variables are automatically initialized in Java. The default variable value depends on the type, and they are initialized as follows:

- Boolean types are initialized to false.
- Primitives holding numbers (short, byte, int, double, and float) are initialized to zero.
- Char types are initialized to space.
- Class types are initialized to null.

It is better practice to explicitly initialize instance variables yourself in the class constructor. More on constructors in later sections of this chapter. Different from double, when you initialize float, you include the letter "f" in the value, e.g., *float f = 123.4f;*

In Java, you can define and initialize multiple variables of the same type in one line. For example, this is correct in Java: int x =2, y =4, z =5; variable declarations are separated from each other by a comma. This is possible only when all the variables are of the same type; in this example, the type is int.

Note that local variables declared inside methods are not automatically initialized. It is the programmer's responsibility to initialize local variables.

1.2.5   Typecasting

A typecast takes a value of one type and produces a value of another type with an "equivalent" value. For example, you can declare:

```
int x;
double y;
y= (double)x;
```

Here, the x value is changed from int to double before being assigned to y.

When casting, the desired type is placed inside parentheses immediately in front of the variable to be cast. The type and value of the variable cast do not change.

If x and y are integers to be divided, and the fractional portion of the result must be preserved, at least one of the two variables must be a typecast to a floating-point type before the division operation is performed. Here is an example:

```
int x =5;
int y =2;
double result = x / (double)y;
the code will become 5/2.0 and the result would be 2.5.
```

When typecasting from a floating-point to an integer type, the number is truncated, not rounded. For example, **(int)2.9** evaluates to **2**, not **3**. When the value of an integer type is assigned to a variable of a floating-point type, Java performs an automatic typecast called type coercion, e.g., **double d = 5;** would be converted to **double d = 5.0;**

1.2.6   Type Assignment Example

In Java, not all types can be assigned to other types without explicit typecasting. Run the code in Listing 1.3 to see when variables of different types can be assigned to each other (e.g., int to double, long to double) and when to do explicit typecasting.

Listing 1.3 Java primitive data type assignments.

```
package lesson01;
public class VariableAssignment {
   public static void main (String args []) {
      int x = 2; double y;
      y = x; // this is possible
      x = y; // this is a mismatch error cannot assignment double to int
      x = (int) y; // explicit type casting
      byte b; short s;
      s = b; // correct
      b = s; // mismatch type
```

```
   s = x; // mismatch type
   b = x; // mismatch type
   x = b; // correct assignment
   x = s; // correct assignment
   long l;
   x = l; // mismatch type
   l = x;
   double d; float f;
   d = l;
   l = d; // mismatch type
   f = l;
   l = f; // mismatch type
   char c = 'a';
   char a = 97;
   System.out.println (a); // prints character a
   int charvalue = (int) c;
   boolean bool1 = true;
   boolean bool2 = false;
   bool1 = 0; // type mismatch cannot convert from int to boolean
   bool2 = 1; // type mismatch cannot convert from int to boolean
   bool1 = (boolean) 1; // cannot cast from int to boolean
  }
}
```

1.2.7 Java String Class

String represents character strings, or text, and is often used along with primitive data types to declare Java class fields. But String is a class, not a primitive type. Here is an example of how to use the String class.

```
String str = "hello class";
```

The String class has many methods to perform actions on string literals. These include compareTo (), charAt(index), contains (), equals (), length (), and many more. A simple example of how to use the String class is giving in Listing 1.4. For detailed information on the String class, visit the Oracle API documentation.

1.2.7.1 String Concatenation

In Java, you can use the plus operator (+) on two strings or more to connect them to form one larger string. For example, if the greeting variable is equal to "Greetings" and the javaClass variable is equal to "Class," then greeting + javaClass is equal to "Greetings Class"; see the code in Listing 1.4:

Listing 1.4 Plus sign is used as a text concatenator in Java.

```java
public class StringClass {
  public static void main (String args[]) {
    String greetings = "Greetings ";
    String JavaClass = " Class";
    System.out.println(greetings + JavaClass);
  }
}
```

Any number of Strings can be concatenated together, and when a String is combined with almost any other type, the result is still a String. For example, if the following line of code is executed, the result would be the String "The answer is 2021."

```java
int number = 2021;
  System.out.println ("The answer is " + number);
```

1.2.8   Java Operators

As in most programming languages, in Java, *expressions* can be formed using variables, constants, and arithmetic operators. These operators are + (addition), - (subtraction), * (multiplication), / (division), % (modulo or remainder), and many more. An expression can be fully parenthesized to specify exactly what expression parts are combined with each operator. Java operators, along with a brief description of each operator, are listed in Table 1.1.[1]

If the parentheses in an expression are omitted, Java will follow *precedence* rules. Java executes/evaluates unary operators such as +, -, ++, --, and ! first; binary arithmetic operators, such as *, /, and %, are executed second; and binary arithmetic operators such as + and − are executed last.

1.2.8.1   Associativity Rules

When two operations have equal precedence, the order of operations is determined by the associativity rules as follows:

- The *unary* operators (+, -, ++, --, and !) of equal precedence are grouped from *right to left*. For example, +-+rate is evaluated as +(-(+rate)).

---

[1] https://docs.oracle.com/javase/tutorial/java/nutsandbolts/opsummary.html

Table 1.1 Java operators

Arithmetic operators	+	Additive operator (also used for String concatenation)
	-	Subtraction operator
	*	Multiplication operator
	/	Division operator
	%	Remainder operator also called modulo operator
Unary operators	+	Unary plus operator; indicates a positive value (numbers are positive without the + symbols as well)
	-	Unary minus operator; negates an expression
	++	Increment operator; increments a value by 1
	--	Decrement operator; decrements a value by 1
	!	Logical complement operator; inverts the value of a boolean (e.g., ! true means false)
Equality and relational operators	==	Equal to
	!=	Not equal to
	>	Greater than
	>=	Greater than or equal to
	<	Less than
	<=	Less than or equal to
Conditional operators	&&	Conditional-AND
	‖	Conditional-OR
	?:	Ternary (shorthand for if-then-else statement)
Type comparison operator	**instanceof** Compares an object to a specified type	
Bitwise and bit shift operators	~	Unary bitwise complement
	<<	Signed left shift
	>>	Signed right shift
	>>>	Unsigned right shift
	&	Bitwise AND
	^	Bitwise exclusive OR
	‖	Bitwise inclusive OR

- *Binary* operators of equal precedence are grouped from *left to right*. For example, the expression base + rate + hours is evaluated as (base + rate) + hours.

A string of *assignment operators* is an exception to the rule above and grouped *right to left*. For example, n1 = n2 = n3; is evaluated as n1 = (n2 = n3); when the println statement executes in the code snippet below (c=b=a), it will print hello.

```
String a = "hello ";
String b = "World";
String c = "Say ";
c = b = a;
System.out.println (c);
```
The output is hello.

1.2.8.2   Shorthand Assignment Operators

Shorthand assignment notation combines the *assignment operator* (=) and an *arithmetic operator*. It is used to change the value of a variable by adding, subtracting, multiplying, or dividing by a specified value. The general form is as follows:

Variable Op = Expression,

and is equivalent to:

Variable = Variable Op Expression

For example, *int x += y;* is the same as *int x = x +y;.*

In Listing 1.5, we show how the shorthand operator can be used. We use each variable twice: the first time with the shorthand operator and the second time without the shorthand operator. The call to the print method shows that the shorthand and non-shorthand operators provide identical results.

Listing 1.5 Using shorthand operator in Java.

```java
public class ShorthandAssignmentOperators {
// instance variable declaration
    static int count = 0, sum = 0, bonus = 2, time = 360, rushFactor = 10,
        change = 37, discount = 5, count1 = 5,
        count2 = 12, amount = 4;
    public static void main (String args[]) {
        count += 2;
        sum -= discount;
        bonus *= 2;
        time /= rushFactor;
        change %= 100;
        amount *= count1 + count2;
        print ();
// instance variables are re-initialized.
        count = 0; sum = 0; bonus = 2; time = 360;
        rushFactor = 10; change = 37; discount = 5;
        count1 = 5; count2 = 12; amount = 4;
        count = count + 2;
        sum = sum - discount;
        bonus = bonus * 2;
        time = time / rushFactor;
        change = change % 100;
        amount *= (count1 + count2);
    }
// print method declaration
    public static void print () {
        System.out.println("Shorthand operator is used");
        System.out.println("variable values are " + count +
            " " + sum + " " + time + " "+ bonus + " " + change + " " + amount);
```

```
System.out.println("---------------------");
System.out.println("variables are re- initialized");
System.out.println(
" regular expressions are used and results are identical");
System.out.println("variable values are " + count +
    " " + sum + " " + time + " "+ bonus + " " + change + " " + amount);
}
}
```

The program output when you run the code in Listing 1.5 is as follows:

```
Shorthand operator is used
variable values are 2 -5 36 4 37 68
---------------------
variables are re-initialized
regular expressions are used and results are identical
variable values are 2 -5 36 4 37 68
```

1.2.9 Control Flow Statements

Generally, code is executed top-down, i.e., from top to bottom in the order that they appear. However, the control flow statements, such as *if-else* statements, break up the flow of the execution. They loop and branch, enabling your program to decide which blocks of code will be executed.

The Java programming language supports the following control flow operators:

1. The decision-making statements: if-then, if-then-else, and switch
2. The looping statements: for, while, and do-while
3. The branching statements: break, continue, and return
   Examples of using these control flows will be given in the sections below.

1.2.10 Arrays

An array is the simplest data structure in Java. It is a homogeneous container object that holds a fixed number of values. By homogeneous we mean all the elements of an array are of the same type.

The length of an array is set when the array is created. After creation, an array's length is fixed and cannot be changed. Arrays have certain features:

- All its elements are of the same type.
- Array elements are in *adjacent* memory locations.

The following line of code declares an array (named myArray):

```
private int [] myArray;
```

Like declarations for variables, an array declaration has three components: the access modifier, the array type, and the array name. If an access modifier is not declared, then the variable takes the default access modifier. Brackets can be put before or after the array's name. For example, **float anArrayOfFloats[];** and **float [] anArrayOfFloats;** are both valid syntaxes to declare an array. However, the latter is more appealing.

The *new* operator is used to create arrays. The following line of code allocates an array with enough memory for ten integer elements and assigns the array to the myArray variable.

```
// create an array of 10 integers, the array size needs to be known at this
// point.
 myArray = new int [10];
```

1.2.11   ArrayList

The length of an array is set when the array is created. After creation, its length is fixed and cannot be changed. In many cases, it is useful to have a data structure that has all the properties of the array and is easy to change size. Java has an ArrayList<type> to overcome the fixed size limitation of the array. It is a dynamic array, and array size can grow or shrink at the runtime. It is also a type and can be used in the same way as any other Java type. It can be used:

1. To declare variables, for example, ArrayList<String> namelist;
2. As a type of parameter in a method definition
3. As the return type of a method
4. With the *new* operator to create a dynamic list. For example,
     namelist = new ArrayList<String> ();

ArrayList has instance methods such as:

- *add* for adding a *String* to the list, e.g., namelist.add("Abdul-Rahman");
- *get*(index) for getting the string at index, e.g., namelist.get(1);
- *size* for getting the number of items currently in the list, for example, namelist.size();

You can use *ArrayList* with any user-defined types or Java types. For example, if Student is a class representing students, you can create a list of students as follows:

```
ArrayList<Student> classList = new ArrayList<Student>();
```

Then, to add students like George or Ali to the list just created, we simply have to say *classList.add (Ali)*. You can remove students from the list using array index, e.g., *classList.remove*(i).

1.2.12   Java Iterator Interface

Java provides an interface for going through or traversing all elements in any collection, container, or data structure. The interface is called an Iterator. The syntax of an iteration is generic and applies to any Java class that implements the Iterator interface. Here is an example of iterating through an ArrayList of Strings without using the Iterator.

```
for (int i =0; i <yourList.size();i++) {
String s = yourList.get(i);
//do something with s
}
```

Alternatively, using the Iterator would be:

```
Iterator<String> itr = list.iterator();
while (itr.hasNext()) {
String s = itr.next();
}
```

It is more suitable to use the Iterator interface than the for loop or for-each loop if you are updating the collection, e.g., removing items from the collection, while you iterate over the collection or the list of objects.

1.2.13   For-Each Loop

A new loop construct called for-each loop was added in Java 5 to loop through each item in an array or a collection more clearly. Table 1.2 show examples where for-each loop is used with for loop and the Iterator.

Table 1.2 For-each loop vs. for loop and Iterator

For-each loop

for (Student aStudent: ClassList){
    System.out.println (aStudent) ;
  }

Equivalent for loop and Iterator	

for (int i = 0; i < ClassList.size(); i++)
{
  aStudent= ClassList.get(i);
  System.out.println (aStudent) ;
}
	Iterator<type> iterator;
	for (iterator = collection.iterator();
	  iterator.hasNext();) {
	// *type variable = iterator.next();*
	// *do something;*
	  }

The generic format of the for-each statement is like this:

For (type variable: any_collection) { // *do something;* **}**

Listing 1.6 is a more complete example of how for-each loop is used:

Listing 1.6 Using for-each loop.

```java
package javaReview;
public class ForEachTest {
  public static void main (String args[]) {
    double sum = 0;
    double [] price = {1.5, 2.5, 3.5, 4, 0.5};
    for (int i = 0; i < price. length; i++) {
      sum = sum + price[i];
    }
    System.out.println ("When regular for loop is used sum is " + sum);
    sum = 0;
    for (double p: price)
      sum = sum + p;
    System.out.println ("When For-each loop is used sum is " + sum);
    Collection<String> myCollectionItem = new ArrayList<String> ();
    myCollectionItem.add ("1 - H - Hydrogen");
    myCollectionItem.add ("2 - He - Helium");
    myCollectionItem.add ("3 - Li - Lithium");
    myCollectionItem.add ("4 - Be - Beryllium");
    myCollectionItem.add ("5 - B - Boron");
    System.out.println (
    " When Iterator is used the collection printout is ");
```

```
Iterator iter = myCollectionItem.iterator();
while (iter.hasNext()) {
  System.out.println(iter.next());
}
System.out.println ("When For-each is used instead of the" +
                Iterator the collection printout is");
for (String item: myCollectionItem)
    System.out.println (item);
  }
}
```

The for-each operator should not be used if you need compatibility with versions before Java 5. You also need to be aware of some rules when using the for-each loop. For example,

1. It is not possible to traverse two structures or collections at once.
2. It can be used only for single-element access.
3. It can only iterate forward by single steps.

For more information about Java language basics, we suggest that you refer to the resources listed at the end of this chapter.

1.3 Object-Oriented Programming Concepts in Java

There are similarities between object-oriented programming (a.k.a, OOP) and procedural programming; both involve executing a set of instructions in a specified order. However, OOP is different from procedural programming in the way that code is organized. In this part of the chapter, we will review some of the fundamental object-oriented programming concepts. These include classes, objects, interfaces, packages, abstract classes, inheritance, polymorphism, and exception handling.

1.3.1 Classes

The Java programming style involves organizing code in "chunks" that logically correspond to real-world objects. For example, you may group all your code related to a person into one file (a class), while code related to a car or a bank account would be grouped in separate files (i.e., classes). A class is an essential building block of the Java programming language and other object-oriented programming languages. Without classes, OO programming would not be possible. In Java, every program, library, and programmer-defined type consists of classes. Think of classes as bulky types when compared to primitive data types such as int, double, etc. A primitive type value is a single piece of data. A class can have multiple pieces of data, as well as actions called *methods*. A class determines the types of data that an instance of the class, i.e., an object, can contain as well as the actions it can perform.

You already saw classes, the objects created from classes, and invoked class methods. For example, you have used the String and the System classes. These are system-defined classes; they are included in the Java SDK you download. In this lesson, you will learn how to define your own Java classes, i.e., user-defined classes, their methods, and how to instantiate objects from your own Java classes.

Think of a class as a special programmer-defined type. They are not int, double, or char. They are programmer types. Once you defined your type, you can declare variables of the defined type. The class variable declaration is like the primitive variable declaration. For example, like declaring int x, you can declare Bird flamingo where Bird is a programmer-defined type. In the example below, a Bird class is defined, and the flamingo variable of the type Bird is declared.

```
public class Bird {
   String name;
   String description;
   String family;
}
Bird flamingo;
```

A value of a class type is called an object or *an instance of the class*. For example, if Bird is a class, then the phrases "Flamingo is of type Bird," "Flamingo is an object of the class Bird," and "Flamingo is an instance of the class Bird" all mean the same thing, i.e., here, types, objects, and instances all mean the same thing. All objects of a class have the same methods and pieces of data (i.e., data name, type, and number). For a given object, each piece of data can hold a different value.

A class may be declared with one or more modifiers which affect its runtime behavior. The modifier types that are supported in Java are:

• Access modifiers: public, protected, and private.
• Modifier requiring override: abstract.
• Modifier restricting to one instance: static.
• Modifier prohibiting value modification: final.
• Modifier forcing strict floating-point behavior: strictfp.
• Comments or metadata that you can insert in your Java code, i.e., annotations. It starts with the @ sign.

The access modifier, for example, specifies which external classes can access a given class and its properties, constructors, and methods. Access modifiers can be assigned to class fields, methods, and constructors separately from the class modifier. For example, in most cases, the class modifier is public, but its internal fields are private or protected. Classes, fields, constructors, and methods can have one of these access modifiers: private, default (package), protected, or public.

The code snippet given in Listing 1.7 is an example of a Bank Account class in Java where all information related to a bank account is grouped to form a BankAccount class. The access modifier for the class as well as the two methods, withdraw and deposit, are public. The access modifiers for the instance variables accountNumber, customer name, and balance, however, are private.

Listing 1.7 Java class named BankAccount.

```java
public class BankAccount {
  private String accountNumber = "";
  private String customer_name = "";
  private double balance = 0.0;
  public BankAccount () {
    this.accountNumber = accountNumber;
    this.customer_name = customer_name;
    this.balance = balance;
  }
  public BankAccount (String id, String name, double amount) {
    this.accountNumber = id;
    this.customer_name = name;
    this.balance = amount;
  }
  public double deposit (double amount) {
    balance = balance + amount;
    return (balance);
  }
  public String withdraw (double amount) {
    String customerBalance = "";
    if (amount > balance) {
      balance = balance - amount;
      customerBalance = "your new balance is" + balance;
    } else {
      customerBalance = "no enough fund to withdraw" + amount;
    }
    return customerBalance;
  }
  public String toString () {
    return (" the account number for the customer " +
        customer_name + " is " + accountNumber +
        " and the balance is " + balance);
  }
}
```

1.3.2 Objects

An object is an individual element of the class, i.e., an instance of the class. In Java, objects and instances are used interchangeably; there can be any number of objects of a given class in computer memory at any one time.

The data (i.e., information) is associated with, or defines, the attributes or properties of the object. These attributes represent the state of the object during its lifetime. Since an object is an instance of a class, we call these kinds of variables instance variables.

You may have noticed that the BankAccount class does not have a main method. This is because it is not a complete application; it is just a blueprint for the BankAccount class that might be used in an application. The responsibility of creating and using new BankAccount objects belongs to some other class in the application. In this case, the TestingBankAccount class is taking care of creating BankAccount objects. The code for the TestingBankAccount is shown in Listing 1.8.

Listing 1.8 TestingBankAccount class for creating and testing BankAccount objects.

```java
public class TestingBankAccount {
  BankAccount anAccount;
  public void test1() {
    BankAccount myDefaultAccount = new BankAccount();
    System.out.println(myDefaultAccount);
  }
  public void test2() {
    BankAccount myNonEmptyAccount = new BankAccount(
        "123", "AR Yunis", 100);
    System.out.println(myNonEmptyAccount);
  }
  public static void main (String args[]) {
    TestingBankAccount testingAccount = new
        TestingBankAccount();
    testingAccount.test1();
    testingAccount.test2();
  }
}
```

The code snippet below shows two methods, test1() and test2(), from the TestingBankAccount class. In each method, a BankAccount object has been created. In the first one, the object is called *myDefaultAccount*, and in the second one, the object is called *myNonEmptyAccount*. Both objects are created by calling the constructor method of the BankAccount class. See the code snippet below; the object creation calls are highlighted in boldface font.

```java
  public void test1() {
    BankAccount myDefaultAccount = new BankAccount();
    System.out.println(myDefaultAccount);
  }
  public void test2() {
    BankAccount myNonEmptyAccount = new BankAccount(
        "123", "AR Yunis", 100);
    System.out.println(myNonEmptyAccount);
  }
}
```

The *new* operator is used to instantiate the class objects. In both test methods, the newly created objects are passed to the System.out.println for printing. During instantiation, the following processes take place:

- A chunk of computer memory gets allocated to the newly instantiated object.
- A reference to the newly allocated memory is returned.
- Object constructor is invoked.

The *new* operator takes only one parameter, a call to the class constructor. The name of the constructor is the name of the class to instantiate. Once a reference to the newly created object is returned, the reference is usually assigned to a variable of the proper type for further use.

The BankAccount class created above has two constructors. You can recognize a constructor easily because its declaration uses the same name as the class and the constructor method has no return type. When we run the code, you get the following:

```
javaReview.BankAccount@7852e922
javaReview.BankAccount@4e25154f
```

The output of the above print method is not very meaningful. This is because we have not defined how the object should look like when we print the objects. To do so, you need to override the *toString* method that BankAccount has inherited from the Object class, the top class in the Java class hierarchy. We will provide more information about the properties of the Object class and the inheritance mechanism in later sections. Here is an example of toString() method implementation.

```
public String toString() {
    return (" the account number for the customer " +
        customer_name + " is " + accountNumber +
        " and the balance is " + balance);
}
```

After adding the toString() method to the BankAccount class and re-running the code, we get the following two meaningful outputs.

the account number for the customer is and the balance is 0.0
the account number for the customer AR Yunis is 123 and the balance is 100.0

As expected, the first object has no value for its attributes, and all three attributes for the second object are initialized.

1.3.2.1   Do It Yourself

1. Using any Java IDE, for example, Eclipse, write the BankAccount and TestBankAccount code, and then compile and run the code.
2. Make modifications to the code gradually, and after each change, compile and run the code until you feel you are fluent with class and object concepts.

3. Add two more properties to the BankAccount class and update the toString method to print the properties that have been added.
4. Add two more test cases to the TestBankAccount class for testing the new properties and the toString method.

1.3.3   Interfaces

The Java interface forms the object's *view* to the outside world. It enables other classes and applications to interact with an object without knowing its internal implementation. To define an interface, you use the keyword *interface* and include one or more methods that represent the object's behavior in the interface's definition. The methods will not have a body but only signatures, i.e., name and parameter list.

Like classes, in Java, an interface is a type. However, the interface can only have the following variable modifiers and method information:

1. Constants
2. Method signatures
3. Default methods, introduced in Java 8
4. Static methods
5. Nested types

Default methods and static methods are the only ones that have method bodies. You cannot instantiate an interface; it can only be *implemented* by classes or *extended* by other interfaces. The code snippet in Listing 1.9 is an example of the interface declaration:

Listing 1.9 An example of an interface declaration is called RemoteControl.

```
public interface RemoteControl {
   int turnOn();
   int turnOff();
   int increaseVolume (double value);
   int decreaseVolume (double valu);
   int changeChannel (int chanelNumber);
   int pressTVMenu();
}
```

Note that the method declaration, i.e., the method signature, has no method body braces; instead, they are ended with a semicolon. An interface declaration consists of modifiers (e.g., public, private, protected), the keyword interface, the interface name, and the interface body. If your interface extends other interfaces, then a comma-separated list of other interfaces will be included in the interface declaration. See the code snippet in Listing 1.10 where *MultiInterface* extends three interfaces.

Listing 1.10 An example of interface extending other interfaces.

```
public interface MultiInterface extends FirstInterface,
SecondInterface, ThirdInterface {
    final double pi = 3.14;
    public void doingSomething ();
    public int doingAnotherThing();
}
```

Defining your interface as public says that the interface can be accessed by any class in any package interested to use the interface. If you do not specify any access specifier, then your interface will have default access, and it will be accessible only to classes defined in the same package where the interface is defined.

An interface can extend other interfaces, just as a class can subclass or extend another class. However, there is a difference between the two. While a Java class can extend only one other class, an interface extension is not limited to one. An interface can extend multiple other interfaces.

To use an interface, you write a class that *implements* the interface like this:

```
Public class operateSamsungTV implements RemoteControl {...}.
```

When a non-abstract class implements an interface, it provides a method body for each of the methods declared in the interface. For example, in the code snippet of Listing 1.11, a dummy implementation for each method of the RemoteControl interface is provided.

Listing 1.11 An example of a class implementing an interface

```
public class MySamsungTV implements RemoteControl {
    public int turnOn() {return 0;}
    public int turnOff() {return 0;}
    public double increaseVolume (double value) {return 0;}
    public double decreaseVolume (double valu) {return 0;}
    public int changeChannel (int chanelNumber) {return 0;}
    public int [] pressTVMenu() {return null ; }
}
```

1.3.3.1   Do It Yourself

Implement a SonyTV class to simulate Sony TV operations. To do so, you need to write code, i.e., the signature body, for all the methods included in the RemoteControl interface.

1.3.4   Package

A package is a way to organize your source code and other components of your application properly. It is done by saving related classes and interfaces together in separate folders. Conceptually, you can think of packages as folders for different components of your application. For example, for a Web application, you might keep all HTML pages, images, scripts, data, and source code in separate folders. Because application code can be composed of many individual classes, it is good practice to keep things organized by placing related code, classes, and interfaces into packages. For example, Java API has a separate package for file I/O classes, util classes, gui classes, security classes, network classes, etc.

The first line in any Java source code file should be the package statement. As shown below, for our BankAccount class, a package has been created and is called JavaReview:

```
package javaReview;
```

1.3.5   Inheritance

The Java programming language supports inheritance, that is, classes can be *derived* or subclassed from other classes, *inheriting* data fields, methods, and nested classes from their superclasses. Except for the Object class, which has no superclass, in Java, every class has one and only one direct superclass. This is because Java supports only single inheritance, different from, for example, C++, which supports multiple inheritances. If no superclass is explicitly declared for a class, then the class becomes a subclass of the Object class.

A class can be derived from classes that are subclasses of other classes which in turn are subclasses of other classes and so on which are derived from the topmost class in the Java class hierarchy, the Object class. Such a class is said to be a child of all the classes in the inheritance chain, stretching back to the Object class.

A subclass inherits all the *members*, properties, and behavior from its superclass. Constructors are not class members, so they are not inherited by subclasses. For the constructor of the superclass to be invoked from the subclass, the subclass must use the keyword *super* in front of the constructor's name, e.g., **Super.contructorName ("list of parameters, if any");**

The most general or *generic* class in Java is the Object class, the topmost class in the Java class hierarchy. Classes near the bottom of the Java class hierarchy are *specialized* classes; they are created to provide more specific or custom behavior.

1.3.6 Inheritance Example

Let us define two classes, the Employee and Manager classes. The first one is a base class, and the second one is a subclass of the Employee class. The class definitions are shown in Listings 1.12 and 1.13:

Listing 1.12 Defining a base class called Employee.

```java
public class Employee {
  String name;
  String department;
  int PRINumber ;
  public Employee (String name,
      String department, int pRINumber) {
    super () ;
    this.name = name;
    this.department = department;
    PRINumber = pRINumber;
  }
  public String getName () {
    return name;
  }
  public void setName (String name) {
    this.name = name;
  }
  public String getDepartment () {
    return department;
  }
  public void setDepartment (String department) {
    this.department = department;
  }
  public int getPRINumber () {
    return PRINumber;
  }
  public void setPRINumber (int pRINumber) {
    PRINumber = pRINumber;
  }
}
```

A class declaration for a *Manager* class that is a subclass of an *Employee* class might look like Listing 1.13:

Listing 1.13 An Employee subclass definition called Manager class.

```java
public class Manager extends Employee {
  int numberOfTeams ;
  public Manager (String name, String department,
      int pRINumber, int numberOfTeams) {
    super (name, department, pRINumber) ;
```

```
      this.numberOfTeams = numberOfTeams;
   }
   public int getNumberOfTeams() {
      return numberOfTeams;
   }
   public void setNumberOfTeams(int numberOfTeams) {
      this.numberOfTeams = numberOfTeams;   }
}
```

The Manager class inherits all the fields and methods of the Employee class. A new field called *numberOfTeams* has been added along with a new method to set the numberOfTeams. Except for the constructor, it is as if you had written a new class from scratch with four fields and five methods. Thanks to inheritance, you don't have to do all the work.

Not having to re-write an entirely new class from scratch would be especially valuable if the methods in the Employee class were complex and had taken substantial time to create, test, and debug.

Java inheritance enables a powerful programming technique called polymorphism which is described next section.

1.3.7   Polymorphism

Polymorphism is the ability of a method to do different tasks based on the object that it is operating on. In other words, polymorphism allows you to define one interface of an object and have multiple implementations of the same object. Polymorphism can be explained with a minor modification to the Employee class. For example, a *printDescription* method could be added to the class to display all the data currently stored in an Employee instance. The Employee print method would be as follows:

```
public String printDescription () {
   return "Employee [name=" + name + ", department=" + department + ",
   PRINumber=" + PRINumber + "]";
}
```

After adding the **printDescription** method, the new definition of the Employee class is shown in Listing 1.14:

Listing 1.14 New Employee class with printDescription method.

```java
package javaReview;
  public class Employee {
    String name;
    String department;
    int PRINumber ;
    public Employee (String name,
             String department, int pRINumber) {
      super ();
      this.name = name;
      this.department = department;
      PRINumber = pRINumber;
    }
    public String getName () {
      return name;
    }
    public void setName (String name) {
      this.name = name;
    }
    public String getDepartment () {
      return department;
    }
    public void setDepartment (String department) {
      this.department = department;
    }
    public int getPRINumber () {
      return PRINumber;
    }
    public void setPRINumber (int pRINumber) {
      PRINumber = pRINumber;
    }
    public String printDescription () {
      return ("Employee [name=" + name + ", " + "department=" +
        department + ", " + "PRINumber=" + PRINumber + "]");
  }
}
```

To demonstrate polymorphic features in the Java language, we create two new classes, Manager and TeamLeader, that extend the Employee class. Each of the newly created classes has its customized print method. For the *printDescription* method in the Manager class, we add a field called *numberOfTeams*. The numberOfTeams field would have an int value indicating how many teams a Manager is managing now. See the Manager class definition in Listing 1.15:

```java
package javaReview;
public class Manager extends Employee {
int numberOfTeams ;
  public Manager (String name, String department, int pRINumber,
           int numberOfTeams) {
    super (name, department, pRINumber);
    this.numberOfTeams = numberOfTeams;
  }
  public int getNumberOfTeams() {
    return numberOfTeams;
  }
  public void setNumberOfTeams(int numberOfTeams) {
    this.numberOfTeams = numberOfTeams;
  }
  @Override
  public String printDescription () {
    return ("Manager [numberOfTeams= " + numberOfTeams +
      ", " + super.printDescription() + "]");
  }
}
```

Note that in addition to the original information included in the printDescription method, additional data about the numberOfTeams is included in the printDescription method of the Manager class.

Next, we create another class called the *TeamLeader* class, and we add an attribute, *numberofEmployee*, that indicates the number of employees a team leader supervises. The TeamLeader class definition is shown in Listing 1.16:

Listing 1.16 An Employee subclass definition called TeamLeader class.

```java
package javaReview;

public class TeamLeader extends Employee {
        int numberOfEmployee;
        public TeamLeader(String name, String department,
                   int pRINumber, int numberOfEmployee) {
                super (name, department, pRINumber);
                this.numberOfEmployee = numberOfEmployee;
        }
        public int getNumberOfEmployee() {
                 return numberOfEmployee;
        }
        public void setNumberOfEmployee(int numberOfEmployee) {
                this.numberOfEmployee = numberOfEmployee;
        }
```

```
    @Override
    public String printDescription() {
    return ("TeamLeader [numberOfEmployee= " +
        numberOfEmployee + ", " + super.printDescription());
    }
}
```

Note that again the printDescription method has been customized. This time, information about the *numberOfEmployee* in the team is included in the printDescription method for the display.

To summarize, we now have three classes: Employee, Manager, and TeamLeader. Some properties are common to all three classes, but the two subclasses override the printDescription method to display unique information relevant to their customized properties. The TestEmployee program shown in Listing 1.17 creates three Employee objects – one for each class; then each object is printed.

Listing 1.17 The main class to create and print Employee objects.

```
package javaReview;

public class TestEmployee {
  public static void main (String args[]) {
    Employee employee1 = new Employee  ("AR yunis","BI", 123456 ) ;
    Employee employee2 = new Manager   ("AR yunis","BI", 123456, 5 ) ;
    Employee employee3 = new TeamLeader ("AR yunis","BI", 123456, 12 ) ;

Employee comapnyEmployees [] = {employee1, employee2, employee3} ;
for (Employee emp : comapnyEmployees) {
  System.out.println (emp.printDescription());
 }
 }
}
```

The following is the test result from the test program:

```
Employee [name=AR yunis, department=BI, PRINumber=123456]
Manager [numberOfTeams= 5, Employee [name=AR yunis, department=BI,
        PRINumber=123456]]
TeamLeader [numberOfEmployee= 12, Employee [name=AR yunis,
        department=BI, PRINumber=123456]
```

Note that the type of all three variables, employee1, 2, and 3, is Employee, yet the Java virtual machine (JVM) finds and calls a suitable printDescription method at runtime for the actual objects instantiated which are Employee, Manager, and TeamLeader, respectively. This behavior, i.e., recognizing the object's customized printDescription at runtime, is the polymorphism feature in the Java language.

1.3.7.1 Do It Yourself

1. To practice inheritance and polymorphism, rebuild the example above. Create four Java classes: Employee, Manager, TeamLeader, and TestEmployee. Make both the Manager and the TeamLeader extend the Employee class as described above. Use the Test class to test the printDescription method. Compile and run your code. You should have results like the output listed above.
2. Create a new project called Students to include information about Student, GraduateStudent, UnderGraduateStudent, FulltimeStudent, and ParttimeStudent. Utilize inheritance to minimize code writing and compile, run, and test your code to become more familiar with Java inheritance.

1.3.8 Hiding Fields

Within a subclass, if a field has the same name as a field in the superclass, then the subclass hides the superclass's field. This field hiding happens even if field types of super- and subclasses are different. Thus, within the subclass, the fields in the superclass cannot be referenced simply by their names. Instead, to reference fields from the superclass, the keyword super should precede the field name. The use of the keyword "super" is covered below in detail. You can also use "super" to refer to the superclass field that has not been overwritten in the subclass. Even though we can access the superclass's hidden fields, generally speaking, hiding fields is not recommended as it makes code difficult to read. To avoid hidden fields, name fields in sub- and superclasses uniquely.

1.3.9 Using the Keyword Super

If your method overrides one of its superclass's methods, then you can call the overridden method from the superclass using the keyword "super." See the examples in Listings 1.18 and 1.19:

Listing 1.18 A base class definition.

```
public class SuperClass_A {
 public void print () {
   System.out.println ( "printing inside superclass A");
  }
}
```

Listing 1.19 A subclass definition uses a super keyword to call the superclass.

```java
public class SubClass_B extends SuperClass_A {
  @Override
  public void print () {
        super.print ();
        System.out.println ("printing inside sub class B");
  }
  public static void main (String args []) {
        SubClass_B b = new SubClass_B ().print ();
   }
}
```

In Listing 1.19, a new class called subclass_B is created. It extends SuperClass_A and overrides the print method. Within subclass_B, the name print () refers to the method declared in the subclass which overrides the one in the superclass. This is normal, and nothing is new here. However, to refer to, or reference, the print () method inherited from the superclass, the subclass must use the "*super*" keyword. The call to the superclass print method, super.print(), is highlighted in bold in the subclass_B method. Compiling and running the subclass_B prints the following output:

printing inside superclass A
printing inside subclass B

1.3.10   Subclass Constructors

In the example below, we illustrate how to use the *super* keyword to call a superclass's *constructor*. We use the *Manager* and the *Employee* classes for this example; we have already defined earlier that the Manager class is a subclass of the Employee class. Here, the Manager constructor calls the superclass constructor first and then initializes its field, **numberOfTeams.**

```java
public Manager (String name, String department, int pRINumber,
        int numberOfTeams) {
    super (name, department, pRINumber);
    this.numberOfTeams = numberOfTeams;
}
```

Calling or invoking a superclass constructor must be the first line in the subclass constructor. The syntax for calling a superclass constructor is either *super();* or *super (parameter list);* depending on whether the superclass constructor takes parameters or not. With super(), the superclass's no-argument constructor is called. With super (parameter list), the superclass's constructor with a matching parameter list is called.

If a constructor in a subclass does not explicitly call a superclass constructor, the Java compiler automatically inserts a call to the *default constructor* (also called the no-argument constructor) of the superclass. This automatic call to the default constructor could be problematic. If the superclass does not have a *no-argument constructor*, then you will get a compile-time error saying *Object does not have such a constructor.*

When a subclass constructor calls a constructor of its superclass, either explicitly or implicitly, there will be a whole chain of constructor calls going all the way back to the constructor of the Object class on the top of the Java class hierarchy; this is called constructor chaining. When a constructor chain happens, the code performance might degrade. When coding, you need to be aware of the impact of constructor chaining calls and try to avoid it. To do so, you need to avoid a long line of class descent.

1.3.11   Using Preserved Keyword "this"

When the preserved keyword "*this*" is used inside a class constructor or any other methods of the class, it means the current class in use. You can refer to any instance variable or method of the object in use using the "*this*" operator. The most common reason for using the "*this*" keyword is to remove ambiguity. For example, the *PressButton* class can be written as shown in Listing 1.20. However, the code would be more clear if it had been written in the way shown in Listing 1.21 where the "*this*" keyword is used.

Listing 1.20 A class definition with no clear constructor definition.

```
public class PressButton {
  int width;
  int height;
  public PressButton(int height, int width) {
   super();
   height = height;
   width = width;
  }
}
```

Listing 1.21 A class definition that uses the "this" keyword to differentiate between incoming arguments and class fields.

```java
public class PressButton {
  int width;
  int height;
  public PressButton(int height, int width) {
    super();
    this.height = height;
    this.width = width;
  }
}
```

Arguments passed to the constructor can be used to set values of an object's fields. For example, inside the constructor of Listing 1.21, height is a local copy variable. To refer to the PressButton class field height, the constructor is using *this.height.*

1.3.11.1   Using this with a Constructor

Inside a class constructor, you can also use "this" keyword to call another constructor in the same class. In Listing 1.22, the *MyButton* class uses "*this*" inside the default and two-parameter constructors to explicitly invoke a constructor that has four parameters.

Listing 1.22 Using this keyword to call other constructors in the class.

```java
public class MyButton {
  int height, width, margin;
  String label;
  public MyButton () {
    this (1, 1, 0, null);
  }
  public MyButton (int margin, String label) {
    this (1, 1, margin, label);
  }
  public MyButton (int height, int width, int margin, String label) {
    super ();
    this.height = height;
    this.width = width;
    this.margin = margin;
    this.label = label;
  }
}
```

If you pay close attention to the *MyButton* class in Listing 1.22, you can see that the *MyButton* class has three different constructors. Each constructor initializes some, or all, of MyButton's fields. For example, when the *default constructor*, or non-argument constructor, is called, no parameters are passed. Yet, two out of four fields of the class are given initial values of 1, and the other two fields are given zero and null values, respectively. Thus, a call to the default constructor creates a *MyButton* object with no labels and zero margins using **this (1, 1, 0, null);**.

The constructor with two arguments, on the other hand, calls the four-argument constructor, passing values to both the margin and label fields. Inside the constructor, the values (1,1) are used to initialize the other two fields using **this (1, 1, margin, label);**. Based on the number and the type of arguments, the compiler determines which constructor to call, and if you need to call a constructor inside a constructor, it must be the first line in the constructor.

Note that both the *"this"* and *"super"* operators can't be invoked within the same constructor. To do so, you need to find a way around it. For example, if constructor A uses the *"this"* operator to call constructor B, then constructor B can include the *"super"* operator in its implementation and make a call to the super constructor.

1.3.12   Java Exception Handling

When an exception happens, also called arises, the normal execution of the program stops abruptly, and the alternative piece of code can be executed. It is also possible for the program to end completely. Exceptions are said to be thrown, or raised, at the point of program interruptions and are said to be handled, or caught, at the point when normal program execution proceeds. There are two types of exceptions in Java, checked and unchecked exceptions.

Checked exceptions—is a list of classes that are defined in the Java SDK to handle situations that can cause trouble in normal program execution. These situations are known to the compiler and are checked during code compilation. For example, you may be given an incorrect path to the file that your program is supposed to read, or the file has been removed. Java designers predicted such situations and have a class, file not found exception class, to check for such situations. The Java compiler checks your program during compilation time to find out if you either catch or re-throw the exceptions. The checked class exceptions are subclasses of the Java class Exception, but their parent class is not RuntimeException.

Unchecked exceptions—is a list of classes that are defined in the Java SDK that represent all types of errors your program can encounter; you need to account for these errors to prevent them from happening. The compiler does not check to see that you catch/handle these types of exceptions. For example, the number format exception and division by zero exception are exceptions only checked at runtime and not during the compilation time. It is your responsibility to handle these types of exceptions through proper programming, design, and testing. In addition to the exceptions already defined by the Java language, programmers may create their exception classes by extending Java-provided exception classes.

1.3.12.1 The Try-Catch-Finally Block

Java uses the try, catch, and finally keywords to handle exceptions; the format is shown in the code snippet below. The first catch block has an exception of type *ExceptionTypeX*. If the type of exception thrown in the try block matches *ExceptionTypeX*, it will be executed, and the other catch blocks will be skipped. The finally block is optional and is executed whether an exception is thrown or not.

```
try {
    // program statements
  } catch (ExceptionTypeX exception) {
    // program statements to handle exceptions of type X or any of its
    // subclasses
  } . . . // other catch clauses
  } catch (ExceptionTypeN exception) {
    // program statements to handle exceptions of type N or any of its
    // subclasses
  } finally {
/* executed after the try block or a catch block has been executed. It will
execute whether an exception is thrown or not. */
}
```

1.3.13 Generic Types

To enable class definition reuse, the generics technique enables classes, interfaces, and methods definitions to be parameterized. Just like the way *parameters* are used in the method declarations, the generic structure enables parameters to be used in the class definition. When using generic types, however, the parameters are types or classes and not the values which is the case when passing parameters to methods. The following simple Material class, Listing 1.23, which seems to be a generic class because of the use of the Object type as a parameter, will be changed to show the true generic concept, Listing 1.24.

1.3.13.1 A Simple Material Class

Let us begin by examining a class called Material that works with objects of Solid, Liquid, and Air types; see Listing 1.23.

Listing 1.23 A Java class called Material use properties of type Object to implement generic behavior.

```
public class Material {
  private Object object;
  public Object getObject() {
  return object;
}
  public void setObject(Object object) {
    this.object = object;
  }
}
```

Since the Material methods accept/return the Object type, any object can be passed to the Material class methods without issue during code compilation. This is because the Object type is a superclass for all types and any class is a subclass of the Object class. However, inconsistent use of the Material class could lead to a disaster at runtime, i.e., when it means different things at different parts of the code. For example, a Solid object in one part of the code is treated as a Liquid or Air object in other parts of the code.

1.3.13.2   A Generic Version of the Material Class

The solution to the runtime error that might happen using the above naive generic structure is to use true generic class definition and type parameters. The generic *class* definition format is like this:

```
class name <T1, T2, ..., Tn> {/* ... */}
```

The type parameters are enclosed inside angle brackets (<>) and follow the class name. The angle brackets, <>, are also called a *diamond*. T stands for the *type parameters*, sometimes called *type variables*, T1, T2, ..., and Tn. To turn the Material class listed in 1.23 into a generics class, you need to use a generic type declaration. That is, you need to change:

```
public class Material {} to public class Material <T> {}
```

The type variable T is introduced, and it can be used anywhere inside the class. The new definition of the Material class is shown in Listing 1.24:

Listing 1.24 A generic version of Material class.

```
public class Material <T> {
  // T stands for "Type"
  private T mtype ;
  public void set (T mtype) {this.mtype = mtype ; }
  public T get () {return mtype; }
}
```

As you can see, all occurrences of objects are now replaced by T. The parameter T can be of any type you want to pass, except the *non-primitive* ones, i.e., T can be any class or interface or another T variable you would like to pass. The generic structure is not limited to the class. The same technique can be applied to create generic interfaces.

1.3.14   Type Parameter Naming Conventions

The type parameter names used with the generic class definition are single uppercase letters. This is contradictory to the Java variable naming convention which suggests using lowercase and meaningful names. Nonetheless, the single uppercase letter convention has been accepted and used widely by developers.

The extensively used type parameter names are E, K, N, T, V, S, and U. The E type parameter is used with the collections and represents collection elements; K is used for keys, N for numbers, T for types, and V for values; and S and U are used for the second and third type parameters.

1.3.14.1   Calling and Instantiating a Generic Type

To use the generic Material class from within an application code, you must perform a *generic type call*, which means replacing T with a concrete type, e.g., Solid material, and it will be declared like this: **Material <Solid> marble;**

The statement above does not create a new Material object yet. It simply declares that a marble variable will hold a "Solid" type of Material. To instantiate an object of Solid type, you need to use the usual *new* keyword and place <Solid> between the class name and the parenthesis at the end. Here is an example:

```
Material <Solid> marble = new Material <Solid> ();
```

In Java SE 7 and later, empty diamond <> can be used instead of <T> if a compiler can infer the argument type from the context using an empty diamond. For example, you can create an instance of Material <Air> like this:

```
Material <Air> air = new Material <> ();
```

1.3.14.2 Multiple Type Parameters

A generic class can have one or more parameters. For example, in Listing 1.25, the generic *PeriodicTable* class, which implements the *Elements* interface, has two parameters:

Listing 1.25 Implementing Periodic Table as a generic class.

```java
public interface Elements<K, V> {
  public K getElementKey();
  public V getElementValue();
}
public class PeriodicTable <K,V> implements Elements <K, V> {
  private K aKey;
  private V aValue;
  public PeriodicTable(K key, V value) {
    this.aKey = key;
    this.aValue = value ;
  }
  public K getaKey()  { return aKey; }
  public V getValue() { return aValue ; }
}
```

The following statements create two objects of the PeriodicTable class:

```java
PeriodicTable <String, Integer> AluminiumAtomicNumber =
        new PeriodicTable <String, Integer> ("Al-uminium ", 13);
PeriodicTable <String, String> AluminiumSymbol =
        new PeriodicTable <String, String> ("Aluminium", "AI");
```

The code, new PeriodicTable <String, Integer>, instantiates a new object with K as a String and V as an Integer. Due to *autoboxing*, it is valid to pass a hard-coded String such as "Aluminium" and an *int* primitive value to the class constructor that expects String and Integer objects.

1.3.15 Autoboxing

Autoboxing is about changing Java primitive types to their corresponding Java objects. The conversion, or the change, is done automatically at runtime by the Java compiler. For example, if you pass int when Integer is expected, the compiler automatically generates an Integer type for the int you pass; similar conversion is done by the compiler for other primitive types when needed. An example of autoboxing is shown in Listing 1.26. An int and a hard-coded String are passed to the class constructor to instantiate objects. Due to autoboxing, these values are changed to their corresponding objects, and proper objects are instantiated.

Listing 1.26 Using this keyword to call other constructors in the class.

```java
public class PeriodicTable <K,V> implements Elements <K, V> {
  private K key;
  private V value;

  public PeriodicTable (K key, V value) {
    this.key = key; this.value = value;
  }
  public K getKey () { return key ; }
  public V getValue () { return value ; }

  public static void main (String args) {
      PeriodicTable <String, Integer>elementKeyValue =
             new PeriodicTable <String, Integer>(args, null);

    PeriodicTable <String, String> PotassiumSymbol =
       new PeriodicTable <String, String> ("Potassium", "K");

    PeriodicTable <String, Integer> PotassiumAtomicNumber =
       new PeriodicTable <String, Integer> ("Potassium", 9);

    PeriodicTable <String, Material<Solid>> aSolidMaterial =
       new PeriodicTable <> ("new Material", new Material<Solid> ());
  }
}
```

The above PeriodicTable<String, Integer> statements can be shortened using diamond notation as follows:

```java
PeriodicTable<String, Integer> PotassiumAtomicNumber = new
                   PeriodicTable <> ("Potassium", 9);
PeriodicTable<String, String> PotassiumSymbol=new
                   PeriodicTable <> ("Potassium", "K");
```

This is because the Java compiler can infer the K and V types from the declaration PeriodicTable<String, Integer>. To create a generic interface, follow the same conventions as for creating a generic class.

1.3.16 Parameterized Types

It is also possible to substitute a type parameter such as K or V with a parameterized type such as List<String> or Material<Solid>. That is, instead of K being String, it can be List<String>, and instead of V being integer, it can be ArrayList<Integer>. In this case, for example, using the PeriodicTable<K, V> for Material<Solid> would be:

```
PeriodicTable <String, Material<Solid>> solidMateral = new
PeriodicTable <> ("Solid Material", new Material<Solid> ());
```

Here, the String "Solid Material" and parametrized type "Material<Solid>" are passed to the K and V values in PeriodicTable generic type.

1.3.17 Anonymous Classes

Sometimes you need to create a class that is only going to be used once. In this case, you don't need to create a file for the class which keeps the code concise. If you need to use a class only once, the anonymous class is the answer. Anonymous class expressions allow you to declare and instantiate a class at the same time. They are similar to regular Java classes except that the class does not have a name.

1.3.17.1 Declaring Anonymous Classes

While regular classes are declared, anonymous classes are *expressions* created on the fly, which means that you define the class in an expression. Listing 1.27, the *AnonymousClassExample*, uses anonymous classes to compute the area for the *rectangle* and *square* classes but uses the local *inner class* to compute the area of the *circle* class.

Listing 1.27 An example of an anonymous class.

```
public class AnonymousClassExample {

    interface ComputeAreaForGeometricShapes {
      public void computeArea (double a, double b) ;
      public void printArea (String shape);
    }
      public void computeAreaForDifferentShapes () {

      class CircleShape implements ComputeAreaForGeometricShapes {
        String name = "Circle Area is ";
```

```java
        public void computeArea(double a, double b) {
          printArea(name + (a * (b*b)) + " unit");
        }
        public void printArea(String shape) {
          System.out.println( shape);
        }
    }
    ComputeAreaForGeometricShapes circle = new CircleShape();

    ComputeAreaForGeometricShapes rectangle =
          new ComputeAreaForGeometricShapes() {
        String name = "Rectangle area is ";
        public void computeArea(double a, double b) {
          printArea(name + (a*b) + " units" );
        }
        public void printArea(String shape) {
          System.out.println(shape);
        }
    };
    ComputeAreaForGeometricShapes squar =
                new ComputeAreaForGeometricShapes() {
        String name = "Squar area is ";
        public void computeArea(double a, double b) {
          printArea(name + (a*a) + " units ");
        }
        public void printArea(String shape) {
          System.out.println(shape );
        }
    };
    // call computeArea on three different objects:
    circle.computeArea (3.14, 4) ;
    rectangle.computeArea (3.14, 4) ;
    squar.computeArea (3.14, 4) ;
  }
  public static void main (String... args) {
    AnonymousClassExample anonymousClassExample =
      new AnonymousClassExample();
    anonymousClassExample.computeAreaForDifferentShapes();
  }
}
```

1.3.17.2 Syntax of Anonymous Classes

As mentioned earlier, an anonymous class is an expression that is written like this: new() {...}. You use the new operator and call a class constructor, and you also pass a block of code, a class definition, to the constructor. See the instantiation of the square object in Listing 1.28. The definition of the two methods and the String "square area is" are contained in curly brackets after the expression *new ComputeAreaForGeometricShapes ().*

Listing 1.28 Creating an anonymous class without using a regular class definition and saving it in a file.

```
ComputeAreaForGeometricShapes squar = new Shapes () {
String name = "Squar area is ";

public void computeArea(double a, double b) {
    printArea(name + (a * a) + " units ");
}
  public void printArea(String shape) {
    System.out.println(shape);
  }
};
```

1.3.18   Object Serialization

Java allows you to save an object's state to a file, i.e., to serialize an object. When the object's state needs to be saved for feature retrieval, the object's data is converted into a series of bytes and saved in a file on your machine or other medians. If the object you are trying to save is set up correctly, the other objects that it contains as fields are serialized automatically as well.

There are several situations when object serialization can be used. For example, serialization is used when you want an object to persist, i.e., the value of the object's instance variable can be restored after turning off the Java virtual machine (JVM). It is also used by RMI (Remote Method Invocation) to pass objects between connected machines in a network. In this case, objects are passed either as method arguments or return values from a method invocation. The RMI is an API that acts as a mediator to create distributed applications in Java. The RMI enables an object to call methods of another object which is running in another JVM on a remote computer. In general, serialization is used when you want the object to exist, not only in computer memory but even when JVM is turned off. More information on how to serialize an object is provided below.

1.3.18.1   Serializable Interface

To be able to serialize an object, its class must implement the Serializable interface. The Serializable interface is empty; it has no methods or fields. The interface's sole purpose is to tell the Java compiler that objects of the class might be serialized. If a class is a composed class, i.e., has objects of other classes as an instance variable, those filed variables must also implement the Serializable interface to be serialized.

1.3.18.2   Serialize an Object

To write a serialized object to a file, you need to use an ObjectOutputStream class. This class is designed to enable the serialization process. To write the bytes to a file, a FileOutputStream object is needed as well. How to use these two classes is shown below:

```
FileOutputStream fileOutStream ;
ObjectOutputStream objOutStm =
   new ObjectOutputStream(fileOutStream);
```

To serialize an object and write it to the file, the writeObject() method from class *ObjectOutputStream* is used. Here is an example of how to use the writeObject method:

```
StoreInventory item = new StoreInventory("char", 120);
objOutputFile.writeObject(item);
```

Note that the writeObject method used in the code snippet above throws an IOException which needs to be handled.

1.3.18.3   Deserialize an Object

As you may guess correctly, the deserialization process is the opposite of the serialization process. The process of reading a serialized object's bytes and constructing an object from them is known as deserialization. To deserialize an object, an ObjectInputStream object is used along with a FileInputStream object as follows:

```
FileInputStream inStream = new FileInputStream("Objects.dat");
   ObjectInputStream objtInputFile =
                new ObjectInputStream(inStream);
```

To read a serialized object from the file, the readObject() method from the class *ObjectInputStream* is used as follows:

```
StoreInventory item = (StoreInventory) objtInputFile.readObject();
```

The *readObject()* method returns the deserialized object which you need to cast to a proper class type. The *readObject()* method throws several different exceptions if an error occurs.

1.3.18.4   Code Example

Let us look at a complete object serialization example. In the following sections, we will create an object, serialize it, write it to a file, read the objects back from the file, and recreate the objects in the memory.

The *StoreInventory* class holds simple data about an item in the inventory. A description of the item is stored in the *description* field, and the number of units on hand is stored in the *unit's* field. An example of an inventory item class is shown in Listing 1.29:

Listing 1.29 A simple item inventory class.

```java
public class StoreInventory implements Serializable {
    String itemName ;
    int itemNumber;
    String description;
    public StoreInventory() {
        super();
    }
    public StoreInventory(
    String itemName, int itemNumber, String description) {
        this.itemName = itemName;
        this.itemNumber = itemNumber;
        this.description = description;
    }
    public StoreInventory(String description) {
        super();
        this.description = description;
    }
    public StoreInventory(String description, int itemNumber) {
        super();
        this.description = description;
        this.itemNumber = itemNumber;
    }
    public String getDescription() {
        return description;
    }
    public void setDescription(String description) {
        this.description = description;
    }
    public int getItemNumber() {
        return itemNumber;
    }
    public void setItemNumber(int itemNumber) {
        this.itemNumber = itemNumber;
    }
    public String getItemName() {
        return itemName;
    }
    public void setItemName(String itemName) {
        this.itemName = itemName;
    }
}
```

1.3.18.5   Example of Serializing an Object

Once you create an object that you would like to serialize, the next step is to write the object to a file for future retrieval. Class SerializeObjects, shown in Listing 1.30, serializes the objects in an array. The array elements are of the type StoreInventory.

Listing 1.30 Object serialization steps.

```java
package javaReview;
import java.io.FileNotFoundException;
import java.io.FileOutputStream;
import java.io.IOException;
import java.io.ObjectOutputStream;
import java.io.Serializable;
public class SerializeObjects {
        private static int NUM_ITEMS = 10;
        private static String description ="";
        private static   int units = 0;;
        public static void main(String[] args) {
           FileOutputStream outStream;
           StoreInventory[] instoreIems ;
           try {
              instoreIems = new StoreInventory[NUM_ITEMS];
              for (int i = 0; i < instoreIems.length; i++) {
              instoreIems[i] = new StoreInventory("item" + i, i);
           }
           outStream = new FileOutputStream("Objects.dat");
           ObjectOutputStream objectOutputFile =
                new ObjectOutputStream(outStream);
                   for (int i = 0; i < instoreIems.length; i++) {
              objectOutputFile.writeObject(instoreIems[i]);
           }
                ObjectOutputStream objOutputFile =
                     new ObjectOutputStream(outStream);
                StoreInventory item = new StoreInventory("char", 120);
                objOutputFile.writeObject(item);
                System.out.println ("serialized") ;
           outStream.close() ;
           objectOutputFile.close();
           } catch (FileNotFoundException e) {
             e.printStackTrace();
           } catch (IOException e) {
             e.printStackTrace();
           }
        }
     }
```

1.3.18.6   Example of Deserializing an Object

There are steps you need to follow to read a serialized object from the file. An example of these steps is included in the DeserializeObjects class; see Listing 1.31. It deserializes the objects in the Objects.dat file, recreates the object, and stores them in an array.

Listing 1.31 Object Deserialization steps.

```java
package javaReview;
import java.io.FileInputStream;
import java.io.ObjectInputStream;

public class DeserializeObjects {
public static void main (String [] args) throws Exception {
        final int NUM_ITEMS = 10;
        FileInputStream inStream =
        new FileInputStream("Objects.dat");
        ObjectInputStream objectInputFile =
        new ObjectInputStream(inStream);
        StoreInventory[] instoreItems =
        new StoreInventory[NUM_ITEMS];
        for (int i = 0; i < instoreItems.length; i++) {
            instoreItems[i] =
            (StoreInventory) objectInputFile.readObject();
        }
        inStream.close();
        objectInputFile.close();
        for (int i = 0; i < instoreItems.length; i++) {
                System.out.println("Item " + (i + 1));
                System.out.println(" Description: " +
                    instoreItems[i].getDescription());
                System.out.println(" Units: " +
                    instoreItems[i].getItemNumber());
        }
    }
}
```

In Android, object serialization is carried out using Parcelable objects, a subject that we cover in detail in the later chapters of this book.

1.3.19   Lambda Expressions

In a previous section, Anonymous Classes, we showed how to implement a concise class without giving it a name and its advantages. Starting with Java 8, there is another way to write concise classes. In cases where a class has only one method, you can use the Lambda expression to create a more concise class than a named class. Lambda expressions are even more compact than anonymous classes for classes that have only one method. See the code example below for how to use the Lambda expression.

Lambda is different from a class with one object. A class with one object is called a singleton class which is similar to static variables when you have only one copy of the variable shared among all the objects of the same class. Once you define a constructor to be private and allow only one object to be instantiated, then you have a singleton class. Singleton is used for controlling resources such as socket and database connections. In Listing 1.32, the class definition uses two methods to do the same thing. The methods show the difference in writing code using an anonymous class vs. the lambda expression.

Listing 1.32 Using Lambda vs. anonymous classes.

```java
public class LambdaTest {
  public void test1() {
    // Anonymous Runnable
    Runnable runnable1 = new Runnable() {
      @Override
      public void run() {
        System.out.println("Not using Lambda");
      } };
    runnable1.run();
  }
  public void test2() {
    // Lambda Runnable
    Runnable runnable2 = () -> System.out.println("Once a Lambda
        expression is" + " used, no Explicit Runnable +
        object and its run" + " method are required.");
    runnable2.run();
  }
  public static void main (String [] args) {
    System.out.println("Testing Lambda expression");
    LambdaTest atest = new LambdaTest();
    atest.test1();
    atest.test2();
  }
}
```

1.3.20   Variable Argument (Varargs)

In Java 5, a new feature, variable arguments or varargs for short, has been introduced for passing arguments to the methods of classes. Using the varargs feature, zero or multiple parameters, i.e., a variable number of parameters, can be passed to a method. In practice, this is equivalent to creating multiple methods, i.e., overloading the method, where each method has a different number of parameters. It is also similar to having a method with an array as a parameter.

The added feature is useful. It improves code maintenance since you do not have to write and maintain multiple methods; you have less code to write and maintain. It also enables developers to deal with situations when they do not know ahead of time how many arguments will have to be passed to a method.

1.3.20.1   Syntax of Varargs

To declare a method with varargs arguments, you need to use three dots after the data type, e.g., (String... variable), also called ellipsis. The method signature syntax is like this:

access modifier, return type, method name (data type ... variableName) {// method body}.

An example of how to use varargs in Java is shown in Listing 1.33.

Listing 1.33 An example using varargs in Java.

```java
public class VariableArgumentExample {
  public static void printLength(String... variable) {
    if (variable.length <= 0) {
      System.out.println(" 0 parameter passed");
    } else {
      System.out.println(variable.length + " parameters are passed" + "
          and they are: ");
      for (String s: variable) {
        System.out.print(s + " ");
      }
      System.out.println();
    }
  }
  public static void main (String args[]) {
    // same print method used over and over with need for a method
    // overloading
    VariableArgumentExample.printLength();
    VariableArgumentExample.printLength("amazing coding");
    VariableArgumentExample.printLength("1", "2");
    VariableArgumentExample.printLength("1", "2", "3");
    VariableArgumentExample.printLength("1", "2", "3", "4");
    VariableArgumentExample.printLength("1", "2", "3", "4", "5");
    VariableArgumentExample.printLength("1", "2", "3", "4", "5", "6");
    VariableArgumentExample.printLength("have you noticed" +
    "the power of varargs?");
  }
}
```

When the program is run, the program output would be as follows:

0 parameter passed

1 parameter are passed, and they are:

amazing coding

2 parameters are passed, and they are:

1 2

3 parameters are passed, and they are:

1 2 3

4 parameters are passed, and they are:

1 2 3 4

5 parameters are passed, and they are:

1 2 3 4 5

6 parameters are passed, and they are:

1 2 3 4 5 6

1 parameter are passed, and they are:

have you noticed the power of varargs?

1.3.20.2   Rules for Varargs

There are rules you must follow when using varargs to compile your program successfully. The rules are:

1. There can be only one variable argument in the method.
2. When you have multiple variables in the method, variable argument (varargs) must be the last argument.

Below are two examples when varargs will not compile:

1. void methodName (String... a, int... b) {}

Compile-time error for having *two* varargs arguments (a and b).

2. void methodName (int... a, String b) {}

Compile-time error for varargs being the first argument and not the last argument; Inside the *parenthesis int ... a* comes before *b*. In the example shown in Listing 1.34, varargs is the second parameter and receives four string values.

Listing 1.34 An example using varargs as a second parameter in the method.

```java
class VarargsTest2 {
        static void display (int num, String... values) {
                System.out.print ( num);
            for (String s : values) {
                        System.out.print (s + " ");
                }
```

```
                        System.out.println(); ;
      }
      public static void main (String args[]) {
                  display(500, " varargs is the last argument");
                  display(1000, " one", "two", "three", "four");
      }
}
```

1.4   Chapter Summary

In this chapter, we presented a brief review of Java programming syntax and
concepts as well as object-oriented programming terminologies and concepts. In
this review, the emphasis was put on the parts of Java that are often used in Android
programming and Android application development. These include topics such as
anonymous class, the lambda expression, varargs, generic types, for-each statement,
object serialization, etc. For thorough and recent coverage of the Java language
fundamentals, and Java UI using JavaFX, see [3, 18], and for object-oriented
programming concepts and using Java for application design, see [17].

Check Your Knowledge
Below are some of the fundamental concepts and vocabularies that have been
covered in this chapter. To test your knowledge and your understanding of this
chapter, you should be able to describe each of the below concepts in one or two
sentences.

- Anonymous class
- Arrays and ArrayLists
- Class
- Decision-making
- Encapsulation
- Exceptions
- Generic
- Inheritance
- Interfaces
- Lambda expressions
- Objects
- Polymorphism
- Programming basics
- Serialization
- Variable argument (varargs)
- Variables and objects

Further Reading

For more information about the topics covered in this chapter, we suggest that you refer to the online resources listed below. These links provide additional insight into the topics covered. The links are mostly maintained by Oracle and are a part of the Java language specification. The resource titles convey which section/subsection of the chapter the resource is related to.

Allen B. Downey and Chris Mayfield, **Think Java: How to Think Like a Computer Scientist**, [Online] Available: http://greenteapress.com/thinkjava6/html/index.html

David J. Eck, **Introduction to Programming Using Java**, Eighth Edition, Version 8.1.1, May 2020, [Online] Available: http://math.hws.edu/javanotes/

Essentials of the Java Programming Language, Part 1, [Online] Available: https://www.oracle.com/technetwork/java/basicjava1-135508.html

Essentials of the Java Programming Language, Part 2, [Online] Available: https://www.oracle.com/technetwork/java/index-139917.html

Java™ Platform, Standard Edition 8, API Specification, [Online] Available: https://docs.oracle.com/javase/8/docs/api/index.html

Lesson 8: Object-Oriented Programming, [Online] Available: https://www.oracle.com/technetwork/java/oo-140949.html

The Java™ Tutorials Getting Started, [Online] Available: https://docs.oracle.com/javase/tutorial/getStarted/

The Java™ Tutorials, Java Tutorials Learning Paths, [Online] Available: https://docs.oracle.com/javase/tutorial/tutorialLearningPaths.html

The Java™ Tutorials, Trails Covering the Basics, [Online] Available: https://docs.oracle.com/javase/tutorial/index.html

XML Tutorial, [Online] Available: https://www.w3schools.com/xml/

Widening Primitive Conversion, [Online] Available: https://docs.oracle.com/javase/specs/jls/se7/html/jls-5.html#jls-5.1.2

Chapter 2
Getting Started with Android

What You Will Learn in This Chapter
By the end of this chapter, you should be able to:

- Download and install Android Studio
- Create Android project
- Compile, build, and run Android apps
- Differentiate between the module and top-level Gradle builds
- Manage code versioning
- Describe Android stack and framework

2.1 Introduction

This chapter marks the start of your journey to learn Android programming. It is divided into six parts. Section 2.2 is an introduction to the Android and Android operating system; Sect. 2.3 describes downloading and installing Android Studio and the Android SDK; Sect. 2.4 describes how to create a simple Android project; Sect. 2.5 describes compiling and running Android apps and running a HelloWorld app; Sect. 2.6 describes technologies used for compiling, building, and packaging Android apps; and, lastly, Sect. 2.7 describes Android stack and framework.

2.2 Starting with Android

Let's start this chapter by learning more about Android as a mobile operating system and platform and as a framework for developing apps.

© The Author(s), under exclusive license to Springer Nature Switzerland AG 2022
A.-R. Mawlood-Yunis, *Android for Java Programmers*,
https://doi.org/10.1007/978-3-030-87459-9_2

2.2.1   A Brief Android History

The story of the Android mobile platform begins in October 2003 when Andy Rubin, Rich Miner, Nick Sears, and Chris White started a company called Android, Inc. The company started with the intention to create an advanced operating system for digital cameras, i.e., use the Linux kernel to create an embedded operating system for digital cameras: in other words, to create an Android operating system. However, they changed the direction of the company and started focusing on mobile devices. Google acquired Android, Inc., and with it acquired the Android operating system in August 2005. People consider this date as the date that Google entered the mobile operating system market. In November 2007, several tech companies including Google, Sony, HTC, Samsung, and others created a consortium called the Open Handset Alliance (OHA) to develop open standards for mobile devices. The OHA released the first Android OS open-source software in 2007. One year later, in October 2008, the first Android phone, the HTC Dream, was launched marking the start of the mobile phones we know today.

2.2.2   Android Is Open Source

Android is a mobile operating system based on the Linux kernel. It is an open-source operating system for mobile devices that has been built upon other open-source projects. As a developer, this means you have access to the source code of the platform, which in turn helps you to better understand how the interface and the various other pieces of the platform work. If you happen to find a bug, you can also submit your solution for the issue and get rewarded by being a part of future Android improvement. You can download the Android source code at the Android Open Source Project (AOSP[1]) repository along with the information you need to create custom Android OS, port devices, and other accessories to the Android platform. You can even download the Android OS to your PC and use your PC as an Android device enabling you to use all the apps available for Android on your PC. To build the Android source files, you will need to have a Linux or Mac OS. Building under Windows is not supported yet.

2.2.3   Android Libraries

In addition to phones and tablets, Android powers watches, TVs, and cars and has a library to develop apps for the IoT (internet of things). Android provides users with the interface for touchscreens. Users can interact with the Android devices by

---

[1] https://wladimir-tm4pda.github.io/source/download.html

swiping, tapping, pinching, or using the virtual keyboard and voice. The voice access app for Android lets you control your device with spoken commands, i.e., use your voice to open apps, navigate, and edit text hands-free. Android has built-in support for Bluetooth, USB, and peripherals such as printers. Android has sensors to discover actions such as user moving, phone rotation, tilting steer, etc. Basically, it is a mini-computer and more.

2.2.4 Android Popularity

Android is a very popular operating system. It is used on a large[2] percentage of all smartphones. Based on Google Play Store's statistics, there are billions of active Android devices, and there are millions[3] of Android apps in the Google Play Store, and these numbers grow daily. Android supports the developer community through documentation and sample codes. The fact that Android is an open-source operating system based on Linux and uses the Java programming language gives Android a unique advantage to becoming a popular platform. The Linux operating system made it easier for device manufacturers to develop drivers for their products. Similarly, Java made it easier for developers to develop apps for Android. Many developers prefer Android as it has a large community ready to help and provide useful information. There are well-developed IDEs for developing Android apps that have many integrated tools, for example, quality assurance or QA tools, performance measuring tools, layout tools, etc. that help to develop efficient, secure, and high-quality Android apps fast and easily.

Before developing an app as simple as a HelloWorld for Android devices, we need to install the programming environment. In this chapter, we set up the programming environment that will be used for the rest of the book. After installing the Android Studio IDE, we will run the HelloWorld app on the Android emulator and phone. Running apps on the Android emulator might be slow; this depends on the CPU speed, memory size, and graphic card size of your machine.

2.2.5 Android Development Environment

To develop Android mobile apps, in addition to your knowledge of the Java data types, operations, statements, syntax, and program structures, you need to become familiar with a new set of libraries, classes, and interfaces, i.e., you need to learn to use the Android software development kit (SDK) and Android API. Unlike Java and C++, which have very stable and well-established SDKs and APIs, the Android SDK

---

[2]https://gs.statcounter.com/os-market-share/mobile/worldwide

[3]https://buildfire.com/app-statistics/

and API evolve quickly which puts an extra challenge on your learning path. You not only need to learn a new API but also watch out for the latest updates to avoid your code from becoming obsolete.

When you write code for Android-powered devices, you are working in a restricted environment. Compared to PCs, Android phones, watches, and tablets have low computational power. The screen size and battery power are also limited and pose new constraints on the development environment that you must account for. You need to understand how to stack or pile frames when going back and forth between screens. You also need to understand object lifecycles, system callback methods, layouts, and device rotations, which are all usually of lower concern when developing stand-alone or distributed Java and Web applications.

Mobile devices come with built-in sensors, GPS (Global Positioning System), Wi-Fi, Bluetooth, cameras, USBs, screens, and other components and features used for text messaging, finding device orientation, tracking the user's movements, etc. Writing programs to use these new components and features is relatively novel to Java programmers and is something that they need to learn and get used to.

Compiling, running, and debugging Android code require learning new tools. You might need to learn how to use a new integrated development environment (IDE), such as Android Studio, or new build tools, such as Gradle. You also need to learn how to refactor, profile, inspect, and measure the performance of your code. Additionally, you need to learn how to use and set up Android Virtual Devices (AVD), use layout inspectors and resource managers, and write bilingual or multilingual code. Furthermore, you might also need to learn how to run automatic testing using the JUnit software and how to do code versioning using versioning tools.

2.2.6 Android Developer's Skills

If you know the Java programming language, can run applications on the Linux operating system, and have some basic XML and Linux administration knowledge, you are pretty much set and ready to be an Android developer. The latter is useful because managing apps on Android devices is similar to managing user accounts on the Linux operating system. If you don't know these technologies, you don't need to worry; we will review them in enough detail to enable you to write Android code and apps.

Knowledge of Java, XML, and Linux are helpful and set you up on the path to becoming an Android developer. However, Android programming is a bit more engaging than usual Java application development on the Linux operating system. To be a successful Android programmer, you need to acquire additional skills. The objective of this book is to teach you the skills needed to become a successful Android programmer.

2.2.7 Model View Controller and App Development

Android programming involves not only a clear separation between the visual components and the app's computational logic, or business objects, but also using XML elements to represent the visual objects. You can create all the GUI (graphical user interface) components of your app using XML files. At runtime, the XML files are converted to Java code and linked to the main source code to be executed. The separation between views, logic, and data is essential in the Android app development philosophy, and you must master this concept to be able to code for Android devices.

2.2.8 Android's Main Program

For any program to start, there is a need for an entry point into the program. For Java programs, the main method in a class is the entry point. For Web applications, you type the address of the website in the browser which looks for the index.html file to load the page and display it. To run Android programs, you need to create the *AndroidManifest.XML file.* All Android application programs start with the manifest file.

When you use Android Studio to create a project, the manifest file is automatically created for you. Every time you add an Android Activity class, i.e., screen, to your app, the Activity is automatically added to the manifest file. Inside the manifest file, you declare one of the Activity classes to be the main class, i.e., the starting point for your app. This is very similar to Java where you can have multiple classes, but your program starts with the one class that has the main method.

2.2.9 Java and Android

Android is an adapted Linux operating system that can run on low-energy mobile touchscreen devices. At first, Android development was done in Eclipse with some plugins to enable Android app development. Coding was done in Java and then installed on Android-enabled devices or emulators powered with the Java virtual machine (JVM) for running. Now, Android Studio, based on IntelliJ IDEA,[4] is used for app development with emulators and physical devices.

Android uses the Java API (application programming interface) and supports most Java features. Not only does Android use the Java programming language, but app development for Android devices follows the JavaFX application design as well. Similar to JavaFX, developing Android apps involves using both XML files and

---

[4] https://developer.android.com/studio/

code as well as extending an already defined class to render graphical components of the app. Having said that, there are differences between Java and Android in terms of application programming interfaces (APIs), software development kits (SDKs), and runtimes. In [1], the differences between Java and Android are explored, and an approach is proposed for developing an application that runs on both the Android platform and the Java platform.

Java is one of the two official languages for Android development; the other language is Kotlin. Kotlin depends on JVM and can coexist with Java in the same application. Kotlin aims to solve several limitations of Java. The description of these limitations and Kotlin's potentials to solve them are described in [2, 3]. There are many versions of Android. Newer versions support more features than the older ones and are backward compatible.

2.2.10   Why Use Java for Android?

From a technical perspective, Java is selected as a programming language for Android for three main reasons.

First, Java is a popular programming language [4]. It has been taught in almost all colleges and universities around the world for many years. This enables Java developers to create Android apps without having to learn a new programming language.

Second, Java runs inside the Java virtual machine (JVM) which helps Android apps to run on any Android-powered device regardless of the device's manufacturer. Android apps can run, for example, on Samsung, LG, and Huawei phones. This helps companies to easily develop devices that can run Android apps.

Third, Java is a comprehensive programming language with a large number of libraries, classes, and interfaces that are open source, or mostly open source, and readily available for use. The latter helps developers and companies to utilize Java resources to develop apps and products.

Java will continue to be the programming language for Android for many years to come. Millions of existing Android apps are written in Java. These apps need to be maintained/extended, and new apps are developed in Java daily.

2.2.11   Android and Linux

Android smartphones and tablets contain the Linux kernel to manage active processes and communication between hardware and software components. Instead of writing the kernel from scratch, Android developers from Google modified the Linux kernel for their devices. This is possible because Linux is an open-source operating system. Others used a similar approach, for example, the Sony gaming console PlayStation 4 uses the open-source FreeBSD kernel.

While the Linux kernel is an important component of Android and has helped to build Android, the Android team made many changes to the Linux kernel. These include adding specialized libraries, APIs, drivers, and tools that are written specifically for Android. It is because of these changes that the programs you write on Linux may not run on Android without modifications. In other words, in terms of the operating system, Android is Linux and more.

2.3   Download and Install Android Studio and Android SDK

In this part, we describe downloading the latest Android development environment and Android SDK. We also provide step-by-step instructions to install the Android development environment, update Android files, and apply release notes.

2.3.1   *Download the Android Studio*

Android Studio is the official integrated development environment (IDE) for Android development and is based on IntelliJ IDEA. It is not the only IDE that you can use to develop apps. There are other IDEs such as Eclipse or NetBeans. However, Android Studio includes everything you need to start developing Android apps. These include project and activity templates, a layout editor, testing tools, the Gradle build tool, a log console, a debugger, and virtual devices to emulate phones, tablets, watches, and many more plugins. Basically, you can develop, debug, test, and package apps with Android Studio. A detailed description of Android Studio is provided in [5].

Click on Android Studio (Fig. 2.1) or put this download link (Download Android Studio and SDK tools | Android Developers) into your browser to get

Android Studio provides the fastest tools for building apps on every type of Android device.

Download Android Studio

2020.3.1 for Windows 64-bit (914 MiB)

Fig. 2.1 Link to download Android Studio

started. The latest version of Android Studio for Windows 64-bit is 4.2. You have to make sure that you have enough RAM and disk space to be able to install Android, create apps, and run the emulator. The space requirements continually change as newer versions of Android need more space. At the download time, you need to check the Android documentation to find out the space requirements.

If you have a Mac or Linux computer, you can use Android Studio with Mac or Linux to develop apps. The installation process would be similar to what is described here. While native iOS developers must develop on a Mac, with Android, you can develop on Windows, Mac, or Linux. To get started with Android on a Mac, however, you need to download Android Studio for Mac.

2.3.2 Install Android Studio

Installing Android is straightforward. After downloading Android Studio, go to your download directory, and double-click on the executable file you downloaded to open Android Studio. To complete the installation, press "Yes" for the installation process to start as shown in Fig. 2.2.

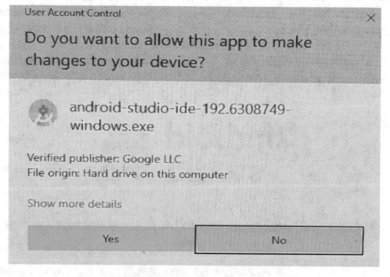

Fig. 2.2 Starting point to download Android

Fig. 2.3   Android welcome setup message

After you click "Yes," a welcome message like Fig. 2.3 will be shown.

Click "Next" to choose components to install, in this case, Android Studio and Android Virtual Device, as shown in Fig. 2.4.

Click "Next" to specify the configuration folder or to specify the installation home of the previous version of Android Studio if you have one and you would like to install the newer version in the same place. The location folder should have enough space to install and run Android projects. The amount of space you need will be shown on the configuration setting window as shown in Fig. 2.5.

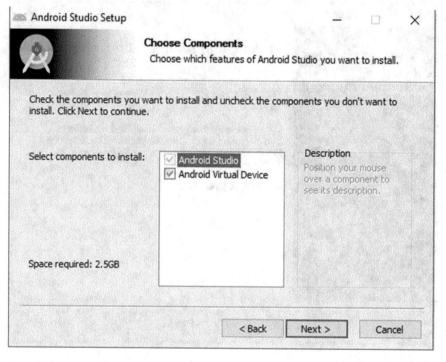

Fig. 2.4 Choose which features of Android Studio you want to install

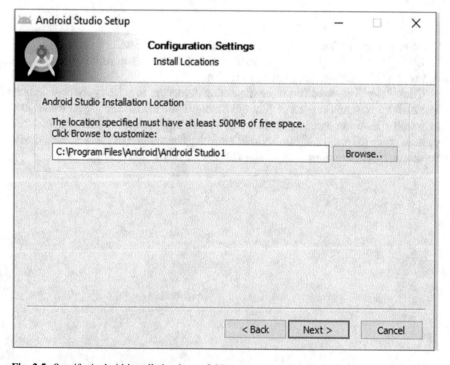

Fig. 2.5 Specify Android installation home folder

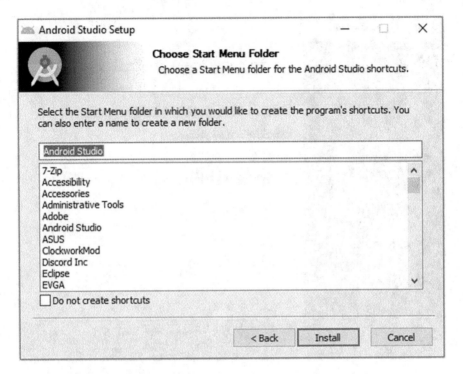

Fig. 2.6 Shortcut to Android Studio home

Click "Next" to start the installation. Clicking Install Android Studio, shown in Fig. 2.6, will automatically install the Android SDK.

Accept all licenses to continue. On Windows, a shortcut will be created on the start menu which points to Android Studio executable in the bin folder (C:\Program Files\Android\Android Studio1\bin). Once the Android SDK installation is complete, you are ready to build and run the HelloWorld app. On the next screen, shown in Fig. 2.7, select Start Android Studio to start Android at the end of the installation process.

To complete installation, you might be asked to import your settings from a previous version of Android Studio, that is, if you have one. This step is shown in Fig. 2.8.

Fig. 2.7 The last step in installing Android Studio

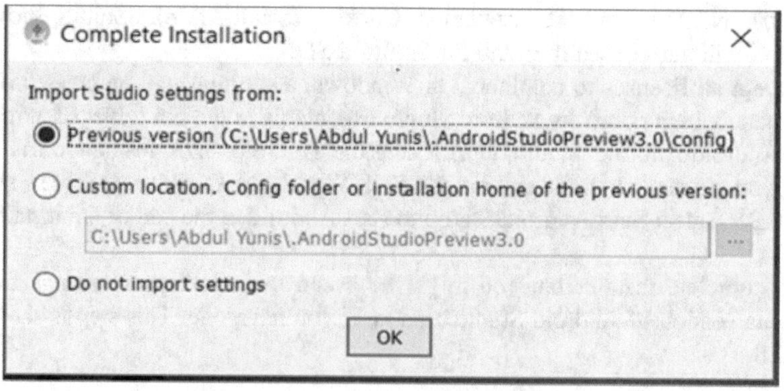

Fig. 2.8 Import previous Android setting step

If you selected Start Android Studio as shown in Fig. 2.7, then it will start, and you will see the Android start screen as shown in Fig. 2.9. You are now ready to start your first app.

Fig. 2.9 Android start

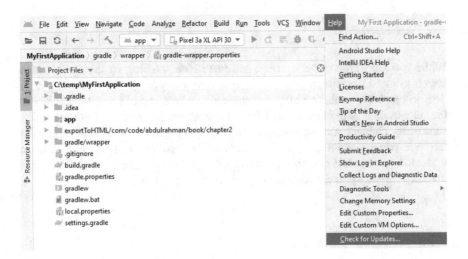

Fig. 2.10 Steps to invoke Android updates

2.3.3 Update Android Files

If Android Studio is missing updates, a message gets displayed to indicate the updates needed. Click on the displayed link and download all of the updates. You can push updates to run in the *background* and continue working. You can check for updates yourself by clicking on the Help tab on the Android Studio toolbar and clicking check for updates as shown in Fig. 2.10.

If new updates exist, you will see a window like the one showing in Fig. 2.11.

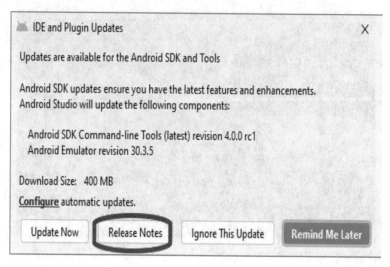

Fig. 2.11 Link to the release note

2.3.4 Release Note

While you are trying to get updates, and just before clicking on the *Update Now* button, click on the *Release Note button* shown on the update window; see Fig. 2.11. This will take you to the Android documentation where you can find what is new in the release. It is important to read the release notes. Sometimes, Android makes substantive changes and improvements that have an impact on your existing code or the code you are about to write. You need to be aware of these changes. In cases where the new updates are related to plugins that you are not using, you don't need to update. This way you can save some space on your machine.

2.3.5 Android SDK

The Android Software Development Kit (Android SDK) consists of a large number of Java classes, interfaces, and packages that are essential to developing apps. These are classes and interfaces that you import to your code during development. The SDK is independent of the Android Studio. However, it is more suitable to work with when used with Android Studio or other IDEs such as NetBeans or Eclipse. On your machine, the SDK is located at *~/Android/sdk*, e.g., C:\Users\username \AppData\Local\Android\Sdk. To see the SDK directories from the Android Studio toolbar, click on Tools followed by SDK Manager as shown below in Fig. 2.12. You can access the SDK directory from the file menu as well. Click file | Settings | Appearance & Behavior | System Settings | Android SDK to see it.

Using SDK Manager, you can access *tools*, *platforms*, and *update sites* as shown in Fig. 2.13. Click on the *SDK tools tab* to find out the available development tools.

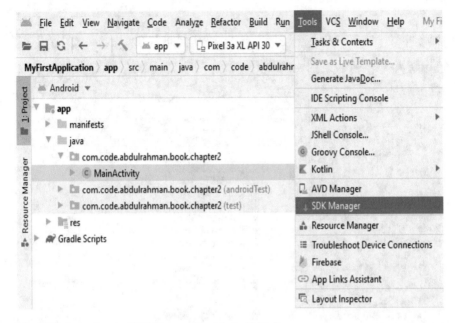

Fig. 2.12 Accessing the SDK Manager from Android Studio

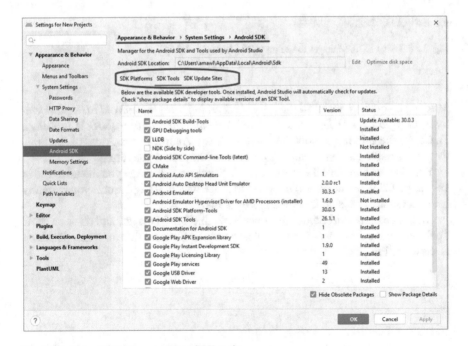

Fig. 2.13 Using SDK Manager to see SDK tools

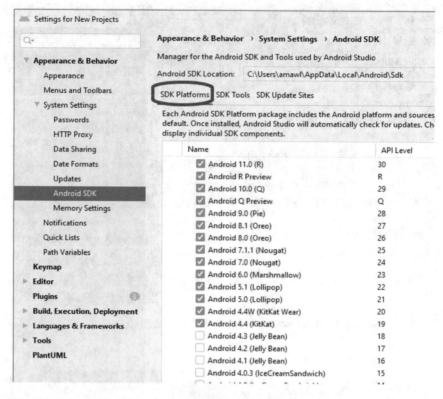

Fig. 2.14 Using SDK Manager to see installed platforms

Make sure you have installed the *Android SDK build-tools*, *Android SDK platform-tools*, *Google USB Driver*, and *Intel x68 Emulator Accelerator (HAXM installer)*. These are the minimum tools you need to create Android apps. Most of the time, these are installed automatically, and you don't have to do anything.

You also need to have the most recent API and any other API you intend to use in your apps. Click on the *SDK platforms* tab to see which SDK platform you currently have access to. This step is shown in Fig. 2.14.

After using Android Studio for a while, open SDK Manager, and click on SDK Tools | optimize disk space button to delete unused files and free up space. This step is shown in Fig. 2.15.

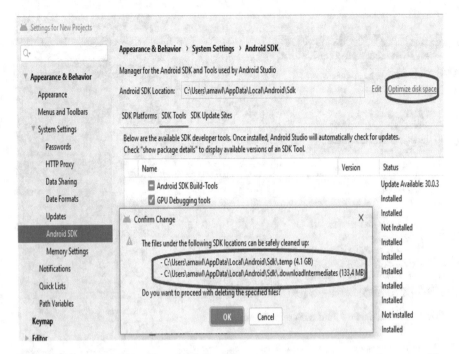

Fig. 2.15 Using SDK Manager to see platforms

2.4 Create a New Android Project

To start a new Android app project for HelloWorld, follow the wizard steps as described in this part.

2.4.1 Start New Project

Click "Create a new Android Studio project" as shown below (Fig. 2.16).

2.4.2 Select an Activity Template

To create an activity, you select an activity template for your app. Activity templates help fast development and best design practices. Android Studios come with multiple code templates. For this exercise, select EmptyActivity as shown in Fig. 2.17, and click next.

Fig. 2.16 Create a new Android project menu

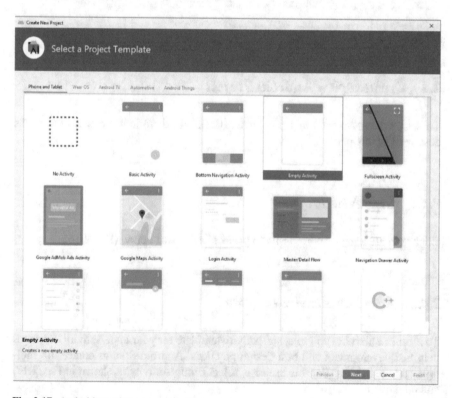

Fig. 2.17 Android templates to choose from

By the time you complete reading this book, you should experiment using all the given templates. This way, you will learn more about the features Android provides to create your desired apps. To make yourself familiar with the Android app templates, I encourage you to read about Android templates that come with Android Studio. For Android templates, see this link: https://developer.android.com/studio/projects/templates.

2.4.3   Fill in Application Requirement

Fill in the application name, package name, and project location as shown below (Fig. 2.18). The package name is the reverse of the company domain. If you want to customize the package name, click *edit* on the right of *Package name*. The project location is where your project files reside. You can choose any location you want. You also have a choice to select Java or Kotlin as a programming language for your coding.

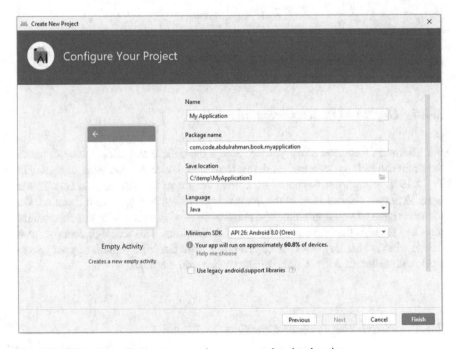

Fig. 2.18 Fill in the application name, package name, and project location

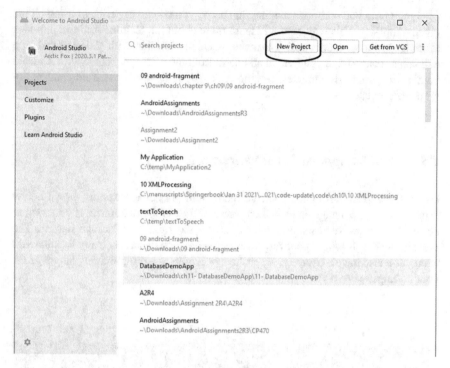

Fig. 2.19 Define a minimum SDK API your app requires

2.4.4 Define SDK Requirements

For Minimum Required SDK, you can accept the default and click *next* or select the desired API for your app, i.e., define the target device for your app, as shown in Fig. 2.19. It is important to choose the correct version of the API for your app. This is because not all phones support the latest version of the API or have it installed. On the other hand, if you don't choose a reasonable version of the API, your app might miss key features that the newer version of APIs offers. This a design decision, you decide what is best for your app, or you build more than one version of your app to work with different APIs. Click *Finish* when you are done.

2.4.5 Finish the Project Creation

Once you have clicked *Finish*, you are presented with the project and all its files as shown in Fig. 2.20.

Open the app/java folder and look at the MainActivity.java code. You should see a Java class similar to the one shown in Listing 2.1. This is a typical Java class file. It

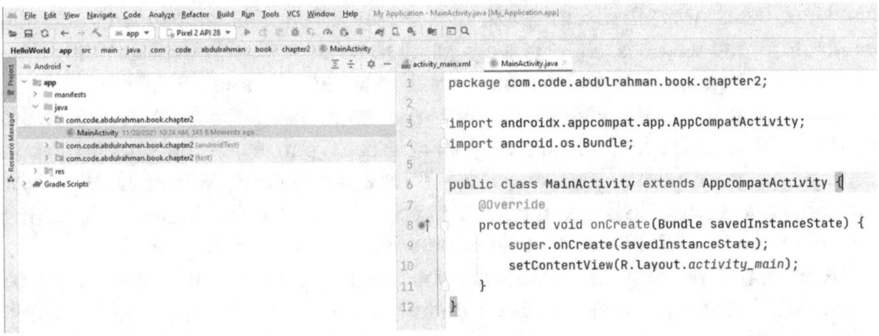

Fig. 2.20 HelloWorld app components

is made of a package name, some import statements, and a class definition. The file is saved as MainActivity.java which has one overwritten method called onCreate(). The meaning of the code components such as AppCompatActivity, setContentView, Bundle, etc. will be explained in the coming chapters.

Listing 2.1 MainActivity.java.

```
package com.code.abdulrahman.book.chapter2;
import androidx.appcompat.app.AppCompatActivity;
import android.os.Bundle;
public class MainActivity extends AppCompatActivity {
  @Override
  protected void onCreate(Bundle savedInstanceState) {
    super.onCreate(savedInstanceState);
    setContentView(R.layout.activity_main);
  }
}
```

2.5 Compiling and Running Android Apps

How you run your app depends on whether you have an Android device or are using an Android emulator. This chapter shows you how to install and run your apps on Android devices as well as on Android emulators. You will also run the HelloWorld app we created in the previous part.

2.5.1 Running HelloWorld on Your Phone

Let's run our code directly on the phone. The biggest advantage of using Android devices for development is that it is fast to load and run programs. In contrast, the emulator, which we will discuss next, runs slowly; it's not recommended to use the emulator for the whole book. If you are going to be an Android developer, it is time to think about getting an Android device and using emulator as a backup.

Before you start, plug your phone into your laptop using the USB port. Android Studio installs the HelloWorld app on your connected phone and starts it. Next, go to Settings on your phone, and select the *Developer options*, shown in Fig. 2.21 (on left), and select USB debugging, shown in Fig. 2.21 (on right). This setting will allow Android Studio to communicate with the phone to program it.

Note that, depending on the device you are going to use, this step might be slightly different than what has been described above. If this is the case, search online, perhaps by visiting the manufacturer's website, to find out information about the developer settings on your device.

If you cannot see the Developer options button, you should tap on the *About phone* button (under settings) and click the *Build number* button seven times. Now you should see the Developer options. Next, go into Developer options and select USB debugging.

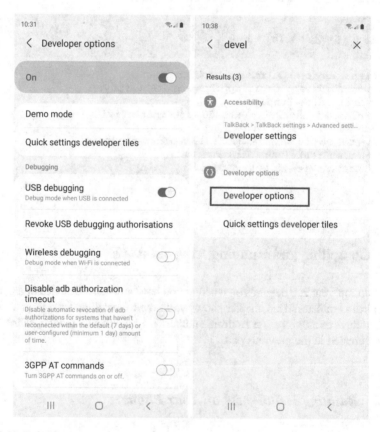

Fig. 2.21 Enabling device developer option

2.5.2 Running the Android App in Android Studio

Click on the *Run* button on the Android Studio toolbar as shown in Fig. 2.22.

The app is downloaded and installed and runs on the phone. You'll see the following "HelloWorld" on your phone (Fig. 2.23).

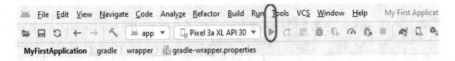

Fig. 2.22 On Android Studio, the run icon is marked

Fig. 2.23 First
HelloWorld app

If you have followed the steps above correctly, congratulations you have developed your first Android app.

2.5.3   Issues Starting First App

If for some reason your app did not run, i.e., you do not see the app running on your phone, make sure that USB has been enabled. Then, make sure that you clicked and enabled the USB debugging option as discussed above. If USB debugging is enabled, unplug the USB cable, and plug it in again. If you see the error message dialog, as shown in Fig. 2.24, on your phone, check "Always allow from this computer," and click OK, as shown below. Now, after re-launching the app, you should see HelloWorld on the phone.

Fig. 2.24 A dialog message indicating phone and Android connection is enabled

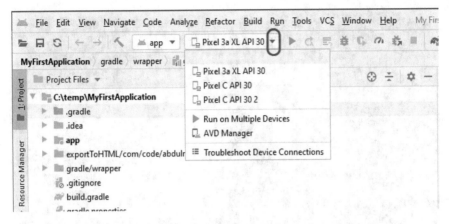

Fig. 2.25 Emulator named My HelloWorld app is selected for running an app

2.5.4 Running HelloWorld on Emulator

Now, let's run the HelloWorld program on the Android emulator which emulates the functionality of the phone as best as possible and allows developers to run, test, and debug code. The code that runs on the emulator runs unchanged on the real device as well.

To run the app, disconnect your phone first, and then click the *run* button in Android Studio. In the *dropdown list* circled in Fig. 2.25, select *Launch Emulator* and click *OK*. Android Studio will install the app (the HelloWorld.apk) on your AVD and start it.

This could take some time, but eventually, you will see the HelloWorld on the emulator as shown in Fig. 2.26.

2.5.5 Setting Up the Emulator

In the previous step, we assumed that you have already set up the emulator. But, in case you didn't or you want to emulate different devices, here we describe how to do it.

There are so many Android devices available that it would be difficult to test your apps on all or many real devices. If you have an Android device, you can use it for testing basic functionalities, and you will have quick results. However, you cannot be sure of how your app will look and behave on every Android device.

Android provides a way to create as many emulated devices as you want using the virtual device manager. The AVD Manager allows you to emulate both the hardware and software part of the devices. Click on the AVD menu as shown in Fig. 2.27, or

Fig. 2.26 HelloWorld app running in an emulator

Fig. 2.27 AVD Manager to
start the virtual emulator

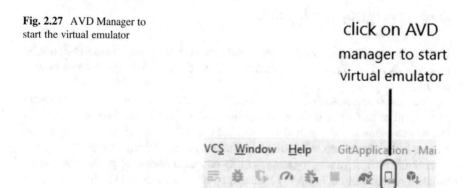

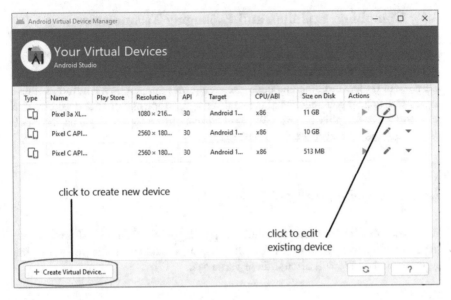

Fig. 2.28 Start Android Virtual Device Manager

click on tools | AVD to start the Android Virtual Device Manager. The AVD Manager is shown in Fig. 2.28.

Click on *Create Virtual Device* and follow the steps to choose a device (phone, tablet, TV, Wear OS, or Automative) and select a system image (Pie or Android 9, Q or Android 10, R or Android 11, etc.) to start the emulator.

Bear in mind that Android emulators can be slow. You can probably do a few things to speed it up a bit. For example, if your app does not use the camera or other components, it doesn't need to be included in the emulator configuration. You can also use third-party emulators such as Genymotion that can be faster than the native emulators or work better with your device especially if you have Mac.

2.5.6 Do It Yourself

Install Android and AVD. Create your first project. Replace the HelloWorld text with some other text and familiarize yourself with Android Studio.

2.6   Compiling, Building, and Packaging Technologies

It is important to understand how your Java code is turned into a .dex (Dalvik Executable) file that will end up on your Android device. Similarly, it is essential to learn about project building and code packaging for publishing. We introduce these topics here to help you understand the Android application and project structures that you will create in this chapter. We will discuss these topics more as the book progresses and wherever we find it necessary.

2.6.1   Compiling Android Code

When you compile Java code for Android apps, it goes through several steps. These steps are summarized below. A few of these steps depend on the version of the system you use. We will discuss these variances.

2.6.1.1   Compiling Java Code

You need a Java compiler, *javac*, to compile the Java code of your application. The javac is included in the Java development kit (JDK) that you need to download separately from downloading Android Studio. Your code and imported codes from the Android API and custom libraries are compiled. The output of this step is Java bytecode files. This is a normal Java compiling process. You are turning *.java classes into *.class bytecode.

2.6.1.2   Minimizing and Obscuring Code

To make it hard to decompile packaged Java code, currently, the Android Gradle plugin uses the R8 compiler to minimize the size of the code and obscure code by changing method names and applying code encryption. Android Gradle used to use the ProGuard plugin to do code optimization. However, starting with Android Gradle 3.4.0, ProGuard is no longer used to perform compile-time code optimization. Instead, Gradle uses the R8 compiler to handle code optimization and code shrinking. The R8 compiler is a replacement for the ProGuard tool. The output of this step is a minimized *.class file.

2.6.1.3   Turning .class into .dex Bytecode

In this step, your bytecode is converted to Dalvik bytecode and stored in a .dex (Dalvik Executable) file. The conversion is done by a command-line tool called D8

(DEX compiler). D8 is a replacement for the DX dexer. Android Studio and the Android Gradle plugin use D8 to compile Java bytecode into DEX bytecode. The .dex bytecode is an optimized bytecode format for Android that can be executed by Dalvik or Android runtime (ART). In this step, you are turning *.class into *.dex. Later, the device's runtime environment will read the .dex file and recompile some of the files to machine code for the fastest possible execution.

The steps we described so far can be summarized as follows:

Source code (*.java) → using javac → Java bytecode (*.class) → using ProGuard or R8 → optimized Java bytecode (*.class) → using D8 or DEX → Dalvik optimized bytecode (*.dex)

2.6.1.4   Packaging DEX Files

The APK Packager combines the DEX files and compiled resources into a single APK file. The APK is a file format designed for distributing Android applications. It is simply just a ZIP archive file similar to the Java JAR package designed for the distribution of Java applications. In addition to the .dex file, APK contains other files, for example, AndroidManifest.xml. In addition to the APK, Android supports another build format, the Android App Bundle (AAB) build format.

2.6.2   Android App Bundle

The Android App Bundle (AAB) is Android's new format to build and release apps. The generated bundle includes all your app's compiled code and resources. However, Google Play defers generating the APK to optimize downloading for each device configuration. That means only the code and resources that are needed for a specific device are downloaded.

To use or switch to the new publishing format, you don't need to refactor your code. When you develop apps using Android Studio 3.2 or higher versions, you can generate AAB builds from Android Studio.

2.6.3   Do It Yourself

Create a new project, and try to generate a .apk using the build APK steps shown in Fig. 2.29. Familiarize yourself with creating APK, signed APK, and AAB files.

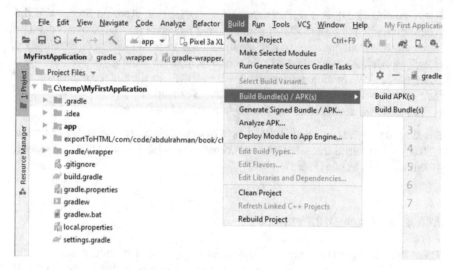

Fig. 2.29 Steps to create APK as shown from Android

2.6.4   Install Android Apps

An Android Package Kit (APK) is similar to a .exe file for Windows PC. The Android operating system uses .apk for the distribution and installation of apps. When you download, or when you get an APK, you're getting an app. Below, we describe how to install APK files posted online and from your computer.

2.6.5   Install APK from Online

The best way to download apps is to get them from trusted sources such as the Google Play Store. However, when needed, you can install apps from any source online. To install APK posted online to your Android device, you need to find the APK file and download it. Once the file is downloaded, you can open **it by** *tapping* on the file and tapping "**yes**" when you are prompted by the installation process. The app should begin installing on your device. We will post one or more .apk for each chapter in this book. You can download these .apk files to your device and run the apps.

2.6.6 Install APK from Files

If you happen to have an APK file on your computer, you can install the APK file on your device. To do so, you need to connect your computer to your Android device and copy the APK file to it. Find the APK file on your device, tap it, and then hit **"install" when you are prompted by the installation process**. To be sure that the newly installed app is working properly, open it from your device. If it is not working, repeat the steps above.

2.6.7 From Dalvik to ART Runtime

Android runtime (ART) is a replacement for the *Dalvik* virtual machine. Dalvik is the original Android runtime implementation. It is a virtual machine specifically created for Android to deal with low-memory devices. Before Lollipop, Dalvik used to translate bytecodes (.classes) to the native code, or machine-level code, (.dex) files. The translation was happening during runtime using the just-in-time (JIT) virtual machine. With ART, the translation from bytecode to machine-level code is done during the app installation which makes apps run faster but takes more memory and time when installing them for the first time.

2.6.8 Gradle Build

Android uses the Gradle build system to build, compile, and package apps. Gradle does the same job as the Apache Ant and Maven toolkits that you are probably familiar with. These are earlier toolkits used for building Java applications. Compared to Ant and Maven tools, Gradle is a faster and more flexible building tool. It allows customized builds enabling you to create APKs that can be uploaded to the emulator for demoing. There are other build tools such as Bazel, which is used by Google to build all its software, and Buck, which is developed and used by Facebook. However, Gradle is the main tool used for building Android apps.

Gradle is a part of the project structure displayed on Android Studio. See Fig. 2.30. It is important to gain some insight into each section of the Gradle structure to understand project configuration and setup. Below will look at a few of these files for their important roles in app development.

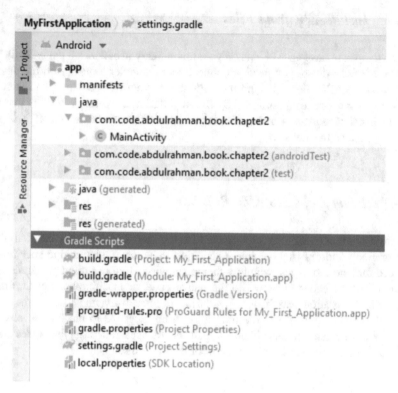

Fig. 2.30 Gradle structure inside project structure

2.6.8.1 Gradle Build Files

Gradle creates two build files, the *module-level build.gradle* file and *top-level build.gradle* file. Each of these files is used for different purposes. If your app is big or complex, for example, it requires more than one team to develop it, then it makes sense for each team to be specialized and work on one part of the app. In this case, each team will create its own *module-level build.gradle* file for the app. Creating app modules can be an effective way to manage your code as it grows as well.

When using Android Studio, the *build* file for each module will be inside the *app* directory and hold configuration information for the module. There will be one build file for each module. The total number of build files in your app will be equal to the number of modules in your project. Table 2.1 shows the content of a module-level build project.

You can see and update the content of the module build files using the Project Structure window. On your Android Studio, click file I Project Structure to open the Project Structure window. Your current build.gradle information will be displayed, and you can use this window to make any changes you want. You can make changes

Table 2.1 Module-level build file

```
plugins {
    id 'com.android.application'
}
android {
    compileSdkVersion 30
    buildToolsVersion "30.0.2"
    defaultConfig {
        applicationId "com.code.abdulrahman.book.chapter2"
        minSdkVersion 26
        targetSdkVersion 30
        versionCode 1
        versionName "1.0"
TestInstrumentationRunner
                    "androidx.test.runner.AndroidJUnitRunner"
    }
    buildTypes {
        release {
            minifyEnabled false
            proguardFiles              getDefaultProguardFile('proguard-android-
optimize.txt'), 'proguard-rules.pro'
        }
    }
    compileOptions {
        sourceCompatibility JavaVersion.VERSION_1_8
        targetCompatibility JavaVersion.VERSION_1_8
    }}
dependencies {
    implementation 'androidx.appcompat:appcompat:1.2.0'
    implementation 'com.google.android.material:material:1.2.1'
    implementation 'androidx.constraintlayout:constraintlayout:2.0.4'
    testImplementation 'junit:junit:4.+'
    androidTestImplementation 'androidx.test.ext:junit:1.1.2'  }
```

directly inside the build XML files, but it is easier to use the Project Structure window to make the changes.

Table 2.2, on the other hand, is an example of the second type of the build file, top-level build.gradle. It holds configuration information for the entire project. It is

Table 2.2 Top-level project build file

```
// Top-level build file where you can add configuration options common to all
sub-projects/modules.
    buildscript {
       repositories {
           google()
           jcenter()
       }
    dependencies {
       classpath "com.android.tools.build:gradle:4.1.1"
       // NOTE: Do not place your application dependencies here; they belong
       // in the individual module build.gradle files
       }
    }
    allprojects {
       repositories {
           google()
           jcenter()
       }
    }
    task clean(type: Delete) {
       delete rootProject.buildDir
    }
}
```

stored in the root directory of your project. There is only one top-level build file for each project.

We will talk more about each task, or component, of the build files as the book progresses. To find out the location of either build files on your PC, right-click on the file inside the project structure, and click on "Show in Explorer" to locate the files.

2.6.8.2 Build Parameters

Gradle creates another five files as shown in Fig. 2.30. These files include information about the Gradle version you are using and the link to the Gradle distribution. There is also a file for inserting rules to *ProGuard*. Other files are used to set project properties such as the parameters passed to the Java virtual machine, whether you are using *AndroidX*, and other information about your project settings and SDK location. Open each of these files, and see their content to become familiar with the Gradle project structure and settings.

2.6.9 Software Versioning Using Local or Remote Repositories

Controlling software versions, also known as source management control (SCM), is an essential part of the software development process. You need to manage your code versions whether you are writing a simple app for your interest or you are a team member working on a large software development project. An open-source version control tool called Git is integrated into the Android Studio and can be used to manage code versioning. Using Git, you can trace the history of your code changes, coordinate work among several programmers working on the same source code, and, if needed, return to previous versions of your code.

Git enables you to develop your code separately from the rest of your team. To do so, you create a *branch* from the main repository. It is a copy of a stable version of your repository which is called *codebase*. Once your part, or changes you made, is ready, you can upload it to the repository and save it, i.e., you *commit* your changes to the codebase. Other tasks you can do with Git include *pulling in commits*, also known as *checkout commits*, from other developers to your repository; *pushing commits*, also known as check-*in commits*, to others; *merging* your commits with the main repository; and finding out who made changes in the code.

Below, we describe the Git setup using Android Studio. However, to be fluent using Git, or using a remote repository such as GitHub or Bitbucket, you need to read the tutorials for these tools provided on their webpages.

2.6.9.1 Create a Git Repository

To create a Git repository for your project, click the VCS menu | **Import into Version Control** menu, and select "**Create Git Repository**" as shown in Fig. 2.31. Then select the repository folder of your Android Studio Project.

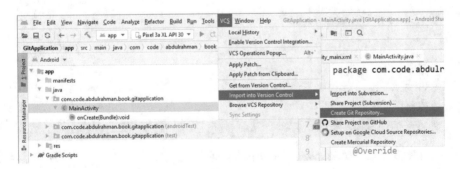

Fig. 2.31 Create a Git repository for your project

The steps above create a .git directory with few subdirectories for objects, refs/heads, refs/tags, logs, info, and template files. An initial HEAD file that references the HEAD of the master branch is also created. To see this file, go to your project root directory, and click on .git file.

While you are creating the .git repository, you will also see a dialog popup asking you to add project configure files to your Git; see Fig. 2.32. Click on *View Files* and select *.gitignore*. You don't need to add project setting files, i.e., .idea files, to the version control repository.

Once you created the Git repository, Android Studio shows the Version Control window as shown in Fig. 2.33. Click on the Git tab (at the bottom left of Android Studio) and explore what you have there.

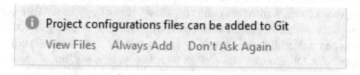

Fig. 2.32   Prompt message to add project files to version control

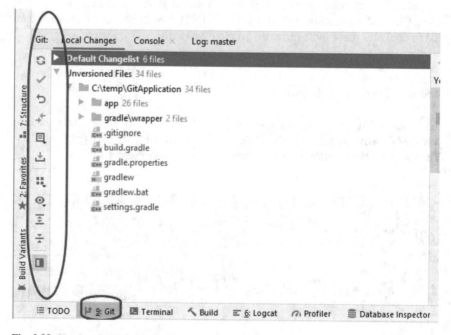

Fig. 2.33   Version Control showing on Android Studio

Fig. 2.34 Pull and push menu showing in Android Studio

By now you should see the pull and push menus on your Android Studio as well as shown in Fig. 2.34.

2.6.9.2 Integrating with GitHub or Bitbucket

Using Android Studio, you can utilize GitHub or Bitbucket or other remote repositories as a storage for your project. To do so, for example, click on File I New I Project from Version Control I GitHub. This will take you to the GitHub login page. Once you have logged in successfully, the Clone Repository dialog window will pop up. This dialog window displays a dropdown menu containing a list of repositories you currently own or have worked on in GitHub. Click Clone to clone the repository to your local machine. Note that you can create a free secure student GitHub account by emailing the GitHub administrators.

2.7 Android Stack and Framework

Understanding Android architecture is an asset that can help you develop high-quality apps. In this part, we describe Android architecture layers. Each layer is briefly introduced, and its components and purposes are explained.

2.7.1 Android Architecture

For developing Android apps, you need to have a high-level understanding of Android architecture. Figure 2.35 shows the major components of the Android development architecture and operating system, also known as the Android stack. The stack is made of the typical layers that you will find in any system platform. The layers are the application layer, the classes and libraries (or API layer), the compiler and runtime environment layer, a layer that connects software to hardware interfaces (or driver layer), and, finally, the physical hardware layer such as the motherboard and other network and hardware components.

Below is a short description of some of the components/layers listed in Fig. 2.35. We start with layer 1.

Fig. 2.35 Android
architecture layers
(Resource source: https://
google-developer-training.
github.io/android-
developer-fundamentals-
course-concepts-v2/unit-1-
get-started/lesson-1-build-
your-first-app/1-0-c-
introduction-to-android/1-0-
c-introduction-to-android.
html)

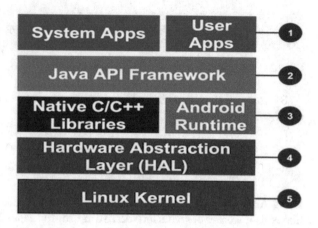

2.7.2   User and System Apps

The apps you will develop will live in *Layer1* along with core *system apps*. This is
the top layer of the Android stack. System apps, such as Clock and Calculator, are
preinstalled on Android devices. Many system apps can't be uninstalled. If you
want, you can enable or disable all system apps. When you disable a system app, that
doesn't mean it has been removed from the system. It just means users and other
apps can't access it. Some system apps are critical for device functionality. You don't
want to disable these critical apps; otherwise, your device will not work. For example,
you can't disallow Bluetooth, contacts, keychain, keyguard, com.android.launcher,
com.android.nfc, com.android.phone, com.android.settings, etc.

2.7.3   Java API Framework

All the classes, interfaces, and other features of Android are available to the
developers through the application programming interfaces (APIs) layer. In other
words, all the classes, interfaces, and packages you import to your code during app
development are from this layer. In addition to Java API, currently, Android supports
Kotlin API as well. The more you know about the Android API, the easier it is to
develop Android apps. However, at the starting point, learning the following is
necessary to be an Android developer:

- View System is used to build apps' user interfaces (UIs), including lists, buttons,
  menus, etc.
- Resource Manager is used to accessing non-code resources such as localized
  strings written in XML, graphics, and layout files.
- Notification Manager is used to displaying custom alerts to the user.
- Activity Manager is used for managing the app's lifecycle.

- Content Provider is used to enable apps to access data from other apps.
- Location Manager is used for providing location information using data from GPS sensors, cell towers, and Wi-Fi networks.

We will study all the above topics and more in the context of this book.

2.7.4   Native Libraries and Android Runtime

Each app runs in its process and with its instance of the Android runtime (ART).

ART is a replacement for the *Dalvik* virtual machine. Before Android Lollipop, Dalvik used to translate bytecodes (.classes) to the native code, or machine-level code, (.dex) files. That translation was happening during runtime using the just-in-time (JIT) virtual machine. With ART, the translation from bytecode to machine-level code is done during app installation which makes apps run faster but takes more memory and time when installing for the first time.

Level 3 of the Android stack also includes native C/C++ libraries. These core libraries help developers create apps using the C/C++ programming language and using NDK (Native Development Kit) libraries. This means you'll be writing code that runs directly on the devices' hardware and your app can access physical components such as sensors and cameras directly. The fact that you don't need to use the Java virtual machine will give you some advantages. For example, you will have better control over memory allocation and memory cleanup, and the app's performance can be improved. This is because many components of the Android system such as ART and HAL are built using native libraries. This is important for performance-intensive apps like games.

2.7.5   Hardware Abstraction Layer (HAL)

It is an abstraction layer between Android's physical hardware and its software. Instead of understanding how the drivers work, or how the hardware is accessed, HAL provides an interface for communication with hardware and drivers. It provides ways for data passing from/to hardware devices to the higher-level Java API framework. This way, you develop software based on the hardware interface without the need to know the implementation of the hardware. The HAL consists of multiple libraries; each library implements access for a specific type of hardware components such as the camera or Bluetooth. Note that, once you implement this layer, it will be hard to change it and make it work for other types of hardware devices and platforms.

2.7.6 Linux Kernel

The basis of the Android platform is the Linux kernel. The four layers above rely on the Linux kernel for underlying functionalities such as threading, memory management, process management, security, networking, etc. You should note that Android is not another Linux version like Red Hat or Ubuntu. Instead, it uses the core of Linux operating system functionalities. For example, the kernel layer contains all the essential hardware drivers. These include drivers for the camera, keyboard, display, USB, audio, etc.

Using the Linux kernel gives Android some advantages. For example, Android inherits the key security features from Linux which are robust and extensively tested worldwide. Device manufacturers can develop hardware drivers for Android easily which in turn has helped the Android devices' popularity. This is because Linux is open-source software that can easily be modified to meet hardware needs. More information on each layer and detailed Android architecture components and modules are listed in Fig. 2.36. For a detailed description of each layer, see the reference section of this chapter.

2.8 Chapter Summary

In this chapter, we put together all the nuts and bolts that set you up for developing Android applications. We covered getting and setting up Android IDE, how to run apps on the Android emulator and the phone, Android SDK components and packages, Android architecture and API framework, and other topics. Once you complete reading this chapter, you will be well on your way to start the journey of learning Android application development. For further information about the topics covered in this chapter, you can see these references [6, 7, 8, 9].

Check Your Knowledge

Below are some of the fundamental concepts and vocabularies that have been covered in this chapter. To test your knowledge and your understanding of this chapter, you should be able to describe each of the below concepts in one or two sentences.

- .dex file
- AndroidX
- APK
- App Bundle
- ART
- AVD
- Dalvik
- Git
- GitHub

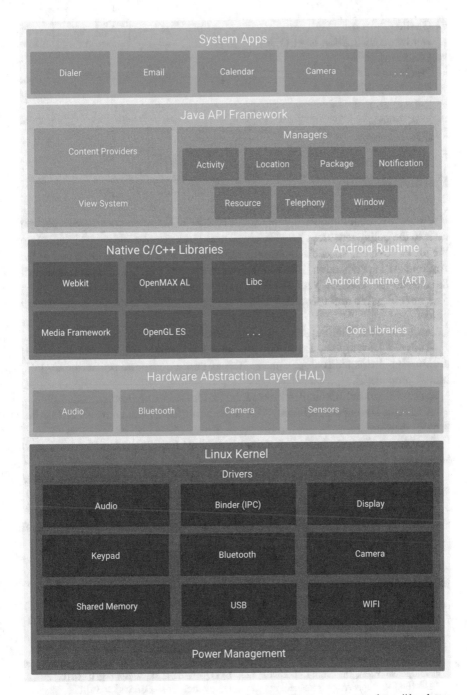

Fig. 2.36 Android architecture components and layers (Resource source: https://developer. android.com/guide/platform/)

- Gradle
- Hardware abstraction layer (HAL)
- Obscuring code
- ProGuard
- R8
- Release note
- SDK Manager
- SDK platforms

Further Reading

For more information about the topics covered in this chapter, we suggest that you refer to the online resources listed below. These links provide additional insight into the topics covered. The links are mostly maintained by Google and are a part of the Android API specification. The resource titles convey which section/subsection of the chapter the resource is related to.

Android guide and tutorial, [Online] Available: https://developer.android.com/guide/.

Android API, [Online] Available: https://developer.android.com/reference/.

Android Developers, Docs, Guides, Build a simple user interface, [online] Available: https://developer.android.com/guide/components/fundamentals.html#Components.

Android Studio, [Online] Available: https://developer.android.com/studio/.

Add App Resources, [Online] Available: https://developer.android.com/studio/write/add-resources.

Developer Documentation, [Online] Available: https://developer.android.com/samples .

What is Gradle?, [Online] Available: https://docs.gradle.org/current/userguide/what_is_gradle.html.

Configure Your Build with Gradle, [Online] Available: https://sodocumentation.net/android-gradle/topic/2161/configure-your-build-with-gradle.

References

1. Y. Cheon, Multiplatform application development for Android and Java, in *2019 IEEE 17th International Conference on Software Engineering Research, Management and Applications (SERA)*, 2019, pp. 1–5. https://doi.org/10.1109/SERA.2019.8886800
2. L. Ardito, R. Coppola, G. Malnati, M. Torchiano, Effectiveness of Kotlin vs. Java android app development tasks. Inf. Softw. Technol. **127**, 106374 (2020). https://doi.org/10.1016/j.infsof.2020.106374. https://www.sciencedirect.com/science/article/pii/S0950584920301439
3. B.G. Mateus, M. Martinez, An empirical study on quality of Android applications written in Kotlin language. Empir. Softw. Eng. **24**, 3356–3393 (2019). https://doi.org/10.1007/s10664-019-09727-4

4. P. Krill, Java programming language celebrates 25 years, in *InfoWorld.com*, San Mateo, 20 May 2020
5. K. Mew, *Mastering Android Studio 3: Build Dynamic and Robust Android Applications* (Packt Publishing, Birmingham, UK, 2017)
6. H.J. Franceschi, *Android App Development* (Jones & Bartlett Learning, LLC, Sudbury, 2017)
7. J. Horton, *Android Programming for Beginners: Build In-depth, Full-Featured Android 9 Pie Apps Starting from Zero Programming Experience*, 2nd edn. (Packt Publishing, Birmingham, UK, 2018)
8. J. Morris, *Hands-On Android UI Development: Design and Develop Attractive User Interfaces for Android Applications* (Packt Publishing, Birmingham, UK, 2017)
9. R. Boyer, K. Mew, *Android Application Development Cookbook*, 2nd edn. (Packt Publishing, Birmingham, UK, 2016)

Chapter 3
Your First Android Application

What You Will Learn in This Chapter
By the end of this chapter, you should be able to:

- Create your first Android app with a user interface
- Navigate between app screens
- Pass parameters between app screens
- Develop Android apps that support multiple languages
- Log information for debugging
- Use Android resources such as string, icon, color, etc.

Check Out the Demo Project
Download the demo app, **MyFirstApplication.zip**, specifically developed to go with this chapter. I recommend that you code this project up from the notes rather than just opening the project in Android Studio and running it; however, if you want to run the code first to get a sense of the app, please do so. The code is thoroughly explained in this chapter to help you understand it. We follow the same approach to all other chapters throughout the book. The app's code will help you comprehend the additional concepts that will be described in this chapter.

How to run the code: unzip the code in a folder of your choice, and then in Android Studio, click **File->import->Existing Android code into the workspace**. The project should start running.

3.1 Introduction

You may have noticed that there were several new ideas in the HelloWorld app presented in Chap. 2 that you usually don't see when running the HelloWorld Java programs. These include using activities, intents, and bundle objects, starting the program from the manifest file, creating a user interface (UI) for the app using an

XML file, and using resources such as layouts and strings. Moreover, an important design principle was presented. In the HelloWorld app, there is a clear separation between the UI implementation, which is written in the XML files, and the program, the Java code.

In this chapter, we will consider a more complex program with multiple UIs, activities, and intent objects. The new program is called *MyFirstApplication*. You can download and run it; the code is on the book page. Before we go deep into the *MyFirstApplication* code and architecture, we start this chapter by studying some important aspects/components of Android and Android application development such as activities, activity context, and the AndroidManifest.xml file.

Note that, in this chapter, you will encounter words, concepts, and technologies that you don't know yet. For example, you will learn later about onCreate, dp, resource files, layouts, etc. For now, just follow the step-by-step instructions to create your first app. These concepts will be introduced gradually throughout the book.

3.2 Android App Development

In this part, we cover a general introduction to Android app development. We describe Android application characteristics and introduce major concepts and components like Android activities, R Files, Android context, AndroidManifest.xml files, opening Android projects in Android Studio, and cleaning Android project builds.

3.2.1 Early Android Development

At first, Android development was done in Eclipse with some plugins to enable Android app development. Coding was done in Java and then installed on Android-enabled devices or emulators powered with the Java virtual machine for running. Now, Android Studio is used for app development, and there is more than one emulator and physical device for running.

In the past, the Jack (Java Android Compiler Kit) toolchain needed to be enabled to support Java 1.8 language features. Now, Jack is deprecated, and native Java 1.8 features are supported as part of the build system.

There are many versions of Android API; some are listed in Fig. 3.1. Newer versions support more features than the older ones and are backward compatible. Only Android Studio version 2.1 and newer ones support Lambda functions. Everything before that uses anonymous classes. Both Lambda and anonymous classes are discussed in Chap. 1.

Android apps use the Android software development kit (SDK), or Android libraries, and the Android Application Framework. The apps are executed by the

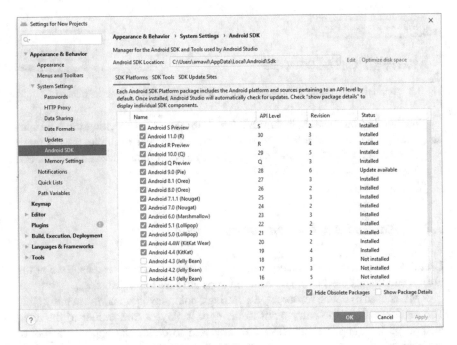

Fig. 3.1 Android versions are listed in Android Studio

Android runtime (ART) virtual machine. The compilation, packaging, and installation of Android apps are different from typical Java applications. These steps were described in Chap. 2, and you are encouraged to review them.

3.2.2   Android Versions

Android versioning reveals the fact that the Android API is continually growing and improving, and this growth is expected to continue for many years to come. Both the users and the developer can feel these improvements. However, their views on the change are different. As a developer, you express these changes as going from API level 25 to API 27 to API 28, etc. However, the user is not aware of these terms. Instead, they see it as going from Nougat to Oreo, to Pie, etc. Only recently Google started to name its APIs as Android 10, Android 11, etc. Below are examples of the Android API levels, or versions, and the features they support.

- AsyncTask was introduced in API 3.
- Download Manager was introduced in API 9.
- GridLayout was introduced in API 14 and is depreciated in the current API version.
- NetworkServiceDiscovery was introduced in API 16.

Fig. 3.2 Android reference page showing when an Android feature has been introduced

You can find out when a feature has been introduced by checking the top right-hand side of the Android reference page for the feature. For example, the reference page for the AsyncTask feature[1] shows that it has been introduced in level 3. See Fig. 3.2.

3.2.3 Android Application Characteristic

Useful Android apps are typically made of multiple interactive screens. Two of the main technologies used to create Android apps are Java and XML files.

XML is used to define resources, e.g., strings, color, layouts, and the manifest file. The manifest file is the entry point to the app. It plays a role similar to the main method of Java applications. Java files are used to define the app's behavior or business logic.

There are multiple challenges when developing Android apps. Android devices come in different kinds of screen sizes and resolutions that you need to account for when developing apps. Your app has to be secure, responsive, and smooth. Android is evolving continuously, and your app needs to be backward compatible as well. These issues and their solutions will be discussed throughout this book.

3.2.4 Android Activity

The Android Activity defines a screen, or a window, in your app, just like an HTML file of a website or a JFrame in a Java Swing application. It is the fundamental building block for creating Android applications. Activities for Android are the same as classes in Java and more. Activities, as the name implies, are activities and are created for a reason, for example, to display information, enable transactions, process business forms, etc. They enable user interactions such as clicking a button or entering text and can start other activities in the same or different apps. It has a lifecycle, i.e., it is created, started, run, paused and resumed, stopped, and destroyed. We will discuss these states in other chapters.

---

[1] https://developer.android.com/reference/android/os/AsyncTask

Just like a JFrame or an HTML page, an Activity usually has a user interface layout to enable arranging components on it. The layout is defined as an XML file. When the app starts, the components on the layout are transformed into visual objects and are arranged according to the layout definition. The components' transformation to visual objects is called inflating.

The following actions take place automatically when a simple Activity is created using Android Studio:

1. An Activity class is created which extends AppCompatActivity. The Activity is saved in a single file with .java extension.
2. An Activity layout is created which will be an XML file inside the layout folder, e.g., activity main.xml, declared inside the layout folder.
3. The Activity's layout is set. In other words, the layout for the screen is set. This is done inside the onCreate() method of the newly created Activity class. The *setContentView(R.layout.activity_main)* method call is used to set the layout and links the Activity code to the XML layout file.
4. A row, or an XML element holding information related to the newly created Activity, is added to the Android manifest.

In the first chapter, we created an Activity named MainActivity while creating a new project. You usually create activities following the steps below:

Right-click on the *app*, or Java folder, in your project, click on *New -> Activity -> Empty Activity* and click to open the create Activity dialog window, and fill in the Activity detail.

The code snippet shown in Listing 3.1 is the definition of the display message activity created for this chapter. The code is saved in a file called MessageDisplayActivity.java, and as you can see, the class is extending the AppCompatActivity class. The screen visual layout is set using the setContentView() method.

Listing 3.1 DisplayMessageActivity.java.

```
public class MessageDisplayActivity extends AppCompatActivity {
  @Override
  protected void onCreate(Bundle savedInstanceState) {
    super.onCreate(savedInstanceState);
    setContentView(R.layout.activity_display_message);
    }
  }
```

ssetContentView is a method in the Activity class that takes a layout object, an XML file declared inside the layout folder, as an input. The statement *R.layout.activity_display_message* is an instruction to the Android system to find inside the *res* folder a *layout* folder and retrieve an XML file named *activity_display_message*.

Another way to interpret the input parameter *R.layout.activity_display_message* passed to the setContentView method is that there is an *R* class that has a static class field called *layout*, which in turn has a static instance variable called *activity_display_message*. This is possible because all the components declared inside the XML file are transformed into visual objects, i.e., GUI type objects, and are presented on the activity screen to form the app screen. More on layout transformations to GUI objects and the R class will be described in the coming sections and chapters.

3.2.4.1   Activity Constructors and Methods

An Activity class has a public default constructor and many methods. These include startActivity(), getIntent(), onCreate(), findViewById(), getResources(), getSupportActionBar(), finish(), getParent(), getTitle(), isChild, setContentView(), and many more methods.

Remember that Java API provides many classes and interfaces to instantiate objects. These classes have one or more constructors, fields, and public methods. Since the Activity is a Java class in the Android SDK, it makes sense to think that it must have one or more constructors, fields, constants, and many public methods.

Activity methods can be classified. Some of these methods are getters and setter methods, for example, the getTitle() and setTitle() methods. Other methods are boolean methods returning true or false, like isChild(), isDestroyed(), isFinishing (), etc. Activities have methods where their names start with "on," for example, onCreate(), onSaveInstanceState(), onStart(), onStop(), onAttachFragment(), etc. These methods are called callback methods. Callback methods are usually invoked by the Android system in response to an event without the user having to directly intervene. We will study these methods as the book progresses.

3.2.5   R File

When compiling an application, the XML files are parsed to generate the R.java class class. For each *folder* **in your res directory,** there will be a static final class with the same name in the R.java file. For example, the layout folder in your app will be represented as a static final class layout. There will be a class for *color, dimen, layout, style, string*, and more in the R.java class.

The **XML files inside the app folders** are also represented in the R.java file. They are represented as a *static final int* instance variable in their corresponding classes (folders). For example, the activity_main.xml file inside the layout folder becomes a static final instance variable inside the layout class, which is an instance variable for the R.java file.

In the early versions of the Android framework, you were able to locate and open the R.java file by searching the *generated* folder of your app. It was located at *app\build\generated\not_namespaced_r_class_sources\debug\r\.* However, this is not the case anymore. New versions of the Android framework transform bytecode into machine code during app installation using ahead-of-time (AOT) compilation and Android runtime (ART), and there is no need to save R.java files anymore to be saved into your device. Nonetheless, inside the *app\build\intermediates \runtime_symbol_list\debug directory* of your project, you can see a file called R. txt with similar content to the R.java file. The R.txt file is used by the Android system for mapping source IDs to the resource name.

After compiling the Android code, the application is put into an "APK" (zip file) and installed on an Android device. Each app on the Android device has a separate Linux account created just for that one app. Each application is protected from other applications the same way that a Linux user is protected from other Linux users on the same machine. All applications can access shared system resources, just like Linux users can.

3.2.6 Android Context

Context is an interface to the app. This is an important class that you are going to use frequently. You can use context to refer to components of your app, for example, your Activity. The Activity class has a method called getContext(), and when called, it returns the reference to the current Activity. In this case, the getContext() method acts similar to the *"this"* construct in Java.

Activity is a subclass of the Context class. Hence, when it is appropriate, you can use Activity in places where Context is expected. For example, within an Activity, you can pass *this* in places where Context is needed.

The same can be applied to the TextView class. TextView is a class in the Android SDK which is the same as the JLable class in Java. The constructor of TextView takes Context as an input. It needs a place where the label can be drawn. In this case, Activity can safely be passed for Context. Here is an example:

```
TextView text = new TextView(this);
```

The getApplicationContext() method returns the context of the entire application and not just the current active Activity. The context of the application is the process holding all the Activities currently running. If you need the context of the entire application and not just the current Activity, use getApplicationContext() instead of getContext().

All Android UI classes are subclasses of the View class which is a class that we will study in other chapters. The View class has a method called getContext() which returns the context. To access the View context in your code, you can use any View component placed on your Activity and call getContext, e.g., *view.getContext()*.

3.2.7 Application Manifest Files

Every application must have a manifest file. The manifest file is the entry point to the app; it acts as the main method in Java. In the manifest file, you declare Activities that are a part of your application. The Activity that launches the app becomes the first screen of your app. When needed, you declare application permissions such as defining permission to use the internet, read files, make calls, etc. inside the manifest file. The parent-child relationship declaration between activities, as well as the app's interaction behavior with other apps on the same device and components within the same app, is also declared inside the manifest file. This information is needed for your build tools, Android OS, and Google Play Store.

3.2.8 Opening Android Project in Android Studio

You should have downloaded the MyFirstApplication.zip by now. If you did not, please do so. Once you have downloaded the .zip file, follow the steps below to open it. To open each of the demo projects given out, you will need to do this:

1. Click on the Application zip file, in this case, the MyFirstApplication.zip file, and download and save the file on your desktop or download folder.
2. Unzip the MyFirstApplication.zip. You will have the MyFirstApplication directory/ project.
3. In Android Studio, click *File → Open* if you have already opened a project.
4. Otherwise, click Open *an existing Android Studio project* at the "Welcome to Android Studio" screen.
5. Find the MyFirstApplication directory and click "Choose." The project should be opened and ready to run.

3.2.9 Cleaning Android Project Builds

If, for some reason, you get errors opening the MyFirstApplication, try to clean the build (go to **Build → clean project**). You also need to synchronize your code with Gradle files. You can do that by clicking on the *Sync Project with Gradle* button on the File menu or just click on the sync button on the menu bar; the Sync button is circled in Fig. 3.3. Cleaning builds and synchronizing your project with Gradle is oftentimes a helpful way to clear out project errors.

Fig. 3.3 Steps to follow to synch project with Gradle files

3.3   Create Your First Mobile App

In this part of the chapter, we will describe how to create your first mobile app. We use our *MyFirstApplication* example to describe the steps. This chapter, along with the previous one, is all that it takes to create your first app.

3.3.1   Your App Specification

Before creating an app, you need to know its specification, i.e., what you are going to build. In this example, the MyFirstApplication app is made of two activities or two screens: the   *MainActivity*   which   starts   the   second   Activity,   called *MessageDisplayActivity*, using an Intent object as a passing parameter between the two Activities. When the user types a message into the input box, or EditText object, on the first Activity and clicks *send button*, the message is bundled up in an intent object and is passed to the second Activity. The second Activity then starts displaying the message on its ViewText object.

Figure 3.4 is the screenshots of the app. The first screen from the left is rendered by the MainActivity; the user enters a message and clicks the send button. The DisplayMessageActivity starts to display the message (the middle screen). You can navigate back to the MainActivity view using the *Back to Main* button from the DisplayMessageActivity view.

To see the application code, open the *app/java* folder, and look at the MainActivity.java code. Again, a Java class with a visual presentation is called an Activity in Android. Below, we describe the steps involved in the app creation.

3.3.2   Create Activity Layout

Earlier in this chapter, we described how to create an Android Activity, specifically, how to create an EmptyActivity. When an Activity is created using the Android Studio, a window pops up, and you will be asked if you want to create a layout file for it. If you checked the *Generate a Layout File* box, a layout file is created. The location of the file would be at *app/res/layout/*. The XML code snippet in Listing 3.2

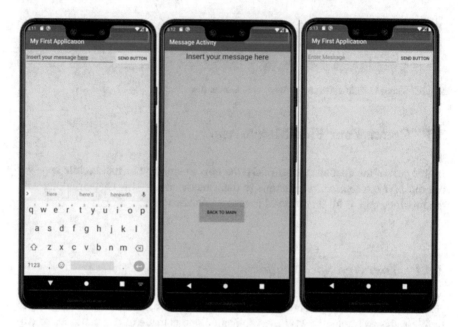

Fig. 3.4 Navigation between activities

is the layout for the MainActivity when you create a project following the default
steps for creating an EmptyActivity.

Listing 3.2 activity_main.xml file.

```
<?xml version="1.0" encoding="utf-8"?>
<androidx.constraintlayout.widget.ConstraintLayout
   xmlns:android="http://schemas.android.com/apk/res/android"
   xmlns:app="http://schemas.android.com/apk/res-auto"
   xmlns:tools="http://schemas.android.com/tools"
   android:layout_width="match_parent"
   android:layout_height="match_parent"
   tools:context=".MainActivity">
</androidx.constraintlayout.widget.ConstraintLayout>
```

As you can see, there are no entries for widget elements between the opening and
closing ConstraintLayout element, i.e., the layout is empty. To make it more
interesting, we need to add some widgets to it. For example, we may need to add
a button, TextView, and labels to make it more appealing. We will also change the
ConstraintLayout to the LinearLayout to simplify the Layout explanation. The
ConstraintLayout is too advanced for this chapter. The ConstraintLayout and other
layout classes will be discussed in Chap. 6. To see the XML layout file for the
MyFirstApplication demo app, check this location: *app/res/layout/activity_main.xml.*

3.3.2.1   Adding an EditText Field to the Layout File

By adding the code snippet below between opening and closing layout elements, we are adding an EditText object to the top left of the main screen of the app. This is a default location for elements added to the linear layout.

EditText is a class with many properties in the Android SDK. In Android, you can use an XML file to declare and initialize classes. In the code snippet below, the EditText class is declared, and four of its properties are initialized using tags. The name of the class becomes an XML element, and class fields are represented using XML element properties.

```
<EditText android:id="@+id/edit_message"
  android:layout_width="wrap_content"
  android:layout_height="wrap_content"
  android:hint="@string/edit_message" />
```

3.3.2.2   Add String to Resource File

By default, an Android project has a strings.xml resource file located *at app/res/values/* directory inside the project structure. Open the file and insert a new string key named "insert_message" and set the value to *"Enter a message."* See the example below:

```
<string name="insert_message"> Enter Message </string>
```

All strings of your app will be added here. So, add another string key, "send_button", for the button you'll soon add called "button_send".

Note that it is important to give your components and variables proper names. Having too many buttons and other variables in your layout without clear names might result in incorrect referencing, which in turn could result in total application failure. After adding strings to the strings.xml file, the content of your final string. xml file should be similar to the one listed below:

```
<resources>
 <string name="app_name">My First Application</string>
 <string name="insert_message"> Enter Message </string>
 <string name="send_button"> Send Button </string>
 <string name="action_settings">Settings</string>
 <string name="title_activity_display_message">My Message</string>
</resources>
```

3.3.2.3   Adding Components to the Layout File

Similar to the EditText class, Button is a class in the Android SDK. Using XML syntax, the Button class is declared below, and three of its properties are initialized. To put both EditText and Button on the same line, add the Button class description to the layout file, and put it under the EditText description.

```
<Button
 android:layout_width="wrap_content"
 android:layout_height="wrap_content"
 android:text="@string/button_send" />
```

To format the EditText input box, add the following attributes to an already declared EditText element in the layout file.

```
android:layout_weight="1"
android:layout_width="0dp"
```

You may think that changing EditText width to 0dp will make it disappear from the screen. However, this does not happen here because we are setting **EditText *layout_weight*** to 1 which will stretch the EditText width to the width of the device screen minus the width of other components that are on the same horizontal line. In this case, there is only one other component on the same line, the send button component. Widget properties will be described in detail in the coming chapters. Now, your end-result activity_main.xml layout file from the res/layout/ directory should be as shown in Listing 3.3:

Listing 3.3 The content of the activity_main.xml file.

```
<?xml version="1.0" encoding="utf-8"?>
<LinearLayout
  xmlns:android="http://schemas.android.com/apk/res/android"
  android:layout_width="match_parent"
  android:layout_height="match_parent"
  android:orientation="horizontal"
  android:background="@color/lightGreen">
  <EditText android:id="@+id/edit_message"
    android:layout_weight="1"
    android:layout_width="0dp"
    android:layout_height="wrap_content"
    android:hint="@string/insert_message"/>
  <Button
    android:layout_width="wrap_content"
    android:layout_height="wrap_content"
    android:text="@string/send_button"
    android:onClick="sendMessage"/>
</LinearLayout>
```

Note that we changed the default ConstraintLayout to LinearLayout to simplify the discussion about the layout. Layout types are described in detail in Chap. 6.

3.3.3 Invoke Message on Activity

Add android:onClick="sendMessage" to the Button definition. By doing so, you are saying that when button_send is pressed, a method called sendMessage() inside the MaintActivity.java class should be executed. The new definition for the Button would be as follows:

```
<Button
  android:layout_width="wrap_content"
  android:layout_height="wrap_content"
  android:text="@string/button_send"
  android:onClick="sendMessage" />
```

Open the MainActivity.java class inside your project, and add sendMessage() definition to the class. The class file is located inside the project's *res* directory. sendMessage is a regular Java class method, and you can add it anywhere in the MainActivity class where the method declaration is acceptable.

The signature for the methods declared inside the layout file has to abide by certain constraints. The return type of the method has to be void, the method should have only one parameter, and the type of the parameter is View. An example of the sendMessage() method implementation is given below.

```
/* This method is called when the user clicks the send button */
  public void sendMessage(View view) {
    // write your code in response to the button click
  }
```

3.3.4 Intent Class

The MainActivity code for the MyFirstApplication example uses the Intent object for starting a second Activity. Let's first explain what the Intent class is. Then, we will describe how you can create and use it.

The Android SDK has a class called Intent, and objects of the Intent class can be passed between Activities. In other words, Intent objects are message objects or links between Activities. You will see what that means when you create an Intent object and used it to start a second Activity and pass data to the second Activity.

You can think of Intent objects as something you would like to do, i.e., your intention, or description, of an operation to be carried out as you request the Android system to do something for you. For example, if you use Intent with the *StartActivity* method (more on StartActivity below), it will launch another Activity. It can also be used to initiate downloading a file and broadcast a message to other components of your app or other apps installed on your device.

There are two types of Intents, explicit Intent and implicit Intent. Both types are described briefly in the subsections below. We will return to this topic as the book progresses.

3.3.4.1   Explicit Intent

Explicit Intents are used to activate other components such as activities explicitly. You use explicit Intent when you know what app components you would like to trigger. Using explicit Intent enables you to pass objects between activities as well.

The code snippet below shows how an explicit Intent object is created. It is an explicit Intent because you pass explicitly the name of the second Activity, i.e., the MessageDisplayActivity.class, that needs to be provided to the intent constructor of the first Activity. As shown, you can also pass data to the next screen using the putExtra (key, value) method from the Intent class. The value of data can be a String, other Java primitive types, or objects.

```
Intent intent = new Intent (this, DisplayMessageActivity.class);
intent.putExtra("key", "value");
startActivity(intent);
```

A complete MainActivity code for the MyFirstApplication example is shown in Listing 3.4.

Listing 3.4 The MainActivity.java class.

```
package code.android.abdulrahman.com.myfirstapplication;
import android.content.Intent;
import androidx.appcompat.app.AppCompatActivity;
import android.os.Bundle;
import android.util.Log;
import android.view.View;
import android.widget.EditText;
public class MainActivity extends AppCompatActivity {
  public final static String EXTRA_MESSAGE =
      "code.android.abdulrahman.com.myfirstapplication.MESSAGE";
  private static final String TAG = "MyActivity";
   @Override
  protected void onCreate(Bundle savedInstanceState) {
    super.onCreate(savedInstanceState);
      setContentView(R.layout.activity_main);
  }
  /** Called when the user clicks the Send button */
```

```
public void sendMessage(View view) {
    // Do something in response to button
    Intent intent = new Intent (this, DisplayMessageActivity.class);
    EditText editText = findViewById(R.id.edit_message);
    String message = editText.getText().toString();
    intent.putExtra(EXTRA_MESSAGE, message);
    Log.d(TAG, "Intent fired ");
    startActivity(intent);
  }
}
```

3.3.4.2   Implicit Intent

There is another type of Intent, implicit Intent. When implicit Intent is used, the Activity that handles the Intent request is not specified; instead, the Android system finds one or more Activities that can handle the request.

To create an implicit Intent, you need two pieces of information: the *action* that needs to be carried out and the *data/information* for the action. The Intent class has multiple actions, or constants, that can be called, for example, *Action_View*, *Action_Dial*, *Action_Answer*, *Action_Call*, *Action_Pick*, *Action_search*, *Action_send*, and many more. The code snippet in Listing 3.5 shows how you can use Action_view to view a webpage and Action_Dial to dial a number using implicit Intent.

Listing 3.5   Using Action_view Action_Dial with implicit Intent.

```
Uri uri = Uri.parse("http://www.wlu.ca");
Intent anIntent = new Intent(Intent.ACTION_VIEW,uri);
startActivity(anIntent );

Uri uri = Uri.parse("tel:8005551234");
Intent telIntent = new Intent(Intent.ACTION_DIAL, uri);
startActivity(telIntent );
```

When using implicit Intent objects, the Uri object is used in two Intent constructors. Hence, it is important to know how to instantiate Uri objects correctly. Uri is a Java class from the net package. It has several methods including the *parse, fromfile,* and *fromParts* method that return Uri object. Both examples above, Listing 3.5, use the parse method to form Uri objects. To create a Uri object using the parse method, you need to know the format of the string passed to the parse method.

Another key step to using implicit Intent is to select a proper constant, or action, from the Intent class to be used with the Uri class. In the examples above, *Action_View* is used to view a webpage, and *Action_Dial* is used to dial a phone number. When you are developing an app with an implicit Intent, you need to check the Android reference page to find the proper string format for the Uri parse method and select the proper action for the Uri.

The Intent has other useful methods. Examples of such methods include PutExtra, putExtras, getIntExtra, etc. It also has multiple constructors; see the table below. We will talk more about these methods and constructors in the coming chapters. Remember that Intent is an important class with many constants, methods, and constructors and is an essential component for creating apps.

3.3.5   Using StartActivity

The Activity class, which is a subclass of Context class, defines multiple versions of the *startActivity* method. To start another Activity from your current Activity, you need to call the **startActivity()** method and pass an Intent object to the method. The Intent object should include the name of the second Activity you would like to launch. These steps are as follows:

1. Create an Intent object, for example, Intent myIntention = new Intent (this, DisplayMessageActivity.class);. The constructor that is used to create the myIntention object is Intent (Context ctx, Class<?> cls). The Intent class has other constructors to instantiate Intent objects. For the list of constructors, see Table 3.1.
2. Put data into the Intent object. Use putExtra() methods to include data about your intention, or the operation about to happen, inside the Intent object. For example, use putExtra(String name, String value) method. The putExtra() method is overloaded, and the intent class provides multiple versions of it.
3. Call startActivity with an Intent object, e.g., startActivity (myIntention);.

    Here we are saying "act upon my intention using the data that has been included in the myIntention object," i.e., start the DisplayMessageActivity screen. The Android system receives the call and starts an instance of the Activity included in the Intent object.

After adding the *startActivity* statement to the *sendMessage* method, the complete code for the *sendMessage()* method that can be invoked by the *Send button* looks as shown below.

Table 3.1 Intent constructors

Intent()	Create an empty intent
Intent(Intent o)	Copy constructor
Intent(String action)	Create an intent with a given action
Intent(String action, Uri uri)	Create an intent with a given action and for a given data url
Intent(Context packageContext, Class<?> cls)	Create an intent for a specific component
Intent(String action, Uri uri, Context packageContext, Class<?> cls)	Create an intent for a specific component with a specified action and data

```
/** Called when the user clicks the Send button */
public void sendMessage(View view) {
  // Do something in response to button
  Intent intent = new Intent(this, DisplayMessageActivity.class);
  EditText editText = findViewById(R.id.edit_message);
  String message = editText.getText().toString();
  intent.putExtra(EXTRA_MESSAGE, message);
  Log.d(TAG, "Intent fired ");
  startActivity(intent);
}
```

When the user presses the send button on the main screen, the sendMessage() method is executed, and the startActivity statement triggers the Activity that has been included in the Intent object, i.e., the Activity that has been passed to the startActivity as a parameter. These steps can be summarized as follows:

Send button → SendMessage () → startActivity (intent) → secondActivity.

Every Activity class inherits the startActivity methods from the Context class. Multiple versions of the *startActivity* method are defined in the Context class. We will use other forms of the startActivity method in other chapters.

Now, you need to create a second Activity, DisplayMessageActivity, for the code above to execute successfully.

3.3.6   Create Second Activity

To create a new activity using Android Studio, do this: Right-click on the app or Java folder, find New -> Activity -> Empty Activity, and click to open the create Activity dialog window; see Fig. 3.5.

Fill in the Activity details; see Fig.3.6.

Finally, click *Finish*. When you are done, Android Studio automatically does the following three things for you:

1. Creates the DisplayMessageActivity file
2. Creates the corresponding activity_display_message.xml layout file given you checked the generate layout activity box
3. Adds the DisplayMessageActivity to the AndroidManifest.xml

The DisplayMessageActivity code is presented in Listing 3.6.

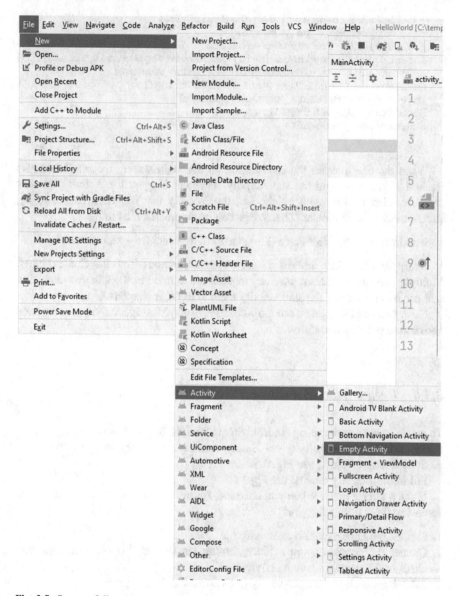

Fig. 3.5 Steps to follow to create a new project in Android Studio

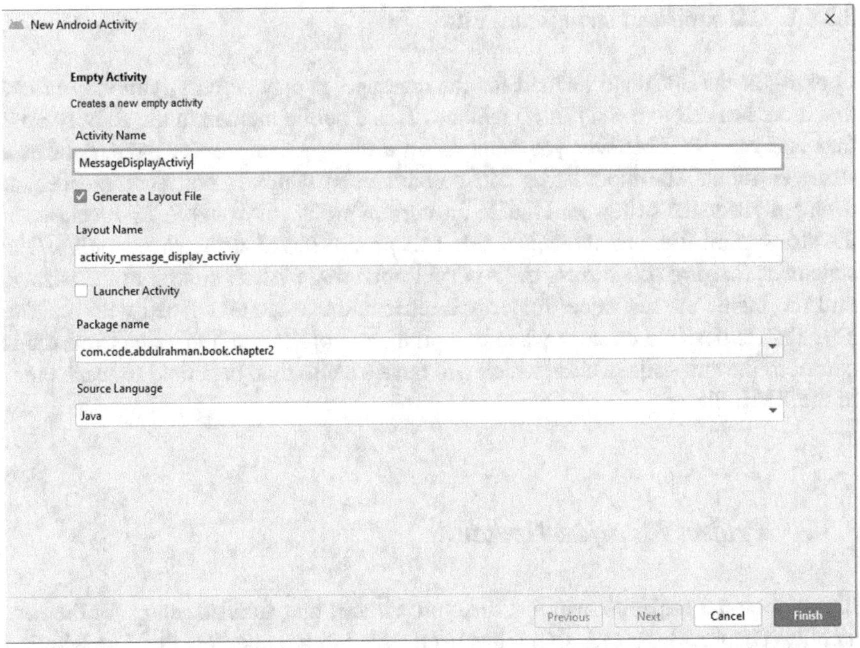

Fig. 3.6 Activity creation temple

Listing 3.6 MessageDisplayActivity.java.

```java
package code.android.abdulrahman.com.myfirstapplication;
import android.content.Intent;
import android.os.Bundle;
import android.support.v7.app.AppCompatActivity;
import android.util.Log;
import android.view.View;
import android.widget.TextView;
public class MessageDisplayActivity extends AppCompatActivity {
  private static final String TAG = "MessageDisplayActivity";
  @Override
  protected void onCreate(Bundle savedInstanceState) {
    super.onCreate(savedInstanceState);
    setTitle(R.string.title);
    setContentView(R.layout.activity_display_message);
    String intentMessage = getString(R.string.intentHasNoData);
}
```

If you created a *non-empty activity*, you would see that several methods have been created for you. We do not use these methods in the current exercise. For example, if you see that an onCreateOptionsMenu(Menu menu) method has been created, you can delete it for now.

3.3.6.1 R.string and strings.xml File

Looking at the onCreate method for the message display activity, you may notice that there is a call to the *setTitle()* method. This a public method in the activity class that you can use whenever you want to set a title for our activity page. It takes a string as input. The input string can be hardcoded which is not recommended or declared inside the strings.xml file. In the current project or example, it is declared in the strings.xml file, and the actual title text gets retrieved using *R.string.title*. The statement *R.string.title* directs the Android operating system to look at the strings. xml file inside the res/value/ folder and retrieve the value associated with the *title* key. This is possible because when compiling an application, the strings.xml file is parsed to the strings.java class which will have a static final data field for each entry in the XML file.

3.3.7 Project Manifest Update

If you open the project's manifest file, you will see that an XML entry for the new activity, DisplayMessageActivity, has been added to the manifest file. The addition is bolded in Listing 3.7.

Listing 3.7 AndroidManifest.xml.

```xml
<?xml version="1.0" encoding="utf-8"?>
<manifest xmlns:android=
  "http://schemas.android.com/apk/res/android"
  package="code.android.abdulrahman.com.myfirstapplication">
  <application
    android:allowBackup="true"
    android:icon="@mipmap/ic_launcher"
    android:label="@string/app_name"
    android:roundIcon="@mipmap/ic_launcher_round"
    android:supportsRtl="true"
    android:theme="@style/AppTheme">
    <activity android:name=".MainActivity">
      <intent-filter>
        <action android:name="android.intent.action.MAIN" />
        <category
        android:name="android.intent.category.LAUNCHER" />
      </intent-filter>
    </activity>
    <activity android:name=".MessageDisplayActivity" />
  </application>
</manifest>
```

3.3.7.1   Intent-Filter and Launcher Screen

We have already mentioned that the manifest file is the first file that gets execute and is an entry point to your app. However, there is much more to it than that. For example, if you have more than one activity, you can define which one will be the starting screen. This can be done by using intent-filter with an action name and category.

In the code snippet below, the intent-filter is part of the MainActivity definition, and both action and category names are used to specify that MainActivity is the starting, or the launcher, activity.

```
<activity android:name=".MainActivity">
  <intent-filter>
    <action android:name="android.intent.action.MAIN" />
    <category
    android:name="android.intent.category.LAUNCHER" />
  </intent-filter>
</activity>
```

If you decide to make, for example, MessageDisplayActivity the starting screen of your app, you need to put the intent-filer element inside the MessageDisplayActivity element declaration and use the action name and category name elements to define the new starting activity.

3.3.7.2   Setting Application Attributes

Application is one of the components of the manifest file. It has subelements and attributes. The subelements, such as Activity, are components of the app. If your app is made of multiple Activities, all Activities have to be defined inside the application element, and then they become the applications' child element.

Application attributes are used to define properties that can be applied to all components of the app. Some of these attributes, such as icon, label, and theme, have default values that can be changed by individual components. Others, such as the debuggable attribute, are applied to the whole application, and once set, it cannot be changed by an individual application component. Some of the attributes that you can set are listed in Listing 3.8.

Listing 3.8 Examples of Application attributes that you can set for your app.

```
<application android:allowTaskReparenting=""
  android:allowBackup=""
  android:allowClearUserData=""
  android:allowNativeHeapPointerTagging=""
  android:backupAgent="string"
  android:backupInForeground=""
  android:banner="drawable resource"
  android:debuggable=""
  android:description="string resource"
  android:directBootAware=""
  android:enabled=""
  android:extractNativeLibs=""
  android:fullBackupContent="string"
  android:fullBackupOnly=""
  android:gwpAsanMode=""
  android:hasCode=""
  android:hasFragileUserData=""
  android:hardwareAccelerated=""
  android:icon="drawable resource"
  android:isGame=""
  android:killAfterRestore=""
  android:largeHeap=""
  android:label="string resource"
  android:logo="drawable resource"
  android:manageSpaceActivity="string"
  android:name="string"
  android:networkSecurityConfig="xml resource"
  android:permission="string"
  android:persistent=""
  android:process="string"
  android:restoreAnyVersion=""
  android:requestLegacyExternalStorage=""
  android:requiredAccountType="string"
  android:resizeableActivity=""
  android:restrictedAccountType="string"
  android:supportsRtl=""
  android:taskAffinity="string"
  android:testOnly=""
  android:theme="resource or theme"
  android:uiOptions=""
  android:usesCleartextTraffic=""
  android:vmSafeMode="" ["true" | "false"] >
. . .
</application>
```

You don't need to learn about all these attributes from the get-go. Instead, based on the needs of the applications you are building, you will study one or more of these attributes. Some of these attributes, like *theme*, *label*, *logo*, and *icon*, are commonly used. Others, like *testOnly* and *supportRtl*, have limited use. When you want to test your app for a certain security feature but don't want to include it in your app, you might want to set the testOnly attribute to true. Similarly, you set supportRtl to true when you want your application to support right-to-left (RTL) layouts.

3.3.8   Running the App

Once you run the demo app and press the send message button on the main Activity, MessageDisplayActivity starts but is empty. This is because the second Activity has an empty layout; see Fig. 3.7. In the following subsections, we will add some elements to the second activity layout to make it more interesting.

Fig. 3.7 The second activity is launched from the first activity

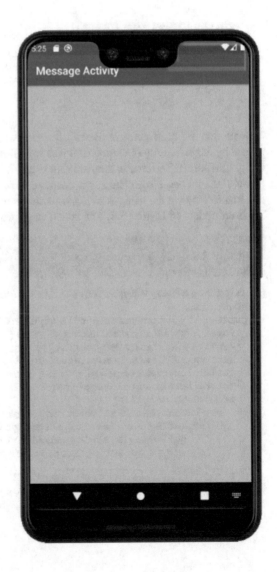

3.3.9   Receiving Messages/Data from an Activity

In the DisplayMessageActivity class and inside the onCreate() method, you can use the getIntent() method to receive the intent object passed by the main activity. The getIntent() method is a public method in the Activity class and can be used like this: **Intent intent = getIntent();.**

The message, or the data delivered by MainActivity, can be extracted as well. The code snippet below shows extracting data from the Intent object received from the caller Activity. You first check to see if the Intent is not null, and then you check to see whether any message or data has been put in the Intent object. If you pass the previous two checks, then you use the getStringExtra() method from the Intent class to retrieve the message.

```
Intent intent = getIntent();
if (intent != null) {
   if (intent.hasExtra(getString(R.string.message))) {
      intentMessage = intent.getStringExtra(
         getString(R.string.message));
      }
}
```

Note that we used getStringExtra() because we know that the type of message passed by MainActivity is a string. If it was something else, for example, int, then we use getIntExtra(). To retrieve the string message, i.e., the string value, you also need to know the message key. The key is declared in the strings.xml file as the *message*, and that is why we are using *R.string.message* as a key to retrieve its value. Listing 3.9 is an update of Listing 3.8. The added steps are highlighted in bold.

Listing 3.9 Using the Intent object, getStringExtra, and R.string.message.

```
public class MessageDisplayActivity extends AppCompatActivity {
   @Override
   protected void onCreate(Bundle savedInstanceState) {
      super.onCreate(savedInstanceState);
      setTitle(R.string.MsgActivity);
      setContentView(R.layout.activity_display_message);
      String intentMessage = getString(R.string.intentHasNoData);
      Intent intent = getIntent();
      if (intent != null) {
         if (intent.hasExtra(getString(R.string.message))) {
            intentMessage = intent.getStringExtra(
               getString(R.string.message));
            Log.d(TAG, getString(R.string.IntentRecieved));
         }
      }
      TextView messageTextView = findViewById(R.id.message);
      messageTextView.setText(intentMessage);
   }
   ...
}
```

3.3.10   Responding to the Messages from an Activity

To display the message on the screen of the second Activity, i.e., the MessageDisplayActivity view, you need to add a TextView element to the display layout of the Activity. To add a TextView, add the following element to the activity display_message.xml file.

```
<TextView
  android:id="@+id/message"
  android:layout_width="match_parent"
  android:layout_height="match_parent"
  android:layout_weight="1"
  android:text="TextView"
  android:textAlignment="center"
  anroid:textAppearance="@style/TextAppearance.AppCompat.Body1"
  android:textSize="24sp"
  android:typeface="normal"
  android:visibility="visible" />
```

Inside the onCreate() method of DisplayMessageActivity, you can access the TextView, which has been newly added to the activity_display_message.xml, using *findViewByID* and passing resource *id* as a parameter, i.e., passing *R.id.message*. The code statement would be like this:

```
TextView messageTextView = findViewById(R.id.message);
```

The message part of "R.id.message" is referencing the id we have included inside the TextView element definition: **android:id="@+id/message"**.

We added the *textAppearance* and *textAlignment* attributes to the description of the TextView for a better look.

The complete code for the onCreate() method for DisplayMessageActivity is shown in Listing 3.10. This is an updated version of Listing 3.8 which includes additional code for the TextView creation and uses. The setMessage() method from the TextView class is used to put the delivered message on the screen. The added code is highlighted in bold.

Listing 3.10 Using TextView and setMessage.

```
@Override
protected void onCreate(Bundle savedInstanceState) {
  super.onCreate(savedInstanceState);
  setTitle(R.string.MsgActivity);
  setContentView(R.layout.activity_display_message);
  String intentMessage = getString(R.string.intentHasNoData);
  Intent intent = getIntent();
```

```
    if (intent != null) {
      if (intent.hasExtra(getString(R.string.message))) {
        intentMessage = intent.getStringExtra(
            getString(R.string.message));
        Log.d(TAG, getString(R.string.IntentRecieved));
      }
    }
    TextView messageTextView = findViewById(R.id.message);
    messageTextView.setText(intentMessage);
  }
```

Once you are done, you can run your first Android application. Enter some text into EditText on the main screen, and then press the send button; see Fig. 3.8, on the left. A new activity should launch displaying the message you entered on the second screen; see Fig. 3.8, on the right.

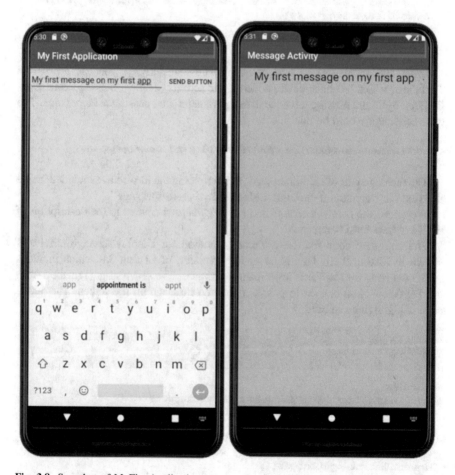

Fig. 3.8 Snapshot of MyFirstApplication screens. On the left is Main Activity; on the right is Display Activity

To make the app a bit more interesting, we added a button on the second activity. When it is pressed, the Display message Activity gets closed, and we return to the main activity. Here is the button description inside activity_display_message.xml.

```
<Button
  android:layout_width="match_parent"
  android:layout_height="60dp"
  android:layout_weight=".5"
  android:background="@android:color/holo_green_dark"
  android:text="Back to Main"
  android:visibility="visible"
  android:onClick="goToMain"/>
```

Note that, inside the button description, there is an entry called *android:onClick* which takes the name of the method that will be executed when the button is pressed. In other words, you name your method inside MessageDisplayActivity, in this example, as "goToMain." The method implementation inside the Activity must be public with a void return type, and it should have one parameter of type View. The method signature is as follows:

```
public void gotoMain(View view) {...}
```

The complete code for MessageDisplayActivity after adding the go back to the main button is shown in Listing 3.11.

Listing 3.11 MessageDisplayActivity.java return messages to the MainActivity.

```
package code.android.abdulrahman.com.myfirstapplication;
import android.content.Intent;
import android.os.Bundle;
import android.support.v7.app.AppCompatActivity;
import android.util.Log;
import android.view.View;
import android.widget.TextView;
public class DisplayMessageActivity extends AppCompatActivity {
  private static final String TAG = "DisplayMessageActivity";
  @Override
  protected void onCreate(Bundle savedInstanceState) {
    super.onCreate(savedInstanceState);
    setTitle(R.string.title_activity_display_message);
    setContentView(R.layout.activity_display_message);
    String message = "no data from intent";
    Intent intent = getIntent();
    if (intent != null) {
      if (intent.hasExtra(
        "code.android.abdulrahman.com.myfirstapplication.MESSAGE")) {
        message = intent.getStringExtra(
```

```
            "code.android.abdulrahman.com.myfirstapplication.MESSAGE");
            Log.d(TAG, "Got Intent");
        }
    }
    TextView messageTextView = findViewById(R.id.message);
    messageTextView.setText(message);
}
public void goToMain(View view) {
    // go back to main page in response to button
    Intent intent = new Intent (this, MainActivity.class);
    startActivity(intent);
}
}
```

The complete layout file for the activity_display_message is shown in Listing 3.12. This layout, along with the code in Listing 3.11, is the complete code for the second activity.

Listing 3.12 The content of the activity_display_message.xml file.

```xml
<?xml version="1.0" encoding="utf-8"?>
<LinearLayout xmlns:android=
 "http://schemas.android.com/apk/res/android"
 xmlns:tools="http://schemas.android.com/tools"
  android:layout_width="match_parent"
  android:layout_height="match_parent"
  android:background="@color/lightBlue"
  android:gravity="top"
  android:orientation="vertical"
  tools:context=".DisplayMessageActivity">
  <TextView
    android:id="@+id/message"
    android:layout_width="match_parent"
    android:layout_height="200dp"
    android:layout_margin="20dp"
    android:text="TextView"
    android:textAlignment="center"
    android:textSize="24sp"
    android:typeface="normal"
    android:visibility="visible" />
  <Button
    android:layout_width="200dp"
    android:layout_height="60dp"
    android:layout_gravity="center"
    android:background="@android:color/holo_green_dark"
    android:onClick="goToMain"
    android:text="Back to Main"/>
</LinearLayout>
```

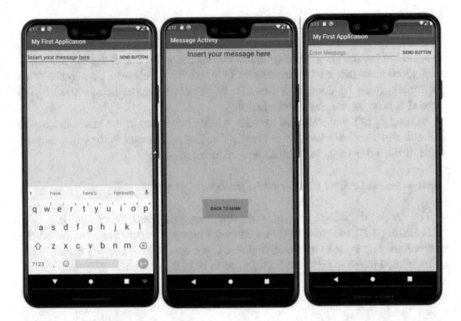

Fig. 3.9 Snapshots of back and forth between Activities

Figure 3.9 shows the back and forth between Main and DisplayMessage activities. First, a send button on the main activity launches the second activity. The second activity displays the content of the message carried inside the Intent object. Lastly, when the *back to the main* button is pressed on DisplayMessageActivity, the Message Activity gets closed, and the MainActivity screen gets opened, i.e., the MainActivity gets launched.

3.4 Debugging Information

The Android SDK has a Log class in the util package to log information and print debugging information to the Logcat window. It has several methods to write different log messages. The Android Log class can be utilized like System.out.println in Java for debugging. By using Logcat, the debugging and monitoring window in Android Studio, you can view the logs and filter log messages during app debugging.

The Log class has five methods for displaying debugging information. The methods are Log.i() for writing information, Log.w() for writing warnings, Log.e() for writing errors, Log.v() for writing verbose or detailed messages, and Log.d() for writing debugging statements. In this part, we will describe how to use the Log class methods in your app.

3.4.1   Debugging Using Log.d()

You use log statements in your code for various purposes. For example, you might want to confirm that an Intent fired by one activity is received by another. This confirmation can be done with Log.d(). In the code snippet below, the Log.d() method is used for message confirmation.

To use Log.d(), you first need to create a TAG in your code and then call Log.d() with the tag. The TAG variable is usually declared as constant in the class, and the value of the TAG variable is the activity name of your app.

```
private static final String TAG = "MainActivity";
```

The syntax of the log methods is like this: *Log.type (TAG, "message");*.

In Listing 3.13, we show how you can use Log class in your app. We import the *android.util.Log* class to the code, define a TAG, and call the Log.d() method. The codes related to the logging are highlighted in bold font.

Listing 3.13 An example showing how to use Log.d in your app.

```
package code.android.abdulrahman.com.myfirstapplication;
import android.content.Intent;
import androidx.appcompat.app.AppCompatActivity;
import android.os.Bundle;
import android.util.Log;
import android.view.View;
import android.widget.EditText;
public class MainActivity extends AppCompatActivity {
  public final static String EXTRA_MESSAGE =
      "code.android.abdulrahman.com.myfirstapplication.MESSAGE";
  private static final String TAG = "MyActivity";
   @Override
  protected void onCreate(Bundle savedInstanceState) {
    super.onCreate(savedInstanceState);
      setContentView(R.layout.activity_main);
  }
    ...
  }
}
```

The Send message method from MainActivity uses Log.d to log debugging information; see the code snippet below.

```
/** Called when the user clicks the Send button */
public void sendMessage(View view) {
  // Do something in response to button
  Intent intent = new Intent (this, DisplayMessageActivity.class);
  EditText editText = (EditText) findViewById(R.id.edit_message);
```

```
String message = editText.getText().toString();
intent.putExtra(EXTRA_MESSAGE, message);
Log.d(TAG, getString(R.string.intent_fired));
startActivity(intent);
}
```

A debug message has been written to the log file. Using Logcat, we can read that the Intent object has been received from MainActivity. The code to show this step is written in Listing 3.14.

Listing 3.14 A code to show Intent object sent by sender is received.

```
Public class MessageDisplayActivity extends AppCompatActivity {
  private static final String TAG = "MessageDisplayActivity";
  @Override
  protected void onCreate(Bundle savedInstanceState) {
    super.onCreate(savedInstanceState);
    setTitle(R.string.MsgActivity);
    setContentView(R.layout.activity_display_message);
    String intentMessage = getString(R.string.intentHasNoData);
    Intent intent = getIntent();
    if (intent != null) {
      if (intent.hasExtra(getString(R.string.message))) {
        intentMessage = intent.getStringExtra(
            getString(R.string.message));
        Log.d(TAG, getString(R.string.IntentRecieved));
      }
    }
    TextView messaView = findViewById(R.id.message);
    messaView.setText(intentMessage);
  }
```

3.4.2 Using Logcat to View Log Messages

You can monitor logs using the Logcat window. Logcat is a command-line tool integrated into Android Studio. You'll find Logcat at the bottom of Android Studio or by clicking the View tab from the Android menu bar followed by the Tool Window and Logcat menu item. The following screenshot, Fig. 3.10, shows viewing and filtering logs from the Logcat window.

We will study code debugging in more detail in the next chapters. What is described here is just a short introduction to Log class and viewing logs in the Logcat window in case you need it while you are creating and running your first app.

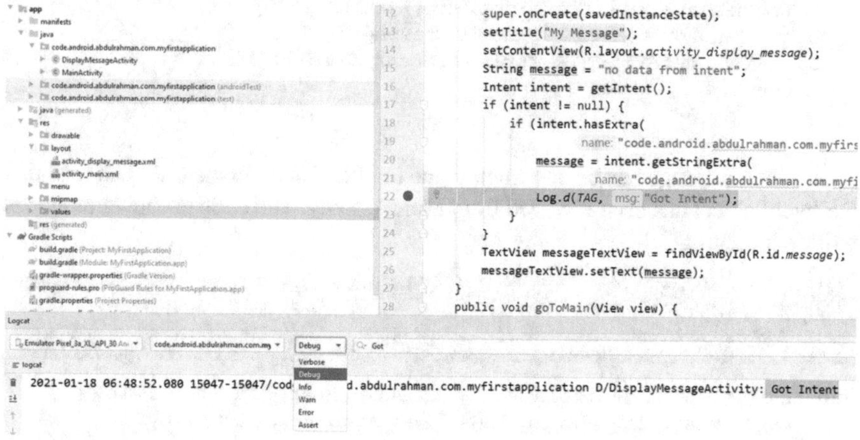

Fig. 3.10 Debugging window is shown with debugging message

3.4.3   Do It Yourself

3.4.3.1   Exercise 1

For this chapter, we have defined TextView and Button inside the Activities' Layout XML files. These objects can be defined as Java code inside your MainActivity and DisplayMessageActivity classes. For example, you can create TextView as follows:

```
TextView = new TextView(this);
textView.setTextSize(40);
textView.setText(message);
```

Re-write the MainActivity and the DisplayMessageActivity classes using Java code only. That is, instead of declaring Android classes inside the XML layout file, use Java code. Study the trade-off between defining UI objects as an XML element vs. Java code.

3.4.3.2   Exercise 2

Familiarize yourself with Android shortcuts. To reduce errors and improve your development time, it is good practice to use Android Studio shortcuts. A comprehensive Android keyboard shortcut is listed on the Android Studio Developers webpage. Put the link below in your browser to see the list of Android shortcuts (https://developer.android.com/studio/intro/keyboard-shortcuts).

3.4.3.3   Exercise 3

Each new version of the Android API adds new features to the prior version. We listed some of the Android APIs and their unique features in this chapter. Search the

Android developer page, to find out what is unique to other APIs that we have not listed in the chapter.

3.5 Localize Your App and Resources

Android runs on a large number of devices and in all countries and regions of the world. For your app to be used by the largest possible number of users, it should at least handle text, numbers, currency, and graphics in ways that is suitable to users in many places. This chapter describes the best practices for localizing Android apps.

3.5.1 Create a Resource File for Second Language

To support texts in other languages in your app, you need to create a strings.xml file similar to the default strings.xml file for the English language for every language you would like to support. To do so, right-click on the "*res*" folder of your app, and select "New" followed by *Android Resource File*. This step is shown in Fig. 3.11. A window, same as the one shown in Fig. 3.12, will open. Select "Locale" from the list, and click the ">>" button to see the list of languages that you can choose from.

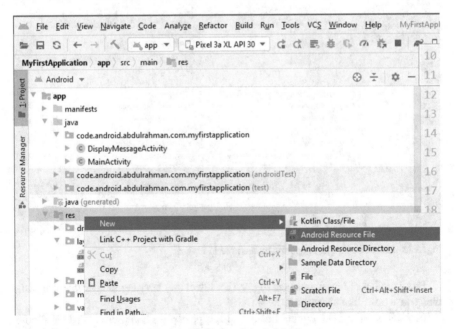

Fig. 3.11 Create a new string resource file for language locale

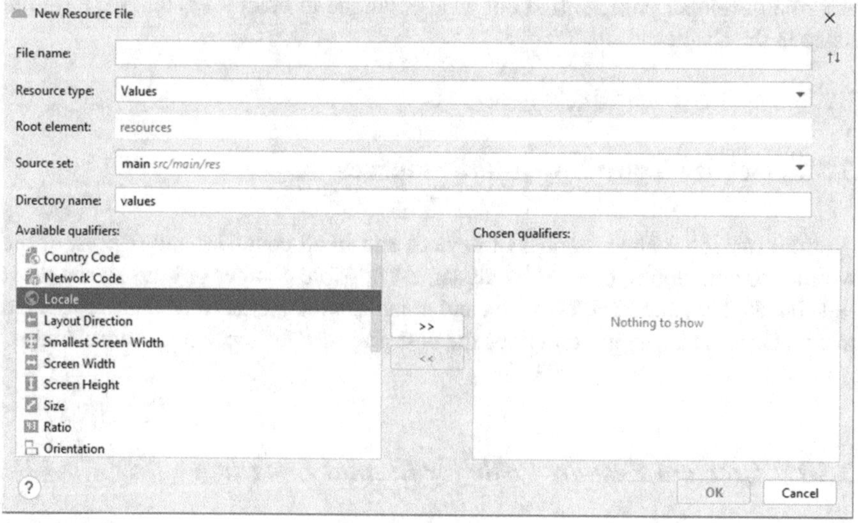

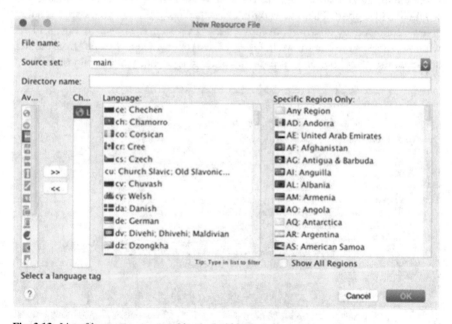

Fig. 3.12 First step to localize your app

Fig. 3.13 List of languages supported by Android is shown

From the list of languages (see Fig. 3.13), select any language, other than English, that you would like to support.

In the file name field, circled in Fig. 3.14, type *strings* and press *OK*. This should create a second "strings.xml" file in the *values* folder. The pattern for the newly

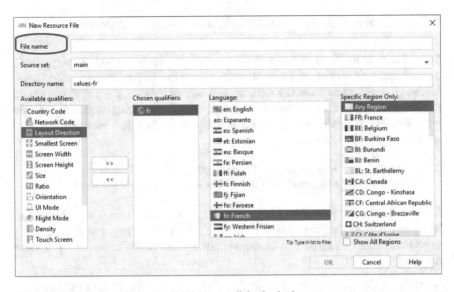

Fig. 3.14 Support for different English language dialectics is shown

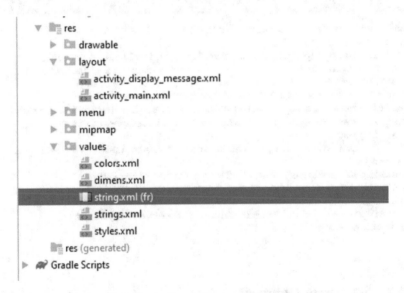

Fig. 3.15 A new strings.xml file for the French language is shown

created file name would be *string(XX-rYY)* where the string is the language like French or Arabic, the first XX is the language qualifier like fr or ab, and the second rYY is the specific region you selected. You also have a choice to not select a specific region. To do so, you leave the Specific Region option to *Any Region*.

In Fig. 3.15, a new string XML file in the values folder is shown for the French language. The file is called french.xml(fr). The file name shows that the French language is selected and is not specified for a specific region.

3.5.2 Create Resource Entries for Languages Supported

To add content to the newly created strings.xml file for the second language, copy
the xml elements between the <resources> tags of the original "values/strings.xml"
file, and paste them between the <resources> tags of the new *strings(xx).xml* file. In
the strings.xml file for the second language, modify the string values to the new
language. For example, the *app name* element in English and French string files
would be as follows, respectively.

```
<string name="app_name">My First Application</string>
<string name="app_name">Ma première application</string>
```

Note that the key part of the XML entry, i.e., app_name, is the same in both files.
It is only the value part, the actual text, of each entry in the strings.xml file that needs
to be translated. Listing 3.15 is an example of a resource file *string.xml(fr)* for our
demo app:

Listing 3.15 strings.xml example for the French language.

```
<?xml version="1.0" encoding="utf-8"?>
<resources>
  <string name="app_name">Ma première application</string>
  <string name="insert_message"> Entrer un message </string>
  <string name="send_button"> Bouton d\'envoi </string>
  <string name="textview">TextView</string>
  <string name="back_to_main">Retour à la page principale</string>
  <string name="MsgActivity">Activité de message</string>
  <string name="message">
      code.android.abdulrahman.com.myfirstapplication.MESSAGE
</string>
  <string name="IntentRecieved">Got Intent</string>
  <string name="intentHasNoData">aucune donnée d\'intention
</string>
  <string name="intentFired">Intention renvoyée</string>
</resources>
```

3.5.3 Set Device Language

To be able to read the content of the second strings.xml you just created, you need to
change the language of your device or the emulator if you are running your app on
the emulator. To do so, click on *Settings -> Language & Input -> Language* menus
or anything equivalent to that. This step may look different on different devices and
different versions of Android. Set the language of the phone to whatever you choose
as your second language for your app. Your app will automatically read the strings

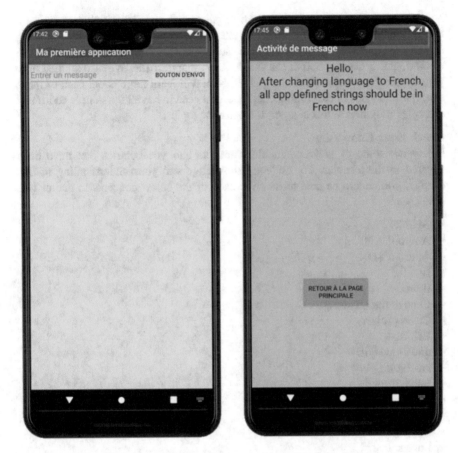

Fig. 3.16 MyFirstApplication is running with support for the French language

from the other strings.xml file you created. Below is an example of supporting the French language in the app; see Fig. 3.16.

3.6 Chapter Summary

In this chapter, we described how to create your first Android app. We defined Activity as a Java class or a component in your app representing a window that fills the screen. We also described both explicit and implicit Intent classes as a message object and a description of the operation that needs to be carried out. We studied the Context class, the Log class, and other classes. We studied how to start a second Activity with an Intent object using the startActivity method, passing data between Activities with extras, and going back and forth between Activities.

We described the fundamental steps to create an app. These include defining a layout in XML, defining an Activity by extending AppCompatActivity, connecting Activity to the XML layout file using the setContentView method in the onCreate() method, and declaring Activity in the Android manifest file. We also studied how your app can support multiple languages. You will learn more about each of these concepts and steps in the coming chapters. You need to run all the sample codes and examples provided in this chapter to master the topics.

Check Your Knowledge

Below are some of the fundamental concepts and vocabularies that have been covered in this chapter. To test your knowledge and your understanding of this chapter, you should be able to describe each of the below concepts in one or two sentences.

- Activity
- Android API
- Android SDK
- Bundle
- Button
- Change the UI string
- Clean project
- EditText
- findViewByID
- hasExtra
- Implicit Intent
- Intent
- Local
- Log class
- Logcat
- OnClick
- OnCreate()
- Open the Layout editor
- getApplicationContext()
- getContext()
- getIntent
- getStringExtra
- intent.putExtra
- Project Sync
- R.java
- setText
- startActivity
- TextView
- Uri

Further Reading

For more information about the topics covered in this chapter, we suggest that you refer to the online resources listed below. These links provide additional insight into the topics covered. The links are mostly maintained by Google and are a part of the Android API specification. The resource titles convey which section/subsection of the chapter the resource is related to.

Build a simple user interface, [online] Available: https://developer.android.com/training/basics/firstapp/building-ui

Localize your app, [online] Available: https://developer.android.com/guide/topics/resources/localization

Keyboard shortcuts, [online] Available: https://developer.android.com/studio/intro/keyboard-shortcuts

Navigation, [online] Available: https://developer.android.com/training/implementing-navigation/ancestral

Intent, [online] Available: https://developer.android.com/reference/android/content/Intent.html

Log, [online] Available: https://developer.android.com/reference/android/util/Log

Chapter 4
Debugging and Testing Using Junit, Espresso, and Mockito Frameworks

What You Will Learn in This Chapter

By the end of this chapter, you should be able to:

- Debug code with the Android Studio Debugger
- Run the Android Profiler to profile your code
- Use the Device File Explorer to manage your app files
- Use the Android Debug Bridge (adb) command-line tool to access Linux shell
- Create Toast and Snackbar messages
- Use Log and the Logcat utility to view log messages from the Logcat window
- Use Junit, Expresso, and Mockito frameworks testing to test your code
- Apply test coverage using Android Studio
- Use a reverse engineering technique to generate a class diagram from the code

Check Out the Demo Project

Download the demo app, **ch04.zip**, specifically developed to go with this chapter. I recommend that you code this project up from the notes rather than just opening the project in Android Studio and running it; however, if you want to run the code first to get a sense of the app, please do so. The code is thoroughly explained in this chapter to help you understand it. We follow the same approach to all other chapters throughout the book. The app's code will help you comprehend the additional concepts that will be described in this chapter.

How to run the code: unzip the code in a folder of your choice, and then in Android Studio, click **File->import->Existing Android code into the workspace**. The project should start running.

© The Author(s), under exclusive license to Springer Nature Switzerland AG 2022

A.-R. Mawlood-Yunis, *Android for Java Programmers*,

https://doi.org/10.1007/978-3-030-87459-9_4

4.1   Introduction

In this chapter, the focus will be put on fault detection (testing and debugging) using the Android Studio Debugger to locate faults and code errors and to fix them. In addition to what Android Studio offers as an IDE to enable debugging and testing, we also study the Android classes and methods that facilitate testing. For example, we will discuss the classes and methods that enable unit testing and how it can be conducted using Android Studio.

Different from the previous chapters, in this chapter, you need to practice what will be described. You need to open Android Studio, run an existing app, follow the instructions provided in each section, and observe the results. You need to be creative and curious to run and find out more about each feature described in this chapter to be fluent in Android debugging and testing. What you are going to learn here will help you throughout your software development career. Each part of this chapter is important and you should not skip it. However, you might not need to read this chapter entirely in one attempt. Instead, you could come back to this chapter as you read other chapters of the book.

4.2   The Android Studio Debugger

In this part, we describe code debugging in Android Studio. We show you how to enable and use the Android Debugger tool to debug your code, inspect and modify variable values during debugging, use the Android Profiler tool to profile the performance of your code, use the Device File Explorer to access and modify files on Android devices, and use the Android Debug Bridge (adb) command-line tool to run Linux commands on an Android device.

4.2.1   Fault Handling Methods

There are various software fault handling methods and approaches. These include preventing fault from happening in the first place, detecting the fault and fixing it, or applying mechanisms to tolerate fault. These methods and techniques can be grouped and classified in various ways. Figure 4.1 shows one way to classify these methods. This is a non-inclusive list of methods. There might be other ways to deal with software bugs, errors, and faults.

From Fig. 4.1, you can draw parallels between software fault handling and fault treatments in other fields of science. For example, in health science, prevention is the best approach to avoid sickness, and once you get sick, you need medication, and when medication is not helpful, you have to live with consequences. As you can see, this is the same approach that is followed in software fault handling: prevention,

Fig. 4.1 Classification for
fault handling approaches

- **Fault Handling**
  - o **Fault Avoidance**
  - o **Fault detection**
    - ▪ **Debugging**
      - • **Correcting code**
      - • **App performance**
    - ▪ **Requirement testing**
  - o **Fault-tolerance**
    - ▪ **Component redundancy**
    - ▪ **N version programming**

fixing, and dealing with consequences. As you progress through this book, you will be introduced to all fault handling approaches listed in Fig. 4.1.

When developing Android apps, the types of bugs that you should watch out for include incorrect or unexpected results, wrong values, crashes, exceptions, freezes, and memory leaks. Android Studio comes with various built-in tools and plugins for app debugging, i.e., finding and fixing errors in code, as well as testing app performance, and verifying/validating the non-functional requirements. Android Studio enables you to debug apps running on the emulator and Android devices. With Android Studio, you can do the following:

- Set a debugging device.
- View the system log.
- Set breakpoints in your code.
- Check the variables and evaluate expressions at runtime.
- Run the debugging tools to debug your code.
- Capture screenshots and videos of your app using Logcat or Android monitor. Android monitor is used in early versions of Android Studio.

The features above enable you to find incorrect or unexpected results, wrong values, crashes, exceptions, freezes, and memory leaks.

4.2.2 Enable Debugger

To debug code, i.e., find and fix errors, you need to enable the debugging option on your device. It is enabled for the emulator by default. As for your device, use *settings* to find developer options. If you cannot find developer options, it means it is hidden by default. Follow the instructions below to enable it.

First, on your device, go to *Settings* → *About <device>* → *build number*, and then tap *build number seven times* or more to make developer options available. On

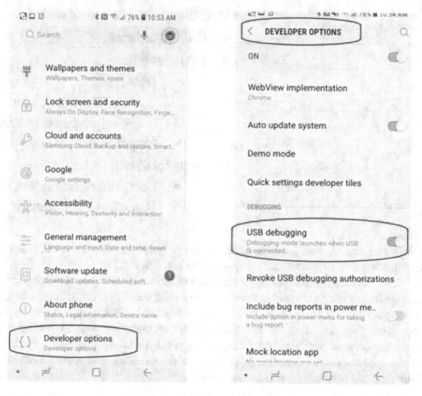

Fig. 4.2 The developer and USB debugging options that you need to enable for debugging

newer Android devices, you need to go to *Settings → System → about <device> → build number*. You also need to enable the USB debugging option. Figure 4.2 shows the developer and USB debugging options that you need to enable.

Now that you have enabled the developer and USB debugger options, do the following to start debugging:

1. Open the project in Android Studio.
2. Select a hardware device, an emulator, or your connected device, for debugging code.
3. Click on the debug icon on the toolbar (circled in red in Fig. 4.3), or click *run → debug* on the menu bar. The app starts on the selected device, and the debugging window opens. Once you see the debugging window, highlighted in black in Fig. 4.3, it indicates that the debugger is attached to your development environment.

Now, you can step through your code and execute it line by line, using the debugging buttons circled in green in Fig. 4.3.

Fig. 4.3   Android Studio debugging windows

While debugging, you can execute code by clicking on the step buttons or using the shortcuts such as F8 for Start Over and F7 for Step Into. The step buttons are circled in green in Fig. 4.3.

During debugging, you can highlight any variable or expression by right-clicking on it and pressing *Evaluate Expression* or *Add to Watch* to find out the value of the variable and the value of the expression when it is executed.

The debugger also allows you to see the execution stack. This is shown in Fig. 4.4. The execution stack and the frame that responds to the current breakpoint are shown below.

4.2.3   Inspecting and Modifying Variable Values

While you are running your code in the debugging mode with breakpoints set, if you execute your code one step at a time using the step buttons, you can see the state of each class variable and object in the Logcat window. Figure 4.5 shows the inspecting variable window.

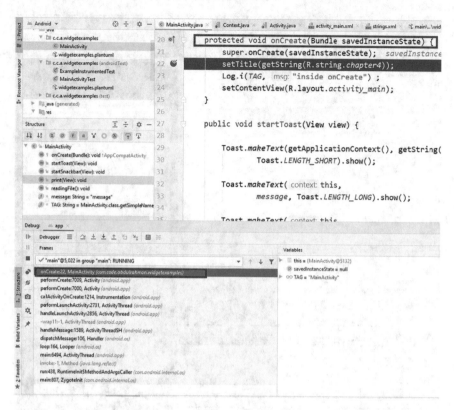

Fig. 4.4 View of the debugger window for inspecting the execution stack

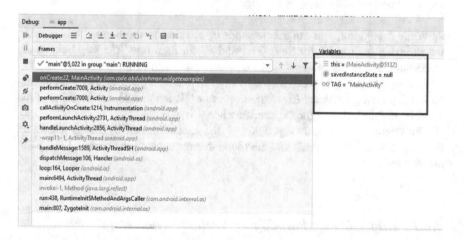

Fig. 4.5 Variables view of the debugger window

Note that, when your app is ready to be published, you need to remove the logging statements and any calls to Toast and Snackbar debugging messages. This cleanup is needed to avoid app hanging and crashes.

4.2.4   Android Profiler

Quality assurance (QA) requirements, such as performance, usability, robustness, security, privacy, and other non-functional requirements, are essential parts of almost all apps. The Android Profiler provides you with the ability to profile your code, i.e., verify/validate the non-functional requirement such as the performance and usability of your app.

Code profiling provides you with real-time data on how much your app uses CPU, memory, network, and battery resources. Using the captured data, you can inspect CPU activity and traces, Java heap and memory allocation, network traffic, energy usage, etc. Table 4.1 summarizes these activities.

To open the Profiler window, on the Android Studio's menu bar, click *View* → *Tool Windows* → *Profiler*, or click on the Profile icon, shown in Fig. 4.6, in the toolbar. Run the app, and press on the plus sign to start profiling (see Fig. 4.7).

Figure 4.7 is a snapshot of the app profiling window. The four components that you can profile, as well as the session ending button, are circled. Once started, the Android Profiler continues collecting data until you either disconnect the device or click the ***end session button***.

On the right-hand side of Fig. 4.7, the graphical representation of the apps' resource usages (CPU, memory, network, energy) is shown. This information can be utilized to determine an app's non-functional behavior. More information about each of the graphs can be found by clicking on it. The ability to extract data about an app's behavior is not only useful for managing device resources but could also be the base for developing various useful apps, for example, having an app that examines all apps, i.e., profiling all the apps running on your device to return information about the CPU time, memory, network, and battery usage for each app.

Table 4.1 Profile activities

CPU profiler	CPU activity and traces
Memory profiler	Java heap and memory allocations
Network profiler	Network traffic
Energy profiler	Battery usage

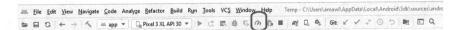

Fig. 4.6 Profile icon is shown

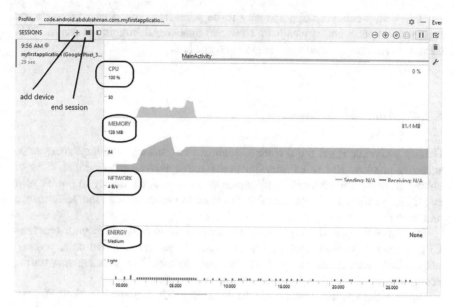

Fig. 4.7 App profiling snapshot

4.2.5   Device File Explorer

The *Device File Explorer* allows you to view, edit, copy, and delete files on an Android device. To use the Device File Explorer on the Android Studio's menu bar, click *View → Tool Windows → Device File Explorer*, or click the Device File Explorer button if it is visible in the window toolbar. File Explorer can be used to examine the files you created or copy files from one device to another.

To practice with the Device File Explorer, run your app and select a device, and open the Device File Explorer window to see the files stored on the device. For example, in Fig. 4.8, Emulator Pixel_3_XL_AP1_30 has been selected to see its content. Figure 4.8 shows some of the device's directories.

If you open the *data directory*, you might be able to see all the apps that you have run on this emulator; an example is shown in Fig. 4.9. The location of where the apps are stored is emulator-dependent.

It is important to be able to access the data directory of your emulator/device and be able to, for example, delete some of the apps/files you no longer use to free up space. Using the Device File Explorer, you can move and create files and directories and check to see whether the file your app is supposed to create has actually been created.

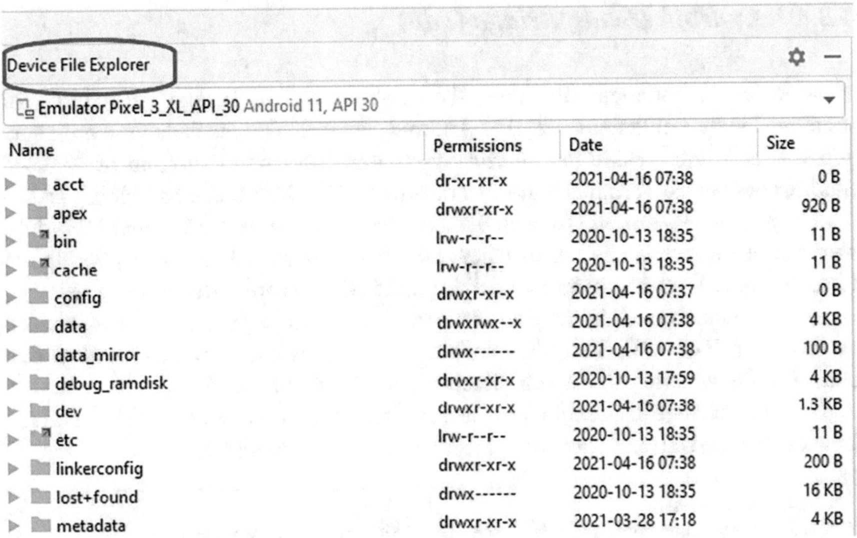

Fig. 4.8 Device File Explorer for an emulator

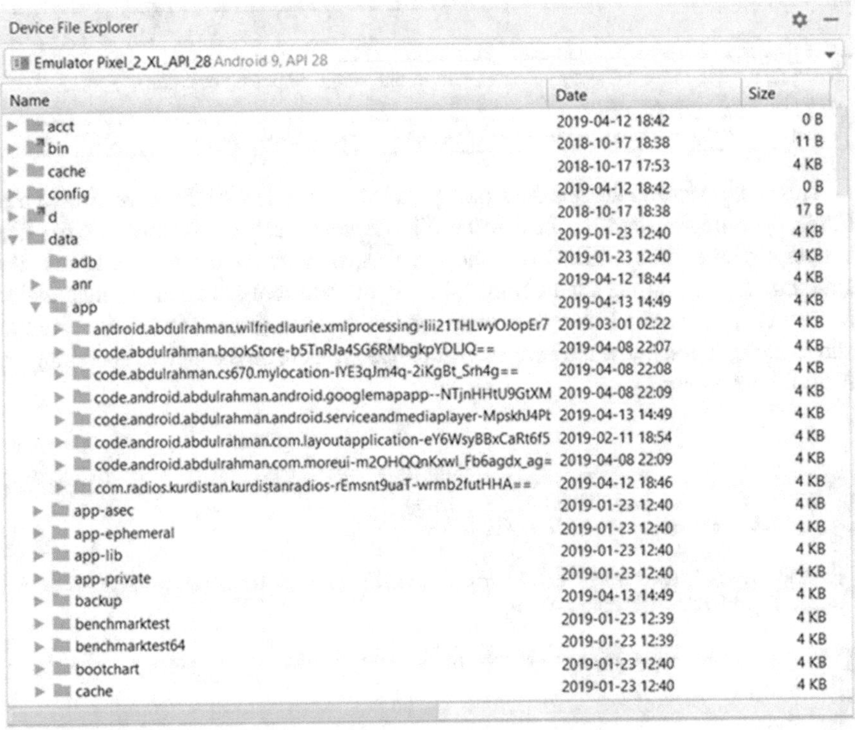

Fig. 4.9 Apps inside the data directory of an emulator

4.2.6 Android Debug Bridge (adb)

Android has a command-line tool, the Android Debug Bridge (adb) tool, for running Linux commands on the Android device. The executable command, adb.exe, is located inside the *platform*-tools directory. At the bottom of Android Studio, click on the Terminal button, or on Android Studio's menu bar, click *View* → *Tool Windows* → *Terminal* to open the Terminal window. In the *Terminal Window*, change the directory, i.e., cd, to where adb.exe is located. It is usually located at **C:\Users\userName\AppData\Local\Android\Sdk\platform-tools\adb.exe.**

Replace "userName" in the path above with *your* user name, in my case, *amawl*, as shown in Fig. 4.10. The steps above, i.e., opening the Terminal window and changing the directory to the adb directory, are shown in Fig. 4.10.

Once you change the directory to the adb directory, you can start adb *shell* and run Linux commands. Below are some examples of shell commands:

To start, type *adb shell:*
C:\Users\AbdulYunis\AppData\Local\Android\Sdk\platform-tools>**adb shell**

Use exit to quit the shell, **generic_x86_64:/ $** *exit*
 and use *ls* to list all the files, **generic_x86_arm:/ $ ls**

To create a shell, make a directory, and exit all in one single command use: *adb shell mkdir /sdcard/app_bkup/.*

To copy a file to the device, use *adb push fragment.apk /sdcard/app_bkup/.*

This section shows that the Android operating system is a modified version of the Linux operating system. In the Device File Explorer section, we saw that the file structure of the Android device is the same as, or very similar to, the Linux file structure. If you run the shell command ls on the adb tool, you can see that again. Moreover, you can run Linux commands on the Android device emulators using the adb tool. So, if you know the Java and Linux OS, you are on the path to becoming an Android developer.

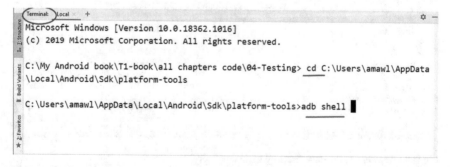

Fig. 4.10 Command-line terminal of Android Studio to run Linux commands using adb

4.2.7   Do It Yourself

In this section, we list a few activities that you need to do to improve your experience and exposure to the Android Studio tools. You will practice using the Android Debugger, the Device File Explorer, the Android Profiler, and the Android Debug Bridge or adb.

1. Debug an app

   Open one of the apps we have created for this course. To pause the normal execution, put breakpoints in your code by clicking on the left side of the editor window next to the line numbers. When a red button next to the line numbers appears, it indicates that a breakpoint has been set. See Fig. 4.11 for an example. Run your code by pressing the debug icon or Run → debug. A window like the one shown in Fig. 4.3 should open. Press on the step button (circled in green in Fig. 4.3, also shown Fig. 4.11), and observe the result.

   Experiment with five buttons (Step Over, Step Into, Force Step Into, and Step Out functions and Run to Cursor), and observe and record the execution behavior of each button.

2. Profile an app

   Open one of the apps developed in this course. Run the app and the profiler, and find out how much CPU time, memory, and energy the app uses. Check to see whether the app is causing any network traffic.

3. Use the Device File Explorer

   Run one of the apps developed in this course, and use the Device File Explorer to find where the apps have been installed on the emulator or your device file system. Try to find the location of all the apps you run on your device or on the emulator. See what is inside the data and *sdcard* folders.

4. Running Linux command using the adb shell

   To familiarize yourself with the file structure of your device or your emulator, run the following Linux file management commands on the adb shell. You need to run the following commands carefully to avoid unwanted results. For example, the *rm* command is used to delete files, the *mv* command is used for moving files, etc.

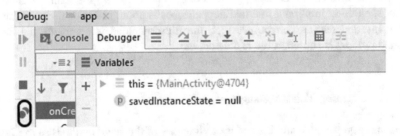

Fig. 4.11 Debugging step buttons and breakpoints

Run *Pull*, *push*, *ls*, *cd*, *rm*, *mkdir*, *touch*, *pwd*, *cp*, *mv*, and *adb device*, and observe the results. You can find other adb commands using *adb shell ls system/bin*.

5. Access apps installed on a device

Create an app that allows you to access all the apps installed on a device. To do so, you need to access the Data directory on the device. Your app should be able to display the name of all the apps listed in the Data directory, delete apps, and create new files and directories.

4.3   Toast and Snackbar Messages

In Android, the *Toast* and *Snackbar* classes are used to give users feedback messages on events that occurred. You can use these classes to identify where in your code something went wrong. For example, you can create snackbar/toast messages inside the catch block of exception handling to find out where the exception happened and its type. We have developed an app to demonstrate how to implement toasts and snackbars in your app. The main interface of the demo app developed for this chapter is presented in Fig. 4.12. The app has three buttons on the main page, one for displaying the toast messages, one for displaying the snackbar messages, and one for displaying information about the current or parent layout.

4.3.1   Toast Messages

In programming languages such as Java, System.out.println is heavily used by programmers for debugging. Developers use the print and println methods to print messages to the console and learn what their code is doing. Similarly, C/C++ developers use the "printf" and "cout" commands to print messages to the console.

In Android, the *Toast* class in the android *widget* package can be used as print, printf, and cout in Java and C/C++, to display a brief message to the developer or user. When the toast message is shown, it appears as a floating text over the screen. It does not block user interaction with the device. Similar to the System.out.print and cout, Toast messages can be a part of an application giving feedback to the user about something important that had happened or is about to happen. For example, when inserted data is correct/incorrect, the file download is complete, the background process is started, a file is deleted, etc.

4.3.1.1   Creating Toast Messages

Toast messages are usually created by calling one of the static methods of the Toast class, for example, *makeText*. The method signature of makeText is as follows:

Fig. 4.12 The main
interface of the demo app

```
public static Toast makeText (Context context, CharSequence text, int
duration);
```

MakeText is a standard toast and takes three parameters: the object, or the view, that displays the toast message, the text of the message, and the duration that the message stays displaying. Android uses CharSequence in places where String is used in Java, but you can still use String. This is because String is CharSequences, i.e., the String class implements the CharSequence interface.

There is another MakeText method that takes the resource id as a second parameter instead of the CharSequence type for the text of the message, meaning that the text is from a resource folder. The signature for the second MakeText method is shown below:

```
public static Toast makeText(Context cxt, int resId, int duration);
```

When you call the second version of the makeText method, you can use *getString(R.string.toastText)* for the *resId*.

The *getString()* method is a public method in the Activity class, and *R.string.toastText* can be interpreted as follows: the *R* class references its static field *res* (res directory), *string* refers to the strings.xml file inside the *values* directory, and *toastText* is a key for a string element inside the resource tag. The steps of referencing the *R.string.toastText* text are shown in Fig. 4.13.

Note that the context parameter in the MakeText method is usually "*this*"; the duration can have any of these constants:

- Toast.LENGTH_SHORT
- Toast.LENGTH_LONG

Android had another constant called LENGTH_INDEFINITE for use with the MakeText() method. In newer versions of Android, this is not supported directly. The code snippet in Listing 4.1 shows how Toast can be coded in your app.

Fig. 4.13 The R.string.toastText components

Listing 4.1 MainActivity.java class.

```java
import android.widget.Toast;
public class MainActivity extends AppCompatActivity {
...
  public void startToast(View view) {
    Toast.makeText(getApplicationContext(),
        getString(R.string.app_name),
               Toast.LENGTH_SHORT).show();
    Toast.makeText(this,
        message, Toast.LENGTH_LONG).show();
    Toast.makeText(this,
        "some text", Toast.LENGTH_LONG).show();
    Toast.makeText(this, getString(R.string.app_name),
               Toast.LENGTH_SHORT).show();
  }
}
```

There are a few things that you should note about the example above.

1. In the code above, both long and short constants are used for showing a Toast message. Of course, you just need one to use in your code, but the example shows how you can use each of them.
2. The example shows that you can change the first parameter of the makeText() method from the getApplicationContext() method to *this*. It is possible to do so because *this* refers to the Activity which is a subclass of the Context class. When using *this* with the makeText() method, the method call will become as follows:

```java
Toast.makeText(this, getString(R.string.app_name),
        Toast.LENGTH_SHORT).show();
```

3. The example shows that the toast message can be hardcoded, a class field, or referenced from the strings.xml file.
4. You need to call the *show* method on the makeText() method to display the actual Toast message. Without calling the show message, you will make a Toast object, but you are not displaying the actual Toast. This is because the makeText() method returns the Toast object and only when you call the show method on it will it display the Toast message on the View.

Figure 4.14 shows the Toast message on the View once the Toast button of the demo app is pressed.

Fig. 4.14 App snapshot
with toast message being
displayed

4.3.2 Snackbar Messages

Similar to Toast messages, the Android SDK has another class called *Snackbar* in
the package android.support.design.widget for displaying messages. It can be used
to display a brief message to the user at the *bottom of the phone and lower left on
large devices*. The message automatically goes away after a short period making it
different from Toast which goes away only when the display time expires.

The Snackbar is ideal for brief messages the user doesn't necessarily need to act
on. For example, a file management app could use a Snackbar to tell the user that the
app successfully downloaded a file. The Snackbar class is *newer* than the Toast class
and provides more features, e.g., it can handle some forms of user input and can be
dismissed by swiping. It is considered as the replacement to the Toast class.

4.3.2.1 Creating Snackbar Messages

Displaying the Snackbar message in your app involves a few steps.

1. Create a Snackbar object with the message text by calling the static method make(). The Snackbar object creation is shown below.

```
Snackbar snackbar = Snackbar.make(view, resouceID, duration);
```

2. Call the show how method to show the message to the user. For example,

```
Snackbar.show();
```

You also need to import *android.support.design.widget.Snackbar* to your code and have the *com.android.support:design* support library in your *build.gradle* file.

Below is an example of a build.gradle file with a support library for the Snackbar. Depending on the API level used, your support library can be the same or different from the example below:

```
dependencies {
  implementation fileTree(dir: 'libs', include: ['*.jar'])
  implementation 'com.android.support:appcompat-v7:28.0.0'
  implementation 'com.android.support:design:28.0.0'
  implementation 'com.android.support.constraint:constraint
                       -layout:1.1.3'
  testImplementation 'junit:junit:4.12'
  androidTestImplementation 'com.android.support.test:runner:1.0.2'
  androidTestImplementation
          'com.android.support.test.espresso:espresso-core:3.0.2'
}
```

The parameters for the Snackbar.make (View view, int resouceID, int duration) method are View, resouceID, and the duration. The purpose and the description of the parameters are as follows:

1. **View**: The view that the Snackbar should be attached to. The view object can be obtained in different ways.

   A. View parentLayout = findViewById(R.id.*content*). *R.id.content* returns the root of the current View. On some devices, R.id.*content* returns null. If you experienced a null return, use
   getWindow().getDecorView().findViewById(android.R.id.*content*) ;
   B. You can always assign an id to the Activity layout and use the given id to access the View of an Activity. Here is an example:

View parentLayout = findViewById(R.id.*myLayout*); where **myLayout** is an id of a screen layout that you would like to display the Snackbar message on.

2. **resouceID**: The *resource ID* of the message you want to display. The description of the resouceID is same as the resouceID we discussed for MakeText in the Toast class. It refers to the text that can be obtained from the strings.xml file inside the res/values folder. For example, you can pass R.string.***app_name*** or any other string you would like to display as a method parameter.
3. **duration**: It can be any one of these three static constants: **LENGTH_LONG, LENGTH_SHORT, or LENGTH_INDEFINITE.**

The code snippet in Listing 4.2 shows how the Snackbar class can be used in your coding:

Listing 4.2 SnackbarActivity.java.

```
public class SnackbarActivity extends AppCompatActivity {
  @Override
  protected void onCreate(Bundle savedInstanceState) {
    super.onCreate(savedInstanceState);
    setContentView(R.layout.activity_main);
    View parentLayout = findViewById(R.id.content);
    Snackbar snackbar = Snackbar.make(parentLayout,
                R.string.app_name, Snackbar.LENGTH_INDEFINITE);
    snackbar.show();
  }
}
```

If you want to specify a View for your snackbar, i.e., if you want to replace *R.id.content,* for example, with *R.id.myLayout* where myLayout is the id of your rootView, you can do it using a statement like this:

```
findViewById(R.id.myLayout).
```

Listing 4.3 is an example where we have defined a rootView, meaning we have assigned an id called myLayout to the LinearLayout object. In this case, the LinearLayout object is a rootView because it is a top element in the layout file holding all Views or Buttons in it.

Listing 4.3 Assigning an id to a view (LinearLayout).

```
<?xml version="1.0" encoding="utf-8"?>
<LinearLayout
    xmlns:android="http://schemas.android.com/apk/res/android"
    xmlns:tools="http://schemas.android.com/tools"
    android:id="@+id/myLayout"
    android:layout_width="match_parent"
    android:layout_height="match_parent"
    android:background="@color/lightgold"
    android:orientation="vertical"
    tools:context=".MainActivity">
```

```
<Button
  android:layout_width="match_parent"
  android:layout_height="wrap_content"
  android:onClick="startToast"
  android:text="@string/click_to_toast"
  android:textStyle="normal" />
<Button
  android:layout_width="match_parent"
  android:layout_height="wrap_content"
  android:onClick="startSnackbar"
  android:text="@string/click_to_get_snackbar"
  android:textStyle="normal" />
<Button
  android:layout_width="match_parent"
  android:layout_height="wrap_content"
  android:onClick="parent_or_current_layout"
  android:text="@string/parent_or_current_layout"
  android:textStyle="normal" />
</LinearLayout>
```

Once you have assigned an id to your root view, you can replace
`View parentLayout=findViewById(R.id.content);` in listing 4.2 with
`View parentLayout = findViewById(R.id.myLayout);` and use the
parentLayout variable as the first parameter to the *make* method as follows:

```
Snackbar = Snackbar.make (parentLayout, R.string.app_name,
  Snackbar.LENGTH_SHORT);
```

Figure 4.15 shows an app snapshot with a Snackbar message displayed at the
bottom of a phone emulator.

In addition to the method *make(View view, int resId, int duration),*
Snackbar has another version of the make method to display messages, i.e.,
make(View view, CharSequence text, int duration). Here the *CharSequence* is
used in place of ResouceID. Accepting the CharSequence instead of the resId is
useful for displaying hardcoded debugging messages quickly.

To use something for debugging, it has to be simple and quickly done. The
second version of the make method can be utilized to quickly print a debugging
message. For example, the two lines of code below are good enough to produce a
debugging message:

```
Snackbar.make (R.id.content,"some text", Snackbar.LENGTH_SHORT);
Snackbar.show();
```

In the code snippet below, we make use of the *make* method to develop a *print*
method that you can use anywhere in your code during debugging. To use the
method, you simply call the print method and pass the debugging message and a
View, i.e., the place where you want the message to be printed.

Fig. 4.15 App snapshot
with Snackbar message
being displayed at the
bottom

```
public void print (View view, CharSequence message) {
  View parentLayout = findViewById(R.id.content);
  if (null != parentLayout) {
    Snackbar snackbar = Snackbar.make
        (parentLayout, message, Snackbar.LENGTH_INDEFINITE);
    snackbar.show();
  }
}
```

The code for the *print* method, along with how to show the Snackbar and Toast
messages that can be used for debugging purposes, is included in Listing 4.4.

Listing 4.4 MainActivity.java.

```java
package com.code.abdulrahman.widgetexamples;
import android.os.Bundle;
import android.util.Log;
import android.view.View;
import android.widget.Toast;
import androidx.appcompat.app.AppCompatActivity;
import com.google.android.material.snackbar.Snackbar;
import java.io.FileInputStream;
import java.io.FileNotFoundException;
public class MainActivity extends AppCompatActivity {
  String message = "message";
  @Override
  protected void onCreate(Bundle savedInstanceState) {
    super.onCreate(savedInstanceState);
    setTitle("Chapter 4: Android Widgets and Debug");
    setContentView(R.layout.activity_main);
  }
  public void startToast(View view) {
    Toast.makeText(getApplicationContext(),
        getString(R.string.app_name),
    Toast.LENGTH_SHORT).show();
    Toast.makeText(this,
        message, Toast.LENGTH_LONG).show();
    Toast.makeText(this,
        "some text", Toast.LENGTH_LONG).show();
  }
  public void startSnackbar(View view) {
    // View parentLayout = findViewById(R.id.content);
    View parentLayout2 =
    getWindow().getDecorView().findViewById(android.R.id.content);
    Snackbar snackbar = Snackbar.make
        (parentLayout2, R.string.app_name,
          Snackbar.LENGTH_INDEFINITE);
    snackbar.show();
  }
  public void print (View view) {
    View parentLayout = findViewById(R.id.myLayout);
    if (null != parentLayout) {
      Snackbar snackbar = Snackbar.make
          (parentLayout, message, Snackbar.LENGTH_INDEFINITE);
      snackbar.show();
    }
  }
  public void readingFile() {
    final String logTAG = "ParentLayout";
    final String FILE_NAME = "fileName.txt";
    try {
      FileInputStream fis = openFileInput(FILE_NAME);
      // do something with the file
    } catch (FileNotFoundException exception) {
      String errorMsg = FILE_NAME + " not found";
```

```
        Log.e(logTAG, errorMsg, exception);
        Toast toast = Toast.makeText(this, errorMsg,
                    Toast.LENGTH_SHORT);
        toast.show();
    }
  }
}
```

There are also methods for setting the text and text color of the Snackbar messages. If you would like to explore more about the Snackbar and Toast classes, see the reference provided at the end of this chapter.

4.3.3   Do It Yourself

Write a method called *print* with the void return type. The method should take one String as an incoming parameter. Include the Snackbar/Toast creation code inside the *print* method. The code should Toast the incoming message parameter. During debugging, call the print method whenever you need to print a debugging message.

4.3.4   The Log Class and Logcat Window

We have introduced the Log class and Logcat tool in the previous chapter. Here, we provide more details about the Log class and Logcat window.

The Log class is included in the android.util package and can be used to log messages at runtime. The Log class has multiple static methods that can be utilized to create and filter proper messages. The methods are *Log.e, Log.w, Log.i, Log.d, Log.v*, and *Log.wtf.* As a developer, you use these methods to log proper messages: *error, warning, information, debugging messages, verbose,* and *what a terrible failure,* respectively. These methods take two parameters; the first one is the TAG, and the second one is the message information.

To help where the issue is, the TAG parameter is usually the name of the activity, for example, **private static final String TAG = "MainActivity";**.

To avoid hardcoding, or to avoid long Activity names (when the activity name includes the package name, it becomes a long name), you can use the getSimpleName () method from the Class class to name your TAG. Here is an example:

```
static String TAG = MainActivity.class.getSimpleName();
```

There is a second version of each logging method listed above that takes three parameters each. The second version of the methods logs the error messages and the exceptions that can be thrown. Exceptions and exception handling are an essential part of programming in Java and any object-oriented programming. The second versions of the log methods recognize this role and provide you with the ability to log the exceptions, thus helping you to recognize errors and exceptions in your code. An example of the Log method signature with three parameters is as follows:

```
Log.e(String TAG, String message, Throwable exception);
```

4.3.4.1 Logging Class Exception

The code snippet in Listing 4.5 shows how the Log class can be used to log the exceptions to the Logcat window for error handling. When an exception is thrown, it will be caught inside the catch block. The log statement inside the catch block is then used to log the exception.

Listing 4.5 Logging class and exception.

```
public void readingFile() {
      final String logTAG = "MainActivity";
      final String FILE_NAME = "fileName.txt";
      try {
       FileInputStream fis = openFileInput(FILE_NAME);
       // do something with the file
      } catch (FileNotFoundException fileNotFound) {
       String errorMsg = FILE_NAME + " not found";
       Log.e(logTAG, errorMsg, fileNotFound);
       Toast toast = Toast.makeText(this, errorMsg,
                               Toast.LENGTH_SHORT);
       toast.show();
     }
  }
```

4.3.4.2 Using adb with Log Messages

You can view Log messages in Android Studio by clicking on the "Logcat" icon on the bottom of Android Studio. If it is not shown, click on *View*→ *tool Windows*→ *Logcat*. The Logcat window is shown in Fig. 4.16. The log message can be filtered based on message type (error, warning, verbose, etc.) or by the TAG specified in the log method calls.

Log messages can also be viewed in the debugger by using the Android Debug Bridge (adb). The command *adb logcat* launches the Logcat window.

You can redirect the output of the adb to a file using >> operator. For example, to redirect your log message to a text file in c:\temp directory, cd to platform-tools, and type this:

```
\Android\Sdk\platform-tools> adb logcat >> c:\temp\log.txt
```

The command line creates a text file with all log messages for further analysis.

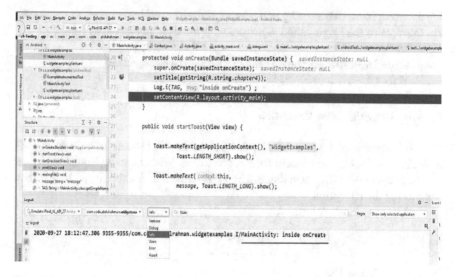

Fig. 4.16 The Logcat window with filtering options dropdown list is showing

Table 4.2 Logcat icons and their description

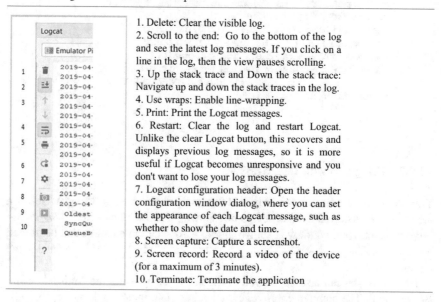

1. Delete: Clear the visible log.
2. Scroll to the end: Go to the bottom of the log and see the latest log messages. If you click on a line in the log, then the view pauses scrolling.
3. Up the stack trace and Down the stack trace: Navigate up and down the stack traces in the log.
4. Use wraps: Enable line-wrapping.
5. Print: Print the Logcat messages.
6. Restart: Clear the log and restart Logcat. Unlike the clear Logcat button, this recovers and displays previous log messages, so it is more useful if Logcat becomes unresponsive and you don't want to lose your log messages.
7. Logcat configuration header: Open the header configuration window dialog, where you can set the appearance of each Logcat message, such as whether to show the date and time.
8. Screen capture: Capture a screenshot.
9. Screen record: Record a video of the device (for a maximum of 3 minutes).
10. Terminate: Terminate the application

There are multiple icons on the left-hand side of the Logcat debugging window. The icons are numbered and their description are provided on the right-hand side of Table 4.2. When clicked, each icon on the list does an action to help developers debug code more efficiently. Below is a brief description of each icon.

4.4   Android App Testing

Testing is a fundamental step in the software development process. As a matter of fact, there is a software developing process that depends entirely on testing. This framework, or methodology, is called test-driven development (TDD). A good review of the TDD framework and tools that enable such an approach is provided in [1].

When developing Android apps, various elements need to be tested. In [2], five of these important elements are identified for testing Android apps. The elements are Intent, Activity lifecycles, event handlers, XML files, and null handling. For an overview of state-of-the-art works on Android app testing challenges and trends, see [3].

You need to test your code to make sure it works the way you expect. There are various testing types. Depending on the application development stage, you will have a different type of testing. For example, when different components developed by different teams are integrated together, you need to do integration testing. To deliver software to the user, you need to do user acceptance testing. Unit testing is the testing type performed by the developers. While they develop a solution, they have to test their code. The piece of the code that is tested during a unit test is the smallest one. It is either a method, part of a method, a class, or few classes.

The type of testing we consider in this section is unit testing. We also consider using the Junit framework which enables us to do automatic testing and re-run existing tests to make sure that previous tests are still working and that you are not breaking any previously tested code.

For the projects you create, you need to develop *unit tests* to make sure that you are handling fundamental error checking. For example, you need to check for invalid input types and logical errors in your code. When reading/writing files, you need to handle unexpected file types and file not found exceptions. You also need to check for correct interactions with activities, etc.

When you create a new Android project, Android Studio generates two folders for testing, the ***instrumental folder (androidTest)*** and a ***unit test (test) folder***. The first one, *instrumental testing*, is used to run tests that need to be run on Android devices or Android Virtual Devices. The second one is used for *unit testing*, tests that require only a Java virtual machine to run. Both types are described below.

4.4.1   Create a Test Class

It is easy to create test cases and test your code in the Android Studio. Once the Java class you want to unit test has a focus in the editor, on computers with the Windows operating system, click anywhere inside the class you want to test, and press **Ctrl+Shift+T**; a window pops up to help you with the creation of a new test (see Fig. 4.17).

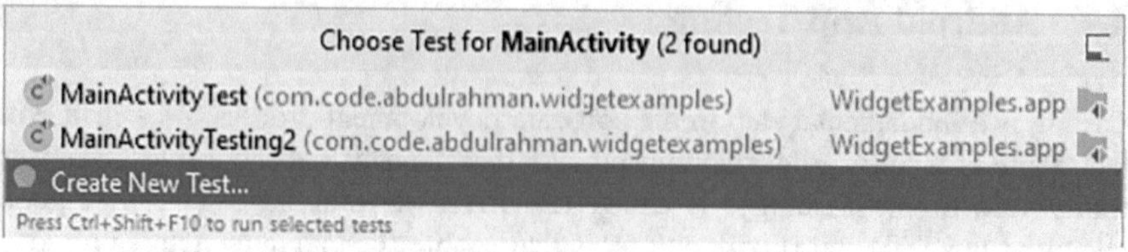

Fig. 4.17 Window for creating a new test class

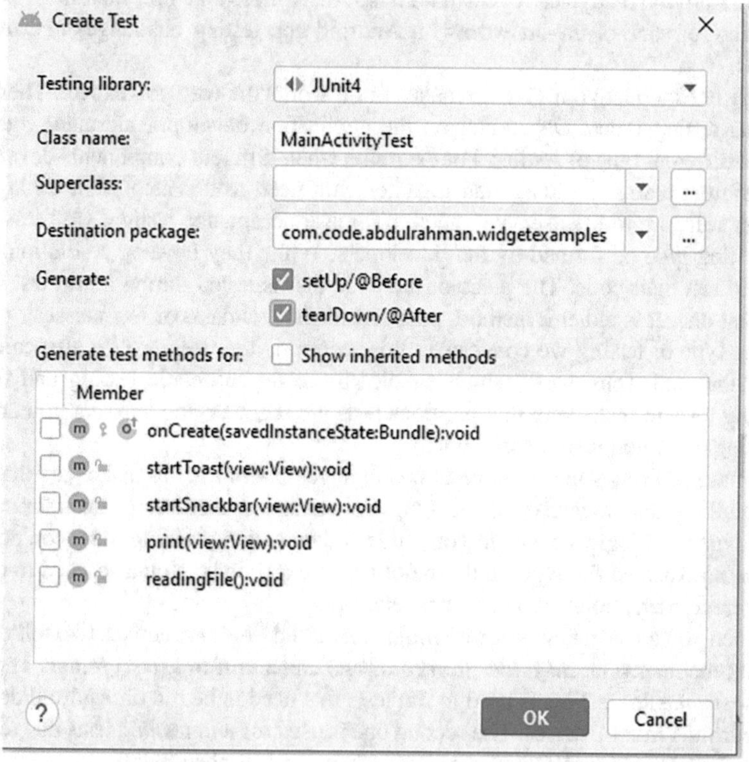

Fig. 4.18 New test class template

In the menu that appears, click *Create New Test*; a test window will pop up for creating a test class (see Fig. 4.18). Select the methods you want to test, and press OK.

The previous steps will generate a test class inside the Android Test directory, the instrumental directory. A snapshot of the generated class is listed below, Fig. 4.19. It is a skeleton class that needs to be completed.

You can also create a test class following a regular way of creating classes. Right-click on the directory where you want to create your testing class, and create a class.

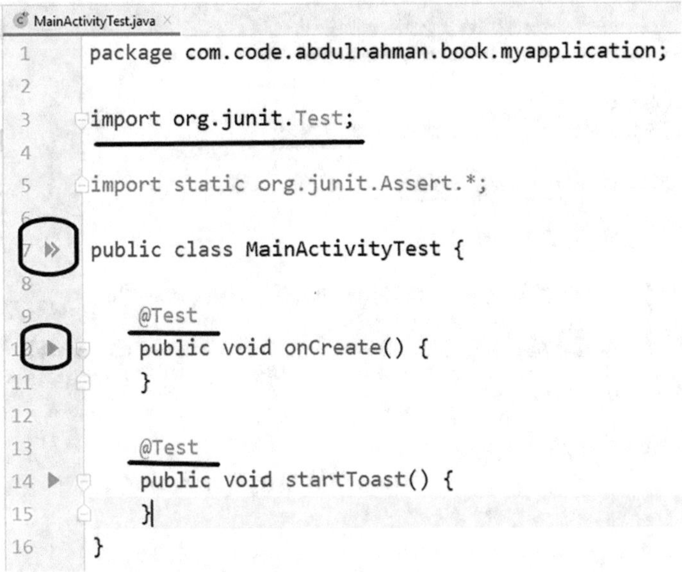

Fig. 4.19 Test class skeleton generated using CTRL + Shift + T

Inside your testing class, declare your test methods. The method must be public with a void return type. Each test method should start with annotation @test.

In Listing 4.6, the bodies for the tested methods are completed. These are just examples. You write the test that meets your needs.

Listing 4.6 MainActivityTest.java.

```
package com.code.abdulrahman.widgetexamples;
import org.junit.Test;
import static org.junit.Assert.assertTrue;
public class MainActivityTest {
  @Test
  public void onCreate() {
    assertTrue(MainActivity.message.compareTo(
        "Hello World") != 0);
  }
  @Test
  public void startToast() {
    assertTrue(MainActivity.message.compareTo(
        "message") == 0);
  }
...
}
```

```
  MainActivity.java      ExampleInstrumentedTest.java      MainActivityTest.java
1     package com.code.abdulrahman.widgetexamples;
2
3     import org.junit.Test;
4     import static org.junit.Assert.assertTrue;
5
6     public class MainActivityTest {
7         @Test
8         public void onCreate() {
9
10            assertTrue( condition: MainActivity.message.compareTo(
11                "Hello World") != 0);
12            assertTrue( condition: MainActivity.class.getName().compareTo(
13                "com.code.abdulrahman.widgetexamples.MainActivity") == 0);
14        }
15        @Test
16        public void startToast() {
17            assertTrue( condition: MainActivity.message.compareTo(
18                "message") == 0);
19        }
```

Fig. 4.20 Android test class example

The look of the MainActivityTest inside Android Studio is listed in Fig. 4.20. It includes the necessary libraries and classes needed for running unit tests. All the unique features and requirements for the test class are underlined.

There are a few things to be noted about the simple code in Fig. 4.20. First, the snapshot shows two types of buttons for running the tests, one for testing individual tests and one for running all the methods. Second, each method of the class starts with annotation @test. This tells us that the method should be run as a unit test. Also, both methods use the assertTrue construct. This construct returns true if the expected results from the method and the actual results obtained when running the code are equal. In our example, both tests return true. This is because MainActivity.message is not equal to ("**Hello World**") in the first case and MainActivity.message is equal to the **"message"** in the second case.

Connect to an Android device or emulator to run the Test class. The results of the test cases in the MainActivityTest class are shown below, Fig. 4.21. You can re-run all your test cases by simply clicking on the run all test button or run an individual test by clicking on the button associated with each test any time you want. This is the power of automated testing. You write once and run forever.

A good programming practice is to re-run all your existing tests every time you make changes to code. This will ensure that the changes you made have not introduced unexpected errors in other places in your code.

Fig. 4.21 Unit test results
for methods in
MainActivityTest class

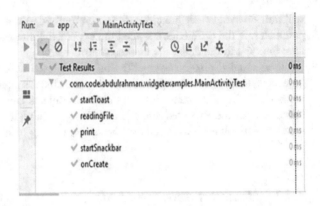

4.4.2   Assert Methods

The assert methods compare the expected results, that is, what the programmer thinks the results will be, with the actual outcome of the program. For example, a programmer can expect that adding two positive numbers will result in a number that is bigger than zero. So, it is possible to write a test case to add two numbers and assert the expected result to be positive. In this case, the assert statement can be **assertTrue (x+y > 0).**

In all the examples above, we used assertTrue(), but that is not the only assert method that Android supports. The org.junit.Assert package provides assert methods for all primitive types, objects, and arrays. The assert pattern is mostly like this: assert* (condition) or assert* (string message, condition). The message part of the assert is only displayed when the assert fails. Below are some useful and commonly used assert methods.

- assertTrue(condition) or assertTrue(string message, condition)
- assertFalse(condition) or assertFalse(string message, condition)
- assertNull(object)
- assertNotNull(object)
- assertEquals(string message, object expected, object actual)
- assertSame(object expected, object actual)
- assertNotSame(object expected, object actual)
- fail(condition)
- assertEquals(double expected, double actual, double delta)

For most of the above-asserted methods, the name is good enough to understand what is the method does. However, you need to pay special attention to a few. For example, the assertEquals() method for the double value is a bit different than the others. This is due to the way double is represented in the Java language. For example, when dividing 1.0/3, you might expect the result to be 0.33, but that is not how the division result is in the computer memory. If you print it, you will see it as 0.3333333333333333. So, if you assert 1.0/3 with a double value of 0.33, the test will fail. To avoid such situations, the assert method uses a third parameter, the delta parameter. If the difference between the expected value and the actual value is less than or equal to the delta, the method returns true.

assertEquals() also behaves differently when used with primitive data types and objects. When used with objects, it invokes the object's equal method. AssertSame() method, on the other hand, is used only with objects and uses the == operator to check if both the expected and the actual object have the same reference, that is, whether both object names refer to the same memory location.

4.4.3   Hamcrest Assert Methods

To test your Android app, you can use a newer version of the assert methods using third-party libraries. For example, you can use the assertThat() method from the *hamcrest* library. The newer forms of the assert methods provide more clarity as to what the methods are supposed to do and they improve the performance.

For most, you don't have to do any additional tasks; these libraries are downloaded with the Android SDK or Android Studio. You just need to learn the new syntax of the methods to apply them and probably check to see if the library is included in the Gradle build file.

In Listing 4.7, we show you how to use assertThat. The first parameter to the *assertThat* method is the *addingTwoInteger()* method which is a method in our *DataOperation* class that we would like to test. The second parameter uses methods from the *org.hamcrest.Matchers* class to enable successful testing. The Matcher classes provide a large number of methods that can be utilized for your testing.

Listing 4.7 UsingAssertThatTest.java.

```
package com.code.abdulrahman.widgetexamples;
import org.hamcrest.Matchers;
import org.junit.Test;
import static org.hamcrest.CoreMatchers.both;
import static org.hamcrest.CoreMatchers.is;
import static org.hamcrest.MatcherAssert.assertThat;

public class UsingAssertThatTest {
  @Test
  public void addingInteger() {
    assertThat(com.code.abdulrahman.widgetexamples.
        DataOperation.addingTwoInteger(3, 4), Matchers.is(7));
  }
  @Test
  public void usingGreaterThan() {
    // greaterThan and lessThan.
    assertThat(com.code.abdulrahman.widgetexamples.DataOperation.
```

```
            addingTwoInteger(10, 20), Matchers.greaterThan(25));
    }
    @Test
    public void UsinglessThan() {
        assertThat(com.code.abdulrahman.widgetexamples.DataOperation.
            addingTwoInteger(10, 20), Matchers.lessThan(30));
    }
    @Test
    public void range() {
        assertThat(com.code.abdulrahman.widgetexamples.DataOperation.
                addingTwoInteger(10, 20),
            both(Matchers.greaterThan(25)).and(Matchers.lessThan(30)));
    }
}
```

4.4.4   Espresso Testing

The third-party software *Espresso* can be used to test the app's user interface (UI) and generate test cases. To do testing, you need to connect the IDE to an Android device or Android Virtual Device, which means it is instrumental testing. You can start recording Espresso testing by clicking on run → record Espresso test. This will result in running your code and recording any actions you perform in your app.

For example, insert some data into an EditText, and click a button to display the content of the EditText screen. While you do these steps, your actions are recorded as shown in Fig. 4.22 (right-hand side). When you press the OK button on the window recording screen, you will be prompted to give a name to your recording, and a test class will be generated. The test class will have all the actions you performed. You can re-run the generated tests as many times as you want. You can also modify the generated code to test different aspects of your GUI elements.

Espresso uses Junit classes and has a small API. To use Expresso, you need to use methods like *withId*, *onView*, *perform*, and *check*. These methods are explained below along with steps you need to follow to create Expresso testing.

Identify the View object or the GUI component, e.g., a Button, or TextEdit, that you would like to test. We will talk more about Views in the coming chapters. You can use *withId* to match the View you would like to interact with, e.g., **withId(R.id.aButton)**. This is like the findViewByID method that we have used in our apps.

To test a GUI component, you start with the onView() or onData() method. For example, you can use onView and withId like this: *onView(withId(R.id.myButton));*

Any View object you have in your app that can be identified with withId can be passed to the onView method. Next, you need to identify the type of action that you would like to have performed on the View object you are testing. For example, if you

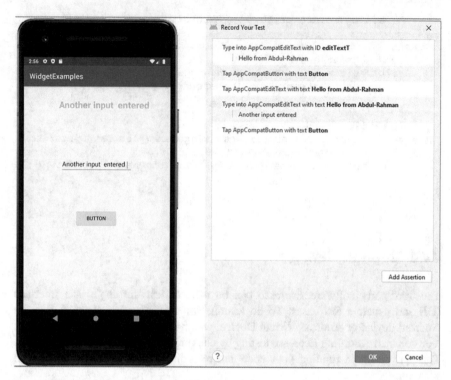

Fig. 4.22 A record of GUI testing using Expresso

want to see a button clicked, then you pass click() to the perform() method from the
ViewInteraction class.

In the code statement below, the onView(withId (R.id.my_view) method returns
the ViewInteraction object. You use the returned object to call the *perform* method
with the click() method to simulate a click on a View.

```
onView(withId(R.id.my_view)).perform(click())
```

The ViewInteraction class has another method called check() that you can use to
check the state of the View object. For example, you can check to see if a View is
being displayed.

```
onView(withId(R.id.my_view))
  .perform(click())
  .check(matches(isDisplayed()));
```

The code in Listing 4.8 shows how you can use all the constructs described above
to do UI testing. The UI components used for testing are EditText and TextView.

Listing 4.8 ExpressoMainActivityTest.java for auto UI testing.

```
package com.code.abdulrahman.widgetexamples;

import androidx.test.ext.junit.rules.ActivityScenarioRule;
import org.junit.Rule;
import org.junit.Test;
import static androidx.test.espresso.Espresso.onView;
import static androidx.test.espresso.action.ViewActions.click;
import static androidx.test.espresso.action.ViewActions.
closeSoftKeyboard;
import static androidx.test.espresso.action.ViewActions.typeText;
import static androidx.test.espresso.assertion.ViewAssertions.
matches;
import static androidx.test.espresso.matcher.ViewMatchers.withId;
import static androidx.test.espresso.matcher.ViewMatchers.withText;

public class ExpressoMainActivityTest {
String inputText = "Hello Abdul-Rahman" ;
    @Rule
    public ActivityScenarioRule<ExpressoMainActivity>
    activityScenarioRule
        = new ActivityScenarioRule<>(ExpressoMainActivity.class);
    @Test
    public void onClick() {
    // Type text and then press the button.
    onView(withId(R.id.editTextT))
        .perform(typeText(inputText), closeSoftKeyboard());
    onView(withId(R.id.buttonT)).perform(click());

    // Check that the text was changed.
    onView(withId(R.id.textViewT)).check(matches(
    withText(inputText)));
  }
}
```

4.4.5 Unit Testing

To run tests without a device or emulator, you use the second directory, the unit test directory in the Android project structure. Here, you write typical unit test cases that can be run on the Java virtual machine. You will test the logic of your methods without the need for an emulator or device to run your code. Android uses the *Junit* framework for unit testing. To use Junit, import org.junit, and use a class package for your test class.

To use Android classes and packages inside unit testing, you have to make sure that you have Android libraries as a dependency on your project. That is, add the

following two lines of code into the dependencies section of your Gradle build file.
dependencies {...
 androidTestImplementation 'com.android.support.test:rules:1.0.2'
 androidTestImplementation 'com.android.support.test:runner:1.0.2' ...}

When developing apps using Android Studio, the libraries are auto imported to the build file, and you don't have to do any extra work. However, you have to be aware that Junit libraries are used for testing, and one way to access these libraries is by including them in the Gradle build file. In the example below, we first create a Java class in the app directory to deal with simple data operations, Listing 4.9. Then, we write a test class in the unit testing directory for testing; see Listing 4.10.

Listing 4.9 DataOperation.java class that takes care of simple data operations.

```
package com.code.abdulrahman.widgetexamples;
public class DataOperation {
  public static int x, y;
  public static int addingTwoInteger(int a, int b) {
    x = a; y = b;
    return (x + y);
  }
  public static int subtractingTwoInteger(int a, int b) {
    x = a; y = b;
    return (x - y);
  }
  public static int mltiplyingTwoInteger(int a, int b) {
    x = a; y = b;
    return (x * y);
  }
}
```

Listing 4.10 DataOperationTests.java. for testing data operation class.

```
package com.code.abdulrahman.widgetexamples;

import org.junit.Test;
import static org.junit.Assert.*;
public class DataOperatoinTests {
  @Test
  public void addingtwoIntegers() {
    assertEquals(20, DataOperation.addingTwoInteger( 10, 10));
    assertTrue(DataOperation.x==10);
    assertTrue(DataOperation.y==10);
  }
  @Test
  public void substractingIntegers() {
    assertEquals(5, DataOperation.subtractingTwoInteger( 50, 45));
    assertTrue(DataOperation.x==50);
```

```
      assertTrue(DataOperation.y==45);
   }
   @Test
   public void multiplyingAndAddingNumbers() {
      assertTrue((DataOperation.mltiplyingTwoInteger(50, 45))!=5);
      assertTrue(DataOperation.x==50);
      assertTrue(DataOperation.y==45);
      assertTrue(DataOperation.y + DataOperation.x > 0);
   }
}
```

4.4.6   Unit Testing with Mockito

Mockito is a mocking framework for Java that allows you to create mock objects for testing purposes [4]. Whether you use Mockito objects or your Stub objects, mock objects are important for testing when the actual object you would like to test is not available yet. You create mock objects when, for example, the database is not ready for your testing, the server is not set up yet, components that are developed by other groups or team members are not available yet, etc. Remember that object mocking is done during the development phase and in the testing environment. It is part of the unit testing, and you should not fake anything in the production environment. All mock objects should be removed from your production code. To use Mockito objects in your project, there are few steps you need to follow:

- Add the Mockito library as a dependency to your project. That is, you need to add the line of code below to the dependency section of your Grade build file.
  testImplementation "org.mockito:mockito-core:3.5.13"
- Add the *@RunWith (MockitoJUnitRunner.class)* annotation to the beginning of the test class:

```
@RunWith(MockitoJUnitRunner.class)
public class MockitoExample {...}
```

This will instruct the Mockito test runner to validate proper usage of the framework's syntax and semantics. It will also help mock object initialization.

- To create a mock object for an actual object or component that has not been written yet, add @mock annotation before the declaration of the variable. See the examples below:

```
@Mock
MyServer server;  or @Mock SQLiteOpenHelper myDatabase ;
```

If you want to mock a method and not an entire class or an object, use @spy instead of @Mock annotation like this:

```
@Spy List<String> alist = new ArrayList<String>();
```

In Mockito, methods like *when()* and *theReturn()* are used to enable object mocking. In Listing 4.11, an example is given to show you how to use the Mockito object. The above steps are also included in the example.

For our example, we first created a class called ClassUnderTesting which has one field of type AppCompatActivity and one method called getPath(). When asked for a file path, it uses its getString() method to get information about a file path from its internal object field and return it. It uses AppCompatActivity to return some results, not necessarily the correct results. See Listing 4.11.

Listing 4.11 ClassUnderTesting .java use mock object AppCompatActivity.

```
package com.code.abdulrahman.widgetexamples;

import androidx.appcompat.app.AppCompatActivity;
public class ClassUnderTesting {
  AppCompatActivity appCompatActivity ;

  public ClassUnderTesting(AppCompatActivity aca) {
    this.appCompatActivity = aca;
  }
  public String getString () {
    System.out.println(ClassUnderTesting.class.getName() +
        appCompatActivity.getString(R.string.filePath));
    return appCompatActivity.getString(R.string.filePath) ;
  }
}
```

In Listing 4.12, a test class called MockitoExample is created to test the ClassUnderTesting. A mock object is created to enable ClassUnderTesting to return a file path which can be any String value. The mock object is created using this statement.

```
ClassUnderTesting testingObject = new ClassUnderTesting
(futureObject);
```

The assertThat statement in the MockitoExample class checks whether ClassUnderTesting can return the file path. The assert statement is like this:

```
String filePath = testingObject.getString();
assertThat(filePath, is(fakePath));
```

If you run the test, it passes; it means a mock object returns the file path.

Note that the current value of the file path is less important. It is a fake value that has been set by a developer for testing. What is more important is that you can continue developing your application without waiting for ClassUnderTesting to be fully implemented. You have tested ClassUnderTesting with a mock object, and it works, i.e., it can return a file path. In other words, using the mock object has cleared the path for you to continue working without waiting for the full implementation of the class under the test. This is the whole idea behind using the mocking and stubbing method.

Listing 4.12 MockitoExample.java testing class using Mockito.

```
package com.code.abdulrahman.widgetexamples;
import androidx.appcompat.app.AppCompatActivity;
import org.junit.Test;
import org.junit.runner.RunWith;
import org.mockito.Mock;
import org.mockito.Mockito;
import org.mockito.junit.MockitoJUnitRunner;
import java.util.ArrayList;
import java.util.List;
import static org.hamcrest.MatcherAssert.assertThat;
import static org.hamcrest.Matchers.is;
import static org.junit.Assert.assertEquals;
import static org.mockito.Mockito.when;


@RunWith(MockitoJUnitRunner.class)
public class MockitoExample {

    private static final String fakePath = "fakePath";
    @Mock
    protected AppCompatActivity futureObject;

    @Test
    public void gettingStringFromSecondActivity() {
        // get filepath from the mock object
        when(futureObject.getString(R.string.filePath))
            .thenReturn(fakePath);
        ClassUnderTesting TestingObject =
          new ClassUnderTesting(futureObject);
        // checking that mock object is returning correct file path
        String filePath = TestingObject.getString();
        assertThat(filePath, is(fakePath));
    }

    @Test
    public void testMockMethod(){
        List mockList = Mockito.mock(ArrayList.class);
        mockList.add("Hello class");
        Mockito.verify(mockList).add("Hello class");
        assertEquals(0, mockList.size());
    }
}
```

Different from the listing above where an object is mocked, in the code snippet below, the *spy* method from the Mockito framework is used to mock a method instead of an object. This approach is useful if you want to mock a method only.

```
@Test
public void testSpyMethod(){
  ArrayList myArrayList = Mockito.spy(new ArrayList());
  myArrayList.add("Hello class");
  Mockito.verify(myArrayList).add("Hello class");
  assertEquals(1, myArrayList.size());
}
```

4.4.7   Code Coverage

Code coverage is a useful metric or measurement for getting information on how well your project is tested. It is used during software development and when you have access to the source code [5]. It allows you to estimate the relevant parts of the source code that have never been executed by your test cases, thus facilitating further testing and improvement of test cases. Android Studio has a built-in capability that allows you to run tests with code coverage. It shows you which parts of code have/ have not been tried out by your test runs.

Right-click on the unit test folder, and select *Run tests with Coverage*. The results will be displayed in a window showing the percentage of the classes, methods, and code lines that have been tested by your test cases. Figure 4.23 shows how to run the code coverage.

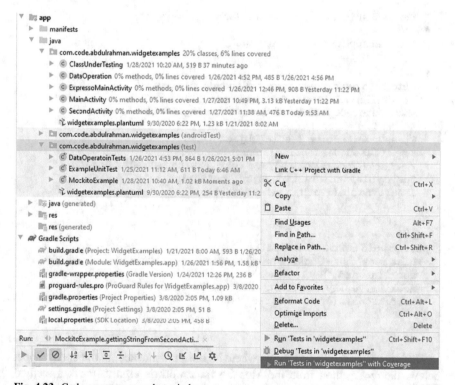

Fig. 4.23 Code coverage snapshot window

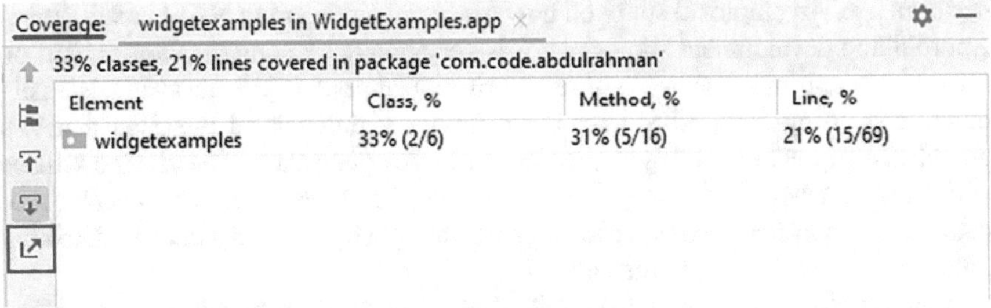

Element	Class, %	Method, %	Line, %
widgetexamples	33% (2/6)	31% (5/16)	21% (15/69)

Fig. 4.24 Coverage window showing test coverage information

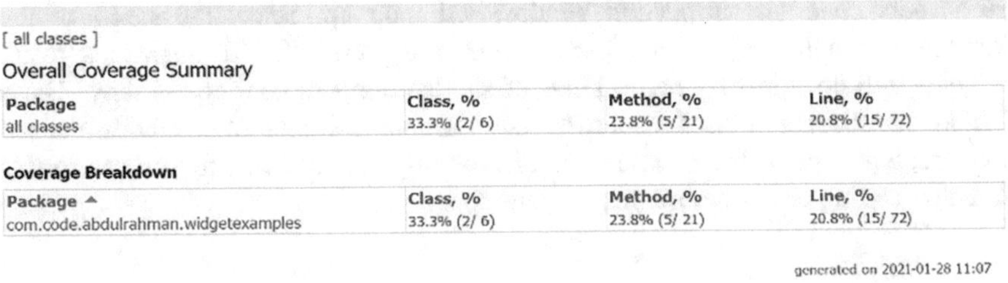
[all classes]

Overall Coverage Summary

Package	Class, %	Method, %	Line, %
all classes	33.3% (2/ 6)	23.8% (5/ 21)	20.8% (15/ 72)

Coverage Breakdown

Package	Class, %	Method, %	Line, %
com.code.abdulrahman.widgetexamples	33.3% (2/ 6)	23.8% (5/ 21)	20.8% (15/ 72)

generated on 2021-01-28 11:07

Fig. 4.25 Test coverage output in the HTML file

Figure 4.24 shows the result of test coverage, i.e., the parts of the code that have been covered by your testing classes and methods.

You can send the coverage result to an HTML file using the output button on the coverage window. This is a useful option for documenting your test results. The output button is squared in red in Fig. 4.24, and the file content is shown in Fig. 4.25.

Using code coverage as the main testing metric, however, does not give a definitive answer to how well your code is tested. For example, if you covered 95% of the test cases but the most important tests are within the 5% that you did not test, then you have not done a good job testing even though the coverage rate is at a very high percent. Regardless, using code coverage to find out about the parts of your code that are untested can still be useful.

4.4.8 Code Inspection and Refactoring

Code refactoring is an important approach to improve the quality of your code. It refers to changing your code during development. For example, you may want to rename your classes, methods, and class attributes or re-organize the structure of your classes by moving classes to different packages and move methods to different classes. All these changes are done to improve the quality of code, for example, to improve the readability of the code, reduce coupling, and improve cohesion and performance. An empirical study on how often code refactoring is conducted during Android app development shows that it is very popular among developers, and on average, an app undergoes 47.79 refactoring operations [6]. Refactoring is easily done when using Android Studio. For example, right-click on the class that you would like to rename, and type the new name for your class. The change will be applied everywhere in your project. Similar to code refactoring, static analysis of code is an important technique to improve the quality of your code by detecting potential bugs and errors in the code [7].

You need to familiarize yourself with these tools to perform code refactoring and code inspection, especially if you are developing code using the Agile framework where you might regularly need to refactor your code to respond to the change requests. To analyze your code, on the Android Studio menu bar, click on *Analyze → inspect code*. An inspection window will pop up. Select the scope of the inspection, whole project, or custom scope, and press OK. An inspection result window will open displaying all kinds of shortcomings in your code if any. These include hardcoding, unused resources, redundant variables, empty methods, unused imports, typos, performance issues, etc. Resolving all or as many as you can results in better coding and better quality of your app.

4.4.9   Reverse Engineering

The last topic of this chapter is about using a *reverse engineering* technique to find out the anomalies in your code structure and design. For small projects, design and implementation most likely go hand in hand; but typically, you have to develop app design first and then code it. Different from the typical software development process, reverse engineering is about decomposing existing codes and programs to understand how it works, its parts, and the structure.

If you find that your code has performance issues, memory leaks, or usability issues and you don't have the proper design documents, generating the class diagram of your code, or parts of your code, will be a useful way to understand the code. For more about reverse engineering and how it is used to detect variability in Android apps, see [8, 9].

Generating the UML (Unified Modeling Language) class diagram for your code, or parts of your code, will help you to understand the relationship between the classes and the structure of your app. This is especially useful if you have inherited some code that you would like to maintain/enhance but you don't have the documentation for it and the developers who created the code are no longer around.

Android Studio allows you to generate UML class diagrams from code. To do so, you need to download UML plugins to generate and show a class diagram. Examples of these tools and their use are given below:

In the Android Studio, click on *File → setting*, and search for plugins. In the plugin search window, type the name of the *PlantUML* plugin. Once the PlantUML plugin is found, press OK, and follow the installation process. The snapshot of the setting and plugin search windows are shown below (see Fig. 4.26).

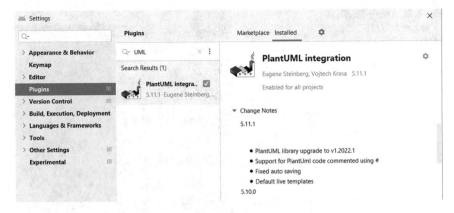

Fig. 4.26 Search window for plugins in Android Studio

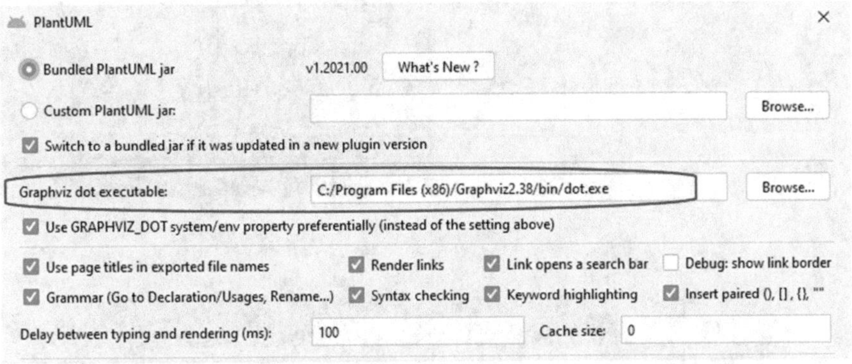

Fig. 4.27 Set PlantUML graph visualization path to the dot executable of Graphviz

To render UML diagrams from the generated PlantUML download, you need to download Graphviz from the GraphVisualize software website[1] and set the PlantUML graph visualization path to the *dot* executable of Graphviz (see Fig. 4.27).

You also need to install the *Sketch It!* plugin similar to the way you install PlantUML. Once you're done installing PlantUML, Graphviz, and Sketch It, select the app folder of your project or an individual class, and on the Android Studio menu bar, click on tools → Sketch It! as shown below, Fig. 4.28, to generate the .PlantUML file.

To open the generated PlantUML file, double click on it, and put the cursor inside the PlantUML text to generate a UML diagram. Figure 4.29 highlights a generated PlantUML file.

---

[1] https://graphviz.gitlab.io/_pages/Download/Download_windows.html

Fig. 4.28 Using Sketch It!
to generate a UML diagram
of your code

Fig. 4.29 A file of type PlantUML is highlighted on the project structure

An example of a generated class diagram is shown below in Fig. 4.30. The diagram should help you understand your code structure and find possible sources of errors or bugs in your code. You can also save the diagram as a part of your code documentation.

If instead of rendering the UML class diagram you experience the below error message, it means the PlantUML software cannot find the Graphviz executable (see Fig. 4.31).

To fix the error, click on the .PlantUML file in the app, and inside the PlantUML window, click on *Open Settings → Browse*, and find the location of the Graphviz executable, i.e., dot.exe file. An example where the Graphviz executable is located

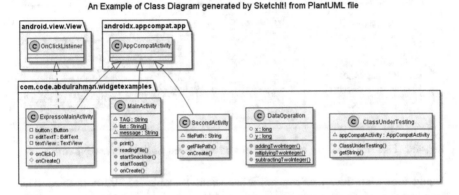

Fig. 4.30 An example of a class diagram generated from code using PlantUML, Graphviz, and Sketch It

Fig. 4.31 A snapshot of error message when PlantUML cannot find Graphviz

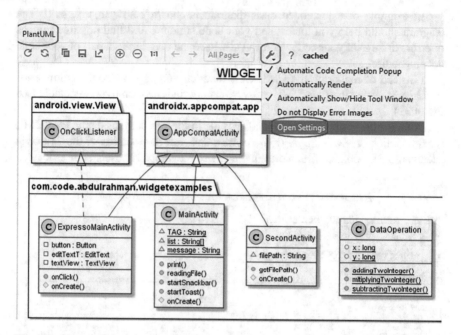

Fig. 4.32 First step in solving PlantUML software cannot find Graphviz executable error

would look like this: **C:\Program Files (x86) \Graphviz2.38\bin\dot.exe**. This should solve the issue, and you should be able to render a UML class diagram for your code. These steps are shown below.

Figure 4.32 shows that PlantUML has been opened and Open Settings has been circled.

Once the Open Settings button is pressed, the PlantUML diagram in Fig. 4.27 will open. Insert the Graphviz dot executable in the box circled.

4.5   Chapter Summary

In this chapter, we described various Android Studio tools and Android classes to debug the app, i.e., find and fixing errors in code, and to profile your code to find out the performance and usability issues of the app. We studied Android Studio Debugger, Android Profiler, Device File Explorer, Android Debug Bridge (adb), Toast and Snackbar classes, the Log class, and the Logcat utility. We also studied unit testing using Junit and Expresso and Mockito tools for testing UI and creating mock objects, as well as code coverage, reverse engineering, code refactoring, and code inspection. The tools and techniques presented in this chapter will help you to correct errors and fix bugs in the code that you are going to develop throughout your career as a developer.

There are other important development tools and Android Studio features that were not covered here. These include infer nullity, backward dependency, etc. You can learn about these tools/features by using them when you re-create the demo projects that come with this book. You need to run all the sample codes and examples provided in this chapter to master the topics.

For additional information about errors and bugs that are the result of bad design and development practices which are also known as *code smells*, you are encouraged to read these papers [10, 11]. There are also my research works related to security and data privacy issues in Android apps. These issues and others are covered in [12].

Check Your Knowledge
Below are some of the fundamental concepts and vocabularies that have been covered in this chapter. To test your knowledge and your understanding of this chapter, you should be able to describe each of the below concepts in one or two sentences.

- Android Debug Bridge
- Code coverage
- Code inspection
- Debugging
- Device File Explorer
- Expresso
- File Explorer
- Graphviz
- Instrumental testing
- Integration testing
- Junit
- Log
- Logcat
- Mockito
- PlantUML
- Profiler
- Refactoring
- Reverse engineering
- Sketch It
- Snackbar
- Toast
- Unit testing
- User acceptance testing

Further Reading

For more information about the topics covered in this chapter, we suggest that you refer to the online resources listed below. These links provide additional insight into the topics covered. The links are mostly maintained by Google and are a part of the

Android API specification. The resource titles convey which section/subsection of the chapter the resource is related to.

ADB, [online] Available, http://adbshell.com/

Debug Your App, [online] Available, https://developer.android.com/studio/debug/

Espresso basics, [online] Available, https://developer.android.com/training/testing/espresso/basics

Espresso, https://developer.android.com/training/testing/espresso

Graph Visualization Software, [online] Available, https://graphviz.gitlab.io/_pages/Download/Download_windows.html

Mockito, [online] Available, https://javadoc.io/static/org.mockito/mockito-core/3.7.7/org/mockito/Mockito.html

Profile Your App Performance, [online] Available, https://developer.android.com/studio/profile/

sketch.it, [online] Available, https://plugins.jetbrains.com/plugin/10387-sketch-it-

Snackbar, [online] Available, https://developer.android.com/reference/android/support/design/widget/Snackbar

Toasts, [online] Available, http://developer.android.com/guide/topics/ui/notifiers/toasts.html

Write and View Logs with Logcat, [online] Available, https://developer.android.com/studio/debug/am-logcat.html

Test your app, [online] Available, https://developer.android.com/studio/test

Tasty mocking framework for unit tests in Java, [online] Available, https://site.mockito.org/

References

1. A. Garcia, V. Farcic, *Test-Driven Java Development: Invoke TDD Principles for End-to-End Application Development* (Packt Publishing, Birmingham, UK, 2015)
2. L. Deng, J. Offutt, P. Ammann, et al., Mutation operators for testing Android apps. Inf. Softw. Technol. **81**, 154–168 (2017)
3. P. Kong, L. Li, J. Gao, et al., Automated testing of Android apps: a systematic literature review. IEEE Trans. Reliab. **68**(1), 45–66 (2019). https://doi.org/10.1109/TR.2018.2865733
4. D. Spadini, M. Aniche, M. Bruntink, et al., Mock objects for testing java systems. Empir. Softw. Eng. **24**, 1461–1498 (2019). https://doi.org/10.1007/s10664-018-9663-0
5. A. Pilgun, O. Gadyatskaya, Y. Zhauniarovich, et al., Fine-grained code coverage measurement in automated black-box Android testing. ACM Trans. Softw. Eng. Methodol. **29**(4), 1–35 (2020). https://doi.org/10.1145/3395042
6. A. Peruma, A preliminary study of Android refactorings, in *2019 IEEE/ACM 6th International Conference on Mobile Software Engineering and Systems (MOBILESoft)*, 2019, pp. 148–149. https://doi.org/10.1109/MOBILESoft.2019.00030
7. L. Li, T.F. Bissyandé, M. Papadakis, S. Rasthofer, A. Bartel, D. Octeau, J. Klein, L. Traon, Static analysis of Android apps: a systematic literature review. Inf. Softw. Technol. **88**, 67–95 (2017). https://doi.org/10.1016/j.infsof.2017.04.00

8. H. Brunelière, J. Cabot, G. Dupé, et al., MoDisco: a model driven reverse engineering framework. Inf. Softw. Technol. **56**(8), 1012–1032 (2014)
9. A. Nirumand, B. Zamani, B.T. Ladani, VAnDroid: a framework for vulnerability analysis of Android applications using a model-driven reverse engineering technique. Softw. Pract. Exp. Source Inf. **49**(1), 70–99 (2019)
10. S. Habchi, N. Moha, R. Rouvoy, Android code smells: from introduction to refactoring. J. Syst. Softw. **177**, 110964 (2021). https://doi.org/10.1016/j.jss.2021.110964
11. F. Palomba, D. Di Nucci, A. Panichella, et al., On the impact of code smells on the energy consumption of mobile applications. Inf. Softw. Technol. **105**, 43–55 (2019)
12. M. Zhang, H. Yin, *Android Application Security: A Semantics and Context-Aware Approach* (Springer, New York, 2016)

Chapter 5
Activity Lifecycle and Passing Objects Between Screens Using Parcelable Interface

Learning Outcome

By the end of this chapter, you should be able to:

- Use the Manifest file for multiple Activities
- Create and use the Launcher Activity
- Understand Activity lifecycle and the creation, running, and destruction of Activities
- Implement the Activity lifecycle callback methods
- Implement the Parcelable interface and pass objects between Activities
- Learn how to pass objects between Activities

Check Out the Demo Project

Download the demo app, **LifeCycleWithParcelable.zip**, specifically developed to go with this chapter. I recommend that you code this project up from the notes rather than just opening the project in Android Studio and running it; however, if you want to run the code first to get a sense of the app, please do so. The code is thoroughly explained in this chapter to help you understand it. We follow the same approach to all other chapters throughout the book. The app's code will help you comprehend the additional concepts that will be described in this chapter.

How to run the code: unzip the code in a folder of your choice, and then in Android Studio, click **File->import->Existing Android code into the workspace**. The project should start running.

5.1 Introduction

It is important to understand what a *state* is to understand the Activity lifecycle. In this chapter, we use the demo app developed specifically for this chapter to explain Activity lifecycles and callback methods, as well as the Parcelable interface. The app

© The Author(s), under exclusive license to Springer Nature Switzerland AG 2022
A.-R. Mawlood-Yunis, *Android for Java Programmers*,
https://doi.org/10.1007/978-3-030-87459-9_5

Fig. 5.1 LifeCycleWith
Parcellable main interface

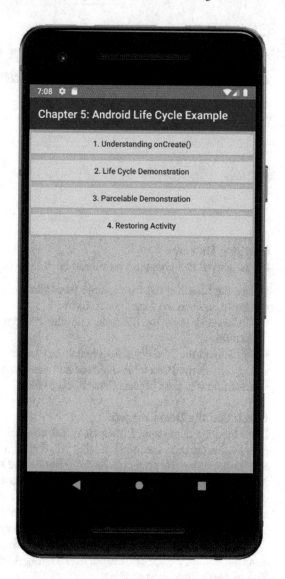

has four buttons on the main page (see Fig. 5.1). When pressed, each button shows one of the app's functionalities. The first button is for demoing the onCreate() method creation and usage, which is an important method of the Android Activity class and Activity lifecycle. The second button is for demoing the Activities' lifecycle. The third button is for passing objects between Activities using the Parcelable interface. The last button is for restoring the Activity states. The implementation details of these methods will be described as well.

5.2 Activity States

In this part, we describe states and Activity lifecycles and why it is important to understand these concepts for app development.

5.2.1 Activity and States

As mentioned earlier, it is important to understand what the *state* is to understand the Activity lifecycle. Activities, like Java objects, can be in different states, where a state is a snapshot of an Activity at a given time. When instance variables of an Activity are holding values and/or its operations are executing, the Activity is in a state. The state can be *starting*, *resuming*, *running*, etc. The set of states that an Activity can go through during its lifetime is called the *Activity lifecycle*. All the states an Activity has, along with transitions from one state to another, form a directed graph. While users navigate in and out of the application or navigate through the Activities (screens) of your app, Activity states change. While this happens, the Android system calls various lifecycle *callback methods*.

You can control how your application behaves as the user interacts with your application and Activity states change. The control is implemented through callback methods. So far, you have only seen the onCreate() callback method. The rest of the lifecycle callback methods and the *Parcelable* interface will be described in this chapter. We use the demo app developed specifically for this chapter to explain activity lifecycle and callback methods as well as the Parcelable interface.

Android apps are different from typical desktop applications. Android apps have limited resources, such as screen size. These limitations put restraints on app design and architecture. Each Android app is made of one or more Activities (screens). Because a phone has a limited size display, the app designer cannot present all the app's views at once on the device's screen. Mobile app views, or screens, overlay one another in the *back stack* as the user navigates through the app, and this leads to Activities being in different states.

An Activity has several states which make up its *lifecycle*. During the lifecycle, Activities change state. For example, the Activity that was put on the back stack hidden from the user might come back into focus and become active. The developer can define, i.e., implement, what kind of actions take place when an Activity transits from one state to another. For example, the developer can *save data* to a database, a file, or another Activity before the Activity is killed by the system so that the next time the app runs, it starts from where it left off. Similarly, the developer can bring into focus the view that was previously running in the foreground. These decisions need to be done at the application design stage, and the implementation of the activity callback methods enables such decisions.

Note the following about an Activity state:

1. An Activity can be in a different state during its lifetime.
2. Typically, an app is made of more than one Activity. Hence, the app can be at different states as the user navigates between different Activities, which in turn puts Activities at different states.

5.2.2   Transition Between States

At any given time, an Activity can be in one of the following three states:

- Running (created, started, resumed): the activity has the focus and is at the top of the activity stack.
- Paused: the device goes to sleep; the activity is partially hidden.
- Stopped: the activity is obscured by another activity. Figure 5.2 shows the transition between Android Activity states.

Activity states are of two types, *static* and *transient* states. When Activities exist or remain for a long period in a state, the state is called a *static state*. If the Activities exist in a state for a very short time, the state is called a *transient state*. For example, after the onCreate() method, the onStart() method is called followed by the onResume() method. When these callback methods are called, the Activity would be in a *transient state*. That is, it will be in these states for a very short time. In these cases, the transition between the states does not require user intervention; the changes happen automatically, i.e., the method calls are initiated by the Android system. When the app is running, e.g., you are browsing the internet on your device, the Activity is running and is in a resumed *static state*.

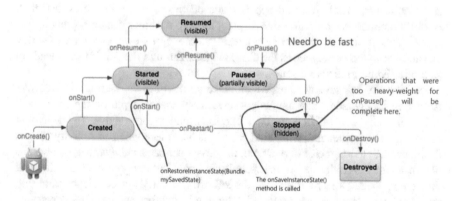

Fig. 5.2 Transition between Activity states (The source of the images is here: https://google-developer-training.gitbooks.io/android-developer-fundamentals-course-practicals/content/en/Unit%201/22_p_activity_lifecycle_&_state.html)

5.2.2.1 Do It Yourself

1. List the three state sequences that an Activity can go through during its lifetime. Hint: See Fig. 5.1 and find out the cycles in the graph.
2. Identify the states that are called only once during an app's lifetime.

Before we go any further, let us discuss an important topic, the *Launcher Activity*. If your app is made of more than one Activity, you must decide which one is the Main Activity, i.e., the Launcher Activity. Our demo apps for this chapter have more than one Activity, and you need to understand the Launcher Activity first.

5.2.3 The Launcher Activity

So far, we have worked with apps that have one or two Activities. However, almost all Android applications will have several Activities. One of these Activities is the Launcher Activity. Each application has only one *Launcher Activity*. It is equivalent to the Java class with the *main* method that starts an application. The Launcher Activity is executed when the user clicks the application icon. The programmer has to decide which Activity is the Launcher Activity and declare it in the AndroidManifest.xml file.

In the Manifest XML file, you will have an element called *application*, where all Activities of your app are children of this element, including the Launcher Activity. Inside the application element and the Activity that you would like to declare as the Launcher Activity, you include a subelement called *intent-filter*. The intent-filter element has two properties, action and category. For your activity to be the Launcher Activity, its intent-filter action name must be MAIN, and its category must be LAUNCHER.

Listing 5.1 is an example of the AndroidManifest.xml file in which the MainActivity has been defined as the LAUNCHER activity and DisplayMessageActivity is the second Activity.

Listing 5.1 AndroidManifest.xml where LAUNCHER activity is identified.

```
<?xml version="1.0" encoding="utf-8"?>
<manifest xmlns:android=
  "http://schemas.android.com/apk/res/android"
  package="code.android.abdulrahman.com.LifeCycleWithParcellable">
  <application
    android:allowBackup="true"
    android:icon="@mipmap/ic_launcher"
    android:label="@string/app_name"
    android:roundIcon="@mipmap/ic_launcher_round"
    android:supportsRtl="true"
    android:theme="@style/AppTheme">
```

```
<activity android:name=".MainActivity">
  <intent-filter>
    <action android:name="android.intent.action.MAIN" />
    <category android:name=
                "android.intent.category.LAUNCHER" />
  </intent-filter>
</activity>
<activity android:name=".DisplayMessageActivity" />
</application>
</manifest>
```

Use the demo app source code to set the *DisplayMessageActivity* as the Launcher Activity. To do so, in the Manifest XML file of the demo app, replace *.MainActivity* with *.DisplayMessageActivity*, and run the app. The DisplayMessageActivity should be the main page of your app now. Now, reverse the changes, and run the app again. This time, the MainActivity should be the main page of your app.

5.2.4   Implementing onCreate()

In studying Activity lifecycle methods, we need to give special attention to the *onCreate()* method. To develop an Android app, you need to implement the onCreate() method for each Activity. It is the only callback method required to be implemented. The onCreate() code executes once for the entire lifetime of the Activity. In the onCreate() method for the Launcher Activity, you implement basic application startup logic, set up an interface, initialize class scope variables, instantiate widgets, etc. The onCreate() method acts as the constructor method in Java classes.

5.2.4.1   Understanding onCreate()

The onCreate() callback method is called when the system creates the Activity for the first time. The method has only one parameter. The type of the parameter is *Bundle*, and its value is null when the app launches. The parameter value changes to store the Activity's previous state if the Activity is recreated for any reason, for example, when the device is rotated or the app's language is changed. The method signature for the onCreate method is as follows:

```
protected void onCreate(Bundle savedInstanceState);
```

Two actions that are done inside the onCreate method for almost all Activities are:
First, using the **super.onCreate(savedInstanceState)** method a call is made to the base class onCreate () method. Second, the activity layout is set using the setContentView(Layout) method call. The code for the onCreate() method below shows the following:

1. The use of the Bundle object.
2. A call to the Base class method using the keyword *super*.
3. The Activity's layout is set using the setContentView method.

```java
@Override
protected void onCreate(Bundle savedInstanceState) {
  super.onCreate(savedInstanceState);
  setContentView(R.layout.activity_main);
  ...
}
```

After calling the onCreate() method, the Android system calls the onStart() and onResume() methods, respectively. If you only have the above few lines of code and run your application, a view will be created. An example in Listing 5.2 shows how onCreate can be used for initializing and setting a display.

Listing 5.2 MainActivity.java class with the onCreate() method.

```java
package abdulrahman.com.code.oneactivityapp;
import android.content.Intent;
import android.os.Bundle;
import android.view.View;
import android.widget.Button;
import android.widget.EditText;
import android.widget.TextView;
import androidx.appcompat.app.AppCompatActivity;
public class MainActivity extends AppCompatActivity {
  EditText name, age, address, course;
  TextView textView;
  @Override
  protected void onCreate(Bundle savedInstanceState) {
    super.onCreate(savedInstanceState);
    setContentView(R.layout.activity_main);
   // assigning widget object declared inside xml file to the local variables
    name = findViewById(R.id.editText1);
    age = findViewById(R.id.editText2);
    address = findViewById(R.id.editText3);
    course = findViewById(R.id.editText4);
    textView = findViewById(R.id.textView);
    Button submit = findViewById(R.id.submit_button);
    submit.setOnClickListener(new View.OnClickListener() {
      @Override
      public void onClick(View v) {
              String aname = name.getText().toString();
        int anAge = Integer.parseInt(age.getText().toString());
        String anAddress = address.getText().toString();
        String courseDescription = course.getText().toString();
        textView.setText(aname + ",  " + anAge + ",  "
            + courseDescription + ",  " + anAddress);
```

```
Intent startNewActivity =
    new Intent(getBaseContext(), StartActivity.class);
startNewActivity.putExtra("main", aname);
startActivity(startNewActivity);
            }
        });
    }
}
```

Once you press the first button on the demo app, a screen with four text areas, a button, and a TextView is created (see Fig. 5.3). Type in some information, and press the submit button. You will see that the TextView is set with the information you

Fig. 5.3 Example of onCreate() method implementation

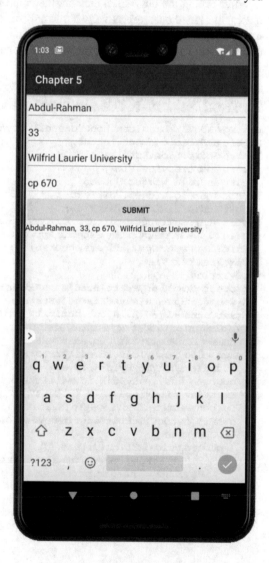

inserted. When you press the phone's back button, the current view will be pushed onto the stack, and the main view starts. In this example, all code was put in the onCreate() method which is not good programming practice. We will see various onCreate implementations in later chapters.

5.2.5 Bundle Class

Bundle is a simple class that acts as a data structure for storing data. It is like a map class in Java that uses a key/value pair to store values. The Bundle object provides the means to save and retrieve the activity's state data. When the first instance of an Activity is created, the Bundle object is null. The Bundle object is used with the *onCreate(Bundle savedInstanceState)*, *onSaveInstanceState(Bundle outState)*, and *onRestoreInstanceState (Bundle outState)* Activity methods. More information on these methods is provided in the below subsection. The Bundle class has several methods. Here are a few of them.

- clear() which removes all elements from the Bundle
- clone() which clones the current Bundle
- deepCopy() which makes a deep copy of the given Bundle
- describeContents() which reports the nature of the Parcelable's contents

Another import method of the Bundle class is getBundle(String key) which returns the value associated with the given key or null if the key doesn't exist. Bundles also have "get" and "put" methods for all the primitive types, Parcelable and Serializable objects. That is, it has getInt(), putInt(), getDouble(), putDouble(), etc.

5.2.5.1 Using Bundle Object with Intent

You can use the Bundle object with Intent in a few different ways. For example, you can use getExtras() to get a Bundle object from the Intent object and use the put methods with the key/values to insert values into the Bundle. The code snippet below shows how to use getExtras() to retrieve the Bundle object from the Intent object and put a value into it using a key.

```
Intent intent = new Intent (this, secondActivity.class);
Bundle extras = intent.getExtras();
extras.putString("key", "value");
```

Note that, if the Intent object is created without the Bundle object added to it, calling getExtras() on the Intent object will return null. Therefore, before using the Bundle object returned from the Intent, you need to check if it is null or not. Here is how you can do it:

```
Bundle extras = intent.getExtras();
       if (extras != null )
           extras.putString("key", "value");
```

You can instantiate the Bundle object and use the putExtras() method to add the Bundle object into the Intent object. See the code snippet below:

```
Bundle bundle = new Bundle();
 bundle.putString("key", "value");
 newIntent.putExtras(bundle);
Intent newIntent = new Intent(this, secondActivity.class);
```

To use putExtra and getExtra in a shortcut way, you can use them as follows:

```
Intent anIntent = new Intent(this, secondActivity.class);
 anIntent.putExtra("key", "value");
 String value = getIntent().getExtras().getString("key");
```

The Bundle object can be used with the StartActivity as well to pass data to the second activity: *startActivity (Intent intent, Bundle bundle).* The second parameter provides additional information for how the Activity should be started.

5.2.5.2 Bundle Object and Activity States

The Bundle object provides the means to save and retrieve the Activity's state data. When the first instance of an Activity is created, the Bundle object is null. The Bundle object is used with the *onCreate(Bundle savedInstanceState), onSaveInstanceState (Bundle outState)*, and *onRestoreInstanceState (Bundle outState)* Activity methods to save and restore Activity states.

When the user rotates their device, changes the device mode to split-screen, or changes the language settings, i.e., changes the configuration of the device, the Android system temporarily destroys the running activity. The method onSaveInstanceState(Bundle outState) is then invoked for saving the Activity's state for recreation. The code snippet in Listing 5.3 shows how you can use Bundle with **onSaveInstanceState** and **onRestoreInstanceState** to save and restore the Activity's state.

Listing 5.3 Using onSaveInstanceState and onRestoreInstanceState to save and restore the Activity's state.

```
@Override
protected void onSaveInstanceState(Bundle outState) {
   super.onSaveInstanceState(outState);
   String nameValue = "Abdul-Rahman";
   int accountNumber = 12345;
```

```
    outState.putString("name", nameValue);
    outState.putInt("accountNumber", accountNumber);
}
@Override
protected void onRestoreInstanceState(
 @NonNull Bundle savedInstanceState) {
    super.onRestoreInstanceState(savedInstanceState);
    String r_name = savedInstanceState.getString("name");
    int r_accountNumber = savedInstanceState.getInt("accountNumber");
    textView.setText("\n" + "Restoring state \n" + r_name + " " +
    r_accountNumber);
 }
```

5.3   Understanding Activity Lifecycle

In this part, we continue to look into the activity's lifecycle callback methods.

5.3.1   Understanding the onDestroy Method

The OnDestroy() method is called when the activity is about to get destroyed. It is usually used to release resources. An Activity gets destroyed either because it is no longer needed or because of configuration changes. When an Activity gets destroyed because of configuration changes, a new Activity is created, and the onCreate() method is called immediately. You can use the finish() method to destroy an Activity and the isFinishing() method to find out if the finish() method has been called. In most cases, you do not need to implement the onDestroy method. This is because most of the code/data cleanup is done using the onPause() or the onStop() method. To decide whether or not to implement the *onDestroy()* method in your code, consider the following:

1. The onDestroy() method is the last lifecycle callback method. It is called when the application is removed from the system memory.
2. If you call the *finish()* method inside the onCreate() method, the onDestroy method can be used for code/data cleanup. This is because the *finish()* method triggers the OnDestroy method.
3. The onDestroy() method can be used to kill long-running processes or when a large amount of resources is released unwillingly.

What is unique about the Activity's finish() method is that it calls the onDestroy() method, and if you come back to the Activity, the onCreate() method is called again. The onCreate() method is supposed to be called only once, the first time you create an Activity. Now, because of the finish() method, if you return to the Activity, the onCreate() method is called again.

5.3.2   Pausing and Resuming an Activity

When a foreground Activity is partially obscured (because of another activity, e.g.), the system calls the **onPause()** method. The state diagram in Fig. 5.2 shows that once an activity is in the paused state, there are two states it can move to: the *resume* or *stop* state. If the user decides to return to the start Activity, the **onResume()** method is called. However, there is a chance that the user will not resume the Activity.

When the **onPause()** method is called, your application is still partially visible. As an app developer, it is here that you should take action, e.g., release resources. Your app should not consume resources while it is in the paused state. The *onPause()* implementations must not take a long time as well. This is because the next Activity will not resume until this method returns, i.e., is completed. If applicable to your app, inside the onPause() method, do the following:

- Stop animations if you have any.
- Release system resources such as Wi-Fi locks, broadcast receivers, and close files.
- Release resources that consume battery life such as background services.

Any other action similar to the ones above should be stopped while your app is in the onPause() state. When the user resumes activity from the paused state, the system calls **onResume()**. The **onResume()** method is called every time an application comes to the foreground, including the first time. If the *OnResume* method is called, you need to initialize resources released previously in the *onPause()* method. In the *onResume()* state, the user can interact with the Activity; the Activity has moved to the top of the Activity stack and accepts user input.

Note that calling AlertDialog, Toast, Date/Time pickers, and similar objects will bring new windows on top of the current one, but they will not lead to executing the onPause() method. Only launching a new Activity will push the current running Activity to the background and result in executing the onPause() callback method. The fourth button on the demo app enables you to practice what we just described, obscuring the running window without calling the onPause() method.

5.3.3   Stopping and Restarting an Activity

An application might be stopped and restarted because:

1. The user switches apps
2. The user performs an action that starts a new Activity
3. The user receives a phone call while using an app
4. The app is doing a complex task, such as a database write

The **onStop()** callback is called when an Activity becomes hidden, i.e., is fully obscured (instead of partially obscured). That is, the user's focus is on another Activity. While stopped, the Activity instance still lives in the system memory. If the Android system runs out of memory space or experiences memory shortages, it

might destroy the stopped Activity. For that reason, you often need to only implement the **onPause()** and **onResume()** methods and **not the onStop() method.** The
onRestart() method is called when an Activity comes to the foreground from a
stopped state. The *OnRestart()* method is not called when the application first starts.
The *onStart()* method is called in two cases: after *onCreate()* when an Activity
becomes visible and after *onRestart()* calls. Generally, you only need to handle the
onStart() method. The Activity states and the callback method order diagram
provided by Google are shown in Fig. 5.4.

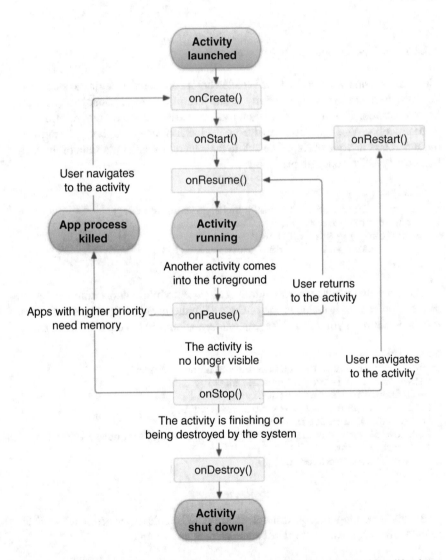

Fig. 5.4 An illustration of the activity lifecycle (The source of this figure is here: https://developer.
android.com/reference/android/app/Activity#ActivityLifecycle)

5.3.4   Restoring Activity State

By default, the Android system only saves limited state information. These include Views with a unique id, scroll positions in a ListView object, etc. If you want to restore more than the default values when an Activity is recreated, then you need to take care of it. That is, the developer is responsible for saving user progress data. You can do that using either the onSaveInstanceState() or onRestoreInstanceState() callback methods.

5.3.4.1   onSaveInstanceState()

The *onSaveInstanceState()* method is called before an Activity begins to stop. Here, you have a chance to save the Activity's state information to the Bundle object using key/value pairs. The saved information can be used for the Activity recreation after its destruction. When you override the onSaveInstanceState() method, you must call the superclass in your coding. The call to the superclass saves the state of the View hierarchy; see the code snippet below:

```
@Override
public void onSaveInstanceState(Bundle outState) {
  super.onSaveInstanceState(outState);
  outState.putString("name",
      String.valueOf(nameView.getText()));
}
```

There are two places where you can retrieve state information from the Bundle object. You can do it inside in the onCreate(Bundle mySavedState) method. If the Bundle is not null, you can retrieve state information; see the code snippet below:

```
@Override
protected void onCreate(Bundle savedInstanceState) {
  super.onCreate(savedInstanceState);
  setContentView(R.layout.activity_main);
  mShowCount = findViewById(R.id.show_count);
  if (savedInstanceState != null) {
    String count = savedInstanceState.getString("count");
    if (mShowCount != null)
      myView.setText(count);
  }
}
```

By implementing the onRestoreInstanceState(Bundle mySavedState) callback method, you can retrieve the saved state. Here is an example:

```
@Override
public void onRestoreInstanceState (Bundle mySavedState) {
  super.onRestoreInstanceState(mySavedState);
  if (mySavedState != null) {
    String count = mySavedState.getString("name");
    if (count != null)
      nameView.setText(count);
  }
}
```

To practice restoring the Activity state, run the demo app, and press the fourth button. Rotate your device to change the devices' configuration. This leads to destroying the running Activity and recreating it. Since the onRestoreInstanceState () method is implemented, the object's state will be restored. The code for restoring the Activity state, button four on the demo app's main menu, is shown in Listing 5.4.

Note that saving instance state information keeps state information within the current session only. If you need to save and retrieve state information after closing your app, you need to save it into a persistence object or file. For example, use shared preferences or a database, which will be described in later chapters.

Listing 5.4 Complete code for restoring activity (RestoringActivity.java).

```
package code.android.abdulrahman.com.LifeCyleapplication;
import android.app.DatePickerDialog;
import android.os.Bundle;
import android.util.Log;
import android.view.View;
import android.widget.Button;
import android.widget.DatePicker;
import android.widget.TextView;

import androidx.annotation.NonNull;
import androidx.appcompat.app.AlertDialog;
import androidx.appcompat.app.AppCompatActivity;
import java.util.Calendar;

public class RestoringActivity extends AppCompatActivity {
  TextView textView;
  Calendar currentDateAndTime = Calendar.getInstance();
  @Override
  protected void onCreate(Bundle savedInstanceState) {
    super.onCreate(savedInstanceState);
    setContentView(R.layout.activity_restoring);
    textView = findViewById(R.id.r_textView);
    final Button button = findViewById(R.id.restoreButton);
    final Button dateButton = findViewById(R.id.fragmentBtn);
```

```java
button.setOnClickListener(new View.OnClickListener() {
  public void onClick(View v) {
    // create alert dialog
    AlertDialog.Builder builder =
        new AlertDialog.Builder(RestoringActivity.this);
    builder.setTitle("Alert Dialog title with Icon");
    builder.setIcon(R.drawable.ic_baseline_airport_shuttle_24);
    builder.show();
  }
});
dateButton.setOnClickListener(new View.OnClickListener() {
  public void onClick(View v) {
    DatePickerDialog.OnDateSetListener dListener = new
                          DatePickerDialog.
        OnDateSetListener() {
      @Override
      public void onDateSet(DatePicker view, int yr, int mth, int dy) {
          currentDateAndTime.set(Calendar.YEAR, yr);
          currentDateAndTime.set(Calendar.MONTH, mth);
          currentDateAndTime.set(Calendar.DAY_OF_MONTH, dy);
      }
    };
    new DatePickerDialog(RestoringActivity.this, dListener,
        currentDateAndTime.get(Calendar.YEAR),
        currentDateAndTime.get(Calendar.MONTH),
        currentDateAndTime.get(Calendar.DAY_OF_MONTH)).show();
  }
});
}


@Override
protected void onPause() {
  super.onPause();
  Log.i("pause", "onpause");
}
@Override
protected void onStop() {
  super.onStop();
  Log.i("onstop", "onstop");
}
@Override
protected void onResume() {
  super.onResume();
}
@Override
protected void onRestart() {
  super.onRestart();
}
@Override
protected void onStart() {
  super.onStart();
}
@Override
protected void onSaveInstanceState(Bundle outState) {
  super.onSaveInstanceState(outState);
```

```
    String nameValue = "Abdul-Rahman";
    int accountNumber = 12345;
    outState.putString("name", nameValue);
    outState.putInt("accountNumber", accountNumber);
  }
 @Override
protected void onRestoreInstanceState(
   @NonNull Bundle savedInstanceState) {
  super.onRestoreInstanceState(savedInstanceState);
  String r_name = savedInstanceState.getString("name");
  int r_accountNumber = savedInstanceState.getInt("accountNumber");
  textView.setText("\n" + "Restoring state \n" + r_name + " " +
  r_accountNumber);
  }
}
```

5.3.5   Do It Yourself

For each activity state listed in Fig. 5.3, identify the in-state (previous state) and the out-state (next state). For example, for the onCreate() method, the in-states are Launcher Activity or the stop state, and its out-state is the running state.

5.4   Lifecycle Illustration App

In our demo app, the **LifeCycleWithParcellable**, we demonstrate the callback method calls and the order of the calls. In this part, we present the implementation details of these methods.

5.4.1   Lifecycle Callback Methods

The lifecycle callback methods implemented in the demo app are listed below.

```
protected void onCreate(Bundle savedInstanceState);
protected void onStart();
protected void onRestart();
protected void onResume();
protected void onPause();
protected void onStop();
protected void onDestroy();
protected void onSaveInstanceState(Bundle outState);
```

Press the second button on the first screen of the app to run the MainActivity. When executed, the LifeCycleWithParcellable demo app does the following:

1. At each callback method, some text, or a string, is appended to a class variable. The class variable is called the MainActivity_called. The added text indicates which method of the MainActivity has been called, which also indicates the Activity state.
2. Once the user presses the send button, the values of the class variable are passed to the DisplayMessageActivity and are displayed on the screen showing the order of the method calls. For example, the first time you press the send message button, the following messages are displayed on the second screen.

from MainActivity, onCreate method invoked 0.
from MainActivity, onStart method invoked 1.
from MainActivity, onResume method invoked 2.

The numbers show the order of the message execution in the starter Activity. This is consistent with what we said about the order of the callback methods: *onCreate →* *onStart → onResume.*

Once on the second screen, that is, when the DisplayMessageActivity is displayed, press the *Back to Main Activity* button to find out the order of the message calls on the DisplayMessageActivity. You will see that the callback methods for the DisplayMessageActivity are executed in the same order as the MainActivity: *onCreate → onStart → onResume.*

Using the *submit* and *back to Main Activity* buttons, along with clear and close buttons, should enable you to test all the possible paths of the Activity lifecycle. The *clear* button cleans what is currently posted on the display. The *close* button closes the app and returns to the home menu. When the close button or the home button of the Android device is used, you will see that the onRestart() method gets called. In the subsection below, the sequence of the method calls is demonstrated.

5.4.2 Callback Methods for the MainActivity

When you open the app and select the second option, the Lifecycle demonstration option, the sequence *onCreate()→ onStart()→ onResume()* is called. These calls append texts "onCreate method invoked," "onStart method invoked," and "onResume method invoked" to a static class variable called *MainActivity_called* in the order of the method calls.

When you press the *start message display* button, the appended text is inserted into the Intent object and passed to the *MessageDisplayActivity* to be displayed. The OnPause() and OnStop() methods are called as well, but the texts for these two methods are not included in the Intent for passing to the MessageDisplayActivity. This is because the startActivity(intent) is called before the onPause() and onStart() methods are executed. The *DisplayMessageActivity* presents the texts inside the Intent Object and is as follows (see Fig. 5.5):

Fig. 5.5 DisplayMessage
Activity displaying the text
messages of callback
methods

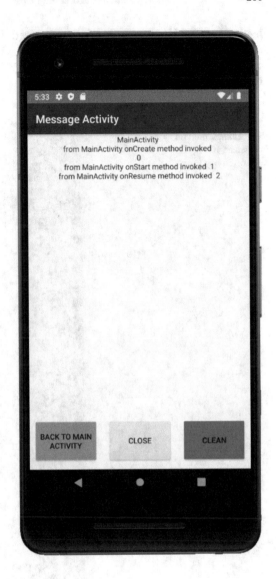

5.4.3 Callback Methods for the DisplayMessageActivity

Similar to the call order of the MainActivity callback methods, when
DisplayMessageActivity starts, the onCreate() → onStart() → onResume() methods
are called. When the *Back To Main Activity* button is pressed, the texts for these three

methods are put into the Intent object and passed to the MainActivity followed by a call to the onPause() and OnStop() methods. The onCreate() → onStart() → onResume() method information for the DisplayMessageActivity are displayed on the MainActivity screen. See Fig. 5.6.

Fig. 5.6 Text messages in the callback method presented on the MainActivity

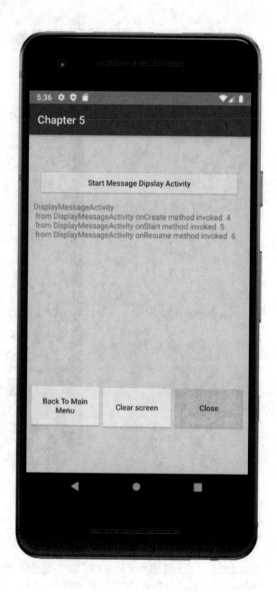

Fig. 5.7 Closing and re-launching the app

To continue with demoing the app, press the home button of the phone/emulator to close the app, and re-launch the app as shown below in Fig. 5.7. The actions above result in a new sequence of method calls. The sequence of the method calls is shown in Fig. 5.8.

We are using a static variable for appending text at each method. The method sequence calls are presented in Fig. 5.8 and can be explained as follows:

1. The onCreate() → onStart() → onResume() is for starting the app.
2. The onPause() → onStop() sequence is appended to the first method sequence calls. This happens after the MainActivity becomes hidden completely and the DisplayMessageActivity starts.

Fig. 5.8 The order of callback methods

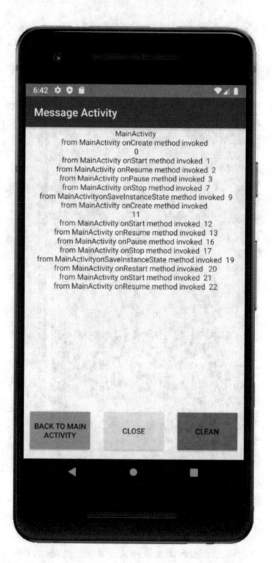

3. The onCreate() → onStart() → onResume() sequence is for starting the DisplayMessageActivity.
4. The onPause() → onSaveInstanceState() → onStop() texts are appended to an already collected call once the home button is pressed on the phone, i.e., the app is closed.
5. The OnRestart→ onStart() → onResume () sequence calls are appended to the previous texts when the app reopens.
6. When the *Start Message Display Activity* button is pressed, the methods onPause() → onSaveInstanceState() → onStop() are called again followed by OnRestart() → onStar () → onResume().

5.4.4 Do It Yourself

Run the LifeCycleWithParcellable app that comes with this chapter, and reproduce the method order calls that are displayed on the screen snapshot in Fig. 5.9.

Fig. 5.9 The order of callback methods for the DisplayMessageActivity

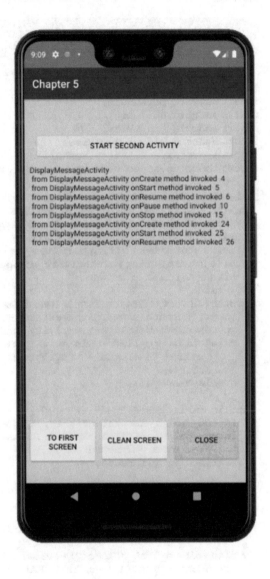

5.4.5   Callback Method Implementations

The code snippet in Listing 5.5 shows the callback method implementations for the MainActivity where important steps are bolded for your attention as you go through the code.

Listing 5.5 MainActivity.java.

```java
package code.android.abdulrahman.com.LifeCyleapplication;
import android.content.Intent;
import android.os.Bundle;
import android.util.Log;
import android.view.View;
import android.widget.TextView;
import androidx.annotation.NonNull;
import androidx.appcompat.app.AppCompatActivity;

public class MainActivity extends AppCompatActivity {
    public static final String EXTRA_MESSAGE =
        "code.android.abdulrahman.com.LifeCycleapplication.MESSAGE";
    public String message = "No data from intent";
    private static final String MainTAG = "MainActivity";
    public static String MainActivity_called = MainTAG;
    public static int order = 0;
    @Override
    protected void onCreate(Bundle savedInstanceState) {
        super.onCreate(savedInstanceState);
        setContentView(R.layout.activity_lifecycle);
        MainActivity_called = MainActivity_called +
            "\n from " + MainTAG + " onCreate method invoked \n " +
            order++;
        displayMessage();
    }
    public void sendMessage(View view) {
        Intent intent = new Intent(this, DisplayMessageActivity.class);
        intent.putExtra(EXTRA_MESSAGE, MainActivity_called);
        Log.d(MainTAG, "Intent fired ");
        startActivity(intent);
    }
    public void clean_main_display(View view) {
        order = 0;
        MainActivity_called = "";
        setContentView(R.layout.activity_lifecycle);
    }
    public void to_first_screen(View view) {
        startActivity(new Intent(this, MainActivity.class
        )
);
    }
```

```java
public void exit_app(View view) {
  MainActivity_called = "";
  Intent intent = new Intent(Intent.ACTION_MAIN);
  intent.addCategory(Intent.CATEGORY_HOME);
  startActivity(intent);
}
@Override
protected void onSaveInstanceState(Bundle outState) {
  super.onSaveInstanceState(outState);
  Log.d("tag", "onSaveInstanceState() called" + order ++);

  MainActivity_called = MainActivity_called +
    "\n from " + MainTAG + "onSaveInstanceState method invoked"
    + order++;
}
@Override
protected void onRestoreInstanceState(
  @NonNull Bundle savedInstanceState) {
  super.onRestoreInstanceState(savedInstanceState);
  MainActivity_called = MainActivity_called +
  "\n from " + MainTAG + "onRestoreInstanceState method invoked"
    + order++;
}
@Override
protected void onStart() {
  super.onStart();
  MainActivity_called = MainActivity_called +
    "\n from " + MainTAG + " onStart method invoked  "
    + order++;
}
@Override
protected void onRestart() {
  super.onRestart();
  MainActivity_called = MainActivity_called +
    "\n from " + MainTAG + " onRestart method invoked   "
    + order++;
}
@Override
protected void onResume() {
  super.onResume();
  MainActivity_called = MainActivity_called +
    "\n from " + MainTAG + " onResume method invoked  "
    + order++;
}
@Override
protected void onPause() {
  super.onPause();
  MainActivity_called = MainActivity_called +
    "\n from " + MainTAG + " onPause method invoked  "
    + order++;
}
@Override
protected void onStop() {
  super.onStop();
```

```
    MainActivity_called = MainActivity_called +
        "\n from " + MainTAG + " onStop method invoked  " +
        order++;
}
@Override
protected void onDestroy() {
  super.onDestroy();
  MainActivity_called = MainActivity_called +
      "\n from " + MainTAG + "onDestroy method invoked  " +
      order++;
}
public void displayMessage() {
  Intent intent = getIntent();
  if (intent != null) {
    if (intent.hasExtra(getString(R.string.appmessage))) {
      message = intent.getStringExtra(
          getString(R.string.appmessage));
      Log.d(MainTAG, "Got Intent");
    }
  }
  TextView messageTextView = findViewById(R.id.messageTextArea);
  messageTextView.setText(message);
}
}
```

5.4.6   Trigger the onPause() Method

We said earlier that Snackbar and Dialog box will not cause onPause() method to be triggered even though they will come up on top of the activity and cover the main activity for some time. The same thing is true when you attached fragment views to the activity's layout. To demonstrate how you can trigger the onPause() method and without going back and forth between activities, you can create an Activity as a Dialog box. That is, you create an activity but apply the dialog theme to it and treated it like a dialog. To do that, inside the AndroidManifest.xml, you need to add theme property to the activity. See the code snippet below.

```
<activity android:name=".ActivityAsDialog"
  android:theme="@android:style/Theme.Holo.Dialog"></activity>
```

Also note that your activity needs to *extend Activity* class and not AppCompatActivity as like this: **public class ActivityAsDialog extends Activity {...}**. A complete code for triggering onPause() method is shown in Listings 5.6 to 5.10. In Listings 5.6 and 5.7, a simple Activity class and its layout are shown. In Listings 5.8 and 5.9, a simple activity that would be used as a dialog box and its layout is shown. In Listing 5.10, AndroidManifest.xml file where dialog theme is assigned to Activity is shown.

Listing 5.6 MainActivity.java.

```java
import androidx.appcompat.app.AppCompatActivity;
import android.content.Intent;
import android.os.Bundle;
import android.view.View;
public class MainActivity extends AppCompatActivity {
  @Override
  protected void onCreate(Bundle savedInstanceState) {
    super.onCreate(savedInstanceState);
    setContentView(R.layout.activity_main);
  }
  public void startDialog (View view) {
    startActivity(new Intent (this, ActivityAsDialog.class)) ;
  }
}
```

Listing 5.7 Main activity layout file.

```xml
<?xml version="1.0" encoding="utf-8"?>
<androidx.constraintlayout.widget.ConstraintLayout
 xmlns:android="http://schemas.android.com/apk/res/android"
  xmlns:app="http://schemas.android.com/apk/res-auto"
  xmlns:tools="http://schemas.android.com/tools"
  android:layout_width="match_parent"
  android:layout_height="match_parent"
  tools:context=".MainActivity">
  <Button
    android:layout_width="wrap_content"
    android:layout_height="wrap_content"
    android:text="start dialog"
    app:layout_constraintBottom_toBottomOf="parent"
    app:layout_constraintLeft_toLeftOf="parent"
    app:layout_constraintRight_toRightOf="parent"
    app:layout_constraintTop_toTopOf="parent"
    android:onClick="startDialog"/>
</androidx.constraintlayout.widget.ConstraintLayout>
```

Listing 5.8 An activity class that would be used as a dialog.

```java
import android.app.Activity;
import android.os.Bundle;
import android.util.Log;
```

```java
import android.view.View;
import android.widget.Button;
public class ActivityAsDialog extends Activity {
  Button oKbutton;
  Button cancelButton;
  @Override
  protected void onCreate(Bundle savedInstanceState) {
    super.onCreate(savedInstanceState);
    setContentView(R.layout.activity_as_dialog);
    oKbutton = findViewById(R.id.Ok);
    oKbutton.setOnClickListener(new View.OnClickListener() {
      @Override
      public void onClick(View v) {
        finish();
      }
    });
    cancelButton = findViewById(R.id.Cancel);
    cancelButton.setOnClickListener(new View.OnClickListener() {
      @Override
      public void onClick(View v) {
        finish();
      }
    });
  }
  @Override
  protected void onPause() {
    super.onPause();
    Log.i("log", "AR on pause is called ");
  }
}
```

Listing 5.9 A layout file for the activity class that would be used as a dialog.

```xml
<?xml version="1.0" encoding="utf-8"?>
<androidx.constraintlayout.widget.ConstraintLayout
  xmlns:android="http://schemas.android.com/apk/res/android"
  xmlns:app="http://schemas.android.com/apk/res-auto"
  xmlns:tools="http://schemas.android.com/tools"
  android:layout_width="200dp"
  android:layout_height="200dp"
  tools:context=".ActivityAsDialog">
  <Button
    android:id="@+id/Ok"
    android:layout_width="76dp"
    android:layout_height="41dp"
    android:layout_marginTop="60dp"
    android:layout_marginEnd="28dp"
    android:text="OK"
    app:layout_constraintEnd_toStartOf="@+id/Cancel"
```

```
      app:layout_constraintTop_toBottomOf="@+id/textView" />
    <Button
      android:id="@+id/Cancel"
      android:layout_width="75dp"
      android:layout_height="38dp"
      android:layout_marginTop="64dp"
      android:layout_marginEnd="16dp"
      android:text="Cancel"
      app:layout_constraintEnd_toEndOf="parent"
      app:layout_constraintTop_toBottomOf="@+id/textView" />
    <TextView
      android:id="@+id/textView"
      android:layout_width="wrap_content"
      android:layout_height="wrap_content"
      android:layout_marginTop="44dp"
      android:text="continue or not ?"
      app:layout_constraintEnd_toEndOf="parent"
      app:layout_constraintStart_toStartOf="parent"
      app:layout_constraintTop_toTopOf="parent" />
</androidx.constraintlayout.widget.ConstraintLayout>
```

Listing 5.10 AndroidManifest.xml file where dialog theme is assigned to Activity.

```
<?xml version="1.0" encoding="utf-8"?>
<manifest xmlns:android=
  "http://schemas.android.com/apk/res/android"
  package="com.code.abdulrahman.onpauseexample">
  <application
    android:allowBackup="true"
    android:icon="@mipmap/ic_launcher"
    android:label="@string/app_name"
    android:roundIcon="@mipmap/ic_launcher_round"
    android:supportsRtl="true"
    android:theme="@style/Theme.OnPauseExample">
    <activity android:name=".ActivityAsDialog"
      android:theme="@android:style/Theme.Holo.Dialog"></activity>
    <activity android:name=".MainActivity">
      <intent-filter>
        <action android:name="android.intent.action.MAIN" />
          <category android:name="android.intent.category.LAUNCHER" />
      </intent-filter>
    </activity>
  </application>
</manifest>
```

5.5   Creating and Using Parcelable Objects

Java is an object-oriented programming language, and except for primitive data types, almost everything is an object; hence, you need to be able to pass objects between activities. So far, we have passed data from one activity to another via the Intent object. This is accomplished by putting (key/value) pairs in Intent objects using the putExtra() method. In this part, we describe how you can pass user-defined objects between Activities using the Parcelable interface.

5.5.1   Passing User-Defined Objects Between Activities

The Intent class puts restrictions on the type of values that can be passed between the Activities. The value types are restricted to primitives, arrays, CharSequence, String, Parcelable, or Serializable objects. In other words, the Intent object does not accept any object as a parameter to be passed between the Activities unless the object is a Parcelable or Serializable object. You have already seen one example of passing objects between Activities by inserting the Bundle object into the Intent object. This is possible because the Bundle object is a Parcelable object.

To pass a user-defined object between Activities, the object must be Serializable or Parcelable. Android recommends using Parcelable rather than Serializable for performance. We will follow the recommendation from Android and implement the Parcelable interface for passing objects between Activities.

The method signatures for the putExtra methods from the Intent class that take objects are shown below. The method definitions specify that the objects must be Parcelable or Serializable to be used with the Intent class.

```
public Intent putExtra (String name, Parcelable value);
public Intent putExtra (String name, Serializable value);
```

Let's assume you have a class called Grades: **Public class Grades {...}**. If you want to create an Intent object and try to insert a Grades object into the Intent object to pass between Activities, it will not work. The code snippet below will not work because the Grades object is not Parcelable.

```
Intent intent = new Intent();
Grades grades = new Grades ();
String name = " a student";
intent.putExtra(name,grades);
```

To make the code snippet above work, you need to change the definition of the Grades class and let it implement the Parcelable interface:

Public class Grades implements Parcelable {...} or you cast the grades object to the Parcelable object: **intent.putExtra(name, (Parcelable) grades);**

In the first chapter, we described object serialization and the Serializable interface. The Serializable interface has no method to be implemented. It is merely an instruction to the compiler telling it that the object state can be written to persistent storage such as a hard drive for future retrieval. Different from the Serializable interface, the Parcelable interface has methods and a field. Instances of classes that implement the Parcelable interface can be written and restored from the Parcel class. The Parcelable interface and its use will be described in this section.

5.5.2 LifeCycle with Parcelable Object

We added new activities to our lifecycle app to pass a *Parcelable object* between Activities. This approach is different from appending Strings together and passing a long String between Activities like we have done earlier in this chapter. We created a new Java class called *MyDataObject* to represent the *data object* that goes back and forth between Activities. We also created two more Activities, ParcelableActivity and ParcelableDisplayMessageActivity, and a new Java class to illustrate how you can create and use Parcelable objects. These classes are shown in Fig. 5.10.

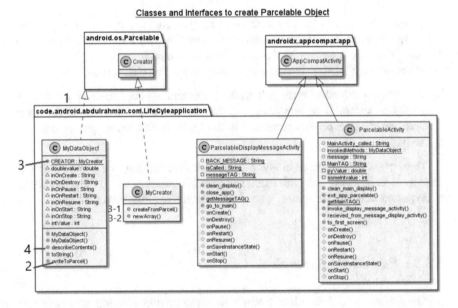

Fig. 5.10 New activities add to the lifecycle app to pass *Parcelable objects* between activities

5.5.2.1   Parcelable Class Creation

For an object to become Parcelable, it needs to comply with certain requirements. Its class needs to implement the Parcelable interface, have a public static final field of type Parcelable.Creator, and override two methods from the Parcelable interface. The methods are writeToParcel and describeContents. These requirements are described below.

1. Implement the Parcelable interface. The implementation would be like this: **public class** MyDataObject *implements Parcelable* { . . .}.
2. Override the **writeToParcel()** method to flatten your object into a parcel object, i.e., add all of the data in your class fields to a Parcel object.
3. Include a **public static final** field of type **Parcelable.Creator** in the class definition. The Creator field is an Interface with two methods, *createFromParcel* and *newArray*. These methods can be implemented as follows:

```
public MyParcelable createFromParcel(Parcel in) {
      return new MyParcelable(in);
   }
   public MyParcelable[] newArray(int size) {
    return new MyParcelable[size];
   }
```

   You use the *createFromParcel(Parcel source)* method to create a new Parcelable object and return it. The object is instantiated from the given Parcel class whose data had previously been written by the *writeToParcel* method.
   The newArray(int size) creates a new array of the Parcelable class.

4. Override the **describeContents() method.** The method implementation can be as simple as returns 0 or any integer value that can be used as an id for some description of the objects contained in the Parcelable instances passed between Activities.

   These steps are numbered in Fig. 5.10. The requirements above indicate that you cannot associate *any* object with Intent and pass it between Activities. For any object to be passed between Activities, it needs to meet the requirements above.

5.5.3   Parcelable Example

MyDataObject is a Java class created to illustrate the creation and usage of Parcelable objects, i.e., the class objects that can be sent back and forth between Activities. Below, we implemented all requirements that are needed to create a Parcelable object. MyDataObject implements the four constraints listed earlier.

5.5.3.1 Implement the Parcelable Interface

For an object to be Parcelable, its class must implement the Parcelable interface. MyDataObject implements the Parcelable interface as follows:

```
public class MyDataObject implements Parcelable {...}.
```

5.5.3.2 Declaring the Parcelable.Creator Interface Field

MyDataObject class has a special *field* of type interface. Usually, Java fields are declared in lower case. However, here the class field CREATOR is declared in upper case to attract your attention. The field, which is of an interface type, has two methods that need to be implemented. The interface implementation is done in a separate class called MyCreator. These steps are shown below.

```
public class MyDataObject implements Parcelable {
...
   public static final MyCreator CREATOR = new MyCreator();
...
}
```

The *MyCreator* class implements the *Parcelable.Creator interface*. This step is done in a separate class for clarity. If you wish, you can implement the *Parcelable.Creator interface* class as an inner class. The implementation of the *Parcelable.Creator interface* is presented in Listing 5.11.

Listing 5.11 MyCreator.java implements the *Parcelable.Creator interface.*

```
package code.android.abdulrahman.com.LifeCyleapplication;
import android.os.Parcel;
import android.os.Parcelable;
public class MyCreator implements Parcelable.Creator <MyDataObject> {
  @Override
  public MyDataObject createFromParcel(Parcel source) {
    return new MyDataObject(source);
  }
  @Override
  public MyDataObject[] newArray(int size) {
    return new MyDataObject[size];
  }
}
```

5.5.3.3 Implementing the describeContents Method

The MyDataObject class overrides the describeContents methods with a simple implementation, i.e., it returns zero. See the code snippet below:

```
@Override
public int describeContents() {
  // TODO Auto-generated method stub
  return 0;
}
```

5.5.3.4 Implementing the writeToParcel Method

The code snippet in Listing 5.12 is the override implementation for the **writeToParcel** method. In this method, you put any value you need to be passed between Activities inside the Parcel object using methods like writeString, writeInt, WriteDouble, etc. See Listing 5.12.

Listing 5.12 Overriding writeToParcel method.

```
@Override
public void writeToParcel(Parcel destination, int flags) {
  destination.writeString(inOnCreate);
  destination.writeString(inOnStart);
  destination.writeString(inOnRestart);
  destination.writeString(inOnResume);
  destination.writeString(inOnPause);
  destination.writeString(inOnStop);
  destination.writeString(inOnDestroy);
  destination.writeInt(intValue);
  destination.writeDouble(doublevalue);
}
```

So far, we have implemented all requirements to have a Parcelable object, and the object is ready to be used in an Activity. The code snippet below shows how the ParcelableActivity uses a Parcelable object, *MyDataObject*. The object is created, its fields are set, and it is ready to be sent back and forth between Activities.

```
public class ParcelableActivity extends AppCompatActivity {
  ...
  public static MyDataObject MyDataObject = new MyDataObject();
  ...
  MyDataObject.setInOnCreate("onCreate");
  ...
  intent.putExtra("MyDataObject", MyDataObject);
        startActivity(intent);
  ...
}
```

Note that both the *writeToParcel* method and the constructor of the MyDataObject take *Parcel* as an input parameter. This is because an instance of MyDataObject will be written to and restored from a Parcel object. The MyDataObject constructor code is shown in Listing 5.13.

Listing 5.13 The constructor method for MyDataObject class.

```
public MyDataObject (Parcel source) {
  this.inOnCreate = source.readString();
  this.inOnStart = source.readString();
  this.inOnRestart = source.readString();
  this.inOnResume = source.readString();
  this.inOnPause = source.readString();
  this.inOnStop = source.readString();
  this.inOnDestroy = source.readString();
  this.intValue = source.readInt() ;
  this.doublevalue = source.readDouble() ;
}
```

5.5.3.5   CREATOR Interface Constructs a Parcelable Object

The code snippet below shows how the *createFromParcel* method from the *Parcelable.Creator* interface is used to call the MyDataObject constructor, i.e., the CREATOR interface is used to create a Parcelable object, in our example, the myDataObject object.

When you create/use a Parcelable object, for example, when you invoke StartActivity with an Intent object that has a Parcelable object in it, you trigger the createFromParcel method which then leads to the creation of a Parcelable object. This step, triggering the myDataObject object creation, consists of a few method calls. The code snippet below shows these steps.

```
Intent intent = new Intent (
    this, ParcelableDisplayMessageActivity.class);
 intent.putExtra("MyDataObject", MyDataObject);
 Log.d(MainTAG, "Intent fired ");
 startActivity(intent);
```

For the Parcelable object to be created, first, its fields need to be written to a Parcel object. The writeToParcel implementation in Listing 5.14 shows this step.

Listing 5.14 Parcelable object fields are written to the Parcel object.

```
@Override
public void writeToParcel(Parcel destination, int flags) {
 destination.writeString(inOnCreate);
 destination.writeString(inOnStart);
 destination.writeString(inOnRestart);
 destination.writeString(inOnResume);
 destination.writeString(inOnPause);
 destination.writeString(inOnStop);
 destination.writeString(inOnDestroy);
 destination.writeInt(intValue);
 destination.writeDouble(doublevalue);
}
```

Once the Parcel object is created, the createFromParcel method uses the Parcelable constructor to create a Parcelable object and return it. These two method calls are shown below.

```
@Override
    public MyDataObject createFromParcel(Parcel source) {
     return new MyDataObject(source); // returns a new Parcelable object
    }

public MyDataObject(Parcel source) {
   this.inOnCreate = source.readString();
   this.inOnStart = source.readString();
   this.inOnRestart = source.readString();
   this.inOnResume = source.readString();
   this.inOnPause = source.readString();
   this.inOnStop = source.readString();
   this.inOnDestroy = source.readString();
   this.intValue = source.readInt();
   this.doublevalue = source.readDouble();
}
```

The sequence of the above steps can be summarized as follows:

StartActivity → writeToParcel() → createFromParcel() → call to the Parcelable constructor.

Putting all the code snippets together, the code for the MyDataObject class, which implements the Parcelable interface, is shown in Listing 5.15.

Listing 5.15 MyDataObject.java is a Parcelable object that can be passed between Activities.

```java
package code.android.abdulrahman.com.LifeCyleapplication;
import android.os.Parcel;
import android.os.Parcelable;
public class MyDataObject implements Parcelable {
  String inOnCreate = "";
  String inOnStart = "";
  String inOnRestart = "";
  String inOnResume = "";
  String inOnPause = "";
  String inOnStop = "";
  String inOnDestroy = "";
  int intValue ;
  double doublevalue ;
 public static final MyCreator CREATOR = new MyCreator();
  @Override
  public int describeContents() {
    // TODO Auto-generated method stub
    return 0;
  }
  /*
   * MyDataObject data to Parcel object
   * all the field values you need to be passed
   * between activities are put inside the Parcel object
   */
  @Override
  public void writeToParcel(Parcel destination, int flags) {
    destination.writeString(inOnCreate);
    destination.writeString(inOnStart);
    destination.writeString(inOnRestart);
    destination.writeString(inOnResume);
    destination.writeString(inOnPause);
    destination.writeString(inOnStop);
    destination.writeString(inOnDestroy);
    destination.writeInt(intValue);
    destination.writeDouble(doublevalue);
  }
  public MyDataObject(int ivalue, double dvalue) {
    this.intValue = ivalue ;
    this.doublevalue = dvalue ;
  }
  public void setIntValue(int intValue) {
    this.intValue = intValue;
  }
  public void setDoublevalue(double doublevalue) {
    this.doublevalue = doublevalue;
  }
  /**
   * the constructor of your class. Here you create object
```

```
 * with multiple fields that could be of any
 * type for passing between activates.
 * @param source
 */
public MyDataObject(Parcel source) {
  this.inOnCreate = source.readString();
  this.inOnStart = source.readString();
  this.inOnRestart = source.readString();
  this.inOnResume = source.readString();
  this.inOnPause = source.readString();
  this.inOnStop = source.readString();
  this.inOnDestroy = source.readString();
  this.intValue = source.readInt() ;
  this.doublevalue = source.readDouble() ;
}
public String getInOnCreate() {
  return inOnCreate;
}
```

5.5.3.6   Passing a Parcelable Object to Second Activity

To pass a Parcelable object to an Activity via an Intent, you use a key/value pair with the putExtra() method. The key argument is a String and is used to get the object in the receiving Activity. The value argument is the Parcelable object that you want to pass, i.e., an instance of the MyDataObject class.

The code snippet in Listing 5.16 shows how to pass an object between Activities. The DataObject creation, the object value setting, and the passing and receiving of the Parcelable object are emphasized in bold in the code snippet below.

Listing 5.16 ParcelableActivity.java starts a second activity and passes an object.

```
public class ParcelableActivity extends AppCompatActivity {
  public String message = "" ; // "initialize intent data";
  private static final String MainTAG = "ParcelableActivity";
  public static String MainActivity_called = MainTAG;
  public static MyDataObject myDataObject =
                           new MyDataObject() ;
  @Override
  protected void onCreate(Bundle savedInstanceState) {
    super.onCreate(savedInstanceState);
    setContentView(R.layout.activity_parcelable);
    myDataObject.setInOnCreate("onCreate");
    recieved_from_message_display_activity() ;
  }
  ...
  /** Called when the user clicks START SECOND ACTIVITY button */
```

```
public void invoke_display_message_activity(View view) {
    Intent intent = new Intent(
    this, ParcelableDisplayMessageActivity.class);
    intent.putExtra("MyDataObject", myDataObject);
    Log.d(MainTAG, "Intent fired ");
    startActivity(intent);
}
public void recieved_from_message_display_activity() {
    Intent intent = getIntent();
    if (intent != null) {
        if(intent.hasExtra("code.android.abdulrahman.
                        com.paracelableLifeCycle.MESSAGE")) {
            message = intent.getStringExtra(
                "code.android.abdulrahman.com.
                        paracelableLifeCycle.MESSAGE");
            Log.d(MainTAG, "Got Intent");
        }
    }
    TextView messageTextView = (TextView) findViewById(
                                    R.id.messageTextArea);
    messageTextView.setText(message);
}
}
```

In Listing 5.16, we used the default constructor to create a MyDataObject object. Then, we used the newly created object with the putExtra() method. You can use the parameterized constructor to create a MyDataObject object as well.

Since the MyDataObject class implements the Parcelable interface, its instances are serialized and can be sent back and forth between Activities. The code snippet in Listing 5.17 shows how the inOnStart and the inOnRestart fields of the MyDataObject class are set in the callback methods for the ParcelableActivity.

Listing 5.17 Setting the inOnStart and the inOnRestart fields of the MyDataObject class.

```
@Override
protected void onStart() {
    super.onStart();
    myDataObject.setInOnStart("onStart");
}
@Override
protected void onRestart() {
    super.onRestart();
    myDataObject.setInOnRestart("onRestart");
}
```

5.5.3.7   Receiving a Parcelable Object from an Activity

You can get the Parcelable object in the receiving Activity using key with either *getIntent().getExtras().getParcelable()* or *getIntent().getParcelableExtra()* as shown in Listing 5.18. You need to check that the key/value pair exists in the Bundle by using the hasExtra() method before trying to retrieve the Parcelable object from it.

Listing 5.18 Code for retrieving Parcelable object from the receiver object.

```
@Override
  protected void onCreate(Bundle savedInstanceState) {
    super.onCreate(savedInstanceState);
    setTitle("Parcelable Display Message");
    setContentView(R.layout.activity_parcelable_display_message);
    isCalled = isCalled + "\n from " + messageTAG +
        " onCreate method invoked ";
    Intent intent = getIntent();
    if (intent != null) {
      if (intent.hasExtra("myDataObject")) {
        ParcelableActivity.MyDataObject =
            getIntent().getParcelableExtra("myDataObject");

        MyDataObject porecieved =
            getIntent().getParcelableExtra("myDataObject");
...
    TextView messageTextView = findViewById(R.id.TextMessage);
    messageTextView.setText(
        ParcelableActivity.myDataObject.toString());
}
```

5.5.3.8   Logging Callback Method Invocation

In the previous subsection, we called the toString() method on the object *ParcelableActivity.myDataObject* and passed the String result to the MessageTextView to be displayed using this statement:

```
messageTextView.setText(ParcelableActivity.myDataObject.toString());
```

In the code snippet below, we show a different way to deal with received objects. Instead of using the toString() method from the MyDataObject class to turn the returned object into a String to be displayed on the Activity screen using setText(), you can get individual fields of the received object and log the field's value.

A field value is an indication that a callback method has been called. This is because each field is initialized inside a callback method. This is another way to debug object states and callback methods. To log object fields, you need to do the following:

1. Declare a local variable. In our example, it is called *porecieved*.
2. Initialize the variable using getParcelableExtra.
3. Access objects' fields using the get methods.
4. Log the fields for debugging and displaying the sequence of method calls.

The code snippet in Listing 5.19 shows the steps described above:

Listing 5.19 Code for retrieving Parcelable object from the receiver object.

```java
public class ParcelableDisplayMessageActivity extends AppCompatActivity {
...
  @Override
  protected void onCreate(Bundle savedInstanceState) {
    Intent intent = getIntent();
    if (intent != null) {
      if (intent.hasExtra("MyDataObject")) {
        MyDataObject porecieved =
            getIntent().getParcelableExtra("MyDataObject");
        Log.d(messageTAG, "Got Intent");
        Log.d("A----", porecieved.getInOnCreate());
        Log.d("B----", porecieved.getInOnStart());
        Log.d("C---", porecieved.getInOnResume());
        Log.d("D----", porecieved.getInOnRestart());
        Log.d("F----", porecieved.getInOnStop());
        Log.d("G----", porecieved.getInOnPause());
        ...
}
```

5.5.3.9 Testing LifecycleParcelable App

The snapshots below show the testing results of our modified Lifecyle example app using a Parcelable object instead of a class variable to pass data between Activities. When the user selects option 3 from the menu on the first screen and presses the START SECOND ACTIVITY button, the myDataObject object gets created, and the onCreate, onStart, and OnResume variables are initialized in their corresponding methods. The ParcelableDisplayMessageActivity displays the method execution order in the ParcelableActivity. See Fig. 5.11.

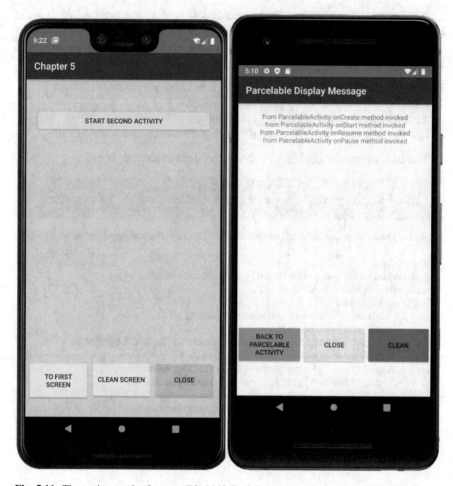

Fig. 5.11 The testing result of our modified LifeCycleExample app using Parcelable Object

Figure 5.12, the left-hand side, shows the case when the Back to Parcelable button on the ParcelableDisplayMessageActivity is pressed. The onCreate, onStart, and onResume methods from ParcelableDisplayMessageActivity are executed, and the result is sent back to the ParcelableActivity to be displayed.

Click on another app on your phone, or go back to the home screen. Once you have done so, re-launch the ParcelableActivity. There will be two additional method calls, onPause and onStop. The app snapshot on the right-hand side of Fig. 5.12 shows the two additional method calls.

Fig. 5.12 A sequence of callback method calls when a Parcelable object is passed between Activities

5.6 Chapter Summary

To summarize, in this chapter, we covered two important topics. First, we studied the lifecycle of Android Activities, i.e., the states an Activity goes through during its lifetime before it gets destroyed. We also studied how the lifecycle callback methods can be used to control and manage Android device resources to create a robust application. Second, we studied how to pass not only the primitive data types between Activities but objects as well.

Java is an object-oriented programming language, and except for primitive types, almost everything is an object. Hence, you need to be able to pass objects between Activities. Android allows Bundle objects to be passed between Activities. This is because the Bundle object is a Parcelable object. But, to be able to pass any user-defined object between Activities, your class needs to implement a Parcelable interface. We studied how to create a Parcelable object in detail. We also created a demo app to go with this chapter to help you learn how to code Parcelable objects and use lifecycle Activities.

Check Your Knowledge

Below are some of the fundamental concepts and vocabularies that have been covered in this chapter. To test your knowledge and your understanding of this chapter, you should be able to describe each of the below concepts in one or two sentences.

- Activity Lifecycle callback methods
- Activity states
- Back-stack
- Bundle
- Finish()
- isFinishing()
- Launcher Activity
- Managing the Activity lifecycle
- OnDestroy()
- OnPause()
- OnRestoreInstanceState()
- OnResume()
- OnSaveInstanceState()
- OnStart()
- OnStop()
- Parcel
- Parcelable.Creator interface
- Parcelable interface

Further Reading

For more information about the topics covered in this chapter, we suggest that you refer to the online resources listed below. These links provide additional insight into the topics covered. The links are mostly maintained by Google and are a part of the Android API specification. The resource titles convey which section/subsection of the chapter the resource is related to.

Activity [online] Available, https://developer.android.com/reference/android/app/Activity#ActivityLifecycle

Parcel [online] Available, https://developer.android.com/reference/android/os/Parcel

Parcelable [online] Available, https://developer.android.com/reference/android/os/Parcelable

Activity Lifecycle and Instance State [online] Available, https://google-developer-training.github.io/android-developer-fundamentals-course-practicals/en/Unit%201/22_p_activity_lifecycle_&_state.html

Chapter 6
User Interface Essential Classes, Layouts, Styles, Themes, and Dimensions

What You Will Learn in This Chapter

By the end of this chapter, you should be able to:

- Design several common user interface layouts
- Use XML and the design tool for design layouts
- Create layouts programmatically
- Define and use styles and themes
- Use phone dimensions properly
- Use View operations and attributes

Check Out the Demo Project

Download the demo app, **LayoutApplication.zip**, specifically developed to go with this chapter. I recommend that you code this project up from the notes rather than just opening the project in Android Studio and running it; however, if you want to run the code first to get a sense of the app, please do so. The code is thoroughly explained in this chapter to help you understand it. We follow the same approach to all other chapters throughout the book. The app's code will help you comprehend the additional concepts that will be described in this chapter.

How to run the code: unzip the code in a folder of your choice, and then in Android Studio, click **File->import->Existing Android code into the workspace**. The project should start running.

6.1 Introduction

From your personal experience using mobile apps, you may have noticed that the user interface is an important part of the app and is vital in its success. It is a large topic that would be difficult to cover in-depth in one or two chapters—it could be a book on its own.

© The Author(s), under exclusive license to Springer Nature Switzerland AG 2022
A.-R. Mawlood-Yunis, *Android for Java Programmers*,
https://doi.org/10.1007/978-3-030-87459-9_6

We will only investigate some aspects of it, specifically aspects related to the user interface component we used in our demo app. We will study Views, Layouts, Widgets, and other components that enable the creation of nice-looking and user-friendly interfaces for Android apps. We will also study phone styles and themes as well as phone dimensions.

This chapter is divided into four parts: user interface (UI) components, writing XML layouts, app styles and themes, and user interface Layout components.

6.2   Essential UI Classes and Properties

In this part, we introduce a few simple and widely used UI classes, class attributes, and methods as a starting point to learn Android UI. As the book progresses, more classes, containers, and other UI components will be introduced along with code samples on how to create and use them. We start by trying to understand the directory structure of an app project in Android Studio and user interface classes that are widely used in all apps, including our demo app.

6.2.1   Android Project Structure

In Fig. 6.1, the fundamental components of our demo app, i.e., the project directory structure, are shown. The two main parts of the app are code and resources, and they are saved in separate directories.

The Java folder holds the MainLayoutActivity and another six activities, one for each button on the demo app's main screen. The data and other resource components are kept separate from Java code. The resource files are stored in the *"res"* folder, and they are *strings, dimensions, images, menu text, colors*, and *style* files. The *strings.xml* file is used to support localization. Localization was discussed in detail in Chap. 2. The project directory structure also includes the manifest XML file which *wires* all components and resources together to make the app work.

6.2.2   Views

In Java, we use the object to refer to almost everything. When developing Android apps, however, you are dealing with UI components, and almost everything is a visual object; hence, you can use View instead of using the object to refer to any UI component of an app. *View* is an Android class that is an essential building

Fig. 6.1 Android project structure

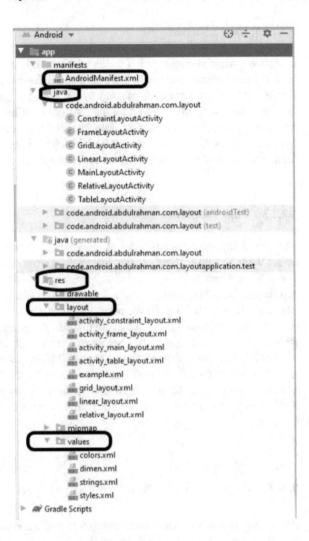

block of Android's user interface. It allows you to create a layout or display an area of your app to put View subclasses and UI components inside it. It occupies the rectangular area of your device and is in charge of drawing and handling user interactions. In Android, every UI element is a View, i.e., is a subclass of the View class.

There is a set of operations (methods) and attributes associated with Views that you need to set and know when creating UI elements. For example, the View class has attributes such as id, width, height, background color, etc. View attributes such as width and height are required when drawing a View.

6.2.2.1 View Listeners

Oftentimes when you include a View in your app, it is used to interact with the user. You as a programmer will set up listeners that will be called when an event gets fired. For example, when a button is pressed by the user, the input data can be saved. For dealing with event firing and handling, Android follows the exact Java listener handling approach. That is, first, you register the component that will fire the event, and second, you write the method which will get executed once the event is fired. This method execution is called event handling.

6.2.2.2 View Properties

Each View has multiple attributes or properties. Some of these properties need to be set when defining View objects inside the layout. Examples of properties that you can set when defining a View object include setting text, positions, margins, padding, dimensions, background colors, text font size, style, etc. These properties can be set in the XML layout file or programmatically in the code. The decision to set the properties using the XML layout file or programmatically depends on whether you know the properties before runtime or not. If you know the properties of your UI elements before runtime, use the XML layout file. Otherwise, if your UI remains unknown until runtime, i.e., you want to set these properties dynamically, use code to set them. Keep in mind that defining Views and their properties in the XML layout file keeps the code clean and compact and is the most common practice.

6.2.3 View Class Examples

Below, we look at two examples to learn more about some of the View attributes and how they can be set in the XML layout file.

6.2.3.1 EditText

Let us look at the EditText class attributes included in the layout file, main_activity.xml, for our demo app. EditText is a user interface class for entering text. The EditText definition is listed below.

```
<EditText
   android:id="@+id/editName"
   android:layout_width="match_parent"
   android:layout_height="wrap_content"
   android:layout_margin="5dp"
   android:hint="@string/name_hint"
   android:inputType="textCapWords"
   android:singleLine="true" >
</EditText>
```

You can see several View attributes are used to define the class. These include *id*, *width*, *height*, *hint*, *inputType*, and *singleLine*. The values of these attributes are "*@+id/editName*", "*match_parent*", "*wrap_content*", "*5dp*", "*@string/ name_hint*", "*textCapWords*", and "true". These attributes and their values are described below:

android:id = "@+id/editName". To define an id attribute, i.e., assign a View or a resource id, you need to include the at-symbol "@" and "+" signs in the attribute declaration. This is language syntax for defining an id in Android, where the plus-symbol (+) means a new resource name must be created and added to the R.java file. In other words, it means that editName does not exist and needs to be created as a static field of the R.java class. The part of id definitions that you refer to in your code, however, is the name part only. For example, you can reference the EditText object above in your code like this:

```
EditText editText = findViewByID(R.id.editName);
```

When referencing a view id (just the id and not the resource object), there is no need to use the plus-symbol "+," but it does require the at-symbol "@" and the Android namespace, for example, **android:id="@android:id/editName**. For example, inside a layout file, you can use android:layout_below="@id/editName". Here, you are referring to an existing view.

android:layout_width="match_parent". The match_parent attribute value means that the view will be as wide as its parent minus any padding that there may be.

android:layout_height="wrap_content". This means that the view is big enough (width and high) to enclose its content plus any padding.

android:layout_margin="5dp". This is the space outside of the border of the view (e.g., a button) and between what is next to and around the view.
android:hint="@string/name_hint. This is a hint of what the user should enter into EditText. For example, you can use android:hint= "enter your email here," on a form to hint the user that the field is for inserting an email address.

android:inputType="textCapWords". This is the user input where the letter of each word will begin with capital by default, for example, Bill Gates. There are other types of input as well. These include textEmailAddress and textAutoComplete.

android:singleLine="true". The input by the user is restricted to a single line.

6.2.3.2 TextView

Another widely used user interface View is TextView which displays text to the user. It is similar to JLabel in Java. It is widely used with EditText. For example, when you create a form, the first field usually is TextView followed by EditText where the user can insert text. The following code sample shows a typical use of TextView and some of its common attributes when defined in an XML layout file.

```
<TextView
android:id="@+id/r_textView"
android:layout_width="wrap_content"
android:layout_height="wrap_content"
android:layout_marginStart="100dp"
android:layout_marginEnd="100dp"
android:text="hello world"
app:layout_constraintEnd_toEndOf="parent"
app:layout_constraintStart_toStartOf="parent" />
```

6.2.4 Widget

A View class has several widget subclasses. These classes are grouped in a package called Widgets. They are fundamental control elements of the graphical user interface of an app. It is through these elements that the user can interact with the app. Examples of Widget elements that are widely used in Android apps include Button, Checkbox, RadioButton, ProgressBar, RatingBar, ImageView, ListView, Switch, etc. Using Android Studio, developers can drag and drop these elements into the editor space and use them for app development.

In this book, we will use most of these Widgets to develop our apps. The Keywords section at the end of this chapter provides links to descriptions and uses of the widgets highlighted in Fig. 6.2. Refer to these links on Android documents to learn more about the use and properties of Android widgets.

See Fig. 6.3 for more information on the View and Widget classes and the relationship between them. Some of the classes are highlighted to show that Widget classes are subclasses of the View class.

Each Widget class has its unique attributes and usages. I suggest you look at the View and Widget classes on the Android developer page to become familiar with the Android View class and its subclasses.

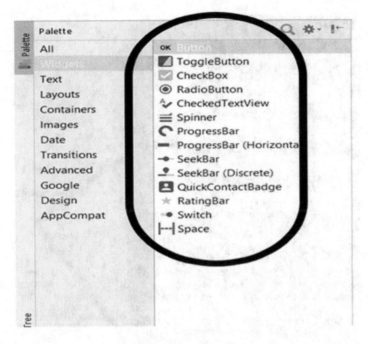

Fig. 6.2 The most widely used Widget element in Android

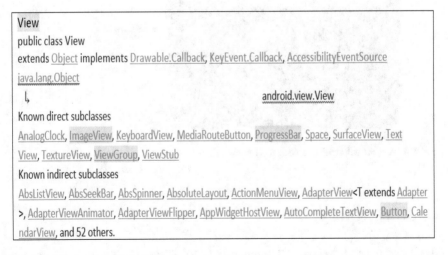

Fig. 6.3 View and its subclasses

For more clarity, the background area in Fig. 6.4 represents the View, and individual buttons drawn on the View are Widgets.

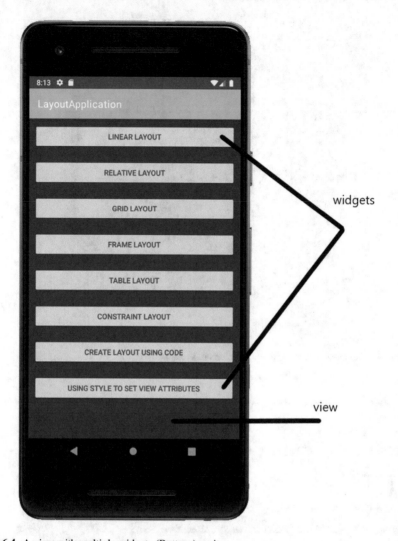

Fig. 6.4 A view with multiple widgets (Buttons) on it

6.2.5   ViewGroup

Another important Android UI component is ViewGroup. *ViewGroup objects* are *invisible* containers that can contain other Views and ViewGroups. The Views that reside inside a ViewGroup are called a child View. ViewGroups are abstract classes and cannot be instantiated. However, they have many subclasses that can be instantiated. Examples of ViewGroups include ScrollView, ListView, and

Fig. 6.5 Examples of
ViewGroup containers

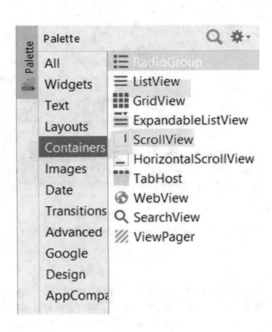

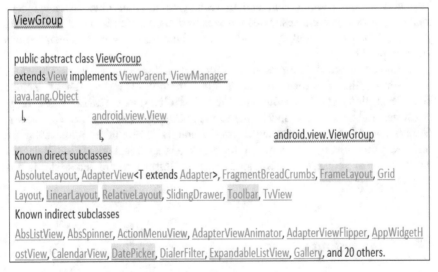

Fig. 6.6 ViewGroup and its subclasses

RadioGroup. Other common ViewGroup classes are Layout classes. Figure 6.5
presents and highlights a few ViewGroups that you can access from the Palette
window of the Android Studio layout manager.

ViewGroup is a base class for Layout classes such as *LinearLayout*, *RelativeLayout*,
FrameLayout, etc. It is used to organize and control the layout of a screen. In Fig. 6.6,
the relationship between Views, ViewGroups, and Layouts is shown.

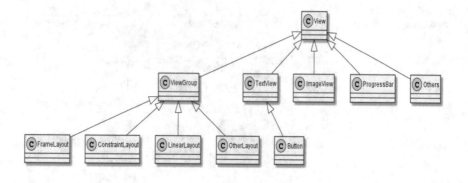

Fig. 6.7 Partial illustration of the View class hierarchy

Figure 6.7 is a partial illustration of the View class hierarchy. The figure shows that buttons are subclasses of TextView and are Views. It also shows that Layouts are ViewGroups and are Views as well. Understanding these relationships will help you in app development and in reusing code. Individual classes inherit methods from other classes, which means writing less code when developing your apps. It will also help you understand when class casting between various views is possible.

A simple user interface is presented in Fig. 6.8. In this example, the user interface is a simple linear vertical layout holding multiple Widgets. These include TextViews, EditTexts, RadioButtons, a dropdown list (i.e., a Spinner where users can select an item, currently indicating *Apples and Pears*), and a button with the text *Go Back to Main View*. The app layout container is arranging Widgets on the surface; in this case, they are arranged linearly and in a vertical orientation. It defines the structure of your app. We will study Layout classes in more detail later in this chapter.

6.2.6 App Layout

Install and run the demo app, LayoutApplication.apk; *apk* stands for Android application package; it is the app's executable code. You can download it from the book webpage. We use the layout of the demo app to explain different UI layouts, click handling, pickers, toasts, and more. Make sure you don't just load and run the code; you'll not learn much from that. Rather, connect the dots. Check each Activity and its corresponding Layouts and resource files. Once you install **LayoutApplication**, you should see six buttons on its start

Fig. 6.8 Linear vertical layout

screen. The buttons are arranged linearly, one after another in a vertical orientation. See Fig. 6.9:

Once clicked, the buttons create linear layout, relative layout, grid layout, and other layouts, respectively. Some of the layout types that Android support are depicted in Fig. 6.10, and they are:

- ConstraintLayout
- LinearLayout (horizontal)
- LinearLayout (vertical)
- RelativeLayout
- TableLayout
- FrameLayout
- GridLayout

Fig. 6.9 The start screen for the Layout app

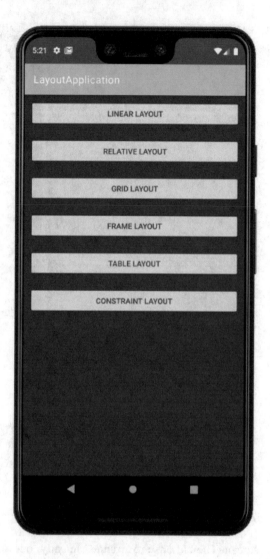

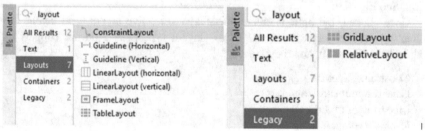

Fig. 6.10 Visual Studio Palette showing Layout object

Both *GridLayout* and *RelativeLayout* are considered as legacy layouts, which means that their use is not encouraged anymore. This is because Android has introduced a more powerful layout, i.e., ConstraintLayout. However, they are kept, and the Android compiler is still able to compile them to support existing apps.

When you create your app, you can have nested layouts. That is, a layout can have a child which is a layout itself. However, you should limit the nesting and keep the hierarchy flat with a minimal number of Views and ViewGroups. This is because the arrangement of the View hierarchy and the number of Views in the app has an impact on the app's performance.

6.3   Writing XML Layouts

A layout is a ViewGroup object, i.e., an invisible container object that defines which part of an Activity screen will be occupied by which View or Widget objects, such as Button, TextView, EditText, or another Layout object such as FrameLayout or ConstraintLayout. In Android, the user interface objects can be created using XML tags, programmatically at runtime, or a combination of both. When a combination of both approaches is used, you create your View and ViewGroup objects using XML elements and modify them at runtime in your code. Below, both approaches, using XML files and programming, are described.

6.3.1   Declare UI Elements in XML

As mentioned before, you can use XML files to create UI and Layout objects in your app. When you use XML files to create UI objects and Layouts for your Activities, the name of the UI class will become an element in the XML file. For example, if you have decided to create a layout file that organizes your UI objects linearly with a Button and a TextView in it, you need to create an XML file where LinearLayout is the root element. Both the Button and TextView will then become elements inside the LinearLayout root element, i.e., they will become child elements of the root element.

Listing 6.1 is a layout file for the first screen of the demo app for this chapter. As you can see, for every Android View/ViewGroup class and class attribute, there is a corresponding XML element and element attribute in the XML file. For example, for the Android LinearLayout class, we have a corresponding LinearLayout element in the XML file, and for the class fields, such as width, height, background, and orientation, there are corresponding element attributes: android:layout_width, android:layout_height, android:background, and android:orientation.

Listing 6.1 Activity_main_layout.xml file for the first screen of the demo app.

```xml
<LinearLayout xmlns:android=
"http://schemas.android.com/apk/res/android"
  xmlns:tools="http://schemas.android.com/tools"
  android:layout_width="match_parent"
  android:layout_height="match_parent"
  android:background="@color/maroon"
  android:orientation="vertical"
  tools:context=".MainLayoutActivity">
  <Button
    android:id="@+id/button_linear_layout"
    android:layout_width="match_parent"
    android:layout_height="wrap_content"
    android:layout_margin="10dp"
    android:onClick="onLinearLayoutClicked"
    android:text="@string/button_linear_layout" />
  <Button
    android:id="@+id/button_relative_layout"
    android:layout_width="match_parent"
    android:layout_height="wrap_content"
    android:layout_margin="10dp"
    android:onClick="onRelativeLayoutClicked"
    android:text="@string/button_relative_layout" />
  <Button
    android:id="@+id/button_grid_layout"
    android:layout_width="match_parent"
    android:layout_height="wrap_content"
    android:layout_margin="10dp"
    android:onClick="onGridViewLayoutClicked"
    android:text="@string/button_grid_layout" />
  <Button
    android:id="@+id/frame_layout"
    android:layout_width="match_parent"
    android:layout_height="wrap_content"
    android:layout_margin="10dp"
    android:onClick="onFrameLayoutClicked"
    android:text="@string/button_frame_layout" />
  <Button
    android:id="@+id/table_layout"
    android:layout_width="match_parent"
    android:layout_height="wrap_content"
    android:layout_margin="10dp"
    android:onClick="onTableLayoutClicked"
    android:text="@string/button_table_layout" />
  <Button
    android:id="@+id/constraint_layout"
    android:layout_width="match_parent"
    android:layout_height="wrap_content"
    android:layout_margin="10dp"
    android:onClick="onConstraintLayoutClicked"
    android:text="@string/button_constraint_layout" />
</LinearLayout>
```

Note that, in the layout XML file, the UI element id names and the method names closely match the name of the class they belong to and the methods they fire. For example, a button id name is btn_linear_layout, and a method name is OnLinearLayoutClicked. This naming convention becomes crucial for debugging and understating code as the app's code becomes increasingly complicated.

6.3.2   Android Studio's Layout Editor

Android Studio as an IDE is improving continually. This makes the *Design and Layout Editor*, which is embedded in Android Studio, more and more useful for creating UI. You can use the Design and Layout Editor to build your UI screens using a drag-and-drop interface. In Fig. 6.11, we are numbering some options that the Layout Editor provides to design the layout of your Activities, and they are:

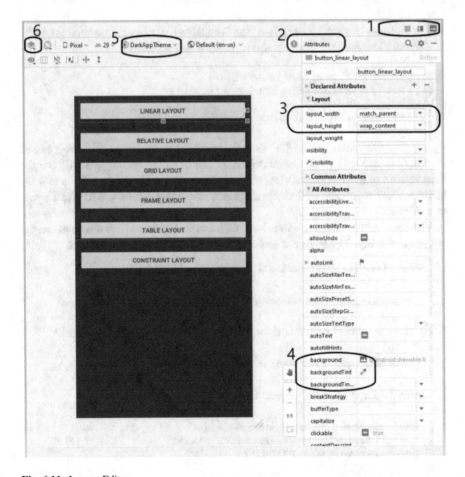

Fig. 6.11 Layout Editor

- Option 1: Toggle between layout code, layout design, and split screen to show code and design.
- Option 2: Set widget attributes such as width, length, background color, etc. Examples of such settings are numbered 3 and 4.
- Option 5: Set the app's theme.
- Option 6: Select the design surface to show the design, the blueprint, or both.

The XML layout that corresponds to Listing 6.1 is presented in Fig. 6.11.

6.3.3 Defining UI Programmatically

In addition to defining your UI Layout in XML files, you can define your UI Layout and other UI components programmatically in your code. Let's look at an example where the Layout is created programmatically. Recall the setContentView() statement is where you set or tell the Activity which layout XML file is going to be a screen Layout.

The Activity class and its subclass AppCompatActivity have three versions of the setContentView method. The method signatures are as follows:

```
public void setContentView (View view) ;
public void setContentView (int layoutResID) ;
public void setContentView (
View view, ViewGroup.LayoutParams params) ;
```

So far, we have used the second version of the method. We passed R.layout.layoutName to setContentView. In the example below, we will use the third version of the setContentView method. The input parameter is not a layout file id, but a View object and its dimensions. The View object will be turned into a layout root element.

The code below uses *setContentView* with *LinearLayout*, which has been created programmatically. The steps are self-explanatory, and they are as follows:

1. Create a LinearLayout object. This can be done like this:

```
LinearLayout linearLayout = new LinearLayout(this) ;
```

2. Specify the vertical orientation for the Layout. This can be done like this:

```
linearLayout.setOrientation(LinearLayout.VERTICAL) ;
```

3. Create the *LayoutParams* object. This can be done like this:

```
LayoutParams linearLayoutParam = new
LayoutParams(LayoutParams.MATCH_PARENT,
LayoutParams.MATCH_PARENT) ;
```

4. Set LinearLayout as a root element of the screen. This can be done like this:
setContentView(linearLayout, linearLayoutParam);

The steps above can be included in the onCreate() method of an Activity, and it would be as shown in Listing 6.2.

Listing 6.2 Creating app layout programmatically.

```
public class MainLayoutActivity extends AppCompatActivity {
@Override
 public void onCreate(Bundle savedInstanceState) {
  super.onCreate(savedInstanceState);
  LinearLayout linearLayout = new LinearLayout(this);
  // specifying vertical orientation
  linearLayout.setOrientation(LinearLayout.VERTICAL);
  // creating LayoutParams
  LinearLayout.LayoutParams linearLayoutParam = new
    LinearLayout.LayoutParams
    (LinearLayout.LayoutParams.MATCH_PARENT,
       LinearLayout.LayoutParams.MATCH_PARENT);
  // set LinearLayout as a root element of the screen
  setContentView(linearLayout, linearLayoutParam);
  }
  ...
}
```

Creating UI elements programmatically is not recommended. This is because one of the fundamental principles of good programming is the separation of code from view, i.e., separating your code from app UI components. This will enable you to change your code without changing the view of your application. Using XML files to draw your app screen layouts and define your View objects using the XML element makes it easy to provide different layouts for different screen sizes and orientations.

While there is a clear advantage of using XML files for creating views, when you code your app's View objects, just like regular Java coding, it shows your coding skills and helps you understand what is beneath the Android XML resource files. Below, we show two examples of Java classes and their corresponding Android elements and attributes.

6.3.4 LinearLayout Java Class

We mentioned earlier that a LinearLayout is a Java class that arranges its children's Views either horizontally in a single column or vertically in a single row. Here, we would like to emphasize that LinearLayout, and other Layouts that we will discuss later in this chapter, can be dealt with as regular Java classes. These classes have constructors, public fields, and public and protected methods and inherit methods

Table 6.1 Examples of linear layout class methods

int getGravity()	Returns the current gravity
int getOrientation()	Returns the current orientation
void setGravity(int gravity)	Sets the positions of the child Views; defaults to GRAVITY_TOP
void setHorizontalGravity(int horizontalGravity)	Controls the alignment of the children
void setOrientation(int orientation)	Sets the orientation, and the layout can be a column or a row
void setShowDividers(int showDividers)	Sets how dividers should be shown between items in this layout

Table 6.2 XML attributes and their corresponding Java class instance variables

XML attribute <LinearLayout>	Class LinearLayout fields
android: divider	Divider
android: gravity	Gravity
android: orientation	Orientation

from their base classes. For example, LinearLayout has four different constructors to instantiate LinearLayout objects. The constructor signatures are listed below. We used the second constructor to create a LinearLayout object in the subsection above.

1. **LinearLayout(Context context)**
2. **LinearLayout(Context context, AttributeSet attrs)**
3. **LinearLayout(Context context, AttributeSet attrs, int defStyleAttr)**
4. **LinearLayout(Context context, AttributeSet attrs,**
                              int defStyleAttr, int defStyleRes)

The LinearLayout class has multiple constants. The most widely used constants are HORIZONTAL and VERTICAL. The other constants are about showing the divider or not between items and where to show it, at the beginning or end of the ViewGroups. The LinearLayout class also has multiple useful methods for setting and retrieving Layout properties. Examples of such methods are listed in Table 6.1.

As mentioned earlier in this chapter, when you use XML files to represent classes, for every class constant and field, there is a corresponding XML attribute. In Table 6.2, examples of LinearLayout attributes that correspond to the LinearLayout class constants and attributes are shown.

6.3.5   LayoutParams Java Class

Another important Android class for defining UI programmatically is LayoutParams. The LayoutParams class is used by Views such as Layout containers to tell Activities how they want to be set on the content view. For example, an Activity class can use

LayoutParams like this: **setContentView(LinearLayout, LayoutParam);**. This will set the Activity's content view linearly with height and width provided in LayoutParams.

Similar to the LinearLayout class, LayoutParams has constructors, class fields, constants, and methods. A LayoutParams constructor is shown below. It describes how big the View can be for both width and height.

```
LayoutParams(int width, int height);
```

The LayoutParams base class has two fields, *MATCH_PARENT* and *WRAP_CONTENT*, that can be used with width and height dimensions.

MATCH_PARENT sets the View to be as big as its parent (minus padding), and WRAP_CONTENT sets the View to be just big enough to enclose its content (plus padding).

When you use LayoutParams with classes other than Layout classes, you might need more than just height and width fields. There are other classes of LayoutParams for various subclasses of ViewGroups. These classes extend the base LayoutParams class and have additional fields of their own. Examples of the ViewGroup subclasses that have their implementation of the LayoutParams include AbsListView.LayoutParams, AbsoluteLayout.LayoutParams, ActionBar. LayoutParams, ActionMenuView.LayoutParams, FrameLayout.LayoutParams, GridLayout.LayoutParams, RelativeLayout.LayoutParams, TableLayout. LayoutParams, etc.

When LayoutParams is used in the XML file, the XML attributes corresponding to the LayoutParams height and width are **android:layout_height**, to specify the basic height of the View, and **android:layout_width**, to specify the basic width of the View.

6.4   Details of the LayoutApplication Demo

In this part, to demonstrate how you can use a Layout in your app, we go through the LayoutApplication code created for this chapter.

6.4.1   MainActivity Layout

Figure 6.12 shows that for each Activity there is a corresponding Layout and all the layout files are in the res/layout folder. This makes sense because Activity is mostly used as a screen. Even though you can create an Activity that is not a screen and that doesn't have a Layout, it is hardly used this way. Instead, screen elements will be put in the Activity's Layout, and together they form an interactive screen.

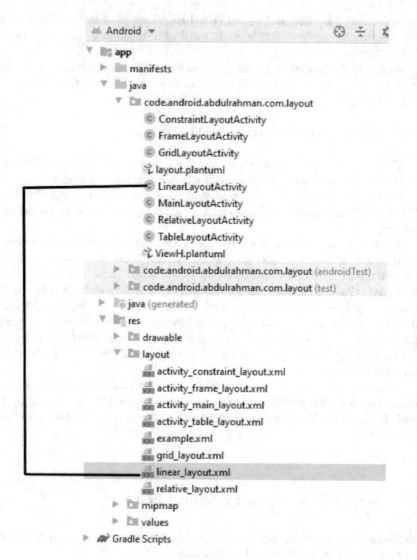

Fig. 6.12 The association between the activity_main_layout.xml and MainActivityLayout code

The XML snippet shown in Listing 6.3 is the *activity_main_layout.xml* which is associated with the *MainActivityLayout* Java code. The layout is a simple linear layout with a root element <LinearLayout> and vertical orientation. By default, the LinearLayout orientation is horizontal.

```xml
<LinearLayout xmlns:android=
  "http://schemas.android.com/apk/res/android"
   xmlns:tools="http://schemas.android.com/tools"
   android:layout_width="match_parent"
   android:layout_height="match_parent"
   android:background="@color/maroon"
   android:orientation="vertical"
   tools:context=".MainLayoutActivity">
   <Button
     android:id="@+id/button_linear_layout"
     android:layout_width="match_parent"
     android:layout_height="wrap_content"
     android:layout_margin="10dp"
     android:onClick="onLinearLayoutClicked"
     android:text="@string/button_linear_layout" />
   <Button
     android:id="@+id/button_relative_layout"
     android:layout_width="match_parent"
     android:layout_height="wrap_content"
     android:layout_margin="10dp"
     android:onClick="onRelativeLayoutClicked"
     android:text="@string/button_relative_layout" />
  ....
<LinearLayout />
```

The LinearLayout root element represents a *container* for all the buttons. It is a ViewGroup object with several Views/Widgets (child elements). It aligns all children in a single line in a vertical orientation, i.e., one vertical column where each element is on a horizontal row. The layout direction is specified with the ***android:orientation*** attribute. If the *horizontal* value is passed to *android:orientation* parameter, i.e., **android:orientation="horizontal"**, all LinearLayout children will be aligned in one line horizontally. If the line exceeds the screen space, the children will go to the next line, eventually going down the screen vertically as more are added.

The property *tools:context="*.MainLayoutActivity" tells us that this Layout is associated with the MainLayoutActivity code. In the code snippet below, the MainLayoutActivity.java class loads the activity_main_layout.xml in the onCreate() callback method using this line of code:

```java
setContentView(R.layout.activity_main_layout).
```

```java
public class MainLayoutActivity extends AppCompatActivity {
  ...
    @Override
    protected void onCreate(Bundle savedInstanceState) {
      super.onCreate(savedInstanceState);
      setContentView(R.layout.activity_main_layout);
```

```
            Toast.makeText(getApplicationContext(),
                     getString(R.string.i_am_here_message),
        Toast.LENGTH_LONG).show();
    }
    ...
}
```

The code snippet contains an additional line of code to print a message to the screen. In Android, printing messages to the screen can be done using the *Toast object* like this:

```
Toast.makeText(getApplicationContext(),
 getString(R.string.i_am_here_message), Toast.LENGTH_LONG).show();
```

The printout shows that the onCreate() method has been called and *activity_main_layout.xml* has been set.

6.4.2   Activity with Linear Layout

Listing 6.4 shows how you can create an Activity where screen elements are linearly arranged.

Listing 6.4 LinearLayoutActivity.java uses a linear layout.

```
package code.android.abdulrahman.com.layoutapplication;
import android.content.Intent;
import android.os.Bundle;
import androidx.appcompat.app.AppCompatActivity;
import android.view.View;
import android.widget.Toast;
public class LinearLayoutActivity extends AppCompatActivity {
  @Override
  protected void onCreate(Bundle savedInstanceState) {
    super.onCreate(savedInstanceState);
    Toast.makeText(getApplicationContext(),
        getString(R.string.i_am_here_message),
      Toast.LENGTH_SHORT).show();
    setContentView(R.layout.linear_layout);
  }
  public void onGoBackLinearLayoutClick(View v) {
    Intent intent = new Intent(LinearLayoutActivity.this,
        MainLayoutActivity.class);
    startActivity(intent);
  }
}
```

Once the "linear layout" Button is pressed on the main screen and intent is fired, the LinearLayoutActivity gets started, and its content view is set to **layout.linear_layout** using setContentView(). The linear_layout.xml file for LinearLayoutActivity looks complicated and long, but you will be able to identify the ViewGroups, Views, Widgets, and the root element, i.e., LinearLayout.

Several new Views such as the Checkbox, RadioButton, and others are used in this example. You can learn about these classes, their properties, and how to use them by studying the source code of the demo app, both the Java code and the layout files. For example, the LinearLayout.xml file includes information on how to use the RadioButton and RadioGroup containers. It also includes information on how to use the Spinner object and how to populate it using string array defined inside the strings. xml file. The screen for the LinearLayoutActivity is presented in Fig. 6.13, and its corresponding layout XML file is shown in Listing 6.5.

Fig. 6.13 The view for linear_layout.xml file

6.4.3   Linear Layout XML File

The layout file in Listing 6.5 presents a detailed linear layout file which is the screen of the LinearMainActivity for our demo up. It contains multiple Views and Widgets and shows all kinds of attributes that have been defined for them that you can use to define individual Views for your app. It also shows how you can use the strings.xml file with the layout file to define text and labels for your app screen.

Listing 6.5 linear_layout.xml sample file made up of several elements.

```
<LinearLayout xmlns:android=
  "http://schemas.android.com/apk/res/android"
    android:layout_width="match_parent"
    android:layout_height="match_parent"
    android:orientation="vertical">
    <TextView
      android:layout_width="wrap_content"
      android:layout_height="wrap_content"
      android:layout_margin="5dp"
      android:text="@string/name" >
    </TextView>
    <EditText
      android:id="@+id/editName"
      android:layout_width="match_parent"
      android:layout_height="wrap_content"
      android:layout_margin="5dp"
      android:hint="@string/name_hint"
      android:inputType="textCapWords"
      android:singleLine="true" >
    </EditText>
    <TextView
      android:layout_width="wrap_content"
      android:layout_height="wrap_content"
      android:layout_margin="5dp"
      android:text="@string/email" >
    </TextView>
    <EditText
      android:id="@+id/editEmail"
      android:layout_width="match_parent"
      android:layout_height="wrap_content"
      android:layout_margin="5dp"
      android:hint="@string/email_hint"
      android:inputType="textEmailAddress"
      android:singleLine="true" >
    </EditText>
    <TextView
      android:layout_width="wrap_content"
      android:layout_height="wrap_content"
      android:layout_margin="5dp"
      android:text="@string/phone" >
    </TextView>
```

```xml
<EditText
  android:id="@+id/editPhone"
  android:layout_width="match_parent"
  android:layout_height="wrap_content"
  android:layout_margin="5dp"
  android:hint="@string/phone_hint"
  android:inputType="phone"
  android:singleLine="true" >
</EditText>
<TextView
  android:layout_width="wrap_content"
  android:layout_height="wrap_content"
  android:layout_margin="5dp"
  android:text="@string/gender" >
</TextView>
<RadioGroup
  android:id="@+id/radioGender"
  android:layout_width="match_parent"
  android:layout_height="wrap_content"
  android:layout_margin="5dp"
  android:orientation="horizontal" >
  <RadioButton
    android:id="@+id/radioGenderF"
    android:layout_width="wrap_content"
    android:layout_height="wrap_content"
    android:layout_weight="1"
    android:text="@string/gender_female" />
  <RadioButton
    android:id="@+id/radioGenderM"
    android:layout_width="wrap_content"
    android:layout_height="wrap_content"
    android:layout_weight="1"
    android:text="@string/gender_male" >
  </RadioButton>
</RadioGroup>
<TextView
  android:id="@+id/textInputType"
  android:layout_width="fill_parent"
  android:layout_height="wrap_content"
  android:layout_margin="5dp"
  android:text="@string/spinner" >
</TextView>
<Spinner
  android:id="@+id/spinnerID"
  android:layout_width="match_parent"
  android:layout_height="wrap_content"
  android:layout_margin="5dp"
  android:entries="@array/spinner_items" >
</Spinner>
<Button
  android:id="@+id/button_goback"
  android:layout_width="match_parent"
  android:layout_height="wrap_content"
  android:layout_margin="5dp"
  android:background="@color/blue"
```

```
      android:onClick="onGoBackLinearLayoutClick"
      android:text="@string/button_goback_title" />
</LinearLayout>
```

6.4.4 Using Android Studio Design Option

We mentioned earlier that you can use Android Layout Editor to create layouts for your Activities. The editor provides three options to develop your Activity layouts, the coding mode, the design mode, or a combination of both. For example, the properties of a Button object can be set by first dragging and dropping the button inside the LinearLayout root element, highlighting the button, and left-clicking to set the button properties such as layout_width, layout_height, id, text, and the onClick method. In Fig. 6.14, the correspondence properties of the button definition shown in the code below are circled in the Android design tool.

```
<Button
  android:id="@+id/button_goback"
  android:layout_width="match_parent"
  android:layout_height="wrap_content"
  android:layout_margin="5dp"
  android:onClick="onGoBackLinearLayoutClick"
  android:text="@string/button_goback_title" />
```

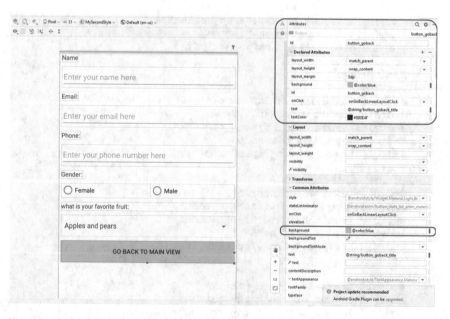

Fig. 6.14 Setting widget properties using a design tool

6.4.5   strings.xml File

The linear layout file for our demo app, which is shown in Listing 6.5, uses the strings.xml file for text strings to avoid hardcoding. The file is in the res/values folder and contains all the texts used inside the demo code. Listing 6.6 is a snippet of the *strings.xml* used in the LayoutApplication showing how to declare an app's text in a file.

Listing 6.6 strings.xml file used with LinearLayout.

```xml
<?xml version="1.0" encoding="utf-8"?>
<resources>
<string name="app_name">LayoutApplication</string>
...
<string name="button_goback_title">go back to main view</string>
<string name="name_hint">Your name here</string>
<string name="name">Name</string>
<string name="email_hint">Your Email here</string>
<string name="email">Email:</string>
<string name="phone_hint">Your phone number here</string>
<string name="phone">Phone:</string>
<string name="gender">Gender:</string>
<string name="gender_male">Male</string>
<string name="gender_female">Female</string>
<string name="profile_date">Date:</string>
<string name="profile_date_hint">MM/DD/YYYY</string>
<string name="spinner">what is your favorite fruit:</string>
  <string-array name="spinner_items">
    <item>Apples and pears</item>
    <item>Citrus - oranges, grapefruits, mandarins, and limes</item>
     <item>Stone fruit - nectarines, apricots, peaches, and plums</item>
    <item>Tropical and exotic - bananas and mangoes</item>
    <item>Berries - strawberries, raspberries, blueberries,
        kiwifruit and passion fruit</item>
    <item>Melons - watermelons, rockmelons and honeydew melons</item>
    <item>Tomatoes and avocados</item>
  </string-array>
....
</resources>
```

You can use the graphical tool to define strings or do it manually. To do it manually, type the first string and its value inside the strings.xml file. Then, cut and paste existing string items into the file, rename them, and use them to declare new strings and their values.

You can use a few HTML tags inside your strings.xml file to declare strings; these are <b>, <u>, and <i> HTML tags for bold, underline, and italics. All other HTML tags are ignored. Another tag that you can use is \n to start a new line or

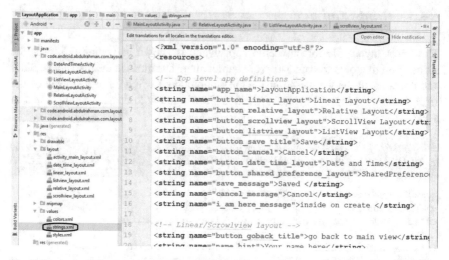

Fig. 6.15 Android Studio String editor

paragraph. Similarly, to write quotations, apostrophes, and any non-ASCII characters, use a backslash (\", \', \é).

6.4.6   String Editor

If you open strings.xml in Android Studio and click on the open tab as shown below in Fig. 6.15, you can view and add to strings using the Resource editor option as shown below. Using the Resource editor is very handy if you need to support multiple languages. You can use the Resource editor to provide translations to the texts in the code. See Fig. 6.16.

6.4.7   String Resources

The strings.xml file can hold a wide set of objects. These include strings, arrays of strings, integer arrays, colors, and styles/themes. We widely use strings, string arrays, and integer arrays for our applications. For example, to list the fruit types using a dropdown menu selection, we used the Spinner object and populated the dropdown list with a set of fruits defined in the strings.xml file, i.e., we used the @array/spinner_items to refer to the list declared inside the strings.xml file. Listing 6.7 is a code snippet from the linear_layout.xml file for declaring the Spinner object and referencing an array of strings defined in the strings.xml file.

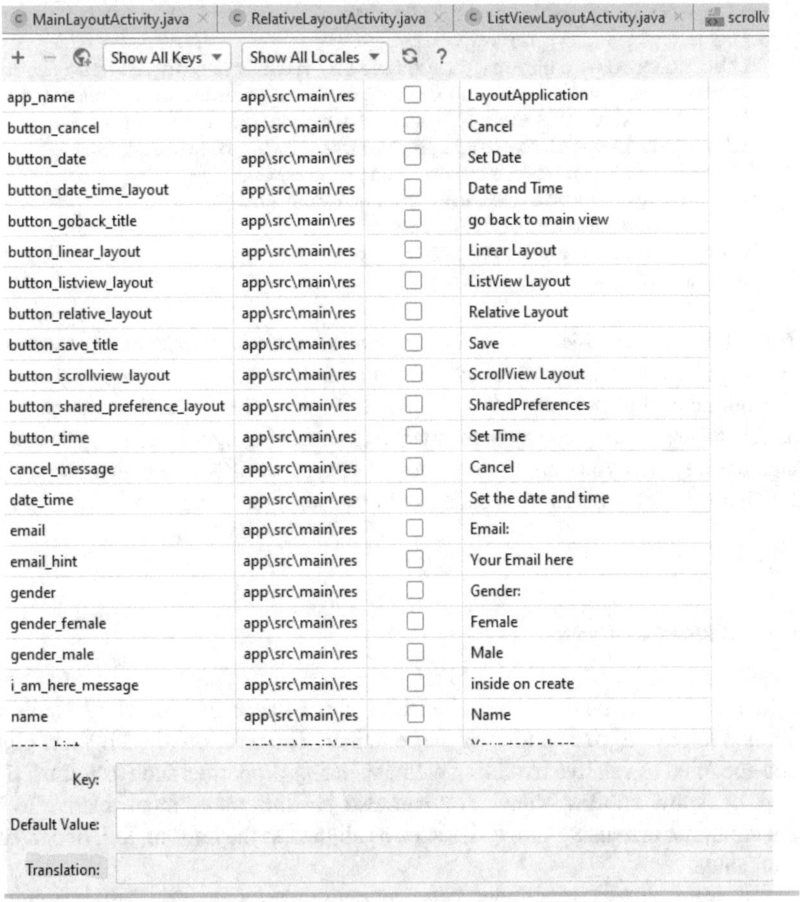
MainLayoutActivity.java
RelativeLayoutActivity.java
ListViewLayoutActivity.java
scrollv
Show All Keys
Show All Locales
app_name app\src\main\res LayoutApplication
button_cancel app\src\main\res Cancel
button_date app\src\main\res Set Date
button_date_time_layout app\src\main\res Date and Time
button_goback_title app\src\main\res go back to main view
button_linear_layout app\src\main\res Linear Layout
button_listview_layout app\src\main\res ListView Layout
button_relative_layout app\src\main\res Relative Layout
button_save_title app\src\main\res Save
button_scrollview_layout app\src\main\res ScrollView Layout
button_shared_preference_layout app\src\main\res SharedPreferences
button_time app\src\main\res Set Time
cancel_message app\src\main\res Cancel
date_time app\src\main\res Set the date and time
email app\src\main\res Email:
email_hint app\src\main\res Your Email here
gender app\src\main\res Gender:
gender_female app\src\main\res Female
gender_male app\src\main\res Male
i_am_here_message app\src\main\res inside on create
name app\src\main\res Name
Key:
Default Value:
Translation:

Fig. 6.16 Android Studio String editor for translation

Listing 6.7 Declaring Spinner and an array of strings using an XML file.

```
<Spinner
   android:id="@+id/spinnerID"
   android:layout_width="match_parent"
   android:layout_height="wrap_content"
   android:layout_margin="5dp"
   android:entries="@array/spinner_items">
</Spinner>
```

The string array defined in the strings.xml is listed below:

```xml
<string-array name="spinner_items">
  <item>Apples and pears</item>
  <item>Citrus - oranges, grapefruits, mandarins and limes</item>
  <item>Stone fruit - nectarines, apricots, peaches and plums</item>
  <item>Tropical and exotic - bananas and mangoes</item>
  <item>Berries - strawberries, raspberries, blueberries,
        kiwifruit and passion fruit</item>
  <item>Melons - watermelons, rock melons and
        honeydew melons</item>
  <item>Tomatoes and avocados</item>
</string-array>
```

Note that Spinner object has a property called *android:entries* which accepts an array as input and to define array inside the string.xml file you use *<type-array name>*. It is recommended to put your app's text and other resources in XML inside res/value folders. This way it will be easy to maintain and extend the app. If later you decided to change entries, then you simply need only to change the XML contents and not the code. This is a nice separation of code from other resources, i.e., data.

6.4.8   RelativeLayout

The RelativeLayout container class enables you to specify how child views are positioned relative to one another or the container. The position of each View object can be specified as relative to sibling elements using properties such as left of, right of, top, or below another View. You can also position an element relative to the parent container area using properties such as aligned to the bottom, left, or center of the container.

In our Application Layout app, RelativeLayout uses a simple relative layout. A more complex relative position of Views and Widgets can be achieved within the layout. We have positioned three objects relative to each other and the parent container. The *AnalogClock* has been put at the bottom of the layout using *layout_alignParentBottom*, the WLU logo has been put at the top of the layout using *ImageView* and *layout_alignParentTop*, and the *RatingBar* is situated in between the two widgets automatically. If you want, you can explicitly position the RatingBar between the other two Widgets using the *below* and *above* layout attributes. You can also use android:paddingBottom and *android:paddingTop* to control the exact position of *RatingBar* or any UI object between the other two Widgets.

RelativeLayout has several properties. These include *match_parent* which will fill the screen and the *padding-left and padding-right* to position Widgets in the container. An example of how to use RelativeLayout is shown in Listing 6.8. In the demo app, when you click the RelativeLayout button, the layout below will be displayed.

Listing 6.8 relative_layout.xml for RelativeLayoutActivity.

```xml
<?xml version="1.0" encoding="utf-8"?>
<RelativeLayout xmlns:android=
 "http://schemas.android.com/apk/res/android"
   android:layout_width="match_parent"
   android:layout_height="match_parent"
   android:paddingLeft="20dp"
   android:paddingRight="20dp">
   <AnalogClock
     android:id="@+id/analogClock1"
     android:layout_width="wrap_content"
     android:layout_height="wrap_content"
     android:layout_alignParentBottom="true"
     android:layout_centerHorizontal="true"
     android:layout_marginBottom="70dp"
     android:paddingBottom="25dp" />
   <ImageView
     android:id="@+id/wluImage"
     android:layout_width="wrap_content"
     android:layout_height="wrap_content"
     android:layout_alignParentTop="true"
     android:layout_centerHorizontal="true"
     android:layout_marginTop="25dp"
     android:clickable="true"
     android:contentDescription="@string/wlu_picture"
     android:onClick="onClickImage"
     android:src="@drawable/wlu" />
   <RatingBar
     android:id="@+id/ratingBar"
     android:background="@color/_yellow"
     android:layout_width="wrap_content"
     android:layout_height="wrap_content"
     android:layout_below="@+id/wluImage"
     android:layout_centerHorizontal="true"
     android:layout_marginTop="150dp" />
</RelativeLayout>
```

The code for the RelativeLayout button in our demo app is in RelativeLayoutActivity.java file and is shown in Listing 6.9. The Activity is a simple Java file with two methods. The first one is *onGoBackRelativeLayoutkClicked*, and the second one is *onClickImage*. Note that, in both cases, a View object is passed to the methods. That is, the method signature for the two methods is **public void onMethodName (View view)**. The first method is triggered when the user clicks on the university logo image, and the second method is triggered when the user clicks on the clock image.

Listing 6.9 RelativeLayoutActivity.java of the demo app.

```
package code.android.abdulrahman.com.layoutapplication;
import androidx.appcompat.app.AppCompatActivity;
import android.content.Intent;
import android.os.Bundle;
import android.view.View;
import android.widget.Toast;
public class RelativeLayoutActivity extends AppCompatActivity {
  @Override
  protected void onCreate(Bundle savedInstanceState) {
    super.onCreate(savedInstanceState);
    setContentView(R.layout.relative_layout);
  }
  public void onGoBacRelativeLayoutkClicked(View v) {
    Intent intent = new Intent(RelativeLayoutActivity.this,
        MainLayoutActivity.class);
    startActivity(intent);
  }
  public void onClickImage(View v) {
    Toast.makeText(this, getString(R.string.wlu_message),
        Toast.LENGTH_LONG).show();
  }
}
```

RelativeLayout is a legacy class now, and its use is no longer encouraged. Currently, Android supports a more sophisticated Layout called ConstraintLayout which will be discussed later in this chapter. ConstraintLayout is a default Layout, i.e., when you create a new Activity, the auto layout for the Activity will be ConstraintLayout. Android keeps supporting RelativeLayout because it is widely used among existing apps.

6.4.9　Other Layouts

The LayoutApplication demo app includes other Layouts, and they are FrameLayout, TableLayout, GridLayout, and ConstraintLayout. Below, we will briefly introduce these layouts. For coding and layout implementation, see the source code of the LayoutApplication demo app.

6.4.9.1　FrameLayout

FrameLayout is shown in Fig. 6.17, on the left-hand side. Elements of *FrameLayout* are stacked on top of each other, and the last element in the layout file is on the top of the stack. We can see this in Fig. 6.17 where the last element,

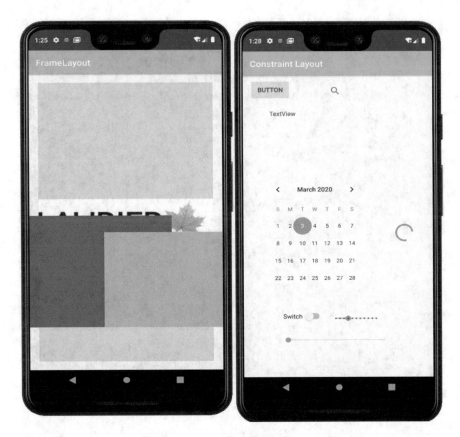

Fig. 6.17 App interface when FrameLayout and Constraint Layout are used

the green frame, is found on top of the others. FrameLayout is often used with the *fragment* View to draw on a part of the Layout. We will study fragments in later chapters.

6.4.9.2 ConstraintLayout

The right-hand side of Fig. 6.17 shows *ConstraintLayout*. It works similar to RelativeLayout except that it is more sophisticated and has more attributes. With ConstraintLayout, you can align and declare a precise position of an element relative to the other elements and the parent element in the Layout. It is a default Layout when you create an activity.

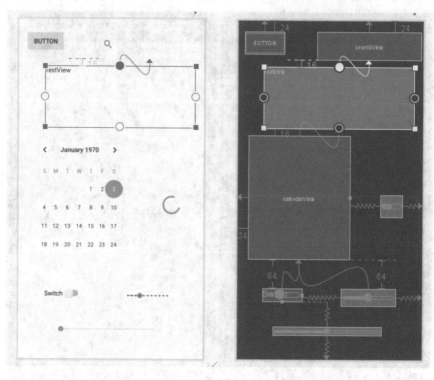

Fig. 6.18 Design and Layout (blueprint) Views when using ConstraintLayout and Layout Editor, respectively

Using the Android Studio Layout Editor and ConstraintLayout, you can create complicated layouts easily. You can do that by simply connecting so-called constraint connectors. Figure 6.18 shows an example of a complicated layout. What is shown on the right-hand side of Fig. 6.18 is called a layout view, or a blueprint, and what you see on the left-hand side is a design view. What you see in the design view is what you get in the final interface of the app. The constraint connectors are showing on the blueprint view. By connecting these connectors, you can define the position of Views relative to other elements and parent Views.

6.4.9.3   Grid and Table Layouts

The Grid and Table layouts are shown in Fig. 6.19, respectively. To create *GridLayout*, you have to declare column and row counts; see the code snippet in Listing 6.10.

Fig. 6.19 Grid and Table layout examples, respectively

Listing 6.10 grid_layout.xml example.

```
<GridLayout xmlns:android=
  "http://schemas.android.com/apk/res/android"
    xmlns:tools="http://schemas.android.com/tools"
    android:layout_width="match_parent"
    android:layout_height="match_parent"
    android:layout_margin="2dp"
    android:background="@color/gold"
    android:columnCount="2"
    android:rowCount="3"
    tools:context=".GridLayoutActivity">
```

To create *TableLayout*, you have to declare rows, and you can have any number of columns in each row. The number of columns in each row does not have to be the same, and that makes it different from the Grid layout. An example of TableLayout code snippet is shown in Listing 6.11.

Listing 6.11 activity_table_layout.xml example.

```xml
<?xml version="1.0" encoding="utf-8"?>
<TableLayout
  xmlns:android="http://schemas.android.com/apk/res/android"
  xmlns:tools="http://schemas.android.com/tools"
  android:layout_width="match_parent"
  android:layout_height="match_parent"
  tools:context="TableLayoutActivity">
  <TableRow
    android:layout_width="match_parent"
    android:layout_height="match_parent">
    <TextView...
....
</TableLayout>
```

6.4.10 Parent-Child Relationship Between Activities

To help navigation between app screens, you can define parent-child relationships between Activities in the manifest file. This results in creating an arrow on the app's menu bar, and when pressed, it will end the current Activity and bring in the parent Activity. To define the parent-child relationship between Activities, add a new entry, i.e., a meta-data entry, to the application element of the manifest file. Inside the meta-data element, declare that the app supports the parent-child relationship, and define which Activity is the parent Activity. This addition to the manifest file is shown below.

```xml
  <application>
...
<meta-data
    android:name="android.support.PARENT_ACTIVITY"
    android:value="MainLayoutActivity" />
  <application>
```

You also need to update the definition of all Activities declared inside the manifest file to tell which Activity is its parent Activity. For example, in the statement below, we are declaring that the parent Activity of ConstraintLayoutActivity is MainLayoutActivity.

```xml
  <activity android:name=".ConstraintLayoutActivity"
    android:parentActivityName=".MainLayoutActivity" />
```

Fig. 6.20 Using the parent-child relationship to create a navigation button

We have revised the manifest file for our demo app, declared MainActivity to be the parent Activity, and declared the other Activities to be a child of MainActivity. The revised file is shown in Listing 6.12, and changes are highlighted in boldface font. The impact of the manifest revision on the user interface is shown in Fig. 6.20.

Listing 6.12 AndroidManifest.xml showing parent-child relationships between activities.

```xml
<?xml version="1.0" encoding="utf-8"?>
<manifest xmlns:android=
 "http://schemas.android.com/apk/res/android"
  package="code.android.abdulrahman.com.layout">
  <application
    android:allowBackup="true"
    android:icon="@mipmap/ic_launcher"
    android:label="@string/app_name"
    android:roundIcon="@mipmap/ic_launcher_round"
    android:supportsRtl="true"
    android:theme="@style/DarkAppTheme">
    <meta-data
      android:name="android.support.PARENT_ACTIVITY"
      android:value="MainLayoutActivity" />
    <activity
      android:name=".ConstraintLayoutActivity"
      android:parentActivityName=".MainLayoutActivity" />
    <activity
      android:name=".TableLayoutActivity"
      android:parentActivityName=".MainLayoutActivity" />
    <activity
      android:name=".FrameLayoutActivity"
      android:parentActivityName=".MainLayoutActivity" />
    <activity android:name=".MainLayoutActivity">
```

```
      <intent-filter>
        <action android:name="android.intent.action.MAIN" />
        <category
          android:name="android.intent.category.LAUNCHER" />
      </intent-filter>
   </activity>
   <activity
      android:name=".LinearLayoutActivity"
      android:parentActivityName=".MainLayoutActivity" />
   <activity
      android:name=".RelativeLayoutActivity"
      android:parentActivityName=".MainLayoutActivity" />
   <activity
      android:name=".GridLayoutActivity"
      android:parentActivityName=".MainLayoutActivity" />
   </application>
</manifest>
```

6.4.10.1   Do It Yourself

1. Modify the existing LayoutApplication to experience different Layout attributes.
2. Re-write the RelativeLayout below to study the impact of match_parent on the width and height. In one example, include only android:layout_width = "match_parent" without android:layout_height. Then, in the next example, include only android:layout_height="match_parent" without android: layout_width, and observe the differences.

```
<RelativeLayout xmlns:android=
 "http://schemas.android.com/apk/res/android"
   android:layout_width="match_parent"
   android:layout_height="match_parent"
   android:paddingLeft="16dp"
   android:paddingRight="16dp">
```

6.5   Styles, Themes, and Dimension

Similar to CSS in HTML programming, the *Android style* specifies the visual properties of the elements that make up the app's interface. In the layout file, you define properties for individual Views on your screen. You can create a style to define properties for multiple Views of the same type in your app. For example, if you use 20 buttons in your app, you can define a style that includes the height, padding, margins, font size, and font colors, i.e., a collection of attributes, that can be applied to all buttons. This enables the reuse of property definitions and a consistent look throughout the app. In this part, we will study UI styles and themes and how to use them to define the format and look of UI elements.

6.5.1 Defining a Style File

To define a style, you give a name to your style and inherit style properties from the existing styles, i.e., the parent styles, that are defined in the Android API. The code snippet below shows how to define a style.

```
<resources>
  <style name=" LightAppTheme"
    parent="Theme.AppCompat.Light.DarkActionBar">
  </style>
</resources>
```

In the code sample above, the style name is **"LightAppTheme",** and it inherits properties from an existing theme, "Theme.AppCompat.Light.NoActionBar".

You customize or add properties to the style by defining <item> entries inside the style elements. The <item> elements are name-value pairs. The name in each item is an Android attribute that you would otherwise use in the layout file to define a View attribute. Examples of name-value pairs that you can use to define your styles are listed below. If you don't provide a proper value, you will get an error such as **"expected reference but got (raw string)"**.

```
<style name="forTextStyle" parent=
  "Theme.AppCompat.Light.DarkActionBar">
  <item name="android:capitalize">characters</item>
  <item name="android:textSize">20sp</item>
  <item name="android:textAppearance">?android:textAppearanceLarge
  </item>
  <item name="android:buttonStyle">
    @style/Widget.AppCompat.Button.Borderless</item>
</style>
```

The value for <item> can be a keyword *string*, a *hex color*, or a reference to another resource type using the at-symbol "@," e.g., @style.

You can define multiple styles in one file using the <style> tag, but each style should have a unique name. Examples of name-value pairs that you can use to define your style, as well as styles using already defined styles, are provided in Listing 6.13.

Listing 6.13 A style file with multiple customized styles.

```
<resources
  xmlns:android="http://schemas.android.com/apk/res/android">

<style name="WithNoActionBar"
     parent="Theme.AppCompat.Light.NoActionBar">
     <!-- Customize your theme here. -->
     <item name="colorPrimary">@color/blue</item>
     <item name="colorPrimaryDark">@color/colorPrimaryDark</item>
     <item name="colorAccent">@color/colorAccent</item>
     <item name="android:textColor">#FF0000</item>
     </style>

 <style name="LightAppTheme"
      parent ="Theme.AppCompat.Light.DarkActionBar">
     <!-- Customize your theme here. -->
     <item name="colorPrimary">@color/blue</item>
     <item name="colorPrimaryDark">@color/colorPrimaryDark</item>
     <item name="colorAccent">@color/colorAccent</item>
     <item name="android:textColor">#000000</item>
      </style>

<style name="forTextStyle" parent=
    "Theme.AppCompat.Light.DarkActionBar">
    <item name="android:capitalize">characters</item>
    <item name="android:textSize">20sp</item>
    <item name="android:textAppearance">
    ?android:textAppearanceLarge</item>
     <item name="android:buttonStyle">
         @style/Widget.AppCompat.Button.Borderless</item>
  </style>

<style name="MyTextViewStyle">
    <item name="android:textColor">@color/colorPrimaryDark</item>
    <item name="android:textStyle">bold</item>
    <item name="android:padding">10dp</item>
    <item name="android:textSize">20sp</item>
    <item name="android:inputType">textMultiLine</item>
    <item name= "android:maxLines">100</item>
    <item name= "android:scrollHorizontally">false</item>
  </style>
<style name="customButtons">
    style="@style/Widget.AppCompat.Button"
    style="@style/Widget.AppCompat.Button.Colored"
    style="@style/Widget.AppCompat.Button.Borderless"
    style="@style/Widget.AppCompat.Button.Borderless.Colored"
  </style>
  </resources>
```

6.5.2 Applying Styles

Depending on which style you refer to in your manifest file, your app's look will be different. A style can be applied to an individual View when referenced inside an element definition in the layout file or to an entire Activity or application when referenced inside the manifest file. In Listing 6.14, we first defined a style called *MyTextViewStyle* for a TextView and referenced it inside the TextView definition in the layout file using @style.

Listing 6.14 A style definition that we reference inside a layout file.

```
<resources>
<style name="MyTextViewStyle">
  <item name="android:textColor">@color/blue</item>
  <item name="android:textStyle">bold</item>
  <item name="android:padding">10dp</item>
  <item name="android:inputType">textMultiLine</item>
  <item name= "android:maxLines">100</item>
  <item name= "android:scrollHorizontally">false</item>
</style>
</resources>
```

The style defined in Listing 6.14, MyTextViewStyle, is referenced in Listing 6.15.

Listing 6.15 A Layout file where style is referenced.

```
<?xml version="1.0" encoding="utf-8"?>
<androidx.constraintlayout.widget.ConstraintLayout
xmlns:android=http://schemas.android.com/apk/res/android ... >
  <TextView
    android:id="@+id/textViewID"
    style="@style/MyTextViewStyle" />
</androidx.constraintlayout.widget.ConstraintLayout>
```

To test Listings 6.14 and 6.15, we added a button to the MainActivity screen. We also created a new Activity called *UsingStyleActivity* and a new layout file called *activity_using_style* with a TextView element inside it. The left-hand side of Fig. 6.21 shows the added button to the MainActivity screen. When the button is pressed, UsingStyleActivity is launched, and the TextView in the activity_using_style file is shown where TextView has been formatted according to style MyTextViewStyle.

Fig. 6.21 Using style within Layout file

6.5.3 Defining the App's Theme

In our demo app, we referenced *LightAppTheme* in the manifest file. The app style in the manifest file is set like this:

```
android:theme="@style/LightAppTheme"
```

LightAppTheme is the name of a style that has been defined in the style file. The at-symbol "@" is an instruction to the Android system to find the style file in the *res* folder.

You create an Android theme by defining a style file with attributes such as Colors, TextAppearance, Dimens, Drawables, Shapes, and Buttons Styles that are

Fig. 6.22 Light.DarkActionBar and AppCompat.NoActionBar themes, respectively

not specific to any individual View type, but rather are applicable more broadly and referenced in the manifest file. For example, you can define a colorPrimary attribute and apply it as a background color to all of your Activities. Similarly, you can define textColor and TextAppearance and apply them to all the texts in your app.

When designing a theme for your app, start by selecting a theme that matches your needs. You can customize your theme later as you learn more about your app's requirements. Figure 6.22 presents a snapshot of an app's appearance when it is run with two different themes.

In the style file for our demo app, we created two new styles by extended Android themes. The first one is created by extending *Theme.AppCompat.Light.NoActionBar* and is called *MyFirstStyle*. The second one is created by extending "Theme.AppCompat.Light.DarkActionBar" and is called *MySecondStyle*. The difference between the two themes is that the first style has no ActionBar and its text is set to red. The primary color for both styles is set to blue. Both styles are listed below.

```xml
<style name="MyFirstStyle"
  parent="Theme.AppCompat.Light.NoActionBar">
  <!-- Customize your theme here. -->
  <item name="colorPrimary">@color/blue</item>
  <item name="colorPrimaryDark">@color/colorPrimaryDark</item>
  <item name="colorAccent">@color/colorAccent</item>
  <item name="android:textColor">#FF0000</item>
  </style>
<style name="MySecondStyle"
  parent="Theme.AppCompat.Light.DarkActionBar">
  <!-- Customize your theme here. -->
  <item name="colorPrimary">@color/blue</item>
  <item name="colorPrimaryDark">@color/colorPrimaryDark</item>
  <item name="colorAccent">@color/colorAccent</item>
  <!-- changed from #0000000 -->
  <item name="android:textColor">#000000</item>
  </style>
```

We re-run the app twice. In the first run, we set the app's theme to *MyFirstStyle*, i.e., android:theme="@style/**MyFirstStyle**", and the impact is shown on the left-hand side of Fig. 6.22. In the second run, we set the app's theme to *MySecondStyle*, i.e., android:theme="@style/**MySecondStyle**", and the impact is shown on the right-hand side of Fig. 6.22.

In the code snippet in Listing 6.16, the definitions for colorPrimary, colorPrimaryDark, and colorAccent are shown. These entries are referenced in the styles we used to set the app's themes. The definitions of these colors are saved in the color.xml file inside the resource folder.

Listing 6.16 colors.xml file where multiple colors are defined.

```xml
<?xml version="1.0" encoding="utf-8"?>
<resources>
  <color name="colorPrimary">#AA0000</color>
  <color name="colorPrimaryDark">#303F9F</color>
  <color name="colorAccent">#00E6E6EE</color>
  <color name="maroon">#990099</color>
  <color name="blue">#0ccef0</color>
  <color name="_yellow">#d7fc03</color>
  <color name="gray">#Afffff</color>
  <color name="graydark">#999999</color>
</resources>
```

Fig. 6.23 A style that is applied to all Activities defining the app's theme

Figure 6.23 shows that the impact of a style that is chosen to be the app's theme, referenced in the manifest file, goes beyond one View and one Activity. The style entries are applied to the entire app. The primary color for all Activities is blue as defined in the color.xml file. We also changed textColor in the LightAppTheme style definition to red to show the impact of the theme on all Activities.

6.5.4   The Difference Between a Theme and Style

A style is a set of properties that specifies the look and format of a single UI View type in your app. Using style, you can specify properties such as height, padding, font color, font size, and background color for all Views of the same type in your app. For example, you can define the format for TextViews, Buttons, EditTexts, etc. and reference them in the layout file to give a similar look to all Views of the same type. A style is an XML resource that is separate from the layout file.

On the other hand, a theme is a style applied to an entire application, instead of an individual View type. When a style is applied as a theme, referenced inside the manifest file, every View in the application will apply each style property that it supports. To have an effective theme, you should create a style that defines widely used attributes such as Colors, TextAppearance, Dimensions, Drawables, and Shapes to format as many Views as possible in one place.

Android provides multiple system themes that you can choose from when building your apps. Examples of such themes include:

- Material (dark version)
- Material Light (light version)
- Material Light with NOActionBar

Multiple Android predefined themes are listed in Fig. 6.24.

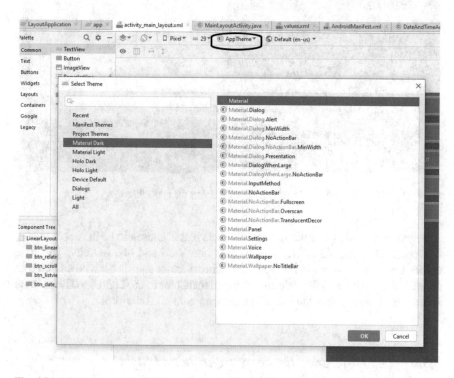

Fig. 6.24 Multiple predefined Themes that are accessible in Android Studio Theme Editor

Fig. 6.25 Padding and
margin attributes of a widget

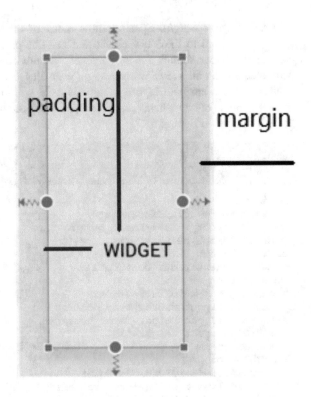

6.5.5   *Padding and Margin View Properties*

View objects have other attributes. For example, several margin attributes can be
applied to Views. The margin attribute names are *android:layout_marginBottom*,
android:layout_marginEnd, *android:layout_marginLeft*, *android:layout_marginRight*,
and *android:layout_marginTop*. They define the extra space around a View on
the bottom, end, left, right, and top, respectively. While margin attributes define
the outside space between the border and the other elements next to the current
View, the attribute *padding* is the inside space between the border and the actual
View's content. Figure 6.25 shows the padding and margin pictorially.

6.5.6   *Gravity and Weight View Properties*

Two important View attributes are *android:layout_gravity* and *android:layout_weight*.
Both are described below and with an example showing how to use them.

   android:layout_gravity. Defines how the child view should be placed or positioned, on both the X and Y axes, within its enclosing layout; some positions include
top, *bottom*, *left*, and *right* and *start*, *center*, and *end*.

android:layout_weight. Specifies how much of the *extra space* in the linear layout is allocated to the View object that has this parameter, for example, zero space if the View should not be stretched. Otherwise, the extra pixels will be distributed among all Views whose weight is greater than zero.

Note that the attribute **layout_weight** is used within the RadioGroup for the Linear Layout in our app; hence, space is equally divided between radio buttons. See the code snippet in Listing 6.17.

Listing 6.17 Using the weight attribute with RadioGroup View.

```
<RadioGroup
  android:id="@+id/radioGender"
  android:layout_width="match_parent"
  android:layout_height="wrap_content"
  android:layout_margin="5dp"
  android:orientation="horizontal" >
  <RadioButton
    android:id="@+id/radioGenderF"
    android:layout_width="wrap_content"
    android:layout_height="wrap_content"
    android:layout_weight="1"
    android:text="@string/gender_female" />
  <RadioButton
    android:id="@+id/radioGenderM"
    android:layout_width="wrap_content"
    android:layout_height="wrap_content"
    android:layout_weight="1"
    android:text="@string/gender_male" >
  </RadioButton>
</RadioGroup>
```

6.5.6.1 Do It Yourself

Create a simple View with three buttons in LinearLayout and with horizontal orientation. Assign each button a different android:layout_weight value, and find the impact of the attribute value on the *space* each button occupies. Now, assign each button a different android:layout_gravity value: top, center, and end, respectively. Find the impact of the property values on the *position* of the buttons.

6.5.7 Dimensions of a Phone and UI

The screen size, both the width and height of a device, as well as the pixel density influence the design of your app. When designing your app's screen, it is helpful if

Fig. 6.26 Google Pixel XL
screen size

you have information about the display characteristics of the device you are designing for.

For example, Fig. 6.26 shows the display properties of the Google Pixel XL. The physical size of the phone is 5.5 inches diagonally, the resolution is 1440 x 2560 pixels, and the pixel density is 534 ppi where ppi is pixels per inch. This information is useful, for example, to determine the resolution of the images your app supports without image deterioration.

Creating and testing your app with a proper AVD emulator and the actual device is the best way to start your app design. However, to be certain about the appropriateness of your application design, you need to be mindful of the dimensions and density of the device you are designing for. Here are some of the scaling units that you need to be aware of when specifying the UI for your app.

- px – screen pixels.
- in – inches based on the physical screen size.
- mm – millimeters based on the physical screen size.
- pt – 1/72 of an inch based on physical screen size.
- dp or dip – device-independent unit relative to a 160 dpi screen.
- sp – similar to dp but used for font sizes.
- dpi – dots per inch; the number of pixels within a physical area of the screen is referred to as dpi.

Most people confuse dp with ppi (pixels per inch); you should not. One dp is equivalent to one pixel on a 160 dpi ((dots per inch)) screen. On a 160 dpi screen, 1dp == 1px == 160/160in, but on a 240dpi screen, 1dp == 240/160= 1.5px.

6.5.7.1   Do It Yourself

Create two AVDs: one with 1080 * 1920 resolution and an LCD density of 480 and the other with 768 * 1280 resolution and an LCD density of 320. Run the demo app created for this chapter on both devices, and study the XML layout look on both screens.

6.6   Chapter Summary

In this chapter, we studied how to create Views, Layouts, Widgets, and other components and their properties that enable you to create a nice-looking and user-friendly interface application. We studied the different types of Layouts that Android supports. These include LinearLayout, ConstraintLayout, RelativeLayout, FrameLayout, GridLayout, TapLayout, and TableLayout. We studied how to define your UI object using XML elements and XML files, as well as how to create Views and Widgets programmatically. To define View objects programmatically, we studied the LinearLayout and LayoutParams classes as well as the setContentView method. Other topics studied in this chapter include phone styles, themes, and phone dimensions. We will continue with the user interface in the next chapter to study ListView, ScrollView, RecyclerView, Pickers, and more.

Check Your Knowledge

Below are some of the fundamental concepts and vocabularies that have been covered in this chapter. To test your knowledge and your understanding of this chapter, you should be able to describe each of the below concepts in one or two sentences.

- android:layout_weight
- Button
- Checkbox
- ConstraintLayout
- dp
- FrameLayout
- GridLayout
- LinearLayout
- Margin
- Padding
- Pickers
- RadioButton
- RadioGroup
- RelativeLayout
- Spinner
- Style
- TableLayout
- TextEditor
- TextView
- Theme
- Toast
- Toggle button
- Tooltips
- View
- ViewGroup

Further Reading

For more information about the topics covered in this chapter, we suggest that you refer to the online resources listed below. These links provide additional insight into the topics covered. The links are mostly maintained by Google and are a part of the Android API specification. The resource titles convey which section/subsection of the chapter the resource is related to.

Build a UI with Layout Editor, [Online] available https://developer.android.com/studio/write/layout-editor

ConstraintLayout, [Online] available https://developer.android.com/reference/android/support/constraint/ConstraintLayout

Design app themes with Theme Editor, [Online] available https://developer.android.com/studio/write/theme-editor

Layouts, [Online] available https://developer.android.com/guide/topics/ui/declaring-layout

Linear Layout, [Online] available https://developer.android.com/guide/topics/ui/layout/linear

Relative Layout, [Online] available https://developer.android.com/guide/topics/ui/layout/relative

User Interface & Navigation, [Online] available https://developer.android.com/guide/topics/ui/

View, [online] Available https://developer.android.com/reference/android/view/View

Chapter 7
ListView, ScrollList, Date and Time Pickers, and RecyclerView

What You Will Learn in This Chapter
By the end of this chapter, you should be able to:

- Create lists and list view layouts
- Use adapters and list listeners
- Use scroll lists
- Use recycler views
- Create time and date picker widgets
- Implement the view holder design pattern

Check Out the Demo Project
Download the demo app, **ListsApplication.zip**, specifically developed to go with this chapter. I recommend that you code this project up from the notes rather than just opening the project in Android Studio and running it; however, if you want to run the code first to get a sense of the app, please do so. The code is thoroughly explained in this chapter to help you understand it. We follow the same approach to all other chapters throughout the book. The app's code will help you comprehend the additional concepts that will be described in this chapter.

How to run the code: unzip the code in a folder of your choice, and then in Android Studio, click **File->import->Existing Android code into the workspace**. The project should start running.

7.1 Introduction

In this chapter, we continue our discussion on the Android user interface and the various layout options we studied in the last chapter. These include list views, scroll views, date and time pickers, and the ViewHolder pattern. This chapter is divided

© The Author(s), under exclusive license to Springer Nature Switzerland AG 2022
A.-R. Mawlood-Yunis, *Android for Java Programmers*,
https://doi.org/10.1007/978-3-030-87459-9_7

into four parts; we study how to create and use list views, date and time pickers, scroll views, and recycler views.

7.2 List Views

In this part, we will study list view implementation using the ListActivity class from Android. If you want to design a user interface (UI) with a long list of items, you can use a ListView class. The *ListView* controller class allows you to vertically scroll up and down through a list of items.

7.2.1 Adapter and ArrayAdapter Classes

Android has an interface called an *adapter* that is implemented by several classes directly or indirectly. These classes include ArrayAdapter<T>, BaseAdapter, CursorAdapter, ListAdapter, SpinnerAdapter, and more. In general, the adapter class is used to enable communication between two incompatible objects. In Android, adapters are used as a bridge between the data and the view. For our demo app, we used ArrayAdapter which is described in more detail below.

7.2.1.1 ArrayAdapter Classes

ArrayAdapter is a simple Java class that can be used between data and the views. The class has several constructors and multiple methods. Some of these methods are listed in Table 7.1. ArrayAdapter can be used with a list view and a spinner. It can be used with a recycler view as well. When used with the recycler view, it has similar results to list views but performs better, e.g., you can scroll up and down lists faster.

7.2.2 ListView and ListActivity

Click on the ListView Layout button from the main page of the ListsApplication app, and check it out. For the demo, we listed Ottawa Senators alumni hockey

Table 7.1 Multiple methods of ArrayAdapter that are widely used

void add (T object)	Adds the specified object at the end of the array
void addAll(T... items)	Adds the specified items at the end of the array
void addAll(Collection<? extends T> collection)	Adds the specified collection at the end of the array
void clear ()	Removes all elements from the list
Context getContext()	Returns the context associated with this array adapter
int getCount()	Gets the number of items in the dataset represented by this adapter
T getItem(int position)	Gets the data item associated with the specified position in the dataset
long getItemId(int position)	Gets the row id associated with the specified position in the list
int getPosition(T item)	Returns the position of the specified item in the array
View getView(int position, View convertView, ViewGroup parent)	Gets a view that displays the data at the specified position in the dataset
void insert (T object, int index)	Inserts the specified object at the specified index in the array
void remove (T object)	Removes the specified object from the array

players[1] (see Fig. 7.1). When you select one of the players from the list, a toast message is displayed for a short time.

To create a list view for your app, you need to follow certain steps. The steps are listed below. We describe these steps in the following subsections.

1. Define the layout for each row in the list.
2. Define the ListViewActivity.
3. Define the data.
4. Select an adapter class.
5. Implement the adapter class.
6. Assign the adapter to the ListView.
7. Assign a listener to the ListView.

7.2.2.1   Define a Layout for the Items on the List

If you look at the **activity_my_list.xml file** in our ListsApplication app, you will see that it includes only a *text view definition. This is a description of one row in the list.* The definition would be applied to each item on the list. You simply need to define a layout for one row in the list; all the items on the list will use that same layout. The row description for our list is defined in Listing 7.1:

---

[1] *Sens Alumni Roster*

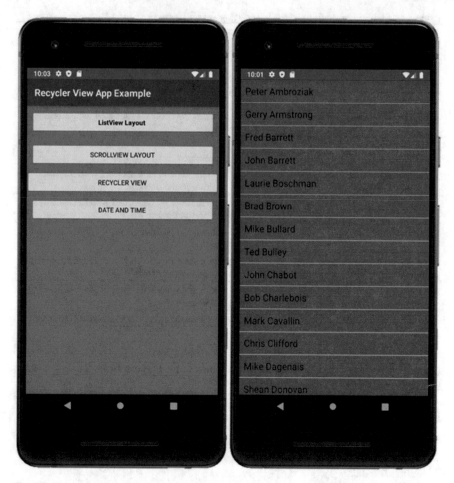

Fig. 7.1 App's main screen on the left and an example of a list on the right

Listing 7.1 listview_layout.xml file representing a row in a list.

```xml
<?xml version="1.0" encoding="utf-8"?>
<TextView xmlns:android=
 "http://schemas.android.com/apk/res/android"
  android:layout_width="match_parent"
  android:layout_height="wrap_content"
  android:padding="10dp"
  android:textSize="20sp"
  android:background="@color/blue">
</TextView>
```

The properties that are defined for the text view in our list are the height, width, padding, text size, and background color. If your list view contains more than just a text, for example, an object with multiple properties, you have to define a different layout in your listview_layout file. We will see an example of that later in this chapter.

7.2.2.2   Create the ListActivity Class

Now that we have a layout for each row in the list, we need to create a Java class, or an activity, to implement the list view and process the list item selections. For our demo app, we created a list view layout activity. The class declaration is as follows:

```
public class ListViewLayoutActivity extends ListActivity {...}
```

Note that, for our app, ListViewLayoutActivity does not extend "Activity"; rather, it extends "**ListActivity**." This is because ListActivity has several methods that help create, manage, and control list views. See the ListActivity class methods in Table 7.2. For our example, we use the getListView and setListAdapter methods.

Since our ListViewLayoutActivity class extends ListActivity, we use getListView() to initialize a ListView object as follows:

```
ListView listView = getListView();
```

Instead of defining a ListView in the XML file, we define it in the code. If you include a ListView in the XML layout file, you need to define a ListView variable in your code and initialize it inside the onCreate() method as follows:

```
ListView listview = findViewById(R.id.listView);
```

Table 7.2 Common methods of ListView class

ListAdapter getListAdapter()
Gets the list adapter associated with this activity's list view
ListView getListView()
Gets the activity's list view widget
Long getSelectedItemId()
Gets the cursor row ID of the currently selected item in the list
Int getSelectedItemPosition()
Gets the position of the currently selected item in the list
Void onContentChanged()
Updates the screen's state (current list and other views) when the content changes
Void setListAdapter(ListAdapter adapter)
Provides the cursor for the list view
Void setSelection(int position)
Sets the currently selected item in the list to a specified position

7.2.2.3 Define Data

Now that we have defined a list view, we need to define or create data and add data to the list. List views use an adapter object to load data onto a list. In our code, we defined a String array for input data; see the code snippets below. The data does not have to be in the code; in fact, it is better to define it in the XML file. However, since our list is small and static, we have done it in code for simplicity and performance as follows:

```
static final String [] Sens_Alumni_Roster = new String [] {
    "Peter Ambroziak",
    "Gerry Armstrong",
    "Fred Barrett",
    "John Barrett",
    "Laurie Boschman",
    "Brad Brown",
    ... };
```

So far, we have the row layout, the list view, and the data. Next, we need to use the adapter class to load data onto the list.

7.2.2.4 Select an Adapter Class

You can use an adapter to provide a view for each object in the array you would like to list. The adapter class is responsible for displaying each item in the array, i.e., it is a bridge between the data and the view. There are several types of adapters to choose from. The choice of which adapter to use depends on the data that you are dealing with. For example, ArrayAdapter displays arrays of Strings, CursorAdapter displays results of SQL queries, and SpinnerAdapter displays data in the spinner and the dropdown list.

In our example, we used ArrayAdapter for its ability to quickly display items in an array. By default, ArrayAdapter creates a view by calling the toString() method on each item in the array and placing the results in a text view. You can customize what view is used for displaying the data objects. We will see an example of a customized view in later chapters.

7.2.2.5 Create an ArrayAdapter Class

ArrayAdapter has several constructors that can be used to create an ArrayAdapter object. Here are two examples of ArrayAdapter constructors:

```
ArrayAdapter (Context ctx, int resource, List<T> objects);
ArrayAdapter (Context ctx, int resource, T [] objects);
```

We used the second constructor for our demo app. The context parameter of the constructor is the Activity that holds the list view. The resource parameter is the ID of a layout with a text view to display the class T's toString() value. The T [] objects are an array of objects, i.e., data, to be loaded onto the list. In our case, the ArrayAdapter constructor would be as follows:

```
ArrayAdapter<String> myArrayAdapter = new ArrayAdapter<String> (
    this, R.layout.activity_my_list, Sens_Alumni_Roster);
```

7.2.2.6   Assign the Adapter to List View

The last step in creating a list is to assign the adapter class to the list view. This is done as follows:

```
setListAdapter(myArrayAdapter);
```

7.2.2.7   Assign a Listener to the List View

If you want to do more than just list data, for example, if you want to display a message when the user clicks on an item on the list, you need to assign listeners to the items. We can do that in two steps:

1. Define a click listener object to handle clicking events for the items on the list. This step can be done using OnItemClickListener as follows:

```
OnItemClickListener itemListener = new OnItemClickListener() {
    public void onItemClick(AdapterView<?> parent,
        View aview, int position, long id) {
        Toast.makeText(getApplicationContext(),
            (TextView) aview).getText() + " is an awesome Sens Alumni!",
            Toast.LENGTH_SHORT).show();
    }
}
```

2. Assign a listener to the list view. This step is done using the statement below:

```
listView.setOnItemClickListener(itemListener);
```

If any entry in the list is clicked, the onItemClick() method is called. The onItemClick() method is implemented to toast, i.e., it displays a message on the screen. You can use the *getSelectedItemID* and *getSelectedItemPosition* methods from the ListActivity class to print out the position in the list and change the toast message to correspond to the selected item.

In Listing 7.2 code snippet, the ListViewLayoutActivity code covers all the steps described so far.

Listing 7.2 ListViewLayoutActivity.java for creating a simple list of items.

```java
package code.android.abdulrahman.com.layoutapplication;
import android.app.ListActivity;
import android.os.Bundle;
import android.view.View;
import android.widget.AdapterView;
import android.widget.AdapterView.OnItemClickListener;
import android.widget.ArrayAdapter;
import android.widget.ListView;
import android.widget.TextView;
import android.widget.Toast;
public class ListViewLayoutActivity extends ListActivity {
// Sens Alumni Roster
// https://www.nhl.com/senators/community/alumni-roster
  static final String [] Sens_Alumni_Roster = new String [] {
      "Peter Ambroziak",
      "Gerry Armstrong",
      "Fred Barrett",
      "John Barrett",
      "Laurie Boschman",
      "Brad Brown",
      "Mike Bullard",
      // ...
  };
  @Override
  public void onCreate(Bundle savedInstanceState) {
    super.onCreate(savedInstanceState);
    // you do not have call setContentView(R.layout.listview_layout);
    //anymore
    // Define a new adapter
    ArrayAdapter<String> myArrayAdapter =
       new ArrayAdapter<String> (this,
                  R.layout.listview_layout, Sens_Alumni_Roster);
    // Assign the adapter to ListView
    setListAdapter(myArrayAdapter);
    // Define the listener interface
    OnItemClickListener itemListener = new OnItemClickListener() {
      public void onItemClick(AdapterView<?> parent, View aview,
                   int position, long id) {
        // When the button clicked, show a toast with the text
        Toast.makeText(getApplicationContext(),
          ((TextView) aview).getText() + " is an awesome Sens Alumni!",
            Toast.LENGTH_SHORT).show();
      }
    };
    // Get the ListView and wired the listener
    ListView listView = getListView();
    listView.setOnItemClickListener(itemListener);
  }
}
```

Once *setListAdapter is executed*, the list view fills the Activity screen. This is because of the `listview_layout.xml` file; see the right-hand side of Fig. 7.1 found at the beginning of this section. This is not a common way to use lists. If you want the list view to occupy only a part of the screen, you have to re-write the **listview_layout.xml file.** An example of such a layout is shown in Listing 7.3.

Listing 7.3 A layout example where a list view occupies only part of the screen.

```xml
<?xml version="1.0" encoding="utf-8"?>
<RelativeLayout xmlns:android=
 "http://schemas.android.com/apk/res/android"
  xmlns:tools="http://schemas.android.com/tools"
  android:layout_width="match_parent"
  android:layout_height="match_parent"
  android:paddingBottom="@dimen/activity_vertical_margin"
  android:paddingLeft="@dimen/activity_horizontal_margin"
  android:paddingRight="@dimen/activity_horizontal_margin"
  android:paddingTop="@dimen/activity_vertical_margin">
  <ListView
    android:layout_alignParentTop="true"
    android:layout_alignParentStart="true"
    android:layout_alignParentEnd="true"
    android:layout_width="match_parent"
    android:layout_height="400dp"
    android:layout_weight="0.5"
    android:id="@+id/listView"/>
  <Button
    android:layout_width="wrap_content"
    android:layout_height="wrap_content"
    android:layout_alignParentBottom="true"
    android:layout_alignParentRight="true"
    android:layout_alignParentEnd="true"
    android:layout_below="@id/listView"
    android:text="Send"
    android:id="@+id/sendButton"/>
  <EditText
    android:layout_alignParentBottom="true"
    android:layout_alignParentLeft="true"
    android:layout_alignParentStart="true"
    android:layout_toLeftOf="@id/sendButton"
    android:layout_width="wrap_content"
    android:layout_height="wrap_content"
    android:hint="enter message"
    android:id="@+id/chatEditText"/>
</RelativeLayout>
```

Fig. 7.2 List layout with
other widgets

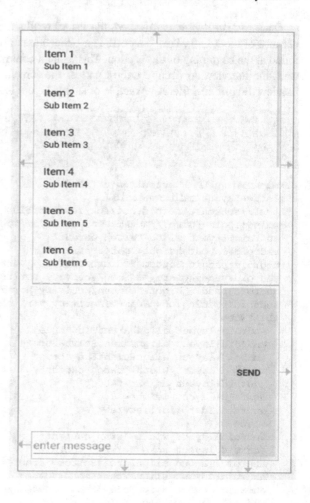

Here, a list view has been put with other widgets in a layout. In Fig. 7.2, the layout
has a list view, an edit text at the bottom left, and a "Send" button on the bottom
right. The end screen for such a layout looks like a normal chat window from
Facebook, Skype, SMS, etc.

7.2.2.8 Do It Yourself

Change the String [] Sens_Alumni_Roster array in the ListViewLayoutActivity
class to an array of item objects. Each item object should have three properties:
name, price, and image. When you run your app, you should have a list like the one
presented in Fig. 7.1 except that each row is made up of three parts, for example, the
name of a device you recently bought, the price you paid, and the image of the
device.

7.3   Date and Time Pickers

In this part of the chapter, we will study date and time pickers. Android provides ways for users to pick a time or date using popup dialogs. Using the date and time pickers helps users pick a time or date that is valid, formatted correctly, and adjusted to the user's local time and date.

7.3.1   Date and Time Pickers

Android provides standard widgets for setting the date and time. These widgets are called pickers. In our demo app, the DateAndTimeActivity.java class uses date and time pickers to set the date and time and display them on text views. Figure 7.3 shows the screen snapshots of the date and time in our demo app.

The layout file for our demo app, date_time_layout.xml, uses a linear layout with a text view and two buttons. The text view is used to display the date and time with a large text size, 30sp. The two buttons are used to call the time and date pickers, respectively. Each button definition includes a call to an onClick() method, and button labels are initialized using text in the strings.xml file. The layout file is shown in Listing 7.4.

Fig. 7.3 Snapshots of Android date and time pickers

Listing 7.4 date_time_layout.xml file for date and time pickers.

```xml
<?xml version="1.0" encoding="utf-8"?>
<LinearLayout
    xmlns:android="http://schemas.android.com/apk/res/android"
    android:layout_width="match_parent"
    android:layout_height="match_parent"
    android:orientation="vertical">
    <TextView
      android:id="@+id/dateTimeID"
      android:layout_marginTop="20dp"
      android:layout_width="match_parent"
      android:layout_height="wrap_content"
      android:text="@string/date_time"
      android:textSize="30sp"
      android:layout_margin="10dp"
      android:background="@color/gray"/>
      <LinearLayout
      android:layout_width="match_parent"
      android:layout_height="match_parent"
      android:layout_margin="10dp">
    <Button
      android:id="@+id/dateBtnID"
      android:layout_width="match_parent"
      android:layout_height="wrap_content"
      android:onClick="onDButtonClicked"
      android:backgroundTint="@color/graydark"
      android:text="@string/button_date"
      android:layout_weight="0.5"/>
    <Button
      android:id="@+id/timeBtnID"
      android:layout_width="match_parent"
      android:layout_height="wrap_content"
      android:onClick="onTButtonClicked"
      android:text="@string/button_time"
      android:backgroundTint="@color/graydark"
      android:layout_weight="0.5"/>
    </LinearLayout>
</LinearLayout>
```

When a user clicks on the Date and Time button on the main screen, a text view is instantiated and initialized inside the onCreate() method. The setTimeAndDateText() method is also called to set the initial date/time for the text view as shown in Fig. 7.4.

The code for the two steps described is:

```
TextView dateAndTimeDisplay = findViewById(R.id.dateTimeID);
    setTimeAndDateText();
```

Fig. 7.4 Date and time on
the picker's main screen

Note that the *setTimeAndDateText()* method is a call to a *local method* that has
been defined in the DateAndTimeActivity class. It uses the *DateUtils* Java class to
format the date and time and uses the *calendar* object with a default time zone. The
dateAndTimeDisplay class is a local variable defined in the DateAndTimeActivity
class. The code for the DateAndTimeActivity is shown in Listing 7.5.

Listing 7.5 The content of the DateAndTimeActivity.java file.

```
public class DateAndTimeActivity extends AppCompatActivity {
  TextView dateAndTimeDisplay;
  Calendar currentDateAndTime = Calendar.getInstance();
  @Override
  protected void onCreate(Bundle savedInstanceState) {
    super.onCreate(savedInstanceState);
    setContentView(R.layout.date_time_layout);
    dateAndTimeDisplay = findViewById(R.id.dateTimeID);
    setTimeAndDateText();
  }
    ...
  private void setTimeAndDateText() {

dateAndTimeDisplay.setText(DateUtils.formatDateTime
        (this, currentDateAndTime.getTimeInMillis(),
DateUtils.FORMAT_SHOW_DATE) + " , " +
DateUtils.formatDateTime(this, currentDateAndTime.getTimeInMillis(),
DateUtils.FORMAT_SHOW_TIME));
  }
}
```

The DateAndTimeActivity view gives the users two options: click on the *set date* button or click on the *time* button. The implementations of the *set date* and *time* buttons are described below.

7.3.2　Set Date Using the DatePicker

When the *set date* button is clicked, a date picker window is presented to the user to select a date and press the OK or Cancel button. Once the OK or Cancel button is pressed, the picker handles the click event (see Fig. 7.5).

The app stores the date and time set by the user after the *OK* button is clicked. The date is stored using the *OnDateSetListener() method*, and the time is stored using the *OnTimeSetListener() method*. The implementation of the DatePickerDialog class for our demo app is shown in Listing 7.6.

Fig. 7.5 Date selection and
confirmation popup window

Listing 7.6 Setting date using the DatePickerDialog and OnDateSetListener
classes.

```
public void onDButtonClicked(View v)
 DatePickerDialog.OnDateSetListener dListener =
   new DatePickerDialog.OnDateSetListener() {
       public void onDateSet(DatePicker view, int yr, int mth, int dy) {
         currentDateAndTime.set(Calendar.YEAR, yr);
```

```
            currentDateAndTime.set(Calendar.MONTH, mth);
            currentDateAndTime.set(Calendar.DAY_OF_MONTH, dy);
            setTimeAndDateText();
        }
    };
    new DatePickerDialog(this, dListener,
            currentDateAndTime.get(Calendar.YEAR),
            currentDateAndTime.get(Calendar.MONTH),
            currentDateAndTime.get(Calendar.DAY_OF_MONTH)).show();
}
```

The code listed above has two important segments, the creation of the DatePickerDialog and the OnDateSetListener objects.

7.3.2.1   The DatePickerDialog Class

The *DatePickerDialog* class is used to create a date picker dialog object for selecting a date. The class has multiple constructors and public methods. The constructor that is used to create the DatePickerDialog object in our demo app is this one:

```
DatePickerDialog(Context context, DatePickerDialog.
OnDateSetListener listener, int year, int monthOfYear, int dayOfMonth).
```

Once you instantiate a DatePickerDialog object, you can display it to the user by calling the *show()* method. The object instantiation and the call to the show() method are listed below.

```
    new DatePickerDialog(this, dListener,
            currentDateAndTime.get(Calendar.YEAR),
            currentDateAndTime.get(Calendar.MONTH),
            currentDateAndTime.get(Calendar.DAY_OF_MONTH)).show();
```

7.3.2.2   The OnDateSetListener Interface

The *OnDateSetListener* interface is used to handle the user's click on the "OK" button, i.e., when the user has finished selecting a date. The OnDateSetListener interface has a single public method called *onDateSet* (DatePicker view, int year, int month, int dayOfMonth) that needs to be implemented. The onDateSet() method is called when the user is done setting a new date, the OK button is pressed, and the dialog is closed.

7.3.3 Set Time Using the TimePicker

Similar to the DatePicker class, the TimePicker class can be used to create a TimePickerDialog window, and the OnTimeSetListener() interface is used to indicate when the user is done selecting the time, that is, they have clicked on the *OK/Cancel* button. The implementation of the TimePickerDialog is shown in Listing 7.7. Note that the time can be configured to be a 24-hour clock or a 12-hour clock with AM/PM. In the 24-hour format, the TimePicker class shows only hours and minutes.

Listing 7.7 Setting time using the TimePickerDialog and OnTimeSetListener classes.

```
public void onTButtonClicked(View v) {
    TimePickerDialog.OnTimeSetListener tListener =
        new TimePickerDialog.OnTimeSetListener() {
            public void onTimeSet(TimePicker view, int hour, int mint) {
                currentDateAndTime.set(Calendar.HOUR_OF_DAY, hour);
                currentDateAndTime.set(Calendar.MINUTE, mint);
                setTimeAndDateText();
            }
        };
    new TimePickerDialog(this, tListener,
        currentDateAndTime.get(Calendar.HOUR_OF_DAY),
        currentDateAndTime.get(Calendar.MINUTE), true).show();

}
```

The code listed above has two important segments, the creation of the TimePickerDialog and the OnTimeSetListener objects.

7.3.3.1 TimePickerDialog Class

The TimePickerDialog class creates a new date picker dialog to select a time. The class has multiple constructors and public methods. The constructor that is used to create the TimePickerDialog object in our demo app is:

TimePickerDialog (Context cxt, TimePickerDialog.OnTimeSetListener callBack, int hour, int mint, boolean is24HourView).

Context is an Activity calling the TimePickerDialog class. TimePickerDialog. *OnTimeSetListener* is a listener object that sets the hours, the minutes, and the time format, i.e., int hour, int minute, and boolean is24HourView. The code snippet below shows how we used the TimePickerDialog class in our demo code.

```
new TimePickerDialog(this, tListener,
        currentDateAndTime.get(Calendar.HOUR_OF_DAY),
        currentDateAndTime.get(Calendar.MINUTE), true).show();
```

The *true* parameter in the code indicates that we want a 24-hour view.

7.3.3.2   OnTimeSetListener Interface

The OnTimeSetListener interface is used to indicate that the user has clicked the
"OK" button, i.e., they have finished selecting a time and the dialog window has
been closed. The TimePickerDialog.OnTimeSetListener class has a single public
method called *onTimeSet(TimePicker view, int hour, int mint)* that needs to be
implemented. We store the time input from the time picker into the calendar object
called dateAndTimeDisplay and call the setTimeAndDateText helper method to
display it.

7.3.3.3   The Calendar Class

In our demo app, we store the time input from the time picker into the calendar
object. Android has a calendar class which is an abstract class. It provides methods
for converting between time instances and has a set of fields such as YEAR,
MONTH, DAY_OF_MONTH, and HOUR. A time instance can be represented by
a millisecond value that is an offset from the epoch January 1, 1970, 00:00:00.000
GMT (Gregorian). The calendar class is locale-sensitive and has a class method
called *getInstance* to get objects of the calendar type. Calendar's getInstance method
returns a calendar object whose calendar fields have been initialized with the current
date and time. Here is an example of how to get an object of the calendar type:
Calendar currentDateAndTime = Calendar.*getInstance*();.

7.3.4   Pickers and Anonymous Classes

For our implementation, we used an anonymous class to define the specialized
listeners for the TimePickerDialog and DatePickerDialog listeners. This approach,
i.e., creating an inner class that implements event handling methods for a component, is widely used by developers. The complete code of the DateAndTimeActivity
class is shown in Listing 7.8.

Listing 7.8 DateAndTimeActivity.java complete code.

```java
import android.app.DatePickerDialog;
import android.app.TimePickerDialog;
import android.os.Bundle;
import androidx.appcompat.app.AppCompatActivity;
import android.text.format.DateUtils;
import android.view.View;
import android.widget.DatePicker;
import android.widget.TextView;
import android.widget.TimePicker;
import java.util.Calendar;
public class DateAndTimeActivity extends AppCompatActivity {
  TextView dateAndTimeDisplay;
  Calendar currentDateAndTime = Calendar.getInstance();
  @Override
  protected void onCreate(Bundle savedInstanceState) {
    super.onCreate(savedInstanceState);
    setContentView(R.layout.date_time_layout);
    dateAndTimeDisplay = findViewById(R.id.dateTimeID);
    setTimeAndDateText();
  }
  public void onTButtonClicked(View v) {
    TimePickerDialog.OnTimeSetListener tListener =
        new TimePickerDialog.OnTimeSetListener() {
      public void onTimeSet(TimePicker view, int hour, int mint) {
        currentDateAndTime.set(Calendar.HOUR_OF_DAY, hour);
        currentDateAndTime.set(Calendar.MINUTE, mint);
        setTimeAndDateText();
      }
    };
    new TimePickerDialog(this, tListener,
        currentDateAndTime.get(Calendar.HOUR_OF_DAY),
        currentDateAndTime.get(Calendar.MINUTE), true).show();
  }
  public void onDButtonClicked(View v) {
DatePickerDialog.OnDateSetListener dListener =
            new DDatePickerDialog.OnDateSetListener) {
      public void onDateSet(DatePicker view, int yr, int mth,
                int dy) {
        currentDateAndTime.set(Calendar.YEAR, yr);
        currentDateAndTime.set(Calendar.MONTH, mth);
        currentDateAndTime.set(Calendar.DAY_OF_MONTH, dy);
        setTimeAndDateText();
      } };
    new DatePickerDialog(this, dListener,
        currentDateAndTime.get(Calendar.YEAR),
        currentDateAndTime.get(Calendar.MONTH),
        currentDateAndTime.get(Calendar.DAY_OF_MONTH)).show();
  }
```

```
private void setTimeAndDateText() {
   dateAndTimeDisplay.setText(
      DateUtils.formatDateTime
      (this, currentDateAndTime.getTimeInMillis(),
      DateUtils.FORMAT_SHOW_DATE) +
      " , " +
      DateUtils.formatDateTime
      (this, currentDateAndTime.getTimeInMillis(),
      DateUtils.FORMAT_SHOW_TIME)) ;
   }
}
```

7.4   Scroll Views

In this part of the chapter, we will study an import Android widget, the scroll view. A scroll view is a view group that allows you to view the hierarchy of widgets placed within it. We will cover how to create and use a scroll view for Android devices in this section.

7.4.1   The ScrollView Class

While developing a mobile app, you may have to design a layout that has too many views and widgets for a simple phone screen. To accommodate such a situation, Android uses a *scrollable view*. Using a scroll view, the user can scroll up and down a list to get to the view of interest. In our ListsApplication demo app, if you click on the ScrollViewLayout button, you will see a screen with a lengthy list of widgets that needs to be scrolled down to see them all. A screenshot of a scrollable screen is shown in Fig. 7.6.

A scroll view may have only one direct child placed within it. To have multiple views within the scroll view, make the direct child a view group, for example, place a linear layout inside the scroll view and place additional views within that linear layout.

Scroll views support vertical scrolling by default. For horizontal scrolling, you can use the HorizontalScrollView class instead. Never add a recycler view or list view to a scroll view. Doing so results in poor user interface performance and a poor user experience.

Fig. 7.6 An example of a
scrollable view

7.4.2 Top-Level XML Element for a Scroll View

To use a scroll view, all you need to do is to make the ScrollView element the top-level XML element, i.e., the wrapper element for your layout. In other words, wrap ScrollView around the layout content. For example, the **scrollview_layout.xml** file in Listing 7.9 shows a linear layout embedded inside the ScrollView element.

Listing 7.9 scrollview_layout.xml where the linear layout is embedded inside the ScrollView element.

```xml
<ScrollView
 xmlns:android="http://schemas.android.com/apk/res/android"
   android:id="@+id/scrollLayout"
   android:layout_width="match_parent"
   android:layout_height="match_parent" >
   <LinearLayout
     android:layout_width="match_parent"
     android:layout_height="wrap_content"
     android:orientation="vertical" >
     <TextView
       android:layout_width="wrap_content"
       android:layout_height="wrap_content"
       android:layout_margin="5dp"
       android:text="@string/name" >
     </TextView>
     <EditText
       android:id="@+id/editName"
       android:layout_width="match_parent"
       android:layout_height="wrap_content"
       android:layout_margin="5dp"
       android:hint="@string/name_hint"
       android:inputType="textCapWords"
       android:singleLine="true" >
     </EditText>
     <TextView
       android:layout_width="wrap_content"
       android:layout_height="wrap_content"
       android:layout_margin="5dp"
       android:text="@string/email" >
     </TextView>
     <EditText
       android:id="@+id/EmailID"
       android:layout_width="match_parent"
       android:layout_height="wrap_content"
       android:layout_margin="5dp"
       android:hint="@string/email_hint"
       android:inputType="textEmailAddress"
       android:singleLine="true" >
     </EditText>
     <TextView
       android:layout_width="wrap_content"
       android:layout_height="wrap_content"
       android:layout_margin="5dp"
       android:text="@string/phone" >
     </TextView>
     <EditText
       android:id="@+id/editPhone"
       android:layout_width="match_parent"
```

```
      android:layout_height="wrap_content"
      android:layout_margin="5dp"
      android:hint="@string/phone_hint"
      android:inputType="phone"
      android:singleLine="true" >
</EditText>
<TextView
   android:layout_width="wrap_content"
   android:layout_height="wrap_content"
   android:layout_margin="5dp"
   android:text="@string/gender" >
</TextView>
<RadioGroup
   android:id="@+id/radioGender"
   android:layout_width="match_parent"
   android:layout_height="wrap_content"
   android:layout_margin="5dp"
   android:orientation="horizontal" >
   <RadioButton
      android:id="@+id/radioGenderF"
      android:layout_width="wrap_content"
      android:layout_height="wrap_content"
      android:layout_weight="1"
      android:text="@string/gender_female" />
   <RadioButton
      android:id="@+id/radioGenderM"
      android:layout_width="wrap_content"
      android:layout_height="wrap_content"
      android:layout_weight="1"
      android:text="@string/gender_male" />
</RadioGroup>
<TextView
   android:layout_width="wrap_content"
   android:layout_height="wrap_content"
   android:layout_margin="5dp"
   android:text="@string/profile_date" >
</TextView>
<EditText
   android:id="@+id/editText1"
   android:layout_width="match_parent"
   android:layout_height="wrap_content"
   android:layout_margin="5dp"
   android:hint="@string/profile_date_hint"
   android:inputType="date" >
</EditText>
<TextView
   android:layout_width="wrap_content"
   android:layout_height="wrap_content"
   android:layout_margin="5dp"
   android:text="@string/rate_department" >
</TextView>
<RatingBar
   android:id="@+id/ratingBar1"
```

```xml
    android:layout_width="wrap_content"
    android:layout_height="wrap_content"
    android:layout_margin="5dp"
    android:background="@color/_yellow"/>
<TextView
    android:layout_width="wrap_content"
    android:layout_height="wrap_content"
    android:layout_margin="5dp"
    android:text="@string/profile_device" >
</TextView>
<ToggleButton
    android:id="@+id/toggleButton1"
    android:layout_width="wrap_content"
    android:layout_height="wrap_content"
    android:layout_margin="5dp" />
<CheckBox
    android:id="@+id/checkBox1"
    android:layout_width="wrap_content"
    android:layout_height="wrap_content"
    android:text="@string/profile_demand" />
<TextView
    android:layout_width="wrap_content"
    android:layout_height="wrap_content"
    android:layout_margin="5dp"
    android:text="@string/signature">
</TextView>
 <EditText
    android:id="@+id/signatureBox"
    android:layout_width="match_parent"
    android:layout_height="wrap_content"
    android:layout_margin="5dp"
    android:hint="@string/signature_hint"
    android:inputType="textCapWords"
    android:singleLine="true"/>
<TextView
    android:layout_width="wrap_content"
    android:layout_height="wrap_content"
    android:layout_margin="25dp"
    android:text="@string/otherWidgets"
    android:textSize="30sp">
</TextView>
<LinearLayout
    android:layout_width="match_parent"
    android:layout_height="match_parent"
    android:orientation="horizontal">
    <Switch
      android:layout_width="0dp"
      android:layout_height="wrap_content"
      android:layout_margin="20dp"
      android:text="on/off Switch"
      android:textSize="25sp"
      android:layout_weight="1"/>
    <SeekBar
```

```
        android:id="@+id/seekBar2"
        style="@style/Widget.AppCompat.SeekBar.Discrete"
        android:layout_width="0dp"
        android:layout_height="52dp"
        android:layout_weight="1"
        android:max="10"
        android:progress="3" />
    </LinearLayout>
    <LinearLayout
      android:layout_width="match_parent"
      android:layout_height="wrap_content"
      android:layout_margin="5dp" >
      <Button
        android:id="@+id/buttonSave"
        android:layout_width="wrap_content"
        android:layout_height="wrap_content"
        android:layout_marginLeft="40dp"
        android:layout_weight="1"
        android:backgroundTint="@color/graydark"
        android:onClick="onSaveClicked"
        android:text="@string/button_save_title" >
      </Button>
      <Button
        android:id="@+id/buttonCancel"
        android:layout_width="wrap_content"
        android:layout_height="wrap_content"
        android:layout_marginRight="40dp"
        android:layout_weight="1"
        android:backgroundTint="@color/graydark"
        android:onClick="onCancelClicked"
        android:text="@string/button_cancel" >
      </Button>
    </LinearLayout>
  </LinearLayout>
</ScrollView>
```

7.4.3 Scroll View Activity

The snippet code for the ScrollViewLayoutActivity class used in our ListsApplication demo app is shown in Listing 7.10. The content view is set to the scrollview_layout file where ScrollView is used as a root element wrapping a linear layout. The code includes two callback methods, onCancelClicked() and onSaveClicked(). These two methods do not do much other than printing messages to the screen using the toast object.

Listing 7.10 ScrollViewLayoutActivity.java.

```java
package code.android.abdulrahman.com.layoutapplication;
import android.content.Intent;
import android.os.Bundle;
import androidx.appcompat.app.AppCompatActivity;
import android.view.View;
import android.widget.Toast;
public class ScrollViewLayoutActivity extends AppCompatActivity {
  @Override
  protected void onCreate(Bundle savedInstanceState) {
    super.onCreate(savedInstanceState);
    setContentView(R.layout.scrollview_layout);
  }
  public void onGoBackScollViewClicked(View v) {
    Intent intent = new Intent(ScrollViewLayoutActivity.this,
        MainLayoutActivity.class);
    startActivity(intent);
  }
  public void onSaveClicked(View v) {
    Toast.makeText(getApplicationContext(),
        getString(R.string.save_message),
            Toast.LENGTH_SHORT).show();

    Intent intent = new Intent(ScrollViewLayoutActivity.this,
        MainLayoutActivity.class);
    startActivity(intent);
  }
  public void onCancelClicked(View v) {
    Toast.makeText(getApplicationContext(),
        getString(R.string.cancel_message),
     Toast.LENGTH_SHORT).show();
    Intent intent = new Intent(ScrollViewLayoutActivity.this,
        MainLayoutActivity.class);
    startActivity(intent);
  }
}
```

7.5   RecyclerView

In this part of the chapter, we will study how to improve the performance of scrolling through a large list of items. The performance improvement is done using the RecyclerView class instead of the ListView class. You supply the data and define how each row in the list should look. The recycler view dynamically creates the views when they are needed. As the name implies, a recycler view recycles individual views when an item scrolls off the screen and does not destroy them. Using a recycler view improves your app's responsiveness and reduces power consumption as well. One popular way of using a recycler view is by implementing the ViewHolder pattern which will be described later in this section. We will try to create a list of books where each book is represented by the title, ISBN, author, and cover image.

7.5.1 Using RecyclerView, Adapter, and ViewHolder Classes

To display a large scrollable list efficiently, you need to use the RecyclerView class. The main idea behind using recycler views is that once you have a large list of identical items to scroll up and down, you do not need to recreate the views, i.e., re-instantiate the view objects, that are holding data, which is the case with a simple list view. Instead, you recycle the views, keep already created objects, and update their content. This is because creating views is a time-consuming task and takes up memory space.

Recycler views are also a more flexible and advanced way to create lists in Android compared to list views. For example, while a list view can only arrange items linearly and in a vertical orientation, a recycler view can arrange items in a grid, in a horizontal or vertical layout orientation, or in staggered grids. In our ListsApplication demo app, the RecyclerView button is used to demonstrate the creation and usage of a recycler view. Remember to use a recycler view only when you have a large list; otherwise, using a list view is easier to implement. To create a recycler view for your app, do the following:

1. Create a class for the objects that will be listed in your recycler view.
2. Create a layout file for one row of your objects.
3. Create an Activity to display objects and to listen to events.
4. Create a layout file for the main Activity, step 3, and include the recycler view in it.
5. Set the layout manager for the RecyclerView view group or container.
6. Create or access data.
7. Link data to the view using the RecyclerView.Adapter class. The RecyclerView.Adapter class enables the binding of data to the views that are displayed within a recycler view. The last step involves creating recycler view and ViewHolder objects.

The steps above are implemented in our demo app using four Java classes and two layout files. The classes are *RecycleViewActivity*, *Book*, *arrayBookAdapter*, and *ViewHolder*, and the layout files are *book_row.xml* and *activity_recyler view.xml*. Below, we will describe the two layout files and the four Java classes.

7.5.1.1 Create Objects for Rows in the List

You need to create a class to hold data that you would like to display in the list. In Java, almost everything is an object. The data fields that form the rows of your list need to be translated to object properties and each row to an object. In our case, we have created a class called *Book*. The book class has three properties, title, authors, and ISBN. The Book.java class is shown in Listing 7.11.

Listing 7.11 Book.java class for the object display in the list.

```java
package code.android.abdulrahman.com.listing;
public class Book {
    String title; int isbn; String author;
    public Book (String title, int isbn, String author) {
      this.title = title;
      this.isbn = isbn;
      this.author = author;
    }
    public String getTitle() { return title; }
    public void setTitle(String title) { this.title = title; }
    public int getISBN() { return isbn; }
    public void setISBN(int isbn) { this.isbn = isbn; }
    public String getAuthor() { return author; }
    public void setAuthor(String author) { this.author = author; }
}
```

Once the recycler view coding is done, the instances, or objects of the book class, will be displayed in the recycler view list.

7.5.1.2 A Layout File for Rows in the List

You also need to create a layout file, e.g., book_row.xml, to define how you would like each book in the list to be displayed. This is a view layout for one row in the list. You saw the use of a one-row layout file before when you created a layout for a list view. Review the listview_layout.xml file described earlier in this chapter to recall how to create and use a one-row layout.

The layout in Listing 7.12, i.e., the book_row.xml file, is a layout for our demo app to hold properties of the Book objects. It includes three text views for the book title, author, and ISBN and an image view object to store the book's cover image.

Listing 7.12 book_row.xml layout to hold properties of the Book objects.

```xml
<?xml version="1.0" encoding="utf-8"?>
<LinearLayout xmlns:android="http://schemas.android.com/apk/res/android"
  android:orientation="horizontal"
  android:layout_width="match_parent"
  android:layout_height="wrap_content">
  <ImageView
    android:id="@+id/cover_page_imgeID"
    android:layout_width="match_parent"
    android:layout_height="100dp"
    android:layout_weight="1"
    android:background="@color/_yellow"
    android:layout_marginTop="10dp"
    android:layout_marginBottom="10dp"
    android:layout_marginLeft="10dp"
    android:gravity="center"/>
  <TextView
    android:id="@+id/row_book_title"
    android:layout_width="match_parent"
    android:layout_height="100dp"
    android:layout_weight="1"
    android:background="@color/red"
    android:layout_marginTop="10dp"
    android:layout_marginBottom="10dp"
    android:layout_marginLeft="10dp"
    android:gravity="center"/>
  <TextView
    android:id="@+id/row_book_isbn"
    android:layout_width="match_parent"
    android:layout_height="100dp"
    android:layout_marginLeft="10dp"
    android:layout_marginTop="10dp"
    android:layout_marginRight="10dp"
    android:layout_marginBottom="10dp"
    android:layout_weight="1"
    android:background="@color/green"
    android:gravity="center" />
  <TextView
    android:id="@+id/row_book_author"
    android:layout_width="match_parent"
    android:layout_height="100dp"
    android:layout_weight="1"
    android:background="@color/blue"
    android:layout_marginTop="10dp"
    android:layout_marginBottom="10dp"
    android:layout_marginRight="10dp"
    android:gravity="center"/>
</LinearLayout>
```

Fig. 7.7 The look of one
row in the list

The pictorial looks for one row of the book list would be as shown in Fig. 7.7.

Note that, in the layout file for a row in the recycler view, e.g., book_row.xml, you need to set the layout_height property for the root element to "wrap_content" and **not** match_parent. That is, you should set **android:layout_height="wrap_content"**. Otherwise, i.e., if *match_parent* is used, one row in the list will occupy all the screen space, something you do not want to happen. See 7.12.

7.5.1.3   RecyclerViewActivity Layout

The layout for the RecyclerViewActivity class is *activity_recyclerview*. This has been set using the setContentView(R.layout.scrollview_layout) method. The RecyclerViewActivity class needs a layout to hold the visual portion of the recycler view along with other view objects if they exist. The code snippet below shows the layout setting for the RecyclerViewActivity class.

```
public class RecyclerViewActivity extends AppCompatActivity {
   ...
   @Override
   protected void onCreate(Bundle savedInstanceState) {
     super.onCreate(savedInstanceState);
     setContentView(R.layout.activity_recyclerview);
     ...
 }
```

A snippet of the activity_recyclerview.xml layout file is shown in Listing 7.13. Note that the layout file contains the recycler view widget, or a container, instead of a list view.

Listing 7.13 The activity_recyclerview.xml layout file that includes the recycler view widget.

```
<?xml version="1.0" encoding="utf-8"?>
<LinearLayout
...
   <androidx.recyclerview.widget.RecyclerView
     android:id="@+id/recycler_id"
     android:layout_width="match_parent"
     android:layout_height="match_parent"
     android:scrollbars="vertical" />
</LinearLayout>
```

Using a recycler view within the layout is the main difference between the layouts we have seen so far, for example, the layouts used in the last two chapters and the one shown in Listing 7.13.

The root element of the *activity_recyclerview* file has three important properties: width, height, and orientation. These properties and their values are as follows:

```
android:layout_width="match_parent"
android:layout_height="match_parent"
android:orientation="vertical"
```

Do not confuse the **android:layout_height** property for the top element in *activity_recyclerview*, the layout that holds an entire list, with the same property for the book_row.xml file, the layout for individual rows. For the latter one, the **android:layout_height** value is "wrap_content."

7.5.1.4   Data Model

For our demo app to be ready to work, we are missing a key ingredient, the actual data, or book instances. The layout file for an individual row, which we have created in previous steps, acts as a table header, or an excel file field header. The book objects, or book instances, are field values, or data. This is what we need to add to the list rows.

In other parts of this chapter and the previous chapter, we created data for our app in different ways. In one case, we put all the data in a string array inside an XML file in the resource folder. That was done when we studied the spinner widget with linear layouts in the previous chapter. In the list view part of this chapter, we included the hockey player names inside an array and used it for the list view, i.e., we hardcoded a shortlist of names. Here, data is created programmatically. An array list is created to hold book objects. The array creation and its initialization are done inside the RecyclerViewActivity.java class as follows:

A call is made to the Book class constructor (String, int, String) with the three parameters below:

1. "title" + i
2. Row_index * 100
3. " author " + row_index

The call is made inside a loop 200 times; see the code snippet below:

```
while (row_index <= number_nubmer_of_rows) {
  bookList.add(new Book("title " + row_index, row_index * 100,
      "author " + row_index));
  row_index++;
}
```

An additional property, i.e., book_cover_image of image view type, will be added to the book properties when binding data to the views. We cannot do it here because in non-GUI Java code we cannot define a variable to hold an image directly. A single image can be added to the image view widget using the Android:src entry inside the layout file. This can be done as follows:

```
<ImageView
   ...
   android:src="@drawable/wlu"/>
```

In the statement above, wlu is an image file inside the drawable folder and has been accessed using the at-symbol "@."

7.5.1.5 RecyclerView.Adapter Class

To complete our app, we need to link the data, the row layout, and the recycler view together. In other words, we need to connect the following:

1. Recycler view, which has been defined inside the layout
2. R.layout.book_row, a layout for one book row
3. bookList, an array list that holds the data

The RecyclerView.Adapter class does the above three steps for us. It binds app-specific data to views that are displayed within a recycler view. Therefore, we need to create a RecyclerView.Adapter class. We have created such a class, and it is called ArrayBookAdapter. The class declaration is listed below. The complete code for the ArrayBookAdapter class is presented in Listing 7.14.

```
public class ArrayBookAdapter extends
                   RecyclerView.Adapter <ViewHolder> {...}
```

We call the ArrayBookAdapter class constructor to create a RecyclerView.Adapter object. The constructor takes three parameters: the layout id for a row, the app context, and the data. It then links the data, the row view, and the recycler view together. The call to the ArrayBookAdapter class constructor is shown below.

```
ArrayBookAdapter arrayBookAdapter =
     new ArrayBookAdapter(
        R.layout.book_row, bookArrayList, getApplicationContext());
```

So far, we have created an array of books and defined how each row should look, and the RecyclerView.Adapter class dynamically creates the elements to link the data and the row view together when they are needed.

Note that our array adapter, i.e., ArrayBookAdapter, is not only a subclass of the recycler view class but is also an array adapter of the view holder objects. In other words, array elements are of type view holder. So, we need to explain what role a view holder object plays in binding data to the recycler view. This will be discussed in the next section.

The implementation of the ArrayBookAdapter class is listed below. It includes implementing the onCreateViewHolder(), onBindViewHolder(), and getItemCount() methods that you need to override when using the RecyclerView.Adapter class. These methods are described in more detail in the next section.

Once the *ArrayBookAdapter constructor* is called, the constructor, in turn, invokes the *onCreateViewHolder* method which leads to linking the *activity_recyclerview layout*, adapter class, and view holder class together. These steps are implemented in the ArrayBookAdapter class as shown in Listing 7.14.

Listing 7.14 ArrayBookAdapter.java.

```java
package code.android.abdulrahman.com.listing;
import android.content.Context;
import android.graphics.Bitmap;
import android.graphics.BitmapFactory;
import android.view.LayoutInflater;
import android.view.View;
import android.view.ViewGroup;
import android.widget.ImageView;
import android.widget.TextView;
import androidx.recyclerview.widget.RecyclerView;
import java.util.ArrayList;
public class ArrayBookAdapter extends
            RecyclerView.Adapter <BookViewHolder> {
  private int book_row_layout;
  private ArrayList <Book> bookList;
  private Context cxt;
  // Constructor of the class
  public ArrayBookAdapter(int book_row_layout_as_id,
            ArrayList <Book> bookList, Context context) {
    book_row_layout = book_row_layout_as_id;
    this.bookList = bookList;
    this.cxt = context;
  }
  // return the size of the list
  @Override
  public int getItemCount() {
    return bookList == null ? 0 : bookList.size();
  }
  //  turning the layout for each row in the list to View object
  @Override
  public BookViewHolder onCreateViewHolder(
            ViewGroup parent, int viewType) {
    // cxt = parent.getContext() ;
    View myBookview = LayoutInflater.from(parent.getContext())
        .inflate(book_row_layout, parent, false);
    // create GUI object equivalent to the Book object
    BookViewHolder myViewHolder =
```

```
            new BookViewHolder(myBookview);
        return myViewHolder;
    }
    // load data to each row in the list
    // for simplicity we used one image for all book cover images.
      @Override
    public void onBindViewHolder(final BookViewHolder holder,
                        final int listPosition) {
        TextView abook = holder.title;
        TextView isbn = holder.isbn;
        TextView author = holder.author;
        // showing book on screen
        author.setText(bookList.get(listPosition).getAuthor());
        abook.setText(bookList.get(listPosition).getTitle());
        isbn.setText("ISBN#: " + bookList.get(listPosition).getISBN());

        // icon is initialized here not when ArrayBook initialized.
        // this demonstrates the Book Object and GUI book object can be
        // different.
        // presenting Book as TextView on the Android device Screen is very
          much
        // like creating toString() method for printing,
        // you can add or remove properties based on the need.
        ImageView coverImage = holder.coverImage;
        Bitmap icon = BitmapFactory.decodeResource(cxt.getResources(),
            R.drawable.fig1);
        coverImage.setImageBitmap(icon);
    }
}
```

You may have noticed that we are passing app context, i.e., getApplicationContext(), to the adapter class, i.e., to the ArrayBookAdapter constructor. We use context inside the adapter class to access app resources, e.g., R.drawable.wlu image. Passing context to the adapter class is one way to access the app's resources. This is because the array adapter class is not a subclass of an Activity class.

Another way to access to the context would be to use the *parent.getContext();* method inside the OnCreateViewHolder method as follows:

```
@Override
publicViewHolder onCreateViewHolder (ViewGroup parent, int viewType) {
        cxt = parent.getContext();
    ...
}
```

You might have also noticed that we used one image for all book cover images. This is done to simplify the presentation. In a commercial application, image IDs can be used to retrieve individual book cover images.

7.5.2   RecyclerViewActivity

Before running the ListsApplication demo app, let us recall what has been implemented in the *RecyclerViewActivity* class. We will then explain some additional concepts including view holder's role in binding data to the recycler view to complete the implementation.

1. Initializing the recycler view

The recycler view field of the RecyclerViewActivity class is initialized. This is done using the RecyclerView element that has been included in the activity_recyclerview_layout file. Both the recycler view definition and the initialization statement are shown below, respectively:

```
<androidx.recyclerview.widget.RecyclerView
    android:id="@+id/recycler_id"
    android:layout_width="match_parent"
    android:layout_height="match_parent"
    android:scrollbars="vertical" />
    recyclerView = findViewById(R.id.recycler_id);
```

2. Setting LayoutManager to the RecylerView

An important step in coding the RecyclerViewActivity class is setting the layout manager for the recycler view. In other words, you need to specify to the recycler view what type of layout is used for each row in the list, i.e., how rows are organized on the recycler view list.

Since we are using a linear layout to display our rows, i.e., book_row.xml uses a liner layout, we set the recycler view's layout manager to a linear layout; see the code statement below:

```
recyclerView.setLayoutManager(new LinearLayoutManager(this));
```

The layout manager is responsible for:

- Measuring and positioning book views within a recycler view
- Determining the policy for when to recycle book views that are no longer visible to the user

Layout manager can be set to standard vertically scrolling lists, uniform grids, staggered grids, horizontally scrolling collections, etc. As mentioned earlier, this is the other advantage of using the recycler view over a simple list.

3. Assigning Adapter class to the RecyclerView

To enable attaching data to the list, after creating the recycler view, we need to assign an adapter to it. In this case, we need to assign ArrayBookAdapter to the recycler view. The adapter setting is done as follows:

```
recyclerView.setAdapter(arrayBookAdapter);
```

The recycler view has many methods to interact with data in the list. These
include:

1. Adding to the list
2. Removing from the list
3. Setting item animator to handle animations involving changes to the items in the
   recycler view
4. Etc.

The three steps described above are shown inside the *RecyclerViewActivity* class
in Listing 7.15, and they are numbered:

Listing 7.15 RecyclerViewActivity.java.

```java
package code.android.abdulrahman.com.listing;
import android.os.Bundle;
import androidx.appcompat.app.AppCompatActivity;
import androidx.recyclerview.widget.LinearLayoutManager;
import androidx.recyclerview.widget.RecyclerView;
import java.util.ArrayList;
public class RecyclerViewActivity extends AppCompatActivity {
  RecyclerView recyclerView;
  private final int number_nubmer_of_rows = 200;
  int row_index = 1;
  @Override
  protected void onCreate(Bundle savedInstanceState) {
    super.onCreate(savedInstanceState);
    setContentView(R.layout.activity_recyclerview);
    ArrayList <Book> bookList = new ArrayList <Book> ();
    // Populating Array book
    while (row_index <= number_nubmer_of_rows) {
      bookList.add(new Book (
          "title " + row_index,
          row_index * 100,
          "author " + row_index));
      row_index++;
    }
ArrayBookAdapter arrayBookAdapter =
new ArrayBookAdapter(R.layout.book_row,
                bookList, getApplicationContext());
  recyclerView = findViewById(R.id.recycler_id); // 1.
  recyclerView.setLayoutManager(new LinearLayoutManager(this)); // 2.
  /recyclerView.setAdapter(arrayBookAdapter); // 3.
  }
}
```

7.5.3 Adapter and ViewHolder

In the section about linking the data, the row layout, and the recycler view together, we mentioned using the ArrayBookAdapter and ViewHolder objects. Let us elaborate more about the role of these objects in making our ListsApplication demo app work.

7.5.3.1 ArrayAdapter

An important step in creating the recycler view is the creation of the adapter class. In our app, what puts everything together is the **ArrayBookAdapter** class. It adds data to the recycler view and uses the ViewHolder objects to display item objects. The ArrayBookAdapter class is created by extending the RecyclerView.Adapter class as follows:

```
public class ArrayBookAdapter extends
            RecyclerView.Adapter <ViewHolder> {...}
```

To be able to use the RecyclerView.Adapter<ViewHolder> class, we need to override the following three methods:

1. onCreateViewHolder(ViewGroup parent, int viewType)
2. onBindViewHolder(RecyclerView.ViewHolder holder, int position)
3. getItemCount()

The implementation of the three methods is described below.

7.5.3.2 onCreateViewHolder

The onCreateViewHolder() method is called by the layout manager when the RecyclerViewActivity class creates an ArrayBookAdapter class to instantiate a new view holder instance. A layout manager class is responsible for measuring and positioning each row within a recycler view layout. It is also responsible for recycling rows that are no longer visible to the user. There are two things to be noted about the onCreateViewHolder() method:

1. It is used to create and initialize the view holder objects.
2. The onCreateViewHolder callback method is called when the adapter, ArrayBookAdapter, is assigned to the recycler view and when the user scrolls the list up and down creating view holder objects for books.

The code snippet for the onCreateViewHolder() method is shown in 7.16.

Listing 7.16 onCreateViewHolder method implementation.

```
// turning the layout for each row in the list to view object
@Override
public ViewHolder onCreateViewHolder(
  ViewGroup parent, int viewType) {
    View myBookview = LayoutInflater.from(parent.getContext())
            .inflate(book_row_layout, parent, false);
    BookViewHolder myViewHolder =
                new BookViewHolder(myBookview);
    return myViewHolder;
}
```

This method inflates the Book object, i.e., it takes a Book definition from the layout file and creates a corresponding view object, a view holder object, from it and returns it. The Book object inflation is done using the LayoutInflater class and its *inflate* method.

7.5.3.3 LayoutInflater and Adapter Class

The LayoutInflater class transforms a layout XML file into its corresponding view object. To access the LayoutInflater class, you can call the getLayoutInflater() method inside an Activity or call the getSystemService() method from the context class. For example, the statement below returns a LayoutInflater object:

```
LayoutInflater.from(parent.getContext());
```

The XML transformation to the corresponding view object is done using the *inflate* method. The use of the LayoutInflater class with the adapter class in our demo code is done as follows. Here is the creation statement (a call to the ArrayBookAdapter constructor):

```
ArrayBookAdapter arrayBookAdapter = new ArrayBookAdapter(
    R.layout.book_row, bookList, getApplicationContext());
```

Note that, in the code statement above, you can use *this* or *RecyclerViewActivity.this* in place of getApplicationContext().

In the RecyclerViewActivity class, when we created an ArrayBookAdapter object, i.e., when we created a RecyclerView.Adapter object, we passed two parameters.

1. R.layout.book_row; is an id of the resource layout, i.e., an id of book_row.xml file.
2. bookList; is an ArrayList of the data.

Inside the *ArrayBookAdapter* class, the id was saved as an *int* in the *book_row_layout variable*. That is, the incoming parameter book_row_layout_as_id is assigned to an int variable, *book_row_layout*. See the code snippet below.

```
public ArrayBookAdapter(int book_row_layout_as_id,
                  ArrayList <Book> bookList, Context context) {
  book_row_layout = book_row_layout_as_id;
  this.bookList = bookList;
  this.cxt = context;
}
```

The *onCreateViewHolder* method of the ArrayBookAdapter class uses the *LayoutInflater* object to turn book_row_layout into a view object as follows:

```
View myBookview = LayoutInflater.from(
      parent.getContext()).inflate(book_row_layout, parent, false);
```

In other words, the layout inflater object turns a layout XML file into its corresponding view object using the layout id received from the ArrayBookAdapter constructor.

7.5.3.4   The Inflate Method

The layout inflater class has more than one version of the inflate method which is used to transform the XML file to its corresponding view object. These include:

```
public View inflate (int resource, ViewGroup root);
public View inflate (XmlPullParser parser, ViewGroup root);
public View inflate (XmlPullParser parser, ViewGroup root,
                            boolean attachToRoot);
public View inflate (int resource, ViewGroup root, boolean attachToRoot);
```

We used the last one in our demo app. We called the inflate method as follows:

```
inflate(book_row_layout, parent, false);
```

There are a few things you should know about the three parameters of the inflate method we used:

The third parameter of the inflate method, i.e., attachToRoot, is about whether or not to *add* the view referenced in the first parameter of the method to the second parameter. For the recycler view, the attach to root parameter should be false. This is because the recycler view, and not the developer, is responsible for determining when to inflate, i.e., instantiate, the list view and to attach the views to it. In general, the attach to root parameter should be false anytime the developer is not responsible for adding a view to a view group. More on the layout inflater class and the inflate method will come when we study *Fragments*, a modular part of an activity.

7.5.3.5   ViewHolder

The last thing to do is to create the view holder class. A view holder class describes an item view, in our case a book view, and metadata about its place within the recycler view. The constructor for the view holder takes a view as an input parameter. See the statement below:

```
ViewHolder myViewHolder = new ViewHolder(myBookview);
```

Remember that the view object passed to the view holder constructor is created from the layout book_row.xml file. Review the code for the onCreateViewHolder method to see how the call to the ViewHolder constructor was made inside that method after inflating the book layout.

Receiving view objects makes it easy for the three text view attributes of the view holder class to be initialized using the **findViewById(R.id.TextViewID)** method. The code for the view holder class is shown in Listing 7.17.

Listing 7.17 ViewHolder.java class.

```
package code.android.abdulrahman.com.listing;
import android.util.Log;
import android.view.View;
import android.widget.ImageView;
import android.widget.TextView;
import androidx.recyclerview.widget.RecyclerView;
public class BookViewHolder extends RecyclerView.ViewHolder
    implements View.OnClickListener {
    // to initialize the views of rows
    public TextView title;
    public ImageView coverImage;
    public TextView isbn;
    public TextView author;

    public BookViewHolder(View bookView) {
        super(bookView);
        coverImage = bookView.findViewById(R.id.cover_page_imgeID);
        title = bookView.findViewById(R.id.row_book_title);
        isbn = bookView.findViewById(R.id.row_book_isbn);
        author = bookView.findViewById(R.id.row_book_author);
        bookView.setOnClickListener(this);
    }
```

```
@Override
public void onClick(View view) {
   Log.d("onclick", "onClick "
      + getLayoutPosition() + " " + title.getText());
   }
}
```

7.5.3.6   onBindViewHolder

The onBindViewHolder method is called by the recycler view. It is called when the recycler view wants to display data at a specified position. The method updates the content of the view item to reflect the item at the given position.

Presenting a book object as TextViews on the Android device screen is similar to creating a toString() method to print an object. This enables the book object and its GUI representation on the screen to be different, i.e., to add or remove properties based on your needs. Listing 7.18 is the code snippet for onBindViewHolder:

Listing 7.18 onBindViewHolder method implementation.

```
@Override
public void onBindViewHolder(final BookViewHolder holder,
   final int listPosition) {
   TextView abook = holder.title;
   TextView isbn = holder.isbn;
   TextView author = holder.author;

   // showing book on screen
   author.setText(bookList.get(listPosition).getAuthor());
   abook.setText(bookList.get(listPosition).getTitle());
   isbn.setText("ISBN#: " + bookList.get(listPosition).getISBN());

   // icon is initialized here not when ArrayBook initialized.
   // this demonstrates the Book object and GUI book object can be different.
   // presenting Book as TextView on the Android device screen is very much
   // like creating toString() method for printing,
   // you can add or remove properties based on the need.

ImageView coverImage = holder.coverImage;
   Bitmap icon =
      BitmapFactory.decodeResource(cxt.getResources(), R.drawable.fig1);
   coverImage.setImageBitmap(icon);
}
```

7.5.3.7 getItemCount()

The getItemCount method returns the size of the collection, ArrayList in our case, which contains the books we want to display. See the code snippet in Listing 7.19.

Listing 7.19 getItemCount method implementation.

```
// get the size of the list
@Override
public int getItemCount() {
  return bookList == null ? 0 : bookList.size();
}
```

7.5.3.8 Recycler View Class Diagram

Figure 7.8 is the class diagram for the recycler view part of our demo app. The diagram shows that the ArrayBookAdapter class is a RecyclerViewAdapter class. It also shows that the ArrayBookAdapter class implements three methods, the getItemCount, onCreateViewHolder, and OnBindViewHolder methods. Similarly, the BookViewHolder class is a subclass of the view holder class and implements an OnClickListener interface. The class diagram also shows that the

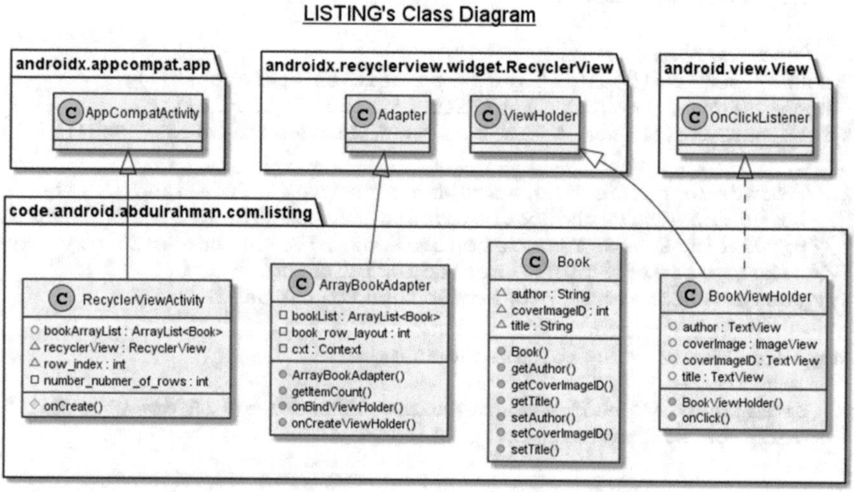

Fig. 7.8 Classes involved in using a recycler view container to display a list

RecyclerViewActivity class is an AppCompatActivity class and that the Book class and the ArrayBookAdapter class are two separate classes.

7.5.4   Using Recycler View with Older SDKs

Using a recycler view requires a compileSdkVersion and/or a targetSdkVersion of 29 or greater. If you choose to use a compileSdkVersion and/or a targetSdkVersion less than 29, you need to declare the following dependency inside the **build.gradle** file of your project.

```
'com.android.support:recyclerview-v7:26.1.0' or a newer version.
```

The support:recyclerview version you are going to use depends on the target device you are building. Below is the code snippet for a build.gradle file where the recycler view library has been added to the list of dependencies:

```
dependencies {
implementation fileTree(dir: 'libs', include: ['*.jar'])
implementation 'com.android.support:appcompat-v7:26.1.0'
implementation 'com.android.support.constraint:constraint-
layout:1.1.3'
testImplementation 'junit:junit:4.12'
implementation 'com.android.support:recyclerview-v7:26.1.0'
compile 'com.android.support:recyclerview-v7:26.1.0'
androidTestImplementation('com.android.support.
             test.espresso:espresso-core:3.0.2', {
exclude group: 'com.android.support', module: 'support-annotations'

})
```

For targetSdkVersions 29 and higher, you need to include this statement in your build.gradle file:

```
implementation 'androidx.recyclerview:recyclerview:1.1.0'.
```

You can migrate your older code to use the androidX library. Using Android Studio, click on the *refactor* button from the menu bar, and press migrate to AndroidX.

Fig. 7.9 The screenshot of
the top part of the recycler
view list

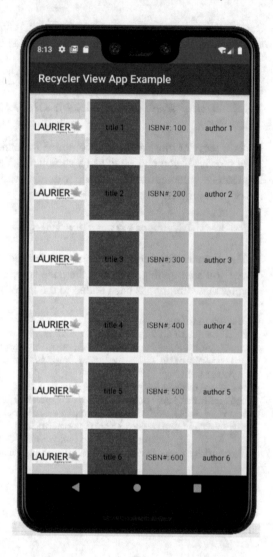

Now, we have completed the creation of the recycler view in our demo app. The
screenshots of our demo app using the recycler view are provided in Figs. 7.8 and
7.9. Two hundred rows are created for this app. The user can easily scroll up and
down. The snapshots show the beginning, middle, and end of the list, respectively;
see Figs. 7.9 and 7.10.

Fig. 7.10 The screenshot of the middle and end of the recycler view list

7.6 Chapter Summary

In this chapter, we studied the instantiation and usage of date and time pickers, list views, scroll views, and recycler views. We also created an app to go with this chapter to help you learn how to code them. For recycler views, we described in detail how the recycler view adapter and view holder classes are created.

Implementing a recycler view involves more than creating a simple list, but it is more efficient when created. The sequence of major steps, or method calls, involved in the creation of recycler views are setLayoutManager() $\rightarrow$ set Adapter (RecyclerViewAdapter) $\rightarrow$ onCreateView $\rightarrow$ Viewholder $\rightarrow$ onBindViewHolder. You also need to create a data object, a layout for a row in the list, and a subclass of the view holder class. When the user scrolls up and down the list, the recycler view triggers an event to update the content of the rows using the position in the list. All these steps and methods are described in this chapter in detail.

Check Your Knowledge
Below are some of the fundamental concepts and vocabularies that have been covered in this chapter. To test your knowledge and your understanding of this chapter, you should be able to describe each of the concepts below in one or two sentences.

- ArrayAdapter
- Date picker
- Inflate
- LayoutInflater
- Layout manager
- ListActivity
- ListView
- onBindViewHolder
- onCreateViewHolder
- OnItemClickListener
- RecylerView
- ScrollView
- Time picker
- ViewHolder

Further Reading

For more information about the topics covered in this chapter, we suggest that you refer to the online resources listed below. These links provide additional insight into the topics covered. The links are mostly maintained by Google and are a part of the Android API specification. The resource titles convey which section/subsection of the chapter the resource is related to.

RecyclerView.Adapter, [online] Available, https://developer.android.com/reference/androidx/recyclerview/widget/RecyclerView.Adapter

LayoutInflater, [online] Available, https://developer.android.com/reference/android/view/LayoutInflater

Pickers, [online] Available, https://developer.android.com/guide/topics/ui/controls/pickers

ListView, [online] Available, https://developer.android.com/reference/android/widget/ListView

ListActivity, [online] Available, https://developer.android.com/reference/android/app/ListActivity

RecyclerView, [online] Available, https://developer.android.com/jetpack/androidx/releases/recyclerview

ScrollView, [online] Available, https://developer.android.com/reference/android/widget/ScrollView

ViewHolder, [online] Available, https://developer.android.com/reference/androidx/recyclerview/widget/RecyclerView.ViewHolder

Chapter 8
Toolbar, Menu, Dialog Boxes, Shared Preferences, Implicit Intent, and Directory Structure

What You Will Learn in This Chapter

By the end of this chapter, you should be able to:

- Create toolbars for putting menus at the top of your app Activity
- Create menus, dd them to the toolbar, and handle item selection action
- Create and use contextual and popup menus
- Create dialog boxes
- Use common Intent to access the camera
- Use Android data storage
- Create shared preferences
- Use and access internal and external file storage
- Use Android Device File Explorer

Check Out the Demo Project

Download the demo app, **MenubarAndMore.zip**, specifically developed to go with this chapter. I recommend that you code this project up from the notes rather than just opening the project in Android Studio and running it; however, if you want to run the code first to get a sense of the app, please do so. The code is thoroughly explained in this chapter to help you understand it. We follow the same approach to all other chapters throughout the book. The app's code will help you comprehend the additional concepts that will be described in this chapter.

How to run the code: unzip the code in a folder of your choice, and then in Android Studio, click **File->import->Existing Android code into the workspace**. The project should start running.

© The Author(s), under exclusive license to Springer Nature Switzerland AG 2022
A.-R. Mawlood-Yunis, *Android for Java Programmers*,
https://doi.org/10.1007/978-3-030-87459-9_8

8.1   Introduction

In this chapter, we will study the creation of toolbars, how to add menus to toolbars, the creation of dialog boxes, and how to access the camera app in your code using implicit intent. We will also study the directory structure and how to store data in apps; for that, we will study shared preferences and file creation in the app's internal and external storages.

8.2   More User Interface

Actionbars, toolbars, menus, and dialog boxes are important components of the user interface. In this part of the chapter, we will learn how to create toolbars and menus and how to add items to menus and menus to toolbars. We will also learn how to create dialog boxes to get user input and display information to the user.

8.2.1   ActionBar

All activities in Android have an actionbar associated with them. It is a menu, but you can associate icons with the menu items. It was introduced in Android version 3. Previously, Android had a dedicated hardware button to make the menu appear.

8.2.2   Toolbar

The toolbar was introduced in Android Lollipop, the API 21 release, and is the spiritual successor of the actionbar. The toolbar is a view group that can be placed anywhere inside your XML layouts. A toolbar's appearance and behavior can be more easily customized than an actionbar's. To use the toolbar class in your app, you need to do the following:

1. Add the androidx.appcompat library to your project build file.
2. Make your activity extend AppCompatActivity.
3. Specify a theme with no actionbar.
4. Add a toolbar element to the activity's layout.
5. Set the activity's toolbar using the setSupportActionBar method.

   Below, we will describe the steps you need to follow to add a toolbar to your app.

8.2.3 Add androidx.appcompat Library to the Project

Adding a library to your app to support the toolbar creation involves two actions.

8.2.3.1 Add the Support Library to the build.gradle

To be able to create a toolbar for your app, you need to add the support library to the dependencies section of your **build.gradle** file. That is, add the below line of code to your build file.

```
implementation 'androidx.appcompat:appcompat:1.0.0'.
```

An example of a build.gradle file with the support library is shown in Listing 8.1.

Listing 8.1 build.gradle.

```
dependencies {
    implementation fileTree(dir: 'libs', include: ['*.jar'])
    implementation 'androidx.appcompat:appcompat:1.0.0'
    implementation 'androidx.constraintlayout:constraintlayout:1.1.3'
    testImplementation 'junit:junit:4.12'
    implementation 'androidx.recyclerview:recyclerview:1.1.0'
    implementation 'com.google.android.material:material:1.0.0'
    androidTestImplementation(
    'androidx.test.espresso:espresso-core:3.1.0', {
    exclude group: 'com.android.support', module: 'support-annotations'
    })
}
```

The version of the support library depends on the *compileSdkVersion* your app is using. Below is an example of a build setting where the **compileSdkVersion** is set to 26. This means that you would like to compile your app code with the SDK version 26. The compile SDK setting is done inside the build.gradle file of your app (Table 8.1).

Here is another example where the compileSdkVersion is set to 29 (Table 8.2).

Note that, if you compile your code with an SDK version of 29 or up, i.e., you specified the compileSdkVersion to 29 or up in your gradle build file, you need to make sure that you are using **androidx**.appcompat to compile your code correctly. If you inherit code that uses older libraries, such as *android.support.v7.widget.Toolbar*, replace the library in your code with androidx.appcompat.widget.Toolbar. You can update older versions of code in Android Studio by clicking on refactor → migrate to AndroidX.

Table 8.1 An example of the build.gradle setting where compileSdkVersion is set to 26

```
android {
compileSdkVersion 26
defaultConfig {
    applicationId "code.android.abdulrahman.com.recyclerviewdemo"
    minSdkVersion 25
    targetSdkVersion 26
    versionCode 1
    versionName "1.0"
    testInstrumentationRunner
        "android.support.test.runner.AndroidJUnitRunner"
}
```

Table 8.2 An example of the build.gradle setting where compileSdkVersion is set to 29

```
android {
    compileSdkVersion 29
    defaultConfig {
        applicationId "code.android.abdulrahman.com.menubarAndMore"
        minSdkVersion 26
        targetSdkVersion 26
        versionCode 1
        versionName "1.0"
        testInstrumentationRunner
            "androidx.test.runner.AndroidJUnitRunner"
    }
```

8.2.3.2   Import Toolbar

The second action that you need to do to support the toolbar creation is to import the toolbar class from the Android library into your code. An example of importing a toolbar class into your code is given below.

```
androidx.appcompat.widget.Toolbar;
public class MainActivity extends AppCompatActivity {...}
```

When using Android Studio, you can import an Android class into your code by pressing the *Alt* and *Enter* keys together.

8.2.4   Extending AppCompatActivity

Make your activity class extend the *AppCompatActivity* class as shown below:

```
... In MyActivity.java...
public class MyActivity extends AppCompatActivity {// ...}
```

AppCompatActivity is a class from the v7 appcompat support library and is now supported by the AndroidX library.

The support libraries are back-compatibility libraries that enable some features of recent versions of Android on older devices. For example, it enables the use of a toolbar for older devices using versions of Android as old as Android 2.1 which uses API level 7.

During app development, if you set the app's minSdkVersion to a low version that does not support the new features in newer APIs, use the support library to enable those features.

Note that starting with Android 9.0 (API level 28), there is a new support library called AndroidX. This new version of the support library contains the existing support library and also includes the latest components. You can still continue to use the older versions of the support libraries, those packaged as android.support.*. However, Google has all the new libraries in the AndroidX package. We recommend using the AndroidX package for all of your projects.

8.2.5   Specify a Theme with NO ActionBar

Once you have decided to use a toolbar in your app, you have to specify that you are not going to use an actionbar. You need to specify that inside your app's manifest file. This is required because a toolbar is an extension/replacement of the actionbar. To do so, you need to set your app's theme to a theme with no actionbar. This step is done inside the manifest file using the **android:theme** attribute inside the application element:

```
android:theme ="@style/MyNoActionBarTheme">
```

An example, where android:theme is set to a no actionbar style, is shown in Listing 8.2.

Listing 8.2 AndroidManifest.xml setting app theme to NoActionBar.

```xml
<?xml version="1.0" encoding="utf-8"?>
<manifest >
  <application
    ...
    android:theme="@style/MyNoActionBarTheme">
    ...
  </application>
</manifest>
```

You also need to make sure that the no actionbar theme you are going to use is defined inside the style file. An example where the app theme defined inside the style file, i.e., the styles.xml file inside the res folder, that has no actionbar is shown below:

```xml
<style name="MyNoActionBarTheme"
          parent="Theme.AppCompat.Light.NoActionBar">
```

8.2.6 Adding Toolbar Element to the Layout

The last step in the toolbar development is to add the toolbar element to the activity layout XML file. Listing 8.3 is an example of the toolbar element declaration inside the layout file:

Listing 8.3 activity_main.xml layout file with Toolbar element.

```xml
<?xml version="1.0" encoding="utf-8"?>
<LinearLayout ...>
...
    <androidx.appcompat.widget.Toolbar
    android:id="@+id/my_toolbar"
    android:layout_width="match_parent"
    android:layout_height="?attr/actionBarSize"
    android:background="@color/colorPrimary"
    />
/LinearLayout>
```

Now, it is time to go back to the MainActivity to put the nuts and bolts together. See the code snippet in Listing 8.4 in which the toolbar object, myToolbar, has been initialized and the activity's toolbar has been set.

Listing 8.4 MainActivity.java where the toolbar is initialized and set.

```
import androidx.appcompat.app.AppCompatActivity;
import androidx.appcompat.widget.Toolbar;
public class MainActivity extends AppCompatActivity {
  @Override
  protected void onCreate(Bundle savedInstanceState) {
    super.onCreate(savedInstanceState);
    setContentView(R.layout.activity_main);
    ...
    Toolbar myToolbar = findViewById(R.id.my_toolbar);
    setSupportActionBar(myToolbar);
  ...
}
```

The activity class has a method called *setSupportActionBar* that you can use to set a toolbar for the activity. By now, the toolbar is integrated with the activity but is empty. The next step is to create a menu and menu items and to add the menu to the toolbar.

8.2.7   Menu Interface

Menus are commonly used in many applications. They provide a familiar and consistent user experience. You need menus to enable users to do actions and have options in your activities. You can create three types of menus, and they are options menu and app bar, context menu and contextual action mode, and popup menu. We will study these menu types and give examples of how to create them.

8.2.8   Options Menu and App Bar

The options menu and app bar is a collection of menu items for an activity. Using the options menu, you use the app bar to present common user actions. It's where you should place actions like Search, Compose an Email, and Settings.

8.2.8.1   Menu Inflater and Click Handling

The menu is a Java interface that can be used to manage menu items. By default, every activity supports a menu of actions or options. You can add items to the menu and handle clicks on menu times.

You can add menu items by inflating an XML file into the menu using the MenuInflater   class   and   handle   item   clicks   by   implementing   the onOptionsItemSelected(MenuItem)   and   onContextItemSelected(MenuItem) methods. Below, we will see an example of how to use the menu inflater class and the onOptionItemSelected method.

8.2.8.2   Define Menu XML File

One way to define the menu is by creating an XML file inside the project's **res/menu/** directory and including the following elements in the file.

  <menu>

Defines a menu, which is a container for menu items. That is, a <menu> element must be the root element for the file and can hold one or more <item> and <group> elements.

  <item>

Represents a single item in a menu. <Item> elements may contain a nested <menu> element in order to create a submenu.

  <group>

Invisible containers for <item> elements. It allows you to categorize your items so that they share properties such as an active state and visibility. <group> elements are an optional element.

8.2.8.3   Menu Item Properties

The menu item has many important properties. These include id, icon, title, orderInCagetory, and showAsAction. These properties are described below.

(a) **android:id**: this is a unique id to the item. It is referenced by the application when used.
(b) **android:icon**: this is a drawable resource, i.e., a PNG file to be used as a menu item icon.
(c) **android:title**: this is a text for the overflow menu.
(d) **android:orderInCategory**: this attribute takes an int value and indicates the item's importance. Since items are drawn in order of importance, the value dictates the order in which the menu items will appear within the menu when it is displayed. The lower the int value, the more important the item becomes.
(e) **app:showAsAction**: this attribute is used to specify whether or not the icon should be drawn. The attribute values are always, ifRoom, and never. One of the three options (always, ifRoom, never) needs to be assigned to the property. Based on the selected option, the icon would be drawn or not. More detail on the valid values for the showAsAction attribute is provided below.

8.2.8.4   orderInCategory Attribute

The attribute *showAsAction* can have one of the following values.

1. **ifRoom**: Only place this item in the app bar if there is room for it. If there is no room for all the items marked "ifRoom," the items with the lowest orderInCategory values are displayed as actions, and the remaining items are displayed in the overflow menu.
2. **withText**: Include the title text (defined by android:title) with the action item. You can include this value along with one of the others as a flag set, by separating them with a pipe-symbol |.
3. **Never**: Never place this item in the app bar. Instead, list the item in the app bar's overflow menu. This is another way to say put the item in the overflow menu.
4. **Always**: Place this item in the app bar. Avoid using this unless the item must always appear in the toolbar. Setting multiple items to always can result in them overlapping with other UIs in the app bar.

The code snippet in Listing 8.5 shows the menu and menu items used in our demo app.

Listing 8.5 main_activity_actions.xml layout file for declaring a menu.

```xml
<?xml version="1.0" encoding="utf-8"?>
<menu xmlns:android="http://schemas.android.com/apk/res/android"
  xmlns:app="http://schemas.android.com/apk/res-auto"
  xmlns:tools="http://schemas.android.com/tools"
  tools:context=".MainActivity">
    <item android:id="@+id/action_one"
    android:title="One"
    android:icon="@drawable/facebook"
    android:orderInCategory="101"
    app:showAsAction="always" />
    <item android:id="@+id/action_two"
    android:title="Two"
    android:icon="@drawable/twitter"
    android:orderInCategory="102"
    app:showAsAction="always" />
    <item android:id="@+id/action_three"
    android:title="Three"
    android:icon="@drawable/setting"
    android:orderInCategory="103"
    app:showAsAction="always" />
    <item android:id="@+id/action_about"
    android:title="About"
    android:orderInCategory="105"
    app:showAsAction="never" />
</menu>
```

Values 101, 102, 103, and 105 represent the menu items' order from left to right. Figure 8.1 summarizes what we have discussed so far about menu creation.

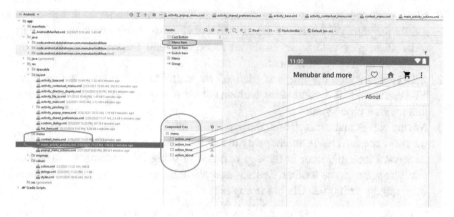

Fig. 8.1 Menu XML file inside the Data Studio showing the elements involved in the Menu creation

8.2.8.5   Methods from the Activity Class for Menu

Below, we describe two activity methods, *onCreateOptionsMenu* and *onMenuItemSelected*, that you can use when dealing with the menu. You can see a full implementation of these two methods in the MainActivity source code of our demo app.

8.2.8.5.1   onCreateOptionsMenu(Menu menu)

To specify the options menu for an activity's toolbar that has been defined inside the res/menu/filename.xml file, you need to implement the onCreateOptionsMenu() callback method. In this method, you *inflate* the menu resource (res/menu/ filename.xml) into the menu passed to the method which will then be displayed in the toolbar. The menu inflation is done using the MenuInflater class and its inflate method. The onCreateOptionsMenu method is automatically called by the activity to initialize the contents of the activity's standard options menu. This is only called once, and the default implementation populates the menu with standard system menu items. For our example, we implemented the onCreateOptionsMenu inside the MainActivity.java class as follows:

```java
@Override
public boolean onCreateOptionsMenu(Menu menu) {
    // Inflate the menu items for use in the Toolbar
    MenuInflater inflater = getMenuInflater();
    inflater.inflate(R.menu.main_activity_actions, menu);
    return true;
}
```

8.2.8.5.2   onMenuItemSelected(MenuItem menuItem)

The onMenuItemSelected(MenuItem menuItem) method needs to be overwritten. This function responds to an item on the menu being selected. A code snippet of our implementation for the second method is shown in Listing 8.6.

Listing 8.6 A onMenuItemSelected() method implementation.

```
@Override
public boolean onOptionsItemSelected(MenuItem mi) {
  int id = mi.getItemId();
  switch (id) {
    case R.id.action_one:
      snackbar.show();
      break;
    case R.id.action_two:
      AlertDialog.Builder builder = new AlertDialog.Builder(this);
      builder.setTitle("Do you want to go back?");
      ...
      break;
    case R.id.action_three:
      AlertDialog.Builder customDialog =
                   new AlertDialog.Builder(this);
      ....
      break
    case R.id.action_about:
     Toast.makeText(this, "Version 1.0," +
              " Abdul-Rahman Mawlood-Yunis",
          Toast.LENGTH_LONG).show();
  }
  return true;
}
```

8.2.8.6   Toolbar Summary

In summary, you need to follow the steps below to add a toolbar to your app:

1. Add a toolbar to your activity layout.
2. In the activity's OnCreate() method, get the toolbar, and call the setActionToolbar() method to set the toolbar for your activity.
3. Create a menu XML file with the items in the res/menu/ directory.
4. Inside the onCreateOptionsMenu() method, inflate the menu resource using the MenuInflater class and inflate method. The onCreateOptionsMenu() method is invoked automatically by the activity.
5. Handle each menu item in the onOptionsItemSelected() method.

Figures 8.2 and 8.3 show the menu and toolbar we have created for our demo app.

Fig. 8.2 Toolbar with four items

Fig. 8.3 App snapshot with Toolbar on the top

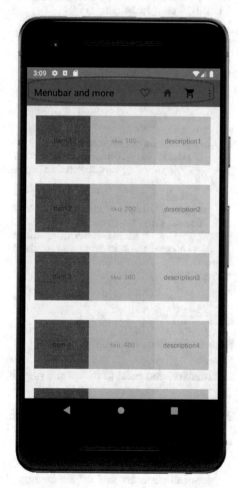

You have probably noticed that we have used the snackbar.show() method in our code. This is another Android widget used to display a short message at the bottom of the screen to provide feedback to the user. In our demo app, if you click on the heart icon on the menu bar, a snackbar notification will appear at the bottom of the screen.

8.2.9 *Context Menu*

A context menu is a floating menu that appears when the user performs *a long click* on a view. It provides actions or options that affect the selected content. The contextual action mode displays action items that affect the selected content in a bar or window at the top of the screen and allows the user to select multiple items.

To create a floating context menu, you need to do three things. *First*, you need to register the view object to which the context menu should be associated with by calling this method *registerForContextMenu*() and pass to it a view object.

If your activity uses a list view or a grid view (we use a list view in our demo app) and you want each item in the list to provide the same context menu, register the context menu for the list view or grid view. This is can be done like this: **registerForContextMenu(getListView());**.

Second, you need to implement the *onCreateContextMenu()* method in your activity. When the registered view receives a long-click event, the system calls the onCreateContextMenu() method. This is where you define the menu items, usually by inflating a menu resource file. The code snippet below shows the onCreateContextMenu implementation where the menu file is inflated. The menu file is called ***context_menu*** and is saved inside the *res/menu* folder of the project.

```
@Override
public void onCreateContextMenu(ContextMenu menu, View v,
                ContextMenu.ContextMenuInfo menuInfo) {
  super.onCreateContextMenu(menu, v, menuInfo);
  MenuInflater inflater = getMenuInflater();
  inflater.inflate(R.menu.context_menu, menu);
}
```

The MenuInflater class allows you to inflate the context menu from a menu resource file. An example of a menu resource is shown in Listing 8.7. The onCreateContextMenu callback method parameters include the view object that the user selected, a context menu object, and a context menu info object. The latter provides additional information about the item selected. If your activity has several views that each provides a different context menu, you can use these parameters to determine which context menu to inflate.

Listing 8.7 An example of a menu context file.

```
<?xml version="1.0" encoding="utf-8"?>
<menu xmlns:android="http://schemas.android.com/apk/res/android"
  android:layout_width="match_parent"
  android:layout_height="wrap_content"
  android:background="@color/gray"
  android:padding="10dp">
  <item android:title="@string/update"
```

```
        android:id="@+id/c_updat"/>
    <item android:title="@string/delete"
        android:id="@+id/c_delete"/>
</menu>
```

Third, you need to implement the onContextItemSelected() method. When the user selects a menu item, the system calls the onContextItemSelected method to perform the appropriate action. The code snippet in Listing 8.8 shows the implementation of the onContextItemSelected() method.

Listing 8.8 An onContextItemSelected() method implementation.

```
@Override
public boolean onContextItemSelected(MenuItem item) {
  super.onContextItemSelected(item);
  AdapterView.AdapterContextMenuInfo info =
      (AdapterView.AdapterContextMenuInfo) item.getMenuInfo();
  switch (item.getItemId()) {
    case R.id.c_updat:
     // your code goes here
      return true;
    case R.id.c_delete:
     // your code goes here
      return true;
    default:
      return super.onContextItemSelected(item);
  }
}
```

For a complete example, see the demo app's source code. Figure 8.4 shows the contextual menu in our demo app. If you perform a long click on any name in the list, the menu should open and give you two options, or actions, to choose from.

8.2.10 Popup Menu

A popup menu displays a list of items in a vertical list to an attached view that has been invoked. The popup menu is useful for providing an overflow of actions that relate to specific content and for providing options for the second part of a command. Actions in a popup menu should not directly affect the corresponding content that is what contextual actions are for. Rather, the popup menu is used to extend actions that relate to parts of your activity.

The code snippet in Listing 8.9 is an example of an XML menu file for the popup menu.

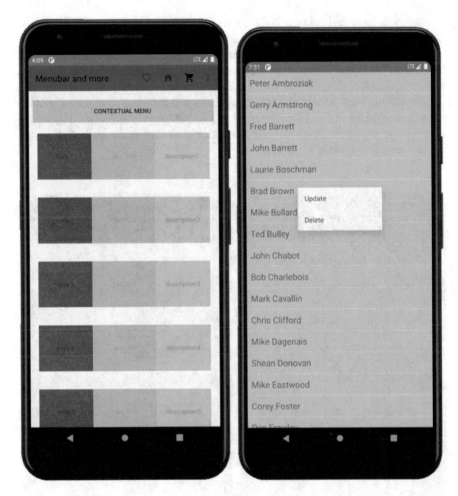

Fig. 8.4 Shows a contextual menu when the user clicks on an item in the list

Listing 8.9 An example of an XML file for a popup menu.

```xml
<?xml version="1.0" encoding="utf-8"?>
<menu xmlns:android="http://schemas.android.com/apk/res/android">
  <item android:title="@string/add"/>
  <item android:title="@string/delete"/>
  <item android:title="@string/update"/>
  <item android:title="@string/cancel_menu"/>
  <item android:title="@string/download_link"/>
  <item android:title="@string/copy_link_address"/>
  <item android:title="@string/share_link"/>
</menu>
```

Once you have defined your XML menu file, you need to follow the three steps below to show the popup menu in your app.

First, instantiate a popup menu with its constructor. The PopupMenu class constructor takes the current application context and the view to which the menu should be attached. *Second*, use the MenuInflater class to inflate your menu resource into the menu object returned by the PopupMenu.getMenu() method. *Third*, call the show() method from the PopupMenu class, i.e., PopupMenu.show(). Figure 8.5 displays the popup menu shown when the user clicks on an image button giving the user multiple options to perform.

Fig. 8.5 Shows a popup menu when the user clicks on an image button

The menu is dismissed when the user selects an item or touches outside the menu area. You can listen for the dismiss event using the PopupMenu.OnDismissListener interface. The steps to create a popup menu button that is used to invoke a popup menu and inflate a menu are implemented in the code snippet in Listing 8.10. For a complete example, see the source code of the app developed for this chapter.

Listing 8.10 A popup menu definition and handling example.

```
<?xml version="1.0" encoding="utf-8"?>
<android.support.constraint.ConstraintLayout ...
 tools:context=".MyPopupMenu">
 <ImageButton
   android:layout_width="wrap_content"
   android:layout_height="wrap_content"
   android:layout_marginStart="10dp"
   android:layout_marginTop="25dp"
   android:layout_marginEnd="10dp"
   android:layout_marginBottom="200dp"
   android:contentDescription="@string/descr_overflow_button"
   android:onClick="showPopupMenu"
   android:src="@drawable/flag"
...
</android.support.constraint.ConstraintLayout>

public void showPopupMenu (View view) {
  android.widget.PopupMenu myPopupMenu =
      new android.widget.PopupMenu(this, view);
  MenuInflater inflater = myPopupMenu.getMenuInflater();
  inflater.inflate(R.menu.popup_menu_actions, myPopupMenu.getMenu());
  myPopupMenu.show();
}
```

8.3   Dialog Boxes and the Camera App

In this part, we will study the creation of dialog boxes and how to access the camera app in your code using the implicit Intent class.

8.3.1   Dialog Boxes

A dialog box is a small box or window that prompts the user to enter additional information or to make yes/ok or no/cancel decisions. A dialog box is normally used for situations that require users to take an action before they can continue. In our example, when the *home* icon on the toolbar is clicked, the dialog box appears as shown below (Fig. 8.6):

Fig. 8.6 A snapshot of the
demo app screen showing a
dialog box

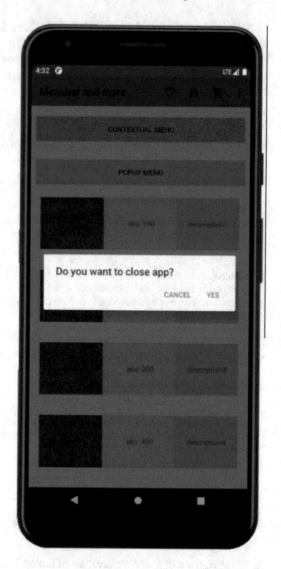

The creation of the dialog boxes is considered flexible. It can be created using the
AlertDialog Java class which existed before Android devices were invented.

You can follow the builder pattern to create a dialog box. Using a builder pattern,
a complex object gets built in multiple steps. In each step, a simple object is created,
and then the newly created object is used in the next step of the creation process. For
the demo app, we follow the builder pattern to create a dialog box and to keep a chain
of function calls as shown in Listing 8.11.

Listing 8.11 Creating an AlertDialog box.

```
{ ...
AlertDialog.Builder builder =
            new AlertDialog.Builder(this);
        builder.setTitle("Do you want to go back?");
        // Add the buttons
        builder.setPositiveButton(R.string.ok,
          new DialogInterface.OnClickListener() {
            public void onClick(DialogInterface dialog, int id) {
                // User clicked OK button, you put Ok code here
                finish();
            } });
        builder.setNegativeButton(R.string.cancel,
            new DialogInterface.OnClickListener() {
            public void onClick(DialogInterface dialog, int id) {
                // User cancelled the dialog, you put cancel code here
            } });
        // Create the AlertDialog
        AlertDialog dialog = builder.create();
        dialog.show();
    ...
}
```

If you need a third button, a neutral button, add the following code to the code snippet above.

```
.setNeutralButton(R.string.Neutral,
        new DialogInterface.OnClickListener() {
            public void onClick(DialogInterface dialog, int id) {
                // What to do on Neutral button goes here
            } });
```

The setPositiveButton() method returns the AlertDialog.Builder object; that is, how you can invoke a chain of method calls on the same object. The method signature for the setPositiveButton is shown below:

```
public AlertDialog.Builder setPositiveButton
            (int textId, DialogInterface.OnClickListener listener);
```

The four important parts of dialog boxes that you need to remember are:

1. Text—What are you telling/asking the user?
2. Positive Button—A button for accepting.
3. Negative Button—A button for rejecting/canceling.
4. Handling the click events—This is done by creating an anonymous class of type DialogInterface.OnClickListener() and implementing the *onClick()* method of the interface. The code for this step can be as follows:

```
new DialogInterface.OnClickListener() {
        public void onClick(DialogInterface dialog, int id) {
            // What to do on the Neutral button goes here
        } });
```

Once a builder has all the information, call the create() method to instantiate the dialog box. Then, call the show() method to draw the dialog box. Both calls can be done in one step like this: builder.create().show().

In our app, we created a text message, positive and negative buttons, when the home icon on the toolbar is clicked. For a complete example, see the source code of the app developed for this chapter.

8.3.2 Custom Dialog Boxes

If your application requires a special action or dialog box design, you can create a custom dialog box. To do so, follow all the steps we described above, and create the special layout that you want your dialog box to have. That is, you need to do the following:

- You must create a specific layout file and inflate it for your dialog box. The layout inflation is done as follows:

```
LayoutInflater inflater = getActivity().getLayoutInflater();
builder.setView(inflater.inflate(R.layout.YourLayout, null));
```

- Set the positive/negative buttons for the builder object:

```
.setPositiveButton( ... )
.setNegativeButton( ... )
.create().show()
```

Before moving to another important topic, take 2 min to think of what we have done so far. Here is what we have discussed so far in this chapter:

- Toolbars allow you to put menus at the top of your activity. There is some work involved in getting it set up, but once you are done, add menu items to your menu resource, and handle item selection in the onOptionsItemSelected() method.
- Dialog boxes allow you to quickly create custom windows to interact with the user. You can also create your layout and attach callbacks.

8.3.3 Access a Phone's Default Camera App

To continue with the interface and design aspect of the app, we will study common or *implicit intent*. So far, we have used the intent object with the StartActivity method to launch a new activity or second activity in our apps, i.e., we used intent explicitly. There are other uses of the intent object where it can be used to start an activity in another app by describing a simple action we would like to happen. For example, an intent can be used to view a map, start an email or an alarm clock app, or start the camera app to take a picture and return the results. This type of intent is called *implicit intent*. It does not explicitly specify another activity to start but instead specifies an action to take place and provides some data to perform the action with.

Below, we show an example where *implicit intent* is used with a *MediaStore* class and its image capture action, i.e., **MediaStore.*ACTION_IMAGE_CAPTURE***, to access a phone's default camera app, take a picture, and return it.

The manifest file is updated to give the MainActivity *permission* to access the default camera from your device. To give permission, add the following line of code to the manifest file.

```
<uses-feature
android:name="android.hardware.camera" android:required="true" />
```

Without permission, your application will crash because a security exception will be thrown. The code snippet shown in Listing 8.12 is a callback handler for the image button. It launches your phone's default camera application by using implicit intent instead of explicitly starting an activity class:

Listing 8.12 A code snippet for taking pictures using a phone camera.

```
public void imageClicked(View imageView) {
    ImageButton btnImg = findViewById(R.id.btn_img);
    Intent takePictureIntent =
        new Intent(MediaStore.ACTION_IMAGE_CAPTURE);
        if (takePictureIntent.resolveActivity(
            getPackageManager()) != null) {
            startActivityForResult(takePictureIntent,
                REQUEST_IMAGE_CAPTURE);
    }
}
```

Now, whenever you press the image button, you should be able to take a picture using your device. The *startActivityForResult* method triggers the *onActivityResult* method which sets the image of the button to the picture taken. The code for the onActivityResult method is shown below.

```
@Override
protected void onActivityResult(
int requestCode, int resultCode, Intent data) {
    if (requestCode == REQUEST_IMAGE_CAPTURE &&
        resultCode == RESULT_OK) {
        Bundle extras = data.getExtras();
        Bitmap imageBitmap = (Bitmap) extras.get("data");
```

```
      ImageButton btnImg = findViewById(R.id.btn_img);
      btnImg.setImageBitmap(imageBitmap);
      try {
        saveImage(imageBitmap);
      } catch (Exception e) {
      }
    }
  }
}
```

The demo app has been updated to include a button to take pictures and add them to the image button (Fig. 8.7).

Fig. 8.7 Updated demo app
to taking pictures

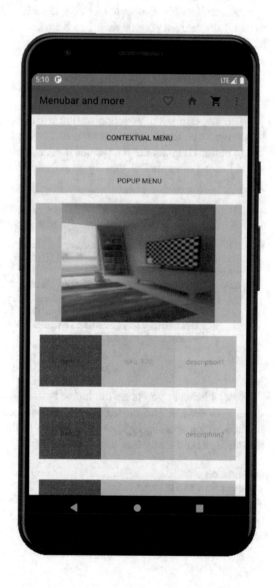

There are several implicit intents that you can use to perform common actions. For example, you can use ACTION_DIAL to call a phone number. In this case, you construct intent as follows:

```
Intent intent = new Intent(Intent.ACTION_DIAL);
   intent.setData(Uri.parse("tel:" + phoneNumber));
```

Similarly, you can use implicit intent to set a timer or clock, insert an entry into a calendar, etc.

8.3.4   Starting Activities for Results

In the example above, we used the *startActivityForResult* method to capture images using the MediaStore.*ACTION_IMAGE_CAPTURE* action. This method is different from the *startActivity* we have seen so far. If you want results back from the activity once it is done, use the startActivityForResult() method instead of the startActivity() method.

The activity class has two versions of the startActivityForResult methods. The signature for the two methods is as follows:

```
public void startActivityForResult (Intent intent, int requestCode,
                             Bundle options);
public void startActivityForResult (Intent intent, int requestCode);
```

In our demo app, we used the startActivityForResult method which takes two parameters. The first one is the *intent*, and the second one is the *caller id* or *request code*. The id would be used to check the caller in the *onActivityResult()* method. This is the method that will be executed after returning from the activity started with the startActivityForResult() method. For the result to be returned from the activity, the request code has to be >=0.

The activity class has two other methods that are commonly used in association with the startActivityForResult method. These methods are *setResult*(int) and *finish*(). The setResult() method is used to send values, e.g., *Result_OK* or *Result_cancelled*, back to the caller activity. The finish() method is used to end the current activity and return to the previous activity (back one in history). When you call the finish() method, you are manually shutting down the activity.

The snippet code below shows how the second activity can use the setResult() and finish() methods from the activity class to end the current activity and return the constant RESULT_OK to the caller activity.

```
Intent resultIntent = new Intent();
   resultIntent.putExtra("name", value);
   ...
   setResult(Activity.RESULT_OK, resultIntent);
   finish();
```

The signature for both methods, the setResult and onActivityForResult methods, is as follows:

```
Public final void setResult(int resultCode) and
 protected void onActivityResult (int requestCode,
                                    int resultCode, Intent data).
```

Once inside the called activity, you use setResult (RESULT_OK). The RESULT_OK sets the value of the resultCode parameter of the caller activity. The sequence of the message calls for the steps above is presented in Fig. 8.8.

8.3.4.1   Do It Yourself

Modify the demo app to invoke other default apps instead of the camera app currently used. For example, invoke Alarm Clock with the *ACTION_SET_ALARM*, or invoke Email with the *ACTION_SENDTO*, *ACTION_SEND*, or *ACTION_SEND_MULTIPLE* instead of the camera app. In the example below, ACTION_DIAL is used to dial a number.

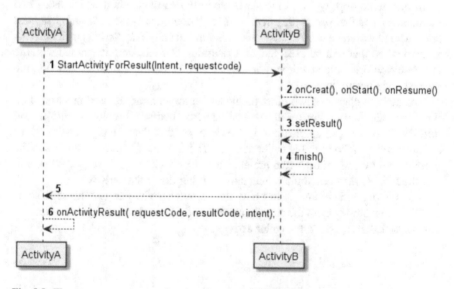

Fig. 8.8 The message sequence calls when StartActivityForResult is used

```
Intent intent = new Intent(Intent.ACTION_DIAL);
  intent.setData(Uri.parse("tel:" + phoneNumber));
```

8.3.5   *Activity Result in AndroidX*

Starting another activity doesn't need to be a one-way operation. You can also start another activity and receive a result back. As described in the previous section, the startActivityForResult() and onActivityResult() methods enable you to do so. The new Android version, however, recommends using the ActivityResult API introduced in AndroidX.

An example of how to use the latest classes and methods is shown in Listings 8.13 and 8.14. The code snippet shows how to use the *ActivityResultLauncher* class, the *registerForActivityResult()* method call, and the *launch()* and *public void onActivityResult(ActivityResult result)* methods to receive a result back from an Activity. Note that, in this example, the *onBackPressed()* method is also implemented. This method is called when the user presses the back button on their device.

Listing 8.13 Using the Activity Result API introduced in AndroidX.

```
package com.code.abdulrahman.activityresult;
import android.app.Activity;
import android.content.Intent;
import android.os.Bundle;
import android.view.View;
import android.widget.Button;
import android.widget.TextView;
import androidx.activity.result.ActivityResult;
import androidx.activity.result.ActivityResultCallback;
import androidx.activity.result.ActivityResultLauncher;
import androidx.activity.result.contract.ActivityResultContracts;
import androidx.annotation.Nullable;
import androidx.appcompat.app.AppCompatActivity;

public class MainActivity extends AppCompatActivity {

  ActivityResultLauncher<Intent> mStartForResult =
      registerForActivityResult(
          new ActivityResultContracts.StartActivityForResult(),
      new ActivityResultCallback<ActivityResult>() {
        @Override
        public void onActivityResult(ActivityResult result) {
          TextView textView = findViewById(R.id.textView);
          if (result.getResultCode() == Activity.RESULT_OK) {
            textView.setBackgroundColor(getResources().
                getColor(android.R.color.holo_blue_light));
```

```
              textView.setText ( "result is recieved in this method") ;
           } else {
             textView.setText (
                "back button pressed, we did not get result ") ;
             textView.setBackgroundColor (getResources ().
                getColor (android.R.color.holo_green_light) ) ;
           }
         }
      }) ;
    @Override
    public void onCreate (@Nullable Bundle savedInstanceState ) {
      super.onCreate (savedInstanceState) ;
      setContentView (R.layout.activity_main) ;
      Button startButton = findViewById (R.id.startButton) ;
      startButton.setOnClickListener (new View.OnClickListener() {
        @Override
        public void onClick (View view) {
          // The launcher with the Intent you want to start
          mStartForResult.launch (new Intent (MainActivity.this
             , SomeActivity.class) ) ;
        }
      }) ;
    }
}
```

Listing 8.14 setResult and finish methods are used with the new Activity Result API.

```
package com.code.abdulrahman.activityresult;
import android.app.Activity;
import android.content.Intent;
import android.os.Bundle;
import android.util.Log;
import android.view.View;
import android.widget.Button;
import androidx.appcompat.app.AppCompatActivity;

public class SomeActivity extends AppCompatActivity {
  @Override
  protected void onCreate (Bundle savedInstanceState) {
    super.onCreate (savedInstanceState) ;
    setContentView (R.layout.activity_some) ;
    Log.i ("SomeActivity", "SomeActivity") ;
    Button return_result_button = findViewById (
      R.id.return_result_button) ;
  return_result_button.setOnClickListener (new View.OnClickListener() {
      @Override
      public void onClick (View view) {
        setResult (Activity.RESULT_OK) ;
```

```
            finish();
        }
    });
}
@Override
public void onBackPressed() {
    super.onBackPressed();
    setResult(Activity.RESULT_CANCELED);
    finish();
}
}
```

8.4 Saving Data with SharedPreferences

Android allows you to store user data in several different ways; these include using files, databases, and content providers. In this part of the chapter, we will study saving data in an XML file using the SharedPreferences interface as well as saving data in text files. In the next chapter, we will study both the SQLite database and the content provider.

8.4.1 SharedPreferences Interface

The activity's default behavior is that if for any reason an activity gets destroyed, i.e., an app screen is closed, any data entered into that screen is lost. Since activities can be destroyed, for example, if the user clicks on the back button or if the Android OS needs to reclaim resources and kills activities that are not in the focus, we need to handle saving preferences/entered data.

Losing data entered into screens, editable text areas, and selection choices are something that should not happen in your app. You should save user preferences data, and if the user decided to re-open the app, previously entered data shouldn't have to be re-entered. The *SharedPreferences* interface enables apps to have such features, saving and retrieving data, by saving a small amount of entered data into an XML file. Your preferences data is saved in an XML file in the key/value pair format. The *SharedPreferences* interface enables accessing and modifying preferences data using methods from the context class. The key/value pair format used by the SharedPreferences interface is similar to the way that the Map and Set classes in Java insert and retrieve data using key/value pairs.

Saving and retrieving data from a local file and without the user having to intervene can be used to add features to your app similar to the caching technique used by the browser, where the app remembers the data you last entered into the app. Furthermore, data entered into forms, user-selected checkboxes, and other user actions can be saved/loaded into/from a file for later use.

In this part, we focus on using the SharedPreferences interface to save a small amount of user data between activity calls.

8.4.1.1 SharedPreferences Creation and Use

There is only one instance of the SharedPreferences interface that all clients can use. To use a SharedPreferences interface, you need a SharedPreferences reference that points to your preferences file. The *getSharedPreferences()* method from the context class can be used to get a reference to the preferences file. Here is how you can do it:

```
SharedPreferences prefs =
    getSharedPreferences(String fileName, int mode);
```

In the statement above, the string *fileName* specifies the name of the file. The *mode* parameter is the security permission. One possible mode option is Context.*MODE_PRIVATE*.

The return type of the getSharedPreferences() method is a SharedPreferences interface to create and read/write data to a file. MODE_PRIVATE is the default mode, where the preferences file can only be accessed by the calling application or all applications sharing the same user id.

To define two apps with a shared user id, both android:**sharedUserLabel** and android:**sharedUserId** entries must have the same values. The code snippet below shows the manifest content for two apps where they share the same user label and id.

```
//Application1
<manifest xmlns:android="http://schemas.android.com/apk/res/android"
    android:sharedUserLabel="@string/label_shared_user"
    android:sharedUserId="com.ar.wlu.example"
    package="com.ar.wlu.example.package1">
//Application2
<manifest xmlns:android="http://schemas.android.com/apk/res/android"
    android:sharedUserLabel="@string/label_shared_user"
    android:sharedUserId="com.ar.wlu.example"
    package="com.ar.wlu.example.package2">
```

The other file creation mode that you might want to know is *MODE_APPEND*. This is used with the openFileOutput(String, int) method. If the file already exists, this mode enables writing data to the end of the existing file instead of erasing it.

8.4.1.2 Editor Interface

To write data to your data preferences file, you must get the *Editor* interface from the SharedPreferences object. The Editor interface is used to access the SharedPreferences file. This is done as follows:

```
SharedPreferences.Editor edit = prefs.edit();
```

Modifications to the shared preferences file must go through an Editor object to ensure that the preferences values remain in a consistent state and to control when they are committed to storage. This is similar to declaring an interface for object A and thus providing a means for other objects to interact with object A without knowing its implementation details to protect the object from undesirable actions.

The Editor interface provides strong consistency; however, it might be slow. If you save and load data often, you should consider other means to save your data. For example, create a data object that will be readily available in the app's memory to save and retrieve data.

The Editor interface has multiple methods to save data to a file. The format of the method is putType(key, value), for example:

- putString(String key, String value)
- putFloat(String key, float f)
- putInt(String key, int i)
- Others

Objects that are returned from the get methods must be treated as *immutable* by the application, i.e., cannot be changed anymore.

8.4.1.3 Commit Method

You must call the Editor's commit() or apply() method when you are ready to save data, e.g., call the edit.apply() or edit.commit() method. Both methods have the same impact and write data to the file. The difference between the two is that the commit method returns a boolean value but the return type for the apply method is void. If you want to be sure that your data is written successfully before executing the next step in your code, use the return value of the commit method to check.

8.4.1.4 SharedPreferences Reading Methods

SharedPreferences has several methods to read data. The format of the methods is getType (key, value), for example:

- getInt(String key, int value) to get an int value related to the key
- getFloat(String key, float value) to get a float value related to the key

Fig. 8.9 Demo update with SharedPreferences button

8.4.1.5   Changes to Our Demo App

A new button called SharedPreferences has been added to the main page of our demo app. See the latest look of our demo app below, Fig. 8.9. The view of the app when the SharedPreferences button is clicked is also shown on the right-hand side.

8.4.1.6   Running and Testing the Demo App

Click on the SharedPreferences button of the demo, and check it out. Try inputting data and then destroying it by exiting the app. Then, start the app again; your data should be saved. Below, we describe the layout and the code for the SharedPreferences activity in detail.

8.4.2 Layout for Shared Preferences Activity

The XML snippet for the activity shared_preferences layout file is shown in Listing 8.15. The content of the file should be familiar to you since we have seen similar layouts earlier in this chapter and in previous chapters. The XML file includes two onClick callbacks methods to "save" data or "cancel" and return to the main page. If "save" is selected, the input data is stored in the SharedPreferences file. If "cancel" is clicked, nothing is saved, and we return to the main view of the app.

Listing 8.15 activity_shared_preferences.xml layout file.

```xml
<LinearLayout
  xmlns:android="http://schemas.android.com/apk/res/android"
  android:layout_width="match_parent"
  android:layout_height="match_parent"
  android:orientation="vertical">
  <TextView
    android:text="@string/email"/ >
  <EditText
    android:inputType="textEmailAddress"
    android:singleLine="true" />
  <TextView
    android:text="@string/gender"/ >
  <RadioGroup
    android:id="@+id/radioGender"
    android:layout_width="match_parent"
    android:layout_height="wrap_content"
    android:layout_margin="5dp"
    android:orientation="horizontal" >
    <RadioButton
      android:text="@string/gender_female" />
    <RadioButton
      android:text="@string/gender_male" />
  </RadioGroup>
  <LinearLayout
    android:layout_width="match_parent"
    android:layout_height="wrap_content"
    android:layout_margin="5dp" >
    <Button
      android:onClick="onSaveClicked"
      android:text="@string/button_save" >
    </Button>
    <Button
      android:onClick="onCancelClicked"
      android:text="@string/button_cancel" >
    </Button>
  </LinearLayout>
</LinearLayout>
```

8.4.3 How SharedPreferencesActivity Code Works

Now, let us discuss how the SharedPreferencesActivity code works. In addition to the onCreate() method and save and cancel buttons, the code has three major methods: load, update, and save user data. We describe each of these methods thoroughly in this section.

8.4.3.1 OnCreate()

The SharedPreferencesActivity code extends AppCompatActivity. The onCreate() method of the activity sets the activity's view and calls a helper method, loadUserData(), to load saved data, if any. You also need to note that the first time the app runs, there is no data to be loaded. See the code snippet in Listing 8.16.

Listing 8.16 SharedPreferencesActivity onCreate method.

```
public class SharedPreferencesActivity extends AppCompatActivity {
  private static final String TAG = "CP670";
  @Override
  protected void onCreate(Bundle savedInstanceState) {
    super.onCreate(savedInstanceState);
    setContentView(R.layout.activity_shared_preferences);
    loadUserData();
  }
  ...
}
```

Once a user inputs data and clicks the save button, the *onSaveClicked()* method calls *saveUserData()* and displays a toast informing the user that their data is saved. See the code snippet in Listing 8.17.

Listing 8.17 Calling save user data method to save data in a file.

```
public void onSaveClicked(View v) {
  saveUserData();
  Toast.makeText(getApplicationContext(),
      getString(R.string.save_message),
      Toast.LENGTH_SHORT).show();
  Intent mIntent = new Intent(SharedPreferencesActivity.this,
      MainActivity.class);
  startActivity(mIntent);
}
```

If the *Cancel* button is clicked, nothing happens other than displaying a toast message and returning to the main menu. The onCancelClickedCode is shown in Listing 8.18.

Listing 8.18 SharedPreferencesActivity onCancelClickedCode method.

```
public void onCancelClicked(View v) {
  Toast.makeText(getApplicationContext(),
    getString(R.string.cancel_message), Toast.LENGTH_SHORT).show();
  Intent mIntent = new Intent(SharedPreferencesActivity.this,
    MainActivity.class);
  startActivity(mIntent);
}
```

An important part of the onCreate() method is loading the preferences. Let us look into the loadUserData() method and learn more about it.

8.4.3.2 loadUserData()

Once the app starts, the onCreate() method invokes loadUserData(). The first time the app starts, no user data is stored in the SharedPreferences file.

The loadUserData() method gets the shared preferences file name from the strings.xml file using the getString() method like this:

```
String file_name = getString(R.string.preference_name);
```

The file name is used to get a reference to the *SharedReference* interface using the getSharedPreferences() method. This step is done like this:

```
SharedPreferences myPrefs =
    getSharedPreferences(file_name, MODE_PRIVATE);
```

Even though it is not recommended to hardcode the file name, you can pass a string name instead of using file_name as shown below.

```
SharedPreferences myPrefs =
getSharedPreferences("my preferences file name", MODE_PRIVATE);
```

As discussed earlier in this chapter, getSharedPreferences() has two parameters, name and mode. The name parameter is the preferences file name, for example, the "my preferences file name" in this case. If a file by this name does not exist, it will be created. The mode parameter is the access mode. The MODE_PRIVATE specifies that the preferences file can only be accessed by the application that created it.

The getSharedPreferences() method returns a reference (e.g., myPrefs) to the file through which you can read/modify the file content. The SharedPreferences interface's behavior is similar to public static class variables. There is only one instance of the SharedPreferences file with a given name. All activities in the app will see the content of the SharedPreferences file.

8.4.3.3 Update SharedPreferences Content

To update or set the value of *preferences*, we first get the key, in our example, **key_email**, from the string.xml file and get the string value for the key. These steps are shown in the code snippet shown in Listing 8.19.

Listing 8.19 A method for retrieving data from SharedPreferences.

```
private void loadUserData() {
    // We can also use log.d to print to the LogCat
    Log.d(TAG, "loadUserData()");
    // Load and update all profile views
    // Get the shared preferences - create or retrieve the activity
    // preferences object
    String preference_file_name = getString(R.string.preference_name);
    SharedPreferences mPrefs =
     getSharedPreferences(preference_file_name, MODE_PRIVATE);
    // Load the user email
    String email_key = getString(R.string.preference_key_profile_email);
    String new_email_value = mPrefs.getString(email_key, " ");
    ((EditText) findViewById(R.id.editEmail)).setText(new_email_value);
    // Please Load gender info and set radio box
    String gender_key = getString(R.string.preference_key_profile_gender);
}
```

Note that, if you try to retrieve data from the preferences file when there is nothing stored with your key, the default value will be retrieved. For example, when using the statement below and no email was saved, an empty string is used as a default value.

```
String new_email_value = myPrefs.getString(email_key, " ");
```

A value, e.g., an email value, stored in the shared preferences file can be used to update the EditText on the device's screen. This is done by getting the view and setting its value to the retrieved data as follows:

```
((EditText) findViewById(R.id.editEmail)).setText(new_email_value);
```

The steps above apply to all widgets, i.e., EditText, RadioButton, Checkbox, etc., from the `shared_preferences layout.xml` file as shown in Listing 8.20.

Listing 8.20 Retrieving user data for multiple views from shared preferences.

```java
private void loadUserData() {
  // We can also use log.d to print to the LogCat
  Log.d(TAG, "loadUserData()");
  // Load and update all profile views
  // Get the shared preferences - create or retrieve the activity
  // preferences object
  String preference_file_name = getString(R.string.preference_name);
  SharedPreferences mPrefs =
   getSharedPreferences(preference_file_name, MODE_PRIVATE);
  // Load the user email
  String email_key = getString(R.string.preference_key_profile_email);
  String new_email_value = mPrefs.getString(email_key, " ");
  ((EditText) findViewById(R.id.editEmail)).setText(new_email_value);
  // Please Load gender info and set radio box
  String gender_key = getString(R.string.preference_key_profile_gender);

  int mIntValue = mPrefs.getInt(gender_key, -1);
  // In case there isn't one saved before:
  if (mIntValue >= 0) {
    // Find the radio button that should be checked.
    RadioButton radioBtn = (RadioButton) ((RadioGroup)
      findViewById(R.id.radioGender))
        .getChildAt(mIntValue);
    // Check the button.
    radioBtn.setChecked(true);
    Toast.makeText(getApplicationContext(),
        "number of the radioButton is : " + mIntValue,
        Toast.LENGTH_SHORT).show();
  }
}
```

Taking a close look to the code above, you will see that the RadioButtons store integer values and −1 is their default value. The default value is used if nothing has already been saved. The 0 and 1 values are stored for the gender buttons (female and male) based on their order in the RadioGroup. The final step, the Toast.makeText()

method call in the loading function, displays a toast with the RadioGroup value. Again, this toast is used to provide feedback to the user.

8.4.3.4 Saving Data in a Shared Preferences XML File

Once the loadUserData() method is completely executed, the screen is updated with the stored data, if there is any. Now, assume that the user enters a new email address and selects a different RadioButton. Once the user clicks the save button, the onSaveClicked() method calls the saveUserData() helper function, which in turn executes code to save the data. The steps for saving data in a SharedPreferences XML file are as follows:

1. Get the SharedPreferences file name.
2. Use the SharedPreferences file name, and obtain a reference to the SharedPreferences object. The code for these two steps are as follows:

```
String file_name = getString(R.string.preference_name);
SharedPreferences myPrefs = getSharedPreferences(
file_name, MODE_PRIVATE);
```

3. Create and clear the SharedPreferences.Editor object. This is done as follows:

```
SharedPreferences.Editor myEditor = myPrefs .edit();
myEditor.clear();
```

4. Get the key of the value you would like to update. To do so, use:

```
myEditor.putString(email_key, new_email_entered);
```

5. Finally, to save all the changes to the preferences file, use:

```
myEditor.commit();
```

Saving data in a SharedPreferences XML file may also include sending a toast to inform the user that the changes, in our example, the new email address and gender selection, have been successfully saved. The saveUserData() method code for our app is shown in Listing 8.21.

Listing 8.21 A code snippet for saving data in shared preferences.

```
private void saveUserData() {
  Log.d(TAG, "saveUserData()");
  // Getting the shared preferences editor
  String preference_file_name = getString(R.string.preference_name);
  SharedPreferences mPrefs = getSharedPreferences(preference_file_name,
                                MODE_PRIVATE);
  SharedPreferences.Editor mEditor = mPrefs.edit();
  mEditor.clear();
  // Save email information
  String email_key = getString(R.string.preference_key_profile_email);
  String new_email_entered = (String) ((EditText)
                  findViewById(R.id.editEmail)).getText().toString();
  mEditor.putString(email_key, new_email_entered);

  String gender_key = getString(R.string.preference_key_profile_gender);
  RadioGroup mRadioGroup = (RadioGroup) findViewById(R.id.radioGender);
  int mIntValue = mRadioGroup.indexOfChild(findViewById(mRadioGroup
      .getCheckedRadioButtonId()));
  mEditor.putInt(gender_key, mIntValue);
  // Commit all the changes into the shared preference
  mEditor.commit();
  Toast.makeText(getApplicationContext(), "saved name: " + gender_key,
      Toast.LENGTH_SHORT).show();
}
```

8.4.3.5   Do it Yourself

In our demo code, we used the onCreate() method to implement the SharedPreferences functionality. Can you think of another callback method where you can implement the same functionality? **Hint**: think of using the onStart() or onResume() method instead of the onCreate method. What is the trade-off?

8.5   Directory Structure and Saving Data in Files

Other data storage options available for Android apps include saving data in the app's internal or external files and folders. In this part of the chapter, we study internal and external file creation and access.

8.5.1   Internal Storage Location

Each app has its private directory on the device like the user account on the Linux and Windows servers. Therefore, the internal storage is a good place for internal app data. When the internal app storage is used, the app's private files are saved on the device file system. The file location is private; other apps, even users, cannot access it directly.

One thing you should remember about the internal storage is that when the user uninstalls an app that has been using the internal storage to save data/files, all the data and files are removed as well. It is for this reason that you should not save data/files on the internal storage when the data needs to be kept after uninstallation. For example, if your app is for drawing pictures or taking photos, and you save the drawings or photos on the internal storage, all your drawings or photos will be gone after uninstalling the app, something you should avoid.

8.5.2   External Storage Location

Every Android device supports storing data/files on the external data storage. To do that, however, your app needs to request read/write file permission. The external data storage can be an external USB storage, a folder outside where the app is installed, or an SD card that can physically be inserted/removed from the SD card port. The external data storage is mostly used when data needs to persist even after the app is uninstalled. They are also useful when data needs to be shared. However, an external storage may not be available all the time, for example, if the user removes the USB storage.

8.5.3   Standard Public Directories for Data/Files

Android provides standard public directories for data/files that should persist after uninstalling the app. For example, the user has one location for all their photos, ringtones, music, and such. Here, we are not talking about removable SD cards or USB drives, but non-removable directories, such as DCIM for storing pictures. That is, we are referring to the Android file system (Linux file directories).

On the Android file system, the root directory for the public external directories is confusingly named sdcard. To remove this confusion, remember that there are two types of external storages, both called sdcard. One is a removable card; you can remove it from the device; hence, it is external. The second one is non-removable; it is a directory on Android's file structure. It is called external because it is outside of the app's local directory.

Fig. 8.10 The location of a file created with the new operator

8.5.3.1   Access Internal Files

Android uses the Linux kernel and is similar to Linux computers. It provides directories where you can save files. For your app to create a file on the internal storage, you can use the following statement:

```
File file = new File(context.getFilesDir(), filename);
```

The statement above will create a file, and the location of the file would be in the *files* folder on the emulator. The path to the files directory is storage → emulated → 0 → Android → data → yourAppPackage → files as shown below in Fig. 8.10. This path can be different on different emulators.

The name of your app package on the path means that the file will be created inside your app's private directory and is not accessible directly.

8.5.3.2   Accessing Files You Create

The Android context class provides several methods to create and access files. These include the *getFilesDir()*, *listFiles()*, *getName()*, and *getAbsolutePath()* methods. In our demo app, we created two files, *TestResults* and *testFiles*, inside the app's directory. That is, we used the internal storage to store data. You can access these file names in the *files* directory as follows:

```
((File)getFilesDir()).listFiles()[0].getName(); // returns TestResult
(File)getFilesDir()).listFiles()[1].getName(); // returns testFiles
```

The code snippet in Listing 8.22 shows how to access the internal storage in our app.

Listing 8.22 Showing how to access the internal storage in our app.

```
String filename = "testFile";
String fileContents = "Some Text";
FileOutputStream outputStream;
File testResult = new File(getFilesDir(), filename);
if (testResult.exists()) {
  Log.i(testResult.getName().toString(), "exists true");
} try {
  outputStream =
  openFileOutput(filename, Context.MODE_PRIVATE);
  outputStream.write(fileContents.getBytes());
  outputStream.close();
} catch (Exception e) {
  e.printStackTrace();
}
// fileList() return files created with openFileOutput(String, int)
// 0 = "myfile"
//1 = "testFile"
String fileNames = "";
for (String fn : fileList()) {
  fileNames = fileNames + fn + "\n";
}
```

In the code above, the getFilesDir() method returns the absolute path to the directory on the file system where the files are created with the openFileOutput(String, int) method. *The fileList()* method lists the file name located at the directory returned by the getFileDir() method. Note that, in the code snippet above, the openFileOutput() method is used to write the file content:

```
outputStream = openFileOutput(
    filename, Context.MODE_PRIVATE);
```

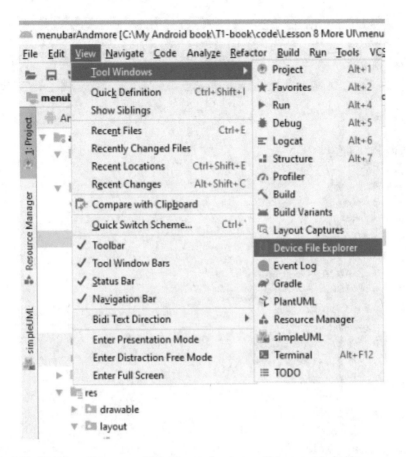

Fig. 8.11 Snapshot of how to use file explorer to locate your file on your Android app

To see the files on the emulator, use the *File.getAbsolutePath()* method in your code to get the file path and print, or log, the path information. Once you have the path info, use the Device File Explorer from the Android Studio to locate the file. Figures 8.11 and 8.12 show how you can use the Device File Explorer to locate the files you created on the Android emulator.

When a file is no longer needed, you should delete it to save space.

The File class has a *delete()* function, and the context class has a *deleteFile(fileName)* function that can be used to delete files. To check if a file exists, call:

```
File aFile = new File ( fileName ) ;
if (aFile.exists ( ) ) // if true, the file exists!
```

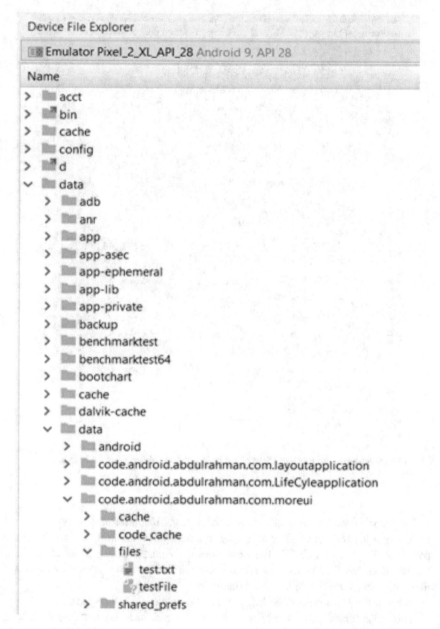

Fig. 8.12 The Android's file system

8.5.4 Android File IO Classes and Methods

We have updated our demo app and included a button called "click for file info." When this new button is clicked, it will start a new page with three buttons to demo the file input/output classes, the file directories, and the app's package name, space, etc. The three buttons for displaying the Android file structure are shown on the left-hand side of Fig. 8.13, and the Android root subdirectories are listed on the right-hand side.

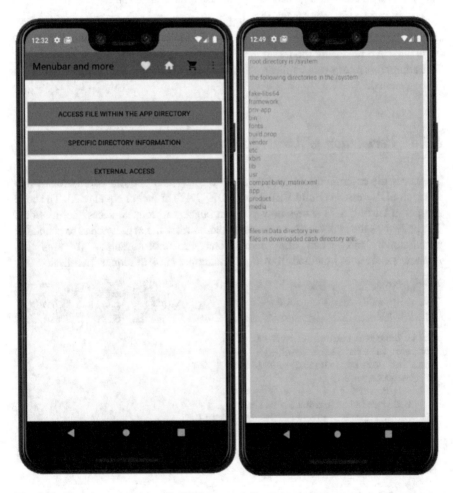

Fig. 8.13 Three buttons to demo file IO classes and directories

8.5.5   Accessing External Storage Files

To have access to files outside of your app's directory, including USB drives and SD cards, use the keyword *external* with the method used for the internal storage. For example, you can use these methods to access the external storages: getExternalFilesDir(), getExternalStorageDirectory(), and getExternalStoragePublicDirectory().

The *getExternalFilesDir()* method returns a File object representing the root of the attached drive. The user may remove the drive, so it might not always be accessible. To avoid app crashes, use the *getExternalStorageState()* method to check the external storage. The external storage can be in one of the three states below:

1. Mounted: this return value indicates that the external drive is available.
2. READ_ONLY: this return value indicates that the external drive is available but is only in a read-only mode.
3. Failure: this return value indicates that the external drive is not available or cannot be reached.

8.5.6   Permission to Access External Directory

To access the external directory, you need to implement request permissions when using an SDK version (Build.VERSION.**SDK_INT**) higher or equal to 23. The code snippet in Listing 8.23 shows how you can check and request access permissions. The code uses the *checkSelfPermission()* method from the activity class to check the permissions, and when the permissions are not granted, it uses the *requestPermissions()* method from ContextCompat class to request permission.

Listing 8.23 A snippet code for checking and requesting access permission.

```
public boolean requestPermission() {
  boolean isPermissionGranted = true;
  final int version = Build.VERSION.SDK_INT;
  if (version >= 23) {
    if (!granted()) {
      isPermissionGranted = false;
      requestPermissions(EXTERNAL_PERMS,
            EXTERNAL_REQUEST);
    }
  }
  return isPermissionGranted;
}
public boolean granted() {
  String permisson =
  android.Manifest.permission.WRITE_EXTERNAL_STORAGE ;
  return (PackageManager.PERMISSION_GRANTED ==
    ContextCompat.checkSelfPermission(this, permisson));
}
```

To read the content of an external file and write to an external file, you need to request read/write permissions. The constants for the write and read permissions are WRITE_EXTERNAL_STORAGE and READ_EXTERNAL_STORAGE. You need to include the permission requests into the manifest file as follows:

```
<uses-permission  android:name =
"android.permission.WRITE_EXTERNAL_STORAGE" />
<uses-permission
  android:name="android.permission.READ_EXTERNAL_STORAGE" />
```

8.5.7 Examples Using External Methods

In our demo app, we use various methods to access external files and directories. These include the *getExternalFilesDir()*, *getExternalStorageDirectory()*, and *getExternalStoragePublicDirectory()* methods, as well as the Android *Environment* methods. In the following subsections, we describe how to use these methods. The code snippets for all the examples below are from the *DirectoryStructureActivity* class in our demo app.

8.5.7.1   getExternalFilesDir

You can use getExternalFilesDir() to return *the absolute path* to the directory on the *primary shared /external storage* device. Similar to the C drive on the PC, every device has only one primary storage volume. You can use the isPrimary() method to check if the volume is the primary shared/external storage or not.

The code snippet in Listing 8.24 shows how you can use getExternalFilesDir() in your code. The code is part of the source code of our demo app and is named as example 1 in the DirectoryStructureActivity class.

Listing 8.24 Using getExternalFilesDir method.

```
{ ...
   String anExFile = ""; // file on internal storage
     File exteranlPath = getExternalFilesDir(null);
     if (null == exteranlPath) {
       exteranlPath = mainActivity.getFilesDir();
     }
     Log.i("path", exteranlPath.getName().toString());
     Log.i("path", exteranlPath.getFreeSpace() + "");
     Log.i("path", exteranlPath.getTotalSpace() + "");
     exteranlPath.list();
   ...
}
```

When the code is executed, the result is *files*, and the absolute path to the files directory is:

/storage/emulated/0/Android/data/code.android.abdulrahman.com.
   menubarAndMore/*files*

8.5.7.2   getExternalStorageDirectory

The getExternalStorageDirectory() method returns the primary shared/external storage directory. Don't be confused by the word "external." This directory can better be thought of as a media/shared storage. In our demo code, we append **"/DCIM/Camera"** to get access to the pictures stored on a device. Note that, when used, the directory may not be accessible for various reasons, for example, if the user accesses the directory on the device from their computer or if the directory has been removed altogether. You can determine the current state of the directory using the getExternalStorageState() method.

In our demo code, we append" **/DCIM/Camera"** to getExternalStorageDirectory(). The code snippet in Listing 8.25 shows the use of getExternalStorageDirectory() with the /DCIM/Camera directory in the DirectoryStructureActivity class.

Listing 8.25 Using getExternalStorageDirectory with /DCIM/Camera directory.

```
{ ...
 String ImageFileNames = "";
    File sdCardRoot = Environment.getExternalStorageDirectory();
    File yourDir = new File(sdCardRoot, "/DCIM/Camera");
    int j = 0;
    if (yourDir != null && yourDir.listFiles() != null) {
      for (File imgfile : yourDir.listFiles()) {
        j++;
        if (j % 20 == 0) // just to limit number of files
          if (imgfile.isFile()) {
            ImageFileNames = ImageFileNames +
            imgfile.getName() + "\n";
          }
      }
    }
 ...
}
```

When the code is executed, it will list all the image files stored on your device. For example, when we ran the code in our device, it generated the following output:

```
20171128_090921.jpg
20171128_090923.jpg
```

```
20171128_090924.jpg
20171128_092709.jpg
20171204_170251.jpg
20171204_183426.jpg
20171215_080819.jpg
20171215_080822.jpg
20171215_080831.jpg
20171215_080931.jpg
Etc.
```

In another example, we used the getExternalStorageDirectory() and list() methods to see the list of subdirectories in the */storage/emulated/0* directory. This is example 8 from the DirectoryStructureActivity class of our demo app. The code snippet is shown in Listing 8.26.

Listing 8.26 Using the getExternalStorageDirectory and list methods.

```
{
 ...
File f3 = getExternalStorageDirectory();
   anExFile = "";
   if (f3 != null && f3.list() != null)
      for (String s : f3.list()) {
         anExFile = anExFile + s + "\n";
      }
fileInfo = fileInfo + "files in External Storage Directory are: " +
anExFile + "\n\n";
 ...
}
```

When the code is executed, it will list all the storage directories on your device. For example, when we ran the code on our device, it generated the following output:

```
path is /storage/emulated/0
0 = "Music"
1 = "Podcasts"
2 = "Ringtones"
3 = "Alarms"
4 = "Notifications"
5 = "Pictures"
6 = "Movies"
7 = "Download"
8 = "DCIM"
9 = "Android"
```

The getExternalStorageDirectory() method was deprecated in API level 29 to improve user privacy. If you want to access content stored on a shared/external storage, you need to use the getExternalFilesDir(String) method from context class, MediaStore, or ACTION_OPEN_DOCUMENT with the intent class.

8.5.8   Environment Class
and getExternalStoragePublicDirectory

Android has a class called *Environment* which provides access to environment variables. It has multiple constants. Examples of these constants include *DIRECTORY_PICTURES*, *DIRECTORY_DCIM*, *DIRECTORY_DOWNLOADS*, etc. You can use these constants with the *getExternalStoragePublicDirectory()* method and obtain information about the file structure and files in the app's external directories. Example 9 from the DirectoryStructureActivity class uses Environment class constants. The code for using these constants is shown in the following sub-sections. The code snippets for all the examples below are from the *DirectoryStructureActivity* class in our demo app.

8.5.8.1   Environment.DIRECTORY_DCIM

In our demo code, we use the DIRECTORY_DCIM constant and the getExternalStoragePublicDirectory method together to retrieve the top-level public directory for pictures and videos; see the code snippet in Listing 8.27.

Listing 8.27 Using Environment class constant and DIRECTORY_DCIM.

```
{  ....
f4 = getExternalStoragePublicDirectory(
   Environment.DIRECTORY_DCIM);
     anExFile = "";
     if (f4 != null && f4.list() != null && f4.list()[0] != null)
       for (String s : f4.list()) {
         anExFile = anExFile + s + "\n";
       } ....
}
```

When the code is executed, it will return the top-level public directory for pictures and videos:

```
0 = "Camera"
1 = "Screenshots"
2 = ".thumbnails"
```

8.5.8.2   Environment.getExternalStorageDirectory

Use the *getExternalStorageDirectory()* and list() methods to see the files in a directory. In our demo code, we use the *getExternalStorageDirectory()* method with *MediaStorage*, i.e., /DICM/Camera/, as shown in Listing 8.28. This is Example 6 in the DirectoryStructureActivity class of our demo app.

Listing 8.28 Using getExternalStorageDirectory() and list methods.

```
{ ...
File sdcardRoot = Environment.getExternalStorageDirectory();
File yourDir = new File(sdcardRoot, "/DCIM/Camera");
if (yourDir != null && yourDir.listFiles() != null) {
    for (File imgfile : yourDir.listFiles()) {
      if (imgfile.isFile()) {
         ImageFileNames = ImageFileNames + imgfile.getName() + "\n";
      }
   }
}
fileInfo = fileInfo + " files in " + yourDir + " are: \n\n" +
    ImageFileNames + "\n\n";
...
}
```

When the code snippet above is executed, the result is:

```
files in /storage/emulated/0/DCIM/Camera are:
IMG_20200224_164220.jpg
IMG_20200224_164233.jpg
```

8.5.8.3 Environment.DIRECTORY_DOWNLOADS

The *getExternalStoragePublicDirectory() method* gets a top-level shared/external storage directory to place files of a particular type. This is a common location where the user will place and manage their files. You should be careful about what you put in this location and ensure that you don't erase user files or get in the way of user file organization.

In our demo code, we use the getExternalStoragePublicDirectory() method with the Environment.DIRECTORY_DOWNLOADS constant as shown in Listing 8.29.

Listing 8.29 Using ExternalStoragePublicDirectory() method to access download directory.

```
{
  ...
  f4 = getExternalStoragePublicDirectory(
    Environment.DIRECTORY_DOWNLOADS);
    anExFile = "";
    if (f4 != null && f4.list() != null)
      for (String s : f4.list()) {
        anExFile = anExFile + s + "\n";
      }
  ...
}
```

The result samples are listed below:

```
result = {String[40]@5316}
 0 = "1 Complete Lesson.pdf"
 1 = "1237805a.pdf"
 2 = "180830_FLX_Cardholder_Agreement_v12_0818_EN.pdf"
 4 = "Contract CP610.docx"
 5 = "Course Design Rubric.pdf"
 6 = "cra-psac-eng-2012.pdf"
 7 = "December12_2018_championship_meet_heat_sheets.pdf"
 8 = "final-thesis-presentation3 (1).ppt"
 9 = "final-thesis-presentation3.ppt"
```

8.5.8.4 Environment.getRootDirectory

The Environment.*getRootDirectory*() method returns the root directory, and when the results of the method call are presented, you will get the list of directories in your device; examples of such directories are listed below. As you can see, the file structure of the Android device is like the Linux file directory.

app
bin
build.prop
camera
data
container
etc
fake-libs
fake-libs64
fonts
framework
hidden
info.extra
lib
lib64
usr
vendor

To see the code for accessing directories in our demo app, open the app → DirectoryStructureActivity → example 8.

8.5.9 Locate Apps on Emulator File System

If you use the Device File Explorer, you will see the location of your app on your device. For example, our menubarAndMore app is stored at sdcard→ Android → Data as shown below in Fig. 8.14.

The sdcard is a symbolic link; the actual path where the apps are stored is **/storage/emulated/0**. See Fig. 8.15:

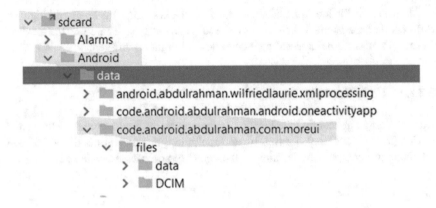

Fig. 8.14 The location of the app on the Android file system

Fig. 8.15 The actual path
where the apps are stored

Note that the file location and structure of the file system on the emulator might be different than the actual device even for the same device type. Therefore, the location of the app on the emulator and the actual device might be different.

8.5.9.1   Do It Yourself

Run the demo app and find the location of the app on the emulator and on the actual device (if you have one). Re-run the app multiple times. Each time use a different emulator and compare the location of the demo app on each emulated device.

8.6   Chapter Summary

In this chapter, we studied some important Android topics for app development. We studied the creation of the toolbar for your apps, adding menus to the toolbar, creating dialog boxes and custom dialog boxes, context menu, popup menu, starting activity for result, the latest ActivityResult from AndroidX, and accessing the camera app in your code using implicit intent. We also studied how to store data in the apps using shared preferences and files. We studied the Android file system and how one can explore the files using the Android Device File Explorer as well as how to access the app package, internal and external storages, and Android files. In Chap. 11, we will explore how to store data using a database and the SQLite database management system and how to query data using the SQL language. We will also look at how to embed queries in the Android app as well as how to use firebase to store data in the cloud.

Check Your Knowledge

Below are some of the fundamental concepts and vocabularies that have been covered in this chapter. To test your knowledge and your understanding of this chapter, you should be able to describe each of the below concepts in one or two sentences.

- ActionBar
- AndroidX
- apply
- commit
- Context.MODE_PRIVATE
- DIRECTORY_PICTURES, DIRECTORY_DCIM
- DIRECTORY_DOWNLOADS
- Editor
- fileList
- finish
- getAbsoluteFile
- getExternalFilesDir

- getExternalStoragePublicDirectory
- getFilesDir
- getSharedPreferences
- immutable
- implicit Intent
- MenuInflater
- onActivityResult
- onContextItemSelected
- onCreateContextMenu
- onCreateOptionsMenu
- onOptionsItemSelected
- openFileOutput
- overflow
- PopupMenu
- READ_EXTERNAL_STORAGE
- refactor
- registerForContextMenu
- sdcard
- setResult
- setSupportActionBar
- SharedPreferences
- sharedUserId
- sharedUserLabel
- startActivityForResult
- support library
- WRITE_EXTERNAL_STORAGE

Further Reading

For more information about the topics covered in this chapter, we suggest that you refer to the online resources listed below. These links provide additional insight into the topics covered. The links are mostly maintained by Google and are a part of the Android API specification. The resource titles convey which section/subsection of the chapter the resource is related to.

ActionBar, [online] Available, https://developer.android.com/reference/android/support/v7/app/ActionBar

Common Intents, [online] Available, https://developer.android.com/guide/components/intents-common

Creating an Options Menu, [online] Available, https://developer.android.com/guide/topics/ui/menus#options-menu

Data and file storage overview, [online] Available, https://developer.android.com/training/data-storage

Data and file storage overview, [online] Available, https://developer.android.com/training/data-storage/files#java

Dialogs, [online] Available, https://material.io/design/components/dialogs.html#
getExternalStorageDirectory, [online] Available, https://developer.android.
com/reference/android/os/Environment#getExternalStorageDirectory().

MediaStore, [online] Available, https://developer.android.com/reference/
android/provider/MediaStore

Menu, [online] Available, https://developer.android.com/reference/android/
view/Menu

SharedPreferences, [online] Available, https://developer.android.com/refer
ence/android/content/SharedPreferences

Take photos, [online] Available, https://developer.android.com/training/camera/
photobasics.html

Chapter 9
Fragments, Dynamic Binding, Inheritance, Pinching, and Screen Swiping

What You Will Learn in This Chapter

By the end of this chapter, you should be able to:

- Describe what a fragment is and the differences between fragments and activities
- Use fragments with varied device sizes
- Explain the lifecycle of fragments and their callback methods
- Apply different layouts for the same device based on its orientation
- Differentiate between dynamic and static fragments
- Subclass activities and apply inheritance
- Reuse toolbars across activities
- Reuse layouts
- Define resource folders with name qualifiers
- Develop apps for different screen densities
- Use screen pinch to zoom images and views
- Use Swiping gestures and events

Check Out the Demo Project

Download the demo app, **android-fragment.zip**, specifically developed to go with this chapter. I recommend that you code this project up from the notes rather than just opening the project in Android Studio and running it; however, if you want to run the code first to get a sense of the app, please do so. The code is thoroughly explained in this chapter to help you understand it. We follow the same approach to all other chapters throughout the book. The app's code will help you comprehend the additional concepts that will be described in this chapter.

   How to run the code: unzip the code in a folder of your choice, and then in Android Studio, click **File->import->Existing Android code into the workspace**. The project should start running.

© The Author(s), under exclusive license to Springer Nature Switzerland AG 2022   379
A.-R. Mawlood-Yunis, *Android for Java Programmers*,
https://doi.org/10.1007/978-3-030-87459-9_9

9.1   Introduction

Up until now, we have used Android Activities to display Views on the screen. That is, in the demo apps for previous chapters, screens were associated with Android Activities to manage user interactions with the widgets and to view the content. Here, we introduce another component to create visual objects in Android apps. In this chapter, you will learn about fragments.

Most applications include one or more Activities and fragments. So, what is a fragment, and why do we use them? In Sect. 9.2 of this chapter, we answer these questions in detail and describe what it takes to create a layout with fragments. We have also developed an app to demonstrate the creation and use of fragments. The app is described in Sect. 9.3 of this chapter. In Sect. 9.4, we show inheritance and layout reuse to achieve layout modularity without using fragments. Lastly, in Sect. 9.5, we describe how to create multiple layout files for devices of various sizes.

9.2   The Fragment Basics

The Fragment class can be used to create visual objects that can be put into the app view, i.e., that can be attached to the app view. It occupies one or more parts of the app screen. Using fragments, you can divide your app screen into multiple independent areas that are hosted within an activity. One difference between fragments and Activities is that fragments are threads, while activities are processes. Each fragment controls its I/O, events, and computational logic.

9.2.1   Fragment Uses

Using fragments, you can divide your app screen into several sections with each section acting as a mini Activity. Fragments are not a replacement for Activities. Your application still needs Activities, but we do not solely depend on them to create Views. You will divide an Activity screen into multiple sections, and all the sections will reside inside an Activity. You can do the following with the fragments:

- Combine multiple fragments in a single activity to build a multi-pane user interface.
- Reuse a fragment in multiple activities.

• Add or remove fragments to/from activities while the activity is running, also called perform fragment transaction.

A fragment must always be included in an activity, and the fragment's lifecycle is directly impacted by the host activity's lifecycle. In other words, a fragment exists within the boundaries of an activity, and an activity is a home container for a fragment. Each fragment has its layout, behavior, or things it can do and lifecycle callback methods.

Fragments can communicate with the host activity, access data held in the activity to which it belongs (the host activity), and send data to the activity which in turn can be sent to other fragments or activities. Fragments may interact with each other using the enclosing activity as a mediator for communication. The communication between the fragment and its host is done using the events and listeners.

You can think of a fragment as a modular section of an activity, with its own lifecycle. Fragments have the normal activity callback methods, i.e., onCreate(), onStart(), onResume(), onPause(), onStop(), onDestroy(), etc. They also have additional callbacks methods: onCreateView(), is where to inflate the user interface (UI); *onAttach(Context c)*, is called when the fragment has been added to the activity; and *onDetach()*, is called when the fragment is detached from the activity after the activity has been destroyed.

9.2.2 Why Using Fragments

Up until now, we have developed apps using Android activities only. A drawback of this approach is that at any given time, one activity fills the whole screen of the device. This is a limitation considering the display area offered by larger devices such as tablets, TV screens, etc. Fragments are the solution to this limitation.

Designing your app layout with fragments enables your app to behave differently based on the size and orientation of the devices; you write the code once and use different layouts to show the content differently on different devices. To elaborate more, let us look at the email app, i.e., email client interface, behavior on the phone and tablet. Phones are typically in portrait mode with limited screen space. If you look at a list of emails on a phone, normally you just see a list. If you select an email, then it opens another screen or activity to view the email content. Tablets, on the other hand, are typically in landscape mode with a lot of screen space. On a tablet, the emails are normally listed on the left side of the screen, and selecting an email will show the email content on the right side of the screen. This is possible when the activity's layout includes fragments.

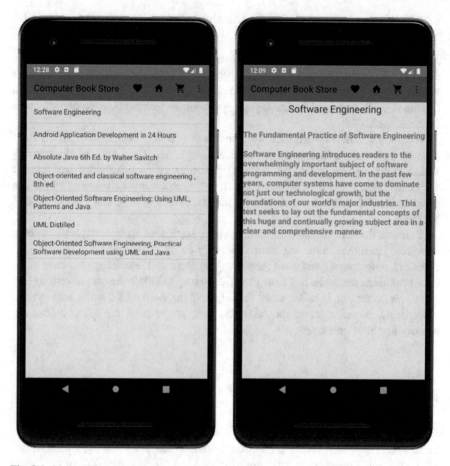

Fig. 9.1 Listing titles on one fragment and title description on another fragment

Figures 9.1 and 9.2 illustrate how designing an app layout with fragments allows the developer to take advantage of the extra space tablets provide and how you can write code once and let your app behave differently based on the device size and orientation.

In Fig. 9.1, there is not enough space for two fragments on the phone screen, so *the activity_main layout that we used* includes only one frame layout which is used as a fragment place holder for the list of book titles (the left-hand side of Fig. 9.1). When the user selects a title, a second fragment is inflated to display a title and its description (the right-hand side of Fig. 9.1). This fragment could be a separate activity as well. So here two different layouts, or screens, are swapped when a user clicks on a book title and then on the back button to return to the book list.

Different from Figs. 9.1 and 9.2 shows the app display when running the app on a tablet. Here, the main_activity layout file resides in the large folder, i.e., the w-600dp folder is used. Since the screen is large enough, the layout embeds two frame

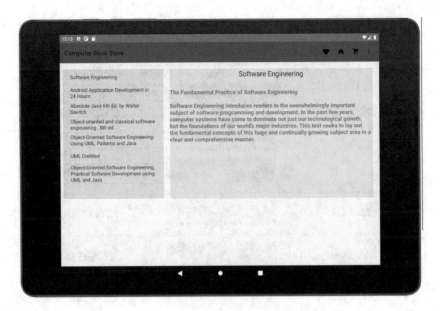

Fig. 9.2 The list title fragment and the detail fragment on one screen

layouts, i.e., embeds placeholders for two fragments. So, when the user clicks on the book title on the left-hand side menu, the description of the book is displayed on the right-hand side, the content of the right-hand side fragment is updated, and the view for the fragment on the left-hand side remains unchanged.

Don't worry if you don't understand the app implementation details yet. The app implementation and coding will be described in the coming sections in detail. For now, you just need to understand the definition and purpose of using fragments.

9.2.3   Fragment Lifecycle

As we stated earlier, fragments have their own lifecycle. Here, we describe the fragment lifecycle flow diagram (see Fig. 9.3) and highlight some details about the fragment lifecycle states, transitions, and flow.

9.2.3.1   Activity Lifecycle Impacts on Fragments

The lifecycle of the activity in which the fragment lives (host activity) directly has an impact on the lifecycle of the fragment, such that each lifecycle callback for the activity results in a similar callback for each fragment. For example, when the activity receives onPause(), each fragment in the activity receives onPause(), and when the activity receives its onCreate() callback, a fragment in the activity receives the onActivityCreated() callback.

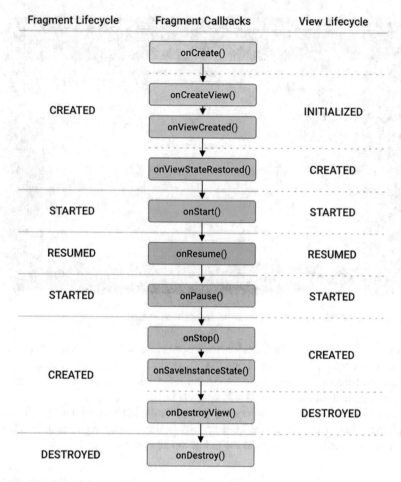

Fig. 9.3 The flow of fragment lifecycle. Retrieved from developer.android.com. Creative Commons Attribution 2.5 license

9.2.3.2 Fragments Extra Lifecycle Callbacks

Think of a fragment as a modular section of an activity, which has its own lifecycle. Thus, fragments have the normal activity callback methods, onCreate(), onStart(), onResume(), onPause(), onStop(), onDestroy(), etc., and they have an additional five callback methods that handle interactions with the host activity in order to perform actions such as building and destroying fragments. These additional callback methods are:

onAttach(): This method is called when the fragment is linked or attached to an activity. The parameter for the attached method is the context, i.e., the host activity. The onAttach() event occurs before the fragment's visually created and before the fragment, or its parent activity, has completed initialization. The syntax for the onAttach() method is as follows.

```
@Override
public void onAttach(Context context) {
super.onAttach(context)
...
}
```

The other fragment methods have a similar method signature to the onAttach() method and are described briefly below.

onCreateView(): This method is called to create the fragment view. It instantiates the fragment by inflating its layout.

onActivityCreated(): This method is called when the activity's onCreate() method has returned, that is, the fragment's activity has been created.

onDestroyView(): This method is called when the fragment is removed.

onDetach(): This method is called when the fragment is disconnected from the activity.

Fragments also have three states; they are fragment is *added*, a fragment is *active*, and a fragment is *destroyed*.

The flow of a fragment's lifecycle as it is affected by its host activity is illustrated in Fig. 9.3 where you can see how each successive state of the activity determines the callback methods a fragment may receive. For example, when an activity receives its onCreate() callback method, a fragment in the activity receives the onActivityCreated() callback method. Once the activity reaches the resumed state, you can add and remove fragments to the activity. When the activity leaves the resumed state, the fragment is again pushed through its lifecycle by the activity. Note that the lifecycle of a fragment can change independently only when the activity is in the resumed state.

9.2.3.3   Overriding Fragment Callback Methods

When implementing fragments, you should consider overriding the following five callback methods:

onAttach(): Invoked when the fragment has been connected to the host activity.

onCreate(): Used for initializing non-visual components needed by the fragment.

onCreateView(): Most of the work is done here. It is called to create the view hierarchy representing the fragment. Usually inflates a layout, defines listeners, and populates the widgets in the inflated layout.

onPause(): The session is about to finish. Here you should commit state data changes that are needed in case the fragment is re-executed.

onDetach(): Called when the inactive fragment is disconnected from the activity.

9.3   Creating an App with the Fragments

In this part, the fragment creation is described. We first list all the steps needed to create a fragment and then describe each step. The class diagram for the app is shown in Fig. 9.4. It should help you understand the explanation provided in this part.

9.3.1   Create a Fragment

Including fragments in your app involves the main steps below:

1. Creating user-defined fragment classes by *extending* the Android fragment class.
2. Implementing the fragment's onCreateView() callback method to instantiate the fragment view by inflating the fragment layout.
3. Instantiating the fragment manager and fragment transactions classes to add, replace, or remove a fragment to the app screen. This takes place inside the onCreate() method of the activity which holds the fragments.

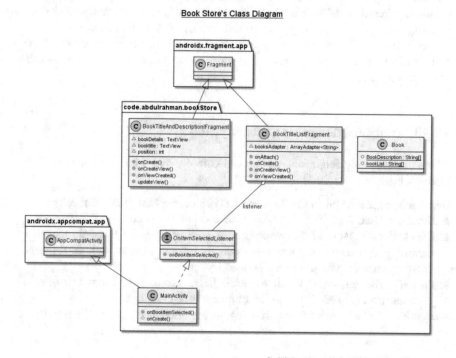

Fig. 9.4 A class diagram of our demo bookstore app

4. Creating one or more layouts for the main activity (e.g., activity_main.xml, activity_main.xml (land), activity_main.xml (w600dp)) for different device sizes and orientations. In Fig. 9.5, three layouts are circled in an orange capsule. These layouts must have one or more *frame layouts* in them. The frame layout is a placeholder for fragments that will be populated at runtime.
5. Creating one or more fragment layouts and fragment classes for fragment instantiation and attachment. In Fig. 9.5, fragment layouts are circled in a black capsule

Fig. 9.5 An app directory structure when the fragment is used

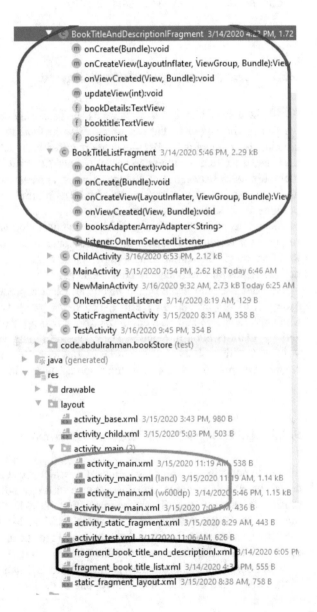

and fragment classes in a red capsule. The fragment layouts represent the fragment's user interfaces, and the fragment classes are used to inflate the layouts, i.e., turn the layouts into the view objects, and attach them to the frame layout in the activity_main layout.

6. Loading a proper main_layout with the right number of fragments to the screen of the device. The last step is particularly important in fragment development. Loading a proper layout is what enables your app to be viewed differently on different device sizes and orientations.

9.3.2 One Activity and Multiple Layouts

For all the apps we have seen so far, we have used only one layout per activity, and we passed the layout to the setContentView method to set up the screen. When creating apps where the apps' views are required to fit screens with different sizes, there needs to be more than one layout per activity to set up the views. This is the main difference between the two types of apps, apps where an activity makes up the entire screen and apps where an activity hosts multiple fragments, smaller screen portions, to fit screens of various sizes.

Since one activity can have multiple layouts, plugging in a proper layout at runtime, for example, based on the devices' screen size or orientation, is one way to differentiate between developing apps made of activities only and apps made of both activities and fragments to create screens.

Android uses the name of the layout to select a proper layout at runtime. For example, to run an app on a tablet, you name your layout activity_main(large). Similarly, to run an app on a device that has a 600 dp width, you name your layout activity_main (w600dp). Once you are done designing your layouts, you need to write your main activity code accordingly. Below, we describe the steps involved in creating an app where the screens are made up of activities and fragments in detail.

9.3.3 Detecting Device Size and Orientation

Similar to detecting an app's locale language which we studied earlier, Android can detect the size and orientation of the device in use. Android has multiple built-in sensors to interact with its environment and provide developers with valuable information. These include device size, orientation, location, etc. The developer can use the information returned from the sensors to check, load, update, and replace a layout. You will learn more about this when we study sensors.

In our demo app, Android detects the size and orientation (portrait or landscape) of the device, and based on this finding, one of the three activity_main layouts will be loaded.

Table 9.1 Design structure of our demo app

Model	View	Controller
Book.java BandDatabase.java	activity_main.xml fragment_book_title_ and_description.xml fragment_book_title_list.xml	MainActivity.java BookTitleAndDescriptionlFragment.java BookTitleListFragment.java

After the initial loading, you use a layout, or the frame layout id, to check which layout is currently loaded. You need to assign an id to the root element of the layout, e.g., layoutID, and check if the layout has been loaded in your activity code. The id can be checked with the findViewByID(R.resouce.**layoutID**) method call, specifically by calling the findViewByID(R.id.**layoutID**) method.

In our demo app, we use layoutID to find out if we need to replace the layout or just update the layout partially. The latter is used when the device is a tablet or is a phone in landscape mode.

The design structure of our demo app is shown in Table 9.1. It is structured following the model-view-controller (MVC) architecture.

9.3.4 Fragment Development Steps in Details

The steps you need to follow to create an app that includes fragments are described in detail below.

9.3.4.1 Extending Fragment Class

To create a fragment class, you need to extend the Android fragment class or an existing subclass of it. We created two fragment classes in our demo app. The class extension is done as follows:

```
public class BookTitleListFragment extends Fragment {...}, and
public class BookTitleAndDescriptionlFragment extends Fragment {...}
```

9.3.4.2 Implement the onCreateView Method

The Android OS calls the onCreateView() method when it is time for the fragment to draw its user interface for the first time. To draw a user interface for your fragment, you must return a **view** object from the onCreateView() method which is a reference to the *root element* of the fragment's layout XML file. The root type can be *LinearLayout*, *RelativeLayout*, **or any other layout** depending on the root element of the fragment layout XML file. Note that you can return null if the fragment does not provide a user interface.

To return a layout view from the onCreateView() method, you inflate the fragment layout using a resource and layout id defined in the layout XML file. What helps you do so is that the onCreateView() method receives the LayoutInflater object as an input parameter which can be used to inflate the fragment layout. The code snippet below shows how onCreateView() is used to inflate the fragment layout and return the reference to the root element of the fragment, i.e., the layout view. It loads fragment_book_title_list.xml layout; inflates it, i.e., creates an object of type LinearLayout; and returns it as a view.

```
@Override
public View onCreateView(LayoutInflater inflater,
    @Nullable ViewGroup parent, @Nullable Bundle savedInstanceState) {
    // Inflate the xml file for the fragment
  return inflater.inflate(
    R.layout.fragment_book_title_list, parent, false);
}
```

Note that you can cast the return object from the inflater.inflate (R.layout. *fragment_book_title_list*, parent, **false) call** to a LinearLayout type; see code snippet below:

```
LinearLayout ln = (LinearLayout) inflater.inflate
              (R.layout.fragment_book_title_list, parent, false);
```

This is because the root element of the *fragment_book_title_list.xml* file is of type LinearLayout.

9.3.4.3 The onCreateView Method Signature

The method signature for the onCreateView() method is as follows.

```
public View onCreateView (LayoutInflater inflater,
        ViewGroup parent, Bundle savedInstanceState);
```

The host activity passes three parameters to the onCreateView() callback method. The parameters are of type *LayoutInflater*, *ViewGroup*, and *Bundle*.

The ViewGroup object is the container, or frame layout, from the activity_main. xml layout where your fragment should reside.

The Bundle object, **savedInstanceState**, provides data about the previous instance of the fragment if the fragment is being resumed.

The LayoutInflater object is used to call the inflate() method to instantiate the fragment object. The inflate() method takes three arguments:

1. The id of the layout you want to inflate, i.e., the id of the layout you defined to create the visual fragment.

2. The view group, the parent, or the container to hold the inflated layout. Often-times, the container is a frame layout from the main layout.
3. A boolean variable indicating whether the inflated layout should be attached to the view group (the second parameter) during the inflation or not.

Note that **if** the system already has inserted the inflated layout into the container, e.g., you have already added a fragment to the frame layout, passing true would create a redundant view group in the final layout.

9.3.4.4   Implement Other Methods

When creating the fragments, in addition to the onCreateView() method, you usually need to implement other lifecycle callback methods as well. This allows you to manage the fragment's state as it is added or removed from the activity and as the activity transitions between its lifecycle states. These include the following methods.

onCreate()

Within your implementation, you should use the onCreate() method to initialize essential components of the fragment that you want to retain when the fragment is paused, or stopped, and then resumed.

onPause()

The system calls the onPause() method as the first indication that the user is leaving the fragment. Leaving a fragment does not always mean that the fragment is being destroyed; it might become active again. Here you should commit any changes that should persist beyond the current user session (because the user might not come back). There are other callback methods you should also use to handle various stages of the fragment lifecycle as described earlier in this chapter.

9.3.4.5   Using FragmentManager and FragmentTransaction Classes

To perform transactions such as add, replace, or remove a fragment, you must use the fragment manager to create a fragment transaction which provides methods to add, remove, replace, and perform other fragment transactions.

Adding, removing, or replacing a fragment using the fragment manager and fragment transactions involves the following steps:

1. A call to the *getSupportFragmentManager()* method to get a *FragmentManager* object. The activity class inherits this method from the activity fragment class; hence, it can be called.
2. A call to the *beginTransaction()* method on the returned object to create a fragment transaction object. The *beginTransaction()* method is a method of the fragment manager class, and its return type is FragmentTransaction.

The code statement below summarizes the two steps described above:

```
FragmentTransaction ft =
    getSupportFragmentManager().beginTransaction();
```

3. A call to the add(), replace(), or remove() method to add, remove, or replace a fragment. Here is an example of how to apply a fragment transaction: **ft.add(R.id.frame1, firstFragment);**.

You can perform multiple fragment transactions for the activity using the same FragmentTransaction. These include adding, replacing, removing, hiding, attaching, detaching, etc. When you're ready to finalize these transactions, you must call the *commit()* method to commit the changes.

4. A call the addToBackStack() method to add fragment transactions to a stack.

Android uses a stack data structure to save fragment states when the user navigates from one screen to another. The stack is called *back stack* and supports push/pop operations. Every back stack entry, i.e., stack data element, is a record of the fragment transaction (remove, add, replace) that occurred.

You can recreate a fragment state by calling the *popBackStack()* method. When the back stack is used, the retrieved fragment is reused instead of being recreated from scratch, and the fragment's state data is restored. Hence, there is no need for input/output state bundles.

When adding an entry to the back stack using the fragment transaction and addToBackStack (String name) method, the name parameter is optional.

Use the back stack if you want to undo the transaction with the back button. Otherwise, pressing the back button changes the activity, and the fragment state can be recreated. Here is how to call addToBackStack():

getSupportFragmentManager().beginTransaction().addToBackStack(null)

Using a back stack leads to a simpler and more efficient solution, and you should call the addToBackStack() method every time you make a fragment transaction.

5. A call to transaction.commit() method to add or replace the fragment, e.g., ft.commit().

The code snippet in Listing 9.1 shows how the steps above are implemented in our demo app:

Listing 9.1 Fragment manager and fragment transaction objects to perform fragment transactions.

```
@Override
protected void onCreate(Bundle savedInstanceState) {
 super.onCreate(savedInstanceState);
 setContentView(R.layout.activity_main);
   BookTitleListFragment firstFragment = new BookTitleListFragment();
   FragmentTransaction ft = getSupportFragmentManager().
   beginTransaction();
   ft.add(R.id.frame1, firstFragment).addToBackStack("bookTitles");
   ft.commit();
}
```

9.3.4.6 Creating Layout Files

You should design different layouts to optimize the available space on various devices, such as phones and tablets, to improve the user experience. For our demo app, we created three alternative layout files: activity_main.xml, activity_main.xml (land), and activity_main.xml (w600dp). The first layout holds space for one fragment, i.e., it has one frame layout entry in it. The second layout holds space for two fragments. The third layout holds space for two fragments as well, but the difference between them is that the third layout is designed for very specific devices, devices with a 600 dp width. You inflate a suitable layout, i.e., create a layout object using the layout file and the inflate method, at runtime based on the current device's size and orientation. The **layout directory** is the place where the main layout files are saved (see Fig. 9.6).

The activity_main.xml file, circled in red in Fig. 9.6, is a layout folder that has neither a **large** nor **w600dp** name qualifier, so activity_main.xml is a default layout. This layout is used when the device screen is small and no more than one fragment fits the screen at the same time. The default layout is also used for the configurations that you have neither accounted for nor anticipated. The code snippet in Listing 9.2, activity_main.xml file, is an example of the default layout configuration for small devices with one frame layout (a place holder for a fragment).

Fig. 9.6 A layout folder with three layout files

Listing 9.2 Activity_main.xml file with one frame layout as a placeholder for a fragment.

```xml
<?xml version="1.0" encoding="utf-8"?>
<LinearLayout xmlns:android=
  "http://schemas.android.com/apk/res/android"
    android:layout_width="match_parent"
    android:layout_height="match_parent"
    android:orientation="vertical"
    android:padding="16dp" >
  <FrameLayout
      android:id="@+id/flContainer"
      android:layout_width="match_parent"
      android:layout_height="match_parent"
      android:background="#33FF00" />
</LinearLayout>
```

Another example where the main layout (main_activity.xml) contains two frame layouts is shown in Listing 9.3. The below layout can be used on large screen devices, such as tables or phone devices in a landscape mode to take advantage of the landscape space of the phone.

Listing 9.3 Activity_main.xml(land) file with two frame layouts.

```xml
<?xml version="1.0" encoding="utf-8"?>
<LinearLayout xmlns:android=
  "http://schemas.android.com/apk/res/android"
          android:orientation="horizontal"
          android:layout_width="match_parent"
          android:layout_height="wrap_content"
          android:layout_marginEnd="10dp"
          android:layout_marginTop="10dp" >
  <FrameLayout
    android:id="@+id/flContainer"
    android:layout_weight="1"
    android:layout_width="0dp"
    android:layout_height="match_parent"
    android:layout_marginLeft="10dp"
    android:layout_marginStart="10dp"
    android:background="#3355" />
  <FrameLayout
    android:id="@+id/flContainer2"
    android:layout_weight="2"
    android:layout_width="0dp"
    android:layout_marginLeft="10dp"
    android:layout_marginStart="10dp"
    android:layout_height="match_parent"
    android:background="#33bbaa" />
</LinearLayout>
```

Fig. 9.7 Layout with large qualifier name

The above layout can be included in the *layout-land* file. The filename would have the *land* name qualifier in it (see Fig. 9.7). To see the layout-land file on your PC, right-click on the layout folder in your project directory, and click *show in explore* to see the file. This layout can be used, i.e., inflated, when the device screen is large enough to fit two fragments. Your main activity code should make this happen.

9.3.4.7 Creating Layout and Fragment Classes

For our demo app, we created two fragment Java classes, BookTitleListFragment and BookTitleAndDescriptionFragment, and two fragment layouts, one for each class. The structure of both fragment classes and their associated layouts are listed, respectively. See Fig. 9.8 and Listing 9.4 for BookTitleListFragment and Fig. 9.9 and Listing 9.5 for BookTitleAndDescriptionFragment.

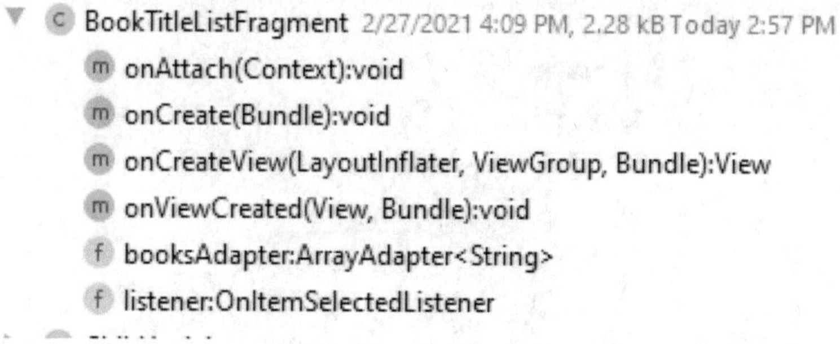

▼ © BookTitleListFragment 2/27/2021 4:09 PM, 2.28 kB Today 2:57 PM

    ⓜ onAttach(Context):void

    ⓜ onCreate(Bundle):void

    ⓜ onCreateView(LayoutInflater, ViewGroup, Bundle):View

    ⓜ onViewCreated(View, Bundle):void

    ⓕ booksAdapter:ArrayAdapter<String>

    ⓕ listener:OnItemSelectedListener

Fig. 9.8 Book fragment class structure

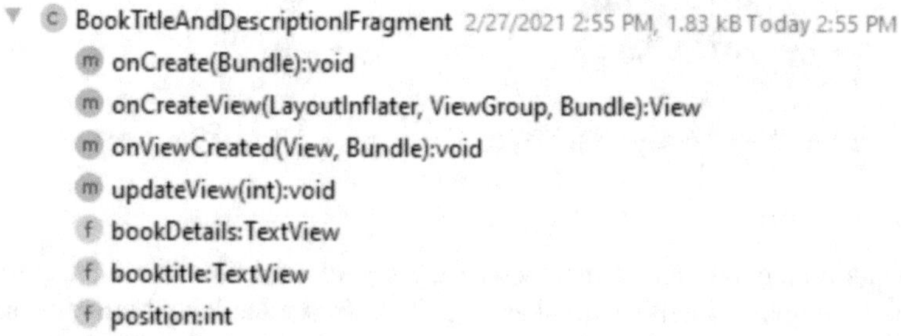

▼ © BookTitleAndDescriptionIFragment 2/27/2021 2:55 PM, 1.83 kB Today 2:55 PM

    ⓜ onCreate(Bundle):void

    ⓜ onCreateView(LayoutInflater, ViewGroup, Bundle):View

    ⓜ onViewCreated(View, Bundle):void

    ⓜ updateView(int):void

    ⓕ bookDetails:TextView

    ⓕ booktitle:TextView

    ⓕ position:int

Fig. 9.9 Book title and description class structure

Listing 9.4 fragment_book_title_and_description.xml layout file.

```xml
<?xml version="1.0" encoding="utf-8"?>
<RelativeLayout
  xmlns:tools="http://schemas.android.com/tools"
  xmlns:android="http://schemas.android.com/apk/res/android"
  android:orientation="vertical"
  android:layout_width="match_parent"
  android:layout_height="match_parent">
  <TextView
    android:layout_width="wrap_content"
    android:layout_height="wrap_content"
    android:id="@+id/bookTitle"
    android:textAppearance="?android:attr/textAppearanceLarge"
    android:text=""
    tools:text="This is a sample title"
    android:layout_alignParentTop="true"
    android:layout_centerHorizontal="true"
```

```
     android:layout_marginTop="30dp"/>
  <TextView
    android:layout_width="wrap_content"
    android:layout_height="wrap_content"
    android:textAppearance="?android:attr/textAppearanceMedium"
    android:id="@+id/bookDetails"
    android:layout_below="@+id/bookTitle"
    android:layout_centerHorizontal="true"
    android:layout_marginTop="30dp"
    android:gravity="left"
    android:scrollbars="vertical"/>
  <TextView
    android:layout_width="wrap_content"
    android:layout_height="wrap_content"
    android:textAppearance="?android:attr/textAppearanceSmall"
    android:id="@+id/textView2"
    android:layout_alignParentTop="true"
    android:layout_alignParentRight="true"
    android:layout_alignParentEnd="true"
    android:scrollbars="vertical"/>
</RelativeLayout>
```

Listing 9.5 fragment_book_title_list.xml layout file.

```
<?xml version="1.0" encoding="utf-8"?>
<LinearLayout
 xmlns:android="http://schemas.android.com/apk/res/android"
        android:orientation="vertical"
        android:layout_width="match_parent"
        android:layout_height="match_parent">
  <TextView
    android:layout_width="wrap_content"
    android:layout_height="wrap_content"
    android:textAppearance="?android:attr/textAppearanceSmall"
    android:id="@+id/textView"
    android:layout_gravity="right"/>
  <ListView
    android:id="@+id/listViewItems"
    android:layout_width="match_parent"
    android:layout_height="match_parent"
    android:choiceMode="singleChoice"
    android:listSelector="#FFCDD2" />
</LinearLayout>
```

Note that the second layout includes a list view entry, but we have not defined a layout for the items in the list. This is because we are using the default layout Android provides, called android.R.layout.*simple_list_item*_1, which is a simple listing. The code snippet in Listing 9.6 shows how the book list array has been set to the array adapter class:

Listing 9.6 BookTitleListFragment.java using ArrayAdapter and default android.R.layout.simple_list_item.

```
public class BookTitleListFragment extends Fragment {
 ArrayAdapter<String> booksAdapter;
 private OnItemSelectedListener listener;
 @Override
 public void onCreate(Bundle savedInstanceState) {
  super.onCreate(savedInstanceState);
  booksAdapter = new ArrayAdapter<String>(getContext(),
      android.R.layout.simple_list_item_1, Book.bookList);
  ...
 @Override
 public void onViewCreated(View view, Bundle savedInstanceState) {
  ListView itemsViewList = view.findViewById(R.id.listViewItems);
  itemsViewList.setAdapter(booksAdapter);
   ...}
 }
```

9.3.4.8 Attaching Proper Layout to the Device View

In our demo app, when the user clicks on a book title in the list, the main activity gets notified that a title was clicked. Then, if the activity is running on a phone, the title description is displayed on the full screen. Otherwise, if it is a tablet, the description of the title will be shown on the right-hand side without occupying the entire screen.

Loading or updating a proper layout is a major step in developing apps with dynamic fragment insertion and updates. Depending on the device size and orientation, different layouts will make up the view of the app. Below, we describe how a suitable fragment is attached to the main activity layout. This step involves carrying out multiple substeps. The substeps are also invoked when the user clicks on the book title to display the title description. The steps are as follows:

1. Declare an interface for communication between the fragment and the main activity. The interface will be implemented by the hosting activity.

    The code snippet below shows the OnItemSelectedListener interface declaration. The interface will help the fragment to access its host activity.

```
public interface OnItemSelectedListener {
  void onBookItemSelected(int position);
}}
```

2. Implementing the interface. The main activity, i.e., the fragment's hosting activity, implements the *OnItemSelectedListener* interface and codes the interface's only method, the onBookItemSelected() method. The code for this step can be as follows:

```
Public class MainActivity extends AppCompatActivity implements
  OnItemSelectedListener {...
  @Override
  public void onBookItemSelected(int position) {...}
}
```

3. Enable communication between the fragment and the main activity. This step is described below.

9.3.4.9 Communication Between Fragment and Its Host Activity

To enable communication between the fragment object and its host activity, a few things need to be done. An interface, e.g., the OnItemSelectedListener interface in the case of our demo app, is used as a type inside of a fragment class, the BookTitleListFragment class in the case of our demo app. In other words, the fragment class will have a field of an interface type, for example, **private OnItemSelectedListener** listener; see the code snippet below.

```
public class BookTitleListFragment extends Fragment {
  private OnItemSelectedListener listener;
  ... }
```

Figure 9.10 shows the relationship between the MainActivity class, the OnItemSelected interface, and the BookTitleListFragment class pictorially. The MainActivity is the context class and of type OnItemSelected because it implements it, and a reference to the MainActivity is stored in the fragment class.

When the onAttach() callback method is called with the host context being a method parameter, you store the host context object (the MainActivity object) in a variable inside the fragment, i.e., the BookTitleListFragment object. The code snippet in Listing 9.7 shows how the onAttach() callback method from the fragment assigns the activity object, i.e., context, to its data field.

Activity and Fragment connection via Interface

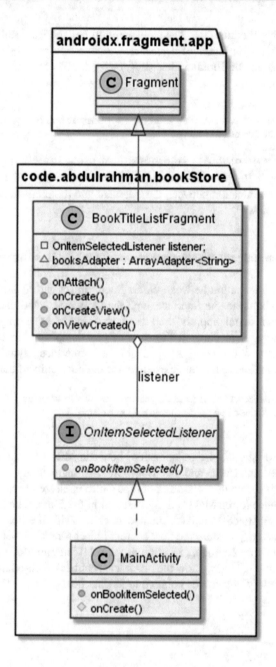

Fig. 9.10 Interface acts as a broker between an activity and a fragment

Listing 9.7 A reference to the MainActivity is stored in the fragment.

```
public class BookTitleListFragment extends Fragment {
   private OnItemSelectedListener listener;
...
@Override
 public void onAttach(Context context) {
  super.onAttach(context);
  if(context instanceof OnItemSelectedListener){
            // assiging context, i.e., MainActivity, to fragment's field
      this.listener = (OnItemSelectedListener) context;
  } else {
   throw new ClassCastException(context.toString()
       + " must implement BookMenuFragment.OnItemSelectedListener");
  }
 }
```

The code shows that the main activity implements the OnItemSelectedListener interface, i.e., the main activity is an OnItemSelectedListener, which makes the statement **if (context instanceof OnItemSelectedListener) to** be true, and context can be assigned to the *listener* field from the fragment class. This assignment is highlighted in bold inside the onAttach() method.

After assigning the context to the listener, i.e., **this.listener = (OnItemSelectedListener) context**, the BookTitleListFragment has access to its host activity and can invoke methods from the main activity class, i.e., communicate with its host activity.

9.3.5 The MainActivity Class and Demo App Demonstration

Now, we have all ingredients to add the fragments to the activity. Let us do just that. The call to add the fragments to the activity is done inside the main activity class; see the code snippet in Listing 9.8.

Listing 9.8 MainActivity.java for adding Fragment to the Activity screen.

```
public class MainActivity extends AppCompatActivity implements
 OnItemSelectedListener {
  @Override
  protected void onCreate(Bundle savedInstanceState) {
     super.onCreate(savedInstanceState);
     setContentView(R.layout.activity_main);
     if (savedInstanceState == null) {
        BookTitleListFragment firstFragment =
        new BookTitleListFragment();
```

```
FragmentTransaction ft = getSupportFragmentManager().
                                        beginTransaction();
ft.add(R.id.frame1, firstFragment);
if (findViewById(R.id.layoutWithDaulFragments) != null) {
    BookTitleAndDescription1Fragment secondFragment = new
            BookTitleAndDescription1Fragment();
    Bundle args = new Bundle();
    args.putInt("position", 0);
    secondFragment.setArguments(args);
    ft.add(R.id.frame2, secondFragment);
}
ft.commit();
    }
}
```

The condition statement if **(findViewById(R.id.layoutWithDaulFragments) != null)** checks to see if the layout with two frame layouts has been loaded or not. This condition can be re-written like this, **if (findViewById(R.id.frame2) != null)**, or like this:

```
if ( isTablet() || getResources().getConfiguration().orientation ==
Configuration.ORIENTATION_LANDSCAPE) {...}
```

The conditional statement is important for finding out whether or not the layout with two frame layouts has been loaded. In other words, the condition indicates whether or not you are using a phone or a larger device and, when using a phone, if it is in portrait or landscape mode.

Because the fragment has been added to the frame layout container at runtime (dynamic binding) instead of being defined in the activity's layout with a <fragment> tag (static binding which we will discuss in next section), the main activity can remove the fragment and replace it with a different one. The code snippet for the fragment replacement or swapping is shown below:

```
if (findViewById(R.id.frame2) != null) {
        .beginTransaction()
        .replace(R.id.frame2, secondFragment) // replace flContainer
        .addToBackStack(null)
        .commit();
}
```

Putting everything together, the code snippet in Listing 9.9 is a complete code for the main activity class.

Listing 9.9 MainActivity.java class in an App using Fragment dynamically.

```java
package code.abdulrahman.bookStore;
import android.os.Bundle;
import android.widget.Toast;
import boolean.appcompat.app.AppCompatActivity;
import boolean.fragment.app.FragmentTransaction;
public class MainActivity extends AppCompatActivity implements OnItem
SelectedListener {
    @Override
  protected void onCreate(Bundle savedInstanceState) {
      super.onCreate(savedInstanceState);
      setContentView(R.layout.activity_main);
  if (savedInstanceState == null) {
      BookTitleListFragment firstFragment = new BookTitleListFragment();
      FragmentTransaction ft =
       getSupportFragmentManager().beginTransaction();
      ft.add(R.id.frame1, firstFragment);
  if (findViewById(R.id.layoutWithDaulFragments) != null) {
      BookTitleAndDescription1Fragment secondFragment = new
                               BookTitleAndDescription1Fragment();
          Bundle args = new Bundle();
          args.putInt("position", 0);
          secondFragment.setArguments(args);
        ft.add(R.id.frame2, secondFragment);
        }
      ft.commit();
  }
}
  @Override
  public void onBookItemSelected(int position) {
     Toast.makeText(this, "Called By Fragment A: position – " +
                 position, Toast.LENGTH_SHORT).show();
     // Load Book Detail Fragment
     BookTitleAndDescription1Fragment secondFragment =
                 new BookTitleAndDescription1Fragment();
     Bundle args = new Bundle();
     args.putInt("position", position);
     secondFragment.setArguments(args);
     if (findViewById(R.id.frame2) != null) {
        getSupportFragmentManager().beginTransaction()
            .replace(R.id.frame2, secondFragment)
            .addToBackStack(null).commit();
     } else {
        getSupportFragmentManager().beginTransaction()
            .replace(R.id.frame1, secondFragment)
            .addToBackStack(null).commit();
     }
   }
 }
```

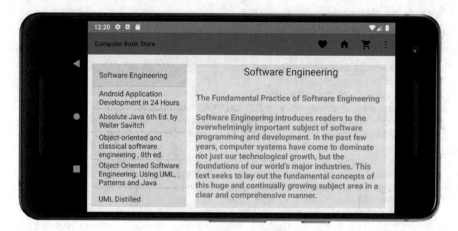

Fig. 9.11 Running the fragment demo app on a phone in landscape mode

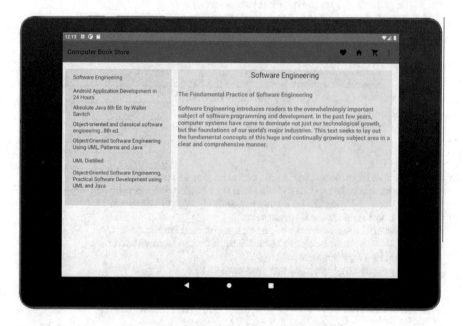

Fig. 9.12 Running the fragment demo app on a tablet in landscape mode

Figures 9.11, 9.12, and 9.13 are snapshots of our fragment app running on a phone and tablet in landscape mode and a tablet in portrait mode, respectively.

9.3.5.1   Do It Yourself

Can you think of another way to determine which device is currently in use and its orientation? Hint: think of using the configuration class.

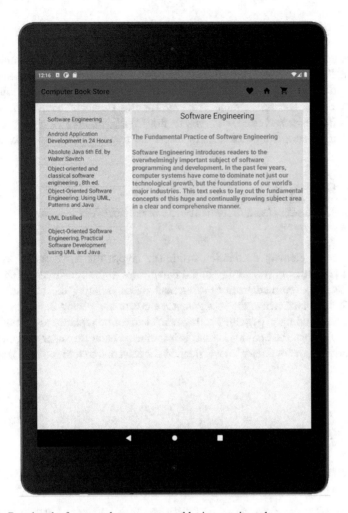

Fig. 9.13 Running the fragment demo app on a tablet in portrait mode

9.3.6   *Inserting Fragments in the Activity*

In general, fragments appear on their enclosing activity's GUI (graphical user interface) using one of the following attachment approaches:

9.3.6.1   Dynamic Binding

The main activity defines a place on its GUI, or layout, for the fragments to be plugged in (or attached). The fragment in the designated area is not permanent. Later, the hosting activity may replace or swap a fragment with another one. We have followed this approach in developing our demo app.

9.3.6.2   Static Binding

When using the static binding approach, an XML element called <fragment> will be included in an activity's layout XML file. The fragment element will have a *name* attribute to define the fragment class, and the value of the attributed will be the fragment class. The name/value property for the fragment element is like this *"android:name=fragmentName"* where the ***fragmentName*** is a fragment class name. Here is an example of how to insert the fragment into the activity layout statically.

```
<LinearLayout
  <fragment android:name=
    "code.abdulrahman.bookStore.BookTitleListFragment"/>
</ LinearLayout>
```

This simple element declaration inside the layout file saves you a call to the fragment constructors (or passing initial parameters to the constructor). The system inserts the **view** returned from the fragment (from inflating the fragment layout) directly in the place where the <fragment> element has been put.

The static binding is permanent; fragments cannot be replaced at runtime. When the system creates the activity layout, it instantiates each fragment specified in the layout and calls the onCreateView() method for each one to retrieve each fragment's layout.

9.3.7   Fragment Static Binding Example

The code snippet in Listing 9.10 is an example of a layout file with two fragment elements statically positioned inside the layout file.

Listing 9.10 Static_fragment_layout.xml file.

```
<?xml version="1.0" encoding="utf-8"?>
<LinearLayout
  xmlns:android="http://schemas.android.com/apk/res/android"
  android:orientation="horizontal"
  android:layout_width="match_parent"
  android:layout_height="match_parent">
  <fragment android:name=
    "code.abdulrahman.bookStore.BookTitleListFragment"
    android:id="@+id/frame1"
    android:layout_weight="1"
    android:layout_width="0dp"
    android:layout_height="match_parent" />
  <fragment android:name=
```

```
    "code.abdulrahman.bookStore.BookTitleAndDescription1Fragment"
    android:id="@+id/frame2"
    android:layout_weight="2"
    android:layout_width="0dp"
    android:layout_height="match_parent" />
</LinearLayout>
```

To test the layout, you can create a simple activity, like the one shown in Listing 9.11, i.e., the StaticFragmentActivity. In our demo app, switch the launcher activity to StaticFragmentActivity, and run the app. The result is shown in Fig. 9.14. As you can see, both fragments are loaded, and the activity screen is divided into two parts.

Fig. 9.14 A screen that is made of two static fragments

Listing 9.11 StaticFragmentActivity.java for testing static fragments.

```
package code.abdulrahman.bookStore;
import android.os.Bundle;
import androidx.appcompat.app.AppCompatActivity;
public class StaticFragmentActivity extends AppCompatActivity implements
OnItemSelectedListener {
  @Override
  public void onCreate(Bundle savedInstanceState) {
    super.onCreate(savedInstanceState);
    setContentView(R.layout.static_fragment_layout);
  }
  public void onBookItemSelected(int position) {
  }
}
```

The hosting activity may at the same time display any number of fragments using a combination of static and dynamic binding.

9.4 Inheritance in Android

We have updated the demo app to create a modular view by using inheritance instead of fragments. At the start of the book, we said that an activity is the same as a class in Java. That means that like Java classes, an activity can extend another activity. In this part of the chapter, we will demonstrate activity subclassing and how to create a modular view using inheritance or subclassing.

9.4.1 Create a Base Activity

Let us create an activity to serve as a base class or superclass for our demo app. The BaseActivity class has two methods, and its associated layout holds a toolbar. The BaseActivity class definition is shown in Listing 9.12. The main components of the class and the way we make use of inheritance are described in the next subsections.

Listing 9.12 BaseActivity.java.

```java
package code.abdulrahman.bookStore;
import android.content.Intent;
import android.net.Uri;
import android.os.Bundle;
import android.view.Menu;
import android.view.MenuInflater;
import android.view.MenuItem;
import android.view.View;
import android.widget.Toast;
import androidx.appcompat.app.AppCompatActivity;
import androidx.appcompat.widget.Toolbar;
import com.google.android.material.snackbar.Snackbar;
public abstract class BaseActivity extends AppCompatActivity {
    Snackbar snackbar;
    View testView;
    String message;
    @Override
    protected void onCreate(Bundle savedInstanceState) {
        super.onCreate(savedInstanceState);
        setContentView(R.layout.activity_base);
        Toolbar myToolbar = findViewById(R.id.in_base_my_toolbar);
//1.
setSupportActionBar(myToolbar);
        snackbar = Snackbar.make(myToolbar, message,
        Snackbar.LENGTH_LONG).setAction("Action", null);
        onViewReady(savedInstanceState, getIntent());
    }
//2.
Protected void onViewReady(Bundle savedInstanceState, Intent intent) {
    // To be used by child activities.
    }
//3.
Protected abstract int getContentView();
    @Override
    public boolean onCreateOptionsMenu(Menu menu) {
        // invoked automatically by activity
        MenuInflater inflater = getMenuInflater();
        inflater.inflate(R.menu.main_activity_actions, menu);
        return true;
    }
    public boolean onOptionsItemSelected(MenuItem menuItem) {
        int id = menuItem.getItemId();
        switch (id) {
          case R.id.action_one:
            Intent intent =
             new Intent(BaseActivity.this, ChildActivity.class);
            startActivity(intent);
            break;
          case R.id.action_two:
            snackbar.setText("You are at home").show();
            break;
```

```
      case R.id.action_three:
        Uri webpage = Uri.parse(
          "http://www.wlu.ca/faculty/abdul-rahman-mawlood-yunis");
        intent = new Intent(Intent.ACTION_VIEW, webpage);
        if (intent.resolveActivity(getPackageManager()) != null) {
           startActivity(intent);
        }
        break;
      case R.id.action_about:
        Toast.makeText(this,
             "Version 1.0," + " Abdul-Rahman Mawlood-Yunis",
             Toast.LENGTH_LONG).show();
    }
    return true;
  }
}
```

9.4.1.1   onViewReady

In our BaseActivity class, we have defined a method called onViewReady() that is called inside the onCreate() method after calling the setContentView() method. The method has an empty body, and its implementation is left for the child class to write. This method allows child activities to attach new widgets or make changes to the layout of the base class.

9.4.1.2   getContentView

We have defined another method called ***getContentView()***. This method is an abstract method that needs to be implemented by the child class. This method will be used by the onViewReady() method to update or make changes to the layout of the base class.

9.4.1.3   Toolbar

The base class also includes a toolbar handling method, i.e., the onCreateOptionsMenu() method. The menu file and the menu handling method will be freely available to any activity that extends the BaseActivity class.

9.4.2   Layout for the BaseActivity

A layout for the BaseActivity class, called activity_base, is created and is shown in Listing 9.13:

Listing 9.13 activity_base.xml.

```xml
<?xml version="1.0" encoding="utf-8"?>
<LinearLayout
  xmlns:android="http://schemas.android.com/apk/res/android"
  xmlns:tools="http://schemas.android.com/tools"
  android:layout_width="match_parent"
  android:layout_height="match_parent"
  android:orientation="vertical"
  tools:context=".BaseActivity">
  <androidx.appcompat.widget.Toolbar
    android:id="@+id/in_base_my_toolbar"
    android:layout_width="match_parent"
    android:layout_height="?attr/actionBarSize"
    android:background="@color/colorPrimary" />
  <LinearLayout
    xmlns:android="http://schemas.android.com/apk/res/android"
    xmlns:tools="http://schemas.android.com/tools"
    android:layout_width="match_parent"
    android:layout_height="match_parent"
    tools:context=".DirectoryStructureActivity"
    android:orientation="vertical"
    android:id="@+id/baseLayout">
  </LinearLayout> </LinearLayout>
```

The activity_base.xml layout file has a toolbar and linear layout element in it. The linear layout element takes the whole screen view without having any components in it. This allows the child activities to update the layout content and attach widgets to it. The following three lines of code represent the main idea behind activity inheritance.

```
linearLayout = findViewById(R.id.baseLayout);
    LayoutInflater layoutInflater = LayoutInflater.from(ChildActivity.this);
    layoutInflater.inflate(getContentView(), linearLayout, true);
```

The code can be explained like this: first, we get the container, the linear layout container, that we have defined in the layout for the base class. It is an empty container, and we can add views to it. The linear layout is retrieved and used to initialize a local liner layout instance variable of the child activity.

Second, we create a LayoutInflater object for the child activity using **LayoutInflater.*from*(ChildActivity.this)**. This is another way to create a LayoutInflater object.

Lastly, we use the inflate method to instantiate a view object. In the last step, we get the child layout we have prepared for the child screen content and put it inside the empty linear layout container. By setting the last parameter of the inflate method to true, we are saying to add the child layout to the linear layout. The ChildActivity class is shown in Listing 9.14.

Listing 9.14 ChildActivity.java.

```java
package code.abdulrahman.bookStore;
import android.content.Intent;
import android.net.Uri;
import android.os.Bundle;
import android.view.LayoutInflater;
import android.view.MenuItem;
import android.widget.LinearLayout;
import android.widget.Toast;
public class ChildActivity extends BaseActivity {
  LinearLayout linearLayout;
  @Override
  protected int getContentView() {
    return R.layout.activity_child;
  }
  @Override
  protected void onViewReady(Bundle savedInstanceState, Intent intent) {
    super.onViewReady(savedInstanceState, intent);
    linearLayout = findViewById(R.id.baseLayout);
    LayoutInflater layoutInflater =
    LayoutInflater.from(ChildActivity.this);
    layoutInflater.inflate(getContentView(), linearLayout, true);
  }
  public boolean onOptionsItemSelected(MenuItem menuItem) {
    int id = menuItem.getItemId();
    String phoneNumber = "613 000 0000";
    switch (id) {
      case R.id.action_one:
        Intent intent = new Intent(Intent.ACTION_DIAL);
        intent.setData(Uri.parse("tel:" + phoneNumber));
        if (intent.resolveActivity(getPackageManager()) != null) {
          startActivity(intent);
        }
        break;
      case R.id.action_two:
        intent = new Intent(ChildActivity.this, NewMainActivity.class);
        startActivity(intent);
        break;
      case R.id.action_three:
        Uri webpage = Uri.parse(
        "http://www.wlu.ca/faculty/abdul-rahman-mawlood-yunis");
        intent = new Intent(Intent.ACTION_VIEW, webpage);
        if (intent.resolveActivity(getPackageManager()) != null) {
          startActivity(intent);
        }
        break;
      case R.id.action_about:
        Toast.makeText(this,
            "Version 1.0," + " Abdul-Rahman Mawlood-Yunis",
            Toast.LENGTH_LONG).show();
    }
    return true;
  }
}
```

In addition to updating the base layout, the child activity inherits the toolbar and overrides its onOptionItemSelected() method. When the toolbar items are clicked, the actions performed are different from the actions performed using the parent class.

9.4.3   No onCreate() Method for Child Class

You may have noticed that the child activity does not implement the onCreate() method; instead, it inherits it from the base class, and by overriding the *onViewReady*() method, it sets a different screen view for the activity.

To run the code above without any disruption to our fragment code, we create a new activity and named *NewMainActivity*. It is a copy of the main activity from our demo app with two minor changes:

(a) The parent class for NewMainActivity is BaseActivity and not AppCompatActivity.
(b) NewMainActivity doesn't have the onCreate() method. The content of the onCreate() from the main activity has been copied to the onViewReady() method.

To run the app and see the changes made, update the AndroidManifest.xml file, and set NewMainActivity to be the launcher activity. Figure 9.15 shows how *NewMainActivity* inherits the toolbar and attaches a new layout to the screen view without using the fragments.

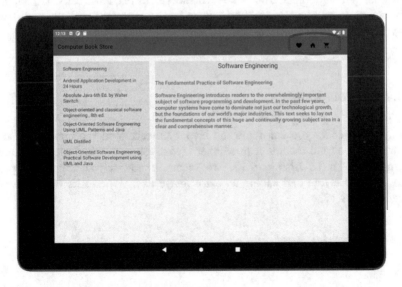

Fig. 9.15 Toolbar inherited from the base activity

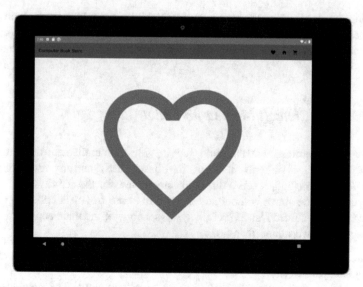

Fig. 9.16 Toolbar inherited from the base activity and view screen update

Clicking on the heart item on the menu bar of the *NewMainActivity screen* opens a new screen shown in Fig. 9.16, i.e., it launches a child activity. Figure 9.16 shows that both the NewMainActivity class and the child activity class inherit the same toolbar from the base class. However, when clicking on menu items of the child activity toolbar, they perform actions differently from the menu items of the NewMainActivity toolbar. The example demonstrates that child activities can have their unique screens and that inherited menu items can work differently in different activities.

9.4.4 Layout Reuse

Like reusing code, you can reuse the layout as well. You can create a base or common layout and include it in another layout using the **"include"** tag. In the example shown in Listing 9.15, we create a new layout by reusing the activity_child layout and adding an extra image to it. When it is loaded, it will produce Fig. 9.17.

Fig. 9.17 Reusing layout
example is shown

Listing 9.15 An example using "include" tag to reuse layout.

```xml
<?xml version="1.0" encoding="utf-8"?>
<LinearLayout xmlns:android=
 "http://schemas.android.com/apk/res/android"
  xmlns:tools="http://schemas.android.com/tools"
  android:layout_width="match_parent"
  android:layout_height="match_parent"
  android:orientation="vertical"
  tools:context=".TestActivity">
  <include
```

```
    layout="@layout/activity_child"
    android:layout_width="match_parent"
    android:layout_height="200dp" />
  <ImageView
    android:layout_width="match_parent"
    android:layout_height="100dp"
    android:src="@drawable/happyface" />
</LinearLayout>
```

To conclude, in this part, we showed that there are different ways to create your app screen. You can use fragments either statically or dynamically, use inheritance, or reuse layouts with the "include" tag.

9.5   Density-Independent Pixel and Screen Sizes

In this chapter, we used fragments to take advantage of the extra space that larger Android devices provide. We did that by creating more than one layout file for a given activity. In this part, we explore how to create and name your layout files.

9.5.1   Naming Scheme

Originally in Android 3.0, you would put the layout file for large devices in the layout-xlarge folder. As of Android 3.2, the folder name needs to follow a certain pattern. In this new format, the pixel size of the display is used to name folders for different devices.

The layout folder for devices in various sizes is named following this format: sw<Number>dp. SW means the smallest width or the smallest possible number of pixels for height or width, for example, layout-sw600dp. Here, for a device to be considered compatible with your app layout, the device's smallest width must be equal to or greater than 600dp. (Usually, the number or value you supply is the "smallest width" that your layout supports, regardless of the screen's current orientation.) In our demo app, we used **layout-sw600dp**.

You can use **w<N>dp**, where w means that your display should be at least N pixels wide. You can also use **h<N>dp**, where **h** is for height instead of width. Table 9.2 summarizes the type of device and the file width you should consider for your app. It also shows the folder names of the layout files.

Table 9.2 The name of the layout folders for different device sizes

320dp	Phone	res/layout/main_activity.xml
480dp	Large phone	res/layout/main_activity.xml
600dp	7 inches tablet	res/layout-sw600dp/main_activity.xml
720dp	10 inches tablet	res/layout-sw720dp/main_activity.xml

To tell Android that your application checks for various screen sizes, you need to define the <**supports-screens**> element in your manifest file. For example, by putting the following statement in your manifest file, you are specifying that the minimum width required for your app is 600 dp.

```
<supports-screens android:requiresSmallestWidthDp="600" />
```

You can also specify a layout for the landscape or portrait mode of the devices using the folder names: *layout-land* and *layout-port*.

9.5.2 Supporting Different Screen Sizes

When you do not provide alternative layouts for your app, Android applies normal resizing. The normal resizing done by Android is fine for most applications. However, it is better if you take care of optimizing your application's UI by yourself. In this chapter, we created alternative layouts for activities to run apps on both phones and tablets ourselves.

To determine if your app supports a given screen size, check to see whether or not your app fills an entire screen when resized. If your application does not appear as desired when resized to fit different screen sizes, you can specify a smaller device screen for your application.

This is done using the <supports-screens> element. Similarly, you can control your UI scaled up to fit larger screens.

It is better to optimize your UI for different screens; otherwise, users will experience blurred UI components, also called pixelation. When your app is not designed for larger screen sizes and the normal resizing does not achieve the appropriate results, the Android screen compatibility mode will scale your UI by emulating a normal size screen and medium density and then zooming in so that it fills the entire screen. This causes the pixelation of your UI, something you can avoid by optimizing your UI for large screens.

9.5.2.1 Create Directory Using Android Studio

To create a new *Android Resource directory* for your app, right-click on the res folder in your project, select new, and click on the Android Resource Directory item in the menu as shown in Fig. 9.18.

The step above results in a popup window as shown in Fig. 9.19. Fill in or select values for the resource file fields as shown in the window below. The new resource file (an XML file) will be created in the specified location with a proper name for your app.

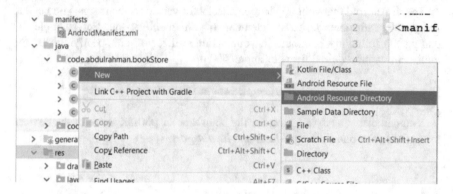

Fig. 9.18 Create a new Android resource directory with Android Studio

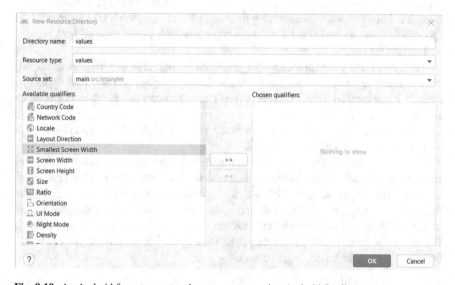

Fig. 9.19 An Android form to create a layout resource using Android Studio

Different from what we described above, you can create an alternative layout in Android Studio using the *Orientation for Preview* tab in the layout editor.

Open your app layout and click *Orientation for Preview* in the toolbar. In the dropdown list, click to create a suggested variant such as *Create Landscape Variant* or *Create Other*. A new layout folder will be created in a proper folder. These steps are shown below in Fig. 9.20.

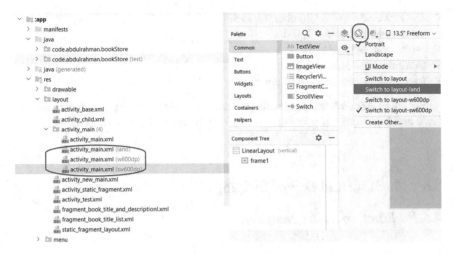

Fig. 9.20 Using orientation for preview in the toolbar in the layout editor

9.5.3 Density-Independent Pixel (dp)

Different devices have different densities or dpi (dots per inch). To express layout dimensions or positions without knowing the density of the device, you need to use dp. dp is a virtual pixel unit and is equivalent to one physical pixel on a 160-dpi screen. For example, if the density of your device is 320 dpi, then every dp you specify in your layout will take two pixels. At runtime, Android scales the dp units based on the actual density of the screen in use.

The conversion of dp units to screen pixels is as follows: $px = dp * (dpi / 160)$. For example, on a 480-dpi screen, the conversion is $px = dp * (480/160)$. That is, a $px = 3$ dp or 1 dp equals to 1/3 physical pixels. The number 160 dpi is the baseline density assumed by Android for a "medium" density screen. You should always use dp units when defining your application's UI to ensure the proper display of your UI on screens with different densities.

9.5.3.1 Various Drawable Sizes

If you specify a bitmap that is 128x128 pixels, it will take up a large part of a small screen but a small space on a large screen. Android has several folder names for drawable resources that you can use for saving images to deal with different screen sizes. The folders are:

- res/drawable-ldpi/ – 120 dots per inch (dpi)
- res/drawable-mdpi/ – 160 dpi
- res/drawable-hdpi/ – 240 dpi
- res/drawable-xhdpi/ – 320 dpi
- res/drawable-xxhdpi/ – 480 dpi

For small size devices, you create your image and save it in the ldpi folder, and for large and high-resolution devices, you save your image in the xxhdp folder.

9.6   Pinching and Screen Swiping

9.6.1   Pinch to Zoom Image

In this part, we look at the pinch gesture, i.e., using two fingers to zoom in and out of a view or image. This can be done using the *ScaleGestureDetector* and *SimpleOnScaleGestureListener* classes. The *SimpleOnScaleGestureListener* class implements the ScaleGestureDetector.OnScaleGestureListener interface. The latter has three callback methods, and they are *onScale*(), onScaleBegin(), and onScaleEnd(). The *onScale*() method responds to scaling events for a gesture in progress, the *onScaleBegin*() method responds to the beginning of a scaling gesture, and the *onScaleEnd*() method responds to the end of a scale gesture. If you want to implement all three callback methods, your class should implement the OnScaleGestureListener interface; otherwise, your class needs to extend the *SimpleOnScaleGestureListener* class. The *SimpleOnScaleGestureListener* class provides empty, or dummy, implementations for all three methods in the OnScaleGestureListener interface. You will only override the methods that you want to implement.

To use pinch gestures in your app, you need to do the following:

1. Create a class that extends the SimpleOnScaleGestureListener class and overrides one or more methods of the SimpleOnScaleGestureListener class that you would like to implement. An example is shown below:

```
public class MyImageScaling extends
      ScaleGestureDetector.SimpleOnScaleGestureListener {
      @Override
      public boolean onScale(ScaleGestureDetector
                             scaleGestureDetector) {
             super.onScale(scaleGestureDetector);
      }
}
```

2. Instantiate a gesture detector object of type ScaleGestureDetector with a listener object of type SimpleOnScaleGestureListener as a parameter to the gesture detector constructor. This step is shown below.

```
public class MainActivity extends AppCompatActivity {
  private ScaleGestureDetector aScaleGestureDetector;
  @Override
  protected void onCreate(Bundle savedInstanceState) {
        new ScaleGestureDetector(this, new MyImageScaling());
  }
```

3. Implement the onTouchEvent() callback method for the enclosing activity. The method implementation should call the onTouchEvent() method of the ScaleGestureDetector class. This is can be done as follows:

```
@Override
public boolean onTouchEvent(MotionEvent event) {
  return aScaleGestureDetector.onTouchEvent(event);
}
```

In Listing 9.16, a simple class is created that implements the SimpleOnScaleGestureListener and overrides the onScale() method.

Listing 9.16 Implements the SimpleOnScaleGestureListener interface.

```
package com.code.abdulrahman.pinchingapp;
import android.view.ScaleGestureDetector;

public class MyImageScaling extends
                ScaleGestureDetector.SimpleOnScaleGestureListener {
  private float sFactor = 0.5f;
  @Override
  public boolean onScale(ScaleGestureDetector scaleGestureDetector) {
    sFactor = sFactor * scaleGestureDetector.getScaleFactor();
    MainActivity.anImageView.setScaleX(sFactor);
    MainActivity.anImageView.setScaleY(sFactor);
    return true;
  }
}
```

Listing 9.17 shows the main activity class where *ScaleGestureDetector* is instantiated and ImageScaling class is used to listen to gestures.

Listing 9.17 Implements the SimpleOnScaleGestureListener interface.

```
package com.code.abdulrahman.pinchingapp;
import android.os.Bundle;
import android.view.MotionEvent;
import android.view.ScaleGestureDetector;
import android.widget.ImageView;
import androidx.appcompat.app.AppCompatActivity;

public class MainActivity extends AppCompatActivity {
  protected static ImageView anImageView;
  private ScaleGestureDetector aScaleGestureDetector;

  @Override
  protected void onCreate(Bundle savedInstanceState) {
    super.onCreate(savedInstanceState);
    setContentView(R.layout.activity_main);
    anImageView = findViewById(R.id.forDirectionView);
    aScaleGestureDetector =
        new ScaleGestureDetector(this, new MyImageScaling());
  }
  @Override
  public boolean onTouchEvent(MotionEvent event) {
    return aScaleGestureDetector.onTouchEvent(event);
  }
}
```

In Listing 9.18, a layout file for the main activity is shown. The layout includes one image view to be scaled in and out by the user.

Listing 9.18 Implements the SimpleOnScaleGestureListener interface.

```
<?xml version="1.0" encoding="utf-8"?>
<LinearLayout xmlns:android=
  "http://schemas.android.com/apk/res/android"
  android:layout_width="match_parent"
  android:layout_height="match_parent">
  <ImageView
    android:id="@+id/forDirectionView"
    android:layout_width="match_parent"
    android:layout_height="match_parent"
    android:layout_centerInParent="true"
    android:src="@drawable/ic_baseline_zoom_out_map_24" />
</LinearLayout>
```

9.6.1.1 Do It Yourself

Create a project using the code given in Listing 9.17. Run the code, and scale the image view to familiarize yourself with using the image and text scale classes and interfaces.

9.6.2 Swiping Gesture

Android supports multiple common gestures that you can implement in your app. These include support for implementing tap down, tap up, swipe from left to right or right to left (also called fling), double-tap, scroll, etc. In this part, we develop an app to show you how to implement some of these gestures.

You can implement gesture functionalities by extending the *SimpleOnGestureListener* class. This class is an adapter class; it provides dummy implementations for all methods of three interfaces, the *OnGestureListener*, *OnDoubleTapListener*, and *OnContextClickListener* interfaces. The *SimpleOnGestureListener* class declaration in the Android API is as follows:

```
public static class GestureDetector.SimpleOnGestureListener extends
    Object
    implements GestureDetector.OnGestureListener,
              GestureDetector.OnDoubleTapListener,
              GestureDetector.OnContextClickListener
```

Since method implementations of the *SimpleOnGestureListener* class are dummies, i.e., do nothing other than returning some values, you need to override some of the class methods, the one's that you would like to listen to but not necessarily all the methods.

9.6.3 Swiping Gesture App

We have created an app where a new screen is created when the user swipes right, left, up, or down on the main screen. The activities created for this app are shown in Fig. 9.21, and they are MainActivity, LeftScreen, RightScreen, UpScreen, and DownScreen. The code snippets for the app are listed in the below subsections.

To handle swipe gestures, you need to register the view that will handle the swipe. For our demo app, the entire screen is registered to respond to the swipe event. This is done in two steps. First, we assign an id to the screen layout. Second, inside the main activity class, the screen layout is referenced using its id, and the layout is set to listen to screen touches using the *setOnTouchListener* method. These two steps are highlighted in boldface font in Listings 9.19 and 9.20.

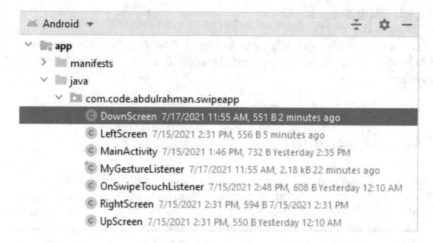

Fig. 9.21 The activities created for this swipe app

Listing 9.19 Assign an id to the screen layout.

```xml
<?xml version="1.0" encoding="utf-8"?>
 <LinearLayout
  xmlns:android="http://schemas.android.com/apk/res/android"
  android:orientation="vertical"
  android:layout_width="match_parent"
  android:layout_height="match_parent"
  android:id="@+id/surface">
  <TextView
    android:layout_width="wrap_content"
    android:layout_height="100dp"
    android:layout_marginHorizontal="70dp"
    android:layout_marginVertical="100dp"
    android:background="@mipmap/ic_launcher"
    android:text="Swipe Right/Left or UP/Down"
    android:textSize="18sp"
    android:textStyle="bold" />
</LinearLayout>
```

To respond to the user screen swipe, i.e., to handle the swipe event, the MainActivity class implements the OnTouchListener interface. This interface has one method that needs to be implemented. The method is called *onTouch*(), and when the user swipes the app screen, it listens to the motion event. The onTouch() method from the MainActivity class calls the *onTouchEvent*() method from the *gestureDetector* class and passes the MotionEvent event as a parameter.

Note that the event parameter here is of type MotionEvent which is different from the type of events associated with, for example, mouse clicks or button presses which are usually of type ActionEvent. Also note that the class that handles all the swipe events is called *MyGestureListener* and is instantiated inside the onCreate() method of the MainActivity class. The code snippet for the MainActivity class is shown in Listing 9.20.

Listing 9.20 Referencing screen layout set it to listen to screen touch.

```
package com.code.abdulrahman.swipeapp;
import android.annotation.SuppressLint;
import android.os.Bundle;
import android.view.GestureDetector;
import android.view.MotionEvent;
import android.view.View;
import android.widget.LinearLayout;
import androidx.appcompat.app.AppCompatActivity;

public class MainActivity extends AppCompatActivity implements
                                        View.OnTouchListener {
    private LinearLayout surface;
    private GestureDetector gestureDetector;

    @SuppressLint("ClickableViewAccessibility")
    @Override
    protected void onCreate(Bundle savedInstanceState) {
        super.onCreate(savedInstanceState);
        setContentView(R.layout.activity_main);
        surface = findViewById(R.id.surface);
gestureDetector = new GestureDetector(this, new MyGestureListener(this));
        surface.setOnTouchListener(this);
    }
    @Override
    public boolean onTouch(View v, MotionEvent event) {
        return gestureDetector.onTouchEvent(event);
    }
}
```

The implementation of the *MyGestureListener* class is shown in Listing 9.21. This class implements two gesture methods, onDown() and onFling(). It also initializes the context, or screen that the gesture is applied to, inside its constructor. It is a good practice to always implement the onDown() method that returns true. This is because all gestures begin with an onDown() message. The onFling() is called when the user drags on the screen with a velocity greater than a user-specified velocity threshold.

Listing 9.21   The implementation of the MyGestureListener class.

```
package com.code.abdulrahman.swipeapp;
import android.content.Context;
import android.content.Intent;
import android.view.GestureDetector;
import android.view.MotionEvent;

public final class MyGestureListener extends
GestureDetector.SimpleOnGestureListener {

  private static final int swipe_value = 80;
  private static final int swipe_velocity_value = 80;
  Context context;

  public MyGestureListener(Context context) {
    this.context = context;
  }
  @Override
  public boolean onDown(MotionEvent e) {
    return true;
  }
  @Override
  public boolean onFling(MotionEvent point1,
                         MotionEvent point2, float vX, float vY) {
    boolean moving = false;
    try {
      float y = point2.getY() - point1.getY();
      float x = point2.getX() - point1.getX();
      if (Math.abs(x) > Math.abs(y)) {
        if (Math.abs(x) > swipe_value && Math.abs(vX) >
            swipe_velocity_value) {
          if (x > 0) {
            onSwipeRight();
          } else {
            onSwipeLeft();
          }
          moving = true;
        }
      } else if (Math.abs(y) > swipe_value && Math.abs(vY) >
        swipe_velocity_value) {
        if (y > 0) {
          onSwipeBottom();
        } else {
          onSwipeTop();
        }
        moving = true;
      }
    } catch (Exception e) {
      e.printStackTrace();
    }
```

```
      return moving;
  }
  public void onSwipeTop() {
    context.startActivity(new Intent(context,
         com.code.abdulrahman.swipeapp.UpScreen.class));
  }
  public void onSwipeRight() {
    context.startActivity(new Intent(context,
         com.code.abdulrahman.swipeapp.RightScreen.class));
  }
  public void onSwipeLeft() {
    context.startActivity(new Intent(context,
         com.code.abdulrahman.swipeapp.LeftScreen.class));
  }
  public void onSwipeBottom() {
    context.startActivity(new Intent(context, DownScreen.class));
  }
}
```

Listings 9.22 and 9.23 are code snippets for simple screens that are displayed when the user swipes to the right and up, respectively. In our demo app, two other screens are used for left and down swipes.

Listing 9.22 Simple screen that is displayed when the user swipes to the right.

```
package com.code.abdulrahman.swipeapp;
import androidx.appcompat.app.AppCompatActivity;
import android.content.Intent;
import android.os.Bundle;

public class RightScreen extends AppCompatActivity {
  @Override
  protected void onCreate(Bundle savedInstanceState) {
    super.onCreate(savedInstanceState);
    setTitle("Right Screen");
    setContentView(R.layout.activity_right_screen);
  }
  @Override
  public void onBackPressed() {
    super.onBackPressed();
    startActivity (new Intent(RightScreen.this, MainActivity.class));
  }
}
```

Listing 9.23 Simple screen that is displayed when the user swipes up.

```
package com.code.abdulrahman.swipeapp;
import androidx.appcompat.app.AppCompatActivity;
import android.content.Intent;
import android.os.Bundle;

public class UpScreen extends AppCompatActivity {

  @Override
  protected void onCreate(Bundle savedInstanceState) {
    super.onCreate(savedInstanceState);
    setContentView(R.layout.activity_up_screen);
  }
  @Override
  public void onBackPressed() {
    super.onBackPressed();
    startActivity (new Intent(UpScreen.this, MainActivity.class)) ;
  }
}
```

The AndroidManifest.xml file is shown in Listing 9.24 to complete the source code for the swipe demo app. It also includes a code for defining the parent-child relationship between activities.

Listing 9.24 The AndroidManifest.xml for the swipe demo app.

```
<?xml version="1.0" encoding="utf-8"?>
<manifest xmlns:android=
 "http://schemas.android.com/apk/res/android"
 package="com.code.abdulrahman.swipeapp"
 android:versionCode="1"
 android:versionName="1.0" >
 <uses-sdk
   android:minSdkVersion="26"
   android:targetSdkVersion="30" />
 <application
   android:allowBackup="true"
   android:appComponentFactory="androidx.core.app.
   CoreComponentFactory"
   android:debuggable="true"
   android:extractNativeLibs="false"
   android:icon="@mipmap/ic_launcher"
   android:label="@string/app_name"
   android:roundIcon="@mipmap/ic_launcher_round"
   android:supportsRtl="true"
   android:testOnly="true"
   android:theme="@style/Theme.SwipeApp" >
```

```
<activity
    android:name="com.code.abdulrahman.swipeapp.DownActivity"
    android:parentActivityName=
        "com.code.abdulrahman.swipeapp.MainActivity" />
<activity
    android:name="com.code.abdulrahman.swipeapp.UpScreen"
    android:parentActivityName=
            "com.code.abdulrahman.swipeapp.MainActivity" />
<activity
    android:name="com.code.abdulrahman.swipeapp.LeftScreen"
    android:parentActivityName=
                "com.code.abdulrahman.swipeapp.MainActivity" />
<activity
    android:name="com.code.abdulrahman.swipeapp.RightScreen"
    android:parentActivityName=
                "com.code.abdulrahman.swipeapp.MainActivity" />
<activity android:name=
    "com.code.abdulrahman.swipeapp.MainActivity" >
    <intent-filter>
        <action android:name="android.intent.action.MAIN" />
        <category android:name="android.intent.category.LAUNCHER" />
    </intent-filter>
</activity>
</application>
</manifest>
```

9.6.3.1 Do It Yourself

Create an app that handles user swipe events to the right, left, up, and down. Reuse the code snippets in Listings 19.19 to 19.24 to develop such an app.

9.7 Chapter Summary

The best way to make your application work well on various devices is to support multiple screens and provide alternative layouts for different screen sizes. Fragments enable you to build an app screen that is made of multiple parts allowing you to support multiple screen sizes. We have described how to use fragments and the fragment manager and fragment transactions classes to create transactions to add, replace, or remove fragments from the app screens using frame layouts. We also explained that device configurations/orientations can change during runtime. When such a change occurs, Android restarts the running activity. We have designed and implemented an app that adapts to the orientation changes by automatically reloading the app with alternative layouts that match the new device orientation.

We also described how to use class inheritance in Android to reuse layouts by including an existing layout into a newly created layout. Lastly, we described how to scale images and text views using screen pinches and how to respond to screen swipe events to the right, left, up, and down.

Check Your Knowledge

Below are some of the fundamental concepts and vocabularies that have been covered in this chapter. To test your knowledge and your understanding of this chapter, you should be able to describe each of the below concepts in one or two sentences.

- BackStack
- Dynamic fragment
- Fragment
- FragmentManager
- FragmentTransaction
- FrameLayout
- Include for including layout
- layout.simple_list_item_1
- onAttach
- onContextClickListener
- onCreateView
- onDetach
- onDoubleTapListener
- onGestureListener
- ScaleGestureDetector
- SimpleOnGestureListener
- SimpleOnScaleGestureListener
- Static fragment

Further Reading

For more information about the topics covered in this chapter, we suggest that you refer to the online resources listed below. These links provide additional insight into the topics covered. The links are mostly maintained by Google and are a part of the Android API specification. The resource titles convey which section/subsection of the chapter the resource is related to.

Advanced Android 01.1: Fragments, [online] Available, https://developer.android.com/codelabs/advanced-android-training-fragments#0

FragmentManager, [online] Available, https://developer.android.com/reference/kotlin/androidx/fragment/app/FragmentManager

Fragments, [online] Available, https://developer.android.com/guide/fragments

Fragment transactions, [online] Available, https://developer.android.com/guide/fragments/transactions

FrameLayout, [online] Available, https://developer.android.com/reference/android/widget/FrameLayout

Layout, [online] Available, https://developer.android.com/reference/android/R. layout#simple_list_item_1

Re-using layouts with <include/>, [online] Available, https://developer. android.com/training/improvinglayouts/reusing-layouts

Support different screen sizes, [online] Available, https://developer.android. com/training/multiscreen/screensizes

Supports-screens, [online] Available, https://developer.android.com/guide/ topics/manifest/supports-screens-element

Understand Tasks and Back Stack, [online] Available, https://developer. android.com/guide/components/activities/tasks-and-back-stack

Chapter 10
Parsing Remote XML and JSON Files, Using HTTPUrlConnection, XmlPullParser, and AsyncTask

Learning Outcome
By the end of this chapter, you will be able to:

- Connect to a remote server using HttpsURLConnection
- Set up an AsyncTask
- Use UI (user interface) threads and run the code in the background
- Parse XML and JSON documents using XMLPullParser
- Save files to the Android device's storage
- Create an app to display real-time weather information in Canada
- Create an app to display real-time Covid-19 information

Check Out the Demo Project
Download the demo app, **xmlProcessingProject.zip**, specifically developed to go with this chapter. I recommend that you code this project up from the notes rather than just opening the project in Android Studio and running it; however, if you want to run the code first to get a sense of the app, please do so. The code is thoroughly explained in this chapter to help you understand it. We follow the same approach to all other chapters throughout the book. The app's code will help you comprehend the additional concepts that will be described in this chapter.

  How to run the code: unzip the code in a folder of your choice, and then in Android Studio, click **File->import->Existing Android code into the workspace**. The project should start running.

10.1 Introduction

In this chapter, we will study how to process data asynchronously using an AsyncTask class. We will describe how to connect your app to a server using HttpsURLConnection and to process remote XML, JSON, and image files stored

© The Author(s), under exclusive license to Springer Nature Switzerland AG 2022   433
A.-R. Mawlood-Yunis, *Android for Java Programmers*,
https://doi.org/10.1007/978-3-030-87459-9_10

on the Web. You will learn about UI threads and running code in the background thread. We will also study XML files, XML elements, attributes, and processing.

10.2   Parsing Remote and Local XML Files

The eXtensible Markup Language (XML) is a set of rules for encoding documents or text in a machine-readable format. It is a popular format for sharing data on the internet. Websites that frequently update their content, such as news sites, stock markets, or blogs, often provide XML feeds so that external programs can have up-to-date information for their users. Uploading and parsing XML data is a common task for network-connected apps. In this section, we explain how to parse and use the data extracted from online XML files.

10.2.1   XML Parser Review

Android has two types of parsers, i.e., XML readers. They are called XML push parser and XML pull parser (XMLPullParser). They are used to parse, i.e., process, the input files. A widely used parser, the Simple API for XML, or SAX, implements the *push parser* model. There are differences between the two parsing models, and each has its advantages and drawbacks. The difference between the two models is mainly in how the data flows during parsing. Below, the two models are described briefly.

10.2.2   Push Parsing

Push parsing refers to a programming model in which an XML parser sends (pushes) XML data to the processing program or client program as the parser encounters XML elements or tags in the documents. Here, the parser sends data to the client program regardless of whether or not the client is ready to use it at that time. That means, the push parser requires you to register or implement the callback methods to handle events generated from the processing. While the parser reads data or loops over the documents, the callback methods are dispatched as the event occurs. During file or XML document parsing, the control remains with the parser until the end of the document is reached, i.e., the end of the loop reached. Since you don't have control over the parser, you have to maintain knowledge of the parser's state; your callback methods need to know where they are called.

10.2.2.1   Push Parser Iterator

As the push parser iterates over all the tags in an XML file, it uses these function handlers: startDocument(), endDocument(), startElement(), endElement(), and characters(). For example, the sequence of function calls for the simple xml document in Listing 10.1 is shown below:

Listing 10.1 Simple XML file.

```
<?XML version="1.0"?>
<Quiz>
  <Title> Quiz 1 </Title>
  <Question>Your name: </Question>
</Quiz>

startDocument(), for starting document.
startElement() for the Quiz opening tag.
startElement() for the Title opening tag.
characters() for the "Quiz 1" text.
endElement() for the Title.
startElement() for the Question.
characters() for the "Your name:" text.
endElement() for the Question.
endElement() for the Quiz.
endDocument() for end document
```

The problem with the push parser model is that it scans the whole document at once and calls element handlers for you. To know which elements have already been processed, for example, if the title element in the listing above has been processed, you must use variables to store the tags that you have already seen.

10.2.3   Pull Parser

The pull parser refers to a programming model in which the client application processes the input XML documents when it needs to interact with them. The client receives, i.e., pulls, the XML data only when it explicitly asks for it. In short, the pull parser works like the push parser, except that you control when the parser advances to the next element. A pull parser is what Google recommends for parsing XML data. For this chapter, we will use the XMLPullParser API to process XML documents received from a remote server. We use our demo app as a running example to explain the concepts and code you need to learn to process online XML files.

10.2.4   Remote XML Parsing

The first step in parsing XML files is to decide which fields of an XML document you are interested in. The parser can extract data for those fields and ignore the rest. In other words, you have to understand your app requirements. Below, we explain the steps involved in parsing an XML file using the pull parser approach.

10.2.4.1   Input File

An example of an XML input file is shown in Listing 10.2. It is similar to the file used in our demo app as input data. The file is retrieved from a remote server and shows the weather information for the city of Kitchener, Ontario, Canada.

Listing 10.2 Weather.xml file retrieved from a remote server.

```
<current>
  <city id="6176823" name="Waterloo">
    <coord lon="-80.52" lat="43.47"/>
    <country>CA</country>
    <timezone>-14400</timezone>
    <sun rise="2020-03-09T11:44:04" set="2020-03-09T23:21:06"/>
  </city>
  <temperature value="12.14" min="10.56" max="15" unit="celsius"/>
  <feels_like value="8.16" unit="celsius"/>
  <humidity value="62" unit="%"/>
  <pressure value="1019" unit="hPa"/>
  <wind>
    <speed value="4.1" unit="m/s" name="Gentle Breeze"/>
    <gusts/>
    <direction value="190" code="S" name="South"/>
  </wind>
  <clouds value="40" name="scattered clouds"/>
  <visibility value="14484"/>
  <precipitation mode="no"/>
  <weather number="802" value="scattered clouds" icon="03n"/>
  <lastupdate value="2020-03-10T00:17:46"/>
</current>
```

For our demo app, we are interested in the values of five elements from the input file, that is, we need to extract data for these elements: current temperature, min temperature, max temperature, wind speed, and weather image. Figure 10.1 shows all the fields we are interested in when the app starts running.

Fig. 10.1 The interface for
weather information app

10.2.4.2   Parser Instantiation Using XmlPullParser Class

After analyzing our input file, the next step in the development process is to instantiate
a parser and start the parsing process. Android has a class called android.util.Xml with
a public static method called newPullParser() to create XmlPullParser objects. You get
an instance of the XmlPullParser by calling the newPullParser() factory method, e.g.,
XmlPullParser parser = Xml.newPullParser();
 The XmlPullParser class has multiple utility methods to process and parse XML
elements. The setFeature() method, for example, is used to change the general

behavior of the parser, i.e., to change the namespace processing or doctype declaration handling. To ask XmlPullParser to not process the XML namespaces, use the
setFeature() method like this.

```
parser.setFeature(
        XmlPullParser.FEATURE_PROCESS_NAMESPACES, false);
```

The XmlPullParser has multiple methods to set the input stream for the parser to
process, for example, **setInput(InputStream inputStream, String inputEncoding)**.
In our demo code, we used **parser.setInput(inputStream, null)** to reset the parser
state and set the event type to the initial value *START_DOCUMENT*. The described
steps can be summarized as follows:

```
XmlPullParser parser = Xml.newPullParser();
parser.setFeature(
XmlPullParser.FEATURE_PROCESS_NAMESPACES, false);
parser.setInput(input, null);
```

10.2.4.3   Connecting to Server Using HTTPUrlConnection

To connect to an HTTP server, Android uses the *HTTPUrlConnection* class. You
can get Facebook updates, weather information, stock prices, tweets, and other
similar services using the HTTPUrlConnection class. Connecting to the server
involves multiple steps. The steps are:

1. The HTTPUrlConnection class starts with a URL object which takes a string in
   the constructor. Here is an example of how to create a URL object.

```
URL url = new URL(
         "https://api.openweathermap.org/" +
             "data/2.5/weather?q=" + this.city +"," +
             "ca&APPID=79cecf493cb6e52d25bb7b7050ff723c&" +
             "mode=xml&units=metric");
```

2. From the URL, you need to call the openConnection() method. This returns a
   URLConnection object that represents a connection to the remote server referred
   to by the URL. The example below starts the connection to the weather network
   passed to the URL class constructor.

```
HttpsURLConnection urlConnection = (HttpURLConnection)
url.openConnection();
```

3. To read an input stream from an open connection, call the getInputStream()
   method from your connection object; here is an example:
   InputStream **in** = urlConnection.**getInputStream()** ;.

4. Pass the InputStream to the XMLPullParser and start processing:

```
parser.setInput (in, null ) ; .
```

Once you have passed the URL to the setInput() method, you are ready to process the parser events. The code snippet in Listing 10.3 shows how to create a URL object and how it is used with the parser.

Listing 10.3 Create a URL object and use it with the parser.

```
@Override
  protected String doInBackground(String... strings) {
    try {
      URL url = new URL(
            "https://api.openweathermap.org/" +
                "data/2.5/weather?q=" + this.city +"," +
                "ca&APPID=79cecf493cb6e52d25bb7b7050ff723c&" +
                "mode=xml&units=metric") ;
          HttpsURLConnection conn =
        (HttpsURLConnection) url.openConnection();
          conn.setReadTimeout(10000) ;
          conn.setConnectTimeout(15000) ;
          conn.setRequestMethod("GET") ;
          conn.setDoInput(true) ;
          conn.connect() ;
          InputStream in = conn.getInputStream() ;
      try {
          XmlPullParser parser = Xml.newPullParser();
          parser.setFeature(
          XmlPullParser.FEATURE_PROCESS_NAMESPACES, false);
          parser.setInput(in, null);
      } ...}
```

10.2.5   Parsing Events

By default, the XML pull parser starts at the first element of the XML file that is being processed. You need to use two parser methods, the getEventType() and next() methods, to iterate over the XML file. To examine each element of the document, you call the *getEventType()* method, and the return result can be either: START_DOCUMENT, START_TAG, TEXT, END_TAG, or END_DOCUMENT. You call the *next()* method to advance to the next tag.

For the start and end tags, you can call getName() method to get the tag's name or the getAttributeValue() method to get the attributes of the start/end tags. The code snippet below shows how to use the getEventType(), getName(), and getAttributeValue() methods to get max and min values for the temperature element in the weather information XML file.

```
if (parser.getEventType() == XmlPullParser.START_TAG) {
    if (parser.getName().equals("temperature")) {
        currentTemp = parser.getAttributeValue(null, "value");
        minTemp = parser.getAttributeValue(null, "min")
        maxTemp = parser.getAttributeValue(null, "max");
    }
}
```

If the tag is a text or a string, call the getText() method to get the string value. In the example below, we read an XML element attribute *id* as a string and cast the value to an integer for further processing.

```
String currentTag =null ;
if (parser.getEventType() == XmlPullParser.START_TAG) {
    currentTag= parser.getName();
}else if (parser.getEventType() == XmlPullParser.TEXT){
    currentTag= parser.getText();
    if ("id".equals(currentTag)){
      int id = Integer.getInteger(parser.getText()) ;
    }
}
```

10.2.5.1 Parsing Loop

The Android parsing algorithm should use a while() loop, where you call next() until you reach the END_DOCUMENT tag. For our sample weather XML file, we used the following while loop to process the XML file, see the code snippet in Listing 10.4.

Listing 10.4 Parsing loop example.

```
while ((type = parser.getEventType()) !=
              XmlPullParser.END_DOCUMENT) {
    if (parser.getEventType() == XmlPullParser.START_TAG) {
        if (parser.getName().equals("temperature")) {
            currentTemp = parser.getAttributeValue(null, "value");
            minTemp = parser.getAttributeValue(null, "min");
            maxTemp = parser.getAttributeValue(null, "max");
            } else if (parser.getName().equals("weather")) {
                ...
            } else if (parser.getName().equals("wind")) {
                ...
            }} parser.next();
    }
```

The first event is of type START_DOCUMENT; hence, we continue reading the input file until we encounter the END_DOCUMENT tag. The stopping condition for the loop is expressed as follows:

```
while((type = parser.getEventType()) !=
        XmlPullParser.END_DOCUMENT) {...}.
```

In each step as the document is processed, we advance to the next event by calling the next() method, i.e., parser.next(). The code simply keeps on advancing to the next event until it encounters the START_TAG which is the beginning of a new element in the XML file. Don't confuse the START_TAG, which represents the start of an element, with the START_DOCUMENT tag, which represents the start of a document.

Once we hit the beginning of a new element, we retrieve the element's local name by calling the getName() method. When namespace processing is disabled, the raw name is returned. The code statement below shows how the getName() method is used to check the start of the new XML element.

```
if(parser.getName().equals("temperature");
```

We then use the *getAttributeValue()* method to retrieve the temperature values, current, min, and max, from the temperature element <temperature value="3.5" unit="metric" max="4" min="3"/>. The method signature for the getAttributeValue() method is as follows:

```
String getAttributeValue (String namespace, String name);
```

The getAttributeValue() method returns the value of the attribute identified by the namespace URI and localName. Since we disabled namespaces URI, we pass null for the first parameter. For the second parameter, we pass the attribute name which returns the string value of the attribute. Here is how the getAttributeValue() method is used:

```
currentTemp = parser.getAttributeValue(null, "value");
minTemp = parser.getAttributeValue(null, "min");
maxTemp = parser.getAttributeValue(null, "max");
```

Similar to temperature value, we used parser.getAttributeValue(**null**, **"value"**); to retrieve the wind speed from the wind element. The wind element is represented as follows:

```
<wind>
    <speed value="4.1" unit="m/s" name="Gentle Breeze"/>
    <gusts/>
    <direction value="190" code="S" name="South"/>
</wind>
```

We treated the attribute extraction of the *weather* element slightly differently from the temperature element. This is because the weather element includes an *icon* attribute. The weather element is like this:

```
<weather number="804" value="overcast clouds" icon="04d"/>
```

We first get an icon attribute from the tag using the getAttributeValue() method and use it to create a file name for the icon image as follows:

```
String iconName = parser.getAttributeValue(null, "icon");
String fileName = iconName + ".png";
```

When you retrieve a weather icon from the weather element, the icon name is included in the URL. For example, the URL to retrieve a cloudy icon from the OpenWeatherMap website API is: https://openweathermap.org/img/w/04d.png. The general URL format for retrieving a weather icon from the OpenWeatherMap website API is like this: **"http://openweathermap.org/img/w/" + iconName + ".png"** where iconName is the name of the icon you would like to retrieve.

10.2.6   Reading Image from Local File

We retrieve each weather icon from the server only one time and save it locally for future use. The OpenWeatherMap website has icons for showing "Cloudy," "Sunny," "Raining," etc. Chances that these images will change sometime soon are unlikely. Hence, it makes sense to retrieve these images only once and save them locally for future use. This will improve the performance of your app. You do not have to download these images every time you visit the weather network; instead, you use the local copy of the images. You should use this strategy whenever you have a similar situation.

Once the file exists locally, you can use both the openFileInput() and BitmapFactory.decodeStream() methods to retrieve the local image. The openFileInput() method can be used to open and read files associated with the application context. The BitmapFactory class creates a Bitmap object from various sources, including files, streams, and byte-arrays, using, for example, the decodeStream() method. The method signature for the decodeStream is as follows:

```
public static Bitmap decodeStream (InputStream is);
```

The method decodes an input stream into a bitmap object. If the input stream is null or cannot be used to decode a bitmap, the function returns null. A code sample for image retrieval using the openFileInput() and decodeStream() methods is shown in Listing 10.5.

> **Listing 10.5** Image retrieval using the openFileInput() and decodeStream() methods.

```
if (parser.getName().equals("weather")) {
String iconName = parser.getAttributeValue(null, "icon");
 // create file name
 String fileName = iconName + ".png";
    if (fileExistance(fileName)) {
           FileInputStream fis = null;
           try { // open the file
                   fis = openFileInput(fileName);
              } catch (FileNotFoundException e) {
                   e.printStackTrace();
              }
                   picture = BitmapFactory.decodeStream(fis);

    }
```

Bitmap, BitmapFactory, BitmapShader, Canvas, Camera, Color, Paint, Point, etc. are important classes in the graphics package for image processing that are used by app developers, and you should familiarize yourself with them.

10.2.7 Retrieving Image from Remote Server

To retrieve images or icons from the net, you need to use the URL and HttpsURLConnection classes and their methods like the *openConnection()*, *connect()*, and *getResponseCode()* methods from HttpsURLConnection class. The code snippet in Listing 10.6 shows how these two classes and their methods are used in our demo app to retrieve an image from the net.

> **Listing 10.6** Using URL and HttpsURLConnection classes to retrieve icons from the network.

```
String iconUrl = "https://openweathermap.org/img/w/" + fileName;
HttpsURLConnection connection =
   (HttpsURLConnection) iconUrl .openConnection();
   connection.connect();
   int responseCode = connection.getResponseCode();
   if (responseCode == 200) {
        return BitmapFactory.decodeStream(connection.getInputStream());
   }
```

Note that the *response code* gets the status code from the HTTP getResponseCodemessage() method, and 200 means the status code is ok. Other status codes include 401 which means that the status code is unauthorized, −1 which means that HTTP is not valid, etc.

10.2.8   An Example of Reading Image File

In Listing 10.7, a code for reading images from the local file system and the remote server is provided. A few things that you should note about the code snippet in this Listing are:

1. To have a clean and easily maintainable code, the image processing is done in a separate method called the *getImage()* method.
2. The FileOutputStream class and compress() method are used to save the image in file. This step is done as follows:

```
picture = getImage (new URL (iconUrl) ) ;
FileOutputStream outputStream = openFileOutput ( fileName, Context.
MODE_PRIVATE) ;
picture.compress (Bitmap.CompressFormat.PNG, 80, outputStream) ;
```

3. The BitmapFactory.**decodeStream**() method is used in two different ways:

   (a) To decode an input stream of a remote image into a bitmap.
       BitmapFactory.decodeStream(connection.getInputStream());
   (b) To decode an input stream of a local file.

   The fileExistance() method returns a boolean value indicating whether or not the file exists. When the file exists, it uses the local file instead of downloading it from the net. This check is done to avoid server connection overheads.

Listing 10.7 Reading an image file from a local file and a remote server.

```
String iconUrl = "https://openweathermap.org/img/w/" + fileName;
picture = getImage (new URL (iconUrl) ) ;
FileOutputStream outputStream = openFileOutput (fileName, Con-text.
MODE_PRIVATE) ;
picture.compress (Bitmap.CompressFormat.PNG, 80, outputStream) ;
Log.i (ACTIVITY_NAME, "Downloaded the file from the Internet") ;
outputStream.flush () ;
outputStream.close () ;
public boolean fileExistance (String fname) {
   File file = getBaseContext ().getFileStreamPath (fname) ;
   return file.exists () ;
}
public Bitmap getImage (URL url) {
   HttpsURLConnection connection = null;
```

```
try {
  connection = (HttpsURLConnection) url.openConnection();
  connection.connect();
  int responseCode = connection.getResponseCode();
  if (responseCode == 200) {
      return BitmapFactory.decodeStream(connection.getInputStream());
  } else
    return null;
} catch (Exception e) {
  return null;
} finally {
  if (connection != null) {
    connection.disconnect();
  }
}
}
```

10.2.9   A Demo App

To display the parsed XML data, we have created a demo app. The app has an activity called WeatherForecast. A button on the main activity page should launch the WeatherForecast activity when the user clicks on it. In the AndroidManifest.xml file, we need to request internet permissions. That is, you need to add the following line code to your manifest file:

```
<uses-permission android:name="android.permission.INTERNET" />
```

In the WeatherForecast activity, we set the activity's layout to the activity_weather_forecast.xml layout file. The layout file has the following widgets:

1. An ImageView to display the current weather icon.
2. A TextVew to display the current temperature.
3. A TextView to display the minimum temperature.
4. A TextView to display the maximum temperature.
5. A TextView to display the wind speed.
6. A progress bar where the initial visibility has been set to "invisible." The style of the progress bar is set to horizontal bar using the style="?android:attr/progressBarStyleHorizontal" parameter.
7. A Spinner, or a dropdown list, to hold the name of all the Canadian cities. When the user selects a city, the weather information for that city will be displayed. A snippet code of the activity_weather_forecast XML layout file is shown in Listing 10.8.

Listing 10.8 Activity_weather_forecast.xml file.

```xml
<?xml version="1.0" encoding="utf-8"?>
<LinearLayout
    xmlns:android="http://schemas.android.com/apk/res/android"
    xmlns:tools="http://schemas.android.com/tools"
    android:layout_width="match_parent"
    android:layout_height="match_parent"
    android:background="@color/colorAccent"
    android:gravity="center"
    android:orientation="vertical"
    android:visibility="visible"
    tools:context=".WeatherForecastActivity">
    <TextView
        android:id="@+id/cityName"
        android:layout_width="wrap_content"
        android:layout_height="wrap_content"
        android:layout_marginLeft="10dp"
        android:layout_marginRight="10dp"
        android:layout_marginTop="25dp"
        android:textColor="@android:color/black"
        android:textSize="@android:dimen/app_icon_size" />
    <TextView
        android:layout_width="wrap_content"
        android:layout_height="wrap_content"
        android:text="@string/select_a_canadian_city"
        android:textSize="18sp"
        android:layout_marginTop="10dp"
        android:layout_marginLeft="10dp"
        android:layout_marginRight="10dp"
        android:textColor="@color/colorPrimary"/>
    <Spinner
        android:id="@+id/citySpinner"
        android:layout_width="match_parent"
        android:layout_height="wrap_content"
        android:layout_marginLeft="30dp"
        android:layout_marginRight="30dp">
    </Spinner>
    <ImageView
        android:id="@+id/image_forecast"
        android:layout_width="140dp"
        android:layout_height="85dp">
    </ImageView>
    ...
</LinearLayout>
```

10.2.9.1 Spinner Initialization and Handling

In the onCreate() method, the app's layout is set, the *progress bar's* visibility is set to visible so that it will be shown while we are retrieving information from the net, and the spinner object is initialized.

The spinner object provides a simple and quick way to select one item from a list. By default, a spinner shows the first item on the list. Clicking the spinner displays a dropdown menu with the list content from which you can select a new one. All the steps you need to create a list of items, i.e., a spinner object, as described in previous chapters, are followed here. These include:

1. Declare a list variable inside an activity. In this case, the variable is cityList.
2. Declare an array of strings to hold data, i.e., the city names. The array is declared inside the strings.xml resource folder like this <**string-array name="cities"**>, and the city list is initialized as follows:

```
List <String> cityList =
    Arrays.asList(getResources().getStringArray(R.array.cities));
```

The asList() method is used to convert an array of strings to a list of strings.

3. Create an adapter class to work with the list as follows:

```
ArrayAdapter <CharSequence> adapter =
    ArrayAdapter.createFromResource (this,
        R.array.cities,android.R.layout.simple_spinner_dropdown_item);
```

The array of city names inside the strings.xml file is referenced using *R.array.cities* where *cities* is the name of the array. The layout for an item on the spinner row is a simple dropdown layout.

The adapter is assigned to the list using the *setAdapter()* method, and a listener, *onItemSelectedListener*, is attached to the spinner object to handle item selection. All the steps above are implemented in the get_a_city() method which is called inside the onCreate() method of the weather forecast activity. The code for the get_a_city() method is shown in Listing 10.9.

Listing 10.9 The code for the get_a_city() method.

```
public void get_a_city () {
cityList = Arrays.asList(getResources().getStringArray(R.array.
cities));
final Spinner citySpinner = findViewById(R.id.citySpinner);
 ArrayAdapter <CharSequence> adapter =
 ArrayAdapter.createFromResource(this, R.array.cities,
                    android.R.layout.simple_spinner_dropdown_item);
citySpinner.setAdapter(adapter);
```

```
citySpinner.setOnItemSelectedListener(new
                        AdapterView.OnItemSelectedListener() {
    @Override
public void onItemSelected(AdapterView<?> adapterView,
        View view, int i, long l) {
            new ForecastQuery(cityList.get(i)).execute();
            cityName.setText(cityList.get(i) + " Weather");
        }
        @Override
        public void onNothingSelected(AdapterView<?> adapterView) {
        }
    });
}
```

You may have noticed that in the code snippet above, we used AsyncTask to connect to the internet to download an XML file and process it in the background thread. What is an AsyncTask and why do we use it? We discuss that in the next part of this chapter.

10.2.9.2   Predefined Layouts

We mentioned in Chap. 2 that the Android R class has an inner class for every folder on the project structure. One of these classes is called the Layout class. The R.Layout class has a set of predefined layouts. These include simple_list_item, simple_list_item_2, simple_selectable_list_item, simple_spinner_dropdown_item, droid.R.layout.simple.spinner_item, etc. When suitable for your app, you can use these layouts instead of defining your own. For example, for listing cities in the spinner in our demo app, we used the *simple_spinner_dropdown_item* which is a standard layout defined in the R.Layout class. Another possible choice for the spinner view that we could have used is *android.R.layout.simple.spinner_item*. For the list of all standard layouts provided by the Android API, see the R.Layout class. A link to the R.Layout class is provided at the end of this chapter.

10.2.10   Parsing Local XML File

If your app needs to parse an XML file residing on the Web, you need to connect to the site. For example, since the content of the XML file in our demo app is dynamic and changes frequently, we connected to the weather network information site, downloaded a file, and processed it.

Once you learn how to process and parse the remote XML files, parsing local ones will be very similar, except that you do not need to connect to the network. The code in the demo app can be reused with minor modifications to process local XML files. The **input stream** parameter of the setInput(**in**, null) method needs to be replaced with the file name as shown below:

```
Parser.setInput(filename, String inputEncoding);
```

Note that, before using a filename in the setInput() method, you also need to open the input file using the InputStream class. This can be done as follows when you have your local XML file inside the asset folder:

```
try {
   InputStream is = getAssets().open("fileName.xml");
} catch (Exception e) {// exception statement goes here}
```

The getAssets() method returns the AssetManager class which has an open method for opening local files saved inside the asset folder. For a complete example, see the code Listing 10.10.

Listing 10.10 Parsing a local XML file.

```java
package android.abdulrahman.wilfriedlaurie.xmlprocessing;
import android.graphics.Bitmap;
import android.graphics.BitmapFactory;
import android.os.Bundle;
import android.util.Xml;
import android.widget.TextView;
import androidx.appcompat.app.AppCompatActivity;
import org.xmlpull.v1.XmlPullParser;
import java.io.File;
import java.io.InputStream;
import java.net.URL;
import javax.net.ssl.HttpsURLConnection;
public class ReadingLocalXMLFileActivity extends AppCompatActivity {
  TextView min ;
  TextView max ;
  TextView current ;
  @Override
  protected void onCreate(Bundle savedInstanceState) {
     super.onCreate(savedInstanceState);
   setContentView(R.layout.activity_reading_local_xml_file);
     current = findViewById(R.id.current);
     min = findViewById(R.id.min);
     max = findViewById(R.id.max);
     InputStream in = null;
     try {
        in = getAssets().open("weather.xml");
        XmlPullParser parser = Xml.newPullParser();
        parser.setFeature(XmlPullParser.
                        FEATURE_PROCESS_NAMESPACES, false);
        parser.setInput(in, null);
        String currenTemp = "" ;
        String minTemp = "";
        String maxTemp = "";
        int type;
```

```
          while (( type = parser.getEventType() ) !=
                            XmlPullParser.END_DOCUMENT) {
        if (parser.getEventType() == XmlPullParser.START_TAG) {
          if (parser.getName().equals("temperature")) {
            currenTemp = parser.getAttributeValue(null, "value");
            minTemp = parser.getAttributeValue(null, "min");
            maxTemp = parser.getAttributeValue(null, "max");
          } else if (parser.getName().equals("wind")) {
            parser.nextTag();
            if (parser.getName().equals("speed")) {
              String windSpeed = parser.getAttributeValue(null,
              "value");
            }
          }
        }
        parser.next();
      }// end of loop
      current.setText ("current temp is" + currenTemp + "\n");
      min.setText ( "min temp is " + minTemp + "\n");
      max.setText ( "max temp is " + maxTemp);
    } catch (Exception ex) {
      ex.printStackTrace();
    } finally {
      try {
        in.close();
      }catch (Exception e) {}
    }
  }
  public boolean fileExistance(String fname) {
    File file = getFileStreamPath(fname);
    return file.exists();
  }
  public Bitmap getImage(URL url) {
    HttpsURLConnection connection = null;
    try {
      connection = (HttpsURLConnection) url.openConnection();
      connection.connect();
      int responseCode = connection.getResponseCode();
      if (responseCode == 200) {
        return BitmapFactory.decodeStream(connection.getInputStream());
      } else
        return null;
    } catch (Exception e) {
      return null;
    }
  }
}
```

10.2.11   Asset Folder

When you have raw, text, HTML, or XML files, you can create an asset folder and save your files in it. When using Android Studio, right-click on the app folder, click → create a new folder → asset folder, and create a new folder. You can use the methods of AssetManager to access and process asset files.

10.3   AsyncTask and Thread Handling

In this part, we study running tasks asynchronously in the background using the Android AsyncTask class.

10.3.1   AsyncTask Class

In Android, an asynchronous task is defined by a computation that runs in the background thread and whose result is published on the app interface. For computationally demanding operations or slow-running operations, the best solution is to run those operations asynchronously separate from the main interface thread. In Android, this can be done using the AsyncTask class. The AsyncTask class is a helper class for thread creation and handling, i.e., it encapsulates the creation of threads and handlers. AsyncTask is not a generic framework for doing threading, and it should ideally be used for operations that take only a few seconds. When AsyncTask is executed, it calls four methods in a predefined order. These methods are: onPreExecute, doInBackground, onProgressUpdate, and onPostExecute. It has another method called publishProgress that can be executed in the background process inside the doInBackground() method. The publishProgress() method helps the background process to send results to the UI thread.

10.3.2   Using AsyncTask Class

To use AsyncTask, you create the class you want to run in the background and make it a subclass of the AsyncTask. Here is how you will subclass AsyncTask.

```
Private class ForecastQuery extends
    AsyncTask<String, Integer, String> {...}
```

AsyncTask is a generic class and uses generic parameters. We studied generic classes when we reviewed Java in the first chapter. If you do not know generic classes, it is a good time to review that part of the chapter.

When subclassing an AsyncTask, you specify the argument types for the class, i.e., you specify the Params, Progress, and Result parameters that will be used by the AsyncTask. The first parameter, *Params*, is used as an input parameter for the thread running in the background. The second parameter, *Progress*, is used for holding intermediate results as the task progresses. The third parameter, *Result*, holds return results from the background thread. In the case above, we defined the parameters to be String, Integer, and String.

Once AsyncTask is instantiated, the background tasks can be executed by calling the execute() method. Here is an example of how to call the execute() method.

```
ForecastQuery fcastQuery = new ForecastQuery().execute();
```

It is important to remember two things when you are about to use the AsyncTask class. One, you need to decide on the number and type of parameters that you will instantiate your object with, and two, you should be aware of the sequence of the callback methods of the class. Below, we will study the AsyncTask class's four methods and its parameters.

10.3.3   AsyncTask and Varargs Type

The AsyncTask class parameters are of the type varargs. The varargs type allows a method to accept zero or multiple arguments. It is like you have written multiple methods all with the same name but with a different argument list. Before adding varargs to Java, programmers used the overload technique or took an array as an input argument to achieve the same result. Using varargs, however, is a better practice; it minimizes code maintenance. If you do not know how many arguments you will have to pass to a method, you should use the varargs type. This way you will write less code. Varargs use ellipsis, i.e., three dots after the data type. The syntax is:

```
return type method name (data type ... variableName) {}
```

We studied the varargs parameters in more detail in Chap. 1. You might want to revisit this part of the book to see an example of how varargs can be used.

10.3.4 Input, Progress, and Result Parameters to AsyncTask

When you define an object of the type AsyncTask class, you need to pass up to three parameters to the class and implement up to five callback methods. The implementation of the long-running tasks will be done in the doInBackground() method. That is, the code that should be executed in a background thread will be put in the doInBackground() method. The method runs automatically in a separate thread, after calling the *.execute()* or *execute(Params... params)* method. The parameters of the *AsyncTask (Input_params, Progress_value, Result_value)* are of type generic varargs and serve different purposes in the method.

The ***Input_params*** is passed into the doInBackground() method as an input. ***Result_value***, the third parameter, is a return value from the doInBackground() method and is passed to the ***onPostExecute()*** method as a parameter. It is used for storing progress information, i.e., holding progress data. The progress data can be published on the UI thread by calling the publishProgress() method. The ***onPostExecute()*** method runs on the user interface thread and allows it to update. It is called by the framework once the doInBackground() method finishes.

For example, if AsyncTask's parameters are String, Integer, and String, i.e., AsyncTask<String, Integer, String> is instantiated; you can infer the following rules:

1. The doInBackground() method accepts String . . . varargs; the first parameter type of the class.
2. The return type of the doInBackground() method is a String. The third parameter in the AsyncTask<String, Integer, String> class declaration is the return type of the doInBackground() method.
3. The publish progress method calls the onProgressUpdate() method and can pass only values of type Integer to it.
4. The input parameter to the onProgressUpdate() method is of type Integer.
5. The input parameter of the onPostExecute() method is of type String which is the return type of the doInBackground() method.

Figure 10.2 shows an example of how you can specify the class parameters for the three callback methods.

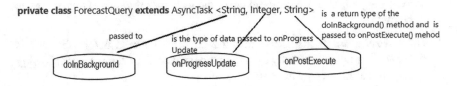

Fig. 10.2 An example of the data types used for the callback methods

10.3.5   AsyncTask Execute Methods

AsyncTask has two versions of the execute method. The method signature for the first one is:

```
public final AsyncTask<Params, Progress, Result>
                    execute (Params... params)
```

You can start a new thread and execute a task by calling the method above with specified parameters. The return type for the method is AsyncTask, i.e., this. This way you can keep a reference to the object itself.

The second version of the execute method is a simpler one and is used with the Runnable object. The method signature is like this:

```
public static void execute (Runnable runnable);
```

We studied the Runnable interface when we reviewed Java in Chap. 1. The Runnable interface is used when you want your class objects to run in a separate thread. The class has one method called *run* which takes no parameters. Any class that implements the runnable interface must implement the run method.

10.3.6   AsyncTask Method Sequence Calls

In the code below, we see how AsyncTask operates, i.e., we describe the sequence of the callback method calls. Again, AsyncTask's generic parameters are *Params*, the type of parameter sent to the task upon execution, *Progress*, the type of progress unit published during the background computation, and *Result*, the type of the result of the background computation. Not all types are always used by an asynchronous task. To mark a type as unused, use the void type. For example, you can declare an AsyncTask like this:

```
private class MyTask extends AsyncTask<void, void, void> {...}
```

When an asynchronous task is executed, the task goes through four steps in the order below:

1. **The onPreExecute()** method is invoked on the UI thread before the task is executed. This step is normally used to set up the task. For example, start showing a progress bar in the user interface.
2. **The doInBackground(Params...)** method is invoked on the background thread immediately after onPreExecute() finishes executing. This step is used to perform background computations. The arguments of the asynchronous task are passed at this stage. The result of the computation, if any, must be returned from this stage and passed to the last step.

This step can also use the *publishProgress(Progress...)* method to publish intermediate results. The progress values are published on the UI thread in the *onProgressUpdate(Progress...)* step.

3. The *onProgressUpdate(Progress...)* method is invoked on the UI thread after a call to publishProgress(Progress...). The timing of the execution is undefined. This method is used to display any form of progress in the user interface while the background process is still executing; for instance, it can be used to animate a progress bar or log text values.

4. The *onPostExecute(Result)* method is invoked on the UI thread after the background computation finishes. The result of the background computation process is passed to this step as a parameter, i.e., the *Result* argument, or the input parameter to *onPostExecute(Result)* is initialized.

Figure 10.3 shows the sequence of the AsyncTask's callback method execution.

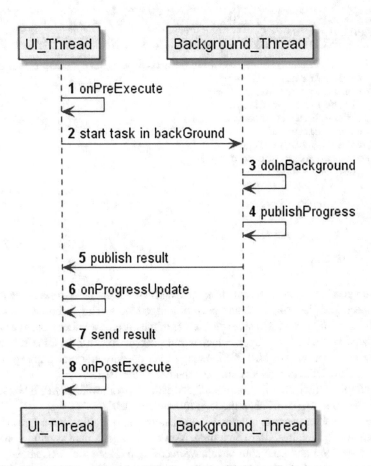

Fig. 10.3 The execution order of the callback methods of the AsyncTask class

10.4   App Implementation Details

So far, we have described all the classes and methods you need to run a task in a background thread as well as how to process remote XML files. Let us look at a concrete app where everything described so far will be used together.

10.4.1   WeatherForecast Class

For our demo app, we created an AsyncTask as an inner class in the WeatherForecast activity and named it ForecastQuery. The class extends the AsyncTask<String, Integer, String> class; see the code snippet shown in Listing 10.11.

Listing 10.11   ForecastQuery is an inner AsyncTask Java class.

```
private class ForecastQuery extends AsyncTask <String, Integer, String> {
    private String windSpeed;
    private String currentTemp;
    private String minTemp;
    private String maxTemp;
    private Bitmap picture;
    protected String city ;
    ForecastQuery(String city) {
    this.city = city;
  }
  ...
 }
```

10.4.1.1   Weather URL

The ForecastQuery class has four string fields. The fields are used to save data for the *wind* speed and the *min*, *max*, and *current* temperatures. The ForecastQuery additionally has a *Bitmap* field to store the picture of the current weather icon. We will be using data posted on the open whether map server to retrieve Canadian cities' weather information. The URL for the map server used in our demo app is provided below and the URL parameters are described in Table 10.1.

http://api.openweathermap.org/data/2.5/weather?q=ottawa,ca&APPID=79cecf4 93cb6e52d25bb7b7050ff723c&mode=xml&units=metric

Open a weather account at https://openweathermap.org/api to get a free APPID. The free APPID expires after some time. You need to get a paid version if you are going to develop and publish a weather forecast app. Paste the URL above into a Web browser. Replace cityname in the link with the name of the city for which you would like to know the weather information. You can see the XML data that is returned. You will be using this data file for your app.

Table 10.1 The description for the parameters used to form the URL

q	Is used to specify the name of the city for which you want the weather information
APPID	Is an API key used to measure how many queries per hour have been submitted using the app key. If you go over the limit for the free service level, it will stop working
Mode	Is used to specify the file return type; it can be a JSON or XML file
Units	Is used to specify the measurement units. For example, use metric to specify that you want units in Celsius and not Kelvin or Imperial units

10.4.1.2 doInBackground()

The *protected String doInBackground(String ...args)* function is created in the ForecastQuery class. The XML parsing is done here. The XML pull parser has a getAttributeValue(String namespace, String name) function that returns the value associated with the given name parameter. The namespace is null in this case, and the attributes that you are looking for are "speed," "value," "min," and "max." For each of the attributes, we call the publishprogress() method with 25, 50, and 75 as the parameters to show the progress of the data retrieval; see the code snippet shown in Listing 10.12.

Listing 10.12 The code for retrieving weather info. from a remote XML file.

```
@Override
 protected String doInBackground(String... strings) {
     try {
         URL url = new URL(
             "https://api.openweathermap.org/" +
                 "data/2.5/weather?q=" + this.city + "," +
                 "ca&APPID=79cecf493cb6e52d25bb7b7050ff723c&" +
                 "mode=xml&units=metric");
         HttpsURLConnection conn =
         (HttpsURLConnection) url.openConnection();
         conn.setReadTimeout(10000);
         conn.setConnectTimeout(15000);
         conn.setRequestMethod("GET");
         conn.setDoInput(true);
         conn.connect();
         InputStream in = conn.getInputStream();
         try {
             XmlPullParser parser = Xml.newPullParser();
             parser.setFeature(XmlPullParser.
                     FEATURE_PROCESS_NAMESPACES, false);
             parser.setInput(in, null);
             int type;
             //While you're not at the end of the document:
```

```
            while ((type = parser.getEventType())
                                != XmlPullParser.END_DOCUMENT) {
            //Are you currently at a Start Tag?
            if (parser.getEventType() == XmlPullParser.START_TAG) {
                if (parser.getName().equals("temperature")) {
                    currentTemp = parser.getAttributeValue(null, "value");
                    publishProgress(25);
                    minTemp = parser.getAttributeValue(null, "min");
                    publishProgress(50);
                    maxTemp = parser.getAttributeValue(null, "max");
                    publishProgress(75);
                } else if (parser.getName().equals("weather")) {
                    String iconName = parser.getAttributeValue(null, "icon");
                    String fileName = iconName + ".png";
                    Log.i(ACTIVITY_NAME, "Looking for file: " + fileName);
                    if (fileExistance(fileName)) {
                        FileInputStream fis = null;
                        try {
                            fis = openFileInput(fileName);
                        } catch (FileNotFoundException e) {
                            e.printStackTrace();
                        }
                        Log.i(ACTIVITY_NAME, "Found the file locally");
                        picture = BitmapFactory.decodeStream(fis);
                    } else {
                        String iconUrl =
                        "https://openweathermap.org/img/w/"
                                + fileName;
                        picture = getImage(new URL(iconUrl));
                        FileOutputStream outputStream =
                          openFileOutput(fileName, Context.MODE_PRIVATE);
                        picture.compress(Bitmap.CompressFormat.PNG,
                                                80, outputStream);
                        Log.i(ACTIVITY_NAME,
                          "Downloaded the file from the Internet");
                        outputStream.flush();
                        outputStream.close();
                    }
                    publishProgress(100);
                } else if (parser.getName().equals("wind")) {
                    parser.nextTag();
                    if (parser.getName().equals("speed")) {
                        windSpeed = parser.getAttributeValue(null, "value");
                    }}}
                parser.next();
            }
        } finally {
            in.close();
        }
    } catch (Exception ex) {
        ex.printStackTrace();
    }
    return "";
}
```

10.4.1.3   onProgressUpdate( )

The *onProgressUpdate(Integer . . .value)* function is implemented so that it sets the visibility of the progress bar to visible. It also sets the progress of the progress bar to value[0]; see the code snippet below.

```
@Override
  protected void onProgressUpdate(Integer... values) {
     progressBar.setProgress(values[0]);
  }
```

10.4.1.4   onPostExecute( )

In the *onPostExecute()* method, the data retrieved from the weather network server is presented. The min, max, and current temperatures are updated. The ImageView object is also updated with a bitmap icon. The visibility of the progress bar is set to invisible, using the setVisibility(View.INVISIBLE) function. The code snippet for this method is listed below.

```
@Override
  protected void onPostExecute(String a) {
     progressBar.setVisibility(View.INVISIBLE);
     imageView.setImageBitmap(picture);
     current_temp.setText(currentTemp + "C\u00b0");
     min_temp.setText(minTemp + "C\u00b0");
     max_temp.setText(maxTemp + "C\u00b0");
     wind_speed.setText(windSpeed + "km/h");
  }
```

10.4.2   Complete Code for Weather Network App Activity

The complete code for the WeatherForecastActivity and its generic AsyncTask inner class, the ForecastQuery class, is shown in Listing 10.13.

Listing 10.13 WeatherForecastActivity.java.

```
package android.abdulrahman.wilfriedlaurie.xmlprocessing;
import android.app.Activity;
import android.content.Context;
import android.graphics.Bitmap;
import android.graphics.BitmapFactory;
import android.os.AsyncTask;
import android.os.Bundle;
import android.util.Log;
import android.util.Xml;
import android.view.View;
```

```java
import android.widget.AdapterView;
import android.widget.ArrayAdapter;
import android.widget.ImageView;
import android.widget.ProgressBar;
import android.widget.Spinner;
import android.widget.TextView;
import org.xmlpull.v1.XmlPullParser;
import java.io.File;
import java.io.FileInputStream;
import java.io.FileNotFoundException;
import java.io.FileOutputStream;
import java.io.InputStream;
import java.net.URL;
import java.util.Arrays;
import java.util.List;
import javax.net.ssl.HttpsURLConnection;
public class WeatherForecastActivity extends Activity {
    private final String ACTIVITY_NAME = "WeatherForecastActivity";
    ProgressBar progressBar;
    ImageView imageView;
    TextView current_temp;
    TextView min_temp;
    TextView max_temp;
    TextView wind_speed;
    List <String> cityList;
    TextView cityName;
    @Override
    protected void onCreate(Bundle savedInstanceState) {
        super.onCreate(savedInstanceState);
        setContentView(R.layout.activity_weather_forecast);
        setTitle("Weather Network Information");
        current_temp = findViewById(R.id.current_temp);
        min_temp = findViewById(R.id.min_temp);
        max_temp = findViewById(R.id.max_temp);
        wind_speed = findViewById(R.id.wind_speed);
        imageView = findViewById(R.id.image_forecast);
        cityName = findViewById(R.id.cityName);
        progressBar = findViewById(R.id.progress_bar);
        progressBar.setVisibility(View.VISIBLE);
        get_a_city();
    }
    public void get_a_city() {
        // Get the list of cities.
        cityList = Arrays.asList(getResources().getStringArray(R.array.
        cities));
        // Make a handler for the city list.
        final Spinner citySpinner = findViewById(R.id.citySpinner);
        ArrayAdapter <CharSequence> adapter =
            ArrayAdapter.createFromResource( this, R.array.cities,
                        android.R.layout.simple_spinner_dropdown_item);
        citySpinner.setAdapter(adapter);
        citySpinner.setOnItemSelectedListener(
            new AdapterView.OnItemSelectedListener() {
        @Override
```

```
      public void onItemSelected(AdapterView <?> adapterView,
                                  View view, int i, long l) {
        new ForecastQuery(cityList.get(i)).execute();
        cityName.setText(cityList.get(i) + " Weather");
      }
      @Override
      public void onNothingSelected(AdapterView <?> adapterView) {
      }
    });
  }
  private class ForecastQuery extends AsyncTask <String, Integer, String> {
    private String windSpeed;
    private String currentTemp;
    private String minTemp;
    private String maxTemp;
    private Bitmap picture;
    protected String city;
    ForecastQuery(String city) {
      this.city = city;
    }
    @Override
    protected String doInBackground(String... strings) {
      try {
        URL url = new URL(
          "https://api.openweathermap.org/" +
            "data/2.5/weather?q=" + this.city + "," +
            "ca&APPID=79cecf493cb6e52d25bb7b7050ff723c&" +
            "mode=xml&units=metric");

        HttpsURLConnection conn = (HttpsURLConnection)
                                  url.openConnection();
        conn.setReadTimeout(10000);
        conn.setConnectTimeout(15000);
        conn.setRequestMethod("GET");
        conn.setDoInput(true);
        conn.connect();
        InputStream in = conn.getInputStream();
        try {
          XmlPullParser parser = Xml.newPullParser();
          parser.setFeature(
          XmlPullParser.FEATURE_PROCESS_NAMESPACES, false);
          parser.setInput(in, null);
          int type;
          //While you're not at the end of the document:
          while ((type = parser.getEventType()) !=
                        XmlPullParser.END_DOCUMENT) {
          //Are you currently at a Start Tag?
          if (parser.getEventType() == XmlPullParser.START_TAG) {
              if (parser.getName().equals("temperature")) {
                  currentTemp = parser.getAttributeValue(null, "value");
                  publishProgress(25);
                  minTemp = parser.getAttributeValue(null, "min");
                  publishProgress(50);
                  maxTemp = parser.getAttributeValue(null, "max");
```

```java
                    publishProgress(75);
                } else if (parser.getName().equals("weather")) {
                    String iconName = parser.getAttributeValue(null, "icon");
                    String fileName = iconName + ".png";
                    Log.i(ACTIVITY_NAME,
                            "Looking for file: " + fileName);
                    if (fileExistance(fileName)) {
                        FileInputStream fis = null;
                        try {
                            fis = openFileInput(fileName);

                        } catch (FileNotFoundException e) {
                          e.printStackTrace();
                        }
                        Log.i(ACTIVITY_NAME, "Found the file locally");
                        picture = BitmapFactory.decodeStream(fis);
                    } else {
                        String iconUrl =
                        "https://openweathermap.org/img/w/" + fileName;
                        picture = getImage(new URL(iconUrl));
                        FileOutputStream outputStream =
                        openFileOutput(fileName, Context.MODE_PRIVATE);
                        picture.compress(Bitmap.CompressFormat.PNG, 80,
                        outputStream);
                        Log.i(ACTIVITY_NAME,
                        "Downloaded the file from the Internet");
                        outputStream.flush();
                        outputStream.close();
                    }
                    publishProgress(100);
                } else if (parser.getName().equals("wind")) {
                    parser.nextTag();
                    if (parser.getName().equals("speed")) {
                        windSpeed = parser.getAttributeValue(null, "value");
                    }
                }
            }
            // Go to the next XML event
            parser.next();
        }
    } finally {
        in.close();
    }
} catch (Exception ex) {
    ex.printStackTrace();
}
return "";
}
public boolean fileExistance(String fname) {
    File file = getBaseContext().getFileStreamPath(fname);
    return file.exists();
}
public Bitmap getImage(URL url) {
    HttpsURLConnection connection = null;
```

```
      try {
        connection = (HttpsURLConnection) url.openConnection();
        connection.connect();
        int responseCode = connection.getResponseCode();
        if (responseCode == 200) {
            return
              BitmapFactory.decodeStream(connection.getInputStream());
          } else
            return null;
    } catch (Exception e) {
      return null;
    } finally {
      if (connection != null) {
        connection.disconnect();
      }
    }
  }
}
```

In Fig. 10.4, the left-hand side shows the first page of the weather app interface, and the right-hand side shows an instance of the weather information. You can click on the dropdown list and select the city for which you would like to know its weather information; see Fig. 10.5.

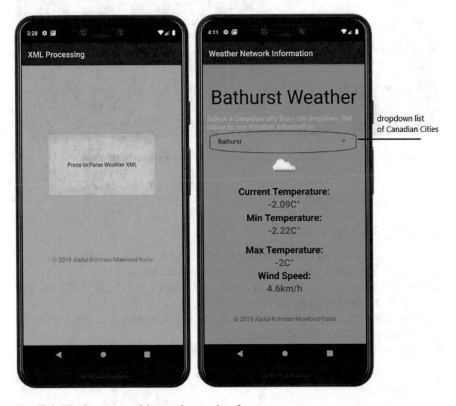

Fig. 10.4 The first screen of the weather app interface

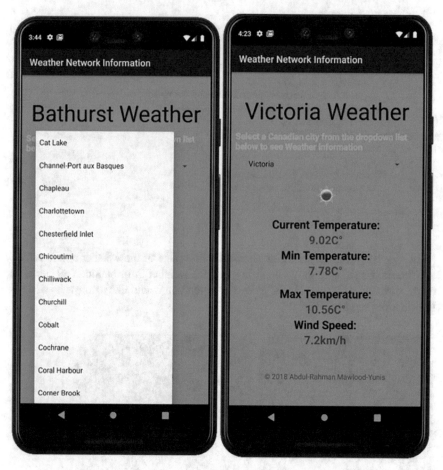

Fig. 10.5 The dropdown list to select a city for retrieving its weather information

10.4.2.1   Do It Yourself

Modify the demo app as follows:

1. Add the date and time to the app display as well as other weather information such as sunset and sunrise, humidity levels, and pressure levels.
2. Change the array list of Canadian cities and regions to a local XML file, and process the file in the app activities.
3. From the URL, change the mode=xml to mode =json, and extract similar weather information in JSON format.
4. Compare the trade-off between processing JSON files and XML files.

   See the section below for information on how to use a JSON file instead of using an XML file.

10.4.3   Parsing JSON Files

If you would like to work with JSON (JavaScript Object Notation) files instead of XML files, you have to process the JSON files. First, in the URL you have to change file mode from mode=xml to mode=json as follows:

   url = "http://api.openweathermap.org/data/2.5/weather?q=ottawa,ca&APPID= 79cecf493cb6e52d25bb7b7050ff723c&mode=xml&units=metric";

The JSON file you would receive from the weather network would be similar to the following text:

Listing 10.14 An example of weather forecast data in JSON format.

```
{
"coord": {
"lon": -75.7,
"lat": 45.41
},
"weather": [
{
"id": 803,
"main": "Clouds",
"description": "broken clouds",
"icon": "04d"
}],
"base": "stations",
"main": {
"temp": -0.44,
"feels_like": -4.32,
"temp_min": -2,
"temp_max": 0.56,
"pressure": 1021,
"humidity": 46
},
"visibility": 24140,
"wind": {
"speed": 1.11,
"deg": 203
},
"clouds": {
"all": 75
},
"dt": 1583959705,
"sys": {
"type": 1,
"id": 872,
"country": "CA",
"sunrise": 1583925722,
"sunset": 1583967809
},
"timezone": -14400,
"id": 6094817,
```

```
"name": "Ottawa",
"cod": 200
}
```

When using result.getJSONObject(**"main"**) you will get {"temp":-3.14,"feels_like":-9.27,"temp_min":-4,"temp_max":-2.22,"pressure":1021,"humidity":68}.

You can extract JSON object property values using keys. To retrieve the current, max, and min temperatures and the pressure and humidity levels, you use the following statements:

```
result.getJSONObject("main").getString("temp")
result.getJSONObject("main").getString("temp_max")
result.getJSONObject("main").getString("temp_min")
result.getJSONObject("main").getString("pressure")
result.getJSONObject("main").getString("humidity")
```

To retrieve an *icon* name, you first retrieve the weather information using the *getJsonArray()* method. This can be done like: *result.getJSONArray("weather")*. You use the *getJsonArray()* method because looking at the JSON file, you can see that the value for the *weather* key is an array; the key is weather, and the value is array as shown below:

```
array:"weather":[{"id":803,"main":"Clouds","description":"broken
clouds","icon":" 04d"}].
```

The result of the getJsonArray() method would be an array with one object. You use getJsonObjet(0) and getString() methods to retrieve the icon name as follows:

```
result.getJSONArray("weather").getJSONObject(0).getString("icon")
to retrieve wind speed, use result.getJSONObject("wind").getString
("speed").
```

As you can see, when using JSON you do not need to use a parser. You can read JSON files using Java objects and methods. The JSON syntax is also shorter than the XML syntax, and both are human-readable files.

10.4.4   Other XML Feeds

Once you learn how to process remote files, there are many interesting sources that you can build an app for. For example, News API provides daily news headlines and articles in XML and JSON that you can use to create apps. Here is the link to the website: https://newsapi.org/. The Bank of Canada provides the daily exchange rate for most currencies in three different formats, XML, JSON, and CVS, which you can equally use to create an app. Here is the link to the website: https://www.bankofcanada.ca/rates/exchange/daily-exchange-rates/M. You can also get information about your local representatives in the government and parliament using his/her name, postal code, or other parameters. For example, to retrieve information about Canadian representatives using a postal code, you can form a URL like this: https://represent.opennorth.ca/postcodes/N2L3C5/?sets=federal-electoral-districts and parse the retrieved JSON file using objects and methods, similar to how we described above.

10.5 An App for Information on Covid-19

In this part, we reuse the structure of the weather information demo app presented earlier in this chapter to create an app for presenting Covid-19 data. The interface for the app is shown in Fig. 10.6.

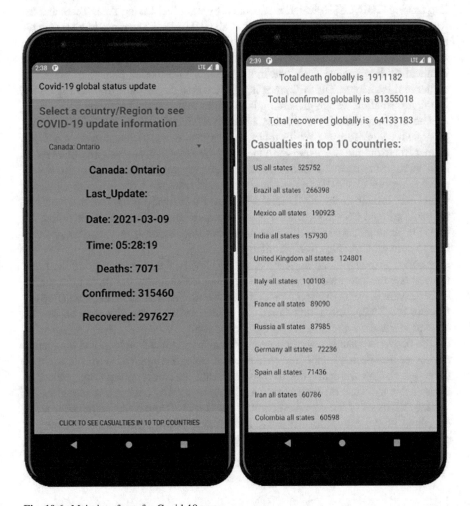

Fig. 10.6 Main interfaces for Covid-19 app

When you run the app, you can select a country/region from a dropdown list to display updated information about Covid-19 in that state/region. An example of this information is shown for Canada/Ontario on the right-hand side of Fig. 10.6. You can also click on a button at the bottom of the app's main view to display the latest information about the casualty and recovery rates for the top ten most affected countries; see the left-hand side of Fig. 10.6.

10.5.1   Covid-19 App Development Steps

The app Data is obtained from the Coronavirus Visual Dashboard which is a public data repository operated by the Johns Hopkins University Center for Systems Science and Engineering (JHU CSSE) which is supported by the ESRI Living Atlas Team and the Johns Hopkins University Applied Physics Lab (JHU APL). The repository is available on the GitHub server at this link: https://github.com/CSSEGISandData/COVID-19.

The steps for the XML parsing and remote connection to the server are almost identical to the ones we described in the weather information demo app presented earlier in this chapter. The difference in this step is in the fields of the two apps. That is, the information we are presenting is different between the two apps.

The data provided by the Johns Hopkins University is in the CSV (comma-separated value) format. While there are various ways of reading the CSV file format, for example, by using the OpenCSV or JavaCSV open-source libraries, it is easier to just reuse our existing code for processing data. Thus, an important step in developing our Covid-19 app is converting data from the CSV (comma-separated value) file format to the XML format. There are software programs that you can utilize to convert CSV files to XML files including ones that are available online for free. For example, we used this webpage https://www.convertcsv.com/csv-to-xml. htm to convert CSV files to XML files for our app.

Another important step in developing our Covid-19 app is identifying the latest file that has the information we need. The data provided includes more information than we want to use in our app. We identified the file we wanted to use, converted the file into the XML format, and stored the data in an XML file. We then posted the converted file onto a remote server for processing.

The converted data is posted on two different environments, testing and production environments. We first put the converted file on a testing environment to test our app with the new data. Once the data is tested and is successful, the data is moved to the production environment to be used as production data, i.e., to be used by our app and seen globally.

One drawback of the current version of our Covid-19 app is that some of the steps described above are done manually. Automating some of the steps involved in creating the Covid-19 app is an interesting future project.

10.5.2   *Data Extraction and Conversion*

We mentioned earlier that we converted the data format provided by the Johns Hopkins University from CVS to XML. More specifically, we converted one file a day, i.e., the daily data about the pandemic, and not all the files. The file covers the latest information about all the countries and regions around the world. A snapshot of the converted data is shown in Listing 10.15. It shows the data for March 09, 2021, for the top five countries from a list of all countries that are organized alphabetically in our demo app.

You may notice that we did not use the latitude and longitude elements of the data. We will return to this app when we study the Android map and location elements in Chap. 13 where we will try to use the latitude and longitude elements for the input data to improve user experience with the app.

Listing 10.15 WeatherForecastActivity.java.

```
<root>
<row>
<FIPS/>
<Admin2/>
<Province_State/>
<Country_Region>Afghanistan</Country_Region>
<Last_Update>2021-03-09 05:28:19</Last_Update>
<Lat>33.93911</Lat>
<Long_>67.709953</Long_>
<Confirmed>55876</Confirmed>
<Deaths>2451</Deaths>
<Recovered>49402</Recovered>
<Active>4023</Active>
<Combined_Key>Afghanistan</Combined_Key>
<Incident_Rate>143.53552852406426</Incident_Rate>
<Case_Fatality_Ratio>4.386498675638915</Case_Fatality_Ratio>
</row>
<row>
<FIPS/>
<Admin2/>
<Province_State/>
<Country_Region>Albania</Country_Region>
<Last_Update>2021-03-09 05:28:19</Last_Update>
<Lat>41.1533</Lat>
<Long_>20.1683</Long_>
<Confirmed>113580</Confirmed>
<Deaths>1956</Deaths>
<Recovered>75887</Recovered>
<Active>35737</Active>
<Combined_Key>Albania</Combined_Key>
<Incident_Rate>3946.7648898464095</Incident_Rate>
<Case_Fatality_Ratio>1.7221341785525621</Case_Fatality_Ratio>
</row>
<row>
```

```
<FIPS/>
<Admin2/>
<Province_State/>
<Country_Region>Algeria</Country_Region>
<Last_Update>2021-03-09 05:28:19</Last_Update>
<Lat>28.0339</Lat>
<Long_>1.6596</Long_>
<Confirmed>114382</Confirmed>
<Deaths>3018</Deaths>
<Recovered>79187</Recovered>
<Active>32177</Active>
<Combined_Key>Algeria</Combined_Key>
<Incident_Rate>260.84214234083333</Incident_Rate>
<Case_Fatality_Ratio>2.6385270409679844</Case_Fatality_Ratio>
</row>
<row>
<FIPS/>
<Admin2/>
<Province_State/>
<Country_Region>Andorra</Country_Region>
<Last_Update>2021-03-09 05:28:19</Last_Update>
<Lat>42.5063</Lat>
<Long_>1.5218</Long_>
<Confirmed>11069</Confirmed>
<Deaths>112</Deaths>
<Recovered>10661</Recovered>
<Active>296</Active>
<Combined_Key>Andorra</Combined_Key>
<Incident_Rate>14326.020837377857</Incident_Rate>
<Case_Fatality_Ratio>1.0118348540970277</Case_Fatality_Ratio>
</row>
...
</root>
```

10.5.3   Testing and Production Development Environments

When developing software, it is especially important to have at least two sets of development environments: one, for example, for testing your code while you are developing your application, and another one for production.

Before making your app or product available for public use or client use, the app needs to be developed and tested thoroughly. This needs to be done on its environment, i.e., testing environment. For example, when we converted data from CSV to XML, we first put it in the testing directory on the server and tested our app with that data. Once we were done testing and were happy with both the converted data and the application, we moved the data to the production directory on the server. Now, both the data and the application are ready for use. That is, external applications can read the files posted on the server, and the app can be published on the app store for users to download and use.

This way you will always have at least two copies of your code. One copy of the code is already published and used by clients. You have to save this code in a separate directory, production directory, or production environment. A second copy of the code is saved in a testing environment where you might work on it to improve it further for subsequent releases or to fix bugs when found. Similarly, you need to test your daily data updates before posting them for public use. Data testing needs to be done in a separate testing environment.

10.5.4   Covid-19 Source Code and Class Structure

The app is made of four main classes, *MainActivity*, *DataObject*, *DataAnalytics*, and *AnalyticDisplay*. The main activity class includes an inner private AsyncTask class for processing remote XML files. The processing is done in the doInBackground class. The main activity displays the latest data on the number of casualties, confirmed cases, and recoveries of Covid-19 for each region/state and country. It can start the AnalyticDisplay activity to present the global state of the pandemic. Figure 10.7 is a simplified class diagram for the app. It shows the main classes, their properties and methods, and the relationship between the classes. For a complete source code, see the demo apps developed for this chapter.

10.6   Chapter Summary

In this chapter, we studied a couple of important topics. These include processing remote XML files using the HTTPUrlConnection and XMLPullParser classes, running tasks asynchronously in the background using the Android AsyncTask class, and processing a large amount of Covid-19 data, analyzing the data, converting the data format, and creating data models.

We studied how the XML pull parser can be instantiated using the Android XML class and the steps involved in processing XML files. We also studied the method sequences for the AsyncTask and the AsyncTask class generic parameters.

We created two real-life apps, the Weather Network and Covid-19 apps, to explain and demonstrate how to use the concepts discussed in this chapter.

Check Your Knowledge
Below are some of the fundamental concepts and vocabularies that have been covered in this chapter. To test your knowledge and your understanding of this chapter, you should be able to describe each of the below concepts in one or two sentences.

Fig. 10.7 A simplified class diagram for the Covid-19 app

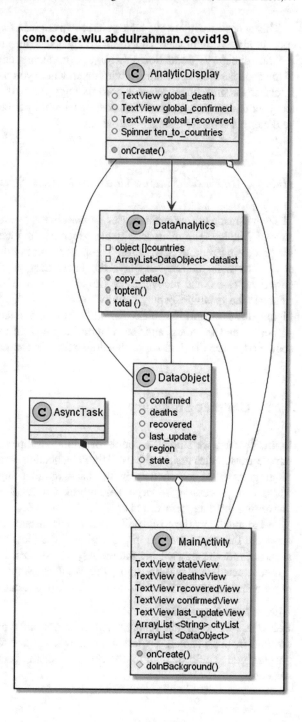

- BitmapFactory
- doInBackground
- END_DOCUMENT
- END_TAG
- execute()
- getName()
- getNamespace()
- getText()
- HttpsURLConnection
- JSON file
- newPullParser
- next()
- nextToken()
- onPostExecute
- onPreExecute,
- OnProgressUpdate
- R.Layout
- setInput(InputStream, String)
- START_DOCUMENT
- START_TAG
- TEXT
- Xml
- XmlPullParser
- XmlPullParserFactory

Further Reading

For more information about the topics covered in this chapter, we suggest that you refer to the online resources listed below. These links provide additional insight into the topics covered. The links are mostly maintained by Google and are a part of the Android API specification. The resource titles convey which section/subsection of the chapter the resource is related to.

AsyncTask, [online] Available, https://developer.android.com/reference/android/os/AsyncTask

BitmapFactory, [online] Available, https://developer.android.com/reference/android/graphics/BitmapFactory

HttpURLConnection, [online] Available, https://developer.android.com/reference/java/net/HttpURLConnection

Interface Runnable, [online] Available, https://developer.android.com/reference/java/lang/Runnable

JSONObject, [online] Available, https://developer.android.com/reference/org/json/JSONObject

Parse XML data, [online] Available, https://developer.android.com/training/basics/network-ops/xml

Pull Parsing versus Push Parsing, [online] Available, https://docs.oracle.com/cd/E19879-01/819-3669/bnbdy/index.html

R.layout, [online] Available, https://developer.android.com/reference/android/R.layout

Weather API, [online] Available, http://api.openweathermap.org

[10] **Xml**, [online] Available, https://developer.android.com/reference/android/util/Xml

Chapter 11
Android SQLite, Firebase, and Room Databases

What You Will Learn in This Chapter

By the end of this chapter, you should be able to:

- Create and use an Android SQLite database
- Open and upgrade an Android SQLite database
- Insert, delete, remove, and query data in the Android SQLite database
- Use ContentValues object
- Use the cursor object
- Understand the uses of Android's content provider
- Use Android's internal and external data storages
- Use the SQLite browser tool
- Use database inspector
- Create and use a Firebase database
- Create and use Room Database

Check Out the Demo Project

Download the demo app, **DatabaseDemoApp.zip**, specifically developed to go with this chapter. I recommend that you code this project up from the notes rather than just opening the project in Android Studio and running it; however, if you want to run the code first to get a sense of the app, please do so. The code is thoroughly explained in this chapter to help you understand it. We follow the same approach to all other chapters throughout the book. The app's code will help you comprehend the additional concepts that will be described in this chapter.

How to run the code: unzip the code in a folder of your choice, and then in Android Studio, click **File->import->Existing Android code into the workspace**. The project should start running.

© The Author(s), under exclusive license to Springer Nature Switzerland AG 2022   475
A.-R. Mawlood-Yunis, *Android for Java Programmers*,
https://doi.org/10.1007/978-3-030-87459-9_11

11.1   Introduction

Android provides diverse ways to store data. In this chapter, we study how to store an app's data into a database. There are many database engines for mobile devices including MongoDB, MariaDB, SQLite, etc. In this part, we investigate using the Android SQLite database to store structured data (a relational database). You will learn how to create, open, and upgrade a database, as well as how to insert, delete, and query data in an Android SQLite database.

SQLite is embedded in the Android SDK (software development kit) download and can be used to save data locally. You will also learn about content values, cursor objects, content providers, and internal and external data storages, as well as how to use the SQLiteBrowser tool, Firebase database, and Room library. The chapter is divided into five parts: the Android SQLite database, content values and cursors, the database demo project, Firebase databases, and other data storage options. Figure 11.1

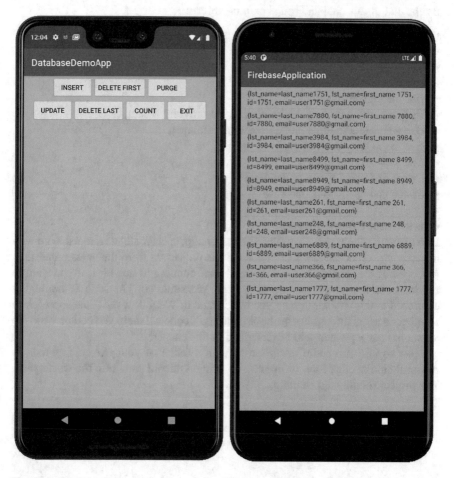

Fig. 11.1 Database demo app interfaces using SQLite on the left-hand side and Firebase on the right-hand side

shows the user interface for the database and Firebase demo apps developed to go with this chapter.

11.2 The Android SQLite Database

The SQLite database is an open-source database engine that Android uses to store small amounts of structured data, such as your list of contacts or SMS (Short Message Service) information. It is a built-in database engine and can create and execute all database operations. To use the SQLite database engine, you first need to create the database and the database tables and then use it to write and read data. Once you are done working with your database operations, you need to close it to avoid any unpredictable behavior. The lifecycle of the Android SQLite database activities can be summarized like this:

1. Create a database.
2. Open the database.
3. Read/write and update the data.
4. Close the database.

11.2.1 SQLiteOpenHelper Class

Android has a package called *android.database.sqlite* which contains all the interfaces and classes that are needed to create and manage a database. Android uses the SQLiteOpenHelper class to create and open databases. The class has multiple constructors and public methods to manage the database. One of the widely used SQLiteOpenHelper constructors is:

```
SQLiteOpenHelper(Context context, String databaseName,
SQLiteDatabase.CursorFactory factory, int version)
```

where the input parameters are:

- **Context** is the activity that opens the database.
- String **databaseName** is the file that will contain the data.
- **CursorFactory** is an object to create cursor objects and normally is null.
- int **version** is the version of your database.

To use a database in your app, you must create a subclass of the SQLiteOpenHelper class for your application. In the code snippet shown in Listing 11.1, MySQLiteHelper is a subclass of SQLiteOpenHelper.

Listing 11.1 Extending MySQLiteHelper class.

```
package com.code.abdulrahman.database;
import android.content.Context;
import android.database.sqlite.SQLiteDatabase;
import android.database.sqlite.SQLiteOpenHelper;
public class MySQLiteHelper extends SQLiteOpenHelper {...}
```

11.2.2 SQLiteDatabase Class

Once you create your database, you need to be able to manage it. That is, you need to be able to run SQL queries on your database to create and delete tables, insert data into tables, remove and update table entries, etc. The SQLiteDatabase class has methods that enable you to run such SQL queries. For our database demo app, we will be using the SQLiteDatabase methods to run queries on the database.

11.2.3 Overriding Methods of the SQLiteOpenHelper Class

There are several essential methods from the SQLiteOpenHelper class that you must override to implement whatever tasks and actions you want your app to do. The methods, or functions, are the *onCreate()*, *onUpgrade()*, and *onOpen*(optional) methods and the class *constructor methods*. Below we describe the roles of each method in the development of SQLite databases for your apps.

11.2.4 The Class Constructor Method

In the subclass you write to create and open a database, you must call a superclass constructor and pass certain information to it. The SQLiteOpenHelper has three constructors. The signatures of these constructors are shown below:

```
SQLiteOpenHelper(Context context, String name,
                 SQLiteDatabase.CursorFactory factory, int version);
SQLiteOpenHelper(Context context, String name,
                 SQLiteDatabase.CursorFactory factory, int version,
                 DatabaseErrorHandler errorHandler);
SQLiteOpenHelper(Context context, String name,
                 int version, SQLiteDatabase.OpenParams openParams);
```

In our Android database demo app, we used the first constructor using the following line of code:

```
super (context, DATABASE_NAME, null, DATABASE_VERSION);
```

The context parameter is DatabaseMainActivity, the database name is myPersonalDatabase.db, CursorFactory is null, and DATABASE_VERSION is an int value, for example, 1 or 2, depending on the version of the database. The code snippet shown in Listing 11.2 shows a call to the superclass constructor for our database demo project. Note that the database file extension is **db**.

Listing 11.2 A call to the MySQLiteHelper superclass database constructor.

```
public class MySQLiteHelper extends SQLiteOpenHelper {
private static final String DATABASE_NAME =
                              "myPersonalDatabase.db";
 private static final int DATABASE_VERSION = 1;
 MySQLiteHelper (Context context) {
    super (context, DATABASE_NAME, null, DATABASE_VERSION);
 }
...
}
```

11.2.5   The onCreate() Method

If the database does not exist, i.e., the onCreate() method of the MySQLiteHelper class has not been called, the onCreate() method is called immediately. The onCreate() method signature would be like this:

```
@Override
 public void onCreate(SQLiteDatabase database) {
    // database is the database object.
 }
```

To elaborate more, in the subclass you create, you call the superclass constructor which in turn calls the onCreate() method to create a database. The call to the superclass constructor should happen only once, the first time you create the database. You do not want to create a new database every time you run the app. Instead, you should use an already created database.

11.2.5.1 Create Table in Database

The onCreate() method can be used to execute SQL table creation statements. The code snippet shown in Listing 11.3 is an example of a table creation statement where the SQL statement is created as a string and saved in a static final string variable named DATABASE_CREATE.

Listing 11.3 An example of creating a table statement.

```
private static final String DATABASE_CREATE = "create table "
    + TABLE_Of_My_ITEMS + " ( " + Item_ID
    + " integer primary key autoincrement, " + ITEM_NAME
    + " text not null);";
```

When executed, the statement above creates a table called *tableOfMyItems* that has two fields, or columns. The columns are *_id* and an *itemName*. The _id type is an integer, and the ITEM_NAME type is text or string. The _id is the primary key for the table and is an auto-increment, i.e., when a record is inserted into the table, a unique number is generated automatically.

The create table statement would be executed only once, when you create a database for the first time. After writing your create table statement, you need to execute it to create tables. The execSQL() method is a function that executes a string SQL statement; see the code snippet below:

```
@Override
public void onCreate(SQLiteDatabase database) {
  database.execSQL(DATABASE CREATE);
}
```

The execSQL() method executes a single SQL statement that is not a *select* or any other SQL statement that returns data.

So far, we have described four steps to create a database in Android using the SQLite database, and they are:

1. Subclassing the SQLiteOpenHelper class.
2. Composing the SQL statement for the database/table creation.
3. Calling the superclass constructor.
4. Calling the execSQL() method with the database create statement. This call is made inside the onCreate() method.

The code snippet in Listing 11.4 summarizes the four steps above.

Listing 11.4 MySQLiteHelper.java.

```
package com.code.abdulrahman.database;
import android.content.Context;
import android.database.sqlite.SQLiteDatabase;
import android.database.sqlite.SQLiteOpenHelper;
import android.util.Log;

// 1. Subclassing SQLiteOpenHelper class
public class MySQLiteHelper extends SQLiteOpenHelper {
  public static final String TABLE_Of_My_ITEMS = "tableOfMyItems";
  public static final String Item_ID = "_id";
  public static final String ITEM_NAME = "itemName";
  private static final String DATABASE_NAME =
                        "myPersonalDatabase.db";
  private static final int DATABASE_VERSION = 2;

  // 2. Table/Database creation statement
  private static final String DATABASE_CREATE = "create table "
      + TABLE_Of_My_ITEMS + " (" + Item_ID
      + " integer primary key autoincrement, " + ITEM_NAME
      + " text not null);";
  // 3. super constructor call
  MySQLiteHelper (Context context) {
   super(context, DATABASE_NAME, null, DATABASE_VERSION);
  }
  @Override
  public void onCreate(SQLiteDatabase database) {
   // 4. Executing SQL command
   database.execSQL(DATABASE_CREATE);
  }
```

11.2.6   onUpgrade Method

The *SQLiteOpenHelper* class calls the onUpgrade() method when the database needs to be upgraded. You update your database if, for example, you change a type of a field in a table, add/remove fields in a table, or add/delete tables.

If you change the database version number inside your code and restart your app, the onUpgrade() method is called. The method signature for onUpgrade() is as follows:

```
public abstract void onUpgrade (SQLiteDatabase db,
                          int oldVersion, int newVersion);
```

Once the onUpgrade() method is invoked, you have a chance to upgrade your data. For example, you can add new columns to an existing table, create a new table, drop a table, or change the table schema. You can also delete all your data using the execSQL() method the with DROP statement as follows:

```
db.execSQL("DROP TABLE IF EXISTS TABLENAME");
```

In our database demo project, when onUpgrade() is called, we will delete all the data in the table and call the onCreate() method with the table name to recreate the table; see the code snippet shown in Listing 11.5.

Listing 11.5 An example of an onUpgrade() method implementation.

```
@Override
public void onUpgrade(SQLiteDatabase db,
                      int oldVersion, int newVersion) {
  db.execSQL("DROP TABLE IF EXISTS TABLE_Of_My_ITEMS");
  onCreate(db); // or database.execSQL("CREATE TABLE...");
}
```

11.2.7   onDowngrade Method

The onDowngrade() method is called when you want to downgrade the database. If you decide to use an *older* version of the database, the onDowngrade() method can be used. The onDowngrade() method implementation may include a create table statement or/and drop a table statement.

Unlike the onCreate() and onUpgrade() methods, the onDowngrade() method is not an abstract method; therefore, you do not have to override it, i.e., its implementation is optional. You do not normally use the onDowngrade() method, but if you need it, it exists and is one of the SQLiteOpenHelper methods.

To invoke the onDowngrade() method, lower the version number of your database. For example, if the current version of your database is 3, change it to 2, and restart your app; you will see that the onDowngrade() function is called. Restarting your app results in calling the MySQLiteHelper class constructor, and when the database version value is lower than the previously provided value, the onDowngrade() method is called.

Since onDowngrade() is an optional method, you do not need to use the @Override keyword when implementing it. An example of how the onDowngrade() method can be implemented is shown in Listing 11.6.

Listing 11.6 An example of an onDowngrade method implementation.

```
public void onDowngrade (SQLiteDatabase db, int oldVersion,
                                    int newVersion) {
  Log.w(MySQLiteHelper .class.getName(),
      "Downgrading database from version " + newVersion + " to "
          + oldVersion);
    db.execSQL("DROP TABLE IF EXISTS  TABLE_Of_My_ITEMS" );
    onCreate(database);
  }
```

Here, the onCreate() method handles the request for downgrading the database.

11.2.8   onOpen() Method

The *onOpen()* method is called when the database has been opened. It is an optional method that you do not have to override. If you decided to override the onOpen() method, you should include the database status check using the isReadOnly() method in the implementation body of your method. The isReadOnly() method returns a true or false value indicating whether the database mode is read-only or read/write, respectively. You should allow database updates only if the database status is read and write. By default, when the onCreate() and onUpgrade()/onDowngrade() methods are called, the onOpen() method gets called last. It can also get called regardless of the onCreate()/onUpgrade() methods, i.e., you can call it separately when needed.

11.2.9   Read and Read/Write Access

Once you create your database, you need to open it to use it. You have the option to open your database in a read-only mode using the getReadableDatabase() method or in a read/write mode. In our demo app, we open the database in a read/write mode as shown below:

```
dbHelper = new MySQLiteHelper (context);
public void open () throws SQLException {
        database = dbHelper.getWritableDatabase();
}
To open a database in read mode only, it can be done as follows:
public void open () throws SQLException {
      database= dbHelper.getReadableDatabase() ;
}
```

The return type of the getWritableDatabase() method is a SQLiteDatabase object. If the database does not exist when either the getWritableDatabase() method or the getReadableDatabase() method is called, the onCreate() method is called to create and return the database.

11.2.10   The execSQL Method from SQLiteDatabase Class

Android uses the execSQL() method from the SQLiteDatabase class to execute a single SQL statement. The statement should not return any data. For example, the execSQL() method cannot be used with the *select* statement.

The SQLiteDatabase class has more than one version of the execSQL() method. The one we used in our demo app has this signature: public void execSQL (String sql);.

The type for the input parameter for the execSQL() method is a string. Hence, the SQL statement you write for your app needs to be formed as a string and passed to execSQL() method to run. We have used the execSQL() method throughout our demo app. Below is an example of how we used the execSQL() method. The input parameter is a *create* table statement.

```
final String contact_table = "create table contacts" + " ( " +
    "firstName" + " text primary key , " +
    "lastName" + " text , " +
    "email"    + " text , " +
    " phoneNumber" + " number " + ") ;";
    database.execSQL(contact_table);
```

In the code above, the SQL statement creates a table called contacts which has four fields: first name, last name, email, and phone number. The type of the first three fields is text, i.e., string, and the phone number type is an integer.

To summarize, implementing the steps above will create a database for your app where your users will be able to apply read, write, and update operations on it. Next, we will describe how your users can interact with the database of your app.

11.3   Content Values and Cursor Objects

In this part of the chapter, we will study how to interact with the data in the database. You will learn how to insert, remove, update, and query data in the database tables. Android has two classes to enable such interactions or transactions. The classes are ContentValues and Cursor; both are described below.

11.3.1   Content Values and Insert Method

The *insert()* method from the SQLiteDatabase class is an easy way to insert a row into the database tables. The signature for the insert method is as follows.

```
public long insert (String table, String nullColumnHack,
                    ContentValues values);
```

The first parameter of the method is the table name into which you want to insert the row. The second parameter is an optional string, which may be null, and the last parameter is an object of type ContentValues. The ContentValues class is a class that you can use to store a set of values using key/value pairs.

If you have multiple fields such as first name, last name, email, and phone number for which you need to insert a row into a table, you first create a ContentValues object and then use the insert() method from the SQLiteDatabase class to add the newly created object into a table row.

You create ContentValues objects by calling the constructor of the class. You can use the put(String ColumnName, String value) method of the ContentValues class to add data into ContentValues objects. Once you have your ContentValues object ready, use the insert() method from the SQLiteDatabase class to add the ContentValues object into a table row. The code snippet below shows the two steps above, i.e., how the ContentValues object is used to insert data into the database using the *put() and the insert() methods*:

```
ContentValues cValues = new ContentValues();
   cValues.put("FristName", "Abdul-Rahman");
   cValues.put("LastName", "Mawlood-Yunis");
   cValues.put("email", "amawloodyunis@wlu.ca");
   dataBaseName.insert("TableName","NullPlaceHolder,",cValues);
```

Note that the second parameter to the insert() method, i.e., the string nullColumnHack of the method, is the column name. If you forgot to provide the column name, the "NullPlaceHolder" will be inserted into the row for the missing column name.

In our demo app, the createItem() method is called with an item object as a parameter to add an item object to the database. The key for the ContentValues objects is MySQLiteHelper.ITEM_NAME, and the values are fields of the incoming parameter. See the code snippet below.

```
public Item createItem(Item item) {
  ContentValues values = new ContentValues();
  values.put(MySQLiteHelper .ITEM_NAME, item.getItem());
  long insertId = database.insert
                (MySQLiteHelper .TABLE_Of_My_ITEMS, null,values);
  ...
}
```

The Item object in our app has only one property of type string which represents the name of the object. Figure 11.2 shows the items that have been inserted into the database after pressing the insert button.

In most cases, the objects that are inserted into the database will have more than one property. This leads us to the exercise below.

Fig. 11.2 Demo screen showing inserted items into a database

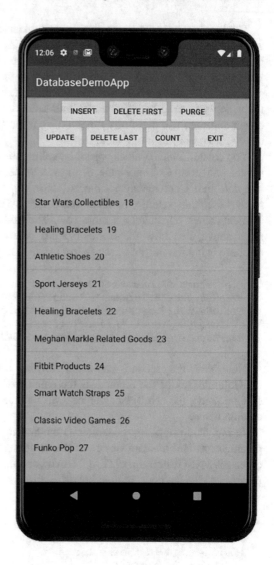

11.3.1.1 Do It Yourself

Exercise 1

Replace the item class with a new class called *Contacts* with three properties, String name, Int phone_number, and String email. Change the database demo project to use the Contacts class instead of the item class. Once you are done inserting the data, the information display of your app should be similar to the information presented below:

ID	Name	Phone number	Email
1	AR Mawlood-Yunis	6135214444	amwloodyunis@wlu.ca
2	SA Mawlood-Yunis	6135214444	amwloodyunis@wlu.ca
3	SI Mawlood-Yunis	6135214444	amwloodyunis@wlu.ca
4	ZY Mawlood-Yunis	6135214444	amwloodyunis@wlu.ca

Exercise 2

Think of some useful applications for the Android database. To make yourself familiar with database usage with the mobile apps, search the Google app store to find out some apps where you think the app developers are utilizing the Android database correctly/wisely. Do some searches to find out popular databases that can be used with mobile apps.

11.3.2   Cursor

Android has a class called cursor. Objects of the cursor class can hold rows returned from a query. Cursor objects can contain a single row or an entire table. You can think of the cursor class as an iterator class in Java or a reference to the result set returned from a query that you can iterate through.

The cursor class has several useful functions. These include methods to move where the cursor is pointing to, for example, moveToNext, moveToFirst, moveToLast, etc. Table 11.1 lists some of these methods and their descriptions.

We used the cursor object in our database demo app in multiple places. The code snippets showing in Listings 11.7 and 11.8 show how it is used inside the *getAllItem()* and *createItem()* methods in our demo app.

Table 11.1 Useful methods of the Cursor class and their description

getCount()	Returns the number of rows a query returned, i.e., the number of rows in the cursor
moveToFirst()	Moves the cursor to the first row
moveToLast()	Moves the cursor to the last row
moveToNext()	Moves the cursor to the next row
moveToPosition(int position)	Moves the cursor to a specified position
close()	Closes the cursor object and releases all its resources

488   11   Android SQLite, Firebase, and Room Databases

Listing 11.7 Using the Cursor object to return all the items in the table.

```
public List<Item> getAllItem() {
 List<Item> items = new ArrayList<>();

 Cursor cursor = database.query (
    MySQLiteHelper .TABLE_Of_My_ITEMS, allItems, null, null, null,
                                                    null, null);
cursor.moveToFirst();
while (!cursor.isAfterLast()) {
    Item item = cursorToItem(cursor);
    Log.d(TAG, "get item = " + cursorToItem(cursor).toString());
    items.add(item);
    cursor.moveToNext();
cursor.close();
  return items;
}
```

Listing 11.8 Creating an Item object and inserting it into a table.

```
public Item createItem(Item item) {
 ContentValues values = new ContentValues();
values.put(MySQLiteHelper .ITEM_NAME, item.getItem());

long insertId = database.insert(
      MySQLiteHelper .TABLE_Of_My_ITEMS, null,values);

 Cursor cursor = database.query(
    MySQLiteHelper .TABLE_Of_My_ITEMS, allItems,
                    MySQLiteHelper .Item_ID +
        " = " + insertId, null, null, null, null);
  cursor.moveToFirst();
  Item newItem = cursorToItem(cursor);
  cursor.close();
  return newItem;
}
```

There are multiple interesting things that one can observe about the two methods above. Both examples show that running queries on the database returns cursor objects, and the cursor objects hold the item object inserted into the table. The createItem() method demonstrates how an id that is returned from the database.insert () method can be reused as part of the query to retrieve an item with the specified id. In both methods, the ContentValues object is used to insert an item object into the database table. We will analyze the database demo code in more detail in the next part of this chapter.

11.3.3   Query Data

The query() method is a convenient function for creating the built-in SQL statements. Android provided three different versions of the query methods. The return type for all three query methods is a cursor object which can be processed by the app. The syntax and components of one of the query methods used in our demo app are as follows:

```
query ( boolean distinct, String tableName, String[] columns,
       String selection, String[] selectionArgs,
       String groupBy, String having, String orderBy, String limit)
```

The meaning of each parameter is as follows:

- distinct is a boolean variable and when set to true, it will return a unique result.
- *The string **tableName*** is the table name for the FROM part of SELECT clause.
- ***Columns []*** is a list of strings, i.e., column names to be used for selection. For example, the new String [] = ["A","B","C"] is the same as saying SELECT (A, B, C) columns.
- ***Selection*** is a string for the WHERE clause without using the WHERE keyword, for example, " firstName like ? AND lastName not ? ". The ? is a placeholder which will be replaced by the *selectionArgs [] array.*
- *selectionArgs[]* is an array of strings to replace the "?" in the selection. The order of replacement is in a left to right order.
- The names of the other parameters explain their purposes.

Below are two test cases using the query clause. The database is called *tableOfMyItems*, and the columns are *id* and *ITEM_NAME*.

Example 1

```
database = dbHelper.getReadableDatabase();
database.query(true, "tableOfMyItems", null,null, null,null, null,
null, null);
```

The query statement above is equivalent to **SELECT * from tableOfMyItems**.

Example 2

```
Cursor c = database.query("tableOfMyItems", new String[]{"*"},
    "_id" + "=?" + " And " + " ITEM_NAME",
    new String[]{"8", "Gift Cards"}, null, null, null, null);
```

The query in example 2 is equivalent to:

```
SELECT * FROM tableOfMyItems WHERE _id=8 AND
                    itemName = Gift Cards ;
```

11.3.4 rawQuery

If you are comfortable with writing the SQL statements yourself, the rawQuery()
construct or method lets you do it. You embed your query inside the rawQuery()
method to run in your app. In Listing 11.9, some examples from our demo app on
how to write and use a rawQuery() method in the app are shown.

Listing 11.9 Examples from our demo app on how to write and use a raw
query.

```
public void test4() {

database = dbHelper.getReadableDatabase();
String q1 = "select itemName from tableOfMyItems where _id=8";
String q2 =
"select _id from tableOfMyItems where itemName='Gift Cards'";
String q3 =
"select _id from tableOfMyItems where itemName like '%Gift%'";

// 1.
    database.rawQuery(q1, null);
    database.rawQuery(q2, null);
    database.rawQuery(q3, null);

//2. Get a specific item
    Cursor c = database.rawQuery(
        "select * from tableOfMyItems where _id = ? ",
        new String[] { " 25 " });

//3. get all table names from the database
    Cursor tables = database.rawQuery(
        "select name from sqlite_master where type= ? ",
        new String [] { " table "}) ;

//4. get count
    Cursor cursor = database.rawQuery("select count(*) " +
        "from tableOfMyItems", null);

//5. to format the output
    Cursor cursor2 = database.rawQuery(String.format(
"select count(*)
from %s", "tableOfMyItems"), null);
}
```

To see the result of the above queries, you need to run the demo app prepared for
this chapter. See the source code of the demo app for more examples of rawQuery().

11.3.5   More Methods of the SQLiteDatabase Class

The SQLiteDatabase class is one of the main classes for interacting with database tables when using the SQLiteDatabase with Android. This class has methods for all types of operations that can be performed on the database. So far, we have used the create(), insert(), query(), and rawQuery() methods, but there are more. Below we describe three more methods of this class that are very relevant to database management.

11.3.5.1   Replace Method

The replace() method from the SQLiteDatabase is used to replace a row in a table. It will insert a new row if a row does not already exist. The signature of the method is as follows:

```
public long replace (String table,
        String nullColumnHack, ContentValues initialValues);
```

11.3.5.2   Update Method

The SQLiteDatabase has a method for updating rows in tables, the update() method. The signature of the method is as follows:

```
public int update (String table,
        ContentValues values,  String whereClause, String[] whereArgs);
```

11.3.5.3   Delete Method

The delete() method is used to delete rows in a table. The signature of the method is as follows:

```
public int delete (String table, String whereClause, String[] whereArgs);
```

The methods replace(), update(), and delete(), which are used in our demo app, will be described in the next part of this chapter.

11.4   DatabaseDemo Project

In this part of the chapter, we will describe how the SQLiteOpenHelper, the SQLiteDatabase, and their methods are used to create an Android database app or to create a database for our app. In our app, we followed the model view controller or MVC design pattern. That is, we created three components:

1. Data and classes to access data: a data component
2. Operational and test driver classes: the middle component, or controller component
3. Presentation and data query classes: the view component

The middle component (component 2) receives commands from the view component (component 3) and sends them to the data component (component 1). Once the middle component receives the results from the data component (component 1), it sends the results back to the view component (component 3). All communication between the database and view components goes through the middle component. Let us dig into each layer in detail:

11.4.1   The Data Component

Almost all apps and computer applications need a database when they need data to work with. In our demo database app, the data that needs to be saved is just a product name: the name of the top 20 items that a business can sell on eBay (this is fictional data; you should not take it as real core business information). The data is saved in an array called *bestThingsToSellOnEBay* inside the SourceData class as shown in Listing 11.10:

Listing 11.10 SourceData.java class for holding data.

```
package com.code.abdulrahman.database;
public class SourceData {
  static String[] bestThingsToSellOnEBay = new String[] {
        "Athletic Shoes",
        "Gift Cards",
        "Marvel Toys",
        "Collectible Coins",
        "BitCoin Collector Coins"
        , "Classic Video Games",
        "New Video Games",
        "Healing Bracelets",
        "Sport Jerseys",
        "Oculus Go",
        "Meghan Markle Related Goods",
        "Yeti Coolers",
        "Healing Bracelets",
```

```
        "Hot Wheels 50th Anniversary Toys",
        "Funko Pop",
        "Star Wars Collectibles",
        "Bobbleheads",
        "Smart Watch Straps",
        "Fitbit Products",
        "Drones"
  };
  public static String[] getBestThingsToSellOnEBay() {
    return bestThingsToSellOnEBay;   }
  public static void setBestThingsToSellOnEBay(String[]
      bestThingsToSellOnEBay) {
    SourceData.bestThingsToSellOnEBay = bestThingsToSellOnEBay;
  }
}
```

We also did the following as part of developing the data component:

1. Created a database helper class named *MySQLiteOpenHelper* which extends the SQLiteOpenHelper class
2. Implemented the functionalities of the onCreate(), onUpgrade(), and onDowngrade() methods
3. Created a third method, a *count() method*, to return the number of rows currently in the item table
4. Developed a table creation statement to create tables and table columns
5. Called a super constructor inside the constructor of our *MySQLiteOpenHelper* class to create a database and assign a database version

Figure 11.3 is a snapshot of the *MySQLiteOpenHelper class* structure in Android Studio.

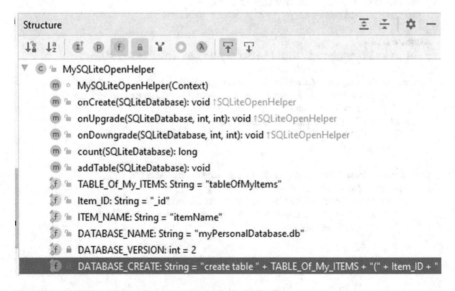

Fig. 11.3 MySQLiteHelper class structure in Android Studio

The implementation of the class structure above is listed in the code snippet shown in Listing 11.11:

Listing 11.11 MySQLiteOpenHelper.java class for creating a database.

```java
package com.code.abdulrahman.database;
import android.content.ContentValues;
import android.content.Context;
import android.database.sqlite.SQLiteDatabase;
import android.database.sqlite.SQLiteOpenHelper;
import android.util.Log;
public class MySQLiteOpenHelper extends SQLiteOpenHelper {

  public static final String TABLE_Of_My_ITEMS = "tableOfMyItems";
  public static final String Item_ID = "_id";
  public static final String ITEM_NAME = "itemName";
  public static final String DATABASE_NAME =
                          "myPersonalDatabase.db";
  private static final int DATABASE_VERSION = 2;
  // Table/Database creation statement
  private static final String DATABASE_CREATE = "create table "
        + TABLE_Of_My_ITEMS + "(" + Item_ID
        + " integer primary key autoincrement, " + ITEM_NAME
        + " text not null);";
  // super constructor call
  MySQLiteOpenHelper(Context context) {
    super(context, DATABASE_NAME, null, DATABASE_VERSION);
  }
  @Override
  public void onCreate(SQLiteDatabase database) {
    database.execSQL(DATABASE_CREATE);
    addTable(database);
  }
  @Override
  public void onUpgrade(SQLiteDatabase db, int oldVersion,
                  int newVersion) {
    Log.w(MySQLiteOpenHelper.class.getName(),
        "Upgrading database from version " + oldVersion + " to "
            + newVersion);
    db.execSQL("DROP TABLE IF EXISTS "
            + TABLE_Of_My_ITEMS);
    onCreate(db);
  }
  public void onDowngrade (SQLiteDatabase database,
      int oldVersion, int newVersion) {
    Log.w(MySQLiteOpenHelper.class.getName(),
        "Downgrading database from version " + newVersion + " to "
            + oldVersion);
```

```
      database.execSQL("DROP TABLE IF EXISTS "
      + TABLE_Of_My_ITEMS);
      onCreate(database);
   }
   public long count(SQLiteDatabase database) {
      long count = 0;
      database.execSQL("select count(*) " + " from "
      + " TABLE_Of_My_ITEMS");
      return count;
   }
   public void addTable (SQLiteDatabase database) {
      database.execSQL("DROP TABLE IF EXISTS " + "contact");
      // Table/Database creation statement
      final String contact_table = "create table " +
          "contact" + " ( " +
          "firstName" + " text primary key , " +
          "lastName" + " text , " +
          "email"   + " text , " +
          " phoneNumber" + " number " + " );";
      database.execSQL(contact_table);
      ContentValues values = new ContentValues();
      values.put( "firstName", "Abdul-Rahman");
      values.put( "lastName", "Mawlood-Yunis");
      values.put( "email", "abdulrahman@mawloodyunis.com");
      values.put ("phoneNumber", "1234567890");
      long insertId = database.insert("contact", null, values);
   }
}
```

11.4.2   The Middle Component

Every request from the user (view component) goes through the middle component to interact with the database. This separates the view component from the data component which in turn enables change in the database without the need for the view component to change and vice versa. The middle component is implemented through the ItemsDataSource class. In this class, all the fundamental database methods (create, open, read/write, and close methods) are implemented. The below code snippets from the ItemsDataSource class show that the methods inside the middle component are merely calls to the methods in the database component. For example, the ItemsDataSource constructor calls the MySQLiteOpenHelper construct to create a database:

```
ItemsDataSource(Context context) {
   dbOpenHelper = new MySQLiteOpenHelper(context);
}
```

After the creation of the database, the open() method calls the getWritableDatabase to open it in a writable mode:

```
public void open() throws SQLException {
      // another option:
      // database = dbOpenHelper.getReadableDatabase();
      database= dbOpenHelper.getWritableDatabase();
}
```

Once the database no longer needs to be open, the close() method calls the database close() method:

```
public void close() {
   dbOpenHelper.close();
}
```

Figure 11.4 shows the structure of the ItemsDataSource class in Android Studio and the database methods that the class implements.

Listing 11.12 is a complete implementation of the ItemsDataSource class:

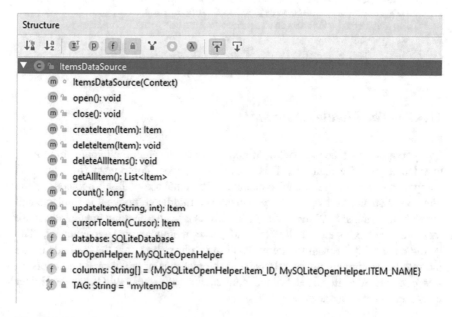

Fig. 11.4 The class structure for ItemsDataSource class showing the database methods it implements

Listing 11.12   ItemsDataSource.java.

```java
package com.code.abdulrahman.database;
import android.content.ContentValues;
import android.content.Context;
import android.database.Cursor;
import android.database.DatabaseUtils;
import android.database.SQLException;
import android.database.sqlite.SQLiteDatabase;
import android.util.Log;
import java.util.ArrayList;
import java.util.List;
public class ItemsDataSource {
  // Database fields
  private SQLiteDatabase database;
  private MySQLiteOpenHelper dbOpenHelper;
  private String[] columns = { MySQLiteOpenHelper.Item_ID,
              MySQLiteOpenHelper.ITEM_NAME };
  private static final String TAG = "myItemDB";
  // call to database constructor
  ItemsDataSource(Context context) {
  dbOpenHelper = new MySQLiteOpenHelper(context);
  }
  public void open() throws SQLException {
   //database = dbHelper.getWritableDatabase();
    database= dbOpenHelper.getReadableDatabase() ;
  }
  public void close() {
    dbOpenHelper.close();
  }
  public Item createItem(Item item) {
    ContentValues values = new ContentValues();
    values.put(MySQLiteOpenHelper.ITEM_NAME, item.getItem());
    long insertId = database.insert(MySQLiteOpen
              Helper.TABLE_Of_My_ITEMS, null, values);
Cursor cursor =
    database.query(MySQLiteOpenHelper.TABLE_Of_My_ITEMS,
    columns, MySQLiteOpenHelper.Item_ID + " = "
                        + insertId, null,    null, null, null);
    cursor.moveToFirst();
    Item newItem = cursorToItem(cursor);
    // Log the item stored
     Log.d(TAG, "item = " + cursorToItem(cursor).toString()
                    + " insert ID = " + insertId);
     cursor.close();
     return newItem;
  }
  public void deleteItem(Item item) {
   long id = item.getId();
    Log.d(TAG, "delete item = " + id);
                    System.out.println("Item deleted with id: " + id);
```

```java
    database.delete(MySQLiteOpenHelper.TABLE_Of_My_ITEMS,
            MySQLiteOpenHelper.Item_ID + " = " + id, null);
}
public void deleteAllItems() {
  System.out.println("Item deleted all");
  Log.d(TAG, "delete all = ");
   database.delete(MySQLiteOpenHelper.TABLE_Of_My_ITEMS,
                null, null);
}
 public List<Item> getAllItem() {
    List<Item> items = new ArrayList<>();
    Cursor cursor = database.query(MySQLiteOpenHelper.
                TABLE_Of_My_ITEMS, columns,
                    null, null, null, null, null);
    cursor.moveToFirst();
          while (!cursor.isAfterLast()) {
            Item item = cursorToItem(cursor);
            Log.d(TAG, "get item = " + cursorToItem(cursor).toString());
             items.add(item);
    cursor.moveToNext();
 }
  // Make sure to close the cursor
  cursor.close();
  return items;
}
public long count () {
  long count = DatabaseUtils.queryNumEntries(database,
       MySQLiteOpenHelper.TABLE_Of_My_ITEMS);
  return count;
}
public Item updateItem (String item, int id) {
   ContentValues values = new ContentValues();
   values.put(MySQLiteOpenHelper.Item_ID, id+"");
   values.put(MySQLiteOpenHelper.ITEM_NAME, item);

   database.update(MySQLiteOpenHelper.TABLE_Of_My_ITEMS,
     values, MySQLiteOpenHelper.Item_ID + " = " + id, null);
     Item it = new Item() ;
     it.setItem(item);
      it.setId(id);
   return it;
}
 private Item cursorToItem(Cursor cursor) {
   Item item = new Item();
    item.setId(cursor.getLong(0));
    item.setItem(cursor.getString(1));
   return item;
 }
}
```

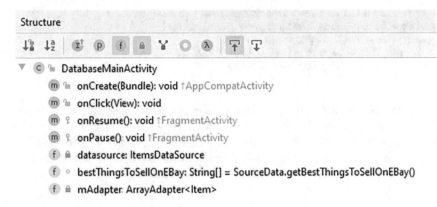

Fig. 11.5 The class structure of the DatabaseMainActivity class

11.4.3   The View Component

The view component is implemented via the DatabaseMainActivity class. The DatabaseMainActivity class contains a reference to the ItemsDataSource class which represents a link to the controller component. The DatabaseMainActivity class implements four methods, onCreate(), onClick(), onResume(), and onPause(). Figure 11.5 is the class structure of the DatabaseMainActivity class.

Inside the onCreate() method of the DatabaseMainActivity class, several method calls are made on the ItemsDataSource class to accomplish three tasks: creating a database, opening the database to write to it, and retrieving data in the database to present on the main screen. The code snippet showing in Listing 11.13 shows the details of the method calls inside the onCreate() method.

Listing 11.13 Method calls to create and use database.

```
@Override
public void onCreate(Bundle savedInstanceState) {
  super.onCreate(savedInstanceState);
  setContentView(R.layout.activity_main);
  ListView mListView = findViewById(R.id.list);

  // 1. call to create database
  datasource = new ItemsDataSource(this);

  // 2. open Database for writing
  datasource.open();
```

```
//3. list all the items in the table on the main screen
List <Item> values = datasource.getAllItem();
mAdapter = new ArrayAdapter <>(this,
    android.R.layout.simple_list_item_1, values);
mListView.setAdapter(mAdapter);
}
```

The DatabaseMainActivity class also implements the onResume() and onPause() activity lifecycle methods. These two methods are used to open and close the database every time the app is re-opened or closed. This is a good demonstration of how one can make use of the activity lifecycle methods properly. Listed below are the code snippets for the onResume() and onPause() methods:

```
@Override
protected void onResume() {
    datasource.open();
    super.onResume();
}
@Override
protected void onPause() {
    datasource.close();
    super.onPause();
}
```

You may have noticed that the ArrayAdapter class has been used to list all the items in the table on the main screen of the app. The constructor that has been used to create the ArrayAdapter object is:

ArrayAdapter(Context context, int resource, List<T> objects).

The constructor uses Android's predefined layout to display one row:

android.R.layout.simple_list_item_1.

The code snippet below shows to use the simple_list_item_1 layout.

```
List <Item> values = datasource.getAllItem();
mAdapter = new ArrayAdapter <>(this,
    android.R.layout.simple_list_item_1, values);
mListView.setAdapter(mAdapter);
```

The bulk of the view component code is inside the *onClick() method* of the DatabaseMainActivity class. The codes for handling all button events are included in this method. It includes a switch statement to handle each button pressed. We have seen event handling in previous chapters, and there is not much new here. A couple of things you might need to pay attention to are:

Fig. 11.6 The database
demo view when the update
button is pressed

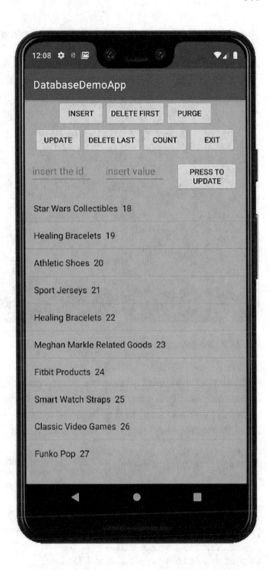

1. When the *update button* is pressed, two edit texts, one to insert the id of the item
   you would like to update and the other to insert a new value, and a button become
   visible (see Fig. 11.6). This is also an example of how you can programmatically
   control Android widgets.
2. The purge button deletes all data in the database.
3. The exit button uses the Android activity finish() methods to close the current
   view and return to where the activity was launched.

   Figure 11.7 shows how an item update method works. In this case, the item that
needs to be updated is "Healing Bracelets" which has an id of 1. The item name is
updated to "New Item Name" in the database and is displayed on the screen.

Fig. 11.7 Snapshot of updating an item in the database

Listing 11.14 shows a complete source code for the DatabaseMainActivity class (view component). If you decide to duplicate the code, the source code below would be handy; you also need to duplicate the activity_main.xml layout file. You can find the activity_main.xml layout in the source file of the database demo app.

Listing 11.14 DatabaseMainActivity.java.

```
package com.code.abdulrahman.database;
import android.content.Context;
import android.os.Bundle;
import android.view.View;
import android.widget.ArrayAdapter;
import android.widget.Button;
import android.widget.EditText;
import android.widget.LinearLayout;
import android.widget.ListView;
import android.widget.Toast;
import androidx.appcompat.app.AppCompatActivity;
import java.util.List;
import java.util.Random;
public class DatabaseMainActivity extends AppCompatActivity {
    private ItemsDataSource datasource;
    String[] bestThingsToSellOnEBay =
            SourceData.getBestThingsToSellOnEBay();
    private ArrayAdapter <Item> mAdapter;
```

```java
@Override
public void onCreate(Bundle savedInstanceState) {
    super.onCreate(savedInstanceState);
    setContentView(R.layout.activity_main);
    ListView mListView = findViewById(R.id.list);
    // 1. call to create database
    datasource = new ItemsDataSource(this);
    // 2. open Database for writing
    datasource.open();
    //3. list all the items in the table on the main screen
    List <Item> values = datasource.getAllItem();
    mAdapter = new ArrayAdapter <>(this,
        android.R.layout.simple_list_item_1, values);
    mListView.setAdapter(mAdapter);
}
// Will be executed via the onClick attribute
// of the buttons in activity_main.xml
public void onClick(View view) {
    try {
        Item item;
        EditText editkey = findViewById(R.id.editKey);
        EditText editvalue = findViewById(R.id.editValue);
        Button updateButton = findViewById(R.id.updateButton);
        LinearLayout ln = findViewById(R.id.group3);
        switch (view.getId()) {
            case R.id.add:
                int nextInt = new Random().nextInt(19);
                // Save the new comment to the database
                item = datasource.createItem(new Item(
                        bestThingsToSellOnEBay[nextInt]));
                mAdapter.add(item);
                break;
            case R.id.delete:
                if (mAdapter.getCount() > 0) {
                    item = mAdapter.getItem(0);
                    datasource.deleteItem(item);
                    mAdapter.remove(item);
                }
                break;
            case R.id.deleteall:
                if (mAdapter.getCount() > 0) {
                    datasource.deleteAllItems();
                    mAdapter.clear();
                }
                break;
            case R.id.update:
                ln.setBackgroundColor(999);
                editkey.setHint("insert the id");
                editvalue.setHint("insert value");
                updateButton.setText("Press to Update");
                editkey.setVisibility(View.VISIBLE);
                editvalue.setVisibility(View.VISIBLE);
                updateButton.setVisibility(View.VISIBLE);
```

```
                break;
            case R.id.updateButton:
                ln.setBackgroundColor(999);
                boolean done = false;
                for (int i = 0; i < mAdapter.getCount() && !done; i++) {
                  Item removedItem = mAdapter.getItem(i);
                  if (removedItem.getId() == new
                    Long(editkey.getText().toString()).longValue()) {
                      done = true;
                      mAdapter.remove(removedItem);
                  }
                }
            item = datasource.updateItem(editvalue.getText().toString(),
                  (new Integer(editkey.getText().toString())).intValue());
                editkey.setVisibility(View.INVISIBLE);
                editvalue.setVisibility(View.INVISIBLE);
                updateButton.setVisibility(View.INVISIBLE);
                mAdapter.add(item);
                break;
            case R.id.delete_last:
                if (mAdapter.getCount() > 0) {
                    item = mAdapter.getItem(mAdapter.getCount() - 1);
                    datasource.deleteItem(item);
                    mAdapter.remove(item);
                }
                break;
            case R.id.count:
                long numOfItems = datasource.count();
                String text = "number of entries in database table is " +
                              numOfItems;
                Context context = getApplicationContext();
                int duration = Toast.LENGTH_LONG;
                Toast toast = Toast.makeText(context, text, duration);
                toast.show();
                break;
            case R.id.exitButton:
                finish();
                break;
        }
        mAdapter.notifyDataSetChanged();
    } catch (Exception e) { }
}
@Override
protected void onResume() {
    datasource.open();
    super.onResume();
}
@Override
protected void onPause() {
    datasource.close();
    super.onPause();
}
}
```

11.4.4 Test Your Database Using SQLiteBrowser

SQLiteBrowser is a simple and free database management application that you can download and use to design and test your Android database. Below, we describe how to use SQLiteBrowser.

11.4.4.1 Locate Your App Database

To view a database stored on your device (or emulator), do the following:

1. Connect your device to your computer using a USB cable.
2. Open Android Studio.
3. Click View - > Tool Windows - > Device File Explorer.

Following these steps, you can also explore files on the Android emulator. Just make sure that the emulator is open when you click on View -> Tool Windows -> Device File Explorer. Figure 11.8 is a snapshot of the file explorer for an Android device using Android Studio.

11.4.4.2 Open Your Database with SQLiteBrowser

In file explorer, do the following:

1. Click data -> data -> [your_app_package_name]->databases.
2. Copy the database file to your PC.
3. Open the database with the SQLite browser.

In the emulator, the location of items.db for our demo app is **/data/user/0/com. code.abdulrahman.database/databases/items.db.**

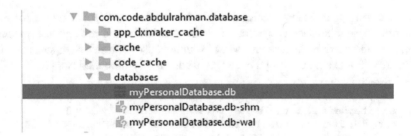

Fig. 11.8 Using file explorer on Android Studio to locate the database of your app

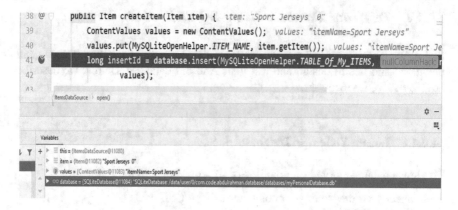

Fig. 11.9 Running your app in the debugging mode to locate the database on the emulator

If you run the app in the debugging mode, you will find the exact location of your database. Figure 11.9 shows the location of the database when running our app in the debugging mode.

11.4.4.3 Test Your Database with SQLiteBrowser

Once you open the database in SQLiteBrowser, do the following:

1. Check the table schemas and data in the database to confirm that your database has been created correctly.
2. Run queries on your database and check the results. Based on your query results, change or update your code.

11.4.5 Use SQLiteBrowser for Database Design

Before coding your database tables and queries, you can use SQLiteBrowser, or any other database management system, to create your tables and run and test queries. Later, when you code the database part of your app, use the tested SQL statement in your code. For example, using the rawQuery construct, Android allows you to write queries such as:

```
select itemName from tableOfMyItems where itemName NOT NULL
select _id, itemName from tableOfMyItems where itemName="Gift Cards"
select _id from tableOfMyItems where itemName='Gift Cards'
select itemName from tableOfMyItems where _id=8 ;
```

If you run both the queries above, or similar ones outside of your app, and the embedded queries in your app and receive identical results, you will be sure of the correctness of your code.

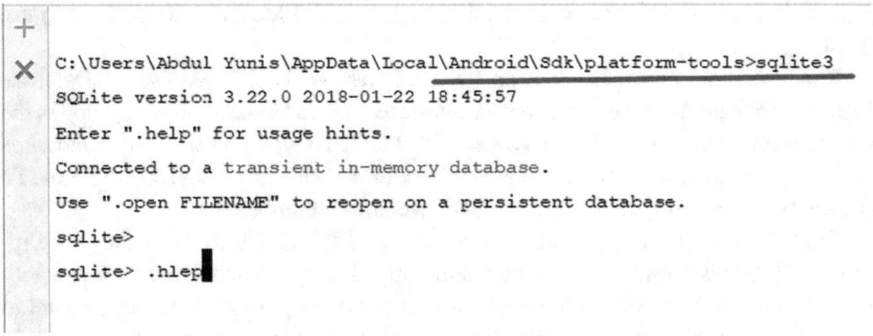

```
+

×   C:\Users\Abdul Yunis\AppData\Local\Android\Sdk\platform-tools>sqlite3

    SQLite version 3.22.0 2018-01-22 18:45:57

    Enter ".help" for usage hints.

    Connected to a transient in-memory database.

    Use ".open FILENAME" to reopen on a persistent database.

    sqlite>

    sqlite> .hlep
```

Fig. 11.10 The location of the sqlite3 inside the Android Studio download folder

11.4.5.1 Sqlite3 Database Tool

The Android SDK includes a sqlite3 database tool which is a simple command-line program that allows you to view table contents and run SQL commands and other useful functions on SQLite databases.

The location of the sqlite3 tool is inside the Android Studio download folder/platform-tools folder, e.g., C:\Users\...\AppData\Local\Android\Sdk*platform-tools*. The screenshot in Fig. 11.10 shows the location of the sqlite3 tool on your PC and how to start sqlite3 program from the Android Studio command line. Once started, you can manually enter and execute SQL statements against an SQLite database.

The sqlite3 tool is not covered in this chapter, but if you want to learn about it, check the references provided at the end of this chapter.

11.4.5.2 Do It Yourself

Do the following exercises to improve your understating of the current project and Android SQLite databases:

1. Add error handling to the update() method of the demo app code. For example, if a user tries to update a non-existent item, the app should handle it and not crash.
2. Currently, when the add button of the demo app is pressed, an item is randomly selected from the data list to be inserted into the database. Change the code to prevent database insert duplication, i.e., prevent an item to be added more than once to the database.

11.4.6 Android Database Inspector

In Android Studio 4.1 and higher, there is a tool called *Database Inspector* that you can use to test and debug your database. It enables you to run queries using regular

SQL statements and inspect your database schema. Below, we describe how to use this tool.

Run your app, and then click on the View tab → Tool Windows → Database Inspector to open the database inspector interface. The database of our demo app in the database inspector window is shown in Fig. 11.11. As you can see, our database is called myPersonalDatabase and contains two tables, contacts and tableOfMyItems. To see the table schemas, click on the head-down arrow, numbered 1.

Click on the query tab icon, numbered 1 in Fig. 11.11, to open the tab. Figure 11.12 shows a query tab for our demo app. The query tab includes a space to write regular SQL queries and run them. You can open as many tabs as you want to run different queries and test your app. The results of your queries will be shown in

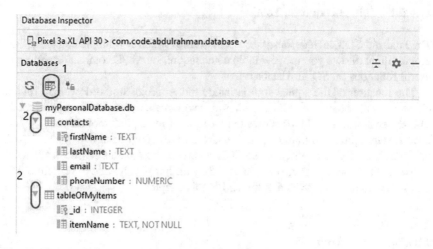

Fig. 11.11 A database is shown in the Database Inspector

	_id		itemName
1	111		Marvel Toys
2	112		Healing Bracelets
3	114		Oculus Go
4	115		Smart Watch Straps
5	116		Yeti Coolers

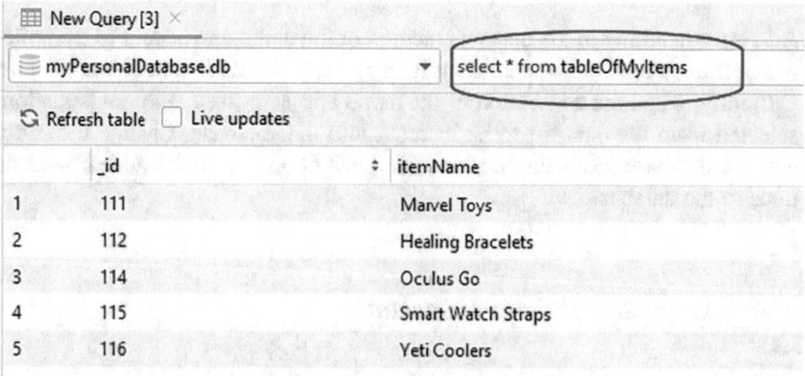

Fig. 11.12 An example of running a query and the query result is shown

the query tab window. An example of where to type the query, running a query, and query results is shown below.

Some examples of SQL queries that you can use to test your database are listed below.

```
select * from contacts
select itemName from tableOfMyItems where _id = 111
delete from tableOfMyItems where _id = 116
select count (*) from tableOfMyItems
insert into tableOfMyItems (_id, itemName) values (30, "new item")
UPDATE tableOfMyItems SET itemName = "updatedItem" WHERE _id = 116
```

11.5 Realtime Firebase Database

Firebase is a Google platform that allows you to build Web, Unity, IOS, and mobile applications without server-side programming. Firebase provides multiple features enabling you to focus on the client-side of your app, while the server-side is taken care of for you. It is a real-time database, i.e., when you update your app data, your clients receive the updated data almost instantly. It has a built-in authentication system and enables you to collect performance data and perform data analytics. You can use Firebase to store images and other files. It can also be a hosting service for the content.

In this section, we will introduce Firebase databases and create an app that inserts, retrieves, queries, and deletes data from a database. To be able to use a Firebase database in your app, you need to do some setup. Below we describe the setup steps.

11.5.1 Firebase and JSON Tree File

When you put your database on the Firebase server, the data is stored as JSON objects. This means there will be no tables and table records. Instead, you will have a JSON tree which is also called a NoSQL database. Every time you add data to your database, it becomes a node in the existing JSON tree structure.

The Firebase real-time database allows deep data nesting, up to 32 levels deep. However, it would be better if you keep the structure of your data as flat as possible. You should store your data in a flat structure for two reasons. First, when you retrieve a node, you are also getting all of its children. Second, when you grant someone access to a node in your database, you also grant them access to all data underneath that node. For these two reasons, when you keep the structure of your database deeply nested, you might put the performance and security of your app at risk.

11.5.2   Firebase Account and Project Setup

To be able to use Firebase in your app, you need to create a Firebase project and connect to the Firebase server. You can start this step within Android Studio or by login into the Firebase console. When using Android Studio, open your project, and click on the Tools tab from the menu bar, and then click Firebase. This will open a pan inside Android Studio on the right-hand side. This is a Firebase assistant workflow that will help you add Firebase to your app. It helps to add the necessary Firebase files, plugins, and dependencies to your Android project. You need to select the type of service you would like to establish and complete the steps required to establish the service.

Below are some of the tasks that you need to do to connect your app to Firebase and use the Firebase database. Some of these tasks are done automatically when you use Firebase assistance.

11.5.3   Register Your Project Using the Firebase Console

Open the Firebase console, and click on the plus sign to add a project to your account. Follow the steps to create your Firebase project. Once you are done creating your firebase project, you need to add your app to the project. From the Firebase console, click on the Android icon, and complete the steps to add your app to the project. You need to download the *google-service.json* file from the Firebase console and put it in the *app* directory of your project to complete this step.

11.5.4   Adding Dependency to Your Project

For your app to be able to use Firebase services, you need to add some dependencies to your Android project. Add the database dependency to your Gradle application level. For example, add **implement com.google.firebase:firebase-database:19.7.0** to your Gradle file. At the time of writing this book, this is the latest Firebase database version. You need to consult Android documentation, https://firebase. google.com/docs/android/setup, to find the latest dependencies for your project. The code snippet below shows how a Firebase database has been added to the Gradle file.

```
dependencies {
    implementation 'androidx.appcompat:appcompat:1.2.0'
    implementation 'com.google.android.material:material:1.3.0'
    implementation 'androidx.constraintlayout:constraintlayout:2.0.4'
    implementation 'com.google.firebase:firebase-database:19.7.0'
    ... }
```

You need to add the classpath and plugin to your project level Gradle; see the examples below:

```
dependencies {
  classpath "com.android.tools.build:gradle:4.1.2"
  classpath 'com.google.gms:google-services:4.3.5'
}
plugins {
  id 'com.android.application'
  id 'com.google.gms.google-services'
}
```

11.5.5   Connecting to Database

Firebase provides multiple classes to connect, read/write, query, and delete data in a database. The most widely used classes are FirebaseDatabase, DatabaseReference, DataSnapshot, DatabaseError, and Query. We will show when and how you are going to use these classes to perform database transactions.

To create an instance of the database, you use the getInstance() method like this: **FirebaseDatabase database = FirebaseDatabase.getInstance();**.

This will return a default database instance that you can use in your app. You call the getReference() method on the returned database to create a child node and set the node value. The code snippet below shows the described steps.

```
FirebaseDatabase database = FirebaseDatabase.getInstance();
DatabaseReference DatabaseRef = database.getReference();
DatabaseRef.child("cp213");
```

Here you are creating a database for students in a class that has a unique name and a root note called cp 213. If you open your database from the Firebase console, you should see the database and the root note.

11.5.6   Inserting Data into Database

By calling the .child("cp 213") method on the database reference, you are creating a reference to a note, i.e., a table called "cp 213." The table is ready for inserting data. You can insert data using the databaseReference.setValue() method as follows.

```
int i = 1;
for (; i <= 10; i++) {
    HashMap <String, String> aStudent = new HashMap <>();
    aStudent.put("student" + i + " Name", "name " + i);
    aStudent.put("student" + i + " number", i * 200 + 25 + "");
    database.getReference("cp 213").child("Class list").
                        child("Student " + i).setValue(aStudent);
}
```

Once the code above is executed, the following JSON tree will be created on the Firebase server. It represents the database of your app. As you can see, it is a NoSQL database where the root note represents a table name and the child elements can be another node or node properties and values. Firebase supports 32 different child levels.

In the code snippet below, we create another node, i.e., a table called User with multiple rows where each row has information about the first name, last name, id, and email address of the user. The code execution results are shown in Fig. 11.11. Both Figs. 11.13 and 11.14 show how you can create multiple tables to form your database.

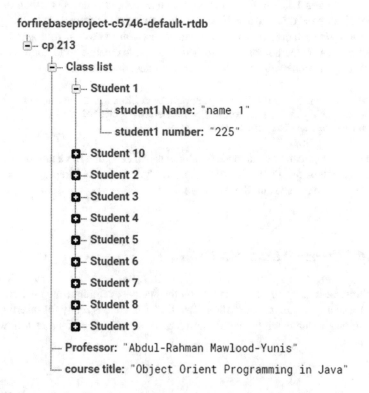

Fig. 11.13 An example of a real-time database created on the Firebase server

Fig. 11.14 A Firebase database with two nodes, User and CP 213, and multiple children in each node

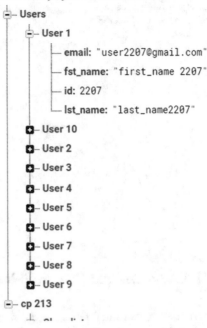

```
Random rand = new Random() ; //instance of random class
int upperbound = 10000;
i = 1;
for (; i <= 10; i++) {
    int id = rand.nextInt(upperbound);
    User user = new User("first_name " + id, "last_name" + id,
        id, "user" + id + "@gmail.com");
    database.getReference("Users").child("User " + i).setValue(user);
}
```

The setValue() method overwrites data at the specified position, including any child nodes. You can use this method to pass JSON types which are String, Long, Double, Boolean, Map<String, Object>, and List.

You can also pass user-defined objects. To do so, you need to define a class with a default constructor that has public getters for the properties to be assigned.

Figure 11.15 is the class structure that we have used in our app for passing user objects.

Fig. 11.15 A user-defined
class structure used as a
parameter to the Firebase
database

11.5.7   Retrieving Data from Database

To retrieve data from Firebase, you can use the ValueEventListener interface to read
values from the database class. Each time the data changes, the listener will be called
with a snapshot of the data. The listener can be added to your database reference
using the addValueEventListener() method. The ValueEventListener has two
methods, *onDataChange()* and *onCancelled()*, that need to be implemented. See
the code snippet shown in Listing 11.15.

Listing 11.15 onDataChange() and onCancelled() method implementation.

```
DatabaseReference UserRef =
 FirebaseDatabase.getInstance().getReference().child("Users");
 UserRef.addValueEventListener(new ValueEventListener() {

  @Override
  public void onDataChange(@NonNull DataSnapshot snapshot) {
    final ArrayList <String> list = new ArrayList <>();
    ArrayAdapter adapter = new ArrayAdapter(getApplicationContext(),
        android.R.layout.simple_list_item_1, list);
    listView.setAdapter(adapter);
    for (DataSnapshot achild : snapshot.getChildren()) {
      list.add(achild.getValue().toString());
    }
    adapter.notifyDataSetChanged();
  }
  @Override
  public void onCancelled(@NonNull DatabaseError error) {
  // Failed to read value
```

```
    Log.w("firebase application", "Failed to read value.",
    error.toException());
  }
});
```

The *onCancelled()* method will be triggered when the listener fails or data is not accessible because of the security and Firebase database rules.

Figure 11.16 shows the student information stored in the Firebase database. The data is retrieved from the Firebase database and put inside a list for presentation.

Fig. 11.16 Data retrieved from the Firebase database are present in the list

11.5.8   Deleting Data from Database

The *removeValue()* method from the DatabaseReference class can be used to remove data from the database. The following code snippet removes ten students from the database we created in our demo app.

```
for (i = 0; i < 10; i++) {
    DatabaseReference Studetns = FirebaseDatabase.getInstance().
    getReference("cp 213").child("Class list").child(
    "Student " + i);
  Studetns.removeValue();
}
    FirebaseDatabase.getInstance().getReference("cp 213").child(
    "Class list").child("Student " + 10).removeValue();
```

Listing 11.16 shows the complete code for creating, using, and deleting data in a real-time Firebase database in an app.

Listing 11.16 Code for creating and using the Firebase database.

```
package com.code.abdulrahman.book.firebaseapplication;
import android.os.Bundle;
import android.util.Log;
import android.widget.ArrayAdapter;
import android.widget.ListView;
import androidx.annotation.NonNull;
import androidx.appcompat.app.AppCompatActivity;
import com.google.firebase.database.DataSnapshot;
import com.google.firebase.database.DatabaseError;
import com.google.firebase.database.DatabaseReference;
import com.google.firebase.database.FirebaseDatabase;
import com.google.firebase.database.ValueEventListener;
import java.util.ArrayList;
import java.util.HashMap;
import java.util.Random;

public class MainActivity extends AppCompatActivity {
  @Override
  protected void onCreate(Bundle savedInstanceState) {
    super.onCreate(savedInstanceState);
    setContentView(R.layout.activity_main);
    ListView listView = findViewById(R.id.listView);

    FirebaseDatabase database = FirebaseDatabase.getInstance();
    DatabaseReference DatabaseRef = database.getReference();

    HashMap <String, String> course = new HashMap <>();
    course.put("course title", "Object Orient Programming in Java");
```

```
      course.put ("Professor", "Abdul-Rahman Mawlood-Yunis");
      DatabaseRef.child ("cp 213").setValue (course);

   int i = 1;
   for (; i <= 10; i++) {
      HashMap <String, String> aStudent = new HashMap <>();
      aStudent.put ("student" + i + " Name", "name " + i);
      aStudent.put ("student" + i + " number", i * 200 + 25 + "");
      database.getReference ("cp 213").child (
             "Class list").child ("Student " + i).setValue (aStudent);
   }

   Random rand = new Random ();
   int upperbound = 10000;
   i = 1;
   for (; i <= 10; i++) {
      int id = rand.nextInt (upperbound);
      User user = new User ("first_name " + id, "last_name" + id,
            id, "user" + id + "@gmail.com");
      database.getReference ("Users").child ("User " + i).setValue (user);
   }
DatabaseReference UserRef = FirebaseData
base.getInstance ().getReference ().child ("Users");
      UserRef.addValueEventListener (new ValueEventListener () {
         @Override
         public void onDataChange (@NonNull DataSnapshot snapshot) {
            final ArrayList <String> list = new ArrayList <>();
         ArrayAdapter adapter = new ArrayAdapter (getApplicationContext (),
            android.R.layout.simple_list_item_1, list);
            listView.setAdapter (adapter);
            for (DataSnapshot achild : snapshot.getChildren ()) {
               list.add (achild.getValue ().toString ());
            }
            adapter.notifyDataSetChanged ();
         }
         @Override
         public void onCancelled (@NonNull DatabaseError error) {
            Log.w ("firebase application", "Failed to read value.",
                        error.toException ()); } });
      // delete
      for (i = 0; i < 10; i++) {
         DatabaseReference Studetns = FirebaseDatabase.getInstance ().
                           getReference ().child ("Student " + i);
         Studetns.removeValue (); }
      FirebaseDatabase.getInstance ().getReference ().child (
"Student " + 10);
   }
}
```

11.5.9   Query Data from Database

The Firebase database API provides multiple classes and methods to retrieve data from the database, i.e., to query a database, in the order that you would like. These include classes like Query and DataSnapshot and methods like orderByChild(), orderByKey(), orderByValue(), etc. These methods can be used along with other methods like limitToFirst(), limitToLast(), startAt(), endAt(), and equalTo() to form complex queries. Below, we describe the DataSnapshot and Query classes and show how to use some of the methods mentioned to run queries.

11.5.10   DataSnapshot and Query Classes

When you query data from the Firebase database, you receive a DataSnapshot object. The DataSnapshot objects are passed to the listener methods that you need to implement, i.e., listen to, in your code. To receive copies of the data when the database is changed, you can register to listen to the database changes using methods like:

```
addValueEventListener(ValueEventListener),
addChildEventListener(ChildEventListener), or
addListenerForSingleValueEvent(ValueEventListener)
```

The code snippet shown in Listing 11.17 shows how to register your database reference to receive data snapshot inside a listener method. Adding a listener to the database reference and receiving a data snapshot inside the listener methods are highlighted in bold.

Listing 11.17 Registering a database reference to receive a data snapshot.

```
public class QueryClass {

  public static void queries1() {
    FirebaseDatabase database = FirebaseDatabase.getInstance();
    final DatabaseReference databaseRef = database.getReference("Users");
    databaseRef.orderByChild("id").addChildEventListener(
         new ChildEventListenerAdapter() {
      @Override
      public void onChildAdded(DataSnapshot dataSnapshot,
      String prevChildKey) {
        User user = dataSnapshot.getValue(User.class);
        System.out.println(dataSnapshot.getKey() + user.id);
      }
    });
  }
  ...
}
```

11.5.11 ChildEventListener Interface

As mentioned earlier, to receive events about changes in the child locations of your database, you need to implement, for example, the *ChildEventListener* interface. This interface has five methods that you need to implement whenever you would like to receive changing events.

To avoid implementing all five methods, we created an Adapter class called ChildEventListenerAdapter that implements all five methods with empty bodies. This way, instead of implementing all five methods in our QueryClass, we simply override the method that we would like to implement from the ChildEventListenerAdapter class. The code for the **ChildEventListenerAdapter** class, shown in Listing 11.18, and how it is used to receive data snapshots in the QueryClass are shown in the code snippet in Listing 11.19.

Listing 11.18 ChildEventListenerAdapter.java class.

```java
package com.code.abdulrahman.firbaseDatabase.firebaseapplication;
import androidx.annotation.NonNull;
import androidx.annotation.Nullable;
import com.google.firebase.database.ChildEventListener;
import com.google.firebase.database.DataSnapshot;
import com.google.firebase.database.DatabaseError;

public class ChildEventListenerAdapter implements ChildEventListener {
    @Override
    public void onChildAdded(@NonNull DataSnapshot snapshot,
                             @Nullable String previousChildName) { }
    @Override
    public void onChildChanged(@NonNull DataSnapshot snapshot,
                               @Nullable String previousChildName) {}
    @Override
    public void onChildRemoved(@NonNull DataSnapshot snapshot) {}

    @Override
    public void onChildMoved(@NonNull DataSnapshot snapshot,
                             @Nullable String previousChildName) {}
    @Override
    public void onCancelled(@NonNull DatabaseError error) {}
}
```

Listing 11.19 QueryClass.java class using ChildEventListenerAdapter class.

```
public class QueryClass {

  public static void queries1() {
    FirebaseDatabase database = FirebaseDatabase.getInstance();
    final DatabaseReference databaseRef = database.getReference("Users");
    databaseRef.orderByChild("id").addChildEventListener(
        new ChildEventListenerAdapter() {
        @Override
        public void onChildAdded(DataSnapshot dataSnapshot,
          String prevChildKey) {
          User user = dataSnapshot.getValue(User.class);
          System.out.println(dataSnapshot.getKey() + user.id);
        }
      });
  }
  ...
}
```

You may have noticed that the ChildEventListenerAdapter class is implemented as an inner class and only one method, the onChildAdded() method, is overridden. Also, both the *orderByChild()* method and *DataSnapshot* class are used to retrieve data from the database, and when the code is executed, the results are written to the console. The query1() method is declared as a static method inside the QueryClass to make it easily accessible inside the MainActivity class.

11.5.12   Querying Firebase Database Using User-Defined Classes

To write to the database, you use set methods like setValue() to set the data and priority to the given values. The data types used by the set methods are of JSON types: Boolean, Long, Double, String, Map<String, Object>, and List<Object>.

You can insert instances of your class into the database. To do so, your class must have a default constructor, i.e., a no argument constructor as well as the getter methods for the properties you would like to save in the database. In the example shown in Listing 11.20, we create a User class that can be used for storing/querying user data in the database. Storing and querying User data is done using the below two statements, and the complete code is presented in Listing 11.21.

```
database.getReference("Users").child("User " + i).setValue(user);
User user = dataSnapshot.getValue(User.class);
```

Listing 11.20 User.java class.

```java
public class User {
 private String fst_name ;
 private String lst_name ;
 protected static int id ;
 private String email ;

 public User() {}

 public User(String fst_name, String lst_name, int id, String email) {
   this.fst_name = fst_name;
   this.lst_name = lst_name;
   this.id = id;
   this.email = email;
 }

 public String getFst_name() {
   return fst_name;
 }
 public String getLst_name() {
   return lst_name;
 }
 public int getId() {
   return id;
 }
 public String getEmail() {
   return email;
 }
 public void setFst_name(String fst_name) {
   this.fst_name = fst_name;
 }
 public void setLst_name(String lst_name) {
   this.lst_name = lst_name;
 }
 public void setId(int id) {
   this.id = id;
 }
 public void setEmail(String email) {
   this.email = email;
 }
 @Override
 public String toString() {
   return "User{" +
        "fst_name='" + fst_name + '\'' +
        ", lst_name='" + lst_name + '\'' +
        ", id=" + id +
        ", email='" + email + '\'' +
        '}';
 }
}
```

Listing 11.21 QueryClass.java class using ChildEventListenerAdapter class.

```
Random rand = new Random();
int upperbound = 10000;
i = 1;
for (; i <= 10; i++) {
  int id = rand.nextInt(upperbound);
  User user = new User("first_name " + id, "last_name" + id,
      id, "user" + id + "@gmail.com");
    database.getReference("Users").child("User " + i).setValue(user);
}
DatabaseReference UserRef =
FirebaseDatabase.getInstance().getReference().child("Users");
UserRef.addValueEventListener(new ValueEventListener() {
 @Override
 public void onDataChange(@NonNull DataSnapshot snapshot) {
   final ArrayList <String> list = new ArrayList <>();
   ArrayAdapter adapter = new ArrayAdapter(getApplicationContext(),
       android.R.layout.simple_list_item_1, list);
   listView.setAdapter(adapter);
   for (DataSnapshot achild : snapshot.getChildren()) {
     list.add(achild.getValue().toString());
   }
   adapter.notifyDataSetChanged();
 }
```

11.5.13   Querying Firebase Database Example

In the code example shown in Listing 11.22, three queries are provided showing how you can query and retrieve data from the Firebase database using the various methods that the Query and DatabaseReference classes provide.

Listing 11.22 QueryClass.java showing how to query Firebase database.

```
package com.code.abdulrahman.firbaseDatabase.firebaseapplication;
import android.util.Log;
import androidx.annotation.NonNull;
import com.google.firebase.database.DataSnapshot;
import com.google.firebase.database.DatabaseError;
import com.google.firebase.database.DatabaseReference;
import com.google.firebase.database.FirebaseDatabase;
import com.google.firebase.database.Query;
import com.google.firebase.database.ValueEventListener;
```

```
public class QueryClass {
  public static void queries1() {
    FirebaseDatabase database = FirebaseDatabase.getInstance();
    final DatabaseReference databaseRef = database.getReference("Users");
    databaseRef.orderByChild("id").addChildEventListener(
                          new ChildEventListenerAdapter() {
      @Override
      public void onChildAdded(DataSnapshot dataSnapshot,
                            String prevChildKey) {
        User user = dataSnapshot.getValue(User.class);
        System.out.println(dataSnapshot.getKey() + user.id);
    }    });
  }

  public static void queries2() {
    FirebaseDatabase database = FirebaseDatabase.getInstance();
    final DatabaseReference databaseRef =
            database.getReference("cp 213").child("Class list");

  databaseRef.addChildEventListener(new ChildEventListenerAdapter() {
      @Override
      public void onChildAdded(DataSnapshot dataSnapshot,

  String prevChildKey) {
        if (dataSnapshot.exists()) {
           Log.v("Students", dataSnapshot.getValue().toString());
        } } });
  }

  public static void query3() {
    FirebaseDatabase database = FirebaseDatabase.getInstance();
    final DatabaseReference databaseRef =
        database.getReference("cp 213").child("Class list");
    Query query = databaseRef.orderByChild(
    "Students").limitToLast(3);
    query.addListenerForSingleValueEvent(new ValueEventListener() {
      @Override
      public void onDataChange(@NonNull DataSnapshot dataSnapshot) {
        //System.out.println("snapp "+dataSnapshot.getChildren());
        if (dataSnapshot.exists()) {
          System.out.println(dataSnapshot.getChildrenCount());
          Iterable <DataSnapshot> iterable =
          dataSnapshot.getChildren();
          for (DataSnapshot snapshot : iterable) {
             System.out.println(snapshot.getValue());
          } } }
      @Override
      public void onCancelled(@NonNull DatabaseError databaseError) { }
    });
  }
}
```

11.6   Other Data Storage Options

To complete this chapter, we will describe other ways to save and access data in Android devices.

11.6.1   Room Database

To simplify the creation, use, and maintenance of databases, Android supports indirect access to SQLite databases using the Room library as a layer on top of the SQLite database. The Room library eliminates the need to work directly with the SQLiteOpenHelper class, the main class involved when working with SQLite databases. The Room library helps you create databases and run full SQL queries using classes and methods defined in the Room library, which is a part of the Android Jetpack libraries. To create databases using the Room library, you need to create at minimum three Java classes: an Entity class, Data Access Object (DAO) abstract class or interface, and an abstract database class that extends the RoomDatabase class. You also need to update both Gradle files of your project and add proper dependencies. In this section, we briefly introduce database creation and usage using the Room library. You can find a complete example of database creation using the Room library by following the link provided at the end of this chapter.

11.6.1.1   Entity Class

The first component that you need to define when using the Room library is the Entity class. For each table you would like to have in your database, define a class, and annotate it with the *@Entity* tag. At runtime, classes and methods from the Room library will take the defined classes and create the corresponding tables to form the database. The instance variables for each Entity class become table column names, and variable types and their properties become table column types and constraints. An example of an Entity class is shown in Listing 11.23.

Listing 11.23   Defining an Entity class for Room database.

```
@Entity(tableName = "book_table")
public class Book {

  @PrimaryKey(autoGenerate = true)
  private int id;

  @NonNull
  @ColumnInfo(name = "book")

  private String book;
```

```
  public Book (@NonNull String book) {
     this.book = book;
  }
  public String getBook () {
     return book;
  }
  public int getId () {
     return id;
  }
  public void setId (int id) {
     this.id = id;
  }
}
```

Note that the getter() and setter() methods are used by Room library classes and need to be included in your Entity class definition.

11.6.1.2 DAO Interface

The second component that you need to define when using the Room library is the DAO abstract class/interface. It is the place where you define all the operations that you need to perform on the database and maps method calls to the database SQL query statements. In your DAO, abstract class/interface, use annotations like @Insert, @query, @primaryKey, and @ColumnInfo with the SQL queries that you would like to execute; the rest will be taken care of by the Room library.

An example of a DAO interface is shown in Listing 11.24.

Listing 11.24 DAO interface for mapping queries to methods.

```
package com.code.abdulrahman.roomdatabase;
import androidx.room.Dao;
import androidx.room.Insert;
import androidx.room.OnConflictStrategy;
import androidx.room.Query;
import java.util.ArrayList;
@Dao
public interface BookDAO {
  @Insert (onConflict = OnConflictStrategy.REPLACE)
  void insert (Book book) ;

  @Query ("DELETE from book_table")
  void deleteAll () ;

  @Query ("SELECT * from book_table")
  ArrayList <Book> getAllBooks () ;
}
```

11.6.1.3 Database Class

The third component that you need to define when using the Room library is the Database class. You create this class by extending the RoomDatabase class. It is an *abstract* class with an abstract method that has a DAO Interface return type. Listing 11.25 shows an example of such a class.

Listing 11.25 Database Java class when using Room.

```
package com.code.abdulrahman.roomdatabase;
import androidx.room.Database;
import androidx.room.RoomDatabase;

@Database(entities = {Book.class}, version = 1)
public abstract class AppDatabase extends RoomDatabase {
   public abstract BookDao bookDao();
}
```

11.6.1.4 App Room Database Class

Once you have all the database components ready, you need to create another class to create and initialize it. An example of such a class is shown in Listing 11.26. The database build statement used to create and initialize the database is shown in boldface font. The database is created using the *databaseBuilder()* and *build()* methods from the Room Builder class. The method signature for the databaseBuilder() method is shown below. The build() method is called on the Builder object returned from the databaseBuilder() method call to create and initialize the database.

```
Builder<T> databaseBuilder (
   Context context, Class<T> yourClass, String name).
```

Listing 11.26 Concrete Room Database class.

```
package com.code.abdulrahman.roomdatabase;
import android.content.Context;
import androidx.room.Room;

public class BookDatabase {
   private Context ctx;
   private static BookDatabase anInstance;
   private AppDatabase appDatabase;
```

```
  private BookDatabase(Context ctx) {
    this.ctx = ctx;
    appDatabase = Room.databaseBuilder(ctx, AppDatabase.class,
        "MyLibrary").build();
  }
  public static synchronized BookDatabase getInstance(Context mCtx) {
    if (anInstance == null) {
        anInstance = new BookDatabase(mCtx);
    }
    return anInstance;
  }
  public AppDatabase getAppDatabase() {
    return appDatabase;
  }
}
```

To complete the app, you need to create additional classes, such as the main class, to interact with the database, instantiate the database, and display query results. The code snippet shown below can be used for inserting data into a table row.

```
BookDatabase.getInstance(getApplicationContext()).
    getAppDatabase().bookDao().insert(book);
```

11.6.1.5   Do It Yourself

All the components needed to create a database using the Room library are described in Sect. 11.6.1. Use the code snippet given in this section to create a complete database app.

11.6.2   Content Provider

If your app manages a data repository and provides access to other apps to use this data, your app is acting as a server that provides the content to multiple clients. In such a situation, you must define how other apps can access the data, i.e., you need to provide a data interface, and what other apps can do with data, i.e., you need to define data access permissions and transaction types. Android provides such a service using content providers. This topic is covered in Chap. 12.

11.6.3   Internal and External Storage

Other data storage options available on Android include internal and external data storages. To cover data storages completely, here we provide a brief review of these two storage types. This topic has been covered thoroughly in Chap. 8.

11.6.3.1   Device File System

When an *internal storage* is used, the app's private files are saved on the device's file system. The file location is private. Other apps (even users) cannot access it. Remember that each app has its private directory on the device, like the user account on Linux or Windows; therefore, internal storage is a good place for internal app data. One thing you should remember about the internal storage is that when the user uninstalls an app that has been using the internal storage to save data/files, all data and files are removed. It is for this reason that you should not save data/files on the internal storage when the data needs to be kept after uninstallation. For example, if your app is for drawing pictures or taking photos and you save the drawings or photos on the internal storage, all your drawings and photos will be gone after uninstalling the app, something you might need to avoid.

11.6.3.2   SD Card, USB Storage, and Standard Public Directories

Every Android device supports storing data/files on external data storages. Your app needs to request read/write permission to be able to work with the external storages. The external data storages can be an sd card that can be physically inserted/removed from the sd card port on the device, an external USB storage, etc. External data storage is mostly used when data needs to persist even after the app is uninstalled. They are also useful when data needs to be shared. External storages might not always be available, for example, if the user removes the USB storage. Another example of an external storage is standard public directories for data/files. Android provides standard public directories for data/files that should persist after uninstalling the app; for example, the user has one location for all their photos, ringtones, music, and such.

11.7   Chapter Summary

Similar to personal computers (PCs), data can be saved in Android devices in multiple different ways, but mostly on a smaller scale since Android devices are meant to have different objectives than PCs. In this chapter, we covered SQLite databases to store structured data in a private database. We studied the SQLiteDatabase and SQLiteDatabaseHelper classes to create, upgrade, and open databases. We also described various methods to interact with the database. These include describing and using the insert(), query(), rawQuery(), replace(), and delete() methods in the demo app. We also described how to test your database using the open-source SQLiteBrowser tool, database inspector, or any other tool.

We covered how to create a Firebase real-time database to store and sync data with a NoSQL cloud database and to enable data to be synchronized across all clients in real time and remain available when your app goes offline.

Lastly, to simplify the creation, use, and maintenance of databases, we described the Room library as a layer on top of the SQLite database.

Check Your Knowledge

Below are some of the fundamental concepts and vocabularies that have been covered in this chapter. To test your knowledge and your understanding of this chapter, you should be able to describe each of the below concepts in one or two sentences.

- @Entity
- addChildEventListener
- Android Database inspector
- autoincrement
- ChildEventListener
- ContentProvider
- ContentResolver
- ContentValue
- Cursor
- DAO
- databaseBuilder
- DatabaseError
- DatabaseReference
- DataSnapshot
- execSQL
- Firebase Database
- getReadableDatabase
- getWritableDatabase
- isReadOnly
- JSON File
- MoveToLast
- MoveToNext
- NoSQL
- onCreate
- onOpen
- onUpgrade
- orderByChild
- rawQuery
- RoomDatabase
- Room
- SQLiteDatabase
- SQLiteOpenHelper

Further Reading

For more information about the topics covered in this chapter, we suggest that you refer to the online resources listed below. These links provide additional insight into the topics covered. The links are mostly maintained by Google and are a part of the Android API specification. The resource titles convey which section/subsection of the chapter the resource is related to. Furthermore, to expand your knowledge about using SQLite database with Android, SQLite performance, and security, see [1, 2].

adb documentation, [online] Available, https://developer.android.com/studio/command-line/adb

Android Room with a View, online] Available, https://developer.android.com/codelabs/android-room-with-a-view#0

Content providers, [online] Available, https://developer.android.com/guide/topics/providers/content-providers

ContentValues, [online] Available, https://developer.android.com/reference/android/content/ContentValues

DatabaseReference, [online] Available, https://firebase.google.com/docs/reference/android/com/google/firebase/database/DatabaseReference

DataSnapshot, [online] Available, https://firebase.google.com/docs/reference/android/com/google/firebase/database/DataSnapshot

firebase-database Reading data, [online] Available, https://sodocumentation.net/firebase-database/topic/9242/reading-data

FirebaseDatabase, [online] Available, https://firebase.google.com/docs/reference/android/com/google/firebase/database/FirebaseDatabase

orderByChild, [online] Available, https://developers.google.com/android/reference/com/google/firebase/database/Query.html#orderByChild(java.lang.String).

Query, [online] Available, https://firebase.google.com/docs/reference/android/com/google/firebase/database/Query

Retrieving Data, https://firebase.google.com/docs/database/admin/retrieve-data

sqlite, [online] Available, https://developer.android.com/reference/android/database/sqlite/SQLiteDatabase

SQLiteOpenHelper, [online] Available, https://developer.android.com/reference/android/database/sqlite/SQLiteOpenHelper

ValueEventListener, [online] Available, https://firebase.google.com/docs/reference/android/com/google/firebase/database/ValueEventListener

References

1. O. Nikola, K. Aleksandar, D. Igor, Performance analysis on Android SQLite database, in *2019 18th International Symposium INFOTEH-JAHORINA (INFOTEH)*, 2019, pp. 1–4. https://doi.org/10.1109/INFOTEH.2019.8717652
2. J.H. Park, S. Yoo, I.S. Kim, et al., Security architecture for a secure database on Android. IEEE Access **6**, 11482–11501 (2018). https://doi.org/10.1109/ACCESS.2018.2799384

Chapter 12
Content Provider, Service, Message Broadcasting, and Multimedia Player

What You Will Learn in This Chapter
By the end of this chapter, you should be able to:

- Create content providers and use content resolvers
- Create and use the Android service and Intent service
- Broadcast messages and use the broadcast receiver
- Use the MediaPlayer object to stream radio stations
- Use MediaView objects to play and stream video content
- Manage Android power and Wi-Fi connections programmatically

Check Out the Demo Project
Download the demo apps, **cprovider**, **ContentProviderClient**, and **LiveStreamingMediaContent.zip**, specifically developed to go with this chapter. I recommend that you code this project up from the notes rather than just opening the project in Android Studio and running it; however, if you want to run the code first to get a sense of the app, please do so. The code is thoroughly explained in this chapter to help you understand it. We follow the same approach to all other chapters throughout the book. The app's code will help you comprehend the additional concepts that will be described in this chapter.

    How to run the code: unzip the code in a folder of your choice, and then in Android Studio, click **File->import->Existing Android code into the workspace**. The project should start running.

12.1 Introduction

In this chapter, you will learn how to create and use the content provider, Android service, message broadcasts, MediaPlayer, and VideoView objects, as well as how to manage Android power and Wi-Fi connections. The chapter is divided into five

© The Author(s), under exclusive license to Springer Nature Switzerland AG 2022   531
A.-R. Mawlood-Yunis, *Android for Java Programmers*,
https://doi.org/10.1007/978-3-030-87459-9_12

parts. In Sect. 12.2, we study the classes and concepts needed to develop and use content provider apps. In Sect. 12.4, we study the main concepts and classes involved in creating and running the Android service. In Sect. 12.5, we study the classes and concepts involved in creating broadcasts to broadcast and receive messages. In Sect. 12.6, we present an app that uses an Android media player, broadcast receiver, and service. Lastly, in Sect. 12.7, we study how to use VideoView to play content remotely and locally.

12.2   Content Provider Component

When your app manages a data repository and provides access to other apps to use this data, your app is acting as a server that provides the content to multiple clients. In such a situation, you must define how other apps can access the data, i.e., you need to provide a data interface, and what other apps can do with data, i.e., you need to define data access permissions and transaction types. Android provides such a service using the ContentProvider, ContentResolver, and URI classes. We will study these classes and how to create and run content providers in this part of the chapter.

12.2.1   Content Provider

Content providers are one of the main components of the Android system related to data sharing. As the name implies, a content provider offers content to others, i.e., enables the sharing of centralized data among apps. It acts as a mediator between data repositories (e.g., SQLite database, text files, image files, etc.) and apps that are interested in the data. For example, multiple apps might need to access your contact information. In this case, data must be accessed through the ContentProvider class. It is a must to prevent data breaches and accidents. Android has several built-in content providers, for example, contacts, media, calendar, and user dictionary.

Using a content provider imposes certain implementations on both the content provider and the client app. Think of content providers as a server or as centralized data. Client apps interested in the data residing underneath a content provider need to implement a standard set of APIs, i.e., transaction protocols, to interact with the data.

Android comes with two classes, ContentProvider and ContentResolver, to securely enable the creation of data-sharing apps. Content provider apps need to extend the ContentProvider class to manage data repositories. Client apps need to use the ContentResolver class to access the shared data.

We have created two demo apps to show you how to create and use content providers. The content provider and the client are separate apps; they are named *cprovider* and *ContentProviderClient*, respectively.

The first app, i.e., the content provider, is used to insert data into a database. It can also display data locally. In other words, we have created a MainActivity class that you can use to query the content provider. This is useful for testing the content provider limitations before making it accessible to other apps.

The second app, i.e., the client app, is used to query the content provider and display the retrieved data in a list. Figure 12.1 shows the interface of both demo apps. The left-hand side of the figure shows the content provider where the user can insert the team contact information (team name, office number, fax number, and email) into an SQLite database. The right-hand side of the figure shows the button used to load the data from the content provider and the area where the retrieved data from the content provider query would be listed.

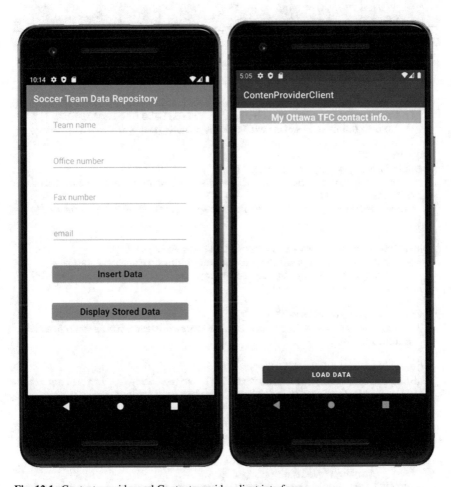

Fig. 12.1 Content provider and Content provider client interfaces

12.2.2   Creating a Content Provider

Creating a content provider involves four steps: designing a URI to do data mapping, inserting a provider element into the manifest file, extending the ContentProvider class, and setting permissions. All these steps will be described in this part.

To create a ContentProvider class, right-click on the app folder from your project → others → content provider. Give a *name* to your provider, and define an *authority*. To keep the authority unique, give it the package name of your app. This will generate a template similar to the one shown in Listing 12.1. You need to implement all six methods listed in the class template to have a content provider. In the following subsections, we will describe each method and its implementation.

Listing 12.1   Content provider class skeleton.

```java
public class MyContentProvider extends ContentProvider {
  public MyContentProvider() {}
  @Override
  public int delete(Uri uri, String selection, String[] selectionArgs) {
    // Implement this to handle requests to delete one or more rows.
    throw new UnsupportedOperationException("Not yet implemented");
  }
  @Override
  public String getType(Uri uri) {
    // TODO: Implement this to handle requests for the MIME type of the data
    // at the given URI.
    throw new UnsupportedOperationException("Not yet implemented");
  }
  @Override
  public Uri insert(Uri uri, ContentValues values) {
    // TODO: Implement this to handle requests to insert a new row.
    throw new UnsupportedOperationException("Not yet implemented");
  }
  @Override
  public boolean onCreate() {
    // TODO: Implement this to initialize your content provider on startup.
    return false;
  }
  @Override
  public Cursor query(Uri uri, String[] projection, String selection,
            String[] selectionArgs, String sortOrder) {
    // TODO: Implement this to handle query requests from clients.
    throw new UnsupportedOperationException("Not yet implemented");
  }
  @Override
  public int update(Uri uri, ContentValues values, String selection,
            String[] selectionArgs) {
    // TODO: Implement this to handle requests to update one or more rows.
    throw new UnsupportedOperationException("Not yet implemented");
  }
}
```

12.2.2.1 Designing a URI

All methods implemented by the content provider have a parameter of type Uri, and that is why before implementing content provider methods, you need to think of designing a Uri for your app. The Uri, i.e., Universal Resource Identifier, is an id that uniquely names a provider and the data in the provider in a way that enables other apps to locate it and communicate with it. For example, the Uri used by the client to locate the provider and the provider data for our demo app is:

"content://com.code.abdulrahman.cprovider/contacts".

The following lines of code show how to define the Uri for your content provider.

```
static final String PROVIDER_NAME = "com.code.abdulrahman.cprovider";
static final String URL = "content://" + PROVIDER_NAME + "/contacts";
static final Uri CONTENT_URI = Uri.parse(URL);
```

The Uri is made of three parts. The first part is the string "content://", also called the schema. The second part is the authority that you declare inside the AndroidManifest.xml file, for example, the authority for our demo app is com.code.abdulrahman.coprovider. The last part is the path to a table in the database, for example, the path in our demo app is contacts.

The Android *UriMatcher* class can be used to match the incoming Uri, i.e., the Uri the app is trying to locate, and the Uri of the content provider. The creation and initialization of the UriMatcher inside the ContentProvider class are as follows:

```
static {
    uriMatcher = new UriMatcher(UriMatcher.NO_MATCH);
    uriMatcher.addURI(PROVIDER_NAME, "contacts", URI_CODE);
    uriMatcher.addURI(PROVIDER_NAME, "contacts/*", URI_CODE);
}
```

This is a static block that is executed when the content provider class is created. The addURI() method has three parameters, the provider's name, path, and return code.

The match() method from the UriMatcher class can be used to match the incoming Uri with the content provider Uri; the matching statement would be like this: **uriMatcher.match(uri)).**

12.2.2.2 onCreate Method Implementation

The onCreate() method implementation can be used to create a database, for example, an SQLite database, for your content provider and to initialize local variables. All the steps involved in creating an SQLite database and the methods used are described in Chap. 11 and are reused here. An example of the onCreate() implementation is shown in the code snippet below. The database instantiation and the access to write to the database statements are in boldface.

```
@Override
  public boolean onCreate() {
    Context context = getContext();
    DatabaseHelper dbHelper = new DatabaseHelper(context);
    db = dbHelper.getWritableDatabase();
    if (db != null) {
        return true;
    }
    return false;
}
```

12.2.2.3 Query Method Implementation

An example of a query() method implementation for the ContentProvider class is shown in Listing 12.2. There are a few things you need to note about the implementation of this method. First, the UriMatcher.match() method is used to match between the client and provider Uris. Second, the database query() method is called to retrieve data from the database. Third, the method calls the *setNotificationUri()* method from the cursor class to notify the observer objects about changes in the content provider. Objects, such as CursorLoader, can register to changes in the content provider data. This is similar to registering listeners to list objects in early chapters; every time the list data changed, the list objects were notified to update their content. The steps described are shown in Listing 12.2.

Listing 12.2 Content provider query implementation.

```
@Override
  public Cursor query(Uri uri, String[] projection, String selection,
            String[] selectionArgs, String sortby) {

  SQLiteQueryBuilder sqLiteQueryBuilder = new SQLiteQueryBuilder();
    sqLiteQueryBuilder.setTables(TABLE_NAME);
    switch (uriMatcher.match(uri)) {
      case uri_code:
        // additonal code goes here
          break;
      default:
        throw new IllegalArgumentException("Unknown URI " + uri);
    }
    // sort result by row id
    if (sortby == null || sortby.isEmpty()) {
      sortby = id;
    }
```

```
  Cursor queryResult = sqLiteQueryBuilder.
     query(db, projection, selection, selectionArgs,
     null, null, sortby);
  queryResult.setNotificationUri
  (getContext().getContentResolver(), uri);
  return queryResult;
}
```

Note that you can have additional code in the switch section of the method implementation. For example, you can have a class variable of type HashMap that can be used to map the column names that the client apps insert into the query to the database column names. This mapping can be done using the **setProjectionMap()** method from the SQLiteQueryBuilder class. In this case, the switch section of your code can be re-written as follows:

```
public class MyContentProvider extends ContentProvider {
private static HashMap <String, String> values;
 ....
  switch (uriMatcher.match(uri)) {
    case uri_code:
      sqLiteQueryBuilder.setProjectionMap(values);
...
}
```

12.2.2.4   Insert Method Implementation

An example of an insert() method implementation for the ContentProvider class is shown in Listing 12.3. The two important code statements that you should be aware of when implementing this method are the database insert() and the ContentResolver's notifyChange() method calls. Both methods are shown in boldface font.

Listing 12.3 Insert implementation.

```
@Override
public Uri insert(Uri uri, ContentValues values) {

  long rowID = db.insert(TABLE_NAME, "", values);
  if (rowID > 0) {
    Uri _uri = ContentUris.withAppendedId(CONTENT_URI, rowID);
    getContext().getContentResolver().notifyChange(_uri, null);
    return _uri;
  }
  throw new SQLiteException("Failed to add a record into " + uri);
}
```

12.2.2.5   Update Method Implementation

The update() method implementation for the ContentProvider class is very similar to that of the insert() method. The most important part of the method implementation is the call to the database update() method. The code snippet in Listing 12.4 is an example of how to implement the update method in an app.

Listing 12.4   Update implementation.

```
@Override
 public int update(Uri uri, ContentValues values, String selection,
          String[] selectionArgs) {
   int count = 0;
   switch (uriMatcher.match(uri)) {
     case uri_code:
       count = db.update(TABLE_NAME, values, selection, selectionArgs);
       break;
     default:
        throw new IllegalArgumentException("Unknown URI " + uri);
   }
   getContext().getContentResolver().notifyChange(uri, null);
   return count;
 }
```

12.2.2.6   Delete Method Implementation

The delete() method implementation for the ContentProvider class is very similar to that of the insert()/update() methods. The most important part of the method implementation is the call to the database delete() method. The code snippet in Listing 12.5 is an example of how to implement the delete() method in an app.

Listing 12.5   Insert implementation.

```
@Override
  public int delete(Uri uri, String selection, String[] selectionArgs) {
    int count = 0;
    switch (uriMatcher.match(uri)) {
      case uri_code:
        count = db.delete(TABLE_NAME, selection, selectionArgs);
        break;
      default:
        throw new IllegalArgumentException("Unknown URI " + uri);
    }
    getContext().getContentResolver().notifyChange(uri, null);
    return count;
  }
```

12.2.2.7   getType Method Implementation

When you create media content, e.g., an image or a text file, it is better to specify the content media type, also called the MIME type, to help applications display the content properly. For example, by creating a website and specifying the content media type as text/html, the browser is better able to display the content. The getType() method implementation returns the content media type of the content provider to the client application. There are several standard content media types such as "text/html" for normal webpages, "text/plain" for plain text, "application/octet-stream," etc. The last one does not specify the content type; it lets the content display application find the content type itself.

Content providers support both the return standard content types and custom ones. The custom MIME type strings, also called "vendor-specific" MIME types, have more complex type and subtype values. When you want to return only one single row, the return type of the getType() method for your app should be **"vnd.android.cursor.item"**. However, when you want to support multiple row retrieval in your content provider app, the return type of your getType() method should be **"vnd.android.cursor.dir"**. This is because the return type of the query is the cursor object. For example, in our method implementation, we will return "vnd.android.cursor.dir/contacts". The contact *subtype* is specific to our app. An example of a getType() method implementation is shown below.

```
@Override
  public String getType(Uri uri) {
     switch (uriMatcher.match(uri)) {
       case uri_code:
          return "vnd.android.cursor.dir/contacts";
       default:
          throw new IllegalArgumentException("Unsupported URI: " + uri);
     }
  }
```

12.2.2.8   ContentProvider Code Example

We put together the implementation of all six content provider methods along with the Uri and database creation in one file to form a complete code for the content provider. The code snippet in Listing 12.6 is the complete code for the ContentProvider class in our demo app.

Listing 12.6 MyContentProvider.java class.

```java
package com.code.abdulrahman.cprovider;
import android.content.ContentProvider;
import android.content.ContentUris;
import android.content.ContentValues;
import android.content.Context;
import android.content.UriMatcher;
import android.database.Cursor;
import android.database.sqlite.SQLiteDatabase;
import android.database.sqlite.SQLiteException;
import android.database.sqlite.SQLiteOpenHelper;
import android.database.sqlite.SQLiteQueryBuilder;
import android.net.Uri;
import java.util.HashMap;

public class MyContentProvider extends ContentProvider {

    static final String PROVIDER_NAME = "com.code.abdulrahman.cprovider";
    static final String URL = "content://" + PROVIDER_NAME + "/contacts";
    static final Uri CONTENT_URI = Uri.parse(URL);
    private static HashMap <String, String> values;

    static final String id = "id";
    static final String contact = "name";
    static final int uri_code = 1;

    private SQLiteDatabase db;
    static final String DATABASE_NAME = "ContactDB";
    static final String TABLE_NAME = "MyContacts";
    static final int DATABASE_VERSION = 1;

    static final String CREATE_DB_TABLE =
          " CREATE TABLE " + TABLE_NAME
        + " (id INTEGER PRIMARY KEY AUTOINCREMENT, "
        + " name TEXT NOT NULL);";

static final UriMatcher uriMatcher;
  static {
    uriMatcher = new UriMatcher(UriMatcher.NO_MATCH);
    uriMatcher.addURI(PROVIDER_NAME, "contacts", uri_code);
    uriMatcher.addURI(PROVIDER_NAME, "contacts/*", uri_code);
  }
  @Override
  public String getType(Uri uri) {
    switch (uriMatcher.match(uri)) {
      case uri_code:
        return "vnd.android.cursor.dir/contacts";
        43 /* you use return "application/octet-stream" ;
        if you don't implement this method */
```

```java
    default:
        throw new IllegalArgumentException("Unsupported URI: " + uri);
    }
}
@Override
public boolean onCreate() {
    Context context = getContext();
    DatabaseHelper dbHelper = new DatabaseHelper(context);
    db = dbHelper.getWritableDatabase();
    if (db != null) {
        return true;
    }
    return false;
}
@Override
public Cursor query(Uri uri, String[] projection, String selection,
            String[] selectionArgs, String sortby) {

    SQLiteQueryBuilder sqLiteQueryBuilder = new SQLiteQueryBuilder();
    sqLiteQueryBuilder.setTables(TABLE_NAME);

    switch (uriMatcher.match(uri)) {
        case uri_code:
            break;
        default:
            throw new IllegalArgumentException("Unknown URI " + uri);
    }
    // sort result by row id
    if (sortby == null || sortby.isEmpty()) {
        sortby = id;
    }
    Cursor queryResult = sqLiteQueryBuilder.
        query(db, projection, selection, selectionArgs,
        null, null, sortby);
    queryResult.setNotificationUri
        (getContext().getContentResolver(), uri);
    return queryResult;
}

@Override
public Uri insert(Uri uri, ContentValues values) {
    long rowID = db.insert(TABLE_NAME, "", values);
    if (rowID > 0) {
        uri = ContentUris.withAppendedId(CONTENT_URI, rowID);
        getContext().getContentResolver().notifyChange(uri, null);
        return uri;
    }
    throw new SQLiteException("Failed to add a record into " + uri);
}
@Override
public int update(Uri uri, ContentValues values,
            String selection, String[] selectionArgs) {
    int count = 0;
```

```
switch (uriMatcher.match(uri)) {
  case uri_code:
    count = db.update
              (TABLE_NAME, values, selection, selectionArgs);
    break;
  default:
    throw new IllegalArgumentException("Unknown URI " + uri);
}
getContext().getContentResolver().notifyChange(uri, null);
return count;
}
@Override
public int delete(Uri uri, String selection, String[] selectionArgs) {
  int count = 0;
  switch (uriMatcher.match(uri)) {
    case uri_code:
      count = db.delete(TABLE_NAME, selection, selectionArgs);
      break;
    default:
      throw new IllegalArgumentException("Unknown URI " + uri);
  }
  getContext().getContentResolver().notifyChange(uri, null);
  return count;
}
private static class DatabaseHelper extends SQLiteOpenHelper {
  DatabaseHelper(Context context) {
    super(context, DATABASE_NAME, null, DATABASE_VERSION);
  }
  @Override
  public void onCreate(SQLiteDatabase db) {
    db.execSQL(CREATE_DB_TABLE);
  }
  @Override
  public void onUpgrade
    (SQLiteDatabase db, int oldVersion, int newVersion) {
    db.execSQL("DROP TABLE IF EXISTS " + TABLE_NAME);
    onCreate(db);
  }
}
}
```

12.2.3 Provider in Manifest File

You need to declare the provider element in the AndroidManifest.xml file to complete your content provider. Otherwise, the app will not run the content provider, and the Android system will not be aware of the class existence. To do so, include the <provider> element in the file; an example is shown in Listing 12.7.

The provider element has multiple items. A complete list of the provider items is shown below. More information on the provider items including their meanings and use are found in the Android documentation. The four element items that we used to define the provider in our demo app are name, authorities, enabled, and exported.

```
<provider android:authorities="list"
     android:directBootAware=["true" | "false"]
     android:enabled=["true" | "false"]
     android:exported=["true" | "false"]
     android:grantUriPermissions=["true" | "false"]
     android:icon="drawable resource"
     android:initOrder="integer"
     android:label="string resource"
     android:multiprocess=["true" | "false"]
     android:name="string"
     android:permission="string"
     android:process="string"
     android:readPermission="string"
     android:syncable=["true" | "false"]
     android:writePermission="string" >
  . . .
</provider>
```

Listing 12.7 MyContentProvider.java class.

```
<?xml version="1.0" encoding="utf-8"?>
<manifest xmlns:android=
 "http://schemas.android.com/apk/res/android"
  package="com.code.abdulrahman.cprovider">
<application
     android:allowBackup="true"
     android:icon="@mipmap/ic_launcher"
     android:label="@string/app_name"
     android:roundIcon="@mipmap/ic_launcher_round"
     android:supportsRtl="true"
     android:theme="@style/Theme.Cprovider">

<provider
 android:name="com.code.abdulrahman.cprovider.MyContentProvider"
     android:authorities="com.code.abdulrahman.cprovider"
     android:enabled="true"
     android:exported="true">
     </provider>
     <activity android:name=".MainActivity"
       android:windowSoftInputMode="adjustPan">
       <intent-filter>
         <action android:name="android.intent.action.MAIN" />
         <category android:name="android.intent.category.LAUNCHER" />
       </intent-filter>
     </activity>
  </application>
</manifest>
```

12.2.4   Run and Test Content Provider

To run and test the ContentProvider class in our demo app, we have created a main class. The main class includes two methods, storeData() and retrieveData(). The storeData() method is used to run the insert() method from the ContentProvider class, and the retrieveData() method is used to run the query() method from the ContentProvider class. The complete code is shown in Listing 12.8.

Listing 12.8 The main class to run and test the content provider app locally.

```
package com.code.abdulrahman.cprovider;
import android.content.ContentValues;
import android.database.Cursor;
import android.net.Uri;
import android.os.Bundle;
import android.view.View;
import android.widget.ArrayAdapter;
import android.widget.EditText;
import android.widget.ListView;
import android.widget.Toast;
import androidx.appcompat.app.AppCompatActivity;
import java.util.ArrayList;
import java.util.StringTokenizer;

public class MainActivity extends AppCompatActivity {
  @Override
  protected void onCreate(Bundle savedInstanceState) {
    super.onCreate(savedInstanceState);
    setContentView(R.layout.activity_main);
    setTitle(getString(R.string.app_title));
  }
  public void storeData(View view) {
   String editText1 =
     ((EditText)findViewById(R.id.editText1)).getText().toString();
   String editText2 =
     ((EditText)findViewById(R.id.editText2)).getText().toString();
   String editText3 =
     ((EditText)findViewById(R.id.editText3)).getText().toString();
   String editText4 =
     ((EditText)findViewById(R.id.editText4)).getText().toString();
   String in = editText1 + "\n" + editText2 + "\n" + editText3 + " \n" +
        editText4 + "\n";

  ContentValues values = new ContentValues();
  values.put(MyContentProvider.contact, in);
  Uri contentResolver =
  getContentResolver().insert
  (MyContentProvider.CONTENT_URI, values);
   if (contentResolver != null)
```

```
      Toast.makeText(getBaseContext(),
         getText(R.string.record_insert), Toast.LENGTH_LONG).show();
  }

  public void reterive_data(View view) {
     StringBuilder strBuild = new StringBuilder();
     Cursor cursor = getContentResolver().query(
         Uri.parse
         ("content://com.code.abdulrahman.cprovider/contacts"),
                   null, null, null, null);
     if (cursor.moveToFirst()) {
       while (!cursor.isAfterLast()) {
         strBuild.append("\n" +
             cursor.getString(cursor.getColumnIndex("name")));
         cursor.moveToNext();
       }
       addToList(strBuild.toString());
     } else {
       addToList(getString(R.string.no_recored_msg));
     }
  }
  private void addToList(String str) {

     ListView resultView = findViewById(R.id.listView);
     ArrayList aList = new ArrayList();
     StringTokenizer stringTonizer = new StringTokenizer(str, "\n");
     while (stringTonizer.hasMoreTokens()) {
       aList.add(stringTonizer.nextToken());
     }
    final ArrayAdapter <String> arrayAdapter = new ArrayAdapter <String>
         (this, android.R.layout.simple_list_item_1, aList);
     resultView.setAdapter(arrayAdapter);
  }
}
```

12.2.4.1   Do It Yourself

In the main class above, we have created two methods to test the insert() and query
methods(). Test the other four methods (the update(), delete(), getType(), and
onCreate() methods) by implementing methods similar to the two created for the
main class.

12.2.5   Content Provider Client

The main objective of content providers is to have an app that can store data where
other apps interested in that data can query and, in some cases, write to and update
it. To show this functionality, we have created a client app that is interested in the

data stored in the content provider app database. The client app queries the content provider using a Uri and displays the retrieved results on its screen.

For the client app to query data from the content provider, it needs to use the *ContentResolver* object and its query() method, *getContentResolver().query()*. The ContentResolver class query() method invokes the ContentProvider.query() method defined by the ContentProvider class, which in turn returns the cursor object. Listing 12.9 shows an example of the query() method from the client app. The left-hand side of Fig. 12.2 shows the content provider client app and the results of querying the content provider. The right-hand side of Fig. 12.2 shows the content provider app and the results of inserting soccer team information into the content provider using the ContentProvider main class.

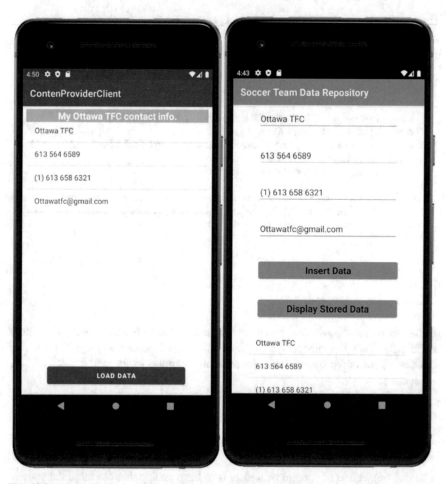

Fig. 12.2 Insert and display team contact info using the content provider and content provider client app

> **Listing 12.9** Query implementation in the client app.

```
public void queryProvider(View view) {

    Cursor cursor = getContentResolver().query( uri,null, null,
        null, null);
    if(cursor.moveToFirst()) {
      StringBuilder stringBuilder=new StringBuilder();
      while (!cursor.isAfterLast()) {
        stringBuilder.append("\n"+
            cursor.getString(cursor.getColumnIndex("name")));
        cursor.moveToNext();
      }
      addToList(stringBuilder.toString());
    }
    else {
      addToList("No Records Found");
    }
  }
private void addToList(String str) {
  ListView resultView = findViewById(R.id.listView);
  ArrayList aList = new ArrayList();
  StringTokenizer stringTonizer = new StringTokenizer(str, "\n");
  while (stringTonizer.hasMoreTokens()) {
    aList.add(stringTonizer.nextToken());
  }
  final ArrayAdapter <String> arrayAdapter = new ArrayAdapter <String>
      (this, android.R.layout.simple_list_item_1, aList);
  resultView.setAdapter(arrayAdapter);
}
```

12.2.5.1 Do It Yourself

Write update(), delete(), and insert() methods for the client content provider app. Note that you need to update the provider's AndroidManifest.xml and add writable access to the provider element in the file.

12.3 Media Content Streaming Apps

Streaming audio and video content locally or from URLs requires multiple Android classes. These include Android Service, BroadcastReceiver, MediaPlayer, VideoView, and other classes. A demo app is developed to demonstrate how to

Fig. 12.3 Demo app's user
interface

use these classes. Figure 12.3 is an interface for the demo app. The app has four buttons to start and stream media content. The app code uses the Android Service, BroadcastReceiver, MediaPlayer, and VideoView classes and demonstrates how to run radio stations using URLs, how to use implicit intent to run videos using URLs, how to use video view to playback remote videos, and how to run embedded videos in your app. The classes and implementation details will be discussed in the following parts.

12.4 Android Service

Having a service component run in the app's background while the user performs other tasks is an essential requirement for many apps, and their popularity depends on this feature. For example, it is because of the service component that you can browse the internet on your phone and listen to your favorite music at the same time. In this part of the chapter, we examine the Android *service* class in detail. We study how it is created, started, stopped, and used, as well as how to send and receive messages to/from the service. We also study the restrictions that Android puts on the service. We additionally study the broadcast receiver object and its uses with the service. Let us start by understanding what the service is.

12.4.1 Service

Service is an Android class that performs long-running tasks in the background with no UI. Since the service runs in the app's background, it does not require an XML layout file. Once the service starts, it continues to run even if the original application is ended or if the user moves to a different application. This might cause some performance issues. We will address these issues later. Service is the right choice to use when an activity does not interact with the user, i.e., it is not the forefront activity. Service can be private or public. When private, it is usable only by the app it belongs to; however, when public, it is also usable by apps other than the app it belongs to.

Service can be used in multiple situations. For example, it can be used to download an app from the app store or any kind of download/upload via the network, and the downloading will continue even when the user leaves the store. It can be used to monitor websites for updates/changes periodically, play music in the background while the user is browsing the device, maintain the connection in a chat app when a phone call is received, etc.

Apps can start a service by calling its API, for example, an application component such as the MainActivity can start service with the **startForegroundService()** method call. The startForegroundService() method is a replacement for the startService() method. Google recently made this change to protect the client's device from resource leaks. When a user starts the service using the foreground service, the user will be notified that a service is running in the background that otherwise the user might forget, leading to the device's battery drain.

The startForegroundService() method is like the startActivity() method used by activities. Once started, the service can run in the background indefinitely. It is the developer's responsibility to prevent resource wastes and stop the service.

Generally, services do not return a result; however, if it is necessary, for example, to notify an activity or other services that the task is done, it can send a local broadcast message. In addition to starting service, the app component and activities can connect (bind) to the service to interact with it through interprocess communication.

12.4.2   Communication with Service

There are two ways to communicate with the service. First, client apps and users can communicate with the service using the *commands*, i.e., method calls, without keeping a connection to the service. For example, when the user or other components initiate the start or end service method calls, they are communicating with the service. Second, the client app can bind to the service. *Binding* follows the subscribe/publish communication pattern between the service and user client. In this approach, the service and other components, such as an activity or another service, register to receive messages from the service.

12.4.3   Services Lifecycle

The Android service has three lifecycle methods. The methods are *onCreate()*, *onStartCommand()*, and *onDestroy()*. The onCreate() method is called to set up the service and is called once. The onStartCommand() method is invoked when a service is explicitly started using the startForegroundService() method. The onDestroy() method is invoked when a service is stopped using the stopService() method. Like the activity and fragments, the service also has lifecycle states which are similar to the activity states.

12.4.4   Creating Service

To create a service, you must create a subclass of the Android *service* or use one of its existing subclasses, e.g., *IntentService*. Here is an example of how to extend the *service* class:

```
public class RadioService extends Service implements
    OnPreparedListener, MediaPlayer.OnErrorListener {...}
```

In your implementation, you must implement the callback methods that are important for the service binding and service lifecycle. These include implementing four methods: onStartCommand(), onBind(), onCreate(), and onDestroy(). Each of these methods is described in this section.

12.4.4.1   OnStartCommand()

When an activity requests the service by calling startForegroundService(), the onStartCommand() method is called, and once the onStartCommand() method is executed, the service starts and can run in the background indefinitely. Since the onStartCommand() is called whenever the service starts with a startForegroundService() call, it may be executed several times during the service's lifetime, and you as a developer need to handle the system response when the service restarts.

The onStartCommand() method returns one of the following three values, predefined constants:

1. **START_STICKY**: If for any reason the Android system terminates the process which is running the service, the service stays in the started state, i.e., remains on, and is later recreated when the process restarts without its state being saved. For example, if the service streams music and you rotate your device, the service terminates and resumes. However, some parts of the music will be lost.
2. **START_REDELIVER_INTENT**: This is like the START_STICKY, but nothing gets lost here, i.e., the original Intent parameter is passed to the onStartCommand() method.

   START_NOT_STICKY: The service runs until its pending works are finished, for example, until it completes downloading a file. When its pending work is done, it will terminate. If this service's process is terminated and is not restarted explicitly, the service will not be recreated.

12.4.4.2   Service and Threads

When running a service, it does not create its running thread by default. Instead, it runs from the main thread of the hosting process. A better approach would be to run the service in a separate thread. For example, create a new thread from the onStartCommand() method to start and stop the service outside the main hosting process. The code snippet shown in Listing 12.10 shows how an app component, RadioMainActivity, starts a service. It also shows the message sequence calls between the main activity and the service. First, a call to the **startForegroundService()** is made in the RadioMainActivity, and then the onStartCommand() method is invoked in the RadioService class.

Listing 12.10   RadioMainActivity is starting a service.

```
public class RadioMainActivity extends ListActivity implements View.
OnClickListener {
  ...
 @Override
 protected void onListItemClick (
 ListView list, View v, int position, long id) {
     try {
        Intent service = new Intent (this, RadioService.class);
        startForegroundService(service);
     } catch (Exception e) { }
       ...
   }
   public class RadioService extends Service implements
      OnPreparedListener, MediaPlayer.OnErrorListener {
      @Override
     public int onStartCommand(Intent intent, int flags, int startId) {
      super.onStartCommand(intent, flags, startId);
      try {
        player.prepareAsync();
        ...
   }
 }
```

If you implement the onStartCommand() method, it is your responsibility to stop the service when its work is complete by calling the **stopSelf()** or **stopService()** method. Note that, if you only want to provide binding, you do not need to implement the onStartCommand() method.

12.4.4.3   Starting Service with the Intent

A service can be started with an explicit or implicit intent. Staring service explicitly would be like this:

```
Intent anIntent = new Intent ("context", "serviceclass");
anIntent.putExtra("key", "value");
startForegroundService(anIntent);
```

We start service explicitly in our demo app as follows:

```
Intent service = new Intent (
RadioMainActivity.this, RadioService.class);
startForegroundService(service);
```

For security reasons, using explicit intent is recommended for starting and binding to the service. If your intent is explicit, your intention is clear; you are specifying which service you would like to start. Once explicit Intent is used, you do not need to worry about the Intent filtering.

Services can start with implicit Intents as well. Using an implicit intent is not secure, and you should not use it. In the newer Android versions, beginning with Android 5.0 (API level 21), Android throws an exception if bindService() is called with an implicit intent.

12.4.4.3.1 Service and Intent-Filter

The IntentFilter class is used to filter client apps that can use a running service by matching the actions, categories, and/or data in the intent object with these properties of the IntentFilter object. IntentFilter objects are often created in XML as a part of the manifest file using the intent-filter tag. It is used with the service tag to tell which client apps can access your service. The intent-filter tag can also have a "priority" value that can be used to order multiple matching filters. An example of declaring an intent filter within the service tag is shown below.

```
<service
  an-droid:name= "com.code.abdulrahman.wlu.
                    serviceandmediaplayer.RadioService"
     <intent-filter>
      <action android:name="com.code.abdulrahman.wlu.
                    serviceandmediaplayer.RadioMainActivity" />
     </intent-filter>
 </service>
```

Here, for example, an intent filter expression specifies that the type of component that can access the service, i.e., start service, is RadioMainActivity.

When your intent is explicit, you are specifying which intent your service can receive; hence, there is no need for extra filtering, i.e., there is no need for an intent filter declaration in your manifest file. In the example below, the intent is created explicitly, and the service object is clear about the intent it is going to receive. Hence, there is no need for intent filtering inside the service tag.

```
Intent service = new Intent(
RadiosMainActivity.this, RadioService.class);
startForegroundService(service);
```

12.4.4.3.2 Intent-Filter and Activity

When you use an intent-filter within the activity tag in your app manifest file, you allow certain specified apps and app components to directly start your activity. When you do not declare any intent-filters for your activity, it can be started only with an explicit intent, and that is what we have been doing for almost all of our examples, except when we studied the implicit intent.

When you use implicit intent, the Android system looks for an appropriate app or component that can handle the intent request. The app selection is done by comparing the contents of the implicit intent to the *intent-filters* declared inside the manifest file of other apps on the device. If multiple intent-filters can handle the request, the system displays a message, so the user selects its favorite app to handle the request. For example, when you implicitly request opening a webpage, all your installed browsers can handle the request, and Android gives you the option to select your favorite.

12.4.5   Service Binding

When an app or component wants to bind, i.e., connect to the service, it needs to call the bindService() method which results in calling the ***onBind()*** method from the service side. Once bound, the app's components can interact with the service (send and receive messages) following the communication protocol. That is, the service must implement the onBind() method and return an IBinder object to the connected client. To return the IBinder object, you need to create an instance of the IBinder class and consider two different cases; we describe these two cases in the two subsections below.

12.4.5.1   Allow Apps to Bind to Service

If you allow other apps to bind to your service, do the following:

1. Create a class by extending the Binder class and implement the getService() method. This step is done as follows:

```
public class MyBinder extends Binder {
  Service getService() {
    return Service.this;
  }
... }
```

2. Override the onBind() method to return the MyBinder instance. This step can be done as follows:

```
@Override
public MyBinder onBind(Intent intent) {
  private final IBinder binder = new MyBinder();
  return binder;
}
```

Note that, inside the onBind() method, the IBinder object is instantiated as follows:

```
private final IBinder binder = new MyBinder();
```

The client app or the client component, such as the RadioMainActivity class, receives the Binder object and can use it to directly access public methods of the Binder and/or the service objects.

12.4.5.2   Prohibit Apps to Bind to Service

If you don't want to allow binding, i.e., other apps or components to connect or communicate with your service, then your onBind() method should return null. The code snippet below shows the onBind() method *returning null* indicating that your service will not accept requests to bind calls, i.e., it is a private service.

```
@Override
public IBinder onBind(Intent intent) {
    return null;
}
```

A service can be both started and bound at the same time as well. That is, if it is not a private service, the service can be started and later bound to other applications.

12.4.6   OnCreate() Method for Service

The Android system invokes the onCreate() method to perform a one-time setup when the service is initially created. If the service is already running, the onCreate method is not called. The OnCreate() method is called before the onStartCommand() or onBind() method is called. In the code snippet shown in Listing 12.11, the onCreate() method of the service class is used to initialize the intent and local variables.

Listing 12.11   RadioService.java initializing the Intent object.

```
public class RadioService extends Service implements
    OnPreparedListener, MediaPlayer.OnErrorListener {
  static MediaPlayer player;
  Intent intentbuf;
  public static final String buffering =
              "com.code.abdulrahman.wlu.serviceandmediaplayer";
  public String NotifiationChannel ="notificationChannel" ;
```

```
@Override
public void onCreate() {
  super.onCreate();
  isRunning = true;
  intentbuf = new Intent(buffering);
}
...
}
```

12.4.7   OnDestroy() Method

The onDestroy() method allows the programmers to do a cleanup. This is the last call that the service receives. The Android system invokes the onDestroy() method when the service is no longer used and is being killed. You should implement this method in your service class to clean up any resources such as threads, registered listeners, or receivers. The code snippet in Listing 12.12 shows how the onDestroy() method can be used to do a resource cleanup.

Listing 12.12   The onDestroy() method is used to clean up resources.

```
@Override
    public void onDestroy() {
      super.onDestroy();
      Log.i(destroy_tag, getString(R.string.destroyed));
      if (player != null) {
        player.stop();
        player.release();
        player = null;
      }
      if (wifiLock != null) {
        wifiLock.release();
        wifiLock = null;
      }
      intentbuf = null;
      stopSelf();
      cancelNotification();
}
```

Putting things together, the code snippet shown in Listing 12.13 is a skeleton for the service class; it shows how the structure of the service class would be with lifecycle callback methods implemented.

Listing 12.13   RadioService.java is the service class skeleton.

```java
public class RadioService extends Service {
  @Override
  public IBinder onBind(Intent intent) {return null; // service is private}
  @Override
  public void onCreate() {/*widget and component initialization*/}
  @Override
  public void onDestroy() {
    super.onDestroy();
    // code cleanup    }
  @Override
  public int onStartCommand(Intent intent, int flags, int startId) {
    super.onStartCommand(intent, flags, startId);
    // start service
    return START_STICKY ;
  }
...
}
```

12.4.8   Stopping Service

To stop a service in your app, two cases need to be differentiated:

- If the **startForegroundService()** method is used by the user client to start the service, which in turn results in a call to the onStartCommand() method, the service continues to run until it stops itself with the **stopSelf()** method or until another component stops it by calling the stopService() method. The code snippet shown in Listing 12.14 shows how the stopService() method is used.

Listing 12.14   An example of using stopService() method.

```java
@Override
public void onClick(View src) {
 switch (src.getId()) {
  case R.id.stopbutton:
    getApplicationContext().stopService(intent);
    break;
case R.id.exitButton:
    getApplicationContext().stopService(intent);
    System.exit(0);
break;
    ...
}
```

- If the user client starts the service by calling the **bindService()** method, and the onBind() method is called instead of onStartCommand(), the service runs only if the client user stays bound to it. After the service is unbound, i.e., disconnected from all its clients and no one is using it, the system destroys it.

12.4.9 Android Rules to End Service

The Android operating system follows the rules below in regard to keeping or destroying a service.

1. It stops a service when the device is running out of memory and when it must recover system resources for the activity that has the user's focus.
2. If the service starts and runs for a long time, the system lowers its priority over time in the list of background tasks, making it susceptible to ending.
3. If the service is bound to an activity that has the user's focus, the chances it will be destroyed are low.
4. If the service is declared to run in the foreground, it keeps running and is rarely killed.
5. If the system kills your service, it restarts it as soon as the resources become available. This also depends on the value that you return from onStartCommand(): **START_STICKY, START_NOT_STICKY,** or **START_REDELIVER_INTENT**.

12.4.10 Declaring a Service in the Manifest

You must declare all services in your application's manifest file just as you do for activities and other components. Otherwise, when the service is started, the app will crash. To declare your service, add a <service> tag as a child of the <application> tag. If you use Android Studio to create a service class, it will be added automatically to your manifest file. The code snippet shown in Listing 12.15 shows how service can be added to the manifest file.

Listing 12.15 AndroidManifest.xml.

```xml
<?xml version="1.0" encoding="utf-8"?>
<manifest
  package="com.code.abdulrahman.wlu.serviceandmediaplayer">
<application ... >
 <activity
  <intent-filter>
  <action android:name="android.intent.action.MAIN" />
  <category android:name="android.intent.category.LAUNCHER" >
 </intent-filter>
```

```
</activity>
<service
       android:name="com.code.abdulrahman.wlu.
          serviceandmediaplayer.RadioService"
          android:description="@string/runningRadio"
          android:enabled="true"
          android:exported="false">
</service>
</application>
```

There are some attributes that you can include in the <**service**> tag to define properties such as the permissions that are required to start the service and the process in which the service should run. The **android:name** attribute is the only required attribute; it specifies the class name of the service. As we mentioned before, to ensure your app is secure, use an explicit intent and no intent-filtering.

You can make your service private, that is, you can ensure that your service is available to only your app, by including the **android:exported** attribute and setting it to **false**. This effectively stops other apps from starting your service, even when using an explicit intent.

Users can see what services are running on their devices. If they see a service that they do not recognize or trust, they can stop the service. To avoid having your service stopped accidentally by users, you need to add the **android:description** attribute to the <service> tag in your app manifest file. In the description, provide a short sentence explaining what the service does and how it is useful. The code snippet in Listing 12.14 shows a service with four properties and no use of an intent-filter.

12.4.11 Intent Service

IntentService is a subclass of service that cannot interact with the GUI and has a simplified lifecycle. It is ideal for one long task on a single background thread. It stops itself once it has handled all the requests. IntentService cannot be interrupted when started, and to use it, you only need to implement the onHandleIntent(intent) method. Beginning with API 26, Android introduced a new service called JobIntentService which does similar work as the IntentService but uses jobs instead of services. The code snippet shown in Listing 12.16 shows how the IntentService implementation would be.

Listing 12.16 IntentService implementation example.

```
package com.code.abdulrahman.wlu.serviceandmediaplayer;
import android.app.IntentService;
import android.content.Intent;
```

```
public class MyIntentService extends IntentService {
  public MyIntentService() {
    super("HelloIntentService");
  }
  @Override
  protected void onHandleIntent(Intent intent) {
    try {   // Do some work
    } catch (Exception e) {
      Thread.currentThread().interrupt();
    }
  }
} // When this method returns, IntentService stops the service.
```

12.4.12   Service Summary

What we have described in this section can be summarized as follows:

1. For service creations, you need to extend the Android service or one of its subclasses.
2. Declare services in the manifest file.
3. Implement the necessary service lifecycle methods, i.e., onCreate(), onStartCommand(), and onDestroy().
4. You can start service by calling the startForegroundService() method with an intent object. This step is similar to starting an activity.
5. Use explicit intent, and do not use the intent-filter with the service.
6. You must stop service before starting up another instance.
7. It is best to start service in the onCreate()/onResume() method and stop it in the onPause() method.

12.4.13   Do It Yourself

To check your knowledge of the service, answer the following questions.

1. In terms of the manifest file, what are services equivalent to?
2. What is the difference between a bound and an unbound service?
3. Give the syntax for declaring a service in the manifest file.
4. How often is "onCreate()" called?
5. How often is "onStartCommand()" called?
6. What are services used for?

12.5 Message Broadcasting in Android

In computer science, broadcasting is about sending messages to interested or registered entities. Broadcasting can be a one-to-one, one-to-many, or many-to-many message exchange between the senders and receivers. Android has a class called BroadcastReceiver for receiving messages when an interesting event happens. For example, when a device is low on battery or disconnected, or when the device screen is turned off, Android broadcasts these events. The message details, i.e., information about what happened, are wrapped in the intent object and broadcasted to the receivers. In this part, we will study message broadcasting in Android.

12.5.1 Android Message Broadcasting Types

Android differentiates between two types of broadcasting, system broadcasting and custom broadcasting. **System broadcasts** are messages sent by the Android system. The Android system broadcasts messages in various situations. These include when the screen turns off, the battery is low, the user is presently using the phone, a picture is captured, etc. The Android system delivers a broadcast Intent to all interested (registered) broadcast receivers. **Custom broadcasts** are broadcasts that your app sends out. Apps can initiate broadcast messages to let other apps know, for example, that some data has been downloaded to the device and is available for them to use. In our demo app, when MediaPlayer is buffering, we send a message to the client to wait until the playing starts. The send message code is shown below:

```
public void startBuffering() {
   intentbuf.putExtra("bufValue", 1);
   sendBroadcast(intentbuf);
}
```

Custom broadcasting can be sent in three different ways, as a *normal broadcast*, an *ordered broadcast*, or a *local broadcast*. When ***normal broadcasting* is used,** the message is sent to all registered receivers in parallel and in an undefined order. This is a one-to-many message broadcasting. Receivers cannot propagate the messages among themselves, and they cannot terminate the broadcast. This approach is used in our demo app. We use the **sendBroadcast()** method to send a normal broadcast.

Ordered broadcasting is delivered to one receiver at a time sequentially. You use the **sendOrderedBroadcast()** method to send ordered broadcasts. Receivers can send the message to the next receiver or terminate it. You can control the message order with the **android:priority** attribute of the intent-filter in the manifest file. Receivers with the same priority run in arbitrary order.

Local broadcasting sends broadcasts to receivers within your app. Local broadcasting is safe, and you do not need to worry about security since message exchanges are done internally inside your app. To send a local broadcast, you need to get an instance of the **LocalBroadcastManager class** and then call the **sendBroadcast()** method on the class instance. Here is an example:

```
LocalBroadcastManager.getInstance(this).
         sendBroadcast(customBroadcastIntent);
```

Senders and receivers must agree on a unique name for the intent they send back and forth. Using the full name of your app as part of the intent name makes your intent name highly likely to be unique. Here is an example of how to name your custom intent.

```
private static final String MY_CUSTOM_BROADCAST =
  "com.code.abdulrahman.wlu.serviceandmediaplayer.My_CUSTOM_
BROADCAT";
```

12.5.2   BroadcastReceiver Class

BroadcastReceiver is an Android class that responds to broadcast announcements, i.e., messages. It receives and handles broadcast intents sent from service by the sendBroadcast(Intent) method. The BroadcastReceiver class does not have a UI, but it can create a status bar notification to alert the user when a broadcast event occurs. The BroadcastReceiver needs to be instantiated and registered to process the broadcasted messages on arrival. This step is like the GUI event handling. In both cases, you must *instantiate* the object, *register* the object that handles the event, and *handle* the events when it is fired. Below, we explain the four steps involved in message broadcasting and receiving which are creating the BroadcastReceiver object, registering the BroadcastReceiver object to receive messages, broadcasting the messages, and performing actions upon receiving the broadcasted messages. These steps are defined in the subsections below.

12.5.2.1   Create a BroadcastReceiver Object

The first step in handling broadcasted messages is to create a BroadcastReceiver object to receive the messages. For our demo app, we created a BroadcastReceiver that is a private inner class inside the main activity class as shown in Listing 12.17.

Listing 12.17 Creating a BroadcastReceiver class as a private inner class.

```
public class RadiosMainActivity extends ListActivity implements
  View.OnClickListener {
...
  private BroadcastReceiver receiver = new BroadcastReceiver() {
    @Override
    public void onReceive(Context context, Intent bufIntent) {
      new CreateProgressDialog(RadiosMainActivity.this, bufIntent);
    } };
...
}
```

12.5.2.2 BroadcastReceiver Registration

For the BroadcastReceiver object to receive messages, it needs to be registered as a listener. There are two ways to register a BroadcastReceiver object to receive broadcasted messages. You can dynamically register an instance of the class with the registerReceiver() method or statically declare it with the <receiver> tag in the AndroidManifest.xml file. The code snippet below shows how in our demo app we dynamically register the receiver object that has been declared inside the main activity.

```
if (!RadioService.isRunning) {
    registerReceiver(receiver, new IntentFilter
    (RadioService.buffering));
    intent = new Intent(RadioMainActivity.this, RadioService.class);
}
```

You can unregister the service when the app is in the paused state and re-register it when the app resumes; see the code snippet below:

```
@Override
protected void onPause() {
    super.onPause();
    unregisterReceiver(reciver);
}
@Override
protected void onResume() {
    super.onResume();
    registerReceiver(reciver, new IntentFilter
    (RadioService.buffering));
}
```

12.5.2.3 Using the sendBroadcast Method

The service can send messages to its listeners about an event that has happened in the background using its sendBroadcast() method. In our demo app, before we call the prepareAsync() method on the MediaPlayer object, we broadcast a message to let the RadioMainActivity (the listener) object know that we are about to play a radio station. This involves doing the following:

1. Creating a constant String:

```
public static final String buffering =
       "com.example.listviewexample.Buffering";
```

2. Creating an Intent object and initializing it with the constant String:

```
Intent intentbuf = new Intent (buffering) ;
```

3. Calling the sendBroadcast() method with the Intent object:

```
sendBroadcast (intentbuf) ;
```

The code snippet shown in Listing 12.18 shows how a service, i.e., the RadioService class, can broadcast messages using the sendBroadcast() method.

Listing 12.18 RadioService.java.

```
public class RadioService extends Service implements
    OnPreparedListener, MediaPlayer.OnErrorListener {
  Intent intentbuf;
  public static final String buffering =
             "com.code.abdulrahman.wlu.serviceandmediaplayer";
  private static final int notification_id = 5005;
  public String NotifiationChannel = "notificationChannel";
  @Override
  public void onCreate() {
    super.onCreate() ;
    intentbuf = new Intent(buffering) ;
  }
  public void bufferingComplete() {
    intentbuf.putExtra("bufValue", 2) ;
    sendBroadcast (intentbuf) ;
  }
...
}
```

12.5.2.4 Receiving Broadcasted Message

The BroadcastReceiver class has a single callback method called onReceive(). The method signature is like this: **public void onReceive(Context context, Intent intentWithmessage)**. When a broadcasted message arrives at a receiver object, the onReceive() method is invoked and receives the Intent object containing the message. You should remember two important things about the onReceive() method.

First, the onReceive() method of the broadcast receiver object in your class is another entry point to your app, similar to how the main method is an entry point to your app. Second, the onReceive() method should do a very minimal amount of work. For instance, it might initiate a service to perform some work. The task that is executed inside the onReceive() method must be complete in less than 10 seconds. If the task takes longer, you must start a new thread to avoid the application crashing.

In our demo app, the receiver class, RadioMainActivity, has an instance variable of type BroadcastReceiver called a receiver for communicating with the service. We use the onReceive() method from the internal BroadcastReceiver class to show the progress dialog informing the users to wait a few seconds before the radio station starts playing. The code snippet shown in Listing 12.19 shows the BroadcastReceiver object instantiation and progress dialog startup.

Listing 12.19 onReceive() is used to show the progress dialog.

```
public class RadiosMainActivity extends ListActivity implements
View.OnClickListener {
  ...
private BroadcastReceiver receiver = new BroadcastReceiver() {
  @Override
  public void onReceive(Context context, Intent bufIntent) {
    new CreateProgressDialog(RadiosMainActivity.this, bufIntent);
  }
};

public class CreateProgressDialog {
  public static ProgressDialog dprogress = null;
  int bufferingResult = 0;
  Context mainactivity = null;
  public CreateProgressDialog(Context mainactivity, Intent bufIntent) {
    this.mainactivity = mainactivity;
    showProgressDialog(bufIntent);
  }

  public void showProgressDialog(Intent bufIntent) {
    bufferingResult = bufIntent.getExtras().getInt("bufValue");
    try {
      if (bufferingResult == 2) {
        if (dprogress != null) {
          dprogress.dismiss();
          //dprogress = null;
        }
      } else if (bufferingResult == 1) {
        dprogress = ProgressDialog.show(mainactivity,
            mainactivity.getString(R.string.msg_title3),
```

```
        mainactivity.getString(R.string.buf_message), true);
    dprogress.setCancelable(true);
    new Thread(new Runnable() {
      volatile boolean running = true;
      public void run() {
        try {
          if (null != dprogress && dprogress.isShowing()) {
            Thread.sleep(20000);
            // dprogress.dismiss();
            if (!running) return;
          }
        } catch (InterruptedException e) {
          Thread.currentThread().interrupt(); }
      }
    }).start();
  }
} catch (Exception e) {
  Log.d("error", e.getMessage()); }
}
}
```

In the next part, we will discuss how we use the service component to play live streaming radio stations using a URL as well as how to use the sendBroadcast() method to notify users of an event.

12.5.3   Do It Yourself

Answer the following questions to test your knowledge.

1. In your own words, what is automatic system broadcasting?
2. Name two ways to register/unregister a BroadcastReceiver.
3. When do you recycle the receiver?

12.6   Android MediaPlayer for Streaming Radio Stations

In this part, you will learn how to create an app using the Android media player, broadcast receiver, and service. You are going to collect your favorite radio station URLs and create an app to stream them on your phone. In [16], we published the first version of this app. The app is cool for two reasons: First, all the radio stations will be grouped in one place, hence, you can easily switch from one station to another one. Second, it is an app to run radio stations on your device. It is very similar to Spotify but on a smaller scale. The app comes with a built-in list of radio stations. You can easily remove and add the stations you would like to listen to. The interface of the app is shown in Fig. 12.4. This is a complete app in itself. However, to access

Fig. 12.4 The interface of
the MyRadioStations app

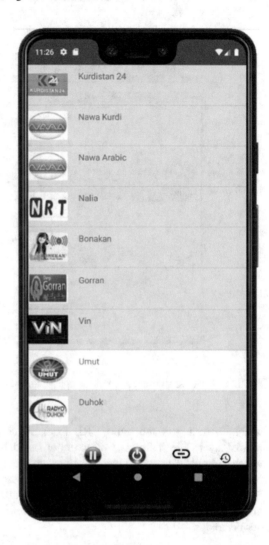

it, you need to click on the first button on the main interface of the app developed for
this chapter.

12.6.1   App Structure

For this part of our demo app, we use the service and MediaPlayer component to
play live streaming radio stations using URLs. We also use BroadcastReceiver to
notify users of an event. RadioMainActivity maintains a reference to the service;
thus, it can make calls on the service just like any other class and can directly access
members and methods inside the service. RadioMainActivity starts the service

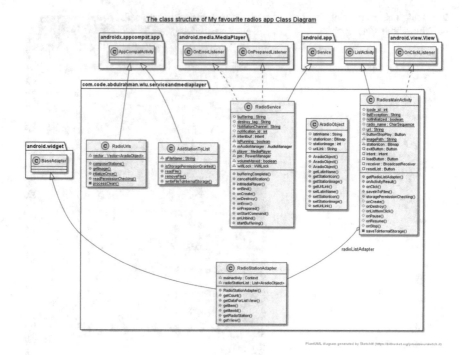

Fig. 12.5 The class structure of our demo app MyRadioStations

which in turn gets the radio URL from the RadioMainActivity and starts the MediaPlayer. The static class structure of our demo app is shown in Fig. 12.5 in which essential classes and their relations are presented. Figure 12.5 reveals that the service component has other member classes. These include MediaPlayer, WifiLock, PowerManager, and AudioManager, and it implements the OnPreparedListener interface. Below, we briefly discuss what role each of these classes plays in making our demo app.

12.6.2   Android Media Player

Android uses the MediaPlayer class to control the playback of audio/video files and streams. MediaPlayer needs to be prepared, started, and released. To understand the lifecycle method of the MediaPlayer, visit Android documentation. For the playback to start, the MediaPlayer must first enter the prepared state. There are two ways for the player to enter the prepared state, the synchronous way using the prepare() method or the asynchronous way using the prepareAsync() method. The difference between the two methods is in what thread they are executed.

The *prepare()* method runs in the UI thread and thus takes a long time to prepare. It will block your UI thread, and the user might get an ANR (Application Not Responding) message. The *prepareAsync()* method, on the other hand, runs in a background thread meaning that your UI thread is not blocked. However, you might end up in a situation where you call the prepareAsync() method but the media player is not ready yet. To avoid such a scenario, you want to implement the onPreparedListener() method to know when the MediaPlayer is ready for use.

The prepareAsync() method is commonly used for playing live data over the stream, and that is why in our app, we use the prepareAsync() method. It allows playing without blocking the main thread. If we use prepare() for live data streaming, it eventually crashes because the data is received in streams. This is because the prepare() method tries to load all the data first and then play it which is not possible. The code snippet shown in Listing 12.20 shows how we create the MediaPlayer object, call the player.prepareAsync() method, handle the onPrepared() method, and **release** all the resources when the onDestroy() method is called.

> **Listing 12.20** Instantiating and using MediaPlayer.

```
public class RadioService extends Service implements
    OnPreparedListener, MediaPlayer.OnErrorListener {
...
@Override
 public int onStartCommand(Intent intent, int flags, int startId) {
   super.onStartCommand(intent, flags, startId);
     try {
       notification(); // private helper method
       initMediaPlayer(); // privte helper method
     player.setOnPreparedListener(this);
     player.setDataSource(RadioMainActivity.url);
       player.setWakeMode(getApplicationContext(),
           PowerManager.PARTIAL_WAKE_LOCK);
   ...
       player.prepareAsync();
     } catch (IllegalArgumentException e) {
   ...
   return START_STICKY;
   }
 public void initMediaPlayer() {
   player = new MediaPlayer();
     player.setAudioAttributes(new AudioAttributes.Builder()
         .setUsage(AudioAttributes.USAGE_MEDIA)
         .setContentType(AudioAttributes.CONTENT_TYPE_MUSIC)
         .build());
 }
   @Override
   public void onPrepared(MediaPlayer mp) {
    new Thread(new Runnable() {
    volatile boolean running = true;
```

```
    public void run() {
      try {
        if (null != MainActivity.url) {
          if (!player.isPlaying()) {
            player.start();
            bufferingComplete();
          }
        }
      } catch (Exception e) { player.reset(); }
  } }).start();
 }
@Override
  public void onDestroy() {
    super.onDestroy();
    player.stop();
    player.release();
    player = null;
    wifiLock.release();
    wifiLock = null;
    intentbuf = null;
    cancelNotification();
  }
}
```

12.6.3   Power Manager and WakeLock

Even though you have code in a BroadcastReceiver or service, it will not run if your
phone goes into a low-power state. To control the power state on the device, you
need to use power management to keep the CPU running, prevent the screen from
dimming or going off, and prevent the backlight from turning on. You need to use a
WakeLock class in your app if the MediaPlayer in your app works fine when your
phone is on and connected to the computer during development, but fails under
normal use, disconnecting your phone from the development environment. The code
snippets presented in Listing 12.21 show how we created the PowerManager object
in our demo app and how we use it with the WakeLock and MediaPlayer.

Listing 12.21 Creating and using PowerManager object.

```
@Override
public int onStartCommand(Intent intent, int flags, int startId) {
  super.onStartCommand(intent, flags, startId);
  try {
   pm = (PowerManager) getSystemService(Context.POWER_SERVICE);
   PowerManager.WakeLock wl = pm.newWakeLock(
        PowerManager.PARTIAL_WAKE_LOCK, "MyWakeLock");
      wl.acquire();
    }
  player.prepareAsync();
...
}
```

The PARTIAL_WAKE_LOCK keeps the CPU running without the screen on. Whenever you want to release the WakeLock, use *wakeLock.release();*.

12.6.4   WifiLock

WifiLock allows an application to keep the Wi-Fi component awake. The Wi-Fi component may turn off when the user has not used the device for a while. Acquiring a WifiLock will keep the Wi-Fi on until the application releases the lock. In our demo app, we have decided to keep the radio stations running even when the device screen is off. Hence, in our app, we acquire the WifiLock. To use a WifiLock, we added the below permission to the AndroidManifest.xml file.

```
<uses-permission android:name="android.permission.WAKE_LOCK" />
```

You also need to add the service foreground permission to your manifest file. This can be done as follows:

```
<uses-permission android:name=
    "android.permission.FOREGROUND_SERVICE" />
```

12.6.5   Other App Components

In the demo app, we also implemented additional features such as the progress dialog when the app tries to connect to the radio station. Users can also delete any listed radio station. This is done by pressing and holding on to an item in the list for a short period and confirming the delete by pressing the OK button on the popup dialog box. Users can add new stations to the list as well. This is done by pressing on the link button at the bottom of the screen and following the wizard which prompts users to enter the station name, link, and icon in sequence. This feature enables users to create a customized list of stations. Lastly, users can populate the list with predefined embedded stations when using the app for the first time or reset the list at any time by pressing the reset button. Figure 12.6 shows both the link and reset buttons at the bottom of the app screen.

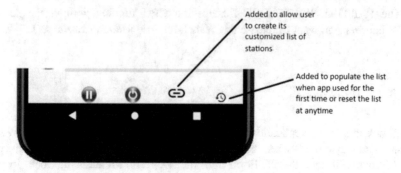

Fig. 12.6 Some app features are highlighted

12.6.6   Stopping and Restarting Service

The app also provides the ability to stop service and MediaPlayer from RadioMainActivity which also demonstrates the communication between activities and service. The code snippet presented in Listing 12.22 shows how to stop and restart the service when the user changes the radio station.

Listing 12.22 Stop and restart the service when stations changed.

```
@Override
 protected void onListItemClick(ListView list, View v, int position,
long id) {
     try {
        url = vector.get(position).getUrlLink();
        icode_id = (vector.elementAt(position)).stationImage;
        radio_name = "\t" + (vector.elementAt(position)).latinName;
        stopService(intent);
        Intent service = new Intent(RadioMainActivity.this,
                       RadioService.class);
        startForegroundService(service);
     } catch (Exception e) {
        Log.d(listException, e.toString());
     }
  }
```

The app can be dismissed or exited, and if this happened, all the resources the app was using are released to prevent resource leaks.

12.6.7 The New Restriction on Background Service

Running multiple apps in parallel puts an extra load on system resources. For example, playing games and listening to music at the same time lead to consuming a lot of RAM which might result in a bad user experience. To avoid this issue, and when your app is using service, you need to use a foreground service.

Starting from Android 8.0, API 26, Android introduced a new method, startForegroundService(), which we have used in our app to start service in the foreground. Android no longer allows apps running in the background to create services in the background. Once an app goes into the background, it has a few minutes to start a service and call startForegroundService() to start a new service in the foreground and create a notification that will be visible to the user. The code snippet in Listing 12.22 shows how to create a foreground service.

Note that the definition of background and foreground used here is not the same definition used in the memory management field. Here, the foreground service is running in the background but with a visible notification.

The code snippet presented in Listing 12.22 shows how to use the foreground service and a notification channel to meet the requirement of using the service in the foreground.

Your app needs to check the API version installed on the device. If the API version is greater than or equal to 26, you need to instantiate the notification channel object. In the code snippet shown in Listing 12.23, a notification channel is created, and a start service foreground is called.

Listing 12.23 NotificationAndForegroundService.java.

```
package com.code.abdulrahman.wlu.serviceandmediaplayer;
import android.app.Notification;
import android.app.NotificationChannel;
import android.app.NotificationManager;
import android.app.PendingIntent;
import android.content.Context;
import android.content.Intent;
import android.os.Build;
import androidx.core.app.NotificationCompat;
public class NotificationAndForgroundService {
  RadioService rService;
  public NotificationAndForgroundService(RadioService rs) {
    this.rService = rs;
  }
  public void notification() {
    CharSequence contentTitle = RadiosMainActivity.radio_name;
    CharSequence contentText = rService.getString
    (R.string.runningRadio);
    Context context = rService.getApplicationContext();
    // Create the NotificationChannel, but only on API 26+ because
    // the NotificationChannel class is new and not in the support library
```

```
if (Build.VERSION.SDK_INT >= Build.VERSION_CODES.O) {
    CharSequence name = rService.getString(R.string.msg_title);
    String description = rService.getString(R.string.runningRadio);
    int importance = NotificationManager.IMPORTANCE_DEFAULT;
    NotificationChannel channel = new NotificationChannel(
        rService.notification_id + "", name, importance);
    channel.setDescription(description);
    NotificationManager notificationManager =
        rService.getSystemService(NotificationManager.class);
    channel.enableLights(true);
    channel.setLightColor(Color.RED);
    channel.enableVibration(true);
    notificationManager.createNotificationChannel(channel);
    Notification notification = new NotificationCompat.Builder(
                        context, channel.getId())
        .setContentTitle(contentTitle)
        .setContentText(contentText)
        .setSmallIcon(R.drawable.ic_launcher)
        .build();
    notificationManager.notify(rService.notification_id, notification);
    rService.startForeground(rService.notification_id, notification);
} else {
    String ns = Context.NOTIFICATION_SERVICE;
    NotificationManager mNotificationManager =
        (NotificationManager) rService.getSystemService(ns);
    Intent notficationIntent = new Intent(rService,
                RadiosMainActivity.class);
    PendingIntent pendingIntent = PendingIntent.getActivity(context,
        0, notficationIntent, 0);
    Notification notification =
        new NotificationCompat.Builder(context,
                    rService.NotifiationChannel)
            .setContentTitle(contentTitle)
            .setContentText(contentText)
            .setSmallIcon(R.drawable.ic_launcher)
            .setContentIntent(pendingIntent)
            .build();
    mNotificationManager.notify(rService.notification_id, notification);
} }}
```

Figure 12.7 shows the notification while an example of the radio station is running.

Fig. 12.7 A notification is
shown while an example of
a radio station is running

12.6.8   *Do It Yourself*

Answer the following questions to test your knowledge and understanding of the
materials discussed in this section.

1. What do you need to do to use MediaPlayer.setWakeMode() in your code?
2. What can you do with the MediaPlayer API?

3. When data is in a file or stream, what method must MediaPlayer use?
4. List the steps to use MediaPlayer.

12.7   Remote and Local Video Playback

In the previous part of this chapter, we discussed the use of the media player and all the essential classes you need to create a live streaming audio app. Android has another class, VideoView, to playback local or live streaming videos, i.e., to enable the creation of Android TV apps. You can also play media content with an implicit intent. These topics are described in this part of the chapter.

12.7.1   Playback Video Using Implicit Intent and URL

To use implicit intent, you need to use Android predefined actions. In this case, the action is **Intent.ACTION_VIEW.** You also need to provide a media URL such as a YouTube link. The example presented in Listing 12.24 shows how you can use implicit intent to play remote videos using URLs.

Listing 12.24 PlayMediaWithIntentActivity.java.

```
package com.code.abdulrahman.wlu.serviceandmediaplayer;
import androidx.appcompat.app.AppCompatActivity;
import android.content.Intent;
import android.net.Uri;
import android.os.Bundle;
public class PlayMediaWithIntentActivity extends AppCompatActivity {
  @Override
  protected void onCreate(Bundle savedInstanceState) {
    super.onCreate(savedInstanceState);
    setContentView(R.layout.activity_play_media_with_intent);
    Intent myMediaIntent = new Intent();
    myMediaIntent.setAction(Intent.ACTION_VIEW);
    myMediaIntent.seData(Uri.parse("https://youtu.be/jxX8olbJZMk"));
      startActivity(myMediaIntent);
  }
}
```

To run the code above, click on the second button, implicit intent action, of the demo app.

12.7.2 Playback Live Streaming Video Using URL and VideoView

To playback a *local* video or *live stream* video using a URL, you need two essential Android classes. That is, you need to use *VideoView* class for the playback and the *MediaController* class to control the view. You also need to use a special VideoView class property, i.e., **app:layout_constraintDimensionRatio property,** to keep the aspect ratio (width ratio to height) the same for all devices. Two popular examples of aspect ratios are 4:3 and 16:9. We use 4:3 in the below code, but you can replace it with 16:9 or any other aspect ratio to see the differences between them and find the best suitable ratio for your app.

Listing 12.25 is an example of the layout file that we used in our demo app, my favorite TVs, which can be activated using the third button on the demo interface. The layout file uses both the VideoView class and the aspect ratio property.

Listing 12.25 A layout file example that uses VideoView tag and aspect ratio.

```
<?xml version="1.0" encoding="utf-8"?>
<android.constraintlayout.widget.ConstraintLayout
  xmlns:android="http://schemas.android.com/apk/res/android"
  android:layout_width="match_parent"
  android:layout_height="match_parent"
  xmlns:app="http://schemas.android.com/apk/res-auto">
  <VideoView
    android:id="@+id/VideoView"
    android:layout_width="0dp"
    android:layout_height="0dp"
    android:layout_margin="8dp"
    app:layout_constraintDimensionRatio="4:3"
    app:layout_constraintBottom_toBottomOf="parent"
    app:layout_constraintEnd_toEndOf="parent"
    app:layout_constraintStart_toStartOf="parent"
    app:layout_constraintTop_toTopOf="parent"/>
</android.constraintlayout.widget.ConstraintLayout>
```

A code example of how VideoView can be used to run live streaming TV stations is shown in Listing 12.26. The *setVideoURI(video)* method is used to set the URL, and the *videoView.start()* method is used to play the video. The media controller, URL setup, and getting the VideoView from layout file are highlighted below in bold.

Listing 12.26 PlayVideoActivity.java uses VideoView object to play back remote video.

```
package com.abdulrahman.mytvs.code;
import android.media.MediaPlayer;
import android.net.Uri;
import android.os.Bundle;
import android.util.Log;
import android.widget.MediaController;
import android.widget.VideoView;
import android.appcompat.app.AppCompatActivity;
public class PlayVideoActivity extends AppCompatActivity {
  VideoView videoview;
  @Override
  protected void onCreate(Bundle savedInstanceState) {
    super.onCreate(savedInstanceState);
    try {
      setContentView(R.layout.activity_play_video);
      MediaController controller = new MediaController(this);
      String VideoURL =
      "https://svs.itworkscdn.net/rudawlive/rudawlive.smil/
      playlist.m3u8";
      videoview = findViewById(R.id.VideoView);
      videoview.setMediaController(controller);
      controller.setMediaPlayer(videoview);
      Uri video = Uri.parse(VideoURL);
      videoview.setVideoURI(video);
    } catch (Exception e) {
      Log.e("Error", e.getMessage());
      e.printStackTrace();
    }
    videoview.requestFocus();
    videoview.setOnPreparedListener
      (new MediaPlayer.OnPreparedListener() {
      public void onPrepared(MediaPlayer mp) {
        videoview.start();
      }
    });
  }
}
```

The VideoView class has multiple methods, for example, start(), pause(), stopPlayback(), getCurrentPosition(), etc. VideoView also has multiple callback methods, for example, the onPrepared() method which is called when the player is ready to play, the onCompletion() method which can be used to inform the user that

Fig. 12.8 An example of VideoView running a live stream TV

the playback has ended, etc. For the complete list of methods that the VideoView class supports, see Android documentation. A link to the documentation is provided in the reference section at the end of this chapter.

Figure 12.8 shows an example where VideoView is used to play live streaming TV stations using URLs. The right-hand side of Fig. 12.9 shows the main interface for an app where one's favorite TV stations are grouped in one place and the user can easily switch between TV stations. This screen is accessible by clicking on the third button of our demo app's main interface. The left-hand side of the Fig. 12.9 shows one of the stations running where the aspect ratio is 4:3. The screen size of Fig. 12.9 is smaller when compared to the screen size of Fig. 12.8 where the aspect ratio is 16:9.

A topic related to live streaming is Android TVs. The features that Android TVs can bring to both TV operators and consumers are described in [19]. These include providing operators with a capable operating system that can help to build a complete TV experience for subscribers, bringing traditional TV broadcasting and streaming services to one place, etc. In this new setting, TVs will have many new features including search, content discovery, personalization, interface customization, Android app store connectivity, and even smart home control as standard features.

Fig. 12.9   The interface for all TV app (left) and running screen for a live TV (right)

12.7.3   Playback Embedded Video in Your App

If your video is embedded in the app, you parse the file path and pass the result to the setVideoUri() method. For example, if the video file is saved in the **res/raw** directory, you compose and run the Uri as follows:

```
Uri video = Uri.parse("android.resource://" +
        getPackageName() + "/raw/" + "videofile");
    videoview.setVideoURI(video);
```

The code snippet shown in Listing 12.27 is a complete code to run a video file embedded in the app. With a simple modification, you can change this part of the demo app to enable users to play their favorite movies stored on their device. This is especially useful when you download your favorite movies while you have access to the internet without using your mobile data so that you can later playback videos without the need for a network connection.

Listing 12.27 PlayLocalVideo.java.

```java
import android.media.MediaPlayer;
import android.net.Uri;
import android.os.Bundle;
import android.util.Log;
import android.widget.MediaController;
import android.widget.VideoView;
import androidx.appcompat.app.AppCompatActivity;
public class PlayLocalVideo extends AppCompatActivity {
  VideoView videoview;
  @Override
  protected void onCreate(Bundle savedInstanceState) {
    super.onCreate(savedInstanceState);
    try {
      setContentView(R.layout.activity_play_local_video);
      MediaController controller = new MediaController(this);
      videoview = findViewById(R.id.videolocal);
      Uri video = Uri.parse("android.resource://" +
          getPackageName() + "/raw/" + "soccer");
      videoview.setMediaController(controller);
      controller.setMediaPlayer(videoview);
      videoview.setVideoURI(video);
    } catch (Exception e) {
      Log.e("Error", e.getMessage());
      e.printStackTrace();
    }
    videoview.requestFocus();
    videoview.setOnPreparedListener
      (new MediaPlayer.OnPreparedListener() {
      // Close the progress bar and play the video
      public void onPrepared(MediaPlayer mp) {
        videoview.start();
      }
    });
  }
}
```

12.7.4 Playback Video Outside Your App Directory

If the video file is outside your app directory, for example, on your device's file system, you must use the environment and external storage directory methods to access the file. You also need to set proper settings permissions in the manifest file to access storages outside of your app directory. Here is an example of how to run a video file in the external file directory.

```
String filepath = Environment.getExternalStorageDirectory() + "/" +
"yourvideofile.mp4;
    File file = new File(fullPath);
    Uri video = Uri.fromFile(file);
    Object mVideoView;
    mVideoview.setVideoUri(video);
```

12.8 Chapter Summary

In this chapter, we covered the creation and usage of the ContentProvider class, ContentResolver class, Android service component, intent server, and BroadcastReceiver. We also covered the creation of the MediaPlayer and VideoView objects to stream radio/TV stations, as well as how to manage Android power and Wi-Fi connections. Additionally, we discussed and described fundamental coding blocks to build an app for audio/video streaming.

The fact that you have learned about content providers, the Android service component, and message broadcasting means that you have completed a major milestone on your way to becoming a professional Android developer.

Check Your Knowledge

Below are some of the fundamental concepts and vocabularies that have been covered in this chapter. To test your knowledge and your understanding of this chapter, you should be able to describe each of the below concepts in one or two sentences.

- ANR
- AudioManager
- bindService
- BroadcastReceiver
- constraintDimensionRatio
- Content provider
- Content resolver
- Custom broadcasts
- *getContentResolver*
- IBinder
- IntentFilter
- IntentService
- MediaController
- MediaPlayer
- MIME-type

- NotificationChannel
- OnPreparedListener
- onStartCommand
- PowerManager
- prepareAsync
- sendBroadcast
- service
- startForegroundService
- START_NOT_STICKY
- START_REDELIVER_INTENT
- START_STICKY
- stopSelf
- stopService
- System broadcasts
- Uri
- UriMatcher
- VideoView
- WakeLock
- WifiLock

Further Reading

For more information about the topics covered in this chapter, we suggest that you refer to the online resources listed below. These links provide additional insight into the topics covered. The links are mostly maintained by Google and are a part of the Android API specification. The resource titles convey which section/subsection of the chapter the resource is related to.

Audio Focus, [online] Available, https://developer.android.com/guide/topics/media-apps/audio-focus

AudioManager, [online] Available, https://developer.android.com/reference/android/media/AudioManager

Broadcasts overview, [online] Available, https://developer.android.com/guide/components/broadcasts

Content provider basics, [online] Available, Content provider basics, [online] Available, https://developer.android.com/guide/topics/providers/content-provider-basics

ContentResolver, [online] Available, https://developer.android.com/reference/android/content/ContentResolver

ContentUris, [online] Available, https://developer.android.com/reference/android/content/ContentUris

IntentFilter, [online] Available, https://developer.android.com/reference/android/content/IntentFilter

IntentService, [online] Available, https://developer.android.com/reference/android/app/IntentService

JobIntentService, [online] Available, https://developer.android.com/reference/androidx/core/app/JobIntentService

MediaControler, [online] Available, https://developer.android.com/reference/android/media/session/MediaController

MediaPlayer Overview, [online] Available, https://developer.android.com/guide/topics/media/mediaplayer

NotificationChannel, [online] Available, https://developer.android.com/reference/kotlin/android/app/NotificationChannel

Notification Overview, [online] Available, https://developer.android.com/reference/kotlin/android/net/wifi/WifiManager

PowerManager, [online] Available, https://developer.android.com/reference/android/os/PowerManager

Service Overview, [online] Available, https://developer.android.com/guide/components/services

UriMatcher, [online] Available, https://developer.android.com/reference/android/content/UriMatcher

VideoView, [online] Available, https://developer.android.com/reference/android/widget/VideoView

WifiManager, [online] Available, https://developer.android.com/reference/kotlin/android/net/wifi/WifiManager

Chapter 13
Sensors, Location-Based Service, and Google Maps

What You Will Learn in This Chapter

By the end of this chapter, you should be able to:

- Describe Android sensor types and their uses
- Use the accelerometer sensor to programmatically find out your phone orientation (in portrait or landscape), which way it is facing (up or down), and whether or not your phone is moving in a linear direction
- Use Location Manager, LocationProvider, and Geocoder to create location-based services
- Use Google Maps in your app

Check Out the Demo Project

Download the demo app, **SensorsLocationAndGoogleMaps.zip**, specifically developed to go with this chapter. I recommend that you code this project up from the notes rather than just opening the project in Android Studio and running it; however, if you want to run the code first to get a sense of the app, please do so. The code is thoroughly explained in this chapter to help you understand it. We follow the same approach to all other chapters throughout the book. The app's code will help you comprehend the additional concepts that will be described in this chapter.

How to run the code: unzip the code in a folder of your choice, and then in Android Studio, click **File->import->Existing Android code into the workspace**. The project should start running.

13.1 Introduction

This chapter covers three important topics, *Sensors*, *Location-based services*, and *Google Maps*. In Sect. 13.2, we will specifically study the *accelerometer* sensor, for it has many applications. In Sect. 13.3, we will study the classes that enable the

© The Author(s), under exclusive license to Springer Nature Switzerland AG 2022
A.-R. Mawlood-Yunis, *Android for Java Programmers*,
https://doi.org/10.1007/978-3-030-87459-9_13

creation of location-based apps. These include Location Manager, LocationProvider, and Geocoders. In Sect. 13.4, we will describe how to include *Google Maps* in your app and point out its many uses.

13.2   Android Sensor

Android has three types of sensors: motion, environment, and position sensors. Motion sensors measure device motion, for example, acceleration, gravity, and rotational moves. Environmental sensors measure environmental conditions such as temperature, pressure, and humidity. Position sensors measure the physical position of a device such as proximity. The left-hand side of Fig. 13.1 lists the different sensors that you might find on your phone, and they include the

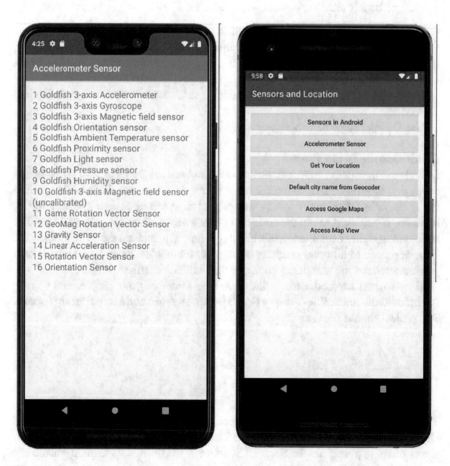

Fig. 13.1 Example of Android sensors and the main interface for the demo app

accelerometer, proximity, gyroscope, magnetic, light, compass, and more. The right-hand side of Fig. 13.1 shows the main interface of the demo app developed for this chapter.

In this part, we will focus on the Android accelerometer, a device used to measure the acceleration force, including the gravitational force.

13.2.1 Accelerometer Sensor

Android uses the accelerometer sensor to measure the acceleration force applied to a device on the (x, y, and z) axes. The data returned from the accelerometer can be used to detect movement, tilts, and vibrations. By measuring the amount of acceleration, you can find the angle your device is tilted at with respect to the earth, and you can analyze the way your device is moving. In general, you can use the accelerometer to determine:

(a) Whether your phone is in the portrait or landscape orientation
(b) Which way your phone is pointed to, facing up or down
(c) Whether or not your phone is moving in a linear direction

Using the accelerometer, you can use your phone to track your steps without having to buy a wearable device, determine if you are speeding up or not, and find out the exact orientation of your phone along the x, y, and z axes.

The value of the x, y, and z axes of the accelerometer is with respect to the phone's coordinates:

1. The x-axis is horizontal and points to the right/left.
2. The y-axis is vertical and points up/down.
3. The z-axis points toward the outside of the front face of your device screen.

In this setting, coordinates behind your screen have negative z values. More detailed information on the phone coordination system is provided on the Android documentation. For more information, see the reference section provided at the end of this chapter.

13.2.2 Accelerometer App

To demonstrate that the accelerometer can capture changes in the x, y, and z axes and how this feature can be used, we have created an app to display the x, y, and z axes readings. Once you install the demo app on your phone, click the accelerometer button on the main interface of the demo app, and shake the app. The app's background changes to a random color in response to the phone's movement. We will study the app's code to demonstrate how the accelerometer can be used in an

Fig. 13.2 App's background color change in response to phone shaking

app. Figure 13.2 shows the x, y, and z values and the changes in the app's background color in response to the user shaking the phone.

13.2.3   Using Accelerometer

The Android API (application programming interfaces) provides multiple classes and interfaces to read data from software and hardware sensors. These include *SensorManager*, *Sensors*, *SensorEvent*, and *SensorEventListener*. To use an accelerometer in your code to read axes in response to device motion, you need to do the following six steps:

13.2.3.1   Sensor Event Listener Implementation

Your activity class needs to implement the SensorEventListener interface. The interface has two methods *onSensorChanged (SensorEvent event)* and *onAccuracyChanged(Sensor sensor, int accuracy)*. The first one is called when there is a new sensor event, and the second one is called when there is a change in the accuracy information that the sensor provides. We have implemented both methods in the main activity class of the demo app. Inside the onSensorChanged() method, we check the event type. If the event is of type Sensor. TYPE_ACCELEROMETER, we retrieve the event values and initialize and display the x, y, and z axes values. See the code snippet shown in Listing 13.1.

> **Listing 13.1** Sensor Accelerometer type event.

```
@Override
public void onSensorChanged (SensorEvent event) {
  int accelerometerType = Sensor.TYPE_ACCELEROMETER ;
  if (event.sensor.getType() == accelerometerType) {
          event.values[0] + " " +
          event.values[1] + " " +
          event.values[2]) ;
    displayAccelerometerVariables (event) ;
    checkForShaking (event) ;
  }
}
```

The onAccuracyChanged() method implementation is used to inform users that the sensor accuracy has changed; this is done using a toast message. See the code snippet shown in Listing 13.2.

> **Listing 13.2** onAccuracyChanged() method implementation.

```
@Override
public void onAccuracyChanged (Sensor sensor, int accuracyValue) {
Toast.makeText(getApplicationContext(),
        R.string.accuracychange , Toast.LENGTH_LONG).show() ;
    Log.i("onAccuracyChanged", " called") ;
}
```

13.2.3.2 Getting Sensor Service and Sensor Manager Objects

To read the accelerometer axes, use the getSystemService() method with the Sensor_Service constant to get the SensorManager object. This can be done using the following two lines of code:

1. **SensorManager sManager = (SensorManager) getSystemService(*SENSOR_SERVICE*);**
2. **sManager.getDefaultSensor(Sensor.*TYPE_ACCELEROMETER*)**

In our demo app, we included the two steps above inside the onCreate() and onResume() callback methods as shown in Listing 13.3.

Listing 13.3 MainActivity.java for using the accelerometer.

```
public class MainActivity extends AppCompatActivity implements
  SensorEventListener {
  SensorManager sManager ;
  @Override
  protected void onCreate(Bundle savedInstanceState) {
    super.onCreate(savedInstanceState) ;
    setContentView(R.layout.activity_main) ;
    sManager = (SensorManager) getSystemService(SENSOR_SERVICE) ;

  @Override
  protected void onResume() {
    super.onResume() ;
    sManager.registerListener(this,
    sManager.getDefaultSensor(Sensor.TYPE_ACCELEROMETER),
        SensorManager.SENSOR_DELAY_NORMAL) ;
  }
}
```

Using the Sensor.TYPE_ACCELEROMETER constant and the set() method, the sensor type is set to accelerometer. You can set your sensor type to other types, such as the ones listed in Fig. 13.1. The code for displaying accelerometer data and calculating the acceleration force would be more clear if they were done inside two separate private helper methods. The code snippet below shows an example of two helper methods called inside the **onSensorchanged()** callback method. These two methods will be explained in the next two sections.

```
  @Override
  public void onSensorChanged (SensorEvent event) {
    int accelerometerType = Sensor.TYPE_ACCELEROMETER ;
    if (event.sensor.getType() == accelerometerType) {
        displayAccelerometerVariables (event) ;
        checkForShaking (event) ;
    }
  }
```

The onSensorChanged(**SensorEvent** event) callback method is called when there is a new sensor event. It is also called when the timestamp is changed, even if the sensor values have not been changed. In the latter case, the same readings will be generated.

13.2.3.3   Display Accelerometer Readings

Once a sensor event is generated, you need to get the axes readings. The readings are passed as an array parameter to the onSensorChanged() callback method. The first element of the array is the x value, and the second and third elements are the y and z values, respectively. In our demo app, these values are retrieved and used to set the values of the x, y, and z axes variables, which are then displayed on the app screen using text views. The code snippet presented in Listing 13.4 shows this step.

Listing 13.4 Getting the axes readings from a sensor.

```
public void displayAccelerometerVariables ( SensorEvent sensorEvent) {
if (null != sensorEvent){
    String coordinateValues [] = new String [3] ;
    String x = new Double (sensorEvent.values[0]).toString() ;
    String y = new Double (sensorEvent.values[1] ).toString() ;
    String z = new Double (sensorEvent.values[2]).toString()  ;
    coordinateValues[0]= R.string.xvalue + x ;
    coordinateValues[1]= R.string.xvalue + y ;
    coordinateValues[2]= R.string.xvalue + z;
    xView.setText(coordinateValues[0] );
    yView.setText( coordinateValues[1]);
    zView.setText(coordinateValues[2] );
  }
 }
```

13.2.3.4 Calculating Acceleration Force

To calculate the acceleration force, we get x, y, and z values from the sensor and use the retrieved values with the acceleration force formula (square root $(x^2 + y^2 + z^2)$/ gravity^2) as follows:

```
double sequreRootOfxyz = (
            xposition * xposition +
            yposition * yposition +
            zposition * zposition ) /
            (SensorManager.GRAVITY_EARTH *
             SensorManager.GRAVITY_EARTH) );
```

Note that, when you hold your device, it is constantly in motion, no matter how hard you try to keep your hand steady. Thus, you are constantly generating new data. That being said, we don't need all this data; it is too much to be useful for our demo app. To avoid the constant reading data situation, we store the system's current time (in milliseconds) and get the next reading only after 200 milliseconds pass. Thus, we set the 200 ms interval between readings. The code snippet presented in Listing 13.5 shows the acceleration force calculation and how the app's background color changes in response to the change in the acceleration forces (device motion).

Listing 13.5 Acceleration force calculation.

```
public void checkForShaking ( SensorEvent sensorEvent) {
    double xposition = sensorEvent.values[0] ;
    double yposition = sensorEvent.values[1] ;
    double zposition = sensorEvent.values[2] ;
    double sequreRootOfxyz = (xposition * xposition +
            yposition * yposition +
            zposition * zposition ) /
            (SensorManager.GRAVITY_EARTH *
            SensorManag er.GRAVITY_EARTH) ;
    long currentTime = System.currentTimeMillis() ;
    if (sequreRootOfxyz >=changeInGravity) {
        if (currentTime - lastUpdateTime < elpasedTime) {
            return;
        }
    lastUpdateTime = currentTime;
    int rand_num = new Random().nextInt(backgroundColors.length) ;
    rootView.setBackgroundColor(backgroundColors[rand_num] *
            new Random().nextInt(colorRange));
    }
}
```

13.2.3.5   Listener Registration

For your activity class to receive the readings, you need to register your activity, e.g.,
MainActivity, as a listener to the events fired by the accelerometer sensor. The code
snippet below shows the registration step.

```
@Override
protected void onResume() {
    super.onResume();
    sManager.registerListener(this,
    sManager.getDefaultSensor(Sensor.TYPE_ACCELEROMETER),
        SensorManager.SENSOR_DELAY_NORMAL);
}
```

13.2.3.6   Unregister Listening

Finally, unregister the accelerometer sensor once you stop or close the app to reclaim
the resources used by your device. The best place to unregister listening to the
accelerometer sensor is inside the onPause() method as shown below:

```
@Override
protected void onPause() {
    // unregister listener
    super.onPause();
    sManager.unregisterListener(this);
}
```

By implementing the six steps above, you are now able to use the accelerometer sensor inside your app to read the x, y, and z axes.

If you haven't done so yet, install and start the demo app. You will receive the x, y, and z values every 200 milliseconds, and when you shake your app, you should see the app's background change to a random color. The code for the accelerometer app is shown in Listing 13.6.

Listing 13.6 AccelerometerActivity.java for using the accelerometer sensor.

```
package com.code.wlu.abdulrahman.sensorsandlocation;
import androidx.appcompat.app.AppCompatActivity;
import android.graphics.Color;
import android.hardware.Sensor;
import android.hardware.SensorEvent;
import android.hardware.SensorEventListener;
import android.hardware.SensorManager;
import android.os.Bundle;
import android.util.Log;
import android.view.View;
import android.widget.TextView;
import android.widget.Toast;
import java.util.Random;

public class AccelerometerActivity extends AppCompatActivity
implements SensorEventListener {
    static final int colorRange = 100 ;
    static final int backgroundColors [] ={Color.GREEN, Color.RED,
            Color.BLUE, Color.CYAN, Color.MAGENTA, Color.YELLOW,
                Color.DKGRAY} ;
    private static final  int changeInGravity = 2;
    SensorManager sManager ;
    TextView xView, yView, zView;
    private View rootView ;
    private long lastUpdateTime ;
    private int elpasedTime = 200 ;

    @Override
    protected void onCreate(Bundle savedInstanceState) {
        super.onCreate(savedInstanceState);
        setTitle("Accelerometer");
        setContentView(R.layout.activity_accelerometer);
        xView = findViewById(R.id.variableX) ;
        yView = findViewById(R.id.variableY) ;
```

```
    zView = findViewById(R.id.variableZ) ;
    rootView = findViewById(R.id.rootLayout) ;
    rootView.setBackgroundColor(Color.CYAN);
    sManager = (SensorManager) getSystemService(SENSOR_SERVICE);
    lastUpdateTime= System.currentTimeMillis() ;
  }
  @Override
  public void onSensorChanged (SensorEvent event) {
    int accelerometerType = Sensor.TYPE_ACCELEROMETER ;
    if (event.sensor.getType() == accelerometerType) {
      Log.i("sensor values", event.values.length + " values are " +
          event.values[0] + " " +
          event.values[1] + " " +
          event.values[2]) ;
      displayAccelerometerVariables (event) ;
      checkForShaking (event) ;
    }
  }
  public void displayAccelerometerVariables (SensorEvent sensorEvent)
{
    if ( null != sensorEvent){
      String coordinateValues [] = new String [3] ;
      String x = new Double (sensorEvent.values[0]).toString() ;
      String y = new Double (sensorEvent.values[1] ).toString() ;
      String z = new Double (sensorEvent.values[2]).toString() ;
      coordinateValues[0] = R.string.xvalue + x ;
      coordinateValues[1] = R.string.xvalue + y ;
      coordinateValues[2] = R.string.xvalue + z;
      xView.setText(coordinateValues[0] ) ;
      yView.setText( coordinateValues[1]);
      zView.setText(coordinateValues[2] );
    }
  }
  public void checkForShaking ( SensorEvent sensorEvent) {
    double xposition = sensorEvent.values[0] ;
    double yposition = sensorEvent.values[1] ;
    double zposition = sensorEvent.values[2] ;
    double sequreRootOfxyz = (xposition * xposition +
        yposition * yposition +
        zposition * zposition ) /
        (SensorManager.GRAVITY_EARTH *
            SensorManager.GRAVITY_EARTH) ;
    long currentTime = System.currentTimeMillis() ;
    if (sequreRootOfxyz >=changeInGravity) {
      if (currentTime - lastUpdateTime < elpasedTime) {
        return;
      }
      lastUpdateTime = currentTime;
      int rand_num = new Random().nextInt(backgroundColors.length) ;
      rootView.setBackgroundColor(backgroundColors[rand_num] *
          new Random().nextInt(colorRange));
    }
  }
```

```
@Override
public void onAccuracyChanged (Sensor sensor, int accuracyValue) {
    // handel sensor accuracy changes.
    //e.g. report the issue to the user.
    Toast.makeText(getApplicationContext(),
            R.string.accuracychange , Toast.LENGTH_LONG).show() ;
    Log.i("onAccuracyChanged", " called") ;
}
@Override
protected void onStart() {
    super.onStart();
}
@Override
protected void onResume() {
    super.onResume();
    // register this class as a listener for the orientation and
    // accelerometer sensors
    sManager.registerListener(this,
        sManager.getDefaultSensor(Sensor.TYPE_ACCELEROMETER),
        SensorManager.SENSOR_DELAY_NORMAL);
}
@Override
protected void onStop() {
    super.onStop();
    sManager.unregisterListener(this);
}
@Override
protected void onPause() {
    super.onPause();
    sManager.unregisterListener(this);
}
}
```

13.2.4   Get List of Sensors

The list of sensors installed on a device depends on the device's model. You can use a sensor manager to find the list of sensors available on a device. The two lines of code below show how you can retrieve the name of the sensors installed on an Android device.

```
SensorManager mSensorManager =
    (SensorManager) getSystemService(Context.SENSOR_SERVICE);
    List <Sensor> sensorList =
    mSensorManager.getSensorList(Sensor.TYPE_ALL);
```

We have created an activity to get the name of the sensors installed on an Android device. The activity code is shown in Listing 13.7, and the results are presented in Fig. 13.3. The result shows that there are 16 different sensors on the Android Pixel 3 XL (API 28) emulator.

Fig. 13.3 List of sensors on
Pixel 3 XL (API 28)

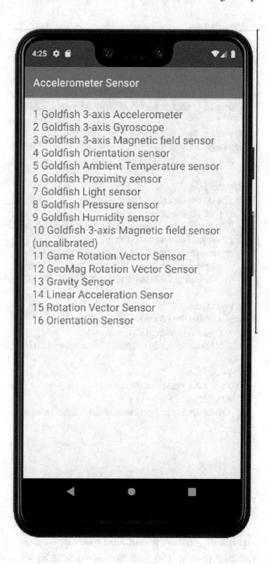

Listing 13.7 SensorNameList.java to retrieve the name of the sensor installed
on a device.

```
package com.code.abdulrahman.cp670.
AccelerometerSignalsASensorManager;
   import androidx.appcompat.app.AppCompatActivity;
   import android.content.Context;
   import android.hardware.Sensor;
   import android.hardware.SensorManager;
   import android.os.Bundle;
```

```
import android.widget.TextView;
import java.util.List;
public class SensorNameList extends AppCompatActivity {
private SensorManager sensorManager;
   @Override
   protected void onCreate(Bundle savedInstanceState) {
      super.onCreate(savedInstanceState);
      setContentView(R.layout.activity_device_sensors);
      sensorManager =
         (SensorManager) getSystemService(Context.SENSOR_SERVICE);
      List <Sensor> sensorList =
         sensorManager.getSensorList(Sensor.TYPE_ALL);
      StringBuilder aSensor = new StringBuilder();
      int i = 1;
      for (Sensor currentSensor : sensorList) {
         aSensor.append(i++ + " " + currentSensor.getName() + "\n");
      }
      TextView sensorTextView = findViewById(R.id.sensor_list);
      sensorTextView.setText(aSensor);
   }
}
```

For information on other types of sensors and Android sensor stack, see [1]. Detailed information about what, why, and how the embedded sensors are used in the current Android is discussed in [2].

13.2.5   Do It Yourself

1. Spend some time familiarizing yourself with the Android sensor types. Refactor the demo code and replace the statement:

   sManager.getDefaultSensor(Sensor.*TYPE_ACCELEROMETER*)

   with other types of sensors and study the results.
2. To receive the axes readings less frequently, change the time interval from 200 ms to 60 seconds; you should receive the x, y, and z readings every minute.

13.3   Location-Based Services

When you search directions for any location, for example, a store address, your phone uses your current location as an input and finds the location you are looking for. These types of apps use Android's location API. Android provides several classes to enable the creation of location-based apps. These include Location Manager, LocationProvider, and Geocoders. In this part of the chapter, we will study these components and their uses. We will also study a demo app to show how these components can be used together to create location-based apps. Remember that, when you are developing location-based apps, you need to account for the user's privacy. That is, you need to abide by, or follow, certain rules, such as:

1. Updating the location only when necessary
2. Letting the user know if you are tracking his/her location
3. Letting the user know where the information is being stored, communicated, and used
4. Allowing the user to disable tracking

13.3.1   Demo App Interface

The demo app, **myCurrentLocation**.zip, is developed for this section. It finds the location as a longitude/latitude and then converts it to a postal address. A snapshot of the demo app is shown in Fig. 13.4. To start the location demo app, click the Get Your Location button from the main interface of the demo app.

13.3.2   Location Service APIs

Android provides two different ways to get the user's location. It can be done using the **android.location.LocationListener** interface and/or the **com.google.android.gms.location.LocationListener** API. The first one is a part of the Android Network Location API, and the second one uses the Google Play Services (GPS) API. In our demo app, we use Android.location.LocationListener to find locations.

Fig. 13.4 MyCurrentLocation view

13.3.3 App Development Steps

Creating location-based service apps involves multiple steps. Below, we describe these steps and the components involved:

13.3.3.1 Permission

For your app to be able to provide location services, it needs to include one of the following two permission types in the AndroidManifest.xml file:

```
<uses-permission
 android:name="android.permission.ACCESS_FINE_LOCATION"/>
<uses-permission
 adroid:name="android.permission.ACCESS_COARSE_LOCATION"/>
```

The difference between the two permission types is in the accuracy and the amount of energy used when getting the location information. The location returned by ACCESS_FINE_LOCATION is more accurate than the location returned by ACCESS_COARSE_LOCATION, but the ACCESS_FINE_LOCATION permission type uses more battery power than ACCESS_COARSE_LOCATION.

13.3.3.2 Obtaining Location Manager

Android uses the LocationManager class to obtain location data. LocationManager gives the location of your phone in terms of longitude and latitude. It uses location providers to return location data. The location providers Android uses are GPS_PROVIDER, NETWORK_PROVIDER, and PASSIVE_PROVIDER, and they are described below.

13.3.3.3 Obtaining Location Providers

Android uses three different providers to get the location. Brief descriptions of these providers are as follows.

1. GPS _PROVIDER: this provider determines the location using satellites. Depending on the weather conditions, this provider may take a while to return a location.
2. NETWORK_PROVIDER: this provider determines the location based on the availability of nearby cell towers and Wi-Fi access points. This is typically faster than GPS.
3. PASSIVE_PROVIDER: this provider returns the locations generated by other apps or service providers installed on your device. When using a passive

provider, your app does not request location; instead, it receives location updates when other apps or services request them.

Depending on the provider you choose for your app, several locations and phone properties will be impacted. These include power consumption, longitude/latitude accuracy, altitude accuracy, and speed and direction information. You can set your provider attributes by creating the Criteria object and assigning it to your provider which we will study later in this chapter.

13.3.3.4   Geocoder

Geocoder is an Android class that does two types of location translations:

- Translating from a location address to a longitude/latitude (forward geocoding)
- Translating from a longitude/latitude to a location address (reverse geocoding)

When doing reverse geocoding, you do not get the exact address of the location. Sometimes, the address is only partially returned. For the Geocoder to work, it needs a backend service available on your phone. If the user has other services, such as a Play Store or Gmail account, they most likely have the backend service as well.

As a developer, use the isPresent() method to check if the user has the backend services on their device or not. The checking can be done as follows:

```
Geocoder geocoder = new Geocoder(this, Locale.getDefault());
  if (geocoder.isPresent()) {...}
```

The Geocoder class uses an internet connection, so you need to add the following permission to your manifest file as well.

```
<uses-permission android:name="android.permission.INTERNET" />
```

13.3.3.5   Register LocationListener

The LocationListener receives notifications from the LocationManager when the user's location changes. This interface has four callback methods each with a special task to perform.

1. onLocationChanged() method is called when a new location can be retrieved.
2. onProviderDisabled() method is called when the location provider is disabled (e.g., the user has turned off the GPS).
3. onProviderEnabled() method is called when the provider is enabled (e.g., the user has turned on the Wi-Fi).
4. onStatusChanged() method is called when the provider status has changed, for example, when a provider is unable to retrieve a location or if the provider has recently become available after a period of unavailability.

The LocationListener needs to be registered with LocationManager to receive notifications of location changes. This is done by calling the requestLocationUpdates() method on the LocationManager object.

The RequestLocationUpdates() method has four parameters. The method signature is like this:

```
requestLocationUpdates(String provider, long minTimeMs,
float minDistanceM, LocationListener listener);
```

and it can be called as follows:

```
locationManager.requestLocationUpdates(
locationProvider, minTime, minDistance, myLocationListener);
```

For example, to receive a notification from the GPS provider every 5 seconds and when the device moves 10 meters, the registration would be as follows:

```
locationManaer.requestLocationUpdates(
LocatonProvider.GPS_PROVIDER, 5000, 10, myLocationListener);
```

The requestLocationUpdates() method is overloaded, i.e., the location manager has multiple versions of this method. The methods are different from each other in the type and number of method parameters.

13.3.4 App Implementation Details

Below, we describe in detail how to implement the steps above. We use our demo app to explain the code, method sequence calls, and class and method implementations.

13.3.4.1 Check and Request Permission

Starting from API 23, you need to ask the user to grant your app permission to track their location right after the app installs and when the app starts to run. In our demo app, for example, this is done by calling the checkPermissions() method which in turn invokes the onRequestPermissionsResult() method. The code snippet presented in Listing 13.8 shows how this step can be implemented.

Listing 13.8 Ask the user to grant your app permission.

```
// setp1
...
private void checkPermissions() {
    if (Build.VERSION.SDK_INT < Build.VERSION_CODES.M)
        return;
    if (checkSelfPermission(
        Manifest.permission.ACCESS_FINE_LOCATION) !=
            PackageManager.PERMISSION_GRANTED) {
// step 2
    requestPermissions(
            new String[]{Manifest.permission
                .ACCESS_FINE_LOCATION}, 0);
    }
}
```

If the access is not granted, you have a chance to briefly explain to the user the benefit of granting it to the app. This is done by using the **shouldShowRequestPermissionRationale()** method. In the code snippet shown in Listing 13.9, the section used to request access after being denied is in boldface font.

Listing 13.9 Request access after being denied implementation.

```
// step 3
    @Override
    public void onRequestPermissionsResult(int request_code,
                        String[] permissions,
                        int[] permissionResults) {
    if (permissionResults[0] != PackageManager.PERMISSION_DENIED) {
        // step 4.
        getMyCurrentLocation();
    } else { // if permission is denied
        // if Build.VERSION_CODES.M is >= 23
        if (Build.VERSION.SDK_INT >= Build.VERSION_CODES.M) {
            if (shouldShowRequestPermissionRationale(
                Manifest.permission.ACCESS_FINE_LOCATION)) {
                buildRequest();
            } }}
    }
```

If the user checks the *do not ask again box* on the request dialog message, the user will not be asked again.

We have built the explanation message in a separate method called *buildRequest( )*; see code snippet in Listing 13.10.

Listing 13.10 The implementation of the access explanation message.

```
public void buildRequest() {
    AlertDialog.Builder builder = new AlertDialog.Builder(this);
    builder.setMessage(R.string.permission_is_important)
        .setTitle(R.string.permission_required);
    builder.setPositiveButton(R.string.ok,
            new DialogInterface.OnClickListener() {
            public void onClick(DialogInterface dag, int id) {
                if (Build.VERSION.SDK_INT
                        >= Build.VERSION_CODES.M) {
                    requestPermissions(new String[]{
                            Manifest.permission.
                                ACCESS_FINE_LOCATION},0);
                }
            }
        }).show();
}
```

13.3.4.2 Location Manager Setup

Once permission is granted, the onRequestPermissionsResult() method invokes the getMyCurrentLocation() method to set up the LocationManager as shown in the code snippet below:

```
public void getMyCurrentLocation() {
    LocationManager locationManager =
        (LocationManager) getSystemService(
            getApplicationContext().LOCATION_SERVICE);
    ...
}
```

Note that getSystemService() uses *LOCATION_SERVICE* as an input and returns the LocationManager object.

13.3.4.3 Specify Location Provider

Even though you can specify the location provider explicitly in your code using the LocationManager.GPS_PROVIDER, LocationManager.NETWORK_PROVIDER, or LocationManager.PASSIVE_PROVIDER constant, you should not rigidly specify the provider. It is better programming practice to let the Android systems choose the available provider for your app based on the criteria you specify.

In our demo app, we specify a location provider for our app using the getBestProvider() method as follows.

```
String locationProvider =
  locationManager.getBestProvider(myLocationCriteria, true);
```

To receive the best provider, we need to define a few parameters to form the criteria, i.e., instantiate a criteria object, for choosing a provider. In our demo app, the parameters to form the criteria are coarse accuracy, low power consumption, and no altitude, bearing, or speed. The code snippet presented in Listing 13.11 shows our app criteria for selecting a location provider.

Listing 13.11 Define the criteria object to choose a location provider.

```
public void getMyCurrentLocation() {
  ...
  Criteria myLocationCriteria = setLocationCriteria();
  ... }
public Criteria setLocationCriteria() {
    Criteria myLocationCriteria = new Criteria();
    myLocationCriteria.setAccuracy(Criteria.ACCURACY_FINE);
    myLocationCriteria.setPowerRequirement(Criteria.POWER_LOW);
    myLocationCriteria.setAltitudeRequired(false);
    myLocationCriteria.setBearingRequired(false);
    myLocationCriteria.setSpeedRequired(false);
    return myLocationCriteria;
}
```

13.3.4.4   Find Your Last Location

The *getLastKnownLocation()* method can be used to find the last location of your device. It returns data about the location attained from the given provider. Once the last location is received, the updateMyLocation(a_lastlocation) method gets called and passes the location to the Geocoder for printing; see the code snippet shown in Listing 13.12.

> **Listing 13.12** Using the getLastKnownLocation() method to find the last location.

```
public void getMyCurrentLocation () {
    ...
    Location a_lastlocation =
      locationManager.getLastKnownLocation (locationProvider);
    updateMyLocation (a_lastlocation);
    ... }
}
public void updateMyLocation (Location location) {
  LinearLayout linearLayout = findViewById (R.id.rooLayout);
  DisplayAddress.displayAddress (linearLayout, location, this);
}
```

Note that you might get the wrong location if your phone has been moved while turned off (it will keep the last known location, i.e., the last location where your phone was on). Furthermore, if the provider or the location is turned off, you might get a null object.

13.3.4.5   Refresh Current Location

An important step in tracking the location of a device is the method calls made to refresh the current location. That is, you need to have a LocationListener object in your code to receive notifications from the LocationManager when the location changes. The LocationManager class has multiple overloaded methods called requestLocationUpdates() for this purpose, and we used the *requestLocationUpdates(String, long, float, LocationListener)* method in our code. The code snippet below shows the method call:

```
locationManager.requestLocationUpdates (locationProvider, minTime,
        minDistance, new MyLocationListener (this));
```

The requestLocationUpdates() method above uses a LocationListener object called *myLocationListener* with two parameters, minTime and minDistance. The definition of the two parameters is as follows.

- minTime: The minimum time needed to pass before receiving the second location update. It is measured in milliseconds.
- minDistance: The minimum distance needed to elapse before receiving the second location update. It is measured in meters and used to control the frequency rate of location updates based on the distance.

Your app will receive an update from the location provider when the location has changed, i.e., when the distance is greater than the minDistance and the time passed is greater than the minTime.

Each location update consumes resources, e.g., battery life. The battery is needed to run the GPS, Wi-Fi, cell, and other components. You need to balance between meeting the app's requirements and reducing resource consumption. Having the right minTime value will help to keep this balance.

The *LocationListener* is used to receive location change notifications from the *LocationManager* class. LocationListener has four callback methods. In our code, we call the *updateMyLocation()* method if the onLocationChanged() method is called. The code snippet below shows how often our demo app updates the location information.

```
public void getMyCurrentLocation() {
...
   locationManager.
            requestLocationUpdates(
            locationProvider, minTime, minDistance,
               new MyLocationListener(this));
}
```

The complete implementation of the location listener interface is shown below in Listing 13.13.

Listing 13.13 MyLocationListener.java implementation.

```
package com.code.abdulrahman.cp670.mycurrentlocation;
import android.location.Location;
import android.location.LocationListener;
import android.os.Bundle;
import android.util.Log;
public class MyLocationListener implements LocationListener {
   final String TAG = "myCurrentLocation";
   MainActivity context ;
   public MyLocationListener(MainActivity context) {
      this.context = context;
   }
   @Override
   public void onLocationChanged(Location location) {
      Log.d(TAG, "onLocationChanged called");
      context.updateMyLocation(location);
   }
   @Override
   public void onStatusChanged(
   String provider, int status, Bundle extras) {
      Log.d(TAG, "onStatusChanged called");
   }
   @Override
```

```
  public void onProviderEnabled(String provider) {
    Log.d(TAG, "onProviderEnabled called");
  }
  @Override
  public void onProviderDisabled(String provider) {
    Log.d(TAG, "onProviderDisabled called");
  }
}
```

13.3.4.6 Do It Yourself

Your app will discover new addresses when you move more than the minDistance away from your last known location and after a time greater than the minTime from the last time you received the change location notification has passed. Write an *updateMyLocation()* method to display the history of the locations visited and the time spent at each location on the screen.

13.3.4.7 Use Geocoding

The updateMyLocation() method in our code uses the *displayAddress()* method from our defined class called *DisplayAddress* to transform the location object into two types of outputs, the longitude and latitude output and a readable address output, like 247 King Street N, Waterloo, Ontario, N2J 2YK, Canada. The first part of the *displayAddress()* method simply prints out the longitude and latitude to the UI. The next output uses reverse geocoding. The Geocoder object is created by calling the Locale.getDefault() method as shown below. The Locale object is used to format the location in the country's custom address.

```
Geocoder geocoder = new Geocoder(cxt, Locale.getDefault());
    The List <Address> addressList =
    geocoder.getFromLocation(latitude, longitude, 1);
```

The *getFromLocation()* method returns a list of addresses that are known to describe the area immediately surrounding the given latitude and longitude. The parameters to the getFromLocation() method are:

- latitude: The latitude at a point for the search.
- longitude: The longitude at a point for the search.
- maxResults: The maximum number of addresses to return; use 1 to 5 for good performance.

In the code snippet above, the maxResults = 1. We are only interested in the top matching address. Once the Address object is returned, we use the StringBuilder object to get and format the address to display on the UI.

The code snippet presented in Listing 13.14 shows the displayAddress() method and the display class:

Listing 13.14 DisplayAddress.java for printing the longitude and latitude and a readable address.

```java
package com.code.abdulrahman.cp670.mycurrentlocation;
import android.content.Context;
import android.location.Address;
import android.location.Geocoder;
import android.location.Location;
import android.widget.LinearLayout;
import android.widget.TextView;
import java.util.List;
import java.util.Locale;
public class DisplayAddress {
  public static void displayAddress(LinearLayout linearLayout,
  Location location, Context cxt) {
    TextView myCurrentLocation =
     linearLayout.findViewById(R.id.myCurrentLocation);
    String youLocationCoordinate =
       cxt.getString(R.string.can_not_find_location);
    String yourAddress = cxt.getString(
    R.string.can_not_find_address);
    if (null != location) {
        double latitude = location.getLatitude();
        double longitude = location.getLongitude();

        youLocationCoordinate = cxt.getString
        (R.string.latitude) + latitude +
           System.getProperty("line.separator") +
           cxt.getString(R.string.longitude) + longitude;
      Geocoder geocoder = new Geocoder(cxt, Locale.getDefault());
      try {
          if (Geocoder.isPresent()) {
            List <Address> addressList = geocoder.getFromLocation(
                               latitude, longitude, 1);
            StringBuilder stringBuilder = new StringBuilder();
            if (addressList.size() > 0) {
              Address anAddress = addressList.get(0);
              for (int i = 0; i <= anAddress.getMaxAddressLineIndex();
              i++) {
                  stringBuilder.append
                  (anAddress.getAddressLine(i)).append("\n");
                  stringBuilder.append(
                  anAddress.getLocality()).append("\n");
                  stringBuilder.append(
                  anAddress.getPostalCode()).append("\n");
                  stringBuilder.append(anAddress.getCountryName());
              }
```

```
                yourAddress = stringBuilder.toString();
            }
        }
    } catch (Exception e) {
        System.out.println(e);
    }
}
String address = cxt.getString(R.string.current_location) +
        System.getProperty("line.separator") +
        youLocationCoordinate + System.getProperty
        ("line.separator") +
        System.getProperty("line.separator")
        + yourAddress;
    myCurrentLocation.setText(address);
    }
}
```

The source code for the location's main activity is shown in Listing 13.15.

Listing 13.15 LocationMainActivity.

```
package com.code.wlu.abdulrahman.sensorsandlocation;
import android.Manifest;
import android.app.AlertDialog;
import android.content.DialogInterface;
import android.content.pm.PackageManager;
import android.location.Criteria;
import android.location.Location;
import android.location.LocationManager;
import android.os.Build;
import android.os.Bundle;
import android.widget.LinearLayout;

import androidx.appcompat.app.AppCompatActivity;
import androidx.core.app.ActivityCompat;

public class LocationMainActivity extends AppCompatActivity
implements LocationListenerParent {

    final int minTime = 200;
    final int minDistance = 10;

    @Override
    protected void onCreate(Bundle savedInstanceState) {
        super.onCreate(savedInstanceState);
        setTitle("Your Location");
        setContentView(R.layout.activity_location_main);
        getMyCurrentLocation();
        checkPermissions();
    }
```

```java
public void updateMyLocation(Location location) {
    LinearLayout linearLayout = findViewById(R.id.rooLayout);
    DisplayAddress.displayAddress(linearLayout, location, this);
}
// setp1
private void checkPermissions() {
    if (Build.VERSION.SDK_INT < Build.VERSION_CODES.M)
        return;
    if (checkSelfPermission(
        Manifest.permission.ACCESS_FINE_LOCATION) !=
                        PackageManager.PERMISSION_GRANTED) {
        // step 2
        requestPermissions(
            new String[]{Manifest.permission
                .ACCESS_FINE_LOCATION}, 0);
    }
}
// step 3
@Override
public void onRequestPermissionsResult(int request_code,
                String[] permissions, int[] permissionResults) {
    if (permissionResults[0] != PackageManager.PERMISSION_DENIED) {
        // step 4.
        getMyCurrentLocation();
    } else {
        // Build.VERSION_CODES.M is 23
        if (Build.VERSION.SDK_INT >= Build.VERSION_CODES.M) {
            if (shouldShowRequestPermissionRationale(
                    Manifest.permission.ACCESS_FINE_LOCATION)) {
                buildRequest();
            }
        }
    }
}
}


public void getMyCurrentLocation() {

    LocationManager locationManager =
        (LocationManager) getSystemService(
        getApplicationContext().LOCATION_SERVICE);

        Criteria myLocationCriteria = setLocationCriteria();
        String locationProvider =
        locationManager.getBestProvider(myLocationCriteria, true);
        if (ActivityCompat.checkSelfPermission(this,
            Manifest.permission.ACCESS_FINE_LOCATION)
            == PackageManager.PERMISSION_GRANTED) {
        Location a_lastlocation =
            locationManager.getLastKnownLocation(locationProvider);
        updateMyLocation(a_lastlocation);
```

```
        locationManager.
            requestLocationUpdates(
            locationProvider, minTime, minDistance,
                new MyLocationListener(this));
    }
}
public Criteria setLocationCriteria() {
    Criteria myLocationCriteria = new Criteria();
    myLocationCriteria.setAccuracy(Criteria.ACCURACY_FINE);
    myLocationCriteria.setPowerRequirement(Criteria.POWER_LOW);
    myLocationCriteria.setAltitudeRequired(false);
    myLocationCriteria.setBearingRequired(false);
    myLocationCriteria.setSpeedRequired(false);
    return myLocationCriteria;
}
public void buildRequest() {
    AlertDialog.Builder builder = new AlertDialog.Builder(this);
    builder.setMessage(R.string.permission_is_important)
        .setTitle(R.string.permission_required);
    builder.setPositiveButton(R.string.ok,
        new DialogInterface.OnClickListener() {
        public void onClick(DialogInterface dialog, int id) {
            if (Build.VERSION.SDK_INT >= Build.VERSION_CODES.M) {
                requestPermissions(new String[]{
                    Manifest.permission.ACCESS_FINE_LOCATION}, 0);
            }
    } }).show();
    }
}
```

13.3.5   Revising Weather App

Now that we know how to retrieve location information using the Android location API, we revisit our weather app from Chap. 10 to use the location API to retrieve the user location and display the weather conditions based on the current location. In other words, if you open the app in Toronto, the app shows you the weather information for Toronto; if you open it in Waterloo, it will show you weather information for Waterloo; etc.

We display the weather information based on the current user location by combing the WeatherForecastActivity class with the myCurrentLocation app. In the myCurrentLocation app, we changed the DisplayAddress class from displaying addresses to initializing static variables. In the WeatherForecastActivity class, we added the current location to the top of the spinner list. The code snippet presented in Listing 13.16 shows these changes.

Listing 13.16 DisplayAddress.java.

```
public class DisplayAddress {
public static String current_city = "";
public static void displayAddress(Location location, Context cxt) {
if (null != location) {
 double latitude = location.getLatitude();
 double longitude = location.getLongitude();
 Geocoder geocoder = new Geocoder(cxt, Locale.getDefault());
 try {
  if (Geocoder.isPresent()) {
    List <Address> addressList =
      geocoder.getFromLocation(latitude, longitude, 1);
           if (addressList.size() > 0) {
              Address anAddress = addressList.get(0);
              current_city = anAddress.getLocality();
           } }
      } catch (Exception e) {
        System.out.println(e); }
    }
 }
}
```

Note that the Android address object has multiple get() methods for retrieving
address fields. The getLocality() method is the method we used to retrieve the city
name. We need the city name to retrieve weather information from the network. The
change made to the WeatherForecastActivity class is highlighted in Listing 13.17 in
boldface font.

Listing 13.17 WeatherForecastActivity.java.

```
public class WeatherForecastActivity extends AppCompatActivity {
...
private class CitySelectListener implements
AdapterView.OnItemSelectedListener {
  @Override
  public void onItemSelected(AdapterView <?> parent, View view,
                    int position, long id) {
      cityList.set(0, DisplayAddress.current_city) ;
      new ForecastQuery(cityList.get(position)).execute();
      cityName.setText(cityList.get(position) + " Weather");
  }
  @Override
  public void onNothingSelected(AdapterView <?> parent) {}
}
```

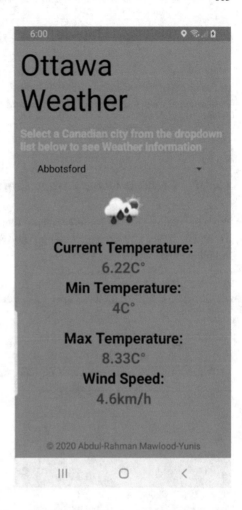

After revising the app, Fig. 13.5 displays the interface of the weather app showing the Ottawa weather information by default. Ottawa is shown because it is the city where the app was tested.

13.3.6   Do It Yourself

In the code above, change the value of maxAddress from 1 to 2 and 3 in this line of code: geocoder.getFromLocation(latitude, longitude,1). Run the app two times, and study the address granularity returned by the second and third addresses associated with the longitude and latitude.

13.4   Use Google Maps in Your App

What we have studied so far can be used to create numerous applications. In this part of the chapter, we will study how to include Google Maps in your apps and how to customize it. We will study the classes and steps involved in creating an app with Google Maps.

13.4.1   Create a Google Maps Project

We will create a Google Maps project to demonstrate how to include it in your app. To do so, create a new project using Android Studio, and select the Google Maps template as shown in Fig. 13.6.

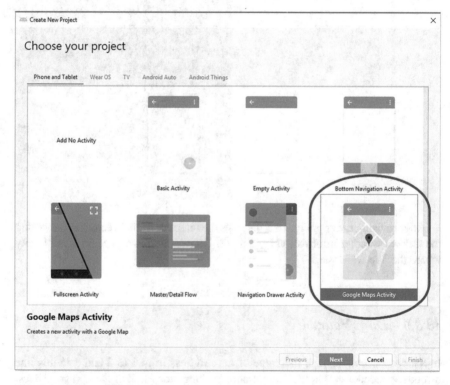

Fig. 13.6   Android template to create a Google Maps project

Fig. 13.7 google_maps_api. xml file location in the project directory

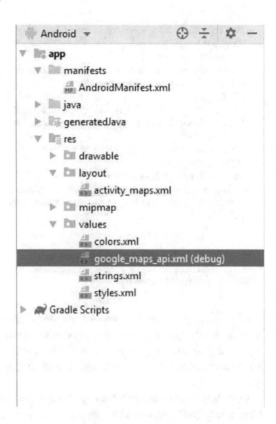

Open the google_maps_api.xml file; the file name and its location in the project directory are shown in Fig. 13.7 inside the values folder.

The content of the google_maps_api.xml file is shown in Listing 13.18. It contains a link to create a free Google Maps API key.

Listing 13.18 google_maps_api.xml file.

```
<resources>
<!--
TODO: Before you run your application, you need a Google Maps API key.

To get one, follow this link, follow the directions and press "Create" at
the end:
 https://console.developers.google.com/flows/enableapi?
apiid=maps_android_backend&keyType=CLIENT_SIDE_ANDROID&r=9A:A9:
0A:46:04:91:11:4D:34:23:22:A5:12:C8:25:A7:B2:B3:29:1C%3Bcom.code.
wlu.abdulrahman.mygooglemapapplication
```

```
You can also add your credentials to an existing key, using these
values:
Package name:
com.code.wlu.abdulrahman.mygooglemapapplication
SHA-1 certificate fingerprint:
9A:A9:0A:46:04:91:11:4D:34:23:22:A5:12:C8:25:A7:B2:B3:29:1C
Alternatively, follow the directions here:
https://developers.google.com/maps/documentation/android/
start#get-key
Once you have your key (it starts with "AIza"), replace the
"google_maps_key"
   string in this file. -->
<string name="google_maps_key" templateMergeStrategy=
"preserve" translatable="false">YOUR_KEY_HERE</string>
</resources>
```

13.4.2   Obtaining App Key

Put the link in your browser, and follow the instructions to obtain a key for your app.
Here is an example where a key has been obtained for our demo app; see Fig. 13.8.
Note that the shown key is usable and is hard to read. The example is shown to help
you to learn about the look and location of the key that you will generate for your
app.

Once you have obtained your key, replace the text **"YOUR_KEY_HERE"** in the
google_map_api.xml file with the key that you have obtained from Google. The
content of the google_map_api.xml file is shown earlier, in Listing 13.18. Below is
an example where "YOUR_KEY_HERE" has been replaced with the key obtained
from Google for our demo app.

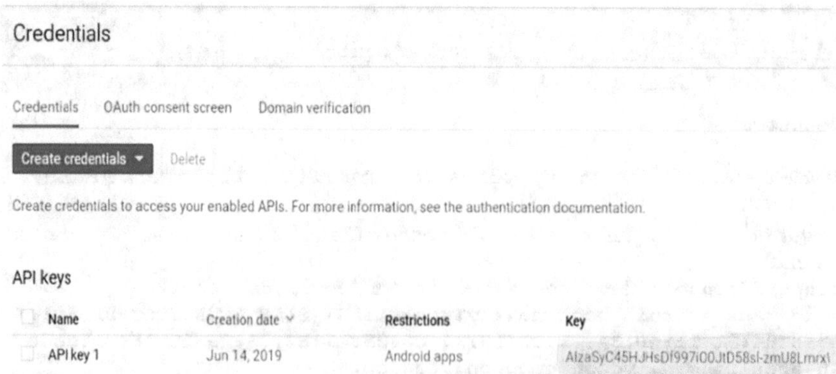

Fig. 13.8 Google Maps key, for example

```
</resources>
    ...
<string name="google_maps_key"
    templateMergeStrategy="preserve"
        translatable="false">YOUR_KEY_HERE</string>
    ...
</resources>
</resources>
    ...
        <string name="google_maps_key"
            templateMergeStrategy="preserve"
            translatable="false">AIzaSyC45HJHsDf997iO0Jt8sl </string>
    ...
</resources>
```

13.4.3   Update Manifest File

The AndroidManifest.xml file should be updated now. Check to see if the meta-data element below has been added to your manifest file. If not, you need to add it for your app to work.

```
<meta-data
  android:name="com.google.android.geo.API_KEY"
  android:value="@string/google_maps_key" />
```

You also need to be sure that the latest version of the 'com.google.android.gms: play-services-maps' has been added to the implementation section of the Gradle module of your app. An example is shown below.

```
dependencies {
implementation fileTree(dir: 'libs', include: ['*.jar'])
implementation 'androidx.appcompat:appcompat:1.1.0'
implementation 'androidx.constraintlayout:constraintlayout:1.1.3'
implementation 'com.google.android.gms:play-services-maps:17.0.0'
testImplementation 'junit:junit:4.12'
androidTestImplementation 'androidx.test.ext:junit:1.1.1'
androidTestImplementation 'androidx.test.espresso:espresso-
core:3.2.0'
}
```

Now, you should have Google Maps displayed in your app; see Fig. 13.9. Your app is now ready to do all kinds of interesting things.

What we did so far can be summarized as follows:

1. Set up the API key and Gradle dependencies.
2. Add a fragment object to an activity to handle the map. This is done by adding the <fragment> element to the layout file of the activity.

Fig. 13.9 Displaying
Google Maps in your app

3. Implement the OnMapReadyCallback interface, and use the onMapReady
   (GoogleMap) callback method to handle the GoogleMaps object.
4. Call the getMapAsync() method on the fragment to register the callback.

The Java code for the myMapsActivity demo app is shown in Listing 13.19. The
class extends the *FragmentActivity* class and implements the *OnMapReadyCallback*
interface. To start the app, click the Access Google Maps button from the main
interface of the demo app.

> **Listing 13.19** MyMapsActivity.java for creating and using GoogleMap.

```java
package com.code.wlu.abdulrahman.sensorsandlocation;
import androidx.fragment.app.FragmentActivity;
import android.os.Bundle;
import com.google.android.gms.maps.CameraUpdateFactory;
import com.google.android.gms.maps.GoogleMap;
import com.google.android.gms.maps.OnMapReadyCallback;
import com.google.android.gms.maps.SupportMapFragment;
import com.google.android.gms.maps.model.LatLng;
import com.google.android.gms.maps.model.MarkerOptions;
public class MyMapsActivity extends FragmentActivity implements
OnMapReadyCallback {

  private GoogleMap mMap;
  @Override
  protected void onCreate(Bundle savedInstanceState) {
    super.onCreate(savedInstanceState);
    setContentView(R.layout.activity_my_maps);
    SupportMapFragment mapFragment =
            (SupportMapFragment) getSupport  FragmentManager()
      .findFragmentById(R.id.map);
    mapFragment.getMapAsync(this);
  }
  @Override
  public void onMapReady(GoogleMap googleMap) {
    mMap = googleMap;
    LatLng sydney = new LatLng(45.2487862,-76.3606792);
    mMap.addMarker(new MarkerOptions().
                      position(sydney).title("Marker in Ottawa"));
    mMap.moveCamera(CameraUpdateFactory.newLatLng(sydney));
    mMap.getUiSettings().setMyLocationButtonEnabled(true);
    mMap.getUiSettings().setCompassEnabled(true);
    mMap.getUiSettings().setMapToolbarEnabled(true);
  }
}
```

13.4.4 Google Maps API

Let us learn few more things about the Google Maps API and the essential Google Maps classes and interfaces before updating our demo app. With the Google Maps API, you can use Google Maps data and display it. You can also provide users with real-time information about the user location and support user interactions by adding markers, polygons, and overlays to your map.

The API has many classes and interfaces. Below, we describe the GoogleMap, MapFragment, MapView, and UiSettings classes, the OnMapReadyCallback interface, and the map's initial state configuration. The complete list of classes, methods, and interfaces can be found in the Google documentation. A reference to the documentation is provided in the references section of this chapter.

13.4.5   GoogleMap Class

The GoogleMap class is the main class to access Google Maps for Android. It has all the essential methods related to creating and dealing with maps and is defined in the com.google.android.gms.maps package.

When you create a Google Maps app using the Google Maps Activity template that Android studio provides, the GoogleMap class becomes a private field of your MainActivity class. The class will implement the OnMapReadyCallBack interface, and its method, onMapReady(), will be included in Google's MainActivity definition. See the code snippet below.

```
public class MyMapsActivity extends FragmentActivity implements
OnMapReadyCallback {
  private GoogleMap mMap;
  @Override
  public void onMapReady(GoogleMap googleMap) {
    mMap = googleMap;
    ...
  }
}
```

13.4.6   OnMapReadyCallback Interface

The OnMapReadyCallback interface is a callback interface with one method, onMapReady(GoogleMap). The onMapReady() method is triggered by the Android system when the map object is not null and is ready to be used. To trigger the onMapReady(GoogleMap) method, the user must have the Google Play Services installed. If you add Google Maps to your app but Google Play Services is not installed on the device, the user will be prompted to install it.

13.4.7   SupportMapFragment Class

We studied fragments in the earlier chapters and created both static and dynamic fragments. We explained that while an activity occupies an entire screen, fragments usually occupy only a portion of the activity screen. The simplest way to place a map in an app is by using fragments. Fragments become a wrapper around a view of a map to automatically handle the necessary lifecycle methods. When you create your main activity using Android Studio's Google Maps activity, the fragment occupies the entire screen. That is, the fragment's width and height are set to match_parent. An example of a layout file for the Google Maps activity is shown in Listing 13.20.

Listing 13.20 An example of a layout file for the Google Maps activity.

```xml
<?xml version="1.0" encoding="utf-8"?>
<fragment
  xmlns:android="http://schemas.android.com/apk/res/android"
  xmlns:tools="http://schemas.android.com/tools"
  android:id="@+id/map"
  android:name="com.google.android.gms.maps.SupportMapFragment"
  android:layout_width="match_parent"
  android:layout_height="match_parent"
  tools:context=".MyMapsActivity" />
```

The fragment element in the layout file includes an entry called *android: name* which specifies the name of the fragment class to be instantiated. In this case, it is the SupportMapFragment class, which is a subclass of the Fragment class.

For our demo app, the SupportMapFragment class is referenced inside the MyMapsActivity class using the getSupportFragmentManager() and findFragmentById() methods. These steps are shown below.

```
SupportMapFragment mapFragment = (SupportMapFragment)
getSupportFragmentManager().findFragmentById(R.id.map);
mapFragment.getMapAsync(this);
```

The getMapAsync() method is used to set a callback object which will be triggered or receive the map when the GoogleMap instance is ready to be used. The method signature for the getMapAsync() method is:

```
public void getMapAsync (OnMapReadyCallback callback),
```

In our example, this method is used like this: mapFragment.getMapAsync(this).

The MyMapsActivity objects are of type OnMapReadyCallback. This is because MyMapsActivity implements the OnMapReadyCallback interface. Hence, the statement mapFragment.getMapAsync(this) means that MyMapsActivity is registered to listen to the map creation event asynchronously and receives the map object when it becomes available.

Note that the getMapAsync() method must be called from the main thread and is executed in the main thread. In cases where the Google Play Services is not installed on the user's device, the callback method will not be triggered until the user installs it.

13.4.8   Map Fragment Layout Example

If you want Google Maps to occupy only a portion of your device screen, you have to set the width and height of the fragment used to hold your map. In the example below, we used ConstraintLayout, some text views, and a fragment to create a layout for the app. The layout is shown in Listing 13.21, and the new look for the app is shown in Fig. 13.10.

Fig. 13.10 Google Maps occupies only a portion of the device screen

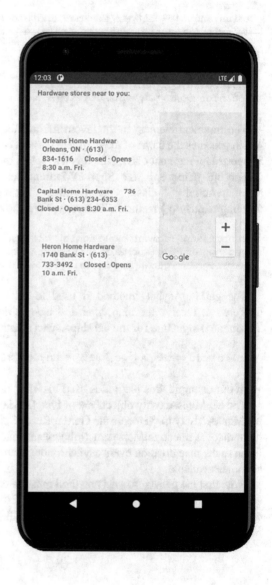

Listing 13.21 A layout file containing a map along with other components.

```xml
<?xml version="1.0" encoding="utf-8"?>
<androidx.constraintlayout.widget.ConstraintLayout
  xmlns:android="http://schemas.android.com/apk/res/android"
  xmlns:map="http://schemas.android.com/apk/res-auto"
  xmlns:tools="http://schemas.android.com/tools"
  android:layout_width="match_parent"
  android:layout_height="match_parent"
  tools:context=".MyMapsActivity">
  <TextView
    android:id="@+id/text"
    android:layout_width="230dp"
    android:layout_height="45dp"
    android:layout_marginStart="16dp"
    android:layout_marginTop="20dp"
    android:layout_marginBottom="50dp"
    android:text="Hardware stores near to you:"
    android:textStyle="bold"
    map:layout_constraintBottom_toTopOf="@+id/text1"
    map:layout_constraintStart_toStartOf="parent"
    map:layout_constraintTop_toTopOf="parent" />

  <TextView
    android:id="@+id/text1"
    android:layout_width="200dp"
    android:layout_height="100dp"
    android:layout_marginStart="16dp"
    android:layout_marginTop="90dp"
    android:padding="10dp"
    android:text="@string/orleans_home"
    android:textStyle="bold"
    map:layout_constraintStart_toStartOf="parent"
    map:layout_constraintTop_toTopOf="parent">
  </TextView>

  <TextView
    android:id="@+id/text2"
    android:layout_width="200dp"
    android:layout_height="90dp"
    android:layout_marginStart="16dp"
    android:layout_marginTop="8dp"
    android:text="@string/capital_home"
    android:textStyle="bold"
    map:layout_constraintStart_toStartOf="parent"
    map:layout_constraintTop_toBottomOf="@+id/text1" />

  <TextView
    android:id="@+id/text3"
    android:layout_width="200dp"
    android:layout_height="90dp"
```

```
    android:layout_marginStart="16dp"
    android:layout_marginTop="8dp"
    android:padding="10dp"
    android:text="@string/heron_home"
    android:textStyle="bold"
    map:layout_constraintStart_toStartOf="parent"
    map:layout_constraintTop_toBottomOf="@+id/text2">
  </TextView>

  <fragment
    android:id="@+id/map"
    android:name="com.google.android.gms.maps.SupportMapFragment"
    android:layout_width="165dp"
    android:layout_height="300dp"
    android:layout_marginEnd="8dp"
    map:layout_constraintEnd_toEndOf="parent"
    map:layout_constraintHorizontal_bias="1.0"
    map:layout_constraintStart_toEndOf="@+id/text2"
    map:layout_constraintTop_toBottomOf="@+id/text"
    map:mapType="normal"
    map:uiCompass="true"
    map:uiZoomControls="true" />
</androidx.constraintlayout.widget.ConstraintLayout>
```

13.4.9   MapView

Different from the MapFragment class, MapView is a view. Specifically, it is a subclass of the FrameLayout container class and is often used as a placeholder for the fragments. MapView is used to display a map with data obtained from the Google Maps Services. Once declared inside the layout file, you can reference it using the findViewByID() method like any other view. When you use the MapView class, you must forward all the lifecycle methods, like the onStart() and onResume() methods, from the activity, or fragment, containing the MapView to the corresponding ones of the MapView class. Listing 13.22 is an example of how to forward the lifecycle onStart() method to its corresponding one in the ViewMap class.

Listing 13.22 A layout file containing a map along with other components.

```
public class MapViewActivity extends AppCompatActivity implements
OnMapReadyCallback {
  private MapView mapView;
  ...
@Override
protected void onStart() {
  super.onStart();
  mapView.onStart();
}
```

The other methods that you must forward to the corresponding ones of the MapView class are onCreate(Bundle), onStart(), onResume(), onPause(), onStop(), onDestroy(), onSaveInstanceState(), and onLowMemory().

To get Google Maps, you need to call the getMapAsync() method. MapView automatically initializes the map system and the view. You should consider the *MapFragment* and *SupportMapFragment* classes for displaying a Map; they are simpler to use than MapView, for example, you don't have to worry about forwarding lifecycle methods. Use the *SupportMapFragment* class if you are looking to target earlier platforms. The code snippet in Listing 13.23 shows how to use the MapView class to include Google Maps in your app.

Listing 13.23 Using the MapView class to include Google Maps in your app.

```
package com.code.wlu.abdulrahman.sensorsandlocation;
import androidx.appcompat.app.AppCompatActivity;
import android.os.Bundle;
import com.google.android.gms.maps.CameraUpdateFactory;
import com.google.android.gms.maps.GoogleMap;
import com.google.android.gms.maps.MapView;
import com.google.android.gms.maps.OnMapReadyCallback;
import com.google.android.gms.maps.UiSettings;
import com.google.android.gms.maps.model.LatLng;
import com.google.android.gms.maps.model.MarkerOptions;

public class MapViewActivity extends AppCompatActivity implements
OnMapReadyCallback {

  private MapView mapView;
  private GoogleMap mMap;
  private static final String MAP_VIEW_BUNDLE_KEY = "bundleKey";
  @Override
  protected void onCreate(Bundle savedInstanceState) {
    super.onCreate(savedInstanceState);
    setContentView(R.layout.activity_map_view);
    Bundle mapViewBundle = null;
    if (savedInstanceState != null) {
      mapViewBundle =
          savedInstanceState.getBundle(MAP_VIEW_BUNDLE_KEY);
    }
    mapView = findViewById(R.id.map_view);
    // the onCreate life cycle methods is forwared t othe MapView
    mapView.onCreate(mapViewBundle);
    mapView.getMapAsync(this);
  }
  @Override
  public void onSaveInstanceState(Bundle outState) {
    super.onSaveInstanceState(outState);

    Bundle mapViewBundle =
    outState.getBundle(MAP_VIEW_BUNDLE_KEY);
```

```java
    if (mapViewBundle == null) {
      mapViewBundle = new Bundle();
      outState.putBundle(MAP_VIEW_BUNDLE_KEY, mapViewBundle);
    }
    mapView.onSaveInstanceState(mapViewBundle);
  }
  @Override
  protected void onResume() {
    super.onResume();
    mapView.onResume();
  }
  @Override
  protected void onStart() {
    super.onStart();
    mapView.onStart();
  }
  @Override
  protected void onStop() {
    super.onStop();
    mapView.onStop();
  }
  @Override
  protected void onPause() {
    mapView.onPause();
    super.onPause();
  }
  @Override
  protected void onDestroy() {
    mapView.onDestroy();
    super.onDestroy();
  }
  @Override
  public void onLowMemory() {
    super.onLowMemory();
    mapView.onLowMemory();
  }
  @Override
  public void onMapReady(GoogleMap googleMap) {
    mMap = googleMap;
    LatLng Ottawa = new LatLng(47.57833,-65.893191);
    mMap.addMarker(new MarkerOptions().position(Ottawa).
      title("Marker in Ottawa"));
    mMap.moveCamera(CameraUpdateFactory.newLatLng(Ottawa));
    mMap.getUiSettings().setMyLocationButtonEnabled(true);
    mMap.getUiSettings().setCompassEnabled(true);
    mMap.getUiSettings().setMapToolbarEnabled(true);
  }
}
```

13.4.10 UiSettings

The UiSettings class is used to set the user interface of a Google Maps. You need to call the getUiSettings() method on the GoogleMap object to retrieve a reference to the UiSettings object and then call the set methods for the retrieved object to set various UI properties for the map. The method signature for the getUiSettings() method is public UiSettings getUiSettings();.

The example below shows how to set Google Maps properties using the UiSettings class.

Listing 13.24 Setting Google Maps properties using the UiSettings class.

```
public class MyMapsActivity extends FragmentActivity implements
OnMapReadyCallback {
...
public void onMapReady(GoogleMap googleMap) {
  mMap = googleMap;
  mMap.getUiSettings().setMyLocationButtonEnabled(true);
  mMap.getUiSettings().setCompassEnabled(true);
  mMap.getUiSettings().setMapToolbarEnabled(true);
}
```

In the example above, the location button, compass, and toolbar are set for the map. There are many more methods from the UiSettings class that you can use to set various properties for the map used in your app. For a complete list of the methods, see the Google documentation. A link to the documentation is provided in the references section of this chapter.

13.4.11 Configure Initial State

You can configure various attributes to the initial map you add to your app using an XML layout file. The Google Maps API provides a set of custom XML attributes for the SupportMapFragment and MapView class which you can use to configure the initial state of the map directly from the layout file.

To use the map attributes within your XML layout file, you must also add the following namespace declaration to your layout file.

```
xmlns:map=http://schemas.android.com/apk/res-auto
```

Instead of naming your xmlns "map," you can name the namespace anything you want, but it is better to name it something meaningful.

In the layout shown in Listing 13.25, three attributes, zoom control, compass, and map type, are configured, and the namespace has been added to the layout. The impact of setting the zoom control to true and the map type to satellite is shown in Fig. 13.11.

Fig. 13.11 Adding UI zoom control to the layout file is shown

Listing 13.25 activity_my_maps.xml layout file is used to set the zoom control, compass, and map type.

```xml
<?xml version="1.0" encoding="utf-8"?>
<fragment xmlns:android=
  "http://schemas.android.com/apk/res/android"
  xmlns:tools="http://schemas.android.com/tools"
  xmlns:map="http://schemas.android.com/apk/res-auto"
  android:id="@+id/map"
  android:name="com.google.android.gms.maps.SupportMapFragment"
  android:layout_width="match_parent"
  android:layout_height="match_parent"
  map:uiCompass="true"
  map:uiZoomControls="true"
  map:mapType="satellite"
  tools:context=".MyMapsActivity" />
```

There are many more attributes that you can use to configure the map in your app. These include attributes to specify the position of the camera, gesture attributes, etc. The XML layout file presented in Listing 13.26 shows how to configure a MapView with some custom options. The same attributes can be applied to a SupportMapFragment as well.

Listing 13.26 Attributes that you can use to configure the map in your app.

```xml
<?xml version="1.0" encoding="utf-8"?>
<androidx.constraintlayout.widget.ConstraintLayout
  xmlns:android="http://schemas.android.com/apk/res/android"
  xmlns:app="http://schemas.android.com/apk/res-auto"
  xmlns:tools="http://schemas.android.com/tools"
  android:layout_width="match_parent"
  android:layout_height="match_parent"
  tools:context=".MapViewActivity"
  xmlns:map="http://schemas.android.com/apk/res-auto">

  <com.google.android.gms.maps.MapView
    android:id="@+id/map_view"
    android:layout_width="match_parent"
    android:layout_height="match_parent"
    app:layout_constraintBottom_toBottomOf="parent"
    app:layout_constraintEnd_toEndOf="parent"
    app:layout_constraintHorizontal_bias="0.498"
    app:layout_constraintLeft_toLeftOf="parent"
    app:layout_constraintRight_toRightOf="parent"
    app:layout_constraintStart_toStartOf="parent"
    app:layout_constraintTop_toTopOf="parent"
    map:uiCompass="false"
    map:uiZoomControls="true"
```

```
      map:mapType="normal"
      map:cameraBearing="112.5"
      map:cameraTargetLat="-33.796923"
      map:cameraTargetLng="150.922433"
      map:cameraTilt="30"
      map:cameraZoom="13">
  </com.google.android.gms.maps.MapView>
</androidx.constraintlayout.widget.ConstraintLayout>
```

Note that using the Maps API for Android with a Google Maps API Premium Plan license is slightly different from using the free one. When you use the Premium Plan license, you must prefix each attribute with m4b_. For example, when specifying the map type attribute, use m4b_mapType instead of mapType. Or, when specifying zoom controls, use m4b_uiZoomControls instead of uiZoomControls, and so on.

13.4.12　Setting Map Initial State Programmatically

You can set various attributes of the map's initial state using your code. You do that if you have added a map to your application programmatically. To do it, you need to use a GoogleMapOptions object. The attributes available to you are the same as those available via an XML layout file. The code snippet below shows how to create a GoogleMapOptions object and use it to set Google map attributes.

```
GoogleMapOptions attribute = new GoogleMapOptions();
attribute.mapType(GoogleMap.MAP_TYPE_SATELLITE)
      .compassEnabled(false)
      .rotateGesturesEnabled(false)
      .tiltGesturesEnabled(false);
```

Now that you have a base app and knowledge of the classes and interfaces that are part of the Google Play Services, you can do all sorts of interesting things with Google Maps in your app. For example, you can change the default street view to the satellite view, control zooming programmatically, move the map's initial location to a specific location instead of Australia on the app start-up, etc.

13.4.13　Covid App Revised

Now that you know how to use the Location class and Google Maps, you can update the Covid-19 app from Chap. 10 to provide Covid information for the user's location. To do so, you need to get the latitude and longitude from the Location object and, as you process the Covid XML file, match the latitude and longitude from the location to the one included in the Covid-19 XML data file. Once you have found one, add the city name to the spinner, and store other related information. This way the user can have updated Covid status information about their area. That is, in addition to the existing information, there should be an option that easily provides Covid data about the user's area.

The code snippet below shows the areas that you should consider updating when revising the Covid-19 app.

First, you need to retrieve the latitude and longitude for each entry in the XML data file.

```
if (parser.getName().equals(getString(R.string.lat))) {
      latitude = parser.nextText();
}else if (parser.getName().equals(getString(R.string.longitude))) {
      longitude = parser.nextText();
```

You also need to get latitude and longitude for where you are using the Location object. An example code is shown in Listing 13.27.

Listing 13.27 Get latitude and longitude for Location object.

```
public void getLocation () {
  LocationManager locationManager =
      (LocationManager) getSystemService(LOCATION_SERVICE);
  Criteria myLocationCriteria = setLocationCriteria();
  String locationProvider =
      locationManager.getBestProvider(myLocationCriteria, true);
  Location a_lastlocation = null;
  if ( !(ActivityCompat.checkSelfPermission(this,
      Manifest.permission.ACCESS_FINE_LOCATION)
      == PackageManager.PERMISSION_GRANTED))  {
    a_lastlocation =
      locationManager.getLastKnownLocation(locationProvider);
  }
  String [] latAndLong = new String [2];
  if (null != a_lastlocation) {
    latAndLong[0] = a_lastlocation.getLatitude()+"";
    latAndLong[1] = a_lastlocation.getLongitude()+"";
  }
  new UpdatedMainActivity.ProcessXML().execute(latAndLong);
}
```

Lastly, you need to match your local information to the one provided in the XML data file.

```
if (parser.getEventType() == XmlPullParser.END_TAG) {
  if (parser.getName().equals(getString(R.string.row))) {

      if ((latitude.compareTo(params[0]) == 0 ) &&
                 (longitude.compareTo(params[1]) == 0)) {
         cityList.add(cityIndex++, region + ": " + state);
         DataObject deo = new DataObject();
         deo.setState(state);
         deo.setRegion(region);
         deo.setLastUpdate(lastUpdate);
         deo.setDeaths(deaths);
         deo.setConfirmed(confirmed);
         deo.setRecovered(recovered);
         list.add(deo);
    }
 }
}
```

A complete app update is left to you as an exercise.

13.5 Chapter Summary

In this chapter, we studied three important Android topics, Android sensors, location-based services, and Google Maps. We studied the main classes needed in your app to access and use sensors and the Location API classes for location-based services. We studied the Accelerometer, LocationManager, LocationListener, Criteria, Permission, and more. We also described how to incorporate Google Maps into your apps.

Check Your Knowledge
Below are some of the fundamental concepts and vocabularies that have been covered in this chapter. To test your knowledge and your understanding of this chapter, you should be able to describe each of the below concepts in one or two sentences.

- Accelerometer
- Address
- checkPermissions
- Criteria
- findFragmentById
- Geocoder
- getBestProvider
- getMapAsync
- getSystemService
- Google Maps
- Location Manager
- LocationProvider

- MapFragment
- MapView
- OnMapReadyCallback
- onRequestPermissionsResult
- SensorEventListener
- SupportMapFragment
- UiSettings

Further Reading

For more information about the topics covered in this chapter, we suggest that you refer to the online resources listed below. These links provide additional insight into the topics covered. The links are mostly maintained by Google and are a part of the Android API specification. The resource titles convey which section/subsection of the chapter the resource is related to.

Address, [online] Available, https://developer.android.com/reference/android/location/Address

Build.VERSION.SDK_INT (your current SDK version), [online] Available, https://developer.android.com/reference/android/os/Build.VERSION

Build.VERSION_CODES.M, [online] Available, https://developer.android.com/reference/android/os/Build.VERSION_CODES

Criteria, [online] Available, https://developer.android.com/reference/android/location/Criteria

Geocoder, [online] Available, https://developer.android.com/reference/android/location/Geocoder

getSystemService, [online] Available, https://developer.android.com/reference/android/content/Context

GoogleMap, [online] Available, https://developers.google.com/android/reference/com/google/android/gms/maps/GoogleMap?hl=en

Location, [online] Available, https://developer.android.com/reference/android/location/Location

LocationListener, [online] Available, https://developer.android.com/reference/android/location/LocationListener

LocationManager, [online] Available, https://developer.android.com/reference/kotlin/android/location/LocationManager

OnMapReadyCallback, [online] Available, https://developers.google.com/android/reference/com/google/android/gms/maps/OnMapReadyCallback

PackageManager, [online] Available, https://developer.android.com/reference/android/content/pm/PackageManager

requestPermissions, onRequestPermissionsResult, shouldShowRequestPermissionRationale, [online] Available, https://developer.android.com/training/permissions/requesting

UiSettings, [online] Available, https://developers.google.com/android/reference/com/google/android/gms/maps/UiSettings

References

1. V. Nagpal, *Android Sensor Programming by Example* (Packt Publishing, Birmingham, UK, 2016)
2. X. Liu, J. Liu, W. Wang, et al., Discovering and understanding android sensor usage behaviors with data flow analysis. World Wide Web **21**, 105–126 (2018)

Index

A
Abstract, 16
Accelerometer, 587
Access modifiers, 12, 16
Actionbar, 326
Action_Dial, 109, 347
Action_View, 109
Activity, 98, 101
Activity lifecycle, 185
addToBackStack, 392
Agile, 174
AlertDialog, 342
AnalogClock, 256
Android, 52
Android API levels, 97
Android App Bundle (AAB), 79
Android Debug Bridge (adb), 144
android:entries, 256
android:layout_gravity, 273
android:layout_weight, 273
AndroidManifest.XML, 55
android:onClick, 107, 121
android:orientation, 247
android.R.layout.*simple_list_item*_1, 398
Android runtime (ART), 89
android:sharedUserId, 352
android:sharedUserLabel, 352
android:src, 310
Android Studio, 57
Android style, 264
android.util.Xml, 437
AndroidX, 327, 329
Annotations, 16
Anonymous, 38
apk, 79, 80, 236

AppCompatActivity, 99
Application, 115
Application Not Responding (ANR), 569
apply(), 353
Array, 11
@array, 254
ArrayAdapter, 284
ArrayList, 12
assertEquals, 163
assertSame, 164
assertThat, 164
assertTrue, 162
Asset folder, 449
AssetManager, 449
Associativity, 8
Asynchronous, 451
AsyncTask, 433, 448, 451
AudioManager, 568
Autoboxing, 36

B
Back stack, 185, 392
Bazel, 81
Binding, 550
bindService, 554
Bitbucket, 85
BitmapFactory, 442
BitmapFactory.decodeStream, 442
Bitmap object, 442
Boolean, 5
Branch, 85
Break, 11
Broadcast, 549, 550
BroadcastReceiver, 567

A.-R. Mawlood-Yunis, *Android for Java Programmers*,
https://doi.org/10.1007/978-3-030-87459-9

Buck, 81
Builder, 526
Bundle, 188, 191
Byte, 3

C

Calendar, 291, 296
Callback methods, 185
Catch, 33
Char, 5
Checked exceptions, 32
Check-*in commits*, 85
Checkout, 85
checkPermissions(), 601
Codebase, 85
Code coverage, 172
Code smells, 179
Comma-separated value (CSV), 468
Commit, 85, 353, 392
compileSdkVersion, 327
constraintDimensionRatio, 577
ConstraintLayout, 104, 258, 259
Constructor chaining, 30
Constructors, 19, 22
Content providers, 532
ContentResolver, 532, 546
ContentValues, 485
Context, 101, 110
Context.*MODE_PRIVATE.*, 352
Continue, 11
createFromParcel, 214, 217
Criteria, 600, 604
Cursor, 487
CursorAdapter, 284
Custom broadcasts, 561

D

Dalvik, 89
Dalvik Executable, 78
Data Access Object (DAO), 524
databaseBuilder(), 526
DatabaseError, 511
database.getReference(), 511
Database Inspector, 507
DatabaseRef.child, 511
DatabaseReference, 511
databaseReference.setValue, 511
Data object, 213
DatePickerDialog, 292
DataSnapshot, 511, 520
DateUtils, 291

Debugging, 137
decodeStream(), 442
Default, 2
Default constructor, 32
Derived, 22
describeContents(), 214
Deserialization, 41
Device File Explorer, 142, 505
doInBackground, 451
Do-while, 11
Dynamic, 12
Dynamic binding, 402
Dynamic fragment, 398

E

Editor, 353
EditText, 103, 105, 230
Ellipsis, 46
endAt(), 518
equalTo(), 518
Espresso, 165
Exception, 32
execSQL(), 480, 484
execute(), 452
Explicit Intents, 108
Explicit typecasting, 4

F

Fields, 2
FileInputStream, 41
fileList(), 364
FileOutputStream, 41
Final, 16
Finally, 33
findFragmentById, 621
findViewByID, 119
finish(), 193
Firebase, 509
FirebaseDatabase, 511
FirebaseDatabase.getInstance, 511
For, 11
For-each, 13
Fragment, 259, 380, 389
Fragment manager, 391
Fragment transaction, 391, 392
FrameLayout, 258, 382

G

Generics, 33
Genymotion, 77

Geocoder, 600
Geodecoders, 597
getApplicationContext(), 101
getAssets(), 449
getAttributeValue(), 441
getBestProvider*()*, 604
GetBundle, 191
getContentResolver(), 546
getFilesDir(), 364
getInstance, 296
getIntent(), 118
getLastKnownLocation(), 604
getLocality(), 612
getMapAsync(), 621, 625
getReadableDatabase(), 483
getSharedPreferences(), 352
getString(), 148
getSystemService(), 603
Git, 85
GitHub, 85
GoogleMap, 619, 620
GoogleMapOptions, 630
GridLayout, 239, 260

H
hamcrest, 164
Hardware abstraction layer (HAL), 89
HorizontalScrollView, 298
HTTPUrlConnection, 433, 438, 443

I
IBinder, 554
If-then, 11
If-then-else, 11
ImageView, 256
immutable, 353
Implements, 13
Implicit intent, 108, 109, 345, 553
Inflates, 316, 317, 390
Inflating, 99
Inheritance, 22
Inner class, 38
insert(), 484
Instance variables, 2
Instrumental testing, 159
Int, 3
Integration testing, 159
Intent, 103, 107
Intent-filter, 115, 187
Intent filtering, 553
IntentService, 550

Interface, 20
isFinishing(), 193
isReadOnly(), 483
Iterator, 13

J
Javac, 78
JavaCSV, 468
Java development kit (JDK), 78
JobIntentService, 559
Junit, 159, 167
Just-in-time (JIT), 89

L
Lambda expression, 45
Launcher Activity, 187
Layout, 104, 448
Layout_alignParentBottom, 256
Layout_alignParentTop, 256
LayoutInflater, 316
Layout manager, 313, 315
LayoutParams, 242, 244, 245
Legacy, 239
limitToFirst(), 518
limitToLast(), 518
LinearLayout, 242
Linux kernel, 90
ListActivity, 283
List view, 279, 280
Local broadcast, 561
LocalBroadcastManager, 562
Locale, 127
Local variables, 2
LocationListener, 600
LocationManager, 597, 599
Location Providers, 597
Log, 123, 156
Logcat, 123, 125
Long, 3

M
Manifest, 102
MapFragment, 619
MapView, 619, 624
Margin, 273
MariaDB, 476
Matcher, 164
MediaController, 577
MediaPlayer, 567, 568
MediaStore, 345

MenuInflater, 331, 334, 337
Mockito, 169
Model-view-controller (MVC), 389
Modifiers, 16
MongoDB, 476
moveToFirst(), 487
moveToLast(), 487
moveToNext(), 487

N
New, 12
newArray, 214
newPullParser(), 437
Non-argument constructor, 32
Normal broadcast, 561

O
Object, 17, 19
ObjectInputStream, 41
Object-oriented programming (OOP), 15
ObjectOutputStream, 41
onActivityCreated(), 385
onActivityResult(), 345, 347
onAttach(), 381, 384
OnContextClickListener, 423
onContextItemSelected, 332, 338
onCreate(), 119, 188, 478
onCreateContextMenu(), 337
onCreateOptionsMenu(), 334
onCreateView(), 381, 385
onCreateViewHolder(), 311
onDateSet(), 294
onDateSetListener(), 292
onDestroy(), 193, 550
onDestroyView(), 385
onDetach(), 381, 385
OnDoubleTapListener, 423
onDowngrade(), 482
OnGestureListener, 423
onItemClick(), 285
onItemClickListener, 285
OnMapReadyCallback, 618, 619, 621
onOpen(), 478, 483
onOptionsItemSelected, 331
onPause(), 194
onPostExecute, 451
onPreExecute, 451
onPreparedListener(), 568, 569
onProgressUpdate, 451
onReceive(), 564
onRequestPermissionsResult(), 601

onResume(), 194
onSaveInstanceState(), 196
onStartCommand(), 550
onStop(), 194
onTimeSetListener(), 292
onTouch(), 424
onTouchEvent(), 424
onUpgrade(), 478, 481
OpenCSV, 468
openFileInput(), 442
openFileOutput(), 364
Open-source, 52
Operators, 8
orderByChild(), 518, 520
orderByKey(), 518
orderByValue(), 518
Ordered broadcast, 561
Overflow, 332, 333
Override, 19, 28

P
Package, 2, 22
Parameters, 2, 33
Params, 452
Parcel, 213, 217
Parcelable, 44, 184, 185, 212
Parcelable.Creator, 214, 217
PARTIAL_WAKE_LOCK keeps,
      571
Paused, 186
perform, 166
Pickers, 279, 289
Pixelation, 417
Polymorphism, 24
Popup menu, 340
PopupMenu.OnDismissListener, 341
PowerManager, 568, 570
Precedence rules, 8
prepare(), 568
prepareAsync, 563, 568
Primitive, 3
Private, 2, 352
Profiler, 141
Progress, 452
ProGuard, 78
Protected, 2
Public, 2
publishProgress(), 451

Q
Query, 511

R
RatingBar, 256
R8 compiler, 78
READ_EXTERNAL_STORAGE, 369
ReadObject, 41
RecyclerView, 304, 305
Refactor, 327
Refactoring, 173
r*egisterForContextMenu()*, 337
RelativeLayout, 239
Remote Method Invocation (RMI), 40
removeValue(), 516
requestLocationUpdates*()*, 601
Result, 452
Return, 11
Reverse engineering, 174
R.java, 100
R.Layout, 448
Room, 524
RoomDatabase, 524, 526
RootView, 152
Runnable, 454
Running, 186
RuntimeException, 32

S
SAX, 434
ScaleGestureDetector, 420, 421
Scroll views, 279
sdcard, 362
SDK Manager, 64
sendBroadcast(), 561–564
sendOrderedBroadcast(), 561
SensorEventListener, 588
Serializable, 40, 212
Serialize, 40
Service, 549
setActionToolbar(), 335
setAdapter, 314
setContentView(), 99, 242
setLayoutManager, 313
setOnTouchListener, 423
setResul()t, 347
setSupportActionBar, 331
setTitle(), 114
SharedPreferences, 351
Short, 3
Shorthand operator, 10
shouldShowRequestPermissionRationale, 602
SimpleOnGestureListener, 423
SimpleOnScaleGestureListener, 420

Singleton, 45
Snackbar, 150
Spinner, 256
SpinnerAdapter, 284
Spy, 171
SQLite, 476, 477
SQLiteBrowser, 505, 506
SQLiteDatabase, 484
SQLiteOpenHelper, 477
sqlite3, 507
StartActivity, 107, 110
startActivityForResult, 345, 347
startAt(), 518
startForegroundService(), 549
startService(), 549
State, 185
Static, 2, 16
Static analysis, 174
Static binding, 402
Static state, 186
Stopped, 186
stopSelf(), 552, 557
stopService(), 550, 552, 557
Strictfp, 16
String, 5, 7
String array, 249
Stub, 169
Style, 264
Subclass, 22
Super, 22, 28
Superclass, 22
Support library, 329
SupportMapFragment, 621
Switch, 11
System broadcasts, 561

T
TableLayout, 262
@test, 162
TextView, 101, 119, 232
Theme, 268
TimePickerDialog, 295
Toast, 146
Toolbar, 326
Tools:context, 247
toString(), 19
Transient state, 186
Try, 33
TV, 576
Type-array name, 256
Typecast, 6

Type coercion, 6
Type parameters, 34
Type variables, 34

U
UiSettings, 619, 627
Unary operators, 8
Unchecked exceptions, 32
Unit testing, 136, 159
Uri, 109, 535
UriMatcher, 535
URL, 443
User acceptance testing, 159
UserRef.addValueEventListener, 514

V
Varargs, 45
Variable arguments, 45
Variables, 2
VideoView, 576

View, 101, 228
ViewGroup, 234
ViewHold, 279
ViewInteraction, 166
ViewText, 103
Virtual pixel unit, 419

W
WakeLock, 570
While, 11
Widgets, 232
WifiLock, 568, 571
WRITE_EXTERNAL_STORAGE,
      369
WriteObject, 41
writeToParcel, 214

X
XML pull parser, 434
XML push parser, 434

Printed in the United States
by Baker & Taylor Publisher Services